LIKING PROGRESS, LOVING CHANGE

A LITERARY HISTORY OF THE PROGRESSIVE WRITERS' MOVEMENT IN URDU

RAKHSHANDA JALIL

OXFORD
UNIVERSITY PRESS

Oxford University Press is a department of the University of Oxford.
It furthers the University's objective of excellence in research, scholarship,
and education by publishing worldwide. Oxford is a registered trademark of
Oxford University Press in the UK and in certain other countries

Published in India by
Oxford University Press
YMCA Library Building, 1 Jai Singh Road, New Delhi 110 001, India

© Oxford University Press 2014

The moral rights of the author have been asserted

First Edition published in 2014

All rights reserved. No part of this publication may be reproduced, stored in
a retrieval system, or transmitted, in any form or by any means, without the
prior permission in writing of Oxford University Press, or as expressly permitted
by law, by licence, or under terms agreed with the appropriate reprographics
rights organization. Enquiries concerning reproduction outside the scope of the
above should be sent to the Rights Department, Oxford University Press, at the
address above

You must not circulate this work in any other form
and you must impose this same condition on any acquirer

ISBN-13: 978-0-19-809673-3
ISBN-10: 0-19-809673-9

Typeset in Adobe Jenson Pro 11/14
by The Graphics Solution, New Delhi 110 092
Printed in India by Akash Press, New Delhi 110 020

*Chalo aao tum ko dikhain hum jo bachaa hai maqtal-e-shahar mein
Ye mazaar ahal-e-safaa ke hain ye hain ahal-e-sidq kii turbatein*
—*Faiz Ahmed Faiz*

*Ghairon se suna tumne, ghairon se kaha tumne
Kabhi hum se suna hota, kabhi hum se kaha hota*
—*Chiragh Hasan Hasrat*

Contents

Acknowledgements — ix
List of Abbreviations — xi
Introduction — xiii

1. The Linkages between Social Change and Urdu Literature: From 1850s till 1920s — 1
2. Rise of Socialist Consciousness: From 1900 till 1930s — 52
3. Analysing *Angarey* — 108
4. The Furore over the Publication of *Angarey* — 146
5. Setting up the All-India Progressive Writers' Association — 190
6. From *Shabab* to *Inquilab*: Progressive Poetry from 1930s till 1950s — 242
7. From *Fasana* to *Afsana*: A Study of Progressive Prose from 1930s till 1950s — 305
8. The Decline of the Progressive Writers' Movement — 339

Annexures 402
Glossary 439
Bibliography 444
Index 466
About the Author 481

Acknowledgements

I am grateful to the Indian Council for Social Science Research for granting me a partial assistance grant for six months, and to the Maulana Abul Kalam Azad Institute of Asian Studies. I am also grateful to the Indian Council for Historical Research for giving me a Foreign Travel Grant that permitted me to work in the British Library for a month; it allowed me to access primary sources that I could not ordinarily have.

I owe a debt of gratitude to my sister, Tabinda J. Burney, and her husband, Khalid Burney, who made my stay in London a pleasant experience. Their warm hospitality and kindness dulled the rigours of long hours of research and reading.

The help rendered by the library staff of the Nehru Memorial Museum & Library, National Archives of India, Sahitya Akademi, Zakir Husain Library, and Academy of Third World Studies at Jamia Millia Islamia has gone a long way in making this study possible. In particular, I wish to thank Ghiyas Makhdumi, the chief librarian, and Shahab Azmi at the Zakir Husain Library, Jamia Millia Islamia. Sushma Zutshi, the then chief librarian of the India International Centre, gave me a cubicle when I needed it the most. That 6 × 10 feet wood-panelled room gave me the necessary space to complete the bulk of writing this study. To her I extend my warm gratitude, as well as to her colleagues who have cheerfully located umpteen books for me through the DELNET. The present librarian of the India International Centre and his staff continue to be a pillar of support.

I take this opportunity to express my gratitude to Professor Mushirul Hasan who agreed to supervise my PhD, upon which this study has been built.

My uncles—A.M.K. Shahryar and Siddiq Ahmad Siddiqui—magically produced books, photocopies, and articles from sources best known to them. Shahryar Mamu is no more; my deep regret will always be that he is not here to see this study in its present form. His help—both practical and intellectual—has strengthened me in ways I cannot enumerate. My mother, Mehjabeen, has been an indefatigable tracker of material, especially out-of-print Urdu texts. She has, patiently and diligently, copied material from libraries and collections in Aligarh and helped me put together a fairly substantial collection of first editions of several Urdu texts studied here. More importantly, she has been a perceptive sounding board for many ideas. I have relied, also, on her reminiscences of some of the progressive writers she has known. It would not be an exaggeration to say that this book, in its present form, would not have been possible without her silent, steady support.

Many friends have offered support and encouragement; among them I wish to acknowledge Shifalika Dalmia, Vishal Kapoor, Anita Samkaria, Humra Quraishi, Vidya Rao, Saibal Roy Choudhury, Seema Jason, Kaushik Ghosh, Ranjan Kaul, Sadia Dehelvi, Mayank Austen Soofi, Sagari Chhabra, Partha Chatterjee, Indira Varma, Sima, and L.K. Sharma. Among those who have offered valuable advice and insights, I offer my profound gratitude to Sharib Rudaulvi, Ali Javed, Arif Naqvi, Najma Baqar, Raza Imam, Munibur Rahman, Zahida Zaidi, Atia Abid, Akhilesh Mitthal, Shahla Haider, Sarwat Rahman, M.M. Mahdi, Bano and Narendar Gupta (in India); and Zehra Nigah, Asif Noorani, Raza Rumi, Intizar Husain, Iqbal Rashid Siddiqui, Asif Farrukhi, Kamran Asdar, Urooj Ahmed Ali, Rahat Saeed, Mushtaq Yusufi, Zafarullah Poshni (in Pakistan). Several dear ones have since passed away: Shahryar, Raza Imam, Zahida Zaidi, Atia Abid, and Sima Sharma. Each helped in different ways; I regret I will never be able to show them this book.

Lastly, I wish to thank my daughters, Aaliya and Insha, for putting up with a mother who has been absent-minded, pre-occupied, and negligent for far too long, preoccupied as she has been with her 'progressives'! And to Najmi, for smiling serenely through it all.

Abbreviations

AICC	All-India Congress Committee
AIPWA	All-India Progressive Writers' Association
AIR	All India Radio
AMU	Aligarh Muslim University
CPGB	Communist Party of Great Britain
CPI	Communist Party of India
CPP	Communist Party of Pakistan
CSP	Congress Socialist Party
DIB	Director, Intelligence Bureau
INC	Indian National Congress
IPC	Indian Penal Code
IPTA	Indian People's Theatre Association
IOL	India Office Library
IOR	India Office Records
MGNREGA	Mahatma Gandhi National Rural Employment Guarantee Act
NAI	National Archives of India
NMML	Nehru Memorial Museum & Library
NWFP	North-West Frontier Province
PPH	People's Publishing House

PWA	Progressive Writers' Association
PWM	Progressive Writers' Movement
SFI	Students' Federation of India

Introduction

> Literary history is an account of the state of learning.
> —Samuel Johnson

The significance of the Progressive Writers' Movement (PWM) is uncontested for most commentators on the literary history of India.[1] It succeeded in bringing to its fold established and emerging writers from almost all the important languages in the Indian subcontinent. From almost its very inception, it succeeded in gaining the attention—and blessings—of the literary stalwarts of the time. Rabindranath Tagore, Mohammad Iqbal, Maulvi Abdul Haq, Hasrat Mohani, Acharya Narendra Dev, Tara Chand, and Sarojini Naidu—while belonging to diverse literary traditions—endorsed the PWM and its objectives. The eminent Hindi writer Premchand addressed the inaugural session of the Progressive Writers' Association (PWA) in Lucknow on 9 April 1936, virtually spelling out

---

[1] Mohan Lal, *The Encyclopaedia of Indian Literature*, vol. IV (New Delhi: Sahitya Akademi, 1991); Muhammad Sadiq, *Twentieth-century Urdu Literature* (Karachi: Royal Book Company, 1983); Ali Jawad Zaidi, *A History of Urdu Literature* (New Delhi: Sahitya Akademi, 1993); among other literary commentators. Aijaz Ahmad has gone so far as to call the PWA a 'hegemonic ideological force'; see his *In the Mirror of Urdu: Recompositions of Nation and Community, 1947–65*, Lectures 102–5 (Shimla: Indian Institute of Advanced Study, 1993).

its agenda in his presidential speech entitled '*Sahitya ka Uddeshya*' (The Aim of Literature).[2]

Some of the greatest Urdu writers were associated with the PWA, namely, Faiz Ahmed Faiz, Sajjad Zaheer, Ismat Chughtai, Krishan Chandar, Kaifi Azmi, and Ali Sardar Jafri, among others. The importance of this movement lies not merely in the intrinsic merits of the writers associated with it or their individual works; it lies instead in the role played by the PWA—and, from 1943 onwards, its partner organization, the Indian People's Theatre Association (IPTA)—in shaping the political consciousness of large numbers of people, in its unequivocal emphasis on the need for social change, and in the relentless portrayal of these twin forces in their literature and, by extension, in all forms of art and popular culture.[3] The PWM and its proponents were a powerful and inescapable force commandeering a space for themselves on the political, social, and literary canvas of India for nearly three decades. In the years before Independence, they influenced the debates on imperialism and decolonization, and in the years after, they were at the centre of the discourses on the nature of the newly independent, post-colonized state and society.[4]

The PWM penetrated into different Indian languages, most notably, Urdu, Hindi, Bengali, Marathi, and Telugu.[5] For the purpose of this literary history, our interest will be in the Urdu writers; and in the use of the acronyms PWM and PWA, I shall allude to *Taraqqui Pasand Tehreek* and *Anjuman-e-Taraqqui Pasand Mussanifin*, respectively. Similarly, I shall use the word 'progressive' for the Urdu expression '*taraqqui pasand*'. The PWA, while in its inception, did indeed have mostly Urdu and some Hindi writers in its fold, I have chosen to use and interpret only Urdu writers primarily because Urdu was, during the period of this study, the

---

[2] The full text of Premchand's address can be found in M.D. Taseer, *The Oxford India Premchand*, translated by Francesca Orsini (New Delhi: Oxford University Press, 2004).

[3] Sudhi Pradhan (ed.), *Marxist Cultural Movements in India: Chronicles and Documents (1936–47)*, vols I and II (Calcutta: National Book Agency, 1979).

[4] Even those who were not a part of the PWM admit to its significance. See, for instance, N.M. Rashid's interview in *Mahfil*, vol. 7, nos 1–2 (Spring–Summer 1971).

[5] Lal, *Encyclopaedia of Indian Literature*.

most widely used language. It was a tensile, growing, alive lingua franca of the people of upper India. It was open to change and ideally suited to the expression of new, even radical ideas.[6] The burst of political consciousness released from the events of 1857, the changes in distant parts of the world at the turn of the century, the Russian revolution and the consequent popularity of socialist thought, the rising nationalism, the growing anti-imperialist sentiments—all this and more found expression in the Urdu language. Urdu literature, therefore, reflected a mind-boggling variety of styles, trends, and voices.[7]

I have attempted to look at Urdu literature, in most cases the literature of the Indian Muslims, in the context of the events and happenings in India, events that affected not Muslims alone though my interest, all along, is on their *effect* on the Indian Muslims. I have devoted two chapters to providing a historical background to the emergence of socially engaged literature in Urdu from the late nineteenth century onwards and setting forth the diversity of responses among the Muslim intelligentsia to the events that shaped their world. In this, I have taken heed of Barbara D. Metcalf's eloquent plea to write 'a history of connections'. Metcalf has urged: 'We need scholars who, unlike my generation, do not study Muslims alone. And, instead of creating difference, we need to draw boundaries around common social and political structures, situating Muslims squarely within

---

[6] Different historians have commented upon the different ways in which Urdu adapted itself to address new concerns. See, for instance, the works of Barbara D. Metcalf, Francis Robinson, and Gail Minault in Christopher Shackle (ed.), *Urdu and Muslim South Asia: Studies in Honour of Ralph Russell* (New Delhi: Oxford University Press, 1991); and Francis Robinson, *Islam and Muslim History in South Asia* (New Delhi: Oxford University Press, 2000). The impact of the Russian revolution and socialist ideology has been studied by several scholars, most notably by Qamar Rais. See Rais, *October Revolution: Impact on Indian Literature* (New Delhi: Sterling Publishers, 1978); and Humayun Khizar Ansari, *The Emergence of Socialist Thought among North Indian Muslims, 1917–1947* (Lahore: Book Traders, 1990).

[7] Ale Ahmad Suroor (ed.), *Tanquid ke Buniyadi Masail* (The Fundamental Issues of Criticism) (Aligarh: Aligarh Muslim University Press [AMU], 1967). In the same volume, Majnooh Gorakhpuri, tracing the evolution of Urdu prose in 'Nazm se Nasr Tak', speaks of the spurt in Urdu prose in the post-1857 period, and the greater freedom enjoyed by prose in terms of scope for expression, form, and content.

the complex world of opportunities and constraints, motivations, and tastes they shared with everyone else.'[8]

While delineating the history of the PWM, I have attempted to posit the Muslim response to events at the national and international fronts. I have attempted to establish the existence of revision, reform, even radicalism among the Muslim intelligentsia as is evident from a study of Urdu literature. At the same time, one must acknowledge that though Urdu literature was not being written by Muslims alone, the great majority of nineteenth-century Urdu writers were indeed Muslims. Notable exceptions such as Pandit Ratan Nath Sarshar (1844–1902) or Daya Shankar Nasim (1811–1843) wrote of Muslim milieus inhabited largely by Muslim characters. By the turn of the century, a new breed of writers such as Durga Sahai Sarur (1873–1910) and Brij Narain Chakbast (1882–1926) set a new trend in poetry by exhorting a pure and sublime love for the motherland; in prose, non-Muslim Urdu writers such as Premchand (1880–1936) followed by Upendranath Ashk (1910–2002) and later Rajinder Singh Bedi (1915–1984) drew attention towards social ills, especially of the lower-middle class. The bulk of Urdu literature, however, remained not just *about* the Muslims, and where not coloured by a quintessentially religious sensibility was, at the very least, influenced by Islamic culture ('Islami ikhlaq').[9]

From establishing the presence of reform-minded individuals and organizations among Indian Muslims,[10] this book will move to the 'idea' of progressivism. Who or what is progressive? Generally speaking, a world view that derides nostalgia is a progressive world view, and an individual who chooses not to look back or hearken to old glories but resolutely look ahead is a progressive. This book will look for some unlikely heroes (and heroines too) apart from reflecting upon the work of the known names among the

---

[8] Barbara D. Metcalf, 'Too Little and Too Much: Reflections on Muslims in the History of India', *The Journal of Asian Studies*, vol. 4 (1995), pp. 951–67. It was originally delivered as the presidential address at the 47th Annual Meeting of the Association of Asian Studies held in Washington, DC, on 7 April 1995.

[9] Ibadat Barelwi, *Urdu Tanquid Nigari* (Delhi: Chaman Book Depot, 1970), p. 274.

[10] For a lucid study of the presence of reform movements, their reflection in Urdu literature, and the growing self-consciousness of the Muslim community, see Annemarie Schimmel, *Islam in the Indian Subcontinent* (Leiden: E.J. Brill, 1980).

PWA. It will do so by first questioning the notion of progressivism. Ghalib was a progressive. He chose to deride Syed Ahmad Khan's laudatory history of the Mughals, *Ain-e-Akbari*, calling it 'self-indulgent'. We will see how definitions of 'progressive' began to merge seamlessly generation after generation. The forward-looking world of Muslim Aligarh was considered progressive during its time, and Syed Ahmed Khan and others who comprised the Aligarh school of thought invited vitriol and invective in much the same measure as Rashid Jahan 'Angareywali' and her fellow writers half a century later. Following in the footsteps of Syed Ahmed Khan, Altaf Husain Hali, Nazir Ahmad, and Maulvi Zakaullah were forward-looking, open to change and progress.[11] In that, they were progressive in their own way and each was laying the groundwork for the progressives—as those writers associated with the PWA came to be called—to make their dramatic on-stage entry in the 1930s.

With the publication of *Angarey* in December 1932, the definition of forward-looking underwent a sea-change and the epithets of irreligious, godless, sacrilegious, even blasphemous, came to be used for a radical, new sort of writing.[12] A few years later, the adoption of a *Manifesto* and the espousal of an iron-clad ideology made the latter-day progressives a force to reckon with, though they were by no means the first to raise their voice

---

[11] For a detailed discussion of this group, its activities, and impact, see Mushirul Hasan, *A Moral Reckoning: Muslim Intellectuals in Nineteenth-century Delhi* (New Delhi: Oxford University Press, 2005). It may be read alongside Hasan's other works such as his Introduction (co-authored with Margrit Pernau) to *Zakaullah of Delhi* by C.F. Andrews (New Delhi: Oxford University Press, 2003) to gain a clearer understanding of the open-mindedness of the Muslim intellectuals of the late nineteenth and early twentieth centuries.

[12] This radical new sort of writing cast a long shadow on Urdu literature for decades to come. In English, see Shabana Mahmud, 'Angare and the Founding of the Progressive Writers' Association', *Modern Asian Studies*, vol. 30, no. 2 (May 1996); Priyamvada Gopal, *Literary Radicalism in India: Gender, Nation and the Transition to Independence* (Oxon: Routledge, 2005); and Talat Ahmed, *Literature and Politics in the Age of Nationalism: The Progressive Episode in South Asia, 1932–56* (New Delhi: Routledge, 2009); and in Urdu, the finest description of the 'effect' of *Angarey* is to be found in Khalilur Rahman Azmi, *Urdu mein Taraqqui Pasand Adabi Tehreek* (Aligarh: Educational Book House, 2002 [1957]). Its historical background is set forth in Khalid Alvi, *Angarey ka Tareekhi Pasmanzar aur Taraqqui Pasand Tehreek* (Delhi: Educational Publishing House, 1995).

against imperialism and oppression. Nor were they the first to call for unequivocal freedom and a new beginning. What set them apart from the others—and what made their voice distinct in that babel of voices that cried for revolution and change—was their use of the word 'progressive', or to be more precise, *taraqqui pasand*, literally meaning those who 'like' progress. Different progressives interpreted the meaning of the word 'progressive' in different ways. Ismat Chughtai, the fiction writer who remained associated with the movement, but on her own terms and not always according to the diktats of the ideologues within the PWA, interpreted progressive literature to mean that which is concerned with humanity, social awareness, and humanism.[13] Others, such as the poet Akhtarul Iman, grew steadily disenchanted with the progressives' increasing concern with issues that, while humane and broad-based, were nevertheless topical and, therefore, unlikely to pass the test of time.[14]

While examining the PWM and the works of its most famous contributors and their role in nation-building, shaping popular consciousness, and defining culture, this book also delves into the reasons that caused such a movement to come into being in the first place. Its central premise is the assertion that the PWM did not spring fully formed out of thin air in the mid-1930s. Contrary to popular perception, as we will see, the PWA was not a foreign plant grafted onto Indian stock rooted in native soil that, with diligent watering, produced strange and exotic fruit. It was, instead, a literary-political-social movement in consonance with the Indian realities of the times. Urdu teacher and critic Ralph Russell has pointed out: 'By the 1920s themes of revolt against imperialism, of nationalism, and of radical social reform were already common in literature (for example, both in the poetry of Iqbal and in the prose of Prem Chand), and the PWA represented simply the continuation and development of such themes.'[15]

And so, while its influences were diverse, the PWM was essentially an Indian phenomenon. The PWA too was a heterogeneous group of writers—some established, others upcoming; some already committed communists, others with socialist leanings and a great many with no discernible

---

[13] See *Mahfil*, vol. 8 (1972).

[14] Akhtarul Iman, *Iss Abad Kharabe mein* (New Delhi: Urdu Academy, 1996).

[15] Ralph Russell, 'Leadership in the All-India Progressive Writers' Movement, 1935–1947', in B.N. Pandey (ed.), *Leadership in South Asia* (New Delhi: Vikas Publishing House, 1977), p. 113.

ideological moorings save an inchoate desire to change the world. They drew their inspiration from the world around them, and from political and social events both within India and the world outside.[16] Ahmed Ali, founder-member of the PWA and fellow traveller in the early years, speaking at the first conference of the All-India Progressive Writers' Association (AIPWA) in April 1936, thus expressed the turmoil of an entire generation of young intellectuals:

The Indian renaissance is beginning to be shocked into frankness about itself. Its old, confused, inconsistent, and contradictory ideology is turning upon itself and today the most significant fact everywhere in India is a process of universal heart-searching—it is a painful process in the throes of which India is finding herself today, finding herself between two worlds, the one dead and the other yet unborn.[17]

The nature of the movement is yet another theme for discussion in this book. We shall see how the PWM was, in its broadest sense, also a social and political movement. In the early years of the PWA, its desire to draw literature closer to social realities and the cause of nation-building drew encouragement from national leaders as well as fellow writers. Invited to address the Allahabad session of the PWA in November 1937, Nehru showed his approval by beginning his address thus: 'In my opinion a writer should not be a mere utopian; for unless he has something fundamental in his mind, and his writing has connection with reality, with actual life, his work cannot prove enduring.'[18]

In the same conference, Rabindranath Tagore sent a message urging writers to mingle with the people and to know them, for 'literature that is not in harmony with mankind,' he warned, 'is destined for failure'. In an address entitled 'Writer Should Not Be a Recluse', the seer exhorted: 'To be able to know the society and to point to its course of progress it is imperative that we feel the pulse of the society and hear its heart beats.'[19]

[16] Sajjad Zaheer, 'A Note on the PWA', in Sudhi Pradhan (ed.), *Marxist Cultural Movements in India: Chronicles and Documents (1936–47)*, vol. I (Calcutta: National Book Agency, 1979), pp. 48–51.

[17] Ahmed Ali, 'Progressive View of Art', *Golden Jubilee Brochure*, Ghulam Rabbani Taban Papers, Nehru Memorial Museum & Library (NMML).

[18] *Selected Works of Jawaharlal Nehru*, vol. 8 (New Delhi: Orient Longman, 1976), p. 859.

[19] Tagore's speech is reprinted in the *Golden Jubilee Brochure*, Ghulam Rabbani Taban Papers, NMML.

The writers associated with this movement were people who wrote not necessarily for the joy of crafting great literature; they wrote because they saw, and were quick to seize, the great inescapable link between literature and socio-political change. Literature for them was a valuable tool in the cause of nation-building and social transformation.[20] It would be futile, therefore, to look merely at the literary merit, or its lack, among the writers associated with this movement. It will be equally futile to do a close textual reading in isolation of the writer's background and beliefs or, for that matter, the time and circumstances during which a particular text was written.

It must also be pointed out that the focus of this book shall be on the Urdu literature of north India. While there were Urdu writers of considerable acclaim in the Deccan, Gujarat, and Kashmir,[21] our prime concern shall be with the Urdu literature produced in upper India, and in India and Pakistan from 1947 till the 1950s. The 1950s have been set as a 'cut-off date' because the decline in the movement had set in, its membership had shrunk, and its influence had decreased. The book begins not with the 1930s that spawned the PWA but almost 80 years prior to its inception. It begins by tracing the release of political consciousness triggered by the First War of Independence and the direct correlation with socially engaged literature being produced in Urdu. From 1857 till the 1930s, many things happened in quick succession that together—and in perfect linear succession—culminated in the emergence of progressive thought among Urdu writers. We will clarify what set them apart from the others, and what made their voice distinct from the other voices that were clamouring to be heard.

The Marxist slogan of 'Workers of the World Unite' was commandeered by the progressives as a weapon of direct attack on the imperialist design of exploitation at home and slavery abroad. With time, certain other preoccupations began to come to the forefront—inequality among the sexes, social injustices, oppression by the powerful, and the latent capacity of the ordinary people to be the agents of change and renewal. These concerns

---

[20] Ahmed, *Literature and Politics in the Age of Nationalism*.
[21] K.M. George, *Comparative Indian Literature*, vols I and II (Trichur: Kerala Sahitya Akademi; and New Delhi: Macmillan India Ltd, 1984).

became evident in the literature, cinema, and theatre associated with the progressives; they were also the single most important reason for the movement's popular appeal.[22] The progressives' strength, and real contribution, lay in their ability to find common cause with a host of related issues such as feminism, secularism, anti-imperialism, anti-fascism, and, most importantly, nationalism.[23] This book shall also attempt to place the history of the PWM in the context of the national framework and the anti-colonial struggle. In doing so, it will endeavour to shed light, perhaps for the first time, on a much neglected theme in historical research.

Certain words, phrases, slogans that arose from the PWM came to be so inexorably associated with it that they are echoed even to this day by those who may not have read progressive literature or know very much about the PWM per se. *Angarey*—a collection of 10 short pieces published in 1932—was one such rhetorical force; its writers came to be associated with radicalism and Rashid Jahan—the only woman member of the *Angarey* quartet—gained notoriety as Rashid Jahan 'Angareywali'. Another was the word 'progressive' itself that came in for much use and abuse. While today it might not be fashionable to call oneself a progressive or, with a sense of smug superiority, dub someone a reactionary, there was a time till the 1950s when these reactions were perfectly commonplace among the literary fraternity. Also, the divide was so clear and so sharp that one was, perforce, one or the other. If one was not a progressive, one was a reactionary. Such was the diktat of the theorists.[24] By the late 1950s a change came about. The theorists went the way of all theorists and the few that remained were

---

[22] Different aspects of the progressives' aesthetics, politics, and concerns have been examined by Ali Husain Mir and Raza Mir, *Anthems of Resistance: A Celebration of Progressive Urdu Poetry* (New Delhi: India Ink/Roli, 2006).

[23] Khalid Hasan (ed.), 'A Conversation with Faiz', *The Unicorn and the Dancing Girl* (New Delhi: Allied Publishers, 1988), p. liv.

[24] One such theorist was Ali Sardar Jafri who, apart from airing the views held by a core ideological group within the PWA, through its organs such as *Naya Adab*, also wrote what he considered a definitive history of the PWM and its aims and objectives entitled *Taraqqui Pasand Adab* (Aligarh: Anjuman-i-Taraqqui Urdu, 1957). In Pakistan, the foremost progressive ideologue was Ahmad Nadeem Qasmi; for details of his role in the post-Partition phase of the PWA, see Hafeez Malik, 'The Marxist Literary Movement in India and Pakistan', *The Journal of Asian Studies*, vol. 26, no. 4 (August 1967), pp. 649–64.

apologetic of the many manifestos and the deteriorating literary standards among the progressives.[25]

This book will attempt to establish how the impact of the PWM cannot be gauged from these random bits of memory stuck in the crevices of public consciousness, random bits that cling in the collective consciousness decades after most of those who were actively associated with the movement are either dead or infirm. The book will explore the many ways in which its impact is felt every time a writer picks up a pen to write about injustice, exploitation, greed—not individual or isolated as an accident or evidence of human frailty—but as proof of social decay, bankruptcy of moral values, and the breakdown of systems of governance and public enterprise. In short, every time a writer advocates the need for a larger social change, the spirit of the PWM is alive and kicking. Ismat Chughtai expressed much the same view when she wrote

It wasn't even as if progressivism was born in the year 1935 or 1940, and died at the dispersal of a group of people. The Progressive Movement's foundation stone was laid when the first man in the history of mankind groaned under the oppression experienced through injustice, the usurpation of his rights, exploitation, inequality and tyranny. As long as there is the possibility of progress on this planet, progressivism will live. Till such time as the big fish swallows the smaller one, progressivism will indeed remain alive.[26]

The study also establishes how the PWM—as a social and political entity—may have waned but its impact remains. The audacious claims of world-transforming achievements may not have come true. The overwhelming sense of righteousness failed to match the conduct of some of the progressives as petty rivalries, groupism, and in-fighting became rampant. Many who were initially taken in by the immediate political and social goals of the PWA rather than the ultimate communist ends of some of its members, eventually expressed dismay at the hold of the Communist Party of India (CPI) over the activities of the PWA. Nevertheless, even the worst detractors of the PWM and its fiercest critics would find it hard to deny its significance in the literary history of this subcontinent. Ahmed Ali,

---

[25] Abdul Alim, 'The Annual Report of the Aligarh PWA', *Mahaul*, Delhi, pp. 13–14.

[26] Sukrita Paul Kumar and Sadique (eds), 'Progressive Literature and I', in *Ismat: Her Life, Her Times* (New Delhi: Katha, 2009), p. 129.

who in later years developed differences with what he termed the political faction, has provided an interesting way of viewing progressivism by giving us his own position vis-à-vis the progressives:

> But what we call leftism is really following the unbeaten path on the left of the road, while those walking on the right of it follow the beaten and commonly accepted way covered with the dust of conventionality and hearsay, the cobwebs of outmoded thought and superstition. I am still a progressive, and try to face the actualities of life, and look at it with unclouded eyes, untrammelled with baseless conservatism or ideality, or the shibboleths of our own making, the tin gods who sit in judgment over our freedom of thought and expression, and restrain us from growth and progress and emancipation....[27]

The first two chapters of this book provide a historical background for the emergence of progressive thought as we understand it today. From 1857 till the 1930s, many voices joined in the chorus—from different ends of the political spectrum—in the clamorous cry for freedom and change that finds such ample reflection in the Urdu literature of this period. Staunch advocates of militant nationalism found common cause with socialism, anarchism, and nihilism. Tagore's memorable words 'Trade and commerce are no longer merely trade and commerce now—they have been wedded secretly to empire'[28] became a clarion call to rise in revolt against imperialism. While the thrust of the many scattered movements that rocked the country all through the 1920s was liberation from foreign rule, certain other preoccupations too began to come to the forefront—social inequities and the ways to find redress by ordinary people. These concerns were seized by the left-leaning writers and activists and given prominent, sometimes flamboyant significance.

The underlying appeal of the *Communist Manifesto*—to the workers of the world to rise in revolt, to throw away their shackles and to unite—had long found an echo in Urdu poetry.[29] A steady stream of revolutionary

---

[27] Ahmed Ali, 'Afterword', in *The Prison-house* (Karachi: Akrash Publishing, 1985), pp. 168–9.

[28] In an article in the journal *Sabuj Patra* (Green Leaf), November–December 1914, cited in Pradhan, *Marxist Cultural Movements in India*, vol. I, p. iii.

[29] Several collections of proscribed poetry, *Zubt Shudah Nazmein* and *Ashob* give a flavour of some of these concerns. See also Norman Gerald Barrier, *Banned*:

literature from the Soviet Union, which wound its way into India through Afghanistan, fuelled the fire that had been lit long years ago by the events of 1857. In places as distant as the Punjab and Bengal, demands of the industrial workers and peasants came to the forefront and were picked up by the Khilafat leaders as yet another example of imperialist brutality.[30] In different parts of India, events conspired to turn attention upon the long-suffering peasants and landless labourers of India's vast hinterland. As the country was rocked by a series of paralysing strikes and labour unrests all through the 1920s and 1930s, Nehru, one of the finest chroniclers of his age, noted:

The crisis in industry spread rapidly to the land and became a permanent crisis in agriculture.... India was under an industrial-capitalist regime, but her economy was largely that of pre-capitalist period, minus many of the wealth-producing elements of that pre-capitalist economy. She became a passive agent of modern industrial capitalism, suffering all its ills and with hardly any of its advantages.[31]

Chapters 1 and 2 in this book are, therefore, in the nature of an extended introduction to the evolution of the progressive strand. They seek to establish the existence and growth of progressive thought in Urdu literature. Chapter 2 sets out to show how the establishment of the CPI in 1920 helped channelize the anti-imperialist sentiments till they acquired a sharper, more focused, more pronounced pro-nationalist hue, while at the same time strengthening the anti-capitalist sentiment that already existed in a large section of educated Indians, especially Muslims. Chapter 3 details the contents of an incendiary book called *Angarey* (meaning 'live embers') written by Sajjad Zaheer and others in 1932, and unfolds the linkages between the literature of this period, nationalism, and socialism. Chapter 4 describes the indignation generated by *Angarey* and also takes into account the response of those who considered the book not merely provocative but blasphemous and its writers a dangerous threat to society,

---

Controversial Literature and Political Control in British India, 1907–1947 (New Delhi: Manohar, 1978).

[30] Gail Minault, *The Khilafat Movement: Religious Symbolism and Political Mobilisation in India* (New Delhi: Oxford University Press, 1982).

[31] Jawaharlal Nehru, *Discovery of India* (New Delhi: Jawaharlal Nehru Memorial Fund, 1982), p. 300.

counterpoising it with the response of the *Angarey* group who advocated the need for self-criticism on the part of the Muslim community.

Chapter 5—drawn as it is almost entirely from primary sources—delineates the circumstances that led to the drawing up of the progressive writers' *Manifesto* in London in the winter of 1934, Sajjad Zaheer's return to India in 1935 and the establishment of branches of the PWA in different cities, the holding of the first All-India Progressive Writers' Conference in April 1936, and the growth of organized communism in India.[32] The next two chapters cover the contested terrain between the Congress, the Muslim League, and the CPI (which had begun to call itself the 'third largest political party in India' or the 'young patriotic party') in the last decade leading up to Partition; simultaneously, these two chapters also reconstruct the history of the PWM during its most productive phase—first from progressive Urdu poetry and then from prose.[33] Historical events—both connected with the PWM as well as Indian national history—run as the warp in the weft of Urdu sources to weave the richly layered and complex tapestry of the freedom movement. The picture that emerges shows the intersections between the PWM and the Indian national movement which is as much my concern in this book as the recreation of a literary history.

While Chapters 6 and 7 examine some of the works of the progressives (something that has hitherto not been attempted in English translation save for a few isolated translations published in journals such as *The Annual of Urdu Studies* for instance), there is also a constant attempt to place the texts in their contexts. The last chapter brings together the many strands of the narrative so far: it looks at the political underpinnings of the PWM, its linkages with the CPI (which had increasingly come to the fore during the War years), the creation of Pakistan, the exodus of many progressives to the new country, and their activities leading up to the Rawalpindi Conspiracy Case which drove the last nail in the coffin of progressivism in

---

[32] Chapter 5 relies upon records and intelligence files in the India Office Records (IOR), British Library, as well as Sajjad Zaheer's reminiscences called *Yaadein* (translated from the Urdu by Khalique Naqvi) in *Marxist Cultural Movements in India*, as well as the history of the early years of the PWM given in his *Roshnai* (New Delhi: Seema Publications, 1985).

[33] I have benefitted enormously from Azmi, *Urdu mein Taraqqui Pasand Adabi Tehreek*, in reconstructing this literary history.

Pakistan.[34] The last section, also in the nature of a conclusion, encapsulates the reasons for the early and widespread success of the PWM followed by reasons for its decline.

Once the harbingers of change—propelled by the twin engines of modernism and socialism—we will see how the relentless energy and ruthless idealism of the early progressives began to dim and sully somewhat. With time, their influence dwindled, their sympathizers began to drift away, and the hold of the Communist Party began to overshadow their literary output. However, the decline of the PWM or the PWA in no way marked an end of progressive thought; it simply marked the gradual disappearance of an organized, energetic, highly driven group of people working in tandem to achieve a set of common goals. After the split of the CPI into two factions—CPI and CPI (Marxist)—and communism itself being rejected as unacceptably authoritarian by large numbers of erstwhile sympathizers, the PWM gradually slipped from public consciousness. Its sister movements—those in the arts and theatre—remained active for some time, notably IPTA which still functions. And while the PWA and the Janwadi Lekhak Sangh are presently active and have a sizeable number of writers within their fold, their influence today is a far cry from the glory days of the 1940s.

As the ingredients of the original *Manifesto*—drafted in London in 1934—began to leach out, party-based ideology and an implacable Unitarian orthodoxy began to take its place. The glue of socialism and nationalism,

---

[34] For an understanding of the Pakistani phase of PWM, I have relied upon the following: Malik, 'Marxist Literary Movement in India and Pakistan'; Atiq Ahmad, '*Taraqqui Pasand Tehreek aur Karachi*', in Qamar Rais and S. Ashoor Kazmi (eds), *Taraqqui Pasand Adab: Pachas Sala Safar* (Delhi: Naya Safar Publications, 1987); M.U. Memon, 'Partition Literature: A Study of Intizar Husain', *Modern Asian Studies*, vol. 14, no. 3 (1980); and Abdulla Malik, *Mustaqbil Hamara Hai* (Lahore: Al-Jadid, 1950). I found cross-references to several crucial events and occurrences in the intelligence reports of IOR, British Library, in these books. For a reconstruction of the events of the Rawalpindi Conspiracy Case, I have found Zafarullah Poshni's memoir very useful. See his *Zindagi Zinda Dilli ka Naam Hai: Rawalpindi Muqadama Sazish ke Aseeron ki Sarguzasht-e-Aseeri*, 4th ed. (Karachi: Fazli Sons Pvt. Ltd, 2001).

a potent combination used with great efficacy for the freedom and anti-colonial movement by political parties of all hues, came unstuck shortly after 1947. The anti-colonial agenda being fulfilled and the new government under Nehru initiating several socialist plans such as land reforms, abolition of the zamindari system, building of roads, dams, infrastructure, schools, and colleges that Nehru called 'the temples of modern India', the PWA found itself on a receding turf. Even the Five Year Plans (based on the Soviet model as a remedy for mass unemployment and cure-all for rampant financial backwardness) were appropriated by the Congress. Increasingly, the PWM found the ground beneath its feet slipping away—its flock dwindling due to deserters, its creative agenda hijacked by mainstream political parties, and its creative output trashed by the literary critics (several of whom were former progressives themselves) as mere propaganda! And, the worst blow of all, the communally divisive forces that arose in the wake of Independence causing many to decry the culmination of their struggle as a chimera, no more than a 'false freedom'. On their part, the left-wing parties too were being forced on the defensive; rise of new and more aggressive conservatism and a growing religious awareness, especially of religious differences, made many notions associated with the progressive ideology seem suddenly outdated. The PWM's ambition of transforming the working class into an organized party seemed incomprehensible to many within their fold. Moreover, the overweening political ambitions of a certain core group within the PWA seemed not quite in consonance with the avowed goals of what was, ostensibly, a literary association.

Yet, the PWM did not die; it simply lost control. There can be no real date or a single reason for its eclipse. It gradually shrank in importance, slipping from public memory, becoming a subject of curiosity to the serious student of social and literary history and a mere byword for liberal humanism to the general public. As this book will attempt to show, no amount of neglect, apathy, or misinformation can, however, undermine the importance of the PWM in the history of political thought and literary trends in India. The portrayal of its own world by some of those most closely associated with the PWA cannot be matched by any historical or literary commentator. The text is the word, and in this case works of those associated with the PWA are faithful, if occasionally cracked, mirrors. They show the world—not the closed, idiosyncratic, highly individual inner world that would interest the writer of the modern and post-modern period in the years to come, but the real world outside. The works of the progressives show the world as it was, sluggishly and fearfully throwing away the shackles of tradition and stepping into a new and changing world order. The mirrors can be said to be flawed insofar as the views they held out were occasionally exaggerated or reflected in words that were not of the highest literary standards.

Having said that, even in a purely literary context, the contribution of the progressives needs be appreciated for they showed the way of singing anthems of resistance—joyfully and with full-throated abandon. Their verses were not as skilfully crafted as the masters from the Golden Age, their words were rough and ready, their metres constrained and awkward and no match to the sophisticated elegies of Mir and Sauda, but what they lacked in craft, they more than made up in energy and enthusiasm. More importantly, the progressive poets wrote rousing and exhilarating songs that promised a new morning and a new beginning where there would be hope and justice for all and not dirge-like plaintive ditties hearkening back to a (largely imaginary) glorious past that had the effect of making people sink into a morass of despair and sorrow. For, it must be remembered that till the progressives burst upon the scene in the mid-1930s, the Urdu poet had been largely content to sing in a melancholy strain. In prose too, the progressives took on themes that showed the brutal realities of their times in a no-holds-barred fashion that had never been attempted before.

Another very important factor to remember is that the glory days of the PWM also spanned the most tumultuous period of modern Indian history—Gandhi's call to Satyagraha, India's response to the rise of fascism, Nehru's Muslim mass contact programme, Gandhi's second civil disobedience movement, the Second World War and its impact on India, the Bengal famine, the rise of Telangana, *tebhaga*, and other movements, Independence, Partition, and the communal disturbances that scarred the nation. As we will see in the following chapters, the progressives faithfully reflected each of these momentous events that shaped the nation's destiny; at the same time, they drew people's attention to events outside the country such as the Rosenberg Trial, the decolonization of Africa, and the emergence of a new world order in which India must, they believed, take its rightful place.

It is to be hoped that this book will revive interest in a largely forgotten segment of Indian political and literary development. It is also hoped that a study such as this will shed some light on the inextricable linkage between literature and social change. While the influence of Marxism has been acknowledged on Indian literature by different literary commentators, the details of that influence, particularly on Urdu literature, have never been spelt out. This study hopes to do that with the intention of establishing a link between political thought and literary form and content.

1

The Linkages between Social Change and Urdu Literature

From 1850s till 1920s

> *Raah-e mazmoon-e taaza band nahin*
> *Ta qayamat khula hai baab-e sukhan*
> (The path of new themes is not closed
> The gateway of languages shall remain open till doomsday)
> —Wali Deccani (1667–1707)

This opening chapter shall link the burst of political consciousness unleashed by the events of 1857 with the heightened social consciousness reflected in the Urdu literature of the late nineteenth century. In the words of the Urdu critic Ale Ahmad Suroor, 'The demands of life after 1857 changed the direction of literature and it became necessary to develop a new way of looking at literary concerns.'[1] We shall trace the new literary trends, the dawn of new styles and new concerns, and, more significantly, a far more radical way

---

[1] Ale Ahmad Suroor (ed.), *Tanquid ke Buniyadi Masail* (Aligarh: Aligarh Muslim University Press, 1967), p. 17.

of looking at the world. We shall also review the responses of the Muslim intelligentsia which, in turn, opened a new chapter in Urdu styles and genres in both prose and poetry. In the last section on 'New Literary Trends: 1857–1920s', we shall link the break from the classical period to the growing influence of writers such as Syed Ahmad Khan (1817–1898), Maulvi Zakaullah (1832–1910), Nazir Ahmad (1836–1912), Altaf Husain Hali (1837–1914), and others who formed a bridge between the old masters and the revivalists. We shall conclude the chapter with some observations on Akbar Illahabadi (1846–1921) and Mohammad Iqbal (1877–1938) who, in turn, marked a departure from the moralists of the previous generation.

The purpose of this extended background is to establish the existence of revision, reform, even radicalism in Urdu literature. Far from being an anemic or moribund body, it was changing and growing, new literary canons were being evolved, and experiments in new forms and styles were being carried out. Having set the stage for the emergence of progressive thought among Urdu writers, Chapter 2 will take the story of the PWM a step further with the introduction of socialist thought in India.

The Revolt of 1857 and Its Aftermath

The Rebellion of 1857, considered by many as the First War of Independence, did not merely mark the end of a way of life; it also, in a sense, marked a departure in the way of *seeing* things. For the purpose of this chapter, what is significant is the Muslim response(s)[2] to the events of 1857, the effect on Muslims in general and Muslim intelligentsia in particular, and the changes ushered in their life and literature as a direct result of this cataclysmic event.

Given the close relationship between social reality and literary texts, it is important to revisit and re-examine the literature(s) produced during times of great social upheaval. Doing so can provide a far more nuanced understanding of historical events than official records and documents. The turbulence of 1857 was witnessed by some of the finest writers of the age—the 'Bloomsbury Group of Delhi'.[3] They saw and commented; yet,

---

[2] The idea of a unified Muslim response has long been rejected; see, for example, Peter Hardy, *The Muslims of British India* (Cambridge: Cambridge University Press, 1972).

[3] Coined by Mushirul Hasan, *A Moral Reckoning* (New Delhi: Oxford University Press, 2005), p. 69.

few scholars and historians have seized upon their testimony. The history of 1857 is still largely being constructed from English-language accounts. In this section I shall attempt to outline the portrayal of actual events and their effect on literary trends by a judicious mixture of primary and secondary sources from *both* Urdu and English. I shall use both translations from contemporary Urdu writers as well as literary commentaries and literary histories crafted by later-day critics. But before I proceed, I will stress that in using Urdu—instead of Persian—these poets were already raising the banner of revolt for, as the literary historian Jameel Jalibi has pointed out, the 'Urdu movement *was* the movement for Independence'.[4] In choosing to write in Urdu, the Indian poets were declaring a break from tradition and fashioning a language that was tensile, robust, capable of expressing a myriad set of moods, and one that was uniquely rooted to the soil.

'Politics and history are interwoven, but not commensurate', said Lord Acton.[5] One can add and say: so also politics and literature. In the Delhi of the nineteenth century, everybody—from the king down to the beggar—was smitten by poetry. Before 1857, poets had dominated the city's cultural and intellectual landscape; they were held in greater esteem than the Mughal emperors whose 'rule' extended no further than the shabby grandeur of the Quila-e-Moalla, or the Exalted Fort, as the Red Fort was then called.[6] After 1857, the political climate became far too volatile for poets and writers to chart the course of the city's fortunes. They could, at best, defend or decry—depending upon their lot after the apocalyptic events of the Revolt—the causes and effects of the annus horribilis that was to change their lives irrevocably. And this they did in prodigious amounts of poetry written in Urdu during and after 1857.

[4] Jameel Jalibi, *Tareekh-e-Adab-e-Urdu*, vol. II (Delhi: Educational Publishing House, 1982), p. 241.

[5] Lord Acton (1834–1902) in his inaugural lecture as Regius Professor at Cambridge in 1895; quoted in Hasan, *A Moral Reckoning*, p. 191.

[6] While the city of Delhi was largely confined within the walls of Shahjahanabad (which were then intact), the 'English peace', as it was called, brought a measure of stability and peace to the citizens of Delhi, according to Percival Spear, *Twilight of the Mughals* (New Delhi: Oriental Books Reprint Corporation, 1969). We get another, less glowing, account in the writings of Urdu writers such as Maulvi Zakaullah. We will examine this in the response of the writers of shehr ashob. For details, see Ehtesham Husain, 'Urdu Literature and the Revolt', in P.C. Joshi (ed.), *Rebellion 1857* (New Delhi: People's Publishing House [PPH], 1957).

Even prior to 1857, there had existed a body of poetry known as *shehr ashob* (literally, 'misfortunes of the city'), to express political and social decline and turmoil.[7] While admittedly much of this genre of poetry was melodramatic, self-pitying, and exaggerated with a great deal of rhetoric and play upon words in the best traditions of elegiac poetry such as *nauha*, *marsiya*, and *soz*, the shehr ashob also provided ample opportunities for the poet to paint graphic word pictures of what he saw and experienced at first hand. Using the conventional imagery of the Persian–Arabic tradition, shehr ashob allowed the poet to speak of his personal sorrows and losses while, ostensibly bemoaning a crumbling social order. Some of the greatest exponents of shehr ashob were the poets Hatim, Sauda, and Mir who, each in his own way, pulled Urdu poetry out of the thrall of romanticism and—while retaining the classical idiom and syntax of the ghazal, masnavi, and *qasidah*—made Urdu poetry speak of newer concerns.[8] Ehtesham Husain notes the existence of 'vague, undefined, unorganized yet intense national sentiments'[9] in the poetry of this period, which would flare up after 1857.

When Nawab Siraj ud-Daulah (1733–1757) of Awadh was killed by the British in the Battle of Plassey, his friend Raja Ram Narain Maozoon expressed his anguish thus:

Ghazaala tum to waaqif ho, kaho Majnun ke marne ki
Diwaanaa to mar gaya aakhir ko virane pe kyaa guzri
(Oh! Where have the mad lovers who once roamed the desert gone?
And where have those days of love vanished?)

---

[7] The first proper shehr ashob is said to have been written by Mir Jafar Zatalli, during Farrukhsiyar's reign. Born in 1685, Farrukhsiyar was the Mughal emperor between 1713 and 1719. Noted as a handsome but weak ruler, easily swayed by his advisers, his rule was in many ways ideally suited to producing writers of wit, satire, and lampoons. The shehr ashob of his period initially had elements of satire and humour and flashes of political insight, but with time the lighter elements leached out, and what was left was highly romanticized, poignant, pathos-laden protest poetry usually about the city the poet dwelt in. For a detailed study of Mir Jafar Zatalli, see 'Burning Rage, Icy Scorn: The Poetry of Ja'far Zatalli' by Shamsur Rehman Faruqi in a lecture delivered under the auspices of the Hindi–Urdu Flagship at the University of Texas at Austin on 24 September 2008.

[8] For a detailed historical background, see Jalibi, *Tareekh-e-Adab-e-Urdu*.

[9] Husain, 'Urdu Literature and the Revolt', p. 237.

(O gazelles, you know. Tell us how Majnun died?
The mad lover died, but what happened to the wilderness?)

Majnun, the legendary lover of Laila–Majnun fame, became a metaphor for Siraj ud-Daulah who fired the imagination of many Indians by his heroic resistance to the British.[10] Yet, such was the overwhelming sense of despair and dejection that pathos overrode protest, melancholy swamped the slightest stirrings of indignation, and an all-pervasive pall of gloom choked the seeds of dissent from sprouting. The poets took note of the disarray, mismanagement, and decline, but they could only bemoan and decry; they could not, to use a modern expression made pejorative by its association with American Republicanism, advocate 'affirmative action'. It would take almost a century and a half for the Urdu poet to emerge from the slough of despondency and despair and begin to rejoice in resistance. For the present, the Urdu poet could do little more than indulge himself in querulous, fretful complaining.

Poetry, it has been said, flourishes when all else withers.[11] When political chaos mars the ordered tenor of everyday life, when the social fabric tears, when corruption and poverty become rampant, when in the words of William Butler Yeats (1865–1939) 'the Centre does not hold', it is, usually, the poet's finest hour. And so it was in the last years of Mughal rule in India. From the middle of the eighteenth century, events conspired to give plenty of fodder to the Urdu elegist's mill. There was the decline and dismantling of the Mughal empire with each successive incompetent ruler, the ransacking of Delhi by Nadir Shah (9 March 1739), the series of invasions by Ahmad Shah Abdali, the Marathas, and the Rohillas, the establishment of British control over Delhi in 1803, and the most cruel blow of all, the annexation of Awadh in 1856, turned even loyal Muslim supporters of the British into discontented, suspicious malcontents if not ardent jehadis. With each fresh catastrophe, the Urdu poet evolved a vocabulary to express his angst, clothing his sorrow in a time-honoured repertoire of images and

---

[10] An account of Siraj ud-Daulah's desperate manoeuvres at Plassey is found in Sushil Chaudhury, *The Prelude to Empire: Plassey Revolution of 1757* (New Delhi: Manohar, 2000).

[11] Hali likened poetry to a 'magic lantern' that shines more brightly when the room—or age—darkens. Quoted in Frances W. Pritchett, *Nets of Awareness: Urdu Poetry and Its Critics* (Berkeley and Los Angeles: University of California Press, 1994), p. 146.

metaphors. Some favourite synonyms for the Beloved—*sitamgar, but, kafir, yaar*—now began to be used mockingly for the British.

To give a sense of the poetry of 1857 and its aftermath, it might be useful to take a quick look at what was being written in the decades leading up to it. The lamentation on the trials and tribulation of the Muslims had already begun. The *zamane ki hawa* (literally, the wind of the times) was being perceived as having turned against the Muslims. Hatim (1699–1792) epitomized the helplessness of the age when he sighed

> How can one describe the ups and downs of the world;
> In the twinkling of an eye the world has been laid waste.[12]

Ashraf Ali Khan Fughan (1725–1772) employed the traditional *gul-o-bulbul* (the rose and the nightingale) image to decry the wilderness of thorns that was now the lot of the nightingale, meaning the Muslims. Mirza Muhammad Rafi Sauda (1706–1781) wrote of the desolation of Shahjahanabad and the poverty, want, and deprivation of its citizens, the lawlessness on its streets, and the shabbiness of its once-splendid houses. His shehr ashob were no mere social satires; they contained minute observations on the hardships suffered by the common man, be it the soldier, trader, farmer, teacher, poet, calligrapher, kotwal, or even the princes of royal blood. His *Tazheek-e-Rozgar* (Mockery of the Age) was a sweeping look at all the ills of contemporary society. Contrasting the Delhi of former times with the present day, Sauda exclaimed

> See the perverted justice of the age
> The wolves roam free: the shepherds are in chains.[13]

Ghulam Hamadani Mushafi (1750–1824) talked of the dacoits that preyed upon the hapless citizens of Delhi, the forced migrations to other cities or to the countryside, the famine-stricken *salatin* for whom every month was the month of Ramazan, and the autumn that ruled over Delhi all the year round. Mir Taqi Mir (1722–1810) wrote plaintively of the desolation of his beloved Delhi:

> What can I say about the desolation of the heart?
> This city has been plundered a hundred times.

---

[12] Muhammad Sadiq, *A History of Urdu Literature (revised and enlarged)* (New Delhi: Oxford University Press, 1984), p. 104.

[13] Ralph Russell and Khurshidul Islam, *Three Mughal Poets* (London: George Allen & Unwin Ltd, 1969), p. 60.

The plunder of Delhi by Nadir Shah in 1739 and the raids by Ahmad Shah Abdali in 1748 had caused writers and poets to flock to Lucknow to seek their fortune in the courts of the Nawabs of Awadh. There too, however, the good life lasted a bare century and the dynastic rule established by Nawab Shuja-ud-daula in 1754 came to an ignominious end in 1856 with the annexation of Awadh by the British.[14] Like Delhi, the plight of Lucknow—looted by rapacious rajahs and talukdars, besieged by famine and disease, and bedeviled by a steady breakdown of law and order—too invited a copious outpouring of lament. Sitting in Matiya Burj, the deposed Nawab Wajid Ali Shah (1822–1887) wrote a largely self-pitying *Huzn-e-Akhtar* (Sorrow of Akhtar, 'Akhtar' being his nom de plume).[15] Mirza Muhammad Raza Barq, who had accompanied Wajid Ali Shah in exile, wrote '*Marsiya-e-Lucknow*', an elegy on the glory and richness of Lucknow's syncretic culture,[16] but one that unwittingly offered a critique of the

---

[14] Abdul Halim Sharar (1869–1926), an essayist and historian of Lucknow, wrote *Guzishta Lucknow*, which has been translated by E.S. Harcourt and Fakhir Hussain as *Lucknow: The Last Phase of an Oriental Culture* (New Delhi: Oxford University Press, 1994). Sharar paints a graphic picture of an Awadh that was at the peak of its glory between the reigns of Asad ud-daula and Wajid Ali Shah. His book is an extended celebration of the Lucknow form of Indo-Muslim culture and a city where scholars flocked and artists were welcomed.

[15] We get an unexpected and altogether delightful reference to Wajid Ali Shah's penchant for writing poetry under the name 'Akhtar Piya', which would later be sung in the semi-classical *dadra* and *thumri* styles of singing, in Vikram Sampath, *My Name Is Gauhar Jan: The Life and Times of a Musician* (New Delhi: Rupa & Co., 2010), p. 107. Wajid Ali Shah's '*Babul mora naihar chuto hi jay*' (O Father, I leave behind my home), at one level, is a bride's lament at leaving her home, but it can also be understood as the anguished cry of a nawab exiled from his beloved Lucknow by his political masters. The composition is still sung by countless musicians, with possibly few being aware of its political sub-text.

[16] With the annexation of Awadh, another dimension was added to its unique pluralist culture; this was the introduction of European ideas of art and civilization. Nawabi Lucknow's response to the presence of the British Resident can still be seen in some of the most stunning examples of neo-gothic architecture dotting the city's landscape. The impact of the British annexation of Awadh on the culture of Lucknow has been comprehensively examined in four excellent books: Rosie Llewellyn-Jones, *A Fatal Friendship: The Nawabs, the British and the City of Lucknow* (New Delhi: Oxford University Press, 1985); Veena Talwar Oldenburg, *The*

excesses, indulgence, and sheer hedonism of nawabi Awadh when precious *kewra* would be sprinkled on the streets for the debauched elite to walk upon. The refrain in Barq's marsiya was one of despair and hopelessness:

> The heart has no strength left
> The sighs can no longer bear fruit.[17]

And it was not just Delhi or Lucknow; everywhere the common man was caught up in the process of change from the decadent Mughal period to the no-less-oppressive British rule. As Sadiq-ur-Rahman Kidwai observes: 'Such were the times! Utter helplessness! The poet was not just the distant observer of the tragedy, he was himself a part of the crumbling edifice and caught in a dilemma: should he accept the change or cling to his former loyalties.'[18]

The writers were torn between submission and adaption; often a thin line differentiated the two and it was a case of being caught between the devil and the deep blue sea, or a rock and a hard place. Some sunk deeper in their gloom, others resorted to satire and humour when the pain became intolerable.

Perhaps the only poet of protest in the pre-1857 period was Nazir Akbarabadi (1735–1830). A people's poet if ever there had been one in Urdu, Nazir joined the ranks of Kabir, Surdas, and Mira, both in his choice of subject and style. Speaking in the voice of the common man, using prosaic words of everyday Hindustani, he wrote of a syncretic culture, of festivals like Holi and Krishna Janmashthami, and chose unconventional subjects such as the person who sells *kakri* in the bazaar of Agra, the baby bear who featured in itinerant road shows, as well as the mullah, pundit, teacher, kotwal, courtesan, and scores of 'real' people facing 'real' problems

---

Making of Lucknow: 1856–1877 (New Jersey: Princeton University Press, 1984); Violette Graff (ed.), *Lucknow: Memories of a City* (New Delhi: Oxford University Press, 1997); and Michael H. Fisher, *A Clash of Cultures: Awadh, the British and the Mughals* (New Delhi: Manohar, 1987).

[17] The verses in this section have been culled from *Nava-i-Azadi* and *Urdu mein Qaumi Shairi ke Sau Saal*, compiled by Abdur Razzaq Qureshi. All translations, unless specified otherwise, are mine.

[18] Sadiq-ur-Rahman Kidwai, 'The Poet Who Laughed in Pain: Akbar Ilahabadi', in Mushirul Hasan (ed.), *Islam in South Asia: The Realm of the Secular*, vol. IV (New Delhi: Manohar, 2009), p. 330.

in '*Banjara Nama*' (The Chronicle of the Nomad), '*Roti Nama*' (The Chronicle of Bread), and '*Aadmi Nama*' (The Chronicle of Man). Nazir's protest poetry, if it may be called that, was a departure from tradition in that he spoke of everyday struggles, sufferings, and failures without resorting to any maudlin sentimentality whatsoever. He differed from the writers of the shehr ashob in his clear-sighted acceptance of contemporary social ills and his refusal to hark back to the imagined glories of the past. In this, Nazir was an *ibn-ul waqt*, a man of his time and age.

Nazir chose to celebrate all those spheres of cultural life that had been disregarded by the highbrow and elitist poets of his time. Quite naturally, therefore, he was marginalized by the upholders of good taste; his poetry was dismissed as sensationalist and his world view, pedestrian. Neither a philosopher nor a satirist, he was, like a poet of the folk tradition, a spectator, one of the crowd, writing for and about the common folk in a language that was simple and spontaneous.[19] Despite being ostracized and excluded from the literary canon,[20] Nazir's poetry continued to be popular not just in his own time but centuries later as well. Aditya Behl offers an explanation:

Nazir is a poet who responds to the concerns of the ordinary people of his day, a poet of sensation, of reaction to real life, of social critique, of popular devotionalism.... Nazir offers us a literary way into the bazaar, to the types of people who frequented that world, their life ... rhythms and celebrations ... sensations, material culture; it is an invitation we cannot afford not to accept.[21]

Shunning the Persianized expressions, complicated conceits, and farfetched similes of conventional Urdu poets, Nazir adopted a style that was unconventional, vivid, and realistic. The following lines, however, give a

---

[19] For a detailed study of Nazir, see Ali Jawad Zaidi, *A History of Urdu Literature* (New Delhi: Sahitya Akademi, 1993); Sadiq, *A History of Urdu Literature*, chapter VIII; and the detailed introduction by Makhmoor Akbarabadi in his edited volume *Rooh-e-Nazir* (Lucknow: Uttar Pradesh Urdu Akademi, 2003).

[20] Both Azad and Hali chose to ignore him when they compiled their histories of Urdu literature.

[21] Aditya Behl, 'Poet of the Bazaars: Nazir Akbarabadi, 1735–1830', in Kathryn Hansen and David Lelyveld (eds), *A Wilderness of Possibilities: Urdu Studies in Transnational Perspective* (New Delhi: Oxford University Press, 2005), pp. 192–222, esp. p. 220.

sense of the richness of his thought and the lucidity of expression clothed, though it was, in the simple and the natural, which is the hallmark of the folk tradition. Here is Nazir writing on a range of subjects that had hitherto figured in the folk literature of upper India, but not in 'classical' or 'high' literature.

On the ghats of Jamuna during Holi:

> The surface of the Jamuna glistens like velvety lawns
> Swimmers glide through its waters like the moon and stars

From the '*Roti Nama*':

> An eyeless fakir was once asked:
> Of what stuff are the moon and stars?
> The fakir smiled and shook his head:
> God bless you, sir, the answer is only bread.

On Krishna Janmashthami:

> Milkmaids away, the little fellow had a field day.
> He stole into houses like a thief much skilled.
> Climbed on a cot and brought down the pot
> That with cream or butter was freshly filled.
> He ate some and wasted some,
> And some he simply spilled.
>
> Fabulous were Krishna's childhood days.
> There are so many tales of his naughty ways!

On the potter:

> Behold the splendour of my pots of clay!
> Like a bed of flowers on a sunny day,
> Which freshen your heart and brighten your way.
> Useful for storing water or milk or whey.
> By tapping on it like this you can play
> Any old rhythm, either sad or gay.
> Behold the splendour of my pots of clay!

And, in the end there is the voice of the *banjara* from '*Banjara Nama*' who says:

> Why do you wander restlessly, why this envy and greed?
> Death will follow wherever you go, a truth you better heed!
> All your wealth and possessions, your cattle of every breed

Those heaps of rice and lentils, every grain and every seed
As you pack your bag to leave there's nothing you will need.[22]

The Revolt of 1857 divided the intelligentsia into two camps: those for it and those against. Some were for Emperor Bahadur Shah Zafar (1775–1862) but against the *ghaddaar*; others vented their ire against the poet-emperor too. Interestingly, the poets of 1857 and the years immediately thereafter not only contradicted each other, often they contradicted themselves too; against the British before and during the siege of Delhi, they turned into fervent admirers of British rule in Hindustan after witnessing the brutality of British vengeance. Many poets referred to the mutineers as *kale* (both in contrast to the *gore* and also as black-hearted scoundrels and lumpens). A collection of 40 poems called *Fughan-e-Dehli* (The Lament of Delhi) presented a graphic picture of the havoc and destruction wrought by the uncouth mutineers from Meerut upon the city that had come to define grace and elegance. Commenting on the different responses to 1857, Gopichand Narang cites the poets' proximity to power and privilege.[23] While admitting that every poet cannot be expected to have the same response to an event or situation, he believes some chose to stay silent on the political implications of the events and contented themselves with lamenting their loss in purely cultural terms, while others saw the political implications of the changing power equation. Some others interpreted the political upheaval in the light of religion. Fazl-i-Haq Khairabadi (1797–1861), in his Arabic text referred to as *Risalah-i-Ghadariya* or *Fitnat-al-Hindiya*, puts the blame squarely on the proselytizing zeal of the Christian British whose sole objective was to turn the populace into 'infidels'.[24]

Where some Muslim intellectuals refused to take sides—with the British or against them and/or with the evanescent Mughal rule or against it—preferring instead to chronicle the end of an age and a way of life, some like Mufti Sadruddin Khan Azurdah (d. 1868), a poet, scholar, and

---

[22] Extracts culled from Akbarabadi, *Rooh-e-Nazir*. Translations mine.

[23] Gopichand Narang, '*Tehreek-e-Azadi aur Urdu Shairi*' (The Movement for Independence and Urdu Poetry), in Vidya Sagar Anand (ed.), *Jang-e-Azadi ke Awwalin Mujahideen aur Bahadur Shah Zafar* (New Delhi: Modern Publishing House, 2007).

[24] Translated by S. Moinul Haq as 'The Story of the War of Independence', *Journal of the Pakistan Historical Society*, vol. 5 (1957), pp. 23–57.

magistrate, in an elegy also called *Fughan-e-Dehli*, directly attacked the people of the Quila and held them responsible for the calamity:[25]

> Calamity befell this city because of the Fort
> Their misdeeds have brought sorrow to Delhi
> The coming of the blacks from Meerut has brought ruin.[26]

In contrast, a staunch 'royalist' Dagh (1831–1905) wrote:

> Calamity has seized the populace, misfortune befallen the city
> The coming of the Purabiyas has spelt God's doom for the city.

Azurdah went on to catalogue the woes of Delhi after the kale were defeated by the gore: the massacre of innocents, men pulled out of their homes on the flimsiest of pretexts (often their being Muslim being reason enough), but his real concern was with people like himself, the aristocracy of Delhi. He mourned the loss of his friends, in particular Imam Bakhsh Sahbai (1802–1857),[27] the teacher, poet, and scholar, the leading light of the 'Dilli Callege' (Delhi College), who was shot dead by the British troops. Azurdah wrote:

> Why shouldn't Azurdah go crazy and run to the wilderness
> When Sahbai is killed so brutally, though he was guiltless.

Different Urdu poets of this period interpreted the notion of 'guilt' differently. One set accused the Indians of being guilty, '*Ujaada tum ne khud gulzar apna baaghbaan ho kar*' ('You have destroyed your garden despite being the gardener'), whereas others such as Maulvi Fazl-i-Haq Khairabadi

---

[25] See Swapna Liddle, 'Azurda: Scholar, Poet, and Judge', in Margrit Pernau (ed.), *The Delhi College: Traditional Elites, the Colonial State, and Education before 1857* (New Delhi: Oxford University Press, 2006), pp. 125–44.

[26] Where not specified the translations are mine. The originals of the verses for this section—those dealing with the poetry of 1857—have been taken from *Azadi ki Nazmein* by Sibte Hasan and *Urdu mein Qaumi Shairi ke Sau Saal* by Abdur Razzaq Qureshi, the latter being an out-of-print book found in the Rare Books collection of the Z.H. Library at Jamia Millia Islamia, New Delhi.

[27] He lies buried under the steps of the mosque in the former Delhi College. For details of this remarkable teacher-poet, see C.M. Naim, 'Shaikh Imam Bakhsh Sahba'i: Teacher, Scholar, Poet, and Puzzle-master', in Margrit Pernau (ed.), *The Delhi College: Traditional Elites, the Colonial State, and Education before 1857* (New Delhi: Oxford University Press, 2006), pp. 145–87.

and Munir Shikohabadi (1814–1880) held the British guilty of unleashing terror upon the hapless Muslims. Writing in his island prison, an unrepentant Fazl-i-Haq declared

> I did not commit any crime except this
> I did not like them [the British], nor was I friendly with them.

Munir Shikohabadi, a poet who was actively involved in the Uprising, was employed by the Nawab of Banda. Like Fazl-i-Haq, he too was arrested and sent to the Andamans, where he wrote prolifically during his imprisonment. Shikohabadi saw himself as a follower of the legacy of Shah Waliullah[28] and exhorted the Muslims to rise in a holy war against the British.

A similar sentiment was echoed in a quatrain written on the occasion of Id-uz-Zuha (which fell on 2 August 1857 on that fateful year) by the poet-emperor Bahadur Shah Zafar (1775–1862) himself:

> O Allah, May the enemy troops be all killed
> May the Gurkhas, Whites, Gujars and Englishmen be all killed
> We shall recognize this day as the Festival of Sacrifice only when
> O Zafar, your murderer is put to the sword today!

In one verse Zafar even urged the rebellious soldiers to ply their swords against the British, and 'reach London' if necessary![29] Depressed by the state of his desolate Delhi and the state he himself had been reduced to, he held the *hakim-e-waqt* (the ruler of the time) responsible:

---

[28] Shah Waliullah Dehelvi (1703–1762) was a reformer who wished to bring Muslims under 'a banner of truth' and rid Indian Islam of the imperfections and impurities it had collected due to centuries of contact with non-Muslims and the Shias. A former student and teacher at the Madrasa Rahimiyya in Delhi, he wrote prodigiously in Persian and Arabic bemoaning the 'decline' of Muslim glory and outlining ways in which the Indian Muslims could reclaim that pristine glory. In 1759 he sought the help of the Afghan invader Ahmad Shah Abdali to 'rescue India for Islam'.

[29] See Aslam Parvez, 'Bahadur Shah Zafar aur Atthara Sau Sattavan' (Bahadur Shah Zafar and 1857), in Vidya Sagar Anand (ed.), *Jang-e-Azadi ke Awwalin Mujahideen aur Bahadur Shah Zafar* (New Delhi: Modern Publishing House, 2007), p. 164. Aslam Parvez credits Zafar not so much with bravado as with pragmatism for encouraging the rebels; if the rebels failed, Zafar and his throne would be the first casualty.

Has anyone heard of such cruelty
That the innocent should be hanged?
From the rows of the devout arise
Clouds from discontented hearts.[30]

On 20 September 1857, Delhi fell. British soldiers entered the Jama Masjid, desecrated it and set about unleashing the most terrible atrocities.[31] In one week, 25,000 people were killed, the rebels and their sympathizers summarily executed, and 160,000 inhabitants driven out of the city limits and forced to camp in the open countryside. Qazi Fazal Husain Afsurdah held the soldiers and spies guilty for the madness that had spiralled out of control and caught both the 'guilty' and the 'innocent':

Calamity came with the coming of the soldiers
The spies added fire to the fury
Both the guilty and the innocent were arrested.

Several felt that Muslims were singled out for the reprisals. Shah Ayatollah Johri rued the desecration of mosques and holy places, claiming that the Brahmins prospered while the Muslims suffered, and the masjids remained desolate while in the temples the conches could be heard:

The House of God lies in darkness whereas the lamps are lit in the temples
The traditions of the infidels thrive whereas the light of faith flickers.

The mystically inclined Syed Ali Tashnah, a much-loved poet of Delhi, blamed the outsiders who robbed and pillaged:

The Tilangas came and looted the entire city
As the saying goes, the naked came to rob the hungry.

Several poets, such as Zaheer Dehlvi, Hakim Agha Jaan Aish, Nawab Mirza Dagh, Qurban Ali Beg Saalik, Mohsin, and Kaukab, spoke of the weeping, homeless men and women, carrying bundles of precious belongings on their heads, who fled Delhi only to be robbed or murdered on the way. Some spoke of unemployment and acute poverty. Dagh wrote 'the only job left for Muslim men is to fill up the prisons'. Bemoaning 'the slaughter of an age' (*ek jahan qatl hua*), Zaheer Dehlvi commented:

---

[30] The originals of these verses are from *Azadi ki Nazmein* by Sibte Hasan and *Urdu mein Qaumi Shairi ke Sau Saal* by Abdur Razzaq Qureshi.

[31] For details of the atrocities, see R.C. Majumdar, *The Sepoy Mutiny and Revolt of 1857* (Calcutta: Firma K.L. Mukhopadhyay, 1957).

People have been pulled out of their homes
Corpses line the road, layers upon layers
Neither grave, nor shroud, nor mourners are left.

Many of these poets belonged to the privileged classes who were the worst hit. So there was an element of personal sorrow and loss mingled with the general lament and mourning. Occasionally, there was also an attempt to shift the 'blame' for the terrors and afflictions on those who opposed the British. Mirza Asadullah Khan Ghalib (1797–1869), the pre-eminent Urdu poet, who stayed all through the siege and fall of Delhi (a bit like the boy on the burning deck who stood 'whilst all but he had fled'), wrote:

Now every English soldier that bears arms
Is sovereign, and free to work his will.

Men dare not venture out into the street
And terror chills their heart within them still.

Their homes enclose them as in prison walls
And in the Chauk the victors hang and kill.

The city is athirst for Muslim blood
And every grain of dust must drink its fill....[32]

A self-confessed *namak-khwar-e-sarkar-e-angrez* (an eater of the salt of the British government on account of his pension, incidentally stopped after 1857 but re-instated in 1860), Ghalib tried to be diplomatic in his Persian Diary called '*Dastambu*'[33] meaning a 'Posy of Flowers'—an incongruous name for a document so grim. He called the rebellious soldiers from Meerut 'faithless to the salt' and 'black-hearted killers'. He termed the revolt 'unwarranted' and expressed joy when Delhi was 'divested of its madmen and conquered by the brave and wise'. But his joy was short-lived, as his letters[34] prove, 'We live in anxious thought for bread and water,

---

[32] Ralph Russell and Khurshidul Islam (trans and eds), *Ghalib: Life and Letters* (New Delhi: Oxford University Press, 1994), p. 149.

[33] All references to '*Dastambu*' taken from the translation by Khwaja Ahmad Faruqi (Delhi: Allied Publishers, 1954).

[34] Taken together Ghalib's letters (written before, during, and after the Revolt) provide an illuminating account of life in the city of Delhi. For a detailed study of these letters, see Aslam Jamshedpuri, '1857 *aur Ghalib ke Khutoot*' (1857 and Ghalib's Letter), in Vidya Sagar Anand (ed.), *Jang-e-Azadi ke Awwalin Mujahideen aur Bahadur Shah Zafar* (New Delhi: Modern Publishing House, 2007).

and die in anxious thought for shroud and grave.' As Delhi turned into a city without a ruler, a garden without a gardener, he wrote, 'By God, you may search for a Muslim in this city and not find one—rich, poor, and artisans alike are gone.' He recorded how Hindus were allowed to return by January 1858 'but on the walls of the homeless Muslim homes the grass grows green, and its tongues whisper every moment that the places of the Muslims are desolate.'

'*Dastambu*' found an unexpected champion in Marxist historian K.M. Ashraf who considered it an important document. While conceding that the book was 'vague' and 'impersonal' in its narration of events and that the author 'took care to see that his diary was not used against him', Ashraf claimed, '… precisely because he has chosen to omit the dramatic incidents and the role of some individuals, Ghalib has unwittingly succeeded in imparting to us, even in this fragment, some of the dynamism of this great movement of national resistance and a glimpse of the new social forces that were involved.'[35]

Apart from '*Dastambu*', several verses too bear testimony to these trying times, albeit obliquely:

> If Ghalib sings in a bitter strain, forgive him;
> Today pain stabs more keenly at his heart

And:

> We kept writing the blood drenched narratives of that madness
> Although our hands were chopped off in the process.

Ghalib's hands were not chopped off. He lived another 12 years after the Revolt and witnessed the confusion and disarray that followed the loss of power and patronage. The Hindus were permitted to return to Delhi in June 1858 and the Muslims in August 1859, almost two years after the Uprising. But the Delhi they returned to was a transformed city. The British had razed to the ground palaces, mosques, parks, libraries, marketplaces, and residential areas to construct a cantonment and clear the way for easy deployment of troops, should the need arise. Many of the monuments that Syed Ahmad Khan had recorded in *Asar us Sanadid*[36] (The

---

[35] K.M. Ashraf, 'Ghalib and the Revolt of 1857', in P.C. Joshi (ed.), *Rebellion 1857* (New Delhi: PPH, 1957), pp. 247–8.

[36] In its first edition, the 600 pages of text were illustrated with over a 100 lithographic illustrations. It listed not just the monuments that lay scattered

Remains of the Past), first published in 1847, were gone. Every tongue that spoke, no matter how timorously, was muffled. Irrespective of the extent of damage or change, the events of 1857 were a clarion call for *all* Muslims. It was time to wake up. Some chose to heed that call; others preferred to pull the blanket of heedlessness more firmly over their ears and hide from the changing world.

With time, two groups of Muslims emerged, who soon established themselves as two opposing camps. One camp made no effort to camouflage their hostility to the British, choosing to do one of two things: either establish cloistered citadels of traditional learning based on religion, or live in the hope that one day their lost glory would be miraculously restored. The other group—and here it must be said that this lot had suffered a mere clipping of wings and not the devastation that one section of Muslims had indeed experienced—took the diametrically opposite view. Believing that the old Muslim elite could never recapture their lost ground, they felt the best they could do, under these irrevocably changed circumstances, was to build bridges between the Muslims and the British and hitch their star to the wagon of Western learning which would, in turn, open the doors to employment in

---

across the many 'Delhis', but also described the city's fairs, festivals, and included a lengthy account of the city's vibrant cultural life. Compiled at real physical risk to life and limb (for its compilation required the venerable Syed to undergo some dexterous footwork), the four-volume work can be regarded as a lasting monument not only to the author's industry, but also to his sense of culture and history and his realization, well ahead of his times, of the need to record and preserve the monuments of Delhi and their inscriptions. The first edition also contained a large section on the sufis, men of learning, and poets and artists of contemporary Delhi. Divided under 10 headings, it also included a listing of 118 eminent citizens of Delhi. Its French translation by Garcin de Tassy was brought out in 1861. Its second edition in 1854 deleted the cultural references and retained only the descriptions of the historical monuments, translations of the epitaphs and plaques, as well as measurements and architectural details of the actual buildings. Scholars such as David Lelyveld and Shamsur Rahman Faruqi have remarked upon this curious deletion from the second edition and attributed it to Syed Ahmad's pragmatic reassessment of the significance of 'culture' in the life of Indian Muslims. It is noteworthy that Syed Ahmad undertook this 'reassessment' well before the Uprising. C.M. Naim, 'Syed Ahmad and His Two Books called "Asar-al-Sanadid"', *Modern Asian Studies*, vol. 45, no. 3 (2011), pp. 669–708 views the two versions as two separate books.

the government. Ghalib, Syed Ahmad Khan, Hali, and Maulvi Zakaullah belonged to this latter group, with Zakaullah, the most idealistic of them all, writing an ode called *Victoria Namah*, which was not merely a paean to the distant British monarch, but a crystallization of all the hopes of a certain section of the Muslim community for 'a rule of peace and settlement such as India had not known since the days of Akbar the Great'.[37]

The British had already introduced Macaulay's scheme of 'modern' education in India in 1835 and several missionary schools were active in different parts of the country imparting an English-medium education. Where the Hindus seized the advantages offered by these new schools, the Muslims by and large preferred the madrasa system for school-level education. The year of the Great Revolt was also, ironically, the year of the establishment of three universities in the three presidencies, namely, Bombay, Calcutta, and Madras. In the next section, we will note the role played by newer institutions of higher learning, most notably the Delhi College, in ushering in at long last an interest in science and technology. We will note, also, how the lack of a 'Protestant'[38] spirit in Islam, an absence of enquiry, and a sense of complacency stemming from unquestioning affirmation of the superiority of Islam were among the contributing factors that caused such disarray among the Muslims and brought the short-lived 'Delhi Renaissance' to an abrupt end. The next section shall reveal how, by the end of the nineteenth century, the *sahiban-i-qalam* (men of pen) came to replace, at least partly, the *sahiban-i-saif* (men of sword) as worthy role models for the Muslim *shurfa*.[39]

So far, we have seen how the events of 1857 were viewed, interpreted, and constructed by those who had either lived through the cataclysmic period or were directly affected by it. It might be useful to get a glimpse

---

[37] Andrews, *Zakaullah of Delhi*, p. 78.

[38] Term coined by Naim in 'Ghalib's Delhi: A Shamelessly Revisionist Look at two Popular Metaphors', in *Urdu Texts and Contexts: Selected Essays* (Delhi: Permanent Black, 2004), pp. 250–73, esp. p. 264.

[39] Naim goes on to state how the men of sword were eclipsed by the Pax Britannica, while the men of pen too suffered due to the loss of employment with the greater use of English; see Naim, ibid., p. 271. I would, however, argue that if the writings of men like Nazir Ahmad, Hali, and Zakaullah are any indices, the sahiban-i-qalam did not lose out entirely; while indeed a minority, they did exercise sufficient influence on the Muslim community as we shall see in the rise and growth of the Aligarh school.

of how latter-day writers, poets, and critics viewed 1857. Claiming he still carries the imprint of those events more than a 100 years later, a modern poet such as Nazeer Banarasi (1911–1995) wrote

> The effect lingers in our heart still
> Though you are gone, your bier carried away
> It has been a hundred years since you were martyred
> Your blood is fresh and red still.[40]

P.C. Joshi, general secretary of the CPI, while editing a volume in the centenary year termed the revolt 'one of the unresolved controversies of Indian history'.[41] In the same volume, K.M. Ashraf theorized that the 'revivalist trend' exemplified by the Wahabis, was the major contributing factor behind the uprising since 'the Wahabis were the only people who came not only armed with a consistent anti-British ideology but also the backing of a network of organized centres spread all over northern India, with contacts in the south and moral influence on the Muslim intelligentsia throughout the country'.[42] Fellow Marxist Ehtesham Husain regretted that the subjective interpretation of historical events (in most cases the events of 1857 were treated as the scourge of God or a result of Muslim misdeeds) diverted attention from the extent and nature of real events. Viewed as a revolt against 'established authority', it took far too long for people to 'link the traditions of the revolt with the national movement'. 'The national spirit,' Husain asserted, 'shrouded in the religious mode of thinking can be discerned if one analyses the literature of the post-1857 period. For a clearer expression of this, however, one shall have to reach for writings of the twentieth century.'[43]

By far, the most authoritative study of the post-1857 Urdu literature has been conducted by Gopichand Narang who has viewed 1857 as a significant milestone in the evolution of *wataniyat* (nationalism) in Urdu poetry.[44] While animosity for the British was becoming increasingly evident in Urdu poetry well before 1857, the *ghadar* was a watershed insofar as hatred for a tyrannical foreign rule coalesced with

---

[40] Nazeer Banarasi, *Ghulami se Azaadi Tak: Qaumi Nazmon ka Majmua* (Lucknow: Uttar Pradesh Soochna Vibhag, 1972), p. 27.
[41] P.C. Joshi (ed.), *Rebellion 1857* (New Delhi: PPH, 1957), p. vii.
[42] Ibid., p. 71.
[43] Ibid., p. 242.
[44] See, for instance, Narang, *'Tehreek-e-Azadi aur Urdu Shairi'*.

mounting frustration at one's helplessness to create an atmosphere of fear and helplessness. Narang cites literary commentaries, various compilations of shehr ashob, volumes such as *Fughan-e-Dehli*, texts and commentaries by Maulvi Zakaullah and Zaheer Dehlvi that paint a picture of defeat and despair when people lived *bejaan* (lifeless) and *berooh* (spiritless) lives. It was only with the dawn of a new century, according to Narang, that *hubb-e-watan* (love for the nation) as we understand it today, was born.[45]

Muslim Responses to 1857

Just as there was no uniform, un-variegated, or one-dimensional reflection in contemporary Urdu literature of what would later be dubbed the First War of Independence, there was no generalized or undifferentiated response to the Revolt of 1857 among the Muslim intelligentsia of the late nineteenth century. The literature of those years reflects a bewildering and often contradictory array of opinions. The Muslim responses are equally, if not more, bewildering and contradictory. Reactions vary from nostalgic lament for a lost age to attaching blame and apportioning responsibility for the terrible misfortunes that had befallen all those who had actively participated in it, and the Muslims who felt they had been singled out for the terrible retribution that came close on the heels of the British victory. In the literature of this period, heroes become villains and vice versa: the mutineering soldiers referred to as *mujahid* (martyrs, or those who bear witness) by some become *balwai* (rioters) for others. So also the Firangi and the Mughals, both of whom invited varying degrees of criticism and approbation.[46]

Two worlds—the decaying and the emergent—fused and merged. Pathos, confusion, and conflict reigned supreme. 'Delhi and Lucknow, the two great centres of Muslim culture in Upper India, the London and the Paris of their milieu, were, in large part, deserted.'[47] Citing 'collective

---

[45] Narang, '*Tehreek-e-Azadi aur Urdu Shairi*', p. 310.

[46] *Azadi ki Nazmein* by Sibte Hasan and *Urdu mein Qaumi Shairi ke Sau Saal* by Abdur Razzaq Qureshi referred to in the previous section, provide ample examples of these fluctuating responses. Some of them have been quoted earlier.

[47] Francis Robinson, 'The Muslims of Upper India and the Shock of the Mutiny', in Mushirul Hasan and Narayani Gupta (eds), *India's Colonial Encounter: Essays in Memory of Eric Stokes* (New Delhi: Manohar, 2004), p. 255.

amnesia' and a fear of 'further British retribution', Francis Robinson called the 1857 revolt a

> watershed in the development of ideas and attitudes of the Muslims of Upper India in the nineteenth century. Before the great upheaval they did not appear to take seriously into account either the challenge of Western civilization or the meaning of British power. After it, they were increasingly concerned to discover how best they could be Muslim under the new dispensation, whether it meant building ideological and institutional bridges between Islam and the West, or developing systems which could enable them largely to ignore Western civilization and the colonial state, or making a point of defending Islam wherever it was threatened in India and the world.[48]

It would take several decades for the clouds of uncertainty to part and the debate on the Old Light versus the New to usher in the Lamp of New Learning. But for that to happen, Delhi—the focus of the 'Dilli Chalo' movement, the worst victim of its worst excesses and also the *markaz* or centre of the finest Urdu writing of its time—had to first rise, phoenix-like, from the ashes of its siege and slaughter.

The Anglo-Arabic Madrasa,[49] or the Delhi College as it came to be called from 1825 onwards, played a crucial role in the re-invention of the city and

---

[48] Ibid.

[49] Both literally and figuratively, the school that stood on this historic site successively built upon the foundations of the traditional madrasa constructed by Ghaziuddin Khan. It began by teaching Arabic and Persian apart from religious discourses and Quranic instruction as madrasas usually did; however, with the introduction of English in 1825, the school was divided into two: the Oriental and the English sections. The Oriental section benefited from an endowment by Nawab Eitmadud-Daula of Lucknow in 1829. In 1843 the Delhi Vernacular Translation Society began to share its premises. From 1857 till 1889 the College was closed down and the building occupied by the police. The Anglo-Arabic School functioned here till the terrible tides of Partition swept across Delhi once again. The military took over the premises in 1947 and in 1949 a portion of the school was given to the refugees who thronged Delhi. At the suggestion of Zakir Husain and Maulana Abul Kalam Azad, a school was started here once again, first called Anglo-Arabic Higher Secondary School and shortly re-christened Delhi College. In 1974 it was renamed Zakir Husain College. A few years ago the Zakir Husain College (affiliated to the University of Delhi) moved to a new building. What remains now is a shell of a building with a grand past but an uncertain future. It is

the appropriation of its intellectual spaces by a new breed of writers and thinkers. Founded in the early eighteenth century by the father of the first nizam of Hyderabad, Ghaziuddin Khan, and known by different names at different times in its history, this madrasa witnessed the earliest linguistic and cultural encounter between English and the languages of the Orient. Never an ordinary school, this was the crucible in which one of the most volatile of experiments was conducted. The best and brightest flocked here to be reckoned amongst equals. The lamp of *Nai Taleem* (New Education) burnt the brightest here, and it was here that the Delhi Renaissance kindled the nation-wide debate on the merits of oriental scholarship versus Western learning. The finest minds taught here setting forth an example of a space where the East and the West could indeed meet. Aloys Sprenger (1813–1893), Master Ram Chander (1821–1880), and Maulvi Zakaullah (1832–1910) were among its leading lights.[50] Its alumni included the who's who of contemporary intellectuals—Nazir Ahmad (1836–1912), the first major Urdu novelist; Mohan Lal Kashmiri (1812–1877), the intrepid traveller and chronicler of the First Anglo-Afghan War; Muhammad Husain Azad (1830–1910), author of *Aab-e-Hayaat* (The Water of Life) and one of the foremost literary critics; amongst scores of others.

C.F. Andrews (1871–1940), the British missionary who worked closely with Gandhi and Tagore, saw the Delhi College as both the cause and the symbol of the Delhi Renaissance. Unlike the renaissance movement lead by Raja Rammohun Roy in Bengal, the Delhi Renaissance or 'efflorescence of modern learning', according to Andrews, was short-lived and 'decay immediately overtook the revival of learning in Delhi, from which it never recovered'.[51] While the renaissance lasted, both staff and students

---

called the Anglo-Arabic Higher Secondary School. The road in front is named the Shraddhanand Marg. The school is presently administered by a trust managed by the Jamia Millia Islamia.

[50] This section on the Delhi College has been obtained from various sources: Margrit Pernau, 'Preparing a Meeting Ground: C.F. Andrews, St Stephens, and the Delhi College', in C.F. Andrews, *Zakaullah of Delhi* (New Delhi: Oxford University Press, 2003); Pernau, *The Delhi College*; Hasan, *A Moral Reckoning*; Barbara Metcalf, *Islamic Revival in British India: Deoband 1860–1900* (Princeton: Princeton University Press, 1982); and Gail Minault's 'Delhi College and Urdu', *Annual of Urdu Studies*, vol. 18 (Chicago: University of Wisconsin-Madison, 2003).

[51] Andrews, *Zakaullah of Delhi*, pp. 43–4.

of the Delhi College championed the cause of Urdu[52] and used this new language in innovative ways, especially in the emerging field of prose writing and journalism. The College played an important role in popularizing Urdu as a medium of instruction instead of Persian as well as encouraging the writing of vibrant, lively prose, making the language a 'cosmopolitan vernacular'[53] as well as a medium for energetic exchanges between oriental and Western-style curricula. During Aloys Sprenger's term as principal,[54] the College also set up a printing press. All these efforts combined to produce an efflorescence, a blossoming of mind and spirit. And Delhi College was also the laboratory where enthusiastic teachers initiated bright-eyed students into the mysteries and marvels of modern science and traditional knowledge. One can say that the seeds of Urdu journalism were sown here and a new impetus given to Urdu prose writings, especially socially engaged, politically driven, scientifically aware works that were, at the same time, stylistically sophisticated.

This spurt in writing was not confined to secular literature. As Barbara D. Metcalf notes, the new lithographic press brought 'a wealth of printed materials that took education out of the privileged relationship between master and select pupil and into a public domain where learning, even religious learning, was widely available.'[55] The reformers among the Muslim ulama, men like Muhammad Qasim Nanotwi (1832–1880) and Rashid Ahmad Gangohi (1828–1905), the founders of the Deoband movement, the learned men of Firangi Mahal in Lucknow, Siddiq Hasan Khan of

---

[52] Persian was the language of official use in the Mughal courts. Urdu, as Gail Minault notes, started by being a 'mediating language between Persian and the regional Indian languages, and between the imperial court and various regional powers'; it played a significant role in, what Minault terms, 'translating cultures'. See Gail Minault, 'Delhi College and Urdu', *Annual of Urdu Studies*, vol. 14 (1999), pp. 119–34, esp p.126.

[53] Sheldon Pollock, 'The Cosmopolitan Vernacular', *Journal of Asian Studies*, vol. 57, no. 1 (1998), pp. 6–37.

[54] For a study of Aloys Sprenger, see M. Ikram Chaghtai, 'Dr Aloys Sprenger and the Delhi College', in Margrit Pernau (ed.), *The Delhi College: Traditional Elites, the Colonial State, and Education before 1857* (New Delhi: Oxford University Press, 2006).

[55] Barbara D. Metcalf, 'Maulana Ashraf Ali Thanawi and Urdu Literature', in Christopher Shackle (ed.), *Urdu and Muslim South Asia: Studies in Honour of Ralph Russell* (New Delhi: Oxford University Press, 1989), p. 93.

the Ahl-e Hadis movement took full advantage of the changing times and emerging technologies to launch a jehad with pen and paper. This profusion of printing activity—both secular and religious—achieved two things. On the one hand, it helped in the development of serious, scholarly prose-writing in Urdu; on the other, it introduced socially relevant issues to a larger readership.

'Even if the Muslim communities did not necessarily adopt the English lifestyle, they recognized foreign rule as an unchanging fact of life',[56] writes Hasan. The reason why Delhi's Muslim elite, he goes on to say, 'retained their position, if not predominance, is because Urdu remained the official language and a necessary qualification for government employment … a specifically Indo-Muslim culture survived the deleterious effects of Muslim rule, and the inner, cultural, moral resilience of the Urdu-speaking elite, though enfeebled, was not beyond repair.'[57] While some former students, teachers, and advocates of the Delhi College who went on to play an active role in setting up the M.A.O. College at Aligarh, notably Syed Ahmad Khan (who was never a pupil though he did pattern the school at Aligarh after the Delhi College), Nazir Ahmad, and Maulvi Zakaullah, embraced Western-style education, a group of Muslim intellectuals in the late nineteenth century were troubled by this proximity to what they considered alien ideas. Any praise of 'Christian' ideas at the cost of Indian Muslims was viewed with scepticism if not outright hostility. While Maulana Nanotwi, the founder of the Deoband school, was himself not averse to modern learning, especially Western science, most *alim* still favoured the seventeenth-century curriculum of traditional madrasas known as *Dars-i-Nizamiyah* and vehemently opposed the introduction of English, whether it was at the Nadwat-ul-Ulama in Lucknow or the Dar-ul-Uloom in Deoband. With Maulana Rashid Ahmad Gangohi, who succeeded Maulana Nanotwi, the schism with Syed Ahmad Khan's 'pro-British' policy widened, and Deoband and Aligarh came to occupy two opposite ends of the intellectual spectrum of Indian Muslims. The next alim to head the Deoband seminary, Maulana Mahmud Hasan, known as Shaikh-ul Hind, was a man with a totally different outlook. His tenure, from 1905 to 1915, saw the seminary exercise an increasingly political role, which we shall examine in greater detail in the next chapter.

[56] Hasan, *Zakaullah of Delhi*, p. x.
[57] Ibid., pp. x–xi.

Here, let us turn towards the career of another remarkable man from Deoband, a scholar who represented a new breed of well-educated, well-born ulama who, while expressing concern over the sort of education being given to the Muslims, spoke of the regeneration of Islam and the need to regain the lost glory of the Muslim elite. This was the charismatic Maulana Ashraf Ali Thanawi (1863–1943) who stressed the importance of family values, upbringing, and background; for instance, he made a distinction between those who came from 'good' families in contrast to those who came from the lower classes such as weavers, tailors, etc. In his scheme of things, those who were not fortunate enough to be born into 'good' families suffered from a natural disadvantage when it came to planning the education of their children, arranging their marriages, or finding new or alternative livelihoods.[58] Thanawi also took a dim view of the new breed of writers like Nazir Ahmad whose writings, he believed, 'weakened faith'.[59] In contrast to Nazir Ahmad's novels, which we shall study in the next section, Thanawi was interested only in the requirements of Muslim women, not *all* women.[60] Thanawi's *Bihishti Zewar* (Heavenly Jewels), commonly given to brides along with their dower, provided a comprehensive compendium of everything a respectable Muslim girl should possess by way of education.[61] Thanawi proposed that *Bihishti Zewar* be read by adolescent girls immediately after they had finished reading the Holy Quran.[62] Fearful that girls would forget their proper place, ulama like Thanawi eschewed formal education for girls. 'Would you turn them into maulvis like men?' they asked. Education, for girls, was simply to make them better Muslims; if in the process they became better wives and mothers that was an added bonus. However, the very fact that here was a book specifically targeted at a female readership meant, at the very least, that women were by now

---

[58] See M. Mujeeb, *Indian Muslims* (London: Allen & Unwin, 1967), pp. 552–3.

[59] Quoted in Barbara D. Metcalf, *Perfecting Women: Maulana Ashraf Ali Thanawi's Bihishti Zewar* (Berkeley: University of California Press, 1990), pp. 379–80.

[60] C.M. Naim, 'Prize-Winning Adab', in *Urdu Texts and Contexts: Selected Essays* (Delhi: Permanent Black, 2004), p. 141.

[61] In Rashid Jahan's play, *Parde ke Peeche*, which has been examined in great detail in Chapter 3, Muhammadi Begum's 13-year-old daughter is reading *Bihishti Zewar*.

[62] Thanawi's syllabus included the Quran, rules of *fiqh*, domestic accounts, health and hygiene, and cooking. See Naim, 'Prize-Winning Adab'.

able to read and write.⁶³ From here, it was still several steps away to more literature *for* women *by* women.

In the preceding section we have discussed the social consciousness increasingly evident in Urdu literature in the post-1857 scenario and how this greater awareness of the lacunae in contemporary society began to be not just felt but more coherently articulated by Muslim writers. Talking of social consciousness, one is equally struck not by the complete absence of, but the much *less* reliance on, religion per se or religious texts in the construction of contemporary social realities. Scholars such as Hasan have argued that the widespread notion that the Muslim response to 1857 was all of a type and that it was uniformly 'revivalist' or 'fundamentalist' was essentially part of the colonial stereotype. It suited the purpose of the imperialist government to perpetuate the myth of Muslims being so steeped in their religion that anything Western or modern was anathema to them.⁶⁴ Whereas a close reading of their texts reveals that men like Syed Ahmad Khan, Ghalib, Nazir Ahmad, Zakaullah, and Hali visualized a world not in terms of Islam, but within the framework of a colonized world where one's claims for survival and prosperity would be buttressed by one's ability to come to terms with Western enlightenment, all the while holding on to the staff of one's own deep-rooted faith. Though no great admirer of oriental scholarship, Syed Ahmad Khan made a vigorous study of Islamic theology and history; 'his primary motive', however, was not so much scholarly research as a reformulation of 'the ideas and practices of Muslims so that they might become full participants in the power and prosperity of the British empire.'⁶⁵

In his epic poem *Musaddas: Madd-o-Jazr-e Islam* (The Ebb and Flow of Islam), Altaf Husain Hali (1837–1914), inspired largely by the reformist ideals of his mentor Syed Ahmad Khan, wrote

---

⁶³ Barbara D. Metcalf points out the inherent irony of a book such as *Bihishti Zewar*: if a girl could read such a book, she could just as well read any other book and thus run the risk of 'serious corruption'. Knowledge, therefore, was a mixed blessing and discretion was as important as the dissemination of knowledge. See Metcalf, 'Maulana Ashraf Ali Thanavi and Urdu Literature', p. 95.

⁶⁴ Mushirul Hasan, 'Resistance and Acquiescence in North India: Muslim Response to the West', in Mushirul Hasan and Narayani Gupta (eds), *India's Colonial Encounter: Essays in Memory of Eric Stokes* (New Delhi: Manohar, 1993), pp. 75–93.

⁶⁵ David Lelyveld, *Aligarh's First Generation: Muslim Solidarity in British India* (Princeton: Princeton University Press, 1978), p. 240.

> No one wishes your religion and faith ill
> No one is hostile to the Traditions and the Quran
> No one damages the pillars of the community
> No one forbids observance of the Holy Laws' commands
> Pray without fear in your places of worship
> Loudly proclaim the calls to prayer in your mosques.[66]

This sort of optimistic Muslim response involved, unlike the revivalist Waliullahi tradition, not the rejection of colonial rule, but its acceptance so that these men arrived at a seemingly 'subservient' position not because they were unquestioning admirers of British rule, but because of their deep engagement with colonial rule and its manifestations. Men like Hali, Zakaullah, and Nazir Ahmad—who had served the British government in one capacity or another—saw colonialism as a necessary evil for it would, they believed most sincerely, pave the way for social re-engineering and open up prospects of growth and prosperity for *all* Indians, in which the Muslims too would partake. On the same page of the *Musaddas*, virtually in the same breath, Hali goes on to say:

> The routes of travel and commerce are open
> Nor are those of industry and craft closed.
> Just as the routes of the acquisition of learning are lit
> So too are those the acquisition of wealth made level.[67]

Hali (his nom de plume originating from the word 'haal' meaning contemporary, or a man of the present) saw the world as one in a constant state of flux. The binaries of rise and fall, progress and decline, development and decay—perennial preoccupations for Hali—caused a yoyo-like tendency in many poets of the late nineteenth century. Like Hali, they vacillated between optimism and despondency. It made them, therefore, sometimes reactionary, sometimes progressive. Making explicit the hortatory character of his poem, Hali wrote in the Introduction to his *Musaddas*: 'This poem has not ... been composed in order to be enjoyed or with the aim of eliciting applause, but in order to make my friends and fellows feel a sense of outrage and shame.'[68]

---

[66] Christopher Shackle and Javed Majeed (eds), *Hali's Musaddas: The Ebb and Flow of Islam* (New Delhi: Oxford University Press, 1997), p. 203.

[67] Ibid.

[68] Ibid., p. 49.

While it can be stated that the Muslim literati—both traditional and modern—were keen to reappraise existing attitudes towards colonial modernity, the results of this reappraisal varied. This introspection produced two sets of reactions: one, a morose dwelling on the largely imaginary glories of the past coupled with scepticism of all things modern; and the other, a need to break away from the decaying feudal culture. Incidentally, Hali in his momentous *Muqadama-e-Sher-o-Shairi* (The Preface to Poetry and Poetics, 1893), also made a distinction between what would soon emerge as the Delhi school of poetry and the Lucknow school. The former, considered superior by Hali, was marked by greater 'realism', 'genuineness of feeling', and 'felicity' of expression while the latter was 'decadent', 'shallow', and 'obsessed with physical-erotic themes'.[69]

Hali's immediate predecessor was Ghalib. His response(s) to the events of 1857, as we have seen earlier, too were contradictory since he was dependent on the pension he received from the British. There is, of course, the blood chilling ghazal he wrote immediately after the Revolt (referred to in the first section of this chapter). Then there are the three couplets he wrote in 1862 said to have been written in response to the Nawab of Farrukhabad who was picked up by the British for aiding the rebels and abandoned on an island off the shore of Arabia. These reflect the hopelessness and escapism that afflicted many Muslims of his generation:

> Let us go and live somewhere where there is no one
> No one who speaks to me in my language, no one to talk to.
>
> I will make something that is like a house
> [But] There won't be any neighbours, nor anyone to guard it.
>
> Were I to fall ill, there will be no one to tend me
> And when I die, no one to mourn me.[70]

It must be stressed that these were not ordinary poets or writers who performed merely in the mini darbars of the rajas and talukdars; they were widely read and copies of their books were sometimes sold out within weeks or months of publications. They were also, for this reason, extremely influential in not just determining literary tastes, but in guiding literary trends.

---

[69] S.R. Faruqi, *Early Urdu Literary Culture and History* (New Delhi: Oxford University Press, 2001), p. 184.

[70] Where not specified, the translations from Urdu here, as elsewhere throughout this book, are mine.

Many of them were also intellectually connected with different organizations as their representatives. Maulvi Nazir Ahmad and Zakaullah were, for instance, close friends of Syed Ahmad Khan and took an active part in his college affairs. Their contributions to Syed Ahmad Khan's journal, *Tehzeeb-ul Akhlaq*, moulded not merely literary tastes but had a profound influence on guiding an entire generation's political sensibility. Launched in 1870, Syed Ahmad Khan described the journal's raison d'etre thus in its inaugural issue, 'The purpose of this journal is to make available to the Indian Muslims the finest that civilization has to offer, so that the disdain with which the civilized communities look upon them may disappear and the Indian Muslims too may count themselves among the civilized peoples of the world.'[71]

While we may quibble over Syed Ahmad's definition of 'civilization' (he uses the English word and gives its meaning as *tehzeeb* and *muhazzab* for being civilized) as indeed his earnest desire to be counted among the so-called civilized people, there is no denying that the Urdu world of letters was, at that crucial point in its history, in sore need of a platform that could take on a broad range of socio-political as well as literary and cultural issues. While the journal (as well as much of Syed Ahmad Khan's other writings and public positions) drew scorn[72] and admiration in equal measure, later-day Urdu critics are unanimous in viewing both the Aligarh school and its organ as influential, if not path-breaking. If Ibadat Barelwi believes 'It [*Tehzeeb-ul Akhlaq*] not only produced a new political awareness among Muslims but also created a turbulence in their mind',[73] Hamid Hasan Qadiri affirms the singular service rendered by the journal to 'religion and the community as well as language and literature'.[74] Ale Ahmad Suroor credits not one or two things associated with the Aligarh school, but the entire Aligarh movement for bringing about radical changes in Urdu literature:

Sir Syed's movement not merely brought to the fore the importance of minority rights, realism, and the needs of society, it also created a new literary language and left a formidable legacy of prose writings. A new 'westernism' (*mashriqiyat*) was

[71] Quoted in Hamid Hasan Qadiri, *Dastan-e-Tareekh-e-Urdu* (Agra: Agra Akhbar Press, 1957), pp. 294–5.

[72] Among Syed Ahmad Khan's bitterest critic was Maulvi Ali Bakhsh Khan, sub-ordinate judge at Gorakhpur, who even went and brought fatwas against the Syed from Mecca and Medina.

[73] Barelwi, *Urdu Tanquid Nigari*, p. 156.

[74] Qadiri, *Dastan-e-Tareekh-e-Urdu*, p. 294.

born as a result of Sir Syed's movement. While this new 'westernism' was quite emotional, it was indebted to the east.[75]

Aziz Ahmad goes a step further and credits Syed Ahmad Khan's entire 'educational programme' as having far-reaching influences that would 'change the intellectual, political and economic destiny of Muslim India'.[76] However, this is not to imply that movements towards the modernization of Muslims were not taking place in other parts of the country; if anything, the Aligarh movement was 'typical' of the modernist movement among Muslims that was unfurling in different forms in different parts of India, be it the Punjab, Hyderabad, or Bombay.[77]

Clearly, the writers of the Aligarh school—and others who were influenced by them—left behind a rich and vibrant intellectual legacy that was appropriated by different people in the early part of the twentieth century. Different people made different 'uses' of this legacy—in this chapter and the next we shall see how the visionary poet Mohammad Iqbal built upon this liberalism and eclecticism; in subsequent chapters we shall see how Syed Ahmad Khan and the Aligarh movement prepared the ground for another movement—the PWM—which, though not as powerful or as large, was nevertheless a significant milestone in the literary history of the Urdu-speaking people. Moreover, as we shall see, it owed a great deal to the reformist trend initiated by the grand old men of Aligarh.

New Literary Trends: 1857–1920s

In this section, we shall seek to evaluate the emergence of new literary trends and new genres of writing in the post-1857 period. We shall also seek to emphasize how the new social and political concerns outlined above manifested themselves in new styles of writing. All of this is directly linked with the emergence of progressive writers in the mid-1930s and their

[75] Ale Ahmad Suroor, 'Urdu Tanquid ke Buniyadi Afkar' (The Basic Thoughts of Urdu Criticism), in *Tanquid ke Buniyadi Masail* (Aligarh: Aligarh Muslim University Press, 1968), p. 21.

[76] Aziz Ahmad, *Islamic Modernism in India and Pakistan, 1857–1964* (London: Oxford University Press, 1967), p. 36.

[77] Yusuf Ali, 'Muslim Culture and Religious Thought', in Mushirul Hasan (ed.), *Islam in South Asia*, vol. II, *Encountering the West: Before and After 1857* (New Delhi: Manohar, 2008), p. 153.

appropriation of a certain style that would, in later years, become their hallmark. Tracing the break from the Urdu literature of the classical period, we will see how the arrival of prose stylists like Muhammad Husain Azad (1830–1910) paved the way for a simple, straightforward style of writing and how the didactic novels of Nazir Ahmad (1836–1912) formed a bridge between the old masters and the revivalists. The emergence of writers such as Premchand (1880–1936) also opened the door for social realism that was to become the cornerstone of all progressive thought and writing. In fact, Premchand's first collection of short stories, *Soz-e-Watan* (1908), was found to be so incendiary and seditious that not only was it banned by the imperial government, but all its copies were also burnt. Undaunted, Premchand kept writing stories that expressed the pain and suffering of the toiling masses that had been suppressed for centuries. While listing the characteristics of this new breed of writers who were willing to raise their voice and demand change, Muhammad Sadiq, the literary historian, noted:

The world, for long considered as unreal or at best, a temporary sojourn, or a preparation ground for an eternal life of bliss hereafter, has [sic] grown wonderfully real and interesting. The idea is not to escape life, or to put up with it as a necessary evil, but to make it better and to have more and more of it.[78]

By the early nineteenth century, the Urdu language had perfected and polished itself to such a sheen that it shone like burnished gold. It had honed its vocabulary to express the noblest of emotions and refined its syntax to convey the most complicated expressions with ease and finesse. As a language, it had come of age. The ghazal, the marsiya, and the qasidah—each an exquisite literary genre, each capable of surpassing the other, each the cause of much astonishment and delight—were the most glittering jewels in its crown. Its concerns were, as Ale Ahmad Suroor puts it, *musarrat* (pleasure); it had little to do with *baseerat* (insight),[79] form took precedence over

---

[78] Sadiq, *A History of Urdu Literature*, p. 320.
[79] Suroor, '*Urdu Tanquid ke Buniyadi Afkar*', p. 17. In the course of a long and illustrious career as a critic, Suroor would often revisit the twin notions of pleasure and insight, as though these were the two poles around which all literature (not merely Urdu literature) must gravitate. He may, perhaps, have been influenced by Matthew Arnold (1822–1888), the Victorian poet and critic who was called the 'critic's critic' and who pointed out the sociological moorings of literary criticism. One of Suroor's later collections of critical essays is called *Mussarat se Baseerat Tak*.

content, and language, idiom, and syntax were not to be trifled with. The novel and the short story, still waiting to be born, would take up the serious business of education, instruction, and, in later years, social realism.

At a time when some fairly sophisticated fiction was being written in English, French, and Russian, the Urdu *fasana-go* were producing what could, at best, be described as romances in the tradition of the picaresque novel.[80] Slowly, almost imperceptibly, things began to change as realism began to creep in and some semblance of plot and characterization began to emerge. Ehtesham Husain, the Marxist critic, makes a connection between growing literacy and the growth of the novel; for while poetry could be recited, *dastan* could be heard from professional *dastan-go* and plays could be watched, the novel had to be read.[81] Slow to gather literary force, the Urdu novel and the short story gradually began to overshadow the other far more stylized genres, eventually proving to be not just more malleable to the needs of modern literary sensibilities, but also far more effective mirrors of society and its needs and aspirations.

Shahryar, one of the foremost Urdu poets of our times, pointed out for me the inextricable link between patronage and poetry, especially in an age when poetry alone held sway. The court, badshah, or feudal aristocracy, being patron of the arts, were not merely the upholders of good

---

[80] The Fort William College was founded at Calcutta in 1800 and John Gilchrist, as its head, set about procuring a band of translators who would produce the finest works from Persian and Sanskrit into Urdu. As a result, *Bagh-o-Bahar* by Mir Amman, *Sakuntala* and *Singhasan Battisi* by Nihal Chand Lahauri, *Araish-e-Mehfil* by Sher Ali Afsos, and a host of other romances became widely available. The establishment of the Naval Kishore Press at Lucknow in about the middle of the nineteenth century further contributed to the development and popularization of Urdu literature. It undertook the translation of the copious series of dastan called *Dastan-i-Amir Hamza* and the *Bostan-i-Khayal*. This frenetic publishing activity had another fall-out, namely, the introduction of a new breed of writer—the translator. Ralph Russell makes the valid point that, though initially meant to be texts for English students, these books eventually reached a much larger audience and it was in the hands of the native readers that they actually showed far-reaching effects; Ralph Russell, *The Pursuit of Urdu Literature: A Select History* (London: Zed Books, 1992), p. 84.

[81] Ehtesham Husain, '*Novel ki Tanquid*' (The Criticism of the Novel), in Ale Ahmad Suroor (ed.), *Tanquid ke Buniyadi Masail* (Aligarh: Aligarh Muslim University Press, 1967), p. 188.

taste; they *defined* literary tastes and the poets felt compelled to defend the values enshrined in traditional, time-honoured systems. With the decay of aristocratic institutions and a steady erosion in the authority of feudal stakeholders, the writer began to address the needs of the common man, the man who bought his books and brought him name, fame, and money. While poetry was slow to extricate itself from the thrall of romanticism, Urdu prose proved more adept at reflecting this changing power equation.

The genesis of this new style of writing can be traced directly to the cataclysmic events of 1857: 'After the revolt of 1857–59 a tremendous change took place, and in the second half of the nineteenth century the impact of British rule and of British Victorian values was so great that the whole character of Urdu literature was changed by it.'[82]

Till 1857, Urdu prose was either didactic or educational. Urdu fiction did not always draw from society; instead it drew the reader *away* from the real, often grim, reality into a magical world of fantasy. The burst of political consciousness released by the Revolt found expression in socially concerned literature. Faced with the challenge of living in a colonized world and making good in an increasingly competitive society, Urdu writers and poets tried to find a modus vivendi with the colonial government; we have seen this in the writings of Syed Ahmad Khan, Hali, and Zakaullah in the previous section. The effort, at this point, was to awaken the Indian Muslims from long years of slumber and to make them fit, as it were, to negotiate the real and much-changed world. The effort was not so much to call for change, certainly not radical change, in the way that writers—especially those who began to display socialist or Marxist leanings and those who came to be known as the progressives—would begin to do from the 1930s onwards. The effort, at this point, was to gradually hold a mirror up to society, a society that though Indian was very Victorian in its social mores. In the process, these writers of the late nineteenth and early twentieth centuries dealt with wide-ranging themes which had been overlooked in the pre-1857 decades. One such writer was Nazir Ahmad who has been regarded as one of the founders of the modern Urdu novel. An alumnus of the Delhi College, he entered government service in the Department of Education in 1854. A powerful orator, he was invited to speak from various public platforms such as the Muhammadan Education

---

[82] Russell, *Pursuit of Urdu Literature*, p. 77.

Conference, Anjuman-e-Himayat-i-Islam (Society for the Support of Islam), and the Delhi Tibbiya College. Already well-known as a translator, an educationist, and a vocal proponent of the Aligarh school, Nazir Ahmad soon established a reputation as a pioneer in his choice of subject: how best to instruct and thereby improve the lot of young Muslim girls who had got left behind in the reformist movement of the Aligarh school which had primarily focused on the education of Muslim men. The cornerstone of Nazir Ahmad's world view was the family and he believed each of its 'constituent members'[83] deserved individual care and attention for the whole to function harmoniously in society. His own life and career exemplified the belief, prevalent among some sections of the Muslim intelligentsia, that '… if only the Indian Muslims made themselves worthy of it, the British government and its officer would provide them with opportunities for getting on in the world. The other side of this optimism was the conviction that the Muslims were listless and unaware of the real conditions of their life.'[84]

Taubat-al-Nasuh, written by Nazir Ahmad in 1874, and translated into English in 1884 as *The Repentence of Nussooh* by M. Kempson,[85] was received by the government and the educated classes as a 'picture of life and manners'.[86] Nazir Ahmad had intended his first book, the much acclaimed *Mirat al-Urus* (The Bride's Mirror) to 'teach ethics and good housekeeping'; the second *Banat al-Nash* (Daughters of the Bier, a name for the constellation Ursa Major) to focus on scientific knowledge; and the third *Taubat al-Nasuh* to deal with the subject of 'religious piety' (*dindari*) through its protagonist Nussooh, whose name meant 'resolutely sincere'. Of the three, it was *Mirat al-Urus*, a cautionary tale of two sisters, that was hailed as the first runaway bestseller in Urdu, given an award by the colonial government, and made a part of the Urdu syllabus in many schools. Its opening lines were, 'No one more thoroughly deserves to be called "stupid" than a human being who does not sometimes ponder over the affairs of the world

---

[83] Naim, 'Prize-winning Adab', p. 137.

[84] Mujeeb, *Indian Muslims*, p. 532.

[85] An officer in the education department in colonial India, he was also the author of a didactic novel in Urdu.

[86] M. Kempson, *The Repentance of Nussoh: The Tale of a Muslim Family a Hundred Years Ago*, translated by M. Kempson and edited by C.M. Naim (Delhi: Permanent Black, 2004 [first published by W.H. Allen & Co., 1884]).

we live in. And although there are fit subjects for meditation in this world of a thousand different kinds, the most fundamental and important of all is human life itself.'[87]

One of the crucial themes that had so far eluded the Muslim writers—but not the reformers in Bengal[88] and Maharashtra—was the status of women, their education, and matters concerning polygamy and divorce. Probably for the first time in the history of Urdu literature, these public issues, debated from different fora, began to occupy some degree of centrality in literary writings. Nor was it any longer a taboo to speculate on, for example, the morality and appropriateness of polygamy in Islam. The letters and novels of Nazir Ahmad are replete with such examples, some of which were drawn from the works of the great educationist from Aligarh[89] and Syed Ameer Ali (1849–1928), the historian-reformer from Calcutta. Describing him as 'mild, courteous and gracious' in manner, but 'formidable in debate', Mushirul Hasan upholds Nazir Ahmad as a 'nineteenth-century liberal humanist within the Islamic frame' and notes, 'With his astounding range of vocabulary and colloquial style, Nazir Ahmad led his readers out of the traditional mode of thinking into new vistas of hope and endeavour.'[90]

Novels like *Taubat al-Nasuh* and *Mirat al-Urus* were, relatively speaking, new voices which invited both criticism and appreciation. Nazir Ahmad talks of the evils of polygamy in *Fasana-e-Mubtila* (Mubtila's Tale) and widow remarriage in *Ayama* (Widows). These new novels, no matter how didactic, were a far cry from the traditional Urdu romances with their heroes meeting moon-like maidens in implausibly adventurous situations. The appeal of these new novels, according to Gail Minault, lay in their

---

[87] Nazir Ahmad, *The Bride's Mirror: A Tale of Life in Delhi a Hundred Years Ago*, translated by G.E. Ward (Delhi: Permanent Black, 2001), p. 4.

[88] It has been pointed out that the leaders of the Bengali Renaissance were all Hindus, see Ralph Russell, 'Strands of Muslim Identity in South Asia', *How Not to Write the History of Urdu Literature and Other Essays* (New Delhi: Oxford University Press, 1999), p. 181.

[89] While Nazir Ahmad identified with most of Syed Ahmad Khan's views, he disagreed on certain theological issues as well as with the Aligarh school's widely perceived advocacy of a Western style of living. Nazir Ahmad's own father was strictly against the learning of English and had vowed that he would rather see his son die or beg on the streets than learn English. For details, see Mujeeb, *Indian Muslims*, pp. 531–2.

[90] Andrews, *Zakaullah of Delhi*, p. xxix.

ability to strike a balance between the wholly stereotypical character-types of the Persian and Indian traditional tale (*dastan*) and a new literary form coming from the West, the novel of manners'.[91] These novels allowed Nazir Ahmad to expound his views on women's education, which went beyond home tutoring for girls and spoke of the need for a carefully monitored but structured school syllabus being devised for a secluded, sheltered sharif household-like atmosphere.[92] The pioneering movement of Shaikh Abdullah in the early years of the twentieth century, which led to the establishment of the girls' school at Aligarh, owed its inspiration to Nazir Ahmad as much as to Altaf Husain Hali and some reformers at the M.A.O. College at Aligarh.[93]

There is no denying that Hali, the Panipat-born poet-writer, lead the crusade despite his mentor Syed Ahmad Khan's reservations on the empowerment of Muslim women by providing them a secular education at par with men. Although Calcutta, Dacca, and Bhopal were beginning to awaken to the need for girls to go to schools and colleges, it was Hali whose impassioned pleas struck a chord in the middle-class families of upper India. His *Majalis un-Nisa* (Conversations among Women, 1904–5) is a remarkable work for it articulates his reformist vision and, at the same time, holds a mirror to contemporary society. Through the *Majalis*, Hali makes two vital points: one, that educated women make better wives and mothers who can, in turn, propel the engine of reform from within Muslim society; and two, educated mothers are far better placed to mould and discipline wayward or slothful sons so that they can survive in an increasingly competitive world. The *Majalis* was given a cash prize of Rs 400 and widely used in girls' schools. Hali's next book, *Chup ki Daad* (In Praise of the Silent, 1906), was a tribute to the unsung virtues of women.

What is more, in the post-1857 period, the reformer and the creative writer came together—often making one indistinguishable from the other—adding weight to the liberal and reformist currents and introducing

[91] Gail Minault, *Secluded Scholars: Women's Education and Muslim Social Reform in Colonial India* (New Delhi: Oxford University Press, 1998), p. 37.

[92] Ibid., p. 35.

[93] The Muslim Educational Conference in its meeting at Aligarh in 1891 passed a resolution to the effect that it was necessary to make efforts for the education of men as well as women. Yet, the Women's College at Aligarh was started by Sheikh Abdullah only in 1906, and the school at Lucknow by Karamat Hussain in 1912.

a discordant note in traditional discourses. Literary historians have not paid adequate attention to this intersection and prefer instead to demarcate boundaries between the interpreters of social realities and the proponents of their creative expression. What is also noteworthy, especially in the context of the post-1857 phase, is the access to various important platforms where the writer and the reformer—or both—could articulate their concerns. In the Punjab, the Anjuman-e-Himayat-i-Islam was one such body; Iqbal is said to have recited his first poem from its platform in 1899 at its annual session.[94] The All-India Muslim Educational Conference, founded by Syed Ahmad Khan in 1886, became a key vehicle for the dissemination of modern scientific learning.[95] Thus, we find eminent Urdu writers and poets like Nazir Ahmad, Zakaullah, Azad, and Hali in the vanguard of the movement for reform and education. In Lucknow the remarkable figure of Karamat Hussain, backed by some rajahs and talukdars, created a stir amongst the Muslim middle classes—who had so far shown no inclination towards secular education—by starting the first-of-its-kind school for Muslim girls in 1912.[96]

If these are any indices we can easily connect the emergence of social consciousness with the writings that were being produced in Urdu in the 1870s and 1880s. We can argue, moreover, that literary writings, whatever their genre, acted as a catalyst for a new awakening that is symbolized in the form of the dynamic movement of a railway train in comparison to a slow-moving ox cart. Exhorting people not to go back to the old, laid-back ways of the feudal aristocracy, Nazir Ahmad said, in one of the public speeches, at the Anjuman-e-Himayat-i-Islam, for which he was increasingly gaining acclaim:

Think Time to be a train, and we a drove of oxen. If we do not know the speed of the train, and wish to resist it, if we cannot keep pace with it, or if we do nothing,

---

[94] L.R. Gordon-Polonskaya, 'Ideology of Muslim Nationalism', Hafeez Malik (ed.), *Iqbal: Poet-Philosopher of Pakistan* (New York: Columbia University Press, 1971), p. 109.

[95] Abdul Rashid Khan, *The All India Muslim Educational Conference: Its Contribution to the Cultural Development of Indian Muslims, 1886–1947* (Karachi: Oxford University Press, 2001).

[96] For details of the school at Lucknow, see Gail Minault, 'Sayyid Karamat Husain and Education for Women', in *Gender, Language and Learning: Essays in Indo-Muslim Cultural History* (Ranikhet: Permanent Black, 2009).

the train will not spare any of us.... Now it is for you to find the speed and force of time.... Will you walk on to the train with the slow and measured steps of the Lucknow men, or resist the train of time, or fly away from it, or blindfold the eyes or put cotton into the ears ... or watch in bewilderment while the train passes over you?[97]

Like the times that were changing, turn-of-the-century literature too was fluid, changing, and incipient. As more and more writers began to try their hand at prose writing—with varying degrees of success—the embryonic Urdu novel began to show a marked ability for taking on a variety of subjects. Munshi Sajjad Hussain (1856–1915), the editor of the immensely popular *Awadh Punch*, introduced humour in novels such as *Haji Baghlol* and *Kaya Palat*. Abdul Halim Sharar (1862–1926) invoked characters and events from Islamic history to conjure tales of heroism and chivalry in novels such as *Firdos-e-Barin*, *Zawaal-e-Baghdad*, and *Husn ka Dakoo Mansoor Mohana*. The most prolific of this new breed of writers was no doubt Rashidul Khairi (1870–1936) who took up virtually every ill that beset Muslim society—widow remarriage, marrying for wealth, the abuse of children at the hands of step-parents, the evil of polygamy, ill-treatment of servants (especially maids), among the many glaring anomalies in typical Muslim households. A member of the 'embryonic middle class', having studied Arabic and Persian, Khairi belonged to the generation that developed Urdu, their mother tongue, 'into a medium of literary expression in prose'.[98]

Another emerging field of literary expression—one that would increasingly dominate the literary scene—was the field of Urdu journalism. The earliest Urdu *akhbar*s (newspapers) had already made their appearance in Delhi by the late 1830s and become popular vehicles for the transmission of news related to culture, literature, society, and politics.[99] Mumtaz Ali

---

[97] From the English translation of *Fitratullah: A Lecture*, delivered in Urdu on the Eighth Anniversary of the Anjuman-e-Himayat-i-Islam, Lahore, 1893, p. 4. Urdu text in *Lekcharon ka Majmua*, vol. 1, pp. 373–4. Nazir Ahmad could not resist a dig at the 'Lucknow men', who in comparison to their counterparts in Aligarh and Delhi, were slow to embrace change.

[98] Gail Minault, '*Ismat*: Rashidul Khairi's Novels and Urdu Literary Journalism for Women', in Christopher Shackle (ed.), *Urdu and Muslim South Asia* (New Delhi: Oxford University Press, 1991), p. 129.

[99] Gail Minault, 'From *Akhbar* to News: The Development of the Urdu Press in Early Nineteenth-Century Delhi', in Kathryn Hansen and David Lelyveld (eds), *A Wilderness of Possibilities: Urdu Studies in Transnational Perspective* (New Delhi: Oxford University Press, 2005).

founded the first women's Urdu newspaper, *Tahzib un-Niswan*, in 1898, in partnership with his wife, Muhammadi Begum.[100] Other voices joined in from different cities such as Bhopal, Hyderabad, Aligarh, Lahore, and Lucknow. Shaikh Abdullah launched the monthly educational journal, *Khatun*, from Aligarh in 1904; it was followed by Rashidul Khairi's literary magazine *Ismat* in 1908. These emerging women's newspapers and magazines not only fostered enlightened housekeeping and debates on women's rights, but also ushered in a new kind of writing. Still, there was nothing in these new writings that seriously threatened the status quo and so, while they occasionally caused ripples of dissent and disagreement, they did not cause the sort of outrage and uproar unleashed by the writers of *Angarey* in 1932.

Ironically, the British—in their own way and for their own ends—moulded and transformed Urdu literature. As we have earlier noted, the new sort of novels by Hali, Nazir Ahmad and others were encouraged by handsome cash awards from the imperial government and promoted in schools as suitable reading material. Frances Pritchett, in her 'Afterword' to Nazir Ahmad's *The Bride's Mirror* says, '... clearly its original impulse was British-influenced, reformist and didactic'.[101] The British patrons of writers like Nazir Ahmad promoted and encouraged this sort of writing—reformist but not radical, enlightened but not extremist, modern but not revisionist. While the education of women was encouraged (for the larger good of the family), patriarchal values were maintained, 'If families are to be reared upon women's earnings, why should there be men.'[102]

Incidentally, in 1868, Sir William Muir, lieutenant-governor of the Western Provinces had made a call for 'useful books' to be published in the vernacular that would be suitably rewarded by the government. This decision was hailed by a section of the Indian intelligentsia, including Hali, and though the awards stopped after a few years, the announcement itself was significant:

Within the heartland of Urdu, it was the first and perhaps the most widely disseminated declaration of official support for 'useful' literature in general, and for

---

[100] Gail Minault, 'Muslim Social History from Urdu Women's Magazines', in *Gender, Language and Learning: Essays in Indo-Muslim Cultural History* (Ranikhet: Permanent Black, 2009), p. 87.
[101] Ahmad, *Bride's Mirror*, p. 220.
[102] Ibid., p. 155.

books on women in particular. It also established the fact that the Government of India was the new patron of learning, and the patronized learning was to be put to use for the general good ... and it had the power not only to approve certain ideas through rewards and disapprove others through neglect, but also to disseminate the approved ones through the educational system....[103]

Colonial Aligarh saw the mushrooming of a variety of journals. Increasing translations from English into Urdu opened the doors to Western literature. Many of these translations were carried out under the aegis of the Scientific Society (set up in 1863) and published in Syed Ahmad Khan's *Tehzeeb-ul Akhlaq*. The Royal Translation Bureau in Lucknow began churning out Urdu translations of scientific works. With the spirit and essence of Western imagination seeping into Urdu literature, literary tastes underwent a change. In Lahore, Colonel Holroyd began to organize new kinds of mushairas that weaned Urdu poetry away from the pre-occupations with courtly love and turn it towards facts and events.[104] Under his influence, Azad and Hali began to exhort poets to look for 'radically new vision of the nature and goal of poetry'. On 9 May 1874, speaking at the Anjuman-e-Punjab in Lahore, Azad stressed the need for reform in Urdu poetry and greater naturalism and realism than the Urdu poet had hitherto displayed. Apart from an eloquent plea for radically new form and content, he also urged the poet to broaden his scope, to look beyond the decadent and decaying fabric of feudalism, and look instead to fresh, new vistas that would bring his readers into closer contact with the natural world. In this, he was encouraged by Syed Ahmad Khan who had, through his *Tehzeeb-ul Akhlaq*, been talking about *nechar* (nature) and natural poetry along the lines of Milton and Shakespeare. Syed Ahmad Khan thus advised Azad, 'Bring your work even closer to nature (*nechar*). The extent to which a work comes close to nature is the extent to which it gives pleasure.'[105]

Azad published his seminal history of Urdu poetry, *Aab-e-Hayaat* (The Water of Life, 1880) and *Nairang-e-Khayal* (The Wonder World of Thought, 1880) which contained translations of 13 allegorical essays by Samuel Johnson and Joseph Addison. Inspired by Azad's style of writing which was akin to painting word pictures, Hali wrote *Muqadama-e-Sher-o-Shairi*. A

---

[103] Naim, 'Prize-winning Adab: Five Urdu Books Written in Response to the Gazette Notification No. 791A (1868)', p. 124.

[104] Pritchett, *Nets of Awareness*, pp. 34–9.

[105] Ibid., p. 38.

pioneering new book, its intention was *islah* (correction); it hoped to offer a 'correct' taste in poetry and, more significantly, stressed in no uncertain terms the close link between poetry and society.[106] Not only did its publication produce many a ripple in the still waters of Urdu criticism, it made the 'Urdu poet look at life and the world squarely in the face'.[107] Urging the poet to discard the artificial (*masnoohi*), Hali—like Azad—drew the readers' attention to Western poetry and encouraged experimentation in both form and content. Hali was especially harsh on the Urdu ghazal, going so far as to declare that either its (the ghazal's) edifice (*imarat*) must undergo repair and renovation (*tarmeem*), or it must go![108]

The new kind of mushairas (nine in all) patronized by Holroyd—and implemented so enthusiastically by Azad—lasted barely a year, but their influence lived on in the new sort of poetry being written. The ghazal did not go away, but it did agree to address issues and concerns that had hitherto been too pedestrian or too real. While some poets did not much care to be 'dictated' by the government or its functionaries and expressed outrage at Hali's diktats, the nudge of government patronage served to encourage, at the very least, a re-evaluation of existing literary values. A new realism began to creep in, whether it was in Hali's depiction of the rainy season (*Barkha Rut*) or his exhortation of patriotism (*Hubb-e-Watan*).[109] The poet began to paint increasingly life-like pictures of the world around him. From there, it was just a step away to talk of social realities and cultural sensitivities.

---

[106] Ale Ahmad Suroor, '*Hali ki Muqadama Sher-o-Shairi ki Manviyat*' (The Importance of Hali's Muqadama Sher-o-Shairi), in *Fikr-e-Roshan* (Aligarh: Educational Book House, 1995), p. 81.

[107] Khurshidul Islam, in Ale Ahmad Suroor (ed.), *Tanquid ke Buniyadi Masail* (The Fundamental Issues of Criticism) (Aligarh: Aligarh Muslim University Press, 1967), p. 250.

[108] While such a pronouncement caused uproar among many of his contemporaries, especially those belonging to the Lucknow school (who in comparison to the new school of thought at Aligarh represented the old school), the ghazal did undergo changes and began to reflect newer concerns. Hali's scathing indictment of the ghazal and the *ghazal-go* of his time, is viewed by later critics, such as Suroor, as evidence of Hali's vision and maturity, one that earns him a pride of place among the serious critics of Urdu literature. See Suroor, '*Yaadgar-e-Hali*' (In Memory of Hali), in *Tanquid Kya Hai?* (New Delhi: Maktaba Jamia, 1972).

[109] Ibid., p. 23.

On the surface, late-nineteenth-century Urdu literature seemed to be the embodiment of Victorian values; there were, however, several reactionary forces at work, pulling and tugging it in different directions. While the bulk of writing was either being produced by writers who belonged to the Aligarh school or were influenced by the prodigiously prolific Syed Ahmad Khan[110] and his younger contemporaries, there were some who made a distinction between British interests and Muslim interests. Shibli Nomani[111] (1857–1914) and Munshi Sajjad Hussain,[112] for instance, began to voice a new concern that would in due course take a distinctly nationalist and anti-British tone. Compared to Syed Ahmad Khan, Shibli was 'more sensitive to the pull of pan-Islamism' and was responsible for the creation of

[110] Sir Syed was knighted by the British in 1879 and remained all through his life a loyal subject of Her Majesty's government. There is no evidence in any of his writings of any criticism of British policies. His analysis of the revolt, *Asbab-i-Baghawat-e-Hind* (Causes for the Indian Revolt), written in 1858, is the closest he comes to giving a candid account of the grievances against British Rule among the common man. But this too is written from the point of view of a loyalist who is at pains to clarify the 'misapprehensions of the intentions of the government' where he hastens to add, 'had there been a native of Hindustan in the Legislative Council, the people would have never fallen into such errors.' Sir Syed Ahmad Khan, 'Causes of the Indian Revolt', chapter 9, in Mushirul Hasan (ed.), *Islam in South Asia*, vol. II, *Encountering the West: Before and After 1857* (New Delhi: Manohar, 2008), p. 180.

[111] One of the 'midnight's children', born as he was in the year 1857, he brought a new readability to historical, scientific, and religious writing. An early alumnus of the College at Aligarh, he began to differ from the Syed on the need for more rigorous religious education for Muslims. This belief was in no way discordant with the increasing nationalist tone of his political writings. His travels in Egypt, Syria, Turkey, and Italy in 1892 (where he visited several madrasas) convinced him that the answer to the Indian Muslims' dilemma lay not in the secular model of education fashioned by the Syed. In his last days he founded the Dar-ul Mussanifien (Academy of Writers) at Azamgarh which later produced several eminent Islamic scholars such as Maulana Suleiman Nadvi. Shibli Nomani, like Iqbal, spoke of the need to bring rationalism closer to Islamic thought.

[112] As editor of the *Awadh Punch*, Munshi Sajjad Hussain, a staunch nationalist and later 'Congressi', did much to propagate a new kind of Urdu journalism, one that had no holy cows. For a detailed study of *Awadh Punch* and its impact on the nationalist movement, see Mushirul Hasan, *Wit and Humour in Colonial North India* (New Delhi: Niyogi Books, 2007).

a 'tradition of Islamic historiography in Urdu' that glorified the religious leaders or heroes of Islam.[113]

Before we conclude this chapter, two writers deserve special mention because each in their own way derived the benefits of the new Western-style education yet deplored the loyalist overtones of its most vocal proponents. More significantly, it is in the writings of these two individuals—poles apart in style and substance, one being a satirist and punster par excellence and the other by far the most stylistically sophisticated poet of the twentieth century—that the word 'revolution' is increasingly begun to be used and the masses exhorted to rise up against their masters as never before. These two—Akbar Illahabadi and Mohammad Iqbal—are of especial interest to us for the purpose of this study primarily because of the revolutionary strain in their poetry and their exhortations to the Muslim masses to rise and, Heaven forbid, rebel!

As the nineteenth century drew to a close, a new voice arose, the satirical doubting voice of Akbar Illahabadi (1846–1921) who could fully support neither the new nor the old, but did feel the need to admonish those who had forgotten the lessons of the Revolt:

> The minstrel and the music—both have changed
> Our sleep has changed, the tale we told has changed.
> The nightingale now sings a different song
> The colour in the cheeks of spring has changed
> Another kind of rain falls from the sky
> The grain that grows upon our land has changed
> A revolution has brought this about
> In all the realm of nature all has changed.[114]

For all his misgivings, this revolution, he felt, was fated, inevitable:

> Understand the poetry of Akbar to be
> The memorial to revolution.[115]

Employing the metaphor of 'Buddhu Miyan' for the Indian Muslim (a confused, none-too-smart sort of Little Fellow) in some places and the

---

[113] Ahmad, *Islamic Modernism in India and Pakistan*, p. 77.

[114] Ralph Russell, *Hidden in the Lute: An Anthology of Two Centuries of Urdu Literature* (New Delhi: Viking, 1995), p. 201.

[115] Akbar Illahabadi, *Kulliyat*, vol. II (Lucknow: Adabi Press, 1931), p. 83. All subsequent translations of Akbar are mine.

'Shaikh' (a pompous, English stooge, occasionally a parody of 'Sir Syed'[116]) elsewhere, Akbar's poetry reflects all the contradictions of his age. On the one hand, he proclaims the arrival of change:

> The revolution is here:
> It's a New World, a new tumult.[117]

On the other, he rues:

> Moderation? It doesn't exist
> Here or there. All have stretched their legs
> Beyond all limits.[118]

Akbar expresses the misgivings of many Muslims who felt that freedom would bring majority rule when he says

> The rule will be British Raj and then Hindu Raj
> Now God alone can save Sallu [meaning the Muslim].

Mockingly, he rubs it in:

> Real goods are those that are made in Europe,
> Real matter is that which is printed in the Pioneer.[119]

And elsewhere:

> Though Europe has great
> Capability to do war,
> Greater still is her power
> To do business. They cannot everywhere
> Install a gun, but the soap
> Made by Pears is everywhere.[120]

---

[116] All Urdu writers routinely refer to Syed Ahmad Khan as Sir Syed, and to Iqbal as just Iqbal and to Akbar as plain Akbar despite their royal honours.

[117] Akbar Illahabadi, *Gandhi Nama* (Allahabad: Kitabistan, 1948), p. 1. Referred to by S.R. Faruqi while delivering the Fourteenth Zakir Husain Memorial Lecture, entitled 'The Power Politics of Culture: Akbar Ilahabadi and the Changing Order of Things', Zakir Husain College, Delhi, January 2002, p. 10.

[118] Akbar Illahabadi, *Kulliyat*, vol. I (Allahabad: Asrar-e Karimi Press, 1931), pp. 161–2.

[119] Ibid., vol. II, p. 62.

[120] Ibid., p. 63.

'*Barq-e-Kalisa*' (Lightning in the Church) is a seemingly over-the-top poem about love at first sight with a young Miss, but is actually a scathing denouement of the Indian Muslims who are blindly in awe of Western civilization, the sort who will gladly say 'Consider my Islam a story of the past' when confronted with the glory of the (Christian) West.

Despite being home-tutored, Akbar had good command over the English language.[121] This got him a job as a *naib tehsildar* and he quickly rose to become first a lawyer and then, in quick succession, a *munsif* (a medium-grade judge), a sessions judge, a district judge, and finally a khan bahadur in 1894. Given his meteoric rise through the ranks of colonial India, his seeming opposition to progress, science, and the enlightened way of living and thinking seems odd, to say the least. But that is because Muslim intelligentsia in general and the Urdu writers in particular had massed themselves into two opposing and irreconcilable groups—those for Syed Ahmad Khan and the Aligarh school of thought, and those against. All those who stood for the Syed's views on education and the prospects for Muslims were automatically assumed to be liberal, progressive, forward-looking, whereas those who opposed them, as Akbar did in biting verse, were taken to be regressive.

Speaking of Akbar's 'passionate engagement with political and social questions in his poetry', S.R. Faruqi sheds light on the duality between his personal life and poetry, what he calls 'the obvious cleavage' between Akbar's life and political opinions:

In his poetry he presents himself as an implacable enemy of all things British. Yet he himself was a fairly senior member of the British official establishment and was apparently quite proud of the high regard in which Thomas Burn, one time Chief Secretary to the Government of U.P. held him. He even wrote an adulatory *qasida* on the golden jubilee of Queen Victoria (1887) at the request of 'Mr. Howell, Judge'. He sent his son Ishrat Husain to England for higher education and on his return suffered him to enter the civil service under the Government of U.P. as Deputy Collector. All this sits ill with the humiliating scorn and trenchant castigation that he pours over the British and the West and their admirers.... Certainly, he knew that no one could really swim against the current, but the tragedy according to him was that those who swam with the current too were drowned. The Indian, in trying to fashion himself like a modern [British]creature, gave up

---

[121] This section on Akbar's career is constructed from Faruqi, 'The Power Politics of Culture'.

his past, his traditions, his belief systems, but could not really become the modern Western individual that Macaulay had expected him to become. The following verse is poignant in its tragic bitterness:

> They became votaries of the Time
> And adopted the style of the West.
> In their ardent desire for a second birth
> They committed suicide.[122]

It would appear that Akbar, far from being a reactionary, expressed the misgivings of an educated colonized Indian Muslim. That these misgivings were often self-contradictory was a symptom of the changing time and age. Moreover, having been a part of the colonial administrative apparatus, Akbar knew perhaps better than others the servility and insignificance of the Indian petty official who was no more than a very small cog in a very large machine, a machine that he kept oiled and working, but one that did not always work to his advantage. One is willing, therefore, to believe that a rational man like Akbar was satirical of Syed Ahmad Khan and the Aligarh school of thought precisely because his own experience after years of service in the provincial administration had taught him that the educated Indian Muslim ought to seek *more* active participation in systems of governance. In this, he showed a generational shift from Nazir Ahmad, who, while similarly employed by the colonial government, showed no desire to ask for more, far less rebel against the hand that fed them. When Akbar mocked at telephones, piped drinking water, printing presses, newspapers, advertisement, railway trains, the teaching of English, etc., one is unwilling to read in it signs of 'backwardness' or 'regression'; instead one sees a fearful man taking recourse to satire to express his worst fears about the potent powers of the colonizer. To my mind, Akbar is not against progress at all or even against the outward symbols of progress as he is against the destruction of traditional life and culture. One sees Akbar as an early nationalist, a trenchant critic of colonialism, and the missing link between poets like Hali and the progressives.

The Urdu critic, Ale Ahmad Suroor, praises Akbar for unfailingly 'pointing to the feet of clay in the new god and the chink in the new armour, and particularly, the comic element in the earnestness of the new leaders of reform, their occasional naiveté and their enthusiasm.' He adds:

---

[122] Faruqi, 'The Power Politics of Culture', pp. 4–5.

For forty years, Akbar acted like a spiritual seismograph, recording every shock and making it into poetry of a high order. Johnson said of Swift that 'the rogue never hazards a metaphor'. Akbar takes every risk, breaks all rules, takes sides, laments the failure of his mission, but does manage to check blind imitation of the west and help in a rediscovery of the east which marches towards progress with a new consciousness of its own heritage. He also sharpens our sensibility by making us aware of the false note in the new harmony which appeared to be perfect to us in the beginning. He has such an 'effectiveness of assertion' and such a telling manner that while his outlook is considered out of date, his art remains a great influence.[123]

By the early twentieth century, Akbar had become a great admirer of Gandhi, the nationalist movement, and Hindu–Muslim unity. His *Gandhi Nama*, a series of brief poems published from 1919–21, is a paean to syncretism and a political movement for independence that could only be propelled by both Hindus and Muslims playing an equal role. Akbar's call for a marriage between faith and modernity was echoed from unexpected quarters—from no less a personage than Iqbal, revered by many as Allama (meaning 'scholar'). As different as apples and oranges, Akbar and Iqbal together helped the Indian Muslim negotiate the choppy waters of a new century and forge a new identity. It would be worthwhile, here, to note M. Mujeeb's assessment of Akbar and Iqbal along with Ghalib, whom we have studied earlier in this chapter, in the context of understanding the Indian Muslim. Mujeeb wrote, '… Ghalib represents the consummation of the humanistic element in Indian Muslim culture, Akbar the harmonization of the values of poetry and humour and Iqbal the beginning of a new age, a new search for values and forms, both of poetry and of life'.[124]

In contrast to the homespun wisdom of Akbar, Iqbal drew on the best resources of a liberal Western education. Upon graduating from the prestigious Government College, Lahore, in 1899, he worked as a lecturer in philosophy at the same college, went on to study philosophy at Trinity College, Cambridge, and in Heidelberg and Munich in Germany, eventually appearing for the Bar-at-Law from 1905 to 1908. Though he returned to teach for two years before quitting government service altogether, he earned no more than a modest livelihood as a lawyer and chose to devote

---

[123] Ale Ahmad Suroor, 'Humour in Urdu', in Nissim Ezekiel (ed.), *Indian Writers in Conference: Proceedings of the Sixth PEN All-India Writers' Conference* (Mysore: PEN, 1964), p. 211.

[124] Mujeeb, *Indian Muslims*, p. 466.

himself entirely to reading and writing. Given his trenchant criticism of the imperial government, he, surprisingly enough, accepted a knighthood in 1922. In 1927, he was elected to the Punjab Legislative Council. The philosophical essence of his writings is distilled in a series of six lectures delivered during 1928–9 at universities in Aligarh, Hyderabad, and Madras entitled 'Reconstruction of Religious Thought in Islam'. In 1931, he attended the Round Table Conference in London as a member of the Indian Muslim delegation led by the Agha Khan.

Where Akbar's quarrel with the West in general and the English in particular was more in the cultural, social, and political realm, Iqbal questioned Western enlightenment and English materialism on philosophical and religious grounds. Both were early patrons of Art for Life's Sake instead of Art for Art's Sake since both were intensely political poets who were, at the same time, acutely aware of the social undercurrents that tugged and towed the Muslim intelligentsia in different directions. No longer content with the crumbs of lowly employment in the colonial administration or even tokens of recognition and appreciation from the imperial government, Iqbal wanted nothing short of an Islamic Renaissance. In soul-stirring verses, he exhorted the Indian Muslims to hearken back to a glorious past, to listen to voices from Islam's history and heed the call of their faith.

While in his early poetry he spoke of a united and free India where the Hindus and Muslims could coexist, this belief in syncretism and pluralism soon gave way to Unitarianism and Individualism. The *'Tarana-e-Hind'* (Ode to Hind) written in 1904 was followed by the *'Tarana-e-Milli'* (Ode to the Religious Community) in 1910 showing the progression from *'Hindi hain hum watan hai Hindostan hamara'* (We are the people of Hind and Hindustan is our homeland) to *'Muslim hain hum watan hai sara jahan hamara'* (We are Muslims and our homeland is the whole world). Two decades later in his presidential address[125] to the Muslim League meeting of 1930 in Allahabad, he propounded the idea of a separate homeland for the Muslims, but his notion of pan-Islamism[126] remained woolly compared

---

[125] For the text of his address, see Annemarie Schimmel, *Islam in the Indian Subcontinent* (Leiden: E.J. Brill, 1980), p. 226. Schimmel also quotes Iqbal's entry in his diary in 1910,'Nations are born in the hearts of poets; they prosper and die in the hands of politicians' (p. 226).

[126] For a detailed study of Iqbal's understanding of pan-Islamism, race, and nationalism, see Javed Majeed, *Muhammad Iqbal: Islam, Aesthetics and Postcolonialism* (New Delhi: Routledge, 2009), chapter 4.

to Jamaluddin Afghani,[127] a man he admired for his insight into the history of Muslim thought. Iqbal's idea of the supra-nationalism of Islam transcended man-made borders (what he called 'this accursed nationalism' in a New Year's radio address on 1 January 1938) to embrace the 'brotherhood of man'. His reproach (in a poem called '*Gila*') with India was:

> Enslaved to Britain you have kissed the rod
> It is not Britain I reproach but you.[128]

Unable to reconcile the differences between east and west, much less reason and faith, unable also to bolster his undoubtedly superlative poetry to a cogent ideology, Iqbal was at his best when he spoke out against injustice and inequality. Addressing the peasant struggling under the yoke of feudalism in '*Punjab ke Dehqan Se*' (To the Farmers of the Punjab), he wrote:

> Break all the idols of tribe and caste
> Break the old customs that fetter men fast!
> Here is true victory, here is faith's crown—
> One creed and one world, division thrown down![129]

And, more famously 'In God's Command to His Angels':

> The field that does not yield bread for its farmer
> Burn every ripening ear of wheat that grows in that field.[130]

Of those seeking government jobs he was unequivocally blunt:

> No slave is given a partnership in England's reign—
> She only wants to buy his brain.[131]

While words mean a great deal in poetry, form can never be all. Content, and the emotions behind the mesmerizing melodies that make poets

---

[127] Jamaluddin Afghani (d. 1897), one of the most vigorous proponents of pan-Islamism, travelled through Egypt, Russia, India, Turkey, and other Muslim lands preaching Islamic revivalism. He spoke of Islam and the West as antagonistic, almost irreconcilable forces and sought to anchor the Muslims of the world in the Khilafat movement.

[128] V.G. Kiernan, *Poems from Iqbal* (Karachi: Oxford University Press, 2004), p. 220.

[129] Ibid., p. 152.

[130] From *Baal-e-Gibril* (Gabriel's Wing); translation mine.

[131] Ibid., p. 196.

popular, are equally important. Perhaps that is why when Iqbal asked, 'Shair tere seene mein nafs hai ke nahi hai?'[132] (O Poet, does the heart beat in your breast, or does it not?), he was asking the poet to heed the voice of his conscience. Perhaps, that is why he considered poetry to be *paighambari*[133] (prophetic) and gave his poetry collections names that are nothing short of messianic. Perhaps that is also what raises his poetry from a 'sweet madness' (*shireen divangi*) to a 'divine madness' (*muqqadas divangi*).[134] However, despite the overwhelming presence of philosophical aesthetics (a result no doubt of his training as a philosopher), most notably the concept of *khudi*, in his poetry, as also in his prose writings and letters, Iqbal spoke out against verse being an 'autonomous and self-referential art' and stressed the need for poetry to be 'politically committed'.[135]

Iqbal's poetry meant different things to different people. What was to the Indian Muslim a talisman to ward off ungodliness was to the British a safer bet, and the lesser of the two evils. Clearly, his call for rebellion, couched as it was in elegant rhetoric and musical word play, seemed far less subversive and less dangerous to the imperial masters than men like Sibte Hasan whose compilation of poems (*Azadi ki Nazmein*) was banned. Was it because a hearkening back to a pure, untainted Islam in no way undermined the grand imperial design and could, therefore, be allowed to grow unchallenged? Communism, on the other hand, directly challenged imperialism. In the next chapter, we shall search for answers as we trace the introduction of socialist thought in India and probe the contours of a fledgling Communist Party which was to become the nursery for the PWM. We shall return once more to Iqbal as we trace the introduction of socialist thought among Indian Muslims. We shall see how his romantic nationalism underwent a change and in the light of influences as diverse as Nietzsche and Bergson and Marx, he produced the 'New Testament of Urdu Poetry'.[136] In collection after collection—from *Baal-e-Jibreel* (1935)

---

[132] Reference in Suroor, *Tanquid Kya Hai?* p. 39.

[133] Ale Ahmad Suroor, 'Iqbal ke Khutoot', in *Tanquid Kya Hai?* (New Delhi: Maktaba Jamia, 1972), p. 97.

[134] Ibid.

[135] Majeed, *Muhammad Iqbal*, p. 2.

[136] Expression coined by Ale Ahmad Suroor in 'In Contemporary Urdu Poetry', *Modernity and Contemporary Indian Literature* (Shimla: Indian Institute of Advanced Study, 1968), p. 193.

to *Zarb-e-Kaleem* (1936) to *Armaghan-e-Hijaz* (1938)—he showed the limitless possibilities of human endeavour. The timing of these visionary verses is significant for this was precisely the time when the progressives were launching their revolution; we will see how the progressives differed and shared Iqbal's vision. While both spoke of revolution and change and both wished to awaken the Indian mind from its thralldom of feudalism, Iqbal chose to do so through a peculiar combination of philosophies that can best be described as 'spiritual socialism' and the progressives derived their version of social realism from the Russian model. Moreover, Iqbal's poetic thinking, heavily influenced as it was by Nietzsche, was centred on the self (khudi) which, in turn, was his interpretation of the life principle that seeks perfection,[137] whereas the progressives shunned any form of individualism or any display of individual will.

We will conclude this chapter by noting the appearance of modern trends in Urdu prose and poetry. Ghalib, the last of the classical and the first of the moderns, had brought Urdu poetry to the point where it was ready to take wing and soar. The poets after him, while still unwilling to try radically new experiments in form, were nevertheless busy pouring new wine in old bottles. We have seen how Syed Ahmad Khan tried to bring about a synthesis of east and west. We have also seen how reform-minded poets like Azad and Hali sensed the spirit of the times and condemned the narrow range and limited concerns popular among the poets of their day and while the hold of tradition was still strong, a transition was indeed becoming evident. In the next chapter, we will take this story further by examining the mingled influence of westernization, industrialization, and modernization along with the increasingly visible presence of socialism in Urdu literature.

---

[137] Carlo Coppola, 'Iqbal and the Progressive Movement', *Journal of South Asian and Middle Eastern Studies*, vol. 1, no. 2 (1977), pp. 49–57.

2

Rise of Socialist Consciousness
From 1900 till 1930s

> *Daur-e-hayat aaega qatil qaza ke baad*
> *Hai ibtida hamari teri inteha ke baad*
> (A period of joy will come most certainly after the martyrdom
> Our beginning will come after your limit)
> —Mohamed Ali (1878–1931)

The Russo-Japanese War (1904–5), the First World War (1914–18), and the developments on the eve of and in the aftermath of the Khilafat movement (1919–22) had a profound effect on Indian politics. These, and several other important political events, are covered in the opening section of this chapter. Creative writers were not unaffected by these events; they gave expression to the sense of disquiet over the repression unleashed by the colonial government. Such sentiments were echoed, with equal vigour and finesse, by the Urdu poets and writers. The second section of this chapter attempts to establish how the nationalist trends[1] in the country as

---

[1] To view the chronological progression of nationalist thought in Urdu poetry, I have studied *Urdu mein Qaumi Shairi ke Sau Saal* (Hundred Years of Nationalistic

a whole strengthened the growth of socialist thought, and how socialistic ideas influenced a cross-section of Urdu writers well before the establishment of the CPI. The establishment of the CPI helped channelize the anti-imperialist sentiments and made them acquire a sharper, more focused, more pronounced pro-nationalist hue, while at the same time strengthening the socialist sentiment that already existed in a large section of educated Indians, especially Muslims. In the third section, we shall review the circumstances and events in the 1930s that lead to the publication of an incendiary book called *Angarey* in 1932, and unfold the linkages between the literature of this period, nationalism, and socialism.

Political Background: 1900–1930s

The introduction of Western education brought in fresh ideas.[2] Educated Indians had access to them through a profusion of printed material.[3] By the second half of the nineteenth century, the writings of the Scottish philosopher and historian J.S. Mill (1806–1873) and the English jurist, philosopher, and legal and social reformer Jeremy Bentham (1748–1832) were being widely read in some of the elite colleges in the presidency towns. Users of public libraries also took to the reading of novels—in English as well as translations; the most popular being Charles Dickens,

---

Poetry in Urdu) and *Nava-i-Azadi* (The Call of Freedom), compiled by Abdur Razzaq Qureshi. Other such compilations include *Azadi ki Nazmein* (Poems of Freedom) by Sibte Hasan and a selection of proscribed poems called *Zabt Shudah Nazmein* (Banned Poetry). Many were written by writers who had to go 'underground' to evade arrest by the colonial government.

[2] Felix Boutros (1796–1863) initiated a programme of translating books suitable for higher education into Urdu. See Annemarie Schimmel, *Islam in the Indian Subcontinent* (Leiden: E.J. Brill, 1980), p. 185.

[3] For a study of the introduction of printing in Muslim South Asia, see Francis Robinson, *Islam and Muslim History in South Asia* (New Delhi: Oxford University Press, 2000). Once the Muslims overcame their resistance to the written word, a spurt in Urdu printing was observed with large numbers of tracts and books being published from the 1830s. Initially led by the ulama, printing activity soon came to embrace secular subjects as the Muslim world view broadened. In tracing the effects of print and religious change, Robinson also speaks of the Indian Muslim's growing affiliation with the ummah and how the Islamic vision was increasingly being used to embrace the Muslim community across the world.

Benjamin Disraeli, William Thackeray, Alexander Dumas, George Eliot, R.L. Stevenson, etc.[4] Along with the dissemination of ideas, manners, and mores came the histories of nationalist and liberation struggles in Italy and Ireland. Soon the Italian mathematician Carlo Antonio Manzini (1599–1677) and the Italian revolutionary Giuseppe Garibaldi (1807–1882) became household names and the saga of Irish revolutionaries was being taught through Indian textbooks.[5]

The opening of the Suez Canal in 1869 increased traffic from Europe—both of people and ideas. A new class of intelligentsia emerged, along with traders and missionaries who had long been plying the eastern sea routes. This was the scholar, the writer, and the professional journalist. English language newspapers began to be increasingly and rapidly available as also books, journals, periodicals, and pamphlets. These brought information from Europe on contemporary and topical events to the readers. This coincided with the rapid growth of the indigenous press.[6] Along with the spread of better rail and road networks and the greater use of telegraphs, news, and news reporting acquired a different and an altogether more contemporary hue.

As the vernacular press became vociferously anti-imperialist and staunchly nationalist, the English press put its weight strongly behind the colonial interests. Virtually from its inception—from the time of Warren Hastings (1732–1818) and Lord Cornwallis (1737–1805)—the scope of the English-language press had been limited. It served British interests. Owned and edited by Englishmen, initially set up to serve the small colony of British residents who carried the White Man's Burden in hot, dusty,

---

[4] The institution of the public library introduced mass reading habits. The Calcutta Public Library (established in 1836) and the Madras Literary Society (1818) allowed common people to walk in and access the wealth of world literature. For details, see Priya Joshi, 'Reading in the Public Eye: The Circulation of Fiction in Indian Libraries, c. 1835–1901', in Stuart H. Blackburn and Vasudha Dalmia (eds), *India's Literary History* (Ranikhet: Permanent Black, 2010), pp. 280–326.

[5] See Surendranath Banerjea, *A Nation in Making* (Calcutta: Oxford University Press, 1963) for the influence of Manzini; and Lala Lajpat Rai, 'Unhappy India', in B.R. Nanda (ed.), *Collected Works of Lala Lajpat Rai*, vol. XIV (New Delhi: Manohar, 2010).

[6] See, Uma Dasgupta, 'The Indian Press 1870–1880: A Small World of Journalism', *Modern Asian Studies*, vol. 11, no. 2 (1977), pp. 213–35.

remote corners and provincial outposts, it made some efforts to change its character after 1857. It took upon itself the onerous task of directing and educating public opinion. But its views did not always find favour with the new breed of politically minded English-educated Indians: 'British assertions of authority met persistent resistance from both regional rulers and the Indian officials employed by the British.'[7]

Many educated Indians launched a number of newspapers and periodicals in English,[8] but these ventures were destined to suffer in a country where the vast majority could not read English. It was left to the vernacular press to not just mould and define public opinion, but steer debates and discussions and focus the reader's attention on social, religious, and literary issues, as well as provide information on political events in India and abroad.[9] From veiled innuendoes through a 'subversive subtext',[10] the Urdu newspapers began to display an increasingly hostile attitude towards the British and a markedly nationalist tone. Moreover, with the far lower

[7] Michael H. Fisher, 'The Office of the *Akhbar Nawis*: The Transition from Mughal to British Forms', *Modern Asian Studies*, vol. 27, no. 1 (1993), p. 45. The *akhbar nawis* (news-writer whose job was to collect and transmit specific kinds of information and who, therefore, also doubled up as an intelligence agent who reported and interpreted events) was institutionalized during Akbar's reign. Fisher traces the changes in his role during the colonial time when he walked a tightrope between objective reporting and intelligence gathering.

[8] The earliest English newspapers, such as *Hicky's Gazette* (1780), *The India Gazette*, *The Calcutta Gazette*, *The Madras Courier* (1785), and *The Bombay Herald* (1789) served British interests. Indian-owned English newspapers such as *The Bengal Gazette* (1816) or *Amrita Bazar Patrika* (1868) served the English-educated Indian elites. It was only in the early twentieth century when the national movement became strong that the Indo-Anglian newspapers began to address Indian nationalist issues. It was the regional press that embraced overtly political and social issues and showed a remarkable commitment to political freedom. For a lucid history of the early years of print in India, see John V. Vilanilam, *Mass Communication in India: A Sociological Perspective* (New Delhi: Sage Publications, 2005), pp. 52–4.

[9] Gail Minault, 'From *Akhbar* to News: The Development of the Urdu Press in Early Nineteenth-Century Delhi', in Kathryn Hansen and David Lelyveld (eds), *A Wilderness of Possibilities: Urdu Studies in Transnational Perspective* (New Delhi: Oxford University Press, 2005), pp. 101–21.

[10] Ibid., p. 117.

prices of dailies such as *Oudh Akhbar, Kohinoor, Akhbar-i-Aam,* and *Paisa Akhbar,* the vernacular newspapers posed a threat to major Anglo-Indian dailies such as *The Pioneer, The Times of India, The Statesman,* etc.

Lord Lytton, the viceroy, introduced the Vernacular Press Act,[11] a draconian law designed to curtail the freedom of the Indian-languages press. It came down especially heavily on the non-English newspapers and muzzled any form of criticism of the government. In the wake of widespread protests, the Act was repealed by Lytton's successor, Ripon, in 1881;[12] however, it marked a cleavage between the English and the non-English press.

Several Indian-owned English newspapers were also started, but their fate was not always good; some survived long enough to establish a regular readership, others folded up as soon as funds dried up.[13] Many were

---

[11] For details, see John Dacosta, *Remarks on the Vernacular Press Law of India, or Act IX of 1878* (London: W.H. Allen & Co., 1878).

[12] Ripon introduced widespread reforms, such as introduction of local representation at district-level elections. See Francis Robinson, *Separatism among Indian Muslims: The Politics of the United Provinces' Muslims, 1860–1923* (Cambridge: Cambridge University Press, 1974) for how some of these reforms, such as the introduction of Nagri script, posed a threat to the Urdu-speaking Muslim elite and lead to the Urdu–Hindi controversy. See also W.S. Blunt, *India under Ripon* (London, 1909).

[13] The *Comrade* was started in 1911. It was founded and edited by Mohamed Ali at Calcutta with the motto 'Comrade of all, partisan of none.' This was followed by *Hamdard* in 1912, also founded by Mohamed Ali but in Urdu, and *Al-Hilal* by Maulana Abul Kalam Azad in the same year. The latter two pioneered a new style of Urdu journalism and took a diametrically opposite position from the 'loyalist' position of the Aligarh school of journalism hitherto prevalent in India. I am indebted to Ziya-ul-Hasan Faruqi's *The Deoband School and the Demand for Pakistan* for an understanding of the role of the Deoband ulama in formulating a new kind of 'anti-loyalist', 'pro-nationalist' form of journalism fashioned by young educated Muslims. I shall quote from Faruqi in greater length in the last section of this chapter. The other major Urdu newspapers of this period were the *Urdu-i-Mualla* founded by Maulana Hasrat Mohani in 1906 at Aligarh, the *Muslim Gazette* started by Maulana Wahiduddin Salim from Lucknow in 1910, and the *Zamindar* founded by Maulana Zafar Ali Khan in Lahore in the same year. Together, these were not only anti-loyalist, but also vigorous and radical in content and style. References to them and their editors shall crop up throughout this chapter.

proscribed by the imperial government and forced to shut shop. Norman Gerald Barrier notes how the 'content of the press reflected the awakening mood of Indian politics'. With a boom in printing presses, vernacular journalism too showed an upward swing. Barrier cites 1,359 newspapers and journals in 1905 serving an estimated 2 million subscribers.[14]

A word about the imperial policy of proscription might be useful here. The link between sedition and immorality has been pointed out as also between censorship and surveillance.[15] The Reporters on Native Newspapers[16] were encouraged to carefully track vernacular press to fathom the public mood and it was believed that heavy censorship could deprive the authority of useful information. Often, instead of an outright ban, the government chose to forfeit securities; this had different effects on different proprietors. Some buckled down; others rose to the challenge. The *Zamindar* of Lahore, for instance, lost a security of Rs 2,000, but since the owner could sustain the loss, it put up Rs 10,000 to continue publication; the result was not to the liking of the proscribers:

[The] paper's notoriety increased subscriptions to 15,000. Similarly, the *Comrade* refused to mute its criticism and lost securities of Rs 2,000 and 10,000. Not only did the sanctions fail to affect the publicists, but to the embarrassment of the British, the publishers fought a running court battle, which challenged application of the Press Act and broadcast the Pan-Islamic message. Ultimately, the Government of India resorted to pre-censorship and, fearing the reaction to public prosecution of leaders, interned them for the duration of the war.[17]

Keenly aware of the damage wrought by the press, the government enforced the Press Act in 1913. As a result, Hasrat Mohani's *Urdu-i-Mualla* was forced out of business, the *Tauhid* had its security confiscated

---

[14] Norman Gerald Barrier, *Banned: Controversial Literature and Political Control in British India, 1907–1947* (New Delhi: Manohar, 1978), p. 9.

[15] C.A. Bayly, *Empire and Information: Intelligence Gathering and Social Communication in India, 1780–1870* (Cambridge: Cambridge University Press, 1996), pp. 340–1.

[16] Like the Akhbar navis, these people were employed to track certain news items in the vernacular press, anything and everything that could be of interest to the empire. Copies of cullings from the Native Newspapers are preserved in the National Archives of India (NAI).

[17] Barrier, *Banned*, p. 70.

in 1913, the *Al-Hilal* and *Comrade* were closed in 1914, the Ali brothers were interned in May 1915 for writing 'The Choice of the Turks', and a year later Hasrat Mohani and Maulana Abul Kalam Azad suffered the same fate for writing/publishing 'seditious' material.[18] Gagged and bound, the agitators could neither be quelled nor wished away. As the agitation simmered away in quiet corners, new voices arose and new names replaced those who were put behind bars. Poet-politicians like Mohamed Ali (who used the nom de plume 'Jauhar') and Hasrat Mohani employed stock images of the caged bird to speak out in defiance of those who sought to curb their freedom:

> My opinions are free and so is my body
> It is useless to lock up the body of Hasrat.[19]

The turn of the century saw changes in many parts of the world. Events in North Africa and the Balkans influenced certain sections of the Muslim community in more ways than one. Western imperialism and its increasing aggressiveness angered them. Italy's aggression in Libya in 1911, the French moves against Morocco in 1912, the Balkan War of 1912, and the gradual shrinking of the once-mighty Ottoman Empire brought fear into the hearts of the Indian Muslims. The First World War broke out in 1914 and ravaged Europe for the next four years. When Turkey entered the fray on the German side, the Indian Muslims found themselves on the horns of a dilemma. On the one hand, they resented the British for their role in dismantling the Ottoman Empire; on the other hand, they were willing to be seduced by the promises held out by the British in return for their support on the Allied war front.[20]

---

[18] Exiled from Calcutta, his press seized under the Defence of India Act, Azad was not allowed to enter the provinces of UP, Punjab, Bombay, and Delhi. The only place left for him was Bihar and so he went to Ranchi where he was promptly placed under house arrest for three years till 1919. For details, see Humayun Kabir (ed.), *Azadi-i-Hind: Maulana Abul Kalam Azad* (Azad Kashmir: Arshad Book Sellers, n.d.).

[19] Quoted in Gail Minault, *Gender, Language and Learning: Essays in Indo-Muslim Cultural History* (Ranikhet: Permanent Black, 2009), p. 110.

[20] The British had promised reforms and greater Indian participation in systems of governance as well as greater Muslim representation. And, they did indeed introduce the much-awaited reforms. However, if the Chelmsford Reforms of

Azad captured the mood of the moment when on 1 November 1914 the government informed its Indian subjects through a widely circulated official announcement of its war with Turkey and its much-laboured keenness to avoid any sacrilege to the holy places: 'Possibly there was no Muslim home left in British India which was unaware of the contents of this announcement.'[21] Azad went on to say, pithily, that the world has seen how the government had fulfilled its promises—from the days of Napoleon till the present time.

Meanwhile, Sharif Husain (1854–1931), the amir of Mecca, proclaimed himself to be the 'king' of Hejaz on 10 June 1916. But, by virtue of a Machiavellian treaty signed between Britain and the House of Saud, Ibn al-Saud (a rival tribesman) was recognized by the former as independent sovereign of Najd, Al-Hisa, Qatif, and Jubayl. Given their virtual monopoly of the steamer ships carrying pilgrims from all over South Asia to the Hejaz as well as their stranglehold on trade and commerce, the British presence in the Middle East caused consternation among the custodians of the holy sites scattered all through the region as well as those who flocked to the holy land.[22] Given also the close affinity between Wahhabism and the fledgling Ahl-e-Hadith movement in India, the rise of the House of Saud caused tripping of power lines from West Asia to India. The rise of the Wahhabis in Arabia was supported by the Ahl-e-Hadith and the Nadwat-ul-ulama, but not by the ulama of Firangi Mahal and Bareilly. The Ali brothers and the Khilafat Party, initially supporters of Ibn Saud, changed their stand in later years and by 1925 had parted ways due to Ibn Saud's dealings with the British. To further complicate matters, Abdul Bari and Mohamed Ali came to a parting of ways over the candidacy of

---

1919 were the benign form of these pre-War promises, the Rowlatt Act of the same year showed the ugly side of British rule in India.

[21] Abul Kalam Azad, *Masala-e-Khilafat* (Lahore: Maktaba-e-Ahbab, n.d.), pp. 287–8.

[22] For details on the geopolitics of the Hejaz, see J.L. Burckhardt, *Travels in Arabia* (London: Frank Cass & Co. Ltd, 1968 [reprint]); F.E. Peters, *The Hajj: The Muslim Pilgrimage to Mecca and the Holy Places* (Princeton: Princeton University Press, 1994); Michael Pearson, *The Indian Ocean* (London: Routledge, 2003); Michael Pearson, *Pious Passengers: The Hajj in Earlier Times* (London: Hurst & Co., 1994); and Mushirul Hasan and Rakhshanda Jalil, *Journey to the Holy Land: A Pilgrim's Diary* (New Delhi: Oxford University Press, 2009).

the Khilafat: Ibn Saud or Husain? All pretence of unity was lost as the Muslim politicians and ulama found themselves in two hostile camps: pro-Wahhabi and pro-Hashemite.[23]

Spurred by news of desecration of the holy places at the hands of the Nejdis and their becoming custodians of Mecca and Medina, the Anjuman-e-Khuddam-i-Kaaba (Society of Servants of Kaaba) was formed as early as 1913 by Abdul Bari and Maulana Shaukat Ali. Earlier still, on 15 December 1912, an Indian medical mission called the Red Crescent Medical Mission had gone to Turkey under the leadership of M.A. Ansari. The purpose of this mission was to extend a hand of friendship on behalf of the Indian Muslims to their Turkish brothers-in-faith. Shibli Nomani[24] had written a paean welcoming Dr Ansari back home called 'Khair Maqdam Ansari'. It was published on 12 July 1913 in *Hamdard* and was promptly proscribed by the imperial government.[25] Earlier still, the same Shibli had written a series of three articles entitled '*Musalmanon ki Political Karwat*' (The Political Turning of the Muslims) in 1912 in the *Muslim Gazette* from Lucknow. An excerpt from the second article makes the following observation: 'Muslims have two characteristics: one, they are subjects of the British government, and two, they are Muslim. As a result, their politics is a combination of these two elements and the first element over-rides the second.'[26]

Mohamed Ali[27] made a distinction between the two sorts of Indian Musalman: the '*deendar*' or men of faith who were helpless to stop the

---

[23] Gail Minault, *The Khilafat Movement: Religious Symbolism and Political Mobilisation in India* (New Delhi: Oxford University Press, 1982), p. 206.

[24] Shibli Nomani was a scholar and researcher, apart from being a theologian and a teacher. His travelogues and historical essays provided an invaluable glimpse into the big world outside India to the Urdu reader of his day. His *Heroes of Islam*, published in 1888, concedes that our own ancient historical works compare poorly with the scholarly tradition of European scientific writings.

[25] Rajesh Kumar Parti (ed.), *Ashob*, vol. 1, *National Archives mein Mahfooz Zabt Sudah Adabiyat se Intekhab* (New Delhi: NAI, 1993), pp. 8–11.

[26] From Abdur Razzaq Qureshi, *Nava-i-Azadi* (New Delhi, Maktaba Jamia); translation mine.

[27] Mohamed Ali devised an ingenious variation of the slogan 'Divide and Rule': 'We Divide, They Rule'. Reference found in the private papers of Ghulam Rabbani Taban, NMML, 446, 78.

progress of an avalanche of *'bedeeni'* or 'irreligiousness' and those who are propelled by *'nai raushni'* or new light. In *My Life*, he wrote, 'The international developments which had resulted in the disintegration of the already enfeebled temporal power of Islam were bound to exercise a great influence on the Musalmans. But few could have prophesied the precise form this reaction was to take. Western education had thrust, so to speak, a wedge into the ranks of Indian Muslim society.'[28]

In the previous chapter, we witnessed the consolidation of British power in India. In this section, we shall attempt to establish the impact of outside events on the emerging Indian Muslim identity; in this part of our narrative the colonizing influence of the British will feature more prominently than it has so far. From here, we will go on, in the next section, to see how socialism combined with the effects of both external and internal events to give rise to a pronounced and proactive nationalism. In the concluding section of this chapter, we shall see the reflection of these events in the Urdu literature of this period.

By the early twentieth century, the impact of socialist thinking was much less felt, though the theme of exploitation—both by the colonial government and its collaborators—had begun to figure quite largely in both prose and poetry. But it was not till the October 1917 revolution that the floodgates of socialism and communistic ideas opened into India. Before that, the Japanese victory over Russia in 1904–5 had been a significant landmark in galvanizing the Asian nations against the hegemony of the European powers. Nehru, writing in his *Autobiography*, captured the excitement of those years, 'Japanese victories stirred up my enthusiasm and I waited eagerly for papers for fresh news daily.... Nationalistic ideas filled my mind. I mused of Indian freedom and Asiatic freedom from the thralldom of Europe.'[29]

The Japanese victory inspired Asian leaders and stiffened their resolve to end colonial domination. In India, the extremists led by B.G. Tilak (1856–1920),[30] felt vindicated, for they had all along rejected the politics

---

[28] Mohamed Ali, *My Life: A Fragment—An Authobiographical Sketch of Maulana Mohamed Ali*, ed. Mushirul Hasan (New Delhi: Manohar, 1999), p. 80.

[29] Jawaharlal Nehru, *An Autobiography* (London: John Lane, 1936), p. 16.

[30] Tilak formed the Home Rule League in 1916 to attain the goal of swaraj. His slogan 'Swaraj is my birthright and I shall have it' inspired millions of Indians. He, along with Bipin Chandra Pal from Bengal and Lala Lajpat Rai from Punjab,

of mendicancy or subservience in favour of radical activism. Tilak and Aurobindo Ghosh began to challenge the existing Congress leadership with a new ideology that combined Hindu revivalism and a far more militant political activism than the stalwarts within the Congress were hitherto used to. Content to secure greater Indian participation in existing systems of governance, the Congress was, till then, an elitist, amorphous sort of organization. The split in the Congress between the moderates and extremists in Surat in 1907 marked a significant watershed. For it was here, in Nehru's words, that 'the Congress broke up in disorder and emerged as a purely moderate group'.[31] A year ago, in 1906 the Congress had adopted the goal of swaraj, self-governance; however, it would take 10 long years for this goal to turn into a mass action programme. For that, India had to await the arrival of Gandhi from South Africa in 1915. On a sea voyage from London to South Africa in 1909, Gandhi had already penned a remarkable document; this was the *Hind Swaraj* written in the form of a dialogue between himself (as editor) and an imaginary reader. In it, Gandhi had outlined his conception of Indian freedom, the need for 'soul force' and passive resistance to win the war against an adversary who was 'splendidly armed'.

Before Gandhi's arrival and his demonstration of the power of satyagraha, several other events happened that deserve a brief mention here for the purpose of this dissertation: the Hindi–Urdu controversy in 1900;[32] the proposed partition of Bengal in 1903 by Curzon (the scheme was enacted in 1906, but in the face of charged communal tensions, annulled in 1911);[33]

---

formed the core group of the extremists within the Congress who called for radical action especially after the British had played the communal card in the partition of Bengal. The trio was called the Bal-Pal-Lal triumvirate.

[31] Nehru, *Autobiography*, p. 23.

[32] Nawab Mohsin-ul Mulk, secretary of the Aligarh College, also the secretary of the newly founded Central Urdu Defence Association, led the agitation against the decision of the Government of the United Provinces sanctioning the use of Hindi in Devanagri script as the official vernacular. In later chapters, we shall see that the progressives, unlike most Muslims, were not against the use of Devanagri. They, in fact, supported the move for a single script for all Indian languages: the Roman script.

[33] The decision to annul the Partition in 1911 nullified the gains secured by the Muslims of East Bengal after Curzon's partition of undivided Bengal in 1906.

the Simla Deputation[34] of 1906 which paved the way for the establishment of the All India Muslim League in 1906 in Dhaka; and the Morley–Minto Reforms[35] of 1909.

Noting the emergence of the Indian Muslims as 'a religiopolitical community' in the wake of the establishment of the Muslim League and the colonial reforms of 1909, Mushirul Hasan writes:

The colonial government reforms of 1909, enacted to defuse the Congress demand for a greater share in administration and decision-making was a calculated masterstroke: it discarded the notion and jettisoned the prospect of secular nationalism. It established separate electorates for Muslims, along with reservations and weightages, and thus gave birth to a religiopolitical community, sections of which began to see themselves in the colonial image of being unified, cohesive, and segregated from the Hindus. Separate electorates put a formal seal of approval on the institutionalized conception of Muslim political identity and contributed to the forging of communitarian identities that were, both in conception and articulation, profoundly divisive and inherently conflict-oriented.[36]

Nehru, in his *Autobiography*, wrote, 'From 1907 onwards for several years, India was seething with unrest and trouble. For the first time since the revolt of 1857 India was showing fight and not submitting tamely to foreign rule.'[37]

---

[34] A group of 70 Muslim representatives, headed by Aga Khan, drew up a plan for separate electorates for their community, and presented it to the Viceroy, Lord Minto, at Simla on 1 October 1906.

[35] It allowed, for the first time, election of Indians to the various legislative councils in India. From the Muslim point of view, it was a significant piece of legislation because it stipulated that they be allotted reserved seats in the municipal and district boards, in the provincial councils and in the imperial legislature; the number of reserved seats be in excess of their relative population (25 per cent of the Indian population); and only Muslims should vote for candidates for the Muslim seats (separate electorates).

[36] Mushirul Hasan, 'The Myth of Unity: Colonial and National Narratives', in David Ludden (ed.), *Contesting the Nation: Religion, Community and the Politics of Democracy in India* (Philadelphia: University of Pennsylvania Press, 1996), pp. 185–210.

[37] Nehru, *Autobiography*, p. 21.

Some of the significant events for the purpose of this chapter are: Gandhi's return to India in 1915; the Lucknow Pact[38] of 1916 between the Congress and the Muslim League; and the Montague–Chelmsford Reforms[39] of 1919. However, the blackest chapter of the period under study (1900–1930s) was the infamous Rowlatt Act passed in March 1919. By indefinitely extending 'emergency measures' (under the Defence of India Regulations Act) enacted during the First World War, ostensibly to control public unrest and root out conspiracy, this piece of legislation effectively authorized the government to imprison, without trial, any person suspected of terrorist activities. Anything that smacked of 'revolutionary' activities could be punished. The Rowlatt Act caused widespread outrage among both Hindus and Muslims and led to the first satyagraha under Gandhi's leadership on 6 April 1919. On 10 April 1919, two Congress leaders were arrested in Amritsar—Satya Pal and Saifuddin Kitchlew—culminating in the worst bloodbath the country had yet known: the Jallianwala massacre, three days later. Here is a sample from Saadat Hasan Manto remembering those days in a short story called *1919 ka Ek Din* (A Day in 1919) written sometime in the late 1930s:

It is about those days in 1919, Brother, when agitations against the Rowlatt Act had sprung up all across the Punjab. I am talking about Amritsar. Sir Michael O'Dwyer had forbidden Mahatma Gandhi from entering the Punjab under the Defence of India Rules. Gandhi ji was on his way when he had been stopped near Palwal, arrested and sent back to Bombay. As far as I can understand, Brother, had the English not committed this grave mistake, the massacre at Jallianwala Bagh, which is the bloodiest chapter in the history of British rule in India, would never have occurred.

Hindus, Muslims, Sikhs—alike—held Gandhi ji in veneration. Everyone considered him to be a 'mahatma', a great man, a truly evolved spirit. When the news

---

[38] This was a historic pact by which the Congress accepted separate electorates for the Muslims and allowed them representation much in excess of their proportion of population in the provinces, except in the Punjab and Bengal. Earlier, in 1913, in its annual session also in Lucknow, the League had declared its objective as a steady reform of the existing system of administration, by promoting national unity, by fostering public spirit among the people of India, and by cooperating with other communities.

[39] These were reforms introduced by the British government in India to introduce self-governing institutions gradually.

of his arrest reached Lahore, all business ground to a standstill. When people in Amritsar heard of this, complete and total strikes paralysed the city within the snap of a finger.[40]

Meanwhile, two important developments need to be noted on the Muslim front: the formation of the Jamiayat-i-Ulama-i-Hind in 1919, and the return of Maulana Mahmud-ul Hasan from British imprisonment in Malta in 1920 and issuance of a fatwa giving religious sanction to the non-violent non-cooperation movement launched by Gandhi in the same year. The dawn of January 1921 saw the Muslims of India 'dizzy with the headiness of *azadi*' blindly willing to follow Gandhi on the long march to freedom.[41] Gandhi's call for non-cooperation mingled with the Muslim's desire to rise in defence of their religion. Syed Mahmud (1889–1971), general secretary of the Central Khilafat Committee from 1921 to 1926, appointing Gandhi as a member of the Committee from Bombay in 1922, wrote, 'It is the hardest time for Islam, and we pray that the Almighty Allah may give you strength and fortitude to stand by righteousness and justice at this hour of trial.'[42]

Unfortunately, the atmosphere of communal camaraderie fostered by the conjoined non-cooperation and khilafat movement proved to be short-lived. The hatred for British rule, that had been steadily mounting, reached such an extent that the slightest stirrings of reform or revivalism within Indian Islam too came to be inseparably intertwined with hatred for the British and—by extension—Christianity. Some Muslim theologians had gone so far as to declare the subcontinent, ruled as it was by the British, to be *Dar-ul-Harb* (literally, 'house or abode of war', but used to refer to enemy territory as opposed to *Dar-ul-Islam*, that is, the 'abode of Islam').[43] The managing committee of the Jamiayat-i-Ulama-i-Hind met at Delhi on 18 October

---

[40] Saadat Hasan Manto, *Naked Voices: Stories & Sketches*, translated by Rakhshanda Jalil (New Delhi: Roli/India Ink, 2008), p. 60.

[41] Qazi Muhammad Adeel Abbasi, *Tehreek-e-Khilafat* (New Delhi: Taraqqui Urdu Board, 1978), p. 174.

[42] V.N. Datta and B. Cleghorn, *A Nationalist Muslim and Indian Politics: Being the Selected Correspondence of the Late Dr. Syed Mahmud* (Delhi: Macmillan, 1974), p. 36.

[43] For a detailed study of jihad in colonial India, see Ayesha Jalal, *Partisans of Allah* (Ranikhet: Permanent Black, 2008).

1922 and decided that since Britain was the only Christian power hostile to the Turks and Islam, it was 'haram (unlawful) for any Moslem on the surface of the world to accord any help to this hostile government'.[44] Some among these ulama also contemplated issuing a fatwa prohibiting enlistment in the Army[45] and to discuss the question of jehad. Other intelligence reports cite the reference from the Netherlands Trading Society and the Imperial Bank of Persia of remittances of £ 10,000 and £ 80,000 by the Sindh and the Central Khilafat Committee for Kemal Pasha at Angora.[46]

Some among the Muslim community interpreted the description of Dar-ul-Harb to be apt also because, apart from the infidel conquerors, there were the Hindu infidels who held positions of power and patronage in India, positions that were, they believed, denied to the Muslims. At the same time, there were some Muslims who felt the need to turn the gaze inwards and look at the reasons for the complete disarray among their numbers. Communitarian politics had so divided the people that small, everyday things that had always been taken for granted now became contentious issues: such as the arti–namaz disputes among temples and mosques. By the 1930s, the rift between the Congress and the Muslim League had grown to such an extent that they were 'like two trees growing on either side of the road'.[47]

To go back to the years immediately after the First World War, the currents of change were sweeping across the Ottoman Empire all through

---

[44] Extract from Weekly Intelligence Summary for week ending 21 November 1922; IOR/L/PJ/12/133, File 6835 (B)/23. Soon after 1920, the Khilafat money scandal began to assume alarming proportions. Things reached such a pass when in January 1923 Seth Chotani admitted to Ansari and Hakim Ajmal Khan that he had invested Rs 16 lakhs of the Khilafat fund into his family business. For details of the Khilafat money scandal, see Minault, *Khilafat Movement*, p. 189.

[45] Ibid., weekly intelligence report ending 14 November 1922, File 6835 (B)/23, 'On 21 September Mohammad Sajjad wrote to Chotani and advised the Central Khilafat Committee to announce to Mohamedan sepoys that further service in the Army is haram (sinful).' Mohammed Sajjad was the vice Amir-i-Shariat in Bihar and Orissa and described in the Report as 'one of the most influential members of the Jamiat-ul-Ulema'.

[46] A hand-written note marked 'secret' by P. Biggani, IOR/L/PJ/12/133 File 6835 (B)/23.

[47] Minault, *Khilafat Movement*, p. 189.

these turbulent times, where the Ottoman Empire was carved up into many small, independent countries and the regime of Sultan Abdul Hameed II was overthrown by the Young Turks. The Young Turks, like their counterparts in India in the Congress, ushered in an era of reform and change. Their revolution too impacted the Indian national movement whose leaders were widely celebrated for their heroism. Events in the Islamic countries had an unsettling effect on India. The Balkan wars in particular stirred the consciousness of educated Muslims, who realized the consequences of Turkey's capitulation to European powers. A pan-Islamic tide with its focus on the Sultan of Turkey who was also the Khalifa of the Sunni Muslims, swept across north India. Poets and writers wrote in white heat about the plight and sufferings of the people in the Balkans. A poem by an unknown writer, Farhat, who wrote *Fughan-e-Kaaba* (The Lament of Kaaba) published in 1920 in *Garya-e-Hind*, placed the blame for the loss of Khilafat squarely on the 'Hindwallon' (the people of Hind):

> The sanctity of the Kaaba is saying:
> The people of Hind have snatched the Khilafat
> How can the Turks protect me now
> The people of Hind have snatched the Khilafat.[48]

By 1919, the pan-Islamic ferment had reached a crescendo with the establishment of the Central Khilafat Committee. Gandhi had been convinced by the Ali brothers that the Khilafat was a cause dearer than life to the Indian Muslims, and for the next four years the Khilafat movement raged across India like a tornado, becoming the first revolutionary mass movement for Indian Muslims. It brought more Muslims together—as it turned out, for slighter reasons—than the later movement for independence. While Muslim opinion and support was divided between the Congress and the League, when it came to the subject of separate electorates, it was unanimous over the Khilafat issue. The peasants who had given whole-hearted support to the non-cooperation and Khilafat movement had done so more out of a sense of impending freedom, a release from the yoke of crushing poverty and oppression rather than any real understanding of the geopolitics of distant Turkey or even any sense of real allegiance—spiritual or otherwise—to a remote khalifa. Nehru,

---

[48] Parti, *Ashob*, p. 152; translation mine.

on his tour of provincial towns and cities in the early 1920s, was quick to grasp this. He wrote:

> Even in remote bazaars the common folk talked of the Congress and Swaraj (for the Nagpur Congress had finally made Swaraj the goal), and what had happened in the Punjab, and the Khilafat—but the word 'Khilafat' bore a strange meaning in most of the remote areas. People thought it came from *khilaf*, an Urdu word meaning 'against' or 'opposed to', and so they took it to mean: opposed to Government![49]

During December 1923, a delegation of Indians comprising Qazi Abdul Ghaffar[50] went to Lausanne with a message for Ismet Pasha on behalf of the Khilafat Committee suggesting that another khalifa be found if the Great National Assembly did not revoke its decree depriving the last khalifa of his temporal powers. Ismet Pasha entrusted Ghaffar to take a message for the Khilafat Committee urging it to provide financial assistance by asking Indian industrialists to invest in Turkish concerns and to continue their support of Turkey.[51] The Anjuman-e-Khuddam-i-Kaaba was also reported to have requested the Turkish government to permit a branch of the society to be opened in Angora and other important Arab towns.[52]

When Mustafa Kemal, the architect of the new Turkish republic and the newly constituted Turkish National Assembly, abolished the Khilafat on 3 March 1924, the Khilafat movement in India collapsed like a house of cards. Not only did the movement lose its raison d'etre, it led to confusion and disarray among Indian Muslims; they were left 'politically all dressed up and nowhere to go'.[53] In equal measure, it made many Hindus question the allegiance and interests of the Indian Muslims.[54] In hindsight,

---

[49] Nehru, *Autobiography*, p. 69.

[50] The author of *Laila ke Khutoot* whom we shall repeatedly encounter in our narrative on the progressives.

[51] Intelligence Report, IOR/l/PJ/12/133, File 6835 (B)/23.

[52] Eastern Summary No. 1192, dated 3.7.23 entitled 'Turkish Pan-Islamic Policy: Propaganda among Pilgrims, etc.': IOR/l/PJ/12/133, File 6835 (B)/23. Note, interestingly enough, the entire file is called 'India: Pan-Islamic Intrigue.'

[53] Peter Hardy, *The Muslims of British India* (Cambridge: Cambridge University Press, 1972), p. 198.

[54] The collapse of the movement left the Hindus with the 'bitter realization that now that the external stimulus of Muslim anti-imperialism had failed, they might have to carry on the struggle alone; and that instead of being allies

it seems a miracle that the movement lasted as long as it did—given the acute dearth of intellectual content in it—and brought so many Muslims together so strongly. Again, in hindsight, it seems evident that the movement was essentially the result of an emotional outburst, stemming from a deep-seated, partly nostalgic, partly emotional response. The enemy in both cases—Muslim Middle East and Muslim India—was common: the British. It must be noted that the growing Muslim antipathy to Pax Britannica took a long time to get fully and coherently articulated. The inchoate distrust of the British presence, distilled and expressed in poetry, pamphleteering, and political speeches did not find a conclusive, intellectually grounded, well-articulated form for a very long time. This was, partly, due to the different shades among the Muslim intelligentsia—from the reactionary to the progressive, the liberal to the traditionalist, the nationalists to the loyalists.

A great ferment, however, was clearly brewing among the Indian Muslims which combined nostalgia for a decaying institution (the Khilafat) with growing anti-colonial sentiments. Urdu poetry and prose mirrored the feelings of what was no doubt a turbulent era. Shibli Nomani's 'Hungama-e-Balqan' (The Turmoil in the Balkans) is a classic exposition in poetry of the trauma experienced by an entire generation of Indian Muslims. Its strength lies in its restraint, self-awareness, and its intuitive cognizance of the far-reaching implications of the trouble in the Balkans:

> When decline has set in over political power,
> The name and banner will stand how long?

> The smoke from the burnt candle of
> A vanished assembly will rise how long?

> When the sky has torn the mantle of power to pieces,
> Its shreds will float in the air how long?

> Gone is Morocco, gone is Persia. We have now to see
> This helpless sick man of Turkey will live how long?

> This tide of woe which is advancing from the Balkans,
> The sighs of the oppressed will stem how long? ...

---

the Muslims might develop into a third force in the triangular fight for the subcontinent's advance towards freedom.' Aziz Ahmad, *Studies in Islamic Culture in the Indian Environment* (Oxford: Clarendon Press, 1964), p. 268.

Shibli! Should you long to migrate, where can you go now?
Syria or Najd or Gyrene are sanctuaries how long?[55]

Like Shibli, another remarkable figure, Hasrat Mohani,[56] eloquently expressed the anxieties of his generation through both poetry and journalism.[57] In a ghazal written in 1917, and published in *An-Nizamiya*, the journal from Lucknow's Firangi Mahal, Mohani made a passionate protest against the British capture of Baghdad in March 1917:

Hasrat's request to the Shah of Jilan[58] is that Islam wishes
That the fate of Baghdad should not have been so decided.

It must be remembered that it was Hasrat Mohani who first recorded in prose, and later used as a rallying cry at a labour rally in Calcutta in 1928, the enduring cry of revolutionaries anywhere in India whatever be the cause or the language of the oppressed: *Inquilab Zindabad!* (Long live the revolution!).[59] Hasrat Mohani, like Shibli Nomani before him was, incidentally, a fervent pan-Islamist as well as nationalist insofar as both

---

[55] Shibli Nomani, *Kulliyat-i-Shibli* (Azamgarh: Maarif Press, 1954), p. 53; translation mine.

[56] Hasrat Mohani (1875–1951) was a poet, journalist, nationalist, and politician. He addressed the first Indian Communist Conference on 26 December 1925 in Kanpur. He was a member of the CPI till 1927. He joined the Muslim League in 1937. He remained in India after Partition as an independent-minded, liberal, devout Muslim who prayed regularly and went for the hajj 13 times, but was also a 'Communist Muslim'.

[57] An excellent biography of Hasrat is available in Urdu: Khaliq Anjum, *Hasrat Mohani* (New Delhi: Publications Division, 1994). Another useful book in Urdu is by Ahmar Lari, *Hasrat Mohani: Hayat aur Karname* (Lucknow: Nami Press, 1973).

[58] The Shah of Jilan refers to the great Sufi master Abdul Qadir Jilani whose shrine is in Baghdad and who is regarded as the founder of the Qadiriya silsila of Sufis.

[59] This Urdu slogan has an interesting history. Said to have been first coined by Iqbal, it has been used by people from across the political, linguistic, socio-cultural spectrum of India from the early decades of the twentieth century till present times. It has crossed the Vindhyas and is heard used by Malayalam and Tamil-speaking people as it is in the north. It is, after Hindi film songs, the best example of the most vibrant use of Urdu by a heterogeneous group of people. Bhagat Singh and his revolutionary comrades popularized the use of this slogan.

believed in a modus vivendi with the Congress.[60] Both wrote prolifically in Urdu and both drew upon world events to inspire, rouse, and challenge the imagination of the Indian Muslims. Shibli's disciple Maulana Abul Kalam Azad[61] was cast in much the same mould. There was much in the lives and careers of these men which inspired their contemporaries and future generations.

The trauma of a generation that Shibli expressed was taken to new poetic heights by the genius of Iqbal, and it was Iqbal who expressed the disquiet that afflicted the Muslim mind in startling ways that no one had ever attempted before. This disquiet found expression in different ways: there was the sorrow over the loss of freedom or power of an Islamic race, both in the distant past and the present; concern about the future of the Islamic countries subject to European hegemony; and suspicion and distrust of Western powers that had, in the first place, plotted and brought about the downfall of Muslim rule everywhere. In a rejoinder to his own famous *Shikwa* (Complaint), *Jawab-e-Shikwa* (Answer to the Complaint, both published in *Bang-e-Dara*, 'The Call of the Road', 1924), Iqbal wrote:

> The tumult caused by the Bulgar onslaught and aggression
> Is to rouse you out of complacency and gird your loins for action.
> Presume not that to hurt your feelings, it is a sinister device
> It is a challenge to your self-respect, it is a call to sacrifice
> Why tremble at the snorting of the chargers of your foes?
> The flame of truth is not snuffed out by the breath the enemy blows.[62]

To return to the troubles inside India, earlier, in 1916, the Lucknow Pact had secured separate electorates for the Muslims and ushered in a short-

---

[60] Mohani, despite brief flirtations with the CPI and Muslim League, chose to be with the Congress; he even stayed back in India after Partition, cast his lot with the Congress, in order to safeguard the interests of the Indian Muslims. It is worth noting that as long ago as 1921, Mohani wanted to move a resolution defining swaraj as 'complete independence', free from all foreign control; it was rejected by the Congress.

[61] See Ian Douglas, *Abul Kalam Azad: An Intellectual and Religious Biography* (New Delhi: Oxford University Press, 1988) for a study of Azad's contribution to intellectual, political, and religious thought in India.

[62] Mohammad Iqbal, *Shikwa and Jawab-i-Shikwa, Complaint and Answer: Iqbal's Dialogue with Allah*, translated by Khushwant Singh (New Delhi: Oxford University Press, 1981), p. 90.

lived period of Hindu–Muslim unity. Relations between the two communities had been strained since the partition of Bengal in 1905. A year later, in 1906, the Muslim League was established in Dhaka under the leadership of the Agha Khan to safeguard Muslim interests. Among Hindus, a movement for the revival of Hindu religious life initiated in the nineteenth century was being strengthened by men like Vivekananda and Sri Aurobindo. Hindi poets like Bharatendu Harishchandra (1850–1885), Pratap Narain Misra (1856–1894), Radha Charan Goswami (1859–1923), Kishorilal Goswami (1866–1932), Mahavir Prasad Dwivedi (1864–1938), and Subhadra Kumari Chauhan (1904–1948), and Bengali writers like Bankim Chandra Chattopadhyay (1838–1894) stoked the fires of an increasingly militant nationalism that many perceived as a Hindu nationalism, for it reviled the Muslims as dominant, oppressive, and destructive.[63] All through the 1920s, the Shuddhi movement and the Arya Samaj gained ground among the Hindu revivalists. Running parallel were the various movements of the Muslim revivalists who kept raising their voice against the dilution and corruption of Islam under the influence of the *kafirs*.[64]

Several attempts were made to not just 'defend' Islam against the combined infidel presence of the British and Hindus, but also, in the bargain, strengthen and bolster Indian Islam. Different voices and movements sprang up in different parts of the country, striving to give the Indian Muslims a measure of self-assurance with varying results. Unfortunately, some sprang from the bedrock of fear and threat; thousands of Muslims migrated to Afghanistan in search of a sanctuary in 1920 in what was called the *hijrat* movement[65] and several thousand more took part in the Moplah

---

[63] Mushirul Hasan, 'Myth of Unity', pp. 220–1.

[64] Paul Brass has argued that *both* the Hindu and Muslim revivalist movements chose to emphasize differences between their communities rather than similarities. Brass also maintains how the religious elites of both communities made an 'explicit choice'; the revivalist movements selected ideals, real or imaginary, from the past to suit their purposes. Paul Brass, *Language, Religion and Politics in North India* (London: Cambridge University Press, 1974), p. 126.

[65] Hijrat, meaning 'exodus', takes its name from the Prophet Muhammad's move from Mecca to Medina in search of a sanctuary. In the summer of 1920, several thousand Muslims, many of whom were illiterate peasants, were encouraged to escape the oppressive rule of the infidels (Dar-ul-harb) and go to the Muslim kingdom of Afghanistan (which could be said to be Dar-ul-Islam). Peasants, many

Uprising[66] on the Malabar Coast in 1921. Some movements sprang from a missionary or proselytizing zeal, such as the Tablighi Jamaat.[67] Others had a relatively more secular 'agenda'. For instance, in July 1929 a group of 'Congress Muslims' organized themselves into a group called the Muslim Nationalist Party with the intention of taking on the communal Muslim leaders. In Nehru's words, while they had 'some success' and a 'large part of the Muslim intelligentsia seemed to be with them', they were 'all upper-middle-class folk, and there *were no dynamic personalities among them*'.[68] The 'communal leaders' who, according to Nehru, being the 'greater adepts' held sway over the masses. The Muslim Nationalist Party proved to be short-lived and had all but collapsed by 1934 leaving the field clear to the greater adepts!

At the end of a decade of growing communal tendencies among both communities, the establishment in 1930 of a group of progressive-minded and socially committed individuals—the Khudai Khidmatgar or Servants of God—seemed like a strange and miraculous occurrence. This group of divergent Pakhtun tribes from the North-West Frontier Province (NWFP), headed by the charismatic Khan Abdul Ghaffar Khan, displayed a remarkable commitment to the cause of Indian nationalism; more importantly, they showed how fighting for freedom from British rule was in no way

---

from Sindh and NWFP, were encouraged to believe by the agitators that the king of Afghanistan was waiting to receive them with open arms and the gift of fertile lands. The number of those who went is put variously at 18,000 to 500,000. Those who reached the Afghan borders were turned back ruthlessly. A few of those who reached Afghanistan later moved on to Russia. Some returned home to India imbued with new ideas of socialism and change.

[66] The Moplahs are poor Muslim peasants along the Malabar Coast. When news of the Khilafat agitation reached them, these poor peasants numbering about a million, rose in rebellion against their British masters. Their uprising was brutally crushed, but like the hijrat movement it is an early example of a mass peasant movement.

[67] The movement was founded in 1926 by Maulana Muhammad Ilyas Kandhelvi (1898–1982) in the Mewat province. The inspiration for devoting his life to Islam came to Ilyas during his second pilgrimage to the Hejaz in 1926. Maulana Ilyas put forward the slogan: '*Ai Musalmano! Musalman bano!*' (O Muslims! Be Muslims!).

[68] Nehru, *Autobiography*, pp. 138–9; italics mine.

discordant with Muslim ideals. Another example of a 'progressive' people's movement is the Ahrar movement which sprang up in the Punjab under the leadership of Chaudhry Afzal Haq (d. 1942) who stressed obedience to the Shariah, but did yeoman's service in the Punjab and Kashmir areas.

While the Indian Muslim was looking at different ways to forge a new identity—one that would be in consonance with the demands of his nationalism and religion, a significant event took place. After the surrender of Turkey's sultan, the communist government of Russia recognized the establishment of a secular government by Mustafa Kemal. This open support of a newly emerging Asian nation state by the largest Western country provided a new way of viewing the East–West conflict. The West, or at least one major Western power, the Soviet Russia, was not only viewing Islam with sympathy, but also extending a helping hand to Muslims. As a result, a new dimension was added to the traditional bipolar world view. This new ingredient was communism. We shall look at it in more detail in the second section of this chapter.

Introduction of Socialist Thought and Setting-up of the CPI

The Russian revolution opened a window to the future.[69] It triggered new debates on state and society. Some of these debates found expression in the establishment of the CPI in 1925 which, in turn, provided a fertile ground for left-leaning writers to gain a stronghold and eventually led to the formation of the PWM a decade later. My contention, in this book, is that the PWA was the manifestation of a movement that was by no means inconsistent with the existing liberal and enlightened trends in Urdu literature; it was, if anything, a logical extension of what was already being debated from social platforms and also, increasingly, being written about by Muslim writers.

However, there were two new developments. One was the strong ideological thrust, and the other was the emphasis on a changeover and not just a re-negotiation with the colonial government. The new breed of socialists exhorted, rather demanded, a break from the past and the conventions—both literary and social—that they felt shackled them and inhibited a move towards the brighter future that awaited the Indian masses. Change would

---

[69] Georg Lukács, *History and Class Consciousness* (Cambridge: MIT Press, 1971), p. xi.

come to the Indian peasants, just as it had to their brethren in Russia after the overthrow of the repressive, regressive Czarist regime.[70] By 1921, a substantial number of books and pamphlets had appeared that gave fairly authoritative information on Lenin and the Russian revolution: there were *Lenin vs. Gandhi* by S.A. Dange in English; *Nicolai Lenin: His Life and Work* by G.V. Krishna Rao; *Socialism* by V.S. Sarawate in Marathi; *Lenin and the Russian Revolution* by Aziz Bhopali in Urdu; *The Liberator of the Poor in Russia—Nicolai Lenin* by Gorakh in Kannada; *Biplab Pathe Russiar Rupantar* by A.C. Sen in Bengali; among others.[71] The influence of the Russian revolution was recognized not just by Indians, but also by the British. Montagu, the British secretary of state to India, and Chelmsford, the viceroy, in their momentous *Report on Indian Constitutional Reforms* noted thus: 'The revolution in Russia in its beginning was regarded in India as a triumph over despotism; and notwithstanding the fact that it has since involved that unhappy country in anarchy and dismemberment, it has given impetus to Indian political aspirations.'[72]

During the First World War, the Ghadar (Revolt) Party and its associates in Berlin had prepared brochures in Urdu and Punjabi which were dropped among Indian soldiers in France by German aircraft. These brochures and pamphlets played up issues such as 'poor pay, racism and British attacks on Indian religion'.[73] Back home, some socialist literature was being made available in the form of British newspapers like *The Herald, Workers' Dreadnaught,* and *Soviet Russia*. The first Urdu translation of the *Communist Manifesto* was serialized in Maulana Abul Kalam Azad's weekly newspaper *Al-Hilal*.[74] The translation was done by Maulana Abdur

---

[70] Ali Ashraf and G.A. Syomin (eds), *October Revolution and India's Independence: Proceedings of the Soviet Land Seminar on 'The Great October Socialist Revolution and India's Struggle for National Liberation'*, New Delhi, August 20–21, 1977 (New Delhi: Sterling Publishers, 1977).

[71] G. Adhikari, *Documents of the Communist Party of India* (henceforth *Documents*), vol. I (New Delhi: PPH, 1971), p. 275.

[72] *Report on Indian Constitutional Reforms, 1918*, p. 14. Cited by M.R. Masani, *The Communist Party of India: A Short History* (London: Derek Vershcoyle, 1954), p. 11.

[73] Barrier, *Banned*, p. 68.

[74] I am grateful to Baidar Bakht who helped locate the reference found in Sajjad Zaheer, *Sajjad Zaheer ke Mazameen* (Lucknow: Uttar Pradesh Urdu Academy, 1979), p. 24. *Al-Hilal* was published during 1912–15 and in 1927. However,

Razzaq Malihabadi (1889–1959). Mushir Hosain Kidwai, the talukdar of Gadia in Barabanki district, influenced by the rising tide of socialism in the West, wrote a pamphlet called *Islam and Socialism*[75] which attempted to prove this radical connection through references from the Holy Quran and the Hadith.[76] Many other scholars and theologians subsequently attempted to prove the link between socialism and Islamic tenets; they did so by stressing that while the Prophet's socialism was 'ethical', the modern breed of socialists was 'materialists' who attacked capitalism, but espoused agnosticism. Earlier, Syed Ahmad Khan and Shibli had already established an intellectual tradition within the framework of religion. *Zamana* and *Muhammadi*, two of the Khilalfatist newspapers of Calcutta, gave further credence to the Bolshevik movement by projecting it as the friend of Islam and the oppressed.[77] Abul Kalam Azad, keeping in mind the demands of the changing times, wrote on matters of faith and religion and provided contemporary commentaries on the Holy Quran. In fact, *Al-Hilal* proved to be so popular and created such a stir among its readers with its revolutionary contents that within the first three months of its appearance, Azad felt constrained to re-publish all the back issues so that readers could maintain a complete set.[78] Later, others attempted to correlate religion with science, but mostly the attempts were rhetorical in nature. It would appear that the

---

according to Humayun Ansari, an Urdu translation of the *Manifesto* appeared in *Madina*. See Humayun Khizar Ansari, *The Emergence of Socialist Thought among North Indian Muslims, 1917–1947* (Lahore: Book Traders, 1990), p. 107.

[75] Mushir Hosain Kidwai, *Islam and Socialism* (London, 1913).

[76] For a detailed study of pan-Islamic groups active in London, see Humayun Khizar Ansari, 'Making Transnational Connections: Muslim Networks in Early-Twentieth Century Britain', in Nathalie Clayer and Eric Germain (eds), *Islam in Inter-War Europe* (New York: Columbia University Press, 2008). 'Like Barkatullah, he [Kidwai] believed that revolutionary socialism was wholly compatible with the achievement of Muslim aim.' Ibid., p. 38.

[77] Ansari, *Emergence of Socialist Thought among North Indian Muslims*, p. 52.

[78] Humayun Kabir (ed.), *Azadi-i-Hind: Maulana Abul Kalam Azad* (Azad Kashmir: Arshad Book Sellers, n.d.), p. 10. Azad goes on to say that two years after its launch the weekly print-run of *Al-Hilal* was an astounding 26,000. He also mentions the conflict with the Aligarh school, which after Syed Ahmad Khan, had fallen in the hands of men who seemed no more than puppets in the hands of the British.

great majority of thinkers who wrote in Urdu seemed afraid of change; when faced with new concepts and new social, economic, and political ideas, they preferred to do so within the comforting confines of religion. This might explain why many theorists, publicists, and intellectuals tried to cast socialism and socialistic ideas in the mould of Islam.

Iqbal introduced modern philosophical concepts, gleaned from his study in Europe, and vastly broadened the scope of the existing intellectual discourse among educated Muslims, yet keeping it all the while tethered to its quintessentially religious moorings. In his passionate protests against the capitalist and imperialist forces, he propounded the message of 'socialism' couched in Islam:

> The capitalist from the blood of workers' veins makes himself a clear ruby;
> Landlords' oppression despoils the villagers' fields: Revolution![79]

And:

> What is the Quran? For the capitalist, a message of death:
> It is the patron of the property-less slave.[80]

Given his own vast reading and early exposure to European philosophy, poets like Iqbal had some understanding of socialism (though not of communism per se, as has been indicated in different ways by Sajjad Zaheer and W.C. Smith). Soon, even the less privileged among the Indian Muslim intelligentsia began to have a steady exposure to socialist thinking through a stream of propagandist literature that was increasingly making its way into India from the 1920s onwards. Most of the Marxist–Communist tomes of the period began to be available in Urdu; some were serialized in the many Urdu-language journals and newspapers that sprang up during this time. A flourishing translator's bureau existed in Tashkent, and Indian mujahidin from Afghanistan (who had set-off to fight beside the Ottoman army, but had either ended up in Turkey or were in the process of finding their way back home) were introduced to socialist literature by men like M.N. Roy and Abdul Rab Peshawari. Led by Akbarjan, another batch of about 100 muhajirs crossed over into Soviet Russia in July–August 1920. The *Azad Hindustan Akhbar* of 1 October 1920 reported that seven delegates from India participated in the Congress of Peoples of the East

---

[79] See *Zabur-i-Ajam*, p. 134.
[80] From '*Paygham-i Afghani ba Millat e Rusiyah*', in *Jawid Nama*, p. 89.

held in Baku.[81] In fact, Indians (again, many of whom were the straggling mujahidin) returning from the Communist University of the Toilers of the East[82] in Moscow introduced Marxism to Indian intellectuals upon their return. In 1922, Soviet Russia set aside funds for promoting the organization of communist groups that would proactively intervene and encourage revolutionary activity in India. M.N. Roy set up a network through which men, ideas, and literature would find its way from Soviet Russia into India. Ghulam Husain, who had translated some of Roy's communist writings into Urdu, was given a substantial sum of money to set up the Urdu daily *Inqilab* (Revolution) from Lahore in 1922; Comintern's magazine *Vanguard* was launched by M.N. Roy from Calcutta in the same year. *Inqilab* came to be known as 'the people's paper' and its office soon became a hub of socialist activity in Lahore. Among those associated with it were Shams al-din Hasan and M.A. Khan who, along with Ghulam Husain, were also office bearers in the North Western Railway Workers' Union.[83] It is significant that a great many of those who were participating in the fledgling communist/socialist activities at various rungs and in different capacities were Muslims. Even a cursory reading of Adhikari's *Documents* throws up a profusion of Muslim names.

Ghulam Rabbani Taban (1914–1993),[84] a communist and active member of the PWA, in an essay entitled 'Some Thoughts on the Soviet Union', recalls:

During the closing years of the 1920s, while still at school, we at times heard some fragmentary stories about Russia that trickled though colonial censors. The news of the Russian revolution and its achievements thrilled us. I had no perception of a revolution but the term had been familiarized by the full-throated cries of 'Long Live Revolution' ringing throughout the country.[85]

---

[81] Adhikari, *Documents*, vol. I, p. 48.

[82] Established on 21 April 1921 in Moscow by the Communist International (Comintern) as a training college for communist cadres in the colonial world.

[83] This paragraph has been largely built from H.K. Ansari's *Emergence of Socialist Thought among North Indian Muslims*.

[84] An important progressive poet and critic, his works include *Saz-e-Larzan*, *Hadees-e-Dil*, *Nawa-e-Awara*, *Shauq-e-Safar*, and a collection of essays in English entitled *Poetics to Politics*. He worked for over two decades as a manager at the Maktaba Jamia from 1949 onwards.

[85] Ghulam Rabbani Taban Papers, 1957–99, NMML, File No. 446, p. 78.

Taban goes on to mention how Nehru's *Soviet Russia* and Tagore's *Letters* written from Moscow were hugely popular with college students because 'they gave a glimpse into a fairytale world.' He also mentions Iqbal, as one of the tall poppies who was also the earliest to introduce socialism and the socialist movement to young people in India through his rousing poetry.

A visceral hatred for English imperialism led the leaders of Comintern and the Indian people to find common cause; it united them in the prospect of a joint campaign against a common enemy. According to E.H. Carr, the left-wing British historian and journalist, Indians were turning perhaps not so much to the communism of Moscow, but towards the political strength of Moscow, and the Comintern was not immune from the temptation of regarding the peoples of the East as pieces on the chessboard of the diplomatic war with Britain and her allies. The thrust of the socialist activities, as well as the brunt of the propaganda literature making its way from Moscow into India via Afghanistan, was anti-imperialist rather than pro-communist or even anti-British. Till 1920 or so, it had little effect on the 'radicalisation of Indian Muslims'.[86] The situation changed after the Second Congress of the Comintern in July 1920. The Russian Revolution had had little impact in Europe; the Bolshevik leaders thus decided to look east. In 1919 at the Second All-Russian Congress of Communist organizations of the East, Lenin declared, 'The socialist revolution will not be only or chiefly a struggle of the revolutionary proletarians in each country against its bourgeoisie—no, it will be a struggle of all colonies and countries oppressed by imperialism, of all dependent countries, against international imperialism.'[87]

The Bolsheviks had been keenly following events in India for a variety of reasons.[88] One, they saw even a threat to British power in India as a way of undermining British hegemony in other parts of the world. Britain represented the biggest obstacle in the global revolution being dreamed of in the new socialist state, and if India were to rise up in revolt against the colonial master it would, they hoped, show the way to other suppressed nations

---

[86] Ansari, *Emergence of Socialist Thought among North Indian Muslims*, pp. 37–8.

[87] Quoted in E.H. Carr, *The Bolshevik Revolution*, vol. 13 (London: Macmillan, 1953), p. 236.

[88] This section has been built from a reading of Gene D. Overstreet and Marshall Windmiller, *Communism in India* (Bombay: Perennial Press, 1960).

such as Arabia, Egypt, China, Tibet, Persia, and large parts of Africa and the Middle East. Moreover, India, the Bolsheviks believed, was ripe for revolution and an ideal vehicle to spring a revolution that could catapult the 'idea' of revolt onto a larger platform. They found many active rebels among scattered émigré groups who could carry the seeds of the Bolshevik ideology. Some of them had settled in Germany after First World War when they had looked towards Germany for arms and money. After the German defeat, they gravitated naturally towards the Bolsheviks in search of similar support. Chief among these were Virendranath Chattopadhyay[89] (1880–1937) and Bhupendranath Dutta (1880–1961), Swami Vivekananda's younger brother, in Berlin; Raja Mahendra Pratap Singh (1886–1979), Ubaidullah Sindhi (1872–1944), and Maulvi Barkatullah (1854–1927) in Kabul; Lala Lajpat Rai (1865–1928) leading the Home Rule League in New York; activists of the Ghadar Party in California; Har Dayal (1884–1939) of the Ghadar Party who had moved from California to Stockholm; Rash Behari Bose (1886–1945) in Japan; and M.N. Roy (1887–1954) in Mexico, who would play a seminal role in setting up the CPI. Usually at loggerheads with each other, they were scattered and of little practical help to each other. On Indian soil, during the second and third decades of the twentieth century, a new brand of revolutionaries had come up, particularly in Bengal, Punjab, and Uttar Pradesh. They were left-leaning, though not yet communists as such, though almost all were influenced by the Russian revolution. They set themselves up in different groupings, such as the Naujawan Bharat Sabha and the Hindustan Socialist Republican Army led by Bhagat Singh, Chandrashekhar Azad, and their comrades; the band of youth led by 'Masterda' (Surya Sen); and the Jugantar and Anushilan groups in Bengal; among others.

Written by Karl Marx and Friedrich Engels in German, the *Communist Manifesto* was first published in 1848 in London; its first English translation by Helen Macfarlane in 1850 seized the imagination of the world. In India, the educated middle classes had long been familiar with it, in parts if not entirely in its sum and substance. The underlying appeal of

---

[89] Virendranath Chattopadhyay set up a body called the League against Imperialism in Berlin. Due to the Nazi putsch it was transferred first to Paris in March 1933 and then to London. The League's main focus was on India and was said to be funded largely by the Comintern. In 1932, the first issue of the *Anti-Imperialist Review* appeared which too took a keen interest in the oppressed people of India.

the *Communist Manifesto*—to the Workers of the World to rise in revolt, to throw away their shackles, and to unite—soon found an echo in Urdu poetry. A steady stream of propagandist literature from the Soviet Union, which wound its way into India through Afghanistan, fuelled the fire that had been lit years ago by the events of 1857. In different parts of India, events conspired to turn attention upon the long-suffering peasants and landless labourers of India's vast hinterland. In places as distant as the Punjab and Bengal, demands of industrial workers and peasants came to the forefront and were picked up by Khilafat leaders as yet another example of imperialist brutality. The Railway Workers' Strike of 1920 in the Punjab coincided with the growth of trade union consciousness among the jute mill workers of Bengal. A wave of strikes assailed India in 1921: 396 strikes in one year alone, involving 600,351 workmen and a loss of 6,994,426 workdays.[90] This involved workers from textile and jute mills of Bombay, Calcutta, Ahmadabad, and Madras; North Western and East Bengal Railways; coalfields of Jharia; Bombay P & T; Assam plantations; Calcutta tramways; among others.

With the establishment of a propaganda base in Mazar-e-Sharif in northern Afghanistan, a steady increase in Russians entering Afghanistan became evident. While the base of their activities was Afghanistan, the target was India. Moscow was at pains to set up a channel of contact with India, a channel that ran through all its eastern border outposts: Tibet, Sinkiang, Persia, and Afghanistan. Mention must be made of two incidents that strengthened the Marxist presence in India even before the formal establishment of the CPI, namely, the Kanpur Conspiracy Case and the Meerut Conspiracy Case. The arrests of communists had begun in Peshawar in 1923. The government had launched a campaign of anti-communist repression by May 1923. Three prominent communists were arrested on slender charges and kept under detention—Shaukat Usmani was arrested from Kanpur, Muzaffar Ahmad from Calcutta, and Ghulam Hussain from Lahore. As Adhikari noted, 'The strategy of the British imperialists in their attempt to destroy the rising communist movement was to discredit the patriotism of communists, show them as agents of a foreign power and drive a wedge between them and the militant left-wing in the Congress and the national movement.'[91]

---

[90] Adhikari, *Documents*, vol. I, p. 273.
[91] Adhikari, *Documents*, vol. II, p. 274.

Scrambling for evidence to link the Bolshevik and communist agencies with 'other foci of disorder', the government embarked upon a lengthy trial. Thirteen people were named in the Kanpur Conspiracy (as the case came to be known since the case was lodged in Kanpur, or Cawnpore as it was then spelt) and complaints were filed against eight 'well-known Bolsheviks'. Referred to as the Bolshevik Conspiracy in official documents, the magisterial inquiry eventually whittled down to four suspects: Muzaffar Ahmad, Shaukat Usmani, S.A. Dange, and Nalini Gupta. The charge was an attempt to secure 'the complete separation of India from imperialistic Britain' by a 'violent revolution' and thus 'deprive the king-emperor of the sovereignty of British India'.[92] The accused were sentenced to four years' rigorous imprisonment. The case attracted a great deal of attention in Britain where the Labour Party had come to power in 1924. Money and help poured in—both from Britain and Russia—for an appeal. Fund drives were launched in Indian papers such as *The Socialist*. The Indian Communist Defence Committee was formed in 1924; its grounds for seeking an appeal were interesting; 'the idea of forming a legal communist party has to be given a trial.'[93] A conference of several loosely coalitioned kisan and workers' unions as well as communist sympathizer groups was held on 25 December 1925 at the same time as the Kanpur session of the Indian National Congress (INC). The foundation of the CPI is said to date from that occasion. Hasrat Mohani, as chairman of the Reception Committee, spoke thus:

The movement of communism is the movement of peasants and workers. The people of India generally agree with the principles and aims and objects of this movement, but owing to certain misunderstandings some weak and nervous people fear the very name of communism ... [our aims and objects] to establish swaraj or complete independence by all fair means ... some evilly-disposed persons incriminate communism as necessarily an antireligious movement. The fact however is that in matters of religion we allow the largest possible latitude and toleration.[94]

The furore over the Kanpur Conspiracy Case had barely died when the government launched the Meerut Conspiracy Case against 31 communist and trade union leaders; this lasted from 1923–33. Upon their release, the

[92] Adhikari, *Documents*, vol. II, p. 274.
[93] Ibid., p. 294.
[94] Ibid., pp. 640–1.

Meerut conspiracy prisoners took to the cause of the trade unions, which had already shown their ability to rock the nation, with great enthusiasm.[95] As we shall see in later chapters, none of the government's various forms of repression could squash the spread of communist ideas; eventually, the government felt constrained to ban the CPI in July 1934 and resorted to mass arrests of communists and militant trade unionists, keeping the suspects under detention without trial under the infamous Preventive Detention Act.

However, the juggernaut of protest had rolled too far to be stopped. The fires of protest raged across the country. The Indian peasant and factory worker, long inarticulate, scattered, and disempowered, increasingly began to find a voice and a platform. The Kanpur Conspiracy Case threw up a new kind of protestor—one who vociferously called out for revolution and would stop at nothing, not even militant terrorist activities, to achieve their end. The country had already witnessed random, scattered acts of nationalist-revolutionary activity during the first phase of the non-cooperation movement (the most famous example being the Kakori Conspiracy Case when a group of young men planned to loot a government treasury from a train in the small *qasbah* of Kakori, near Lucknow on 9 August 1925). From 1925 onwards, examples of armed resistance began to increase; what

---

[95] Intelligence Reports on Communist Influence in India's Trade Unions, IOR/L/PJ/12/137, File 6835 (E)/23 January 1933–December 1934.'The release of the Meerut prisoners lends spice to the situation.... Communism in Bombay will have to be a hardy growth to survive the bickering, pettinesses, and jealousies that have so prominently marked the actions of its leaders hitherto.' Extract from weekly intelligence report of the Director, Intelligence Bureau (DIB), Government of India, dated 28 September 1933, Simla. The very next week, the writer urges the need to take a broader view on the communist situation. The real threat was not so much from the home-grown communists, but from the British comrades who were directing and controlling the movement; the report mentions Hutchinson and Bradley. The writer goes on to say that as is frequently argued, 'India does not provide a suitable soil for Communism', the government would need to keep a careful watch on the activities of those who have recently received communist training in London, Europe, Moscow and have lately returned or are on their way home. Another intelligence report dated 3 February 1934, after giving a brief history of communism in India, concludes thus: 'Perhaps, after all, Bradley has some justification for the remark (written just before he left for England),"Taking everything into consideration, I think things are going very well."'

was different now was the inclusion of the workers and peasants into these militant activities. The year 1925 was rocked by two prolonged strikes—the North West Railway Workers' strike and the Bombay Textile Workers' strike. The days of spontaneous strikes led to organized ones that paralysed industry and, in turn, paved the way for the militant red-flag trade union movement during 1927–9. The leaders of these movements were influenced by Marxist ideology and by developments in the Soviet Union, especially the Five Year Plan which took several things into account in an organized forecast, especially issues related to labour. In 1929, a Royal Commission was appointed to look into the problems of industrial labour that was, in Nehru's words, 'miserable and militant'.[96] The post-war years that had spelt boom time for the Indian industry had brought no respite to the workers. The slight increase in their wages was evened out by the rising inflation. A gulf separated the lives of the workers and the mill owners, 'Semi-naked women, wild and unkempt, working away for the barest pittance, so that a broad river of wealth should flow ceaselessly to Glasgow and Dundee, as well as to some pockets in India.'[97]

A journal called *Langal* (meaning 'plough') was launched from Bengal by the Labour Swaraj Party of the INC in 1925. Among its founders was the legendary Bengali poet, Kazi Nazrul Islam. The first issue of *Langal* carried Nazrul's famous poem '*Samyavadi*' (Communist) and sold a record 5,000 copies within a few hours.[98] *Langal* routinely carried Bangla translations of Marxist texts, short stories by Maxim Gorky and other Russian masters, as well as articles on topical issues such as the Bengal Tenancy Bill. Elsewhere in the country, tumultuous events were taking place which would, in different ways, encourage the publication of radical literature in general. Some of these events were: the Madras Congress (December 1927); the Congress' declaration of complete independence (1929); the boycott of Simon Commission (1928); the launch of civil disobedience (1930); and the Communal Award announced by the British government (1932). The first ever May Day celebrations in 1934 were a major landmark in the growing labour movement in India.[99]

---

[96] Nehru, *Autobiography*, p. 187.
[97] Ibid., p. 188.
[98] Adhikari, *Documents*, vol. II, p. 676.
[99] IOR/L/PJ/12/137, File 6835 (E)/23.

Ideologically driven newspapers were being set up all over the country. *The Socialist* was set up by S.A. Dange from Bombay, first as a weekly in August 1922 and then as a monthly from February 1923. It did yeoman's service in the face of mounting Hindu–Muslim tensions by publishing articles such as 'Proletarian Hindu–Muslim Unity' and exposing the imperialist hand in stoking communal fires. In the wake of the declining influence of both non-cooperation and Khilafat movements, both of which had affirmed Hindu–Muslim unity, newspapers like *The Socialist* tried to show how the capitalists and big landlords were behind the fratricidal conflict that tore the country's secular fabric. *The Socialist* also carried advertisements of books and treatises that dealt with socialist issues and reprints of articles from the *Inprecor*[100] that 'occasionally slipped through the British censorship net'.[101] Many forms of subterfuge were adopted to escape detection—books were wrapped in the dustcovers of popular novels or religious tracts, communist newspapers were slipped in between the pages of mainstream newspapers, and communist agents took great pains to collect safe addresses of firms and shops where proscribed literature could be sent from abroad by ordinary mail. The government saw through many of these ruses and under Section 19 of the Sea Customs Act prohibited the import of any publication issued by or emanating from the Comintern or its affiliates. Writing the Preface to the revised edition of the compiled intelligence reports, H. Williamson, DIB noted that '… Communism as preached by the Third International constitutes the gravest threat to the civilization of the modern world'.[102]

The contact between Moscow and the communist groups in India was initially through the Communist Party of Great Britain (CPGB) which tended to monopolize India as its own 'province', thus ironically strengthening the imperialist relationship that the fledgling organization in India had set out to denounce. R. Palme Dutt, member of the CPGB, became a

---

[100] Inprecor was established by the Third International in the wake of the Russian Revolution to allow communists to read the documents and thoughts of their comrades around the world. Its name was a contraction of International Press Correspondence and indicated that the magazine translated articles and letters from revolutionaries around the world.

[101] Adhikari, *Documents*, vol. II, pp. 191–2.

[102] *India and Communism* (Simla: Government of India Press, 1935), IOR/L/PJ/12/671.

mentor or 'pundit to lay down the law to the Indian Communist Party'.[103] And much against the protestations of men like M.N. Roy who wished to convince Moscow that they alone were the true and faithful repositories of communism in India, Comintern began sending a series of British communists to India. The most notable of these was Philip Spratt, who arrived in India in December 1926 ostensibly on behalf of a bookseller's firm, but actually to open a branch of the Labour Research Department such as the one he had worked for in London through which Soviet money could be received and distributed. Along with financial assistance, Spratt actively helped and guided the workers' and peasants' movements of the cotton mills and railway workers' unions. He is credited with helping set up the Workers and Peasants' Party in the United Provinces, which held its first conference in Meerut in October 1928, and the strengthening of the various scattered units in the Punjab. Spratt was joined in September 1927 by Benjamin Francis Bradley who devoted himself to the cause of the workers and peasants. A file in the British Library entitled *Communist Party of Great Britain: Reports on Members*[104] yielded a mine of information on the activities of British communists and their sympathies (and the reasons thereof) for the Indian masses. The file also contained a pamphlet entitled 'India's Fight for Separation and Independence' written by one W. Rust and issued by the CPGB in 1932. Some extracts from this rousing pamphlet are as follows:

British imperialism is staking everything on drowning the movement in blood.... The number of arrests already exceeds 20,000 and tax and revenue collection in the countryside is carried out with the aid of troops and armed police ... the phrase 'Struggle or Starve', so often used in Britain, has a terrible literal meaning for the Indian peasants, who are dying off by the thousand.

Going to great lengths to extend its support to the Indian communist movement, it ends thus, 'We must resist every attack of British imperialism on India with the burning consciousness that their fight is our fight and that we cannot advance in the struggle against the capitalists unless the slogan of "Indian Independence" is inscribed on our banners.'[105]

[103] Masani, *Communist Party of India*, p. 25.
[104] IOR/L/PJ/12/383, File 198/29, 1931–4.
[105] Ibid., p. 50.

While the CPI was (officially) set up in 1925, it was not till 1927 that its constitution was drafted and attention focused on a single dynamic organization. The Sixth World Congress of Comintern on 1 September 1928 stressed the need to consolidate the party apparatus while working to throw off the imperialist yoke. The Resolution dealing with India under the heading 'Communist Strategy and Tactics' read:

The basic tasks of the Indian communists consists in struggle against British imperialism for the emancipation of the country.... The union of all communist groups and individual Communists scattered throughout the country into a single, independent and centralised Party represents the first task of the Indian communists.... In the Trade Unions, the Indian communists must mercilessly expose the national-reformist leaders.[106]

In December 1930, there appeared first in the *Inprecor* and later in the London *Daily Worker* and the Moscow *Pravda*, a thesis on Indian communism entitled 'Draft Platform of Action of the Communist Party of India'. It was later translated into Urdu and was widely circulated throughout India. Briefly, after a vigorous denunciation of Gandhism and the INC, it set out the following main tasks:

1. The complete independence of India by the violent overthrow of British rule. The cancellation of all debts, confiscation and nationalization of factories, banks, railways, sea, and river transport and plantations.
2. The establishment of a Soviet government. The realization of the right of national minorities to self-determination including separation. The abolition of the native states. The creation of an Indian Federal Workers' and Peasants' Soviet Republic.
3. The confiscation, without compensation, of all lands, forests, and other property of landlords, ruling princes, churches, the British government, officials, and moneylenders, and the handing of them over for use by the toiling peasantry. The cancellation of slave agreements and all indebtedness of the peasantry to moneylenders and banks.
4. An eight-hour working day and the radical improvement of conditions of labour, increase in wages, and state maintenance for the unemployed.[107]

---

[106] Ibid., p. 31.
[107] From *India and Communism*, IOR/L/PJ/12/671, p. 170.

While the Russian influence is evident in this document with its emphasis on 'toiling peasants', it is significant to note the seeds of the communists' acceptance of a separate homeland for the Muslims. We see here an early indicator of the left's alignment with the Muslim League as well as their later demand that the princely states be given the right of self-determination *before* their accession into India. All through the 1930s, there were repeated assertions that a 'general national armed insurrection against the British exploiters' was the only means of winning independence. Also, the 'left' element within the Congress, namely, Jawaharlal Nehru, was viewed as the most dangerous obstacle and a ruthless war, it was exhorted, must be waged on the left national reformists.[108]

On 1 May 1934, the *Bande Mataram*, a newspaper from Lahore, carried a report by Hari Harnath Shastri, president, All-India Trade Union Congress, Kanpur, announcing the establishment of the All-India Socialist Party.[109] It not merely announced its goal of national independence, but also achieving it by means of force. It held its inaugural conference at Patna at the same time as a meeting of the All-India Congress Committee (AICC) and was attended by 100 delegates from all over India. The party declared its objective to be the formation, through a Constituent Assembly, of a socialist state. It was largely propelled by the work of M.R. Masani, a young barrister from Bombay, and Jayaprakash Narain. The fact that they could induce 35 members of the Congress to vote against a resolution moved by Gandhi was a testimony to their strength.

One of the most significant fallouts of the Khilafat movement[110] had been the emergence of Muslim socialist leaders who had the knack of establishing mass contact. Their skills of oratory, the flourishes of their

---

[108] *India and Communism*, IOR/L/PJ/12/671, pp. 170–1.

[109] IOR/L/PJ/12/137, File 6835 (E)/23.

[110] Another off-shoot of the Khilafat movement had been the emergence of several Hindu and Muslim leaders in different parts of the country—men like Muzaffar Ahmad and E.M.S. Namboodripad—who seized the anti-colonial ideology generated by the movement. They were among the first to bring this ideology into the communist movement, which the next generation of communists would harness with the independence movement. Unfortunately, this book does not permit me to explore their contribution at greater length. Mushirul Hasan, in *Nationalism and Communal Politics*, dwells on what he calls the 'radicalisation' of the Khilafat and non-cooperation movement.

pen, and most important of all, their ability to invoke both Islam and the principles of socialism with equal ease made them instantly popular with the people. Industrial hubs like Bombay, Calcutta, and Kanpur, which had a large number of Muslim workers, brought to national prominence leaders like Hasrat Mohani and Azad Subhani.[111] These men did a great deal of work in establishing nationwide peasants' and trade union movements for, given the migratory nature of the industrial workers, both the peasants and the workers, had their roots in the villages. In fact, four-fifths of the population lived in villages, that is, 226 out of 244 million people[112] in British India lived in villages and agriculture was the basic industry of the people. The kisan movements, therefore, acquired a special significance for *all* political parties and regardless of their differences, were engaged in the emancipation of the ryot. While Gandhi took the lead in stirring agrarian consciousness, others were not far behind.

After the Kanpur Conspiracy Case, many Muslim publicists had come to the fore. The career of Azad Subhani deserves some scrutiny.[113] A pan-Islamist and communist, he became principal of the Madrasa-i Ilahiyat, formed to oppose Arya Samajism and protect Islam. Subhani came into prominence in 1913 over the Kanpur mosque case when he was arrested for inciting rioters; after becoming a supporter of the Anjuman-e-Khuddam-i-Kaaba in 1914, he became a prominent extremist Khilafat agitator, a leading non-cooperator, and advocate of complete independence; in 1923 he published a scheme for swaraj which had a distinct communist tone and advocated the establishment of a parallel government. He continued to be involved in Congress activities till 1924, but in 1925 became vice president of the CPI and spent the next several years espousing communism and the cause of labour movements. Arrested on 10 May 1934 for advocating extreme communist doctrines at a meeting of railway union in Lucknow, he went to Mecca for haj along with Hasrat Mohani upon his release. On return, he agitated against the repressive policy of the British in the Hejaz,

---

[111] The Muslim Independent Party was set up in July 1932 with Hasrat Mohani as its general secretary and Azad Subhani and Syed Zahir Ali as assistant secretaries. The party being new and completely without funds, Mohani went on tour to preach the gospel of the new party and collect funds.

[112] These figures are from Masani, *Communist Party of India*, p. 16.

[113] Details of Azad Subhani's career culled from *The United Provinces' Political Who's Who*, IOR/L/PJ/12/672.

and remained irreconcilably anti-British. He toured the United Provinces, 'pouring vitriol, stirring up passions about the politico-religious crisis in Islam'.[114]

Modernists tend to shy away from the past and revile all that was done in the name of tradition. But some men, like Hasrat Mohani, show a strange mingling of the old and the new, a regard for the past, while at the same time harbouring a passionate quest for change. We will see this duality in some of the liberal, forward-looking, educated, middle-class Muslims. In subsequent chapters, we will also see how the *Angarey* group marked a feisty departure from precisely this norm; they carried no duality whatsoever, either in their lives or work. Also, some Indian Muslims were attracted to socialism because it carried the same poetic and romantic appeal of egalitarianism that they were familiar with through the works of well-loved and well-respected poets from the time of Ghalib down to Iqbal and Hasrat. The establishment of the CPI in 1925 and the emergence of a new breed of comrade of the ilk of Rashid Jahan, Mahmuduzzafar, and Sajjad Zaheer put paid to these hazy ideas of romanticism that seemed cozy from the luxury of their well-appointed, Western-style drawing rooms and salons. The writings of this new lot, such as the contributors of *Angarey*, showed how there was no romanticism in poverty, illiteracy, and backwardness. The communists, especially those who were members of the party and were therefore convinced and highly committed ideologues unlike the left-leaning liberals enamoured by fuzzy notions of equality and egalitarianism, were people in a hurry. Not only did they want to call a spade a spade, they also wanted to call out to the masses to rise up in revolt—just as the Russian peasants had done—and bring about a new socio-economic order, one in which religion had no role. In fact, the communist ideology as laid down in the Programme of the Communist International adopted by the First World Congress as early as September 1920 had already dealt with ideologies that were inimical to communism. Among these ideologies, it also included Gandhism:

Tendencies like Gandhism in India, thoroughly imbued with religious conceptions, idealise the most backward and economically most reactionary forms of social life, see the solution of the social problem not in proletarian socialism, but in

---

[114] Robinson, *Separatism among Indian Muslims*, p. 216.

a reversion to these backward forms, preach passivity and repudiate the class struggle, and in the process of the development of the revolution become transformed into an openly reactionary force. *Gandhism is more and more becoming an ideology directed against mass revolution. It must be strongly combated by Communism.*[115]

As the communist ideology got more ingrained, the directive from the party was to expunge religion from revolutionary activities that would bring about the much-needed change. We shall discuss the party's involvement in the work of the PWA in greater detail in later chapters. At this point, it is necessary to take note of two things. One, how communist ideology was sometimes supporting, sometimes opposing nationalist ideology and how it was always opposing Gandhism as an ideology that was reactionary and therefore inimical to communism. Gandhi's talk of God, love, non-violence was anathema to the believers of dialectical materialism. 'To the communist,' wrote Masani, 'the end justifies the means; to Gandhi the means were everything—the means and the end were like the seed and the tree; and so Gandhi pronounced Soviet Communism to be "repugnant to India".... Communism seeks to centralize and collectivise everything; Gandhi preached the need to decentralize and to distribute power both politically and economically.'[116] Gandhi came in for a fair amount of abuse from the CPGB too, especially at the time of the second All-India Round Table Conference in September 1931 where Gandhi claimed to represent all of India; the CPGB even collected funds for this particular purpose.[117]

The Appearance of Socially Engaged Literature

Smarting under British biases since the Revolt of 1857, denied positions in British–Indian services, acutely aware of being unequal beneficiaries in the British system of education, and distant events in Muslim lands fuelled the growing sense of besiegement among India's Muslims. The fate of fellow-Muslims in different parts of the colonized world seemed to carry a portent of worse things in store for them in India. The last section of Chapter 1

---

[115] Cited in Masani, *Communist Party of India*, p. 21; italics mine.
[116] Ibid., p. 234.
[117] *Communist Party of Great Britain: Reports on Members*, IOR/L/PJ/12/383, File 198/29, 1931–4.

has dealt in detail with the poetry of Akbar Illahabadi and Mohammad Iqbal and how it reflected the effects of outside events on the Indian Muslims. Feted and lionized Urdu poets like Iqbal fed this growing paranoia in poems such as '*Masjide-e-Qartaba*' (The Mosque at Cordoba), and 'O *Ghafil Afghan*' (O Heedless Afghan).[118] The emotional tug of tradition, of memories of Islam's glorious past blurred Iqbal's vision of the future. While on the one hand, he remembered the glorious civilization that had produced the splendid mosque at Cordoba, he was reminded also of the abject state of the Muslim in the present time. If one views Iqbal's vast and varied oeuvre, one is struck with how often progressive, even socialist, ideas are quickly negated by regressive, even reactionary ones.[119] Standing before the mosque at Cordoba, he exclaims:

> Destiny's curtain till now muffles the world to be,
> Yet, already, its dawn stands before me unveiled;
> Were I to lift this mask hiding the face of my thoughts,
> Europe could never endure songs as burning as mine![120]

In 'God's Command to His Angels', he exhorts:
> Rise, and from their slumber wake the poor of my world!
> Shake the walls and windows of the mansions of the great!
> Kindle with the fire of faith the slow blood of the slaves!
> Make the fearful sparrow bold to meet the falcon's hate![121]

---

[118] Iqbal proposed a separate homeland for Muslims of north-west India in 1930: '[T]he formation of a consolidated North-West Indian Muslim state appears to me to be the final destiny of the Muslims at least of North-West India.' Quoted by Ralph Russell in 'Iqbal and his Message', *The Pursuit of Urdu Literature*, citing Q.M. Haq and M.I. Waley, *Allama Sir Muhammad Iqbal* (London: British Museum Publications Ltd, 1977), p. 28.

[119] In a letter to Padmaja Naidu, Nehru talks of Iqbal and the 'baneful influence of dogmatic religion which does 'infinite harm' to Iqbal's poetry. Nehru writes, 'He has always been one of the many problems I could not solve. How can a real poet be so extra-ordinarily communal and narrow minded and earthly? And yet he happens to be both.' Nehru then goes on to make a light-hearted reference to Iqbal's clothes and manner of dressing, saying poets must look and act as poets. From the *Selected Works of Jawaharlal Nehru*, vol. 12 (New Delhi: Orient Longman, 1979), p. 641. Letter dated 16 February 1929.

[120] V.G. Kiernan, *Poems from Iqbal* (London: John Murray, 1955), p. 41.

[121] Ibid., p. 43.

In '*Armaghan-i-Hejaz*' (The Gift of Hejaz), in one of his last important works, 'Satan's Parliament' written in 1936, he puts these words in the mouth of Satan:

> ... When Nature's hand
> Has rent the sleeve, no needleworking logic
> Of communism will put the stitches back.
> I be afraid of socialists?—street-bawlers,
> Ragged things, tortured brains, tormented souls!
> No, if there is one monster in my path
> It lurks within that people in whose ashes
> Still glow the embers of an infinite hope.[122]

Yet, it is the same Iqbal who has also written:

> Follow the path of thy ancestors, for that is solidarity
> The significance of religious conservatism is the integration of the community.[123]

And, on the subject of women he is most inconclusive, in a small poem titled '*Aurat*' (Woman):

> I too at the oppression of women am most sorrowful
> But the problem is intricate, no solution do I find possible.[124]

Victor Kiernan, in an essay on Iqbal entitled 'The Prophet of Change' admits: 'Iqbal mirrored the confusions and contradictions of his highly complex environment, and there were to be moments when he could come near the brink of a narrow sectarianism.'[125]

Events abroad and simmering communal tensions at home conspired to heighten a sense of persecution amongst the Indian Muslim intelligentsia. The most visible and direct source of this persecution seemed to be the British imperialistic adventurism and everything that fed and nurtured this grand design, such as capitalism, landlordism, unjust

---

[122] Ibid., p. 83.

[123] From 'Ramuz-i-Bekhudi', in *Asrar-e-Ramuz*, p. 143; translation by W.C. Smith in *Modern Islam in India: A Social Analysis* (Delhi: Usha Publications, 1979), p. 161.

[124] '*Aurat*', in *Zarb-e-Kaleem*, p. 96; translation from Smith, ibid., p. 166.

[125] Prakash Karat (ed.), *Across Time and Continents: A Tribute to Victor Kiernan* (New Delhi: LeftWord Books, 2003), p. 201.

taxation, and monopolistic trade policies, among other repressive measures by the civilian administration. The firebrand revolutionary, Hasrat Mohani, was imprisoned in 1908 for writing an article that criticized the British educational policy in Egypt. He also wrote a poem called 'Ain-e-Soviyat' (Soviet Administration) on the Soviet system. Hasrat continued to write and send articles, poems, and essays for publication even during his internment. When the British government in Kanpur began to demolish a mosque in 1913 in a bid to widen a road, protests broke out and the police fired on the crowds to dispel them. Riots broke out soon thereafter where 23 people were killed and 30 were wounded.[126] This sort of thing had been done before by the British authorities, but this time the discontent among the Muslims was so high that the issue caught fire and, getting mixed up with the Khilafat agitation, it sparked the cry of 'Islam in Danger!' and stirred countrywide indignant protests. Hasrat Mohani wrote a stirring poem on the subject; so did the editor of the *Agra Akhbar*. The latter, called '*Chand Lamhe Shaheedan-e-Sitam ke Saath*' published on 26 August 1913 in *Kanpur ki Khooni Dastan*, concludes on a poignant note:

> Our sorrow is for neither ourselves nor our children
> Our only regret is for the ruined and helpless Muslims.[127]

Syed Sulaiman Nadwi writing in the *Al-Hilal* on the destruction of the Kanpur mosque begins by asking, 'The earth is thirsty. It needs blood. But whose? The Muslims.' The *Al-Hilal*'s security deposit was cancelled upon the publication of this article. Yet, Maulana Azad congratulated its author. Khwaja Hasan Nizami, the *sajjadanashin* of the venerable dargah of the Sufi saint Nizamuddin in Delhi, also wrote a tract called '*Kanpur ki Khooni Dastan*' (The Bloody Tale of Kanpur) in 1913; it too was proscribed.

Several poets, lost in the veils of time and virtually unknown today, made important interventions. Presented ahead is a sampling of the socially conscious, politically aware message of the poets of the times. Not all of these poets are well-known today, nor is their poetry of a high calibre; yet fragments of their work have been included here simply to illustrate the strong yearning for freedom in the Urdu poetry of the

---

[126] Hardy, *Muslims of British India*, p. 184.
[127] Parti, *Ashob*, vol. I, pp. 15–16.

times.[128] Suroor Jahanabadi (aka Durga Sahai) lamented in a poem called 'Khak-e-Watan' (Dust of the Country):

> Once your flag of greatness was flying high
> Now the sign of your greatness lies in the dust.

Brij Narain Chakbast in a poem also called 'Khak-e-Watan' rued the fact that *hubb-e-watan* (love for the country) was no more, though *khak-e-watan* remained the same.[129] In an open letter to Queen Victoria, Sajjad Hussain Kakorvi wrote with sarcasm about the Queen's many advisors who were misguiding her.

Hashmi Faridabadi in 'Chal Balkan Chal' (Come Let's Go to the Balkans) urged his readers to go to the Balkans, if they had the slightest bit of *ghairat* left, for if they were true *momin*, they must go where they were most needed. That the Urdu poet was not content with mere high-flying rhetoric and was rooted—and aware—of immediate contemporary realities becomes evident when Chakbast in 'Awaz-e-Qaum' (The Call of the Nation) declared:

> From the ground to the skies there are cries of Home Rule
> And the youthfulness of nationalism and the urge for Home Rule.

Similarly, Hasrat Mohani in a poem called 'Montagu Reforms' was scathing about the so-called reforms which were mere *kaagaz ke phool* with no *khushboo*, even for name's sake. The poem ended with a fervent plea that the people of Hind should not be taken in by the sorcery of the reforms. Zafar Ali Khan[130] in 'Mazalim-e-Punjab' (The Victims of

---

[128] Culled from Abdur Razzaq Qureshi, *Nava-i-Azadi*. All translations are mine.

[129] Comparing Chakbast and Hasrat, Gopichand Narang finds Chakbast inspired by leaders such as Bipin Chandra Pal, Gokhale, and Annie Besant. His poetry reflects the 'liberal-moderate' aspect of the freedom struggle compared to the more militant Hasrat who wanted nothing short of full freedom and was inspired by Tilak and his demand for sampurna swaraj. See Gopichand Narang, *Urdu Language and Literature: Critical Perspectives* (New Delhi: Sterling Publishers, 1991), p. 67.

[130] As editor of the *Zamindar*, Zafar Ali Khan exerted a powerful role in the Muslim politics of the Punjab. A daily feature of his newspaper was the political verses that reflected popular sentiment and also provided information on topical events. Using stock images of the nightingale and the candle, he spoke out

Punjab) mocked the excesses of the British and jestingly praised the delights of martial law and the brutality of men like General Dwyer. In *'Shola-e-Fanoos-e-Hind'* (The Spark in the Chandelier of Hind), he went on to wish that all the drops of the martyrs' blood may be used to decorate the walls of the *qasr-e-azadi* (the fort of freedom). Hashar Kashmiri in a sarcastic ode to Europe called *'Shukriya Europe'* (Thanks Europe) thanked it for turning the world into a *matamkhana* and for having turned the East into an example of Hell. Another proscribed poet, Ehsan Danish, in his rousing anthem *'Tarana-e-Jihad'* (The Anthem of Jihad) urged his fellow Muslims to go forth (*Badhe chalo, badhe chalo*) using the parameters of religion.

Mention must be made of a remarkable series of mushairas held in Agra Jail from January till May 1922.[131] Home to over 200 political prisoners, including Hindi and Urdu poets, writers, editors, university teachers, lawyers, doctors, etc., the jail authorities permitted the inmates to organize a series of cultural programmes. Some of the country's most distinguished men happened to be serving time in Agra Jail: Mahadev Desai, private secretary to Gandhi; George Joseph, editor of *The Independent* (Allahabad); as well as some literary heavy weights such as Josh Malihabadi, Firaq Gorakhpuri, Arif Hasoi, Khwaja Abdul Hamid Khwaja, among others. The first such mushaira, on 20 January 1922, organized soon after the Friday prayer was presided over by Arif Hasoi. As *tarah*, a line from Hasrat Mohani was chosen: *'Hai yeh woh dard jo sharminda ahsan na hua'* (It is the pain that knows not the gratitude of embarrassment). In his inimitably rousing style, Josh read:

> The chieftains of the community have entered the prison
> May they be kept safe from the harm of enemies
> Their crime is that they are the prophets of their religion
> Their fault is that they obey the commands of their god.[132]

---

powerfully through poems titled 'Martial Law', 'The Central Khilafat Committee', or 'Swaraj'. See Gail Minault, 'Urdu Political Poetry during the Khilafat movement', in *Gender, Language and Learning: Essays in Indo-Muslim Cultural History* (Ranikhet: Permanent Black, 2009), pp. 107–8.

[131] Detailed account of these mushairas as well as press cuttings from contemporary newspapers found in *Mushaira-e-Zindan* (Lucknow: Uttar Pradesh Urdu Akademi, 1982).

[132] Ibid., p. 19; translation mine.

Firaq, serving an eight-month sentence and a fine of Rs 500, declared:

This assembly of the inmates of this prison is proof
Though scattered, this shiraza, has not gone waste.[133]

The *Zamindar* of Lahore carried a detailed coverage of each of the four mushairas and marvelled at the courage of these men, their unabashed fervour, and love for the motherland. The last report, dated 4 May 1922, spoke of the mushairas coming to an end and the inmates transferred to Lucknow where not only would they be treated more strictly, but also be kept in solitary confinement. At the last mushaira in Agra Jail, the *Zamindar* reported, the prisoners outdid themselves in not merely the technical excellence of their poetry but in laying bare their souls.

Each successive milestone—the Rowlatt Act, the first non-cooperation movement, Jallianwala Bagh massacre, amongst others—produced voluminous poetry, polemics, and posters in Urdu. The more virulent ones were proscribed, some of them being: *Ek Khuli Chitthi Benam Asquith Sahib* (An Open Letter to Asquith) on British rule in Egypt, in 1915; *Rowlatt Act ki Asli Mansha* (The Real Intent of the Rowlatt Act), a sarcastic attack on British laws published in 1919; *Waqia-e-Punjab* (The Incident in the Punjab), a collection of poetry, 1920; *Vatan ka Rag* (The Song of the Nation), a collection of poems on revolutionary 'martyrs'; and 'O Lenin, Mazzini, Washington and Napoleon, come and see the future of India's heroes' in 1932; among others.[134]

All these themes expressed by the poets and publicists of the age were taken up by the growing number of Urdu newspapers, journals, and prose writers such as Mehfooz Ali who wrote a humorous column in Mohamed Ali's *Hamdard*. Ale Ahmad Suroor, in an essay on humour and satire, commenting on the proliferation of newspapers and journals during the period between the two wars, writes, 'Q.A. Ghaffar, a journalist shaped by the Balkan war, the first World War and the Khilafat and non-cooperation movement, gave us *Naqsh-i-Firang* (A Picture of Europe), a satirical account of the mission that failed. It is poor reportage but delightful writing.'[135]

---

[133] Ibid., p. 34; translation mine.

[134] Culled from Barrier, *Banned*.

[135] Ale Ahmad Suroor, 'Humour in Urdu', from Nissim Ezekiel (ed.), *Indian Writers in Conference: Proceedings of the Sixth PEN All-India Writers' Conference* (Mysore: PEN, 1964), p. 212.

A number of newspapers were launched to voice the sentiments of the Muslims, notably the *Al-Hilal* from Calcutta (from 1912–15 and again in 1927), the *Zamindar* from Lahore, and the *Comrade* from Delhi. This has been touched upon in the first section of this chapter. It finds a mention here again because these newspapers were a barometer of their times; they had a finger on the pulse of their readers and, in turn, provided themes for the poets to pick up and elaborate.

As we have noted in the first chapter, there was no uniform or unvariegated response among the Muslim intelligentsia to the events of 1857. Similarly, there was no uniform response to domestic and international events that impinged upon the Indian Muslims. For every nationalist there was a defender of the Raj, for every progressive, a reactionary, and so on. Mention must be made of two Muslims who exemplified the Muslim loyalist point of view, loyal that is to the British government: these were Abdullah Yusuf Ali (1872–1953) and Ameer Ali (1849–1928). The former, a commentator on the Holy Quran and the latter, a historian and scholar of Islam were advocates of Anglo–Muslim rapprochement rather than confrontation. Apologetic of the poor intellectual and religious leadership of Muslim India, Yusuf Ali attempted an analysis of the hostility towards British education in a seminal essay 'Muslim Culture and Religious Thought'.[136]

The Muslim intelligentsia of the early twentieth century had been quick to seize upon the writings of a motley group of writers and thinkers, chief among them being John Stuart Mill (1806–1873), Herbert Spencer (1820–1903), Aldous Huxley (1894–1963), and of course Karl Marx (1818–1883). Among Indian writers and thinkers, Iqbal had the most profound influence on a cross-section of writers. In his espousal of an 'activist view of life and the rejection of fatalism', we can see a 'continuation' of Syed Ahmad Khan's ideas and thoughts: 'He [Iqbal] was asking the Muslims, and primarily the Muslim middle-class intelligentsia to develop their 'egos', to stand on their own feet, to get going, in fact. That was the way to create a destiny for the Muslims in India as elsewhere.'[137]

---

[136] In L.S.S. O'Malley (ed.), *Modern India and the West: A Study of the Interaction of Their Civilisations* (London, 1941). Published in Hasan, *Encountering the West*, pp. 137–65.

[137] Iqbal Singh, *The Ardent Pilgrim: An Introduction to the Life & Work of Mohammad Iqbal* (New Delhi: Oxford University Press, 1997 [reprint]), p. 57.

However, such is the duality of Iqbal's message—couched though it is in a language of a Muslim addressing fellow Muslims—that it can be read as the inspiration for both Muslim nationalists and seekers of pan-Islamism as well as by communists and socialists. Despite the overtly Islamic frame of reference of almost all of Iqbal's writings, reams have been written on the socialist content of his thought. Possibly, this is because Iqbal was among the first Indian intellectual to openly and warmly welcome the socialist revolution and the dawn of the era of the workers.[138]

'One of the great paradoxes of the history of Islam in the twentieth century,' writes Humayun Ansari, 'is that many of the first Muslim socialists were men who at earlier stages in their lives had been devout Muslims, often passionately involved with the fate of Islam throughout the world.'[139] Why should this be considered a paradox? Is Islam so antithetical to the notion of socialism? Are a Muslim and a socialist a contradiction in terms? Not really. After all, both Islam and socialism preach equality and brotherhood and advocate an egalitarian society. The best example to illustrate this point is the remarkable and varied career of a man like Hasrat Mohani whom we encountered in the first section of this chapter. A romantic poet in the classic ghazal tradition (remembered today for his sweetly sentimental '*Woh tera kothe pe nange paon aana yaad hai*', immortalized by Ghulam Ali), journalist, politician, parliamentarian, and freedom fighter, Hasrat Mohani was profoundly impressed by the Russian Revolution and carried its imprint on all his later writings.

Several leaders emerged from the Muslim clergy too who worked and wrote passionately in favour of nationalism.[140] Notable among them was the scholar from Deoband, Shaikhul-Hind Maulana Mahmud-ul Hasan and his protégé, the Sialkot-born Sikh convert, Maulana Ubaidullah

---

[138] L.R. Gordon-Polonskaya, 'Ideology of Muslim Nationalism', in Hafeez Malik (ed.), *Iqbal: Poet-Philosopher of Pakistan* (New York: Columbia University Press, 1971), p. 119.

[139] Humayun Khizar Ansari, 'Pan-Islam and the Making of the Early Indian Muslim Socialist', *Modern Asian Studies*, vol. 20, no. 3 (1986), p. 509.

[140] On the Muslim attitude towards the British government, struggle within orthodox parties, conflicts between pan-Islamism and nationalism, splits within the ulama at Firangi Mahal, Deoband, and Bareilly, see Robinson, *Separatism among Indian Muslims*.

Sindhi.¹⁴¹ During the First World War, amongst several leaders of the Deoband school who, led by Maulana Mahmud-ul Hasan, left India to seek support of the Central Powers for a pan-Islamic revolution in India in what came to be known as the Silk Letter Conspiracy, Ubaidullah's career was marked by a 'penchant for high political adventure'.¹⁴² He reached Kabul in 1915 to rally the Afghan amir to attack India, and shortly thereafter, offered his support to Raja Mahendra Pratap's plans for a revolution in India with German support. Always a firebrand, he joined the Provisional Government of India formed in Kabul in December 1915. After several years in Kabul where he met a Turko-German delegation and men like Maulvi Barkatullah, Ubaidullah left for Russia in 1922.¹⁴³ In Moscow, he observed, at first hand, how the socialist ideology was a quick tool for mobilizing people and gaining results. He compared the Russian revolution with the early days of Islam thus, 'I came to understand that Islam in its early period had brought about a similar revolution as the one in which the Russians are now engaged. And the Holy Quran is the book of an identical revolution in the history of mankind.'¹⁴⁴ Subsequently, Ubaidullah Sindhi spent two years in Turkey and, passing through many countries, eventually reached Hejaz where he spent about 14 years learning and pondering the philosophy of Islam in the light of Shah Waliullah's teachings. Upon his return to India, he became not just a vocal anti-imperialist, but, more importantly, the defender of a new social order. Barkatullah Bhopali (1864–1926), prime minister in Mahendra Pratap's government-in-exile, was yet another early socialist. He edited *Islam Fraternity* from Japan and *Naya Islam* from Germany, participated in the anti-imperialist conference held in Brussels in 1927, and lived and worked in Japan, USA, Turkey, Afghanistan, and Germany gathering momentum for a pan-Islamic movement. Barkatullah's writings, like Hasrat's and Mushir Kidwai's were vague,

---

¹⁴¹ For a detailed study of his political thought see, Muhammad Sarwar, *Maulana Obaidullah Sindhi* (Lahore: Sindh Sagar Academy, 1967); and Naseer Habib, 'The Tradition of Deoband and the Pragmatism of Ubaid Allah Sindhi', *Third Frame*, vol. 1, no. 3 (July–September 2008), pp. 30–42.

¹⁴² Jalal, *Partisans of Allah*, p. 203.

¹⁴³ Ziya-ul-Hasan Faruqi, *The Deoband School and the Demand for Pakistan* (Bombay: Asia Publishing House, 1963).

¹⁴⁴ Muhammad Sarwar, *Ifadat-o-Malfuzat* (Lahore: Sindh Sagar Academy, 1972), p. 206.

filled with 'obtuse insinuations to the struggle ahead but to both Hasrat and Barkatullah, the ideology or its practical application is not of immediate concern and even as a righteous dream it is distant.'[145]

Did this dream remain a distant one? Did the Indian Muslim ever get fully drawn into a mass movement? If so when? These questions acquire significance when we see the strands of socialism, communism, nationalism come together to form a grand tapestry of the freedom struggle, a tapestry that drew people from every part of the country and from every walk of life. The first mass contact movement—the non-cooperation movement that had coincided with the Khilafat movement—had been abandoned by Gandhi in 1922 due to scattered incidents of violence; it had seen a sizeable Muslim presence.[146] The second one launched almost a decade later, under Gandhi's control and direction, proved to be a 'protracted and, on the whole, an inconclusive one, and it produced among the politically articulate a dissatisfaction with Gandhian methods and a sympathy for more modern left-wing Marxist-influenced political policies.'[147] Nehru's mass contact campaign launched in 1936—aimed directly at wooing the Muslims away primarily from the Muslim League—was more successful. It, in fact, nibbled away at the socialists' territory and brought back those Muslims who had strayed into the socialist camp back into the Congress' thrall. We shall return to the role and presence of Muslims in the national movement at various points when we examine the reasons for both the success and failure of the PWM in subsequent chapters.

The majority of the Muslim socialist writers came from families who had served the British and knew, therefore, the inequities of the colonial administration at close quarters. Humayun Ansari lists the number of Muslims active in the socialist movement, and a brief look at their family background reveals that almost all had some linkage or the other with the British administration. The suffering that many Muslim families had endured after 1857 perhaps explains the attraction of their descendants towards a new movement that was propelled on the twin engines of anti-colonialism and anti-imperialism. Ahmed Ali, writing in *Twilight of Delhi*,

---

[145] Ali Jawad Zaidi, *A History of Urdu Literature* (New Delhi: Sahitya Akademi, 1993), p. 349.

[146] Mujeeb, *Indian Muslims*, pp. 435–6.

[147] Russell, *Pursuit of Urdu Literature*, p. 193.

speaks of the trauma of his own immediate family in the aftermath of 1857, 'My grandmother was five and my grandfather eleven when the *ghadar* of 1857, the blind persecution and massacre of the citizens of Delhi, took place. The triumphant British held an orgy of blood and terror, all mention of which has been dropped by their historians....'[148]

As Ahmed Ali suggests, the concern was also with the effacement that the British had so successfully implemented and the conspiracy of silence to which some Muslims had themselves been a party. Socialism gave to the Muslims born a couple of generations later the courage of their convictions to speak up and, in a sense, avenge the wrongs done to their ancestors.

The 'disproportionately large' number of Shias[149] among Muslim socialists is also noteworthy: 'whereas Shias formed a mere three per cent of the Muslim population of UP, twenty per cent of the Muslim socialists [surveyed] were Shia, as were forty per cent of the organizers of the PWA [as we shall see later]. Their development was affected by the relatively more privileged position enjoyed by qasbah Shia elites.'[150] Interestingly, the word Shia or Shiah literally means 'followers' or 'members of party', referring to those who joined the group of Ali, the close comrade and son-in-law of the Prophet. The Shias, then, can be seen as the earliest organized group of dissenters, or those who protested against a political stalemate. In India, the Shias have been more organized, that is, more organized in comparison to the Sunni masses (but not more than other Islamic sects such as the Ahmadiyas or the Bohras) and in many ways, more progressive. A sizeable number of Muslims in the PWM, as we shall see later, were indeed Shias. Surely, this had less to do with coincidence and more with the 'separateness' or 'distinctiveness' that marked the Shias in India. Or, perhaps, it had something to do with the Shia consciousness of being a minority within a minority.

Another interesting fact is that despite the larger world view afforded by their 'conversion' to socialism, many Muslim socialists retained their

---

[148] Ahmed Ali, *Twilight in Delhi: A Novel* (New Delhi: Rupa & Co., 2007 [reprint]), pp. xiv–xv.

[149] Sajjad Zaheer, in an interview with Hari Dev Sharma for the NMML's Oral History Project, stated that the Shias remained aloof from the Khilafat movement and, by extension, the first non-cooperation movement.

[150] Ansari, *Emergence of Socialist Thought among North Indian Muslims*, p. 125.

affiliation to their *qasbati* origin by calling themselves Sandelwi, Kirhani, Rudaulvi, Orainvi, and so on. It has, in fact, been argued that it was the qasbati culture that encouraged the propagation of socialist thought among the privileged Muslims of north India.[151] This culture also encouraged the development of wit, humour, satire, ridicule, and lampooning—all valuable skills for a critic of society. One such young man, Wilayat Ali (1885–1918), wrote mostly in English under the nom de plume 'Bambooque'. He mocked the British rule in skits and sketches, published mostly in the *Comrade*, that were modelled on the *Tatler* and the *Spectator*. He also made fun of the imperialist arrogance and cultural superiority with as much tartness as the 'England-returned' natives. In column after column he made fun of the servility of the Indian babus.[152]

In prose, the figure of Premchand (1880–1936) loomed large over his contemporaries. Some of his finest writings, written in the last 20 years of his life, portray the influence of Gandhi and the Russian Revolution in his choice of subjects: widow remarriage, dowry, untouchability, the rich-and-poor divide, the problems of landless labour, the inequalities of the caste system, etc.[153] Some of Premchand's notable works of this period are *Nirmala* and *Narak ka Marg* (The Road to Hell; both appeared in 1925 and both dealt with May–December marriages [marriages where the ages of the spouses are disparate, that is, old men with very young wives] caused due to the problems of dowry); *Rangabhumi* (literally, The Land of Colours, but said to mean the arena of life in all its colours) where a woman leaves her husband for the larger cause of nationalism; *Godan* (The Gift of a Cow, 1936) with its depiction of Malti and Govindi as the ideal traditional Indian women, paragons of devotion and kindness. Premchand, incidentally, supported the Sarda Bill which aimed to raise the age of marriage for girls and advocated the right to give widows a share of their late husband's property. Interestingly enough, unlike women writers of the same period, such as Mahadevi Varma and Subhadra Kumari Chauhan, Premchand made no attempt to portray the woman as a silently suffering

---

[151] Mushirul Hasan, *From Pluralism to Separatism: Qasbahs in Colonial Awadh* (New Delhi: Oxford University Press, 2004), see 'Introduction'.

[152] For details, see Mushirul Hasan, *Wit and Humour in Colonial North India* (New Delhi: Niyogi Books, 2007).

[153] David Rubin, 'Introduction', in *The World of Premchand: Selected Short Stories* (New Delhi: Oxford University Press, 2001).

victim; if anything, his women 'voice the strongest arguments, complaints and feelings'.[154]

As we have seen so far, the Urdu poet and prose writer took up newer, more immediate concerns like never before. No longer was he content to sing of the gul-o-bulbul or traipse around in the magic gardens of the fasanas. This literary 'adventurism' required a new diction and a new vocabulary. For these writers, language became a means, not an end, of a creative exercise. No longer was it necessary to revive the debates on whether—or the extent to which—literature should reflect contemporary realities. Realism *had* crept into the writings of even those who shied away from labels or chose not to belong to schools of thought. These changes were as much evident in popular writings, be they in the form of 'literary' digests, pamphlets, or the novels of respected writers such as Premchand. Individuals apart, Indian society in general and creative men in particular were being swayed by the themes of colonial exploitation and subjugation, on the one hand, and, on the other, the centuries-old injustice and intolerance that had weakened Indian society from within. Freedom from foreign rule became the war cry and liberation from the clutches of landlordism and capitalism the rallying point. Against such a background, the publication of a book like *Angarey* becomes, in retrospect, a fait accompli, an event waiting to happen. In the next chapter, we shall look more closely at the year 1932 and the circumstances in which three young men and one woman put together a collection of 10 ensemble pieces—which were by no means great literature, but which nevertheless redefined what *could* constitute significant literature and, in the process, laid the foundations of the PWM.

Having seen above what was on offer in the literary scene, as reflected in the writings of the Muslims intelligentsia in the first three decades of the twentieth century, one is struck by the intellectual crisis among Indian Muslims. The only major Muslim thinker of any stature during this time was one man: Iqbal. And Iqbal offered the Indian Muslim a vision of the future that was confused, self-contradictory, and profoundly reactionary. The Age of Enlightenment in Europe had successfully brought together the spirit of modern, scientific enquiry and religion. In India, they remained mutually exclusive. Syed Ahmad Khan's 'Aligarh

---

[154] Francesca Orsini, 'Introduction', in *The Oxford India Premchand* (New Delhi: Oxford University Press, 2004), p. xxiv.

Experiment' had not borne the desired result. The marriage of science and faith, progress and tradition had failed to bear fruit. Why did this happen? What was the difference in the crucible of upper India and Europe? Was it the presence of Islam that worked as a contraceptive? Or was it the potent presence of the colonizer that emasculated? Perhaps it was a combination of the two.

Despite the good number of Muslim socialists who, as we have seen above, were active either as publicists or journalists, there was little being written at this time that made a sufficiently deep emotional and intellectual impact on the Indian Muslim—an impact, that is, that could counter the moral and intellectual imperialism of the west. The Deoband Ulama, 'after an initial flurry of anti-British activity',[155] had settled down to the business of weeding out 'false accretions' from 'true' Islam. The *deendar* from Deoband regrettably did not find common cause with the *duniyadar* of Aligarh. They had, briefly, come together during the early, heady days of the Khilafat movement, but that euphoria soon petered out. It is perhaps a great tragedy that these two forces chose not to join hands and produce an intellectual renaissance, one that could have taken the Indian Muslims on another, altogether different trajectory. Even progressive Muslim leaders such as Maulana Abul Kalam Azad, who embodied the liberal face of Indian Islam, could do little to rouse the Muslim community from apathy and torpor. The strident illiberal voices were drowning out the moderate liberals. Ideological rivals were bent upon eroding each other's space rather than creating an ideologically sound, emotionally drawn, intellectually driven movement that could appeal to a cross-section of people. One is tempted to make a comparison with the Hindus who, at this very time, were enjoying the benefits of the Arya Samaj and the Brahmo Samaj movements launched in the 1880s.

I will conclude this chapter with two observations about the Indian Muslims, both by Western scholars. They are important here because they show an understanding of the Indian Muslim which, regrettably, both the reactionaries and the progressives lacked. Once freedom was achieved, the glue of nationalism was no longer required. With nothing else to replace it, with no understanding or empathy for the Muslims and their very real

---

[155] Mushirul Hasan, 'Sharif Culture and Colonial Rule', in Mushirul Hasan and Asim Roy (eds), *Living Together Separately: Cultural India in History and Politics* (New Delhi: Oxford University Press, 2005), p. 328.

fears, the progressives found mere ideology insufficient to hold and sustain their movement. However, more on that in later chapters; first, the observation by W.C. Smith. 'The Indian Muslim is both Indian and Muslim. The existence of this duality, and the endeavour to stress either one or the other fact rather than both, have proven, shall we say, explosive. There has been a failure to intellectualise the duality, to hold the two poles synthetically in creative tension.'[156]

It is precisely this failure that I wish to stress by way of conclusion to this chapter. It would be erroneous to view the Muslim community as a victim of circumstance, more sinned against than sinning, or to suggest that all of its problems stemmed from a hostile or overwhelming colonial power.

I have devoted two chapters to enumerating the fears and insecurities of India's Muslims, articulated through public platforms, journalistic writings, and literature. While these fears and insecurities may have had some grounds, the Muslim community was not without its own shortcomings. It is important, at the very least, to take note of them. Apart from the intellectual failure that Smith refers to, we can see—after having surveyed in this chapter the concerns reflected in Urdu literature in the first three decades of the twentieth century—how indeed there was an intellectual paucity. Along with the shortcomings among Muslim writers and thinkers, there was also the failure of Muslim institutions—both Deoband and Aligarh, representing the two poles of the intellectual spectrum of the Muslims of upper India. The Aligarh of Syed Ahmad Khan that had once held out such high hopes for the Indian Muslim failed to produce any major pedagogue who could capture the imagination of the Muslim masses. One can, then, go so far as to venture that there was indeed an intellectual vacuum, a space that the progressive writers filled only too gleefully. That they went about doing so in a hammer-and-tongs sort of way is another matter; or, even, that their own intellectual agenda was flawed, limited, and ill-conceived. But it is definitely worth considering that in the 1930s, while Urdu literature was reflecting a gamut of concerns—both national and international—the Indian Muslims were an intellectually anemic, listless community. The progressives gave them, quite literally, a shot in the arm.

[156] W.C. Smith, 'Modern Muslim Historical Writing in English', in C.H. Philips (ed.), *Historians of India, Pakistan and Ceylon* (London: Oxford University Press, 1961), p. 330.

The second observation is by Francis Robinson, and it concerns the very real fears of the Muslims which stemmed from the ulama's 'passionate engagement' not just with Islam, but also the Muslim public:

As ulama they are oppressed by their marginalization in the affairs of Muslim India. As Muslims they are oppressed by the marginalization of Islamic power in the world at large. Their security threatened, their very identity questioned, their distress bites ever more deeply as World War One comes to its close. Witness of this fact helps to explain their prolonged, and often frenzied, struggle from 1919 to 1924 to defend the Turkish Khilafat.[157]

This, to my mind, is not inconsistent with the observation made in the preceding paragraphs. It is easy, with hindsight, to look at a community's shortcomings; but we would be guilty of a shortcoming of our own if we fail to at least *acknowledge* their fears. As I shall attempt to show later, it was precisely this *lack of understanding of the fear* that gripped the Muslim which, for all their other strengths of mind and heart, proved to be the undoing of the progressive writers. Completely fearless themselves, by virtue of their inherent advantages of class and education and early exposure to Western ideas, they had no sympathy for those who dwelt in fear.

The two observations above are useful precisely because, as we shall see in the next chapter, when a group of four young writers—all four being Indian *and* Muslim—chose to express one duality at the expense of the other, the result was, to say the least, explosive! *Angarey* is the expression of one fact 'rather than both' in Smith's memorable words. Perhaps its explosive result was, therefore, inevitable.

---

[157] Francis Robinson, 'An-Nizamiya: A Group of Lucknow Intellectuals in the Early-Twentieth Century', in Christopher Shackle (ed.), *Urdu and Muslim South Asia: Studies in Honour of Ralph Russell* (New Delhi: Oxford University Press, 1991), p. 110. Incidentally, the position of scholars such as Robinson and Barbara D. Metcalf in taking a sympathetic view of the ulama has been criticized in recent years by historians such as Mushirul Hasan. Hasan questions the role of the ulama by asking why they could not extricate themselves from Islamic thralldom. He asks what the ulama did for the regeneration of the Muslim community at a time when it most needed their guidance. In India, he says, the ulama were content to rejoice in tradition unlike their counterparts in Egypt and Turkey who initiated debates which lead to change.

3

Analysing *Angarey*

> *Aag dekhi, pani dekha, aur angarey dekhe*
> (We have seen fire, water, and now live embers)
> —*Sarguzasht*, 24 February 1933

Angarey was published some time in December 1932. It was banned in March 1933. In the few short months of its existence, in an age innocent of the Xerox, it was possibly read by few people, especially since the remaining copies were confiscated from the printer. Those who read it did so perforce on the sly adding to the air of secrecy and furtiveness that the very mention of the book evoked for years to come. Yet, it unleashed a storm of controversies. Before we begin to look at the furore created by its publication and the sequence of events culminating in its ban (dealt with in detail in the next chapter), we must look at the contents of the book that caused all the uproar.[1]

---

[1] For the purpose of this study I have used Khalid Alvi's *Angarey* published by Educational Publishing House, Delhi in 1995, which is a sanitized version of one of the original copies saved from imperial proscription. I also have a copy of the original *Angarey*; it was given to me by Asghar Wajahat. Upon reading the original

This chapter shall be devoted to a detailed discussion of each of its 10 contributing segments. Since no complete translation of *Angarey* exists in English, a great deal of space will be given to extracts from each of its 10 segments. This is not only a new initiative, but an important one also because few people have actually read the book and fewer still *know* the book rather than *know of* the book! It must also be noted that *Angarey* was possibly the first anthology of short stories published in Urdu, a collection, that is, of short stories by different authors included within one cover.

Angarey consisted of five short stories by Sajjad Zaheer, namely, *Neend Nahin Aati* (Sleep Doesn't Come), *Jannat ki Bashaarat* (The Glad Tidings of Heaven), *Garmiyon ki Ek Raat* (A Summer's Night), *Dulari*, and *Phir Yeh Hungama* (Again This Commotion); two by Ahmed Ali, namely, *Baadal Nahin Aate* (The Clouds Don't Come) and *Mahavaton ki Ek Raat* (A Night of Winter Rain); one short story by Mahmuduzzafar called *Jawanmardi* (Virility); and a story and play each by Rashid Jahan, namely, *Dilli ki Sair* (A Tour of Delhi) and *Parde ke Peechche* (From Behind the Veil), respectively.[2]

Of the four contributors to *Angarey*, two came from upper-middle-class families and Mahmuduzzafar and Sajjad Zaheer from highly privileged backgrounds; their choice of subjects is, therefore, both interesting and

---

against Khalid Alvi's edited version, I could spot the minor differences, which I have pointed out in footnotes in the course of this chapter. Shabana Mahmud has reprinted *Angarey* with a lengthy introduction under the title *Angarey: Ek Jaiza*. It was published in Sweden by Bokforlag Kitabiat in 1988 but I have not been able to access it. References to the book abound on the Internet, but exhaustive searches through DELNET and other library-based search engines in India have not shown any results. Clearly, the book is not found in any Indian library.

[2] The story by Mahmuduzzafar was apparently in the nature of a 'command performance'; Sajjad Zaheer wanted something to flesh out the rather slender contents of the book and so Mahmuduzzafar, a friend and comrade from Zaheer's London days, was asked to pitch in. It is possible that *Jawanmardi* was first written in English and then translated, possibly by Sajjad Zaheer, into Urdu for inclusion in *Angarey*. Zaheer, in *Roshnai*, indicates how Mahmuduzzafar who had returned in 1931 after many years in England—where he had first attended a private school and then secured a BA from Balliol College—could understand Urdu, his mother tongue, but not write in it. It was several years later that he learnt to read and write in Urdu.

instructive. All four were English-educated, bilingual,[3] affluent, and deeply committed to bringing about an end to colonialism. Given their Western-style education, their knowledge of English and Western literature, given also their fairly well-known penchant for radical and avant-garde movements (literary and otherwise), they lent themselves quite easily to accusations of 'Westernization'. That is, their profligacy could easily be excused as 'the result of cultural and intellectual contact with Europe'.[4] They were accused of being 'intoxicated by English education, brainwashed into attacking Islam and its tenets'.[5]

Sajjad Zaheer (1905–1973),[6] the prodigal son of Sir Wazir Hasan,[7] the chief justice of Oudh, had lately returned from England after completing his BA where he had been greatly influenced by communistic ideas and had also made friends with a wide circle of writers and intellectuals such

---

[3] Aijaz Ahmad has noted how the bilingualism and 'polyglot ease in communication' was, in a sense, 'typical' of the intelligentsia of the late period of colonial India. For a detailed explanation, see *In Theory: Classes, Nations, Literatures* (London: Verso, 1992), p. 76.

[4] Priyamvada Gopal, *Literary Radicalism in India: Gender, Nation and the Transition to Independence* (Oxon: Routledge, 2005), p. 16.

[5] Ibid.

[6] Apart from penning the history of the PWM in *Roshnai*, Sajjad Zaheer wrote in dribs and drabs about his own life. A great deal has been written on him in Urdu, but much of it is hagiographical and repetitive. A comprehensive biographical essay in Urdu was written by Pandit Rahul Sankrityayana, 'Sajjad Zaheer: Nai Nayta', *Naya Daur*, August 1948, Karachi, pp. 8–16. Unfortunately, I have not been able to access it. Sajjad Zaheer's daughter Noor Zaheer in her book, *Mere Hisse ki Roshnai* (Shahadra: Medha Books, 2005), brings to light many lesser-known facets of her father's personality and life.

[7] Sir Wazir Hasan had gone on deputation to England with Mohamed Ali in 1913 to put forth the wrongs done to the Indian Muslims, but according to Sajjad Zaheer his father was more a 'cultural Muslim' who subscribed to a liberal democratic ideology than a religious one. In an interview for the NMML's Oral History Project, Sajjad Zaheer said his father was a product of the wave generated by Syed Ahmad Khan; unfortunately men like Sir Wazir Hasan, he said, found themselves out of the mainstream of the nationalist movement even though the latter joined the Congress after his retirement as a judge. Zaheer also wonders why men like his father, liberals who were more modern in their outlook and more real than the sectarian leaders, were discarded in the larger national arena.

as V.K. Krishna Menon, Mulk Raj Anand, and others. In his first year of BA at New College, Oxford, Zaheer fell ill and had to go to a sanatorium in Switzerland for close to a year. However, he used this time to learn good German and French. On returning to England, he was influenced by the British communist of Indian origin, Shapurji Saklatvala (1874–1936), joined the Oxford Majlis, and attended the Second Congress of the League against Imperialism held in Frankfurt where he met Viren Chattopadhyay, Saumendranath Tagore, N.M. Jaisoorya (Sarojini Naidu's son), and Raja Mahendra Pratap. From the League Congress he took back the message of forging an alliance with nationalistic liberation movements in Indonesia, Egypt, etc. David Guest, the Marxist scholar from Cambridge, introduced him to Marx's *Capital*. During his undergraduate days,[8] he also read Lenin's *What Is To Be Done?* which laid down the essentials in regard to the organization of a communist party, the need of a centralized democratic leadership, discipline, etc., as well as *Left-wing Communism: An Infantile Disorder* and *The State and Revolution* (both by Lenin) and John Stratchey's *The Coming Struggle for Power*. All this was supplemented by regular readings of *Labour Monthly* and *Daily Worker*.[9] Writing in his *Yaadein*, he spoke passionately of the tumult that grew inside him during his student days in England:

We were gradually drifting towards socialism. Our minds searched for a philosophy which would help us to understand and solve the difficult social problems. We were not satisfied with the idea that humanity had always been miserable and would always remain so…. After the end of our university education, this was the beginning of a new and unlimited field of education.[10]

---

[8] Incidentally, in the NMML interview Zaheer claims to have met Gandhi when the latter visited England for the Second Round Table Congress in 1931 as the sole representative of the Congress. Zaheer says he went to meet Gandhi at an apartment in London's East End and asked him why he had chosen to attend the Congress and was his attendance not a compromise with British imperialism? Gandhi, according to Zaheer replied: 'Ek chakki ke neeche hamara haath dab gaya hai, chakki ke patthar ke neeche' (Our hand is stuck under a millstone). He (Gandhi) had come to lift the stone a little so that the hand may be released.

[9] This section has been culled from Zaheer's interview for the NMML's Oral History Project.

[10] Sudhi Pradhan (ed.), *Marxist Cultural Movements in India (1936–1947)*, vol. I (Calcutta: National Book Agency, 1979), p. 36.

Scion of a distinguished family from Rampur and the son of Dr Saiduzzafar, a professor of anatomy at the Lucknow Medical College, Mahmuduzzafar (1908–1956) had lived in England for the greater part of his life till he burst upon the Urdu-speaking world with the publication of *Angarey*. Sent to Sherborune School in Dorset at the age of 12, he completed his graduation from Oxford. Yet, when he returned to India, in 1931, he had become an active nationalist, choosing to wear khadi and refusing to sit for the civil services examinations as was expected of someone of his class and privilege. Betrothed to his cousin Zohra[11] since childhood, he was swept off his feet by Rashid Jahan whom he married in 1934. Together, they weathered the worst of the storm over *Angarey* and became the most committed and active members of the PWA.

Rashid Jahan (1905–1953), the eldest daughter of Shaikh Abdullah, a pioneer among male reformers and the founder of the Muslim Girls' College at Aligarh, had studied medicine at Lady Hardinge College. At the time of writing *Angarey* she was working at the Lady Dufferin Hospital in Lucknow. A committed political organizer, a free-spirited writer whose life was cut short by cancer, the epitaph on her grave in Moscow sums up her extraordinary life quite aptly and succinctly: 'Rashid Jahan: Communist Doctor and Writer'. Being a woman and having written so bravely and boldly about sexual matters in a largely puritanical, patriarchal milieu, she naturally faced the ire of those who most vehemently opposed a book such as *Angarey* and all that it stood for. Obviously, different people viewed her in different ways: 'In progressive families she became a symbol of the emancipated woman; in conservative homes an example of all the worst that can occur if a woman is educated, not kept in purdah, and allowed to pursue a career.'[12]

Lampooned as Rashid Jahan 'Angarewali' by the baser elements in the vernacular press, she became the public face of *Angarey*. As Priyamvada Gopal notes, 'Rashid Jahan—as a woman and a doctor—writing about

---

[11] This information was revealed in an interview with Dr Sarwat Rahman, Mahmuduzzafar's neighbour in Dehradun. Zohra, also belonging to the royal family of Rampur, like Mahmud, later became famous as the dancer-actress Zohra Segal.

[12] Carlo Coppola and S. Zubair, 'Rashid Jahan: Urdu Literature's First "Angry Young Woman"', *Journal of South Asian Literature*, vol. 22, no. 1 (1987), p. 170.

gender, medicine and the politics of space, became an icon of the literary radicalism of *Angarey* itself; decried by some and celebrated by others.'[13]

Ahmed Ali (1910–1994) was a friend of Rashid Jahan's brother, Mohsin, and a frequent visitor to their home in Aligarh.[14] A man of many parts, Ahmed Ali was—in the course of a long and distinguished career—a teacher of English, translator, poet, critic, diplomat, and a highly successful writer. After completing his MA in English from the University of Lucknow in 1931, where he also taught for a year (1931–2), during the *Angarey* drama he was teaching at the Agra College. A prodigiously prolific writer, he later translated, among other things, the Holy Quran. Of the *Angarey* quartet, he is best known to the English reader for his epochal novel *Twilight in Delhi*; he is also the most enigmatic of the four. His varied career showed glimpses of a person who was both a part of the establishment, and against it. Yet, it was Ahmed Ali who gave a lasting definition of progressivism. 'Progressive,' he declared at the very outset of the PWM, 'should not be taken to be synonymous with revolutionary. It does, however, mean trying for the betterment of our social life. It implies the banishment of mysticism and all that which stands in the way of attaining freedom. It also means the acceptance of realism as a primary factor in the arts and literature.'[15] We will return to this definition of progressivism again in later chapters.

Five Stories by Sajjad Zaheer

To begin with, let us look at the five stories by Sajjad Zaheer. The first and most obvious thing that strikes a reader is their true-to-life quality. Each story paints graphic pictures of the poorest and most downtrodden people—servant girls who have been bought as slaves to serve rich masters, down-at-heel poets living on the largesse of rich relatives, a sweeper living in a dirty, smelly hovel on a rich man's estate, as well as 'vulgar lower-class types' such as clerks and orderlies. Sajjad Zaheer

---

[13] Gopal, *Literary Radicalism in India*, p. 42.

[14] Lubna Kazim (ed.), *A Woman of Substance: The Memoirs of Begum Khurshid Mirza (1918–1989)* (New Delhi: Zuban, 2005), p. 81.

[15] Ahmed Ali, 'The Progressive View of Art', address at the First Session of the AIPWA, Lucknow, 10 April 1936. From Pradhan, *Marxist Cultural Movements in India*, vol. I, p. 78.

adopts the stream of consciousness and interior monologue techniques newly popularized in the West by writers such as James Joyce, D.H. Lawrence, Dorothy Richardson, and Virginia Woolf. His stories have the flavour of ostensibly unedited, spontaneous, or live performances. Sajjad Zaheer himself acknowledged the influence of Dadaism[16] on his *Angarey* stories.[17] Incidentally, in sharp contrast, the stories of Rashid Jahan and Mahmuduzzafar are straightforward, almost didactic in their lack of artfulness or technique.

First, let us look at '*Neend Nahi Aati*', written in the stream of consciousness technique. The story—completely free of a plot—begins with a set of alliterative sounds: *Ghaddh Ghaddh, Ghaddh, Ghaddh, Ghaddh, Thakh, Thakh, Chatt, Thakh, Thakh, Thakh, Chatt, Chatt, Chatt*. The opening paragraph is an amateurish attempt at an interior monologue that takes us into the mind of the protagonist who is trying to sleep through a dark and dreary night. His attempt at sleep is constantly interrupted by the sounds from the streets and the incoherent jumble of his own thoughts that tumble out helter-skelter. Sajjad Zaheer, a pampered privileged young man, is attempting to write from the point of view of Akbar, an impoverished young poet who can neither think straight on an empty stomach nor fall into a deep and peaceful sleep. Pangs of hunger interrupt a series of unrelated thoughts—Gandhiji's public speech that is marred by rain ('*Qudrat moot rahihai*'—'Nature is peeing'); the embarrassment of having to go out in sweat-stained grimy clothes and the trauma of genteel poverty; the *ruhani sukoon* offered by prayers; the charms of the courtesan and the sarangi-infused *kotha* culture spawned by the shurfa class; the miseries of Akbar's own state of impoverishment and helplessness that includes an ailing TB-ridden mother racked by bouts of coughing; the fear and horror of watching a parent die and the loathing of having to see well-off relatives treat one's poverty with ill-concealed disdain; the constant headache of having a nagging wife who adds to Akbar's domestic travails; and in

---

[16] Dadaism was a cultural movement that began in Zürich, Switzerland, during the First World War and peaked from 1916 to 1922. The movement primarily involved visual arts, literature, and theatre. Its purpose was to ridicule what its participants considered to be the meaninglessness of the modern world. In addition to being anti-war, it was also anti-bourgeois and anarchistic in nature.

[17] Qamar Rais, *Tanquidi Tanazur* (Aligarh: Educational Publishing House, 1978), p. 73.

between all this there is the steady drone of mosquitoes and the street sounds that keep him awake.

Jostling among his jumbled thoughts are three iconic images—one, the notion of 'Muslim hell' (coinage mine) which is a raging inferno that awaits all sinners; two, the courtesan, Munnijan, who too is consigned to hell, but the punishment meted out to her is that she must forever have two snakes licking away at her breasts; and three, a poet reciting at a mushaira. All three are archetypal 'Muslim' images insofar as they feature, one way or another, in the culture, imagination, and literature of the Indian Muslims; of these, Munnijan's appearance in hell is worth a mention here. She appears from the wisps and shards of Akbar's imagination. With a name like 'Munnijan' she could be a real person, one of the *tawaif*-prostitutes that Akbar had known in the kothas of Lucknow or she could be an archetype of *any* tawaif-prostitutes from *any* of the kothas in old Lucknow. Her first-person account of her first day in hell borders on the ludicrous, yet there is much here that may be considered blasphemous and sacrilegious, as can be seen from the account below:

When I came here, the Darogha saheb said, 'Bi Munnijan! The Sarkar has ordered five scorpions to be pressed into your service.' I was terrified. I have hated scorpions ever since my childhood. I pleaded but the Darogha saheb said that it was his bounden duty to carry out the instructions of Sarkar. Then I said, all right, you take me to the court of Sarkar; I will myself beg for clemency before him. The Darogha saheb was a good man; he called me near him, made me sit down and patted my cheek, and eventually agreed. I had to wait many hours. Darogha saheb told me that Sarkar was holding a Council of Prophets, and I would be presented before him only after it was over. When I heard this I tried to peep in and catch a glimpse of my Prophet's glorious splendour. But the guard at the gate, an awful ogre, shouted and pushed me away. Anyhow, eventually my turn came. My heart was beating fast. I was wondering what awaited me. As soon as I entered the court of Sarkar, I fell on my knees. As I was in no condition to speak with my own tongue, Darogha saheb narrated my case. I heard the command: Stand up! I stood up. Sarkar too stood up and came towards me. A big white beard, a fair glowing complexion. He looked at me and smiled. Then, he took my hand and led me to an adjacent chamber. I could not understand what was going on…. But, huzoor, he only looked elderly! I have not seen such a man in this world, and by your good grace, huzoor, I have entertained some of the biggest and wealthiest men in my time. Anyhow, huzoor, Sarkar later said that punishment would surely be meted out to me because his justice is for everyone, but instead of scorpions I would get two snakes that would forever lick my nipples. If you ask the truth, huzoor, there is no pain in this, only pleasure....[18]

It is worth noting that there is a Darogha saheb in hell, as in all good government offices taking care of the administrative procedures, ensuring due protocol, and maintaining law and order; Satan, who is presumably the Big Boss of the establishment, is referred to by the Darogha saheb as 'Sarkar'; Satan is holding a Council of Prophets where Munnijan's Prophet, the beloved Prophet of all Muslims, is also present; the Council Meeting is guarded by 'an awful ogre' (a *'mua mustanda'* in Munnijan's words); and Satan, who has 'a big white beard, a fair glowing complexion' takes Munnijan to a room where she 'entertains' him and pronounces that he only looks elderly, but is obviously not so when it comes to virility; and because even in hell there must be justice for all, instead of the scorpions that were initially allotted to her she now gets two snakes that forever lick away at her breasts giving her pleasure instead of pain.

The apparition of Munnijan fades away and her place is taken by pangs of hunger. The bottom-line of the story is that for all the *azadi ki hawa* that is blowing about, an empty stomach asks for food; its persistent call cannot be smothered with freedom, or with thoughts of heaven or hell. Asked to choose between death and freedom, he says he wants neither. All he wants is food. '*Koi mera pet bhar de*', he says ('If only someone were to fill my stomach'). The present is all that matters and the present cannot be sated with poetry about gul-o-bulbul or with freedom! Bread, roti, is the only thing that matters in the here and now.

The second story *Jannat ki Bashaarat* is set in Lucknow. It is about Maulvi Dawood who teaches in a madrasa. A deeply religious man who spends entire nights reading from the Holy Quran, the next day, during classes at the madrasa, when he falls into a drowsy stupor, his students thinking their pious teacher to be in a trance quietly leave the classroom. Zaheer, delineating the minutiae of a good Muslim's character and behaviour, stresses how Maulvi Dawood bears the rigours of Ramzan by fasting during the searing hot days of an Indian summer, and notes, 'Obviously, the more hardships a person suffers, the greater is the *savab* he earns' and

---

[18] Unless otherwise specified, all translations are mine. All translations, unless otherwise specified, are from the version of *Angarey* edited by Khalid Alvi.

during these trying days 'every good Muslim is like an enraged lion bent upon undertaking *jihad* in the way of the Lord'. While all the days and nights of the holy month of Ramzan are meant for prayer, Shab-e-Qadar[19] or the Night of Revelation is special. On this night, like countless other Muslims, Maulvi Dawood too plans to pray all night so that he too might accrue some favours and be absolved of his past sins. But while the spirit is strong the body is weak. In his fifties, the Maulvi has a nubile and demanding second wife. On top of that, he has feasted on a rich dinner of *pulao, sheermal,* and *kheer* that is sitting heavily in his stomach. His body racked by yawns, his mind devoured by thoughts of his body, Maulvi Dawood is finding it very hard indeed to stay awake. A terrible war is being waged between his body and his spirit. As only a few hours remain of the precious night, he leaves the mosque where he has been struggling to stay awake and pray, and comes home thinking it might be easier to pray there. But all is dark and still inside his house. He gropes his way in the dark, looking for a matchbox to light a lantern. He finds his young wife, fast asleep in the courtyard under the star-lit summer sky. He wakes her asking for the elusive matchbox, but his wife, as though under a spell of sleep and seduction, tries to pull him to lie down beside her. Images of Adam's first sin and woman's eternal temptation flash before his eyes and somehow Maulvi Dawood resists the lure. His wife, enraged at being denied, spits venom at him, calling him, among other things, an old man! Humiliated, Maulvi

---

[19] While the entire period of Ramzan is a time of fasting and praying (*ibadat*), there is one night that is especially significant for Muslims. For, it is believed that there is one night when Allah first revealed the first verses of the Quran to Muhammad through the angel Gabriel. Muhammad was then 40 years old and unlettered. This most blessed of all nights falls on a night that no one can pinpoint with any certainty. Yet, the faithful who have prayed through the dark watches of the night seeking communion with God say that the heart always knows when communion has been reached. Shab-e-Qadr or *Lailatul-Qadr* (also called *Shab-e-Meraj*), understood variously to mean the Night of Honour and Dignity, the Night of Destiny, or the Night of Power, can fall on any of the odd nights in the last 10 days of the month of Ramzan, that is, on 21, 23, 25, and 27 of Ramzan. Unlike other anniversaries, this is a solemn occasion—a time to reflect and pray, to celebrate the arrival of the Message from Allah not through a feast for the senses but through abstinence and worship. Some go into retreat (*i'tikaf*), spending all their time in a mosque for the last 10 days of Ramzan; others take as much time out as possible on these special nights for prayer and the study of the Quran.

Dawood finds the matchbox, lights a lantern, spreads out his prayer rug, and begins to read from the Holy Quran. Shortly, however, the combined effect of a full stomach and his own melodious reading from the Surah Rehman[20] begins to affect him like a lullaby. Soon, he falls asleep on his prayer mat. In a state of half-sleep, half-wakefulness, he is transported to a strange place that is like a vast empty maidan where a voice bids him to fall into *sajda*. Terrified, the Maulvi does so. A voice then resounds all around him:

My son, I am pleased with you. You have been so engrossed in my worship all your life that you have never attempted to use your brain and your thoughts, the two satanic powers and the root of all *kufr*. Human thought is the enemy of faith and worship. You have well understood this secret and you have never allowed the light of faith to be rusted and darkened by your intellect. Your reward shall be paradise where your every desire shall be fulfilled.

After the voice, presumably a divine one, falls silent, Maulvi saheb finds the courage to look around him. He finds himself not in a deserted maidan, but in a splendid round hall with bejewelled, intricately engraved walls. A cool, soothing light is seeping through the walls. And studded in these amazingly coloured walls is a window and sitting in each window, a *hoor*. In whichever direction Maulvi saheb casts his gaze, he finds a hoor looking at him, smiling and making the most alluring gestures. Initially, the poor man averts his gaze bashfully from these gorgeous creatures because they are—every single one of them—without a stitch of clothing! Eventually, his embarrassment subsides somewhat and the vigour of youth begins to course through his veins, a youth that shall never fade.

Maulvi saheb ran a hand over his beard and moved towards one of the windows. The *hoor* too stepped forward and came closer. He ran his gaze over her from head to toe. The glowing amber of her body, her piercing eyes, her alluring beauty—Maulvi saheb could barely pull his gaze away from this heavenly sight. But man is never satisfied with a good thing. The Maulana's steps rose and moved towards the next window. And in this manner he moved from window to window, stopping beside every window and, after gazing his fill at every bodily part of these heavenly creatures, he would move on to the next one—with the words

---

[20] Surah Rehman is the 55th Surah of the Holy Quran; its recurring verse is 'Then which of the favours of your Lord will you deny?'

of the *durood*[21] on his lips. He would adore the inky blackness of the curls of one, or the pink cheeks of another, the plum-coloured lips of yet another, the shapely legs of one, the slender fingers of another, the intoxicating eyes of yet another, the pointed breasts of one, the delicate waist of another, or the soft stomach of another.

Finally, the bewitching ways of one *hoor* beguiled the Maulana. He climbed into her enclosure and instantly clutched her to his bosom. But, their lips had barely touched, when the sound of coarse laughter came from behind them. The Maulana's anger knew no bounds at this ill-opportune laughter. He woke up. The sun had risen. The Maulana was lying on his belly on the prayer rug and hugging the …[22] to his chest. His wife was standing beside him and laughing.

A full stomach and sleep combine to cause havoc with a man's best intentions in this hilarious account. As in the previous story, the metaphor of the dream recurs here, but now Zaheer plays with the Muslim notion of heaven as he had earlier done with hell. While depicting Maulvi saheb's religiosity, he is mocking the notion of heaven where the pious shall be rewarded with gorgeous naked women; in the process, he is also mocking the very notion of religion. Later, during the thick of the *Angarey* controversy, one of the Urdu papers would say in Sajjad Zaheer's defence that he is making fun of *maulviyat*, not *Islamiyat*, and that the two are not synonymous.

The third story by Sajjad Zaheer is *Garmiyon ki Ek Raat*. It unfolds the tedium of a humdrum, middle-class existence that leads, in the end, to a great escape into a world of fantasy. A compact story, it relies for its effect on realistic dialogue and a crisp, almost abrupt ending. Munshi Barkat Ali is out for a walk in Ameenabad Park on a hot summer evening when he meets Lalaji, the head clerk under whom he works. Meeting Lalaji, who

---

[21] Durood refers to invocations in the form of specific verses from the Holy Quran which rain benediction upon the Prophet. A Muslim should recite the durood whenever he speaks, hears, or reads the name of the Prophet (PBUH).

[22] In Khalid Alvi's version, the text has a series of dashes and an editorial footnote containing two words—'*Kitab ka naam*' (Name of the book). From the context, it seems safe to surmise that the author is referring to the Holy Quran. It is to be noted that the editor/printer/publisher forbore to print the name of the holy book. In the original version of *Angarey*, a copy of which was given to me by Asghar Wajahat, the name of the holy book is given and there is no coy attempt to gloss over it.

looks prosperous and happy, sets him thinking about his own sad lot: how he is finding it increasingly difficult to manage his household comprising his wife and children on a salary of 60 rupees a month and how the little that used to come 'under the table' is getting increasingly hard to come by. As Barkat Ali strolls away from Lalaji and his companions, he ruminates on the rural clients who are growing smarter by the day and how it is becoming increasingly difficult to make them part with even a few small coins. He fulminates as he walks:

These low class types have had their heads turned.... It is us—blue collar types—who suffer. On the one hand, we cannot mix with these lower-class people; on the other hand, our bosses and the government are getting increasingly strict.... It is always the poor who get punished; the worst that is ever done to the senior officer is that he gets transferred.

These doleful ruminations are interrupted by Jumman, the orderly in his office. Barkat Ali does nothing to encourage a conversation with someone who is clearly his social inferior, yet Jumman follows Barkat Ali and unburdens his long and plaintive tale of exploitation, poverty, and injustice: how he (Jumman) works long hours in the office, then goes to serve in the manager's house where the manager's wife makes him do her shopping and when the groceries are not to her liking makes the wretched fellow pay for them from his pocket. Poor Jumman ends up poorer by a rupee because the mangoes he had bought for the manager's wife were not to her liking. Hearing this, Barkat Ali becomes uneasy. Why was Jumman telling him all this? 'Who doesn't know that the poor suffer and go hungry?' Barkat Ali says to himself and, mouthing a few platitudes, walks away. Jumman follows, making Barkat Ali nervously feel the rupee that he had managed to extract as bribe from a client at the office earlier in the day. His unease growing with every step, Barkat Ali launches into a long and winding tale simply to evade any mention of a loan. He narrates a sermon he had heard the day before during Friday prayers and concludes with a mention of the Ben Israel who suffered for 'lesser crimes than ours'. A bit like the maulvis who give the Friday sermons, Barkat Ali too 'didn't know much about the history of the Ben Israel tribe but he could talk about it for hours'.

Actually, Barkat Ali is rather cleverly using the Ben Israelis and their misfortunes as a red herring—to turn poor starving Jumman's attention away from talk of hunger and poverty that might eventually lead to a request for a loan. Sajjad Zaheer puts ostensibly laudatory words in Barkat Ali's mouth to mock the rampant use of the rhetoric that has invaded a true understanding of religion and is used as a crutch by the ill-informed.

Despite the mild fun he is able to have at poor Jumman's expense, Barkat Ali's desire to get rid of him is very real. The more the poor starving orderly follows him from the park to the chowk to the street, Barkat Ali becomes more desperate to get rid of him before the orderly touches him for a loan or makes a public spectacle of himself. While it is not a pleasant thing to run into a poor starving man, especially if one has had one's fill at dinner and is out for a quiet, peaceful walk, Barkat Ali is hardly expected to 'shoo Jumman away like a dog' because 'for one, they had to meet every day at the court where they both worked, and for another, he [Jumman] was after all a low-class person who might, who knows, insult him in full public view'. Clearly, there are several dynamics at work here: poverty is only one; there is also an acute class consciousness running all through the walk in the park. First, there is Barkat Ali's meeting with Lalaji (a Hindu who is a senior and slightly better-off socially and financially), and then there is Jumman (a Muslim like him, but inferior in every other way). Religion brings Barkat Ali and Jumman together momentarily as does the workplace, but it cannot bridge the socio-economic gap between them. Since a chance encounter on a summer evening can only bring one-sided gain (a small loan to help Jumman tide over his acute chronic poverty, but nothing whatsoever to Barkat Ali), it is best therefore to try and lose him at the next crossroad. And so making some excuse Barkat Ali strides off in the direction of Qaisar Bagh cinema hall. Sajjad Zaheer uses this opportunity to make a devastating critique of capitalism that brings prosperity only to some and not all (certainly not 'all of God's creation'). Poor helpless Jumman stands still, not knowing what to do: 'Drops of sweat glistened on his forehead. His eyes looked here and there meaninglessly. The bright glare of electricity, the fountain, the cinema poster, hotels, shops, motor-cars, *tongas*, *ekkas* and above them all the dark sky and the twinkling stars. In short, all of God's creation.'

The unsaid but obvious inference of the above passage is that prosperity in terms of material progress such as electricity, motor cars, hotels, shops, cinemas is: (*a*) actually Man's creation and not God's; and (*b*) comes only to the deserving, that is, the rich. To get back to Barkat Ali, who has used every trick in the book (including all sorts of religious discussions and talk of Judgement Day) to shake Jumman off his trail, finds the poor, hungry, and desperate man still hanging on. And, then, the unexpected happens. A rotund, well-dressed, paan-chewing, cigarette-smoking, prosperous-looking gentleman hails Munshi Barkat Ali on the road. He is a wealthy aristocrat and an old college friend who happens to visit Lucknow in search of entertainment. He urges Barkat Ali to join him in his hedonistic search for pleasure: a *mujra* by the famous and coquettish courtesan Noorjahan, in the courtyard of his house under the stars. The friend is a caricature of a feudal aristocrat who lives off the sweat of the poor on his lands (which he has no doubt inherited) and comes to the big cities periodically to blow up large sums of money by way of having fun. The story ends thus: 'An old friend, a ride in a car, song and dance, the promise of heavenly eyes, a delightful place—Munshi leapt and got into the car. He didn't even think of Jumman. When the car began to pull away he saw Jumman standing still, quiet as before.'

Ending the way it does, *Garmiyon ki Ek Raat* relies for greatest effect on what it leaves unsaid. Jumman's misery is the mute misery of the animal that can do nothing to improve its lot or break free of its tethers. The poor remain as poor as ever; they can do nothing except watch the petit bourgeoisie move up the social and economic ladder.

The fourth story by Sajjad Zaheer, *Dulari*, is about a *laundi*. A laundi is a servant, a slave girl—unlike a paid *naukrani* or a part-time *mama*—who has been bought and is therefore not entitled to wages, but is simply fed and clothed. Both boys and girls were often bought for a pittance and made to serve as family retainers for their entire lives. While for the most part they were badly treated by their masters, in many cases even abused, both physically and sexually, there are rare instances of the laundi becoming the mistress of the household. In *Umrao Jaan*, the novel by Mirza Ruswa, two girls are abducted and sold to two separate households: one is bought by a courtesan and grows up to become the famous Umrao Jaan of Lucknow; the other is bought by a lady from a sharif family and raised well, and by sheer good fortune, ends up marrying the son of the family. But this was an exception. Normally, the laundis were treated a bit like common property by the men of the household and the boys invariably had their rite of passage into manhood through a laundi—either consensually or forcibly. The servant girl figures in much of Urdu fiction—most memorably in *Bhag Bhari* (The Fortunate One) by Hajra Masroor and *Utran* (Hand-Me-Downs, usually clothes) by Wajeda Tabassum. In some cases, the servant girls were not bought; they were the progeny of existing or old servants and so the blood in their veins had a healthy admixture of sharif blood.

Dulari, meaning 'loved one', had been raised from childhood in the home of Sheikh Nazim Ali Khan. No one knew who her parents were. Dulari had grown up with the younger daughter of the family, Hasina Begum who, unlike Dulari, spent her time stitching and sewing, reading and writing. With time, the difference between them becomes a gulf. Dressed in grubby and smelly rags, Dulari is forever sweeping, cleaning, filling water, and doing assorted chores for the Begum saheba (the master's wife). While at one level her lot is better-off than the paid servants, whenever she has a fight with some naukrani or mama who also serves the same household, she has to hear the taunt, 'I am not a laundi like you!'[23]

At 16 or 17 years of age, Dulari is a good-looking girl with long arms and legs and a well-rounded body though normally she smells and looks awful. However, on special occasions when she has to go out with the Begum saheba or the *sahebzadis*, or on festive occasions, she puts on her good clothes and takes some pains with her appearance. On the occasion of *Shab-e-Barat*,[24] she is 'dressed up like a doll'. She is bursting firecrackers in the courtyard when the gaze of Qasim, the 21-year-old eldest son of the family, falls upon her. Qasim is in his last year of college and is

---

[23] In this context, Priyamvada Gopal notes, 'The contractual nature of the work that these women do, as opposed to Dulari's liege labour allows them to "at the slightest grievance, quarrel and leave".' See Gopal, *Literary Radicalism in India*, p. 34.

[24] In *Jannat ki Bashaarat*, Zaheer has pegged his story on Shab-e-Qadar. Now he uses the occasion of Shab-e-Barat to weave a twist in his story. In the process, he not only shows his knowledge and minute observation of such occasions in upper-class households such as his own, but also uses these occasions to mock at religiosity. The festival of Shab-e-Barat is celebrated by making and distributing halwa, decorating homes and mosques with lights, and bursting crackers. It is believed that on the night of Shab-e-Barat, God writes the destinies of all men for the coming year by taking into account the deeds committed by them in the past. The festival is celebrated either on the 13th or on the 14th day of *Shaban*, the eighth month of the Muslim year. This happens to be 15 days before the beginning of Ramadan.

disdainful and distant with his family whom he considers old-fashioned and narrow-minded. For all his disdain, he is however not prepared to do anything about his family's old-fashioned and orthodox ways except show his displeasure by staying aloof and angry. In this, Qasim is a 'type', the sort of young man who knows that some of the old ways are bad, but is unwilling to change them; such men accept the old ways, though angrily, but do nothing to *be* the change. Qasim fancies himself as a social reformer, yet does precious little to prove himself to be anything other than a social malcontent. Perhaps, more than the social order, it is he who is single-handedly responsible for Dulari's ruin.

On the spur of the moment, Qasim takes a sudden fancy to Dulari. A brief tryst takes place between two nubile bodies. Zaheer writes, 'Two people, whose thinking lives were poles apart, suddenly felt as though they were standing on the same shore of desire. Actually, like straws, they were swimming in a sea of dark currents.'

A year passes. Celebrations are underway for Qasim's wedding. The house is full of gaiety and guests when, suddenly, one night, Dulari disappears. Every effort is made to search for her. Even the police are informed, but to no avail. Suspicion falls on one servant who, it is assumed, has helped her escape. Eventually Dulari is found with that servant, but she flatly refuses to return to the household that has always been her home, in fact her only home. A few months later Dulari is spotted in the prostitutes' quarter[25] by one of the old servants who had known her since her childhood. The old man goes up to her and persuades her to return. Dulari agrees. Her return, as abrupt as her disappearance, causes ripples of commotion in the household.

Dulari returns to the house of Sheikh Nazim Ali Khan, her head lowered, her body covered from head to toe in a white sheet, and goes to sit in one corner of a room. The Chhoti sahebzadi, Hasina Begum, who had once been Dulari's childhood playmate, comes near her, but not too near. (Is it because she fears she might be contaminated by Dulari's exposure to the outside world?) Hasina Begum wonders how someone like Dulari, who was raised in this household, would even *think* of running away, forsaking the safety of its four walls for the big bad world outside.

---

[25] Exploited, weak, helpless women turning to prostitution is a familiar theme in Urdu literature, as in Premchand's *Bazar-e-Husn* (The Marketplace of Beauty) and in Manto's stories such as *Sharda* and *Licence*.

'Respectable, pure, virginal Hasina Begum was filled with pity for this poor unfortunate girl.' Why had she run away? Hasina Begum, brought up as she is in the cloistered world of the zenana, cannot fathom the compulsions of the poor, unfortunate, exploited Dulari. And look at the result, Hasina Begum ruminates in her blind, though well-meaning, self-righteousness: 'The sale of her honour, poverty, shame! It is true that she is a *laundi* but how can running away improve her lot?' Moreover, running away from *such* a household, where she had literally been raised, to Hasina Begum's closed, protected mind, smacked of ingratitude. Now that Dulari has returned, soiled and dishonoured, she would be married off to some male servant and afterwards, Hasina Begum reassures herself, 'everything would be all right'. The Begum saheba arrives on the scene, scolds Dulari for running away and blackening her face ('*mooh kala kar ke lauti hai*'), but is pleased nonetheless that she is back for, in her absence, the household chores were not being done properly. The entire household assembles to watch this public berating of the poor hapless Dulari. 'To watch an impure, imperfect being so humiliated made everyone feel bigger and better. The vultures that feed on the dead do not feel that the helpless bodies on which they tear away with their sharp beaks, despite being lifeless are better off than these living beings.' The implication here, as in the previous passage about conventional wisdom as reflected through the attitudes of various members of the household including the venerable Sheikh Nazim Ali Khan himself, is a unanimous verdict for Dulari: a laundi is better-off than a prostitute, and no matter what the provocation or exploitation, her place is within the four walls of the sharif household.

While this berating of Dulari is still underway, Qasim appears with his newly wed beautiful bride in tow. He moves towards his mother, but does not cast even one glance towards Dulari. His face shows anger. In a measured tone he addresses his mother, 'For God's sake, Ammijan, leave this unfortunate creature alone. She has suffered enough. Can't you see the state she is in?' Dulari hears the voice, but cannot look up. Instead, her eyes are filled with visions from the past:

[W]hen she and Qasim had been alone together in the long nights of solitude and her ears had grown accustomed to hearing words of love. Qasim's marriage had pierced her heart like a lance. It was this anguish that had driven her hither and thither and now she must listen to such things from him, too! This state of mind turned Dulari into a figurine of human fortitude. She stood up and looked at those all around her in such a way that one by one everyone began to step back. But it was the last attempt at flight of a defeated, broken bird. That night she disappeared once again.

Her final act of defiance, her flight from the so-called safe haven of respectability as also the manner in which she looks at those around her, is directed as much at Qasim as the rest of the sharif members of the household who have watched her degradation. That she has been brought to such a pass by the emotional and physical exploitation she has suffered at the hands of Qasim is left unsaid; herein lies the impact of the story. A lowly creature brought low by fate and circumstance, is Dulari destined to belong to the lowest of the low and live a life of poverty, ignominy, and namelessness? Or, is her fate sealed after her 'encounter' with the spoilt son of a rich father? Born into poverty, is she to remain poor, and, therefore, helpless all her life? Zaheer studs this simple narrative somewhat clumsily with lugubrious sarcasm and affected truisms that are meant to mock conventional thinking. Here is a sampling:

- 'Upper class people always look after people from the lower classes.'
- 'All this is God's doing: He bestows honour upon whoever he wishes and humiliates whoever he wishes. Why cry about it?'
- 'While it is true that her honour had been trampled in the dust, but for a laundi it is not such an important thing as it is for a *sharifzadi*.'

As Priyamvada Gopal points out, Sajjad Zaheer is 'drawing on the existing literature of social reform'[26] and in taking up the theme of domestic servitude and exploitation, the woman being 'victim of a patriarchal and feudal order', he is following in the footsteps of Premchand, the most celebrated exponent of reformist literature. She then goes on to say:

Progressive fiction and drama in the next two decades were thickly populated by characters such as the female servant whose labour as well as sexuality are

---

[26] By way of examples of economic and sexual politics of domestic servants in Urdu literature, Gopal lists: Premchand's *Penalty*, Rashid Jahan's *Iftar* (The Opening of the Fast), Razia Sajjad Zaheer's *Neech* (Lowly), Ismat Chughtai's *Dil ki Duniya* (The World of the Heart), and Manto's *Ji Aaya, Saab* (Coming, Sir).

vulnerable to exploitation; upper-class women who are either willingly exploitative (as the mother in 'Dulari') or naively benevolent (the daughter of the house); the paterfamilias for whom domestic matters are too small to be of concern; and the young man whose reformist ambitions are most honoured by caddish breaches of trust. Dulari herself stands at the head of a long line of fictional domestic servants, peasant women and prostitutes subject to the most extreme forms of gendered exploitation and yet whose subjectivities emerge insistently to disrupt the narratives that seem to determine their lives.[27]

Khalilur Rahman Azmi sees *Dulari* as the first serious study of the position of women in patriarchal society; it is a subject that will be repeatedly taken up by other Urdu writers who followed in Zaheer's footsteps.[28]

The fifth and last story by Zaheer in this collection, *Phir Yeh Hungama*, is perhaps the weakest link in the chain of *Angarey*. Taking more potshots at religion as in the previous stories, or more particularly conventional, half-baked notions of right and wrong, he makes his characters mouth trite, almost facile statements. Again, using the stream of consciousness technique displayed in the very first story that allows the writer to meander—in the absence of a plot and storyline—holding little more than an idea in his pen, this is in some ways similar to *Neend Nahin Aati*. Again, there is a jumble of random images and mini stories strung together, but unlike *Neend Nahin Aati*, no clear message appears out of them. Zaheer wants to mock religion, but he chooses to do so by praising it, or by making his characters mouth statements that are so patently exaggerated that they convey the reverse of what they purport. Two friends are tossing about vague, incoherent ideas about religion. One says '… when we are searching everywhere like a wounded animal with scared, helpless eyes, where do we get the strength to support our sinking hearts? From religion! And the root of religion is faith. Fear and faith. Religion cannot be praised adequately in words. Nor can we understand it through the intellect. It is an internal state of being….'

The other immediately brings the conversation crashing down from the sublime to the ridiculous by talking about his internal state of being: he has a stomach ache and needs a laxative! And so it goes on…. Zaheer strings

---

[27] Gopal, *Literary Radicalism in India*, pp. 33–4.
[28] Khalilur Rahman Azmi, *Urdu mein Taraqqui Pasand Adabi Tehreek* (Aligarh: Educational Book House, 2002 [1957]), pp. 180–1.

together vignettes that display his powers of observation rather than intellectual dexterity or literary capability. The conversation between the friends dissolves into a kaleidoscope of images: famine, starvation, sunken eyes, pallid faces, cholera, dysentery, flies, death. This brief 'horrorscope' segues into a story about a foreign breed dog called Lion who initially bullies the neighbourhood strays and has a free run with the bitches till, one day, a stray about twice his size appears and begins to challenge his superiority. Overnight, the tables are turned: Lion is bullied by the strays, injured several times, and takes to hiding in his own yard. Under the leadership of the new leader, the strays claim total victory. One day, another fight ensues, but this time Lion's master, a rich gentleman whose sleep is disturbed by the barking of the dogs, fires and kills the big stray dog. The others cower and slink away. Lion—the thoroughbred foreign dog owned by a rich master—is once again the undisputed master of all he surveys. There is a moral in this story: about the rich crushing the poor with the help of brute force (or arms) when they rise in rebellion, but it fails to make an impact buried as it is in a short story that is trying to cram far too many motifs and images. Sajjad Zaheer would have done better to write an allegorical story only about Lion; there is enough meat in this mini-story stuck on the bare bones of a larger, skeletal story. In another stray reference, the angel Gabriel appears, but he is mistaken for Satan.[29] Stuck with the glue of incoherence are several unrelated observations: about the river Gomti, about Kallu Mehtar's son who dies of a snake bite, and Hamid's love for his cousin Sultana that finds fulfilment in marriage. The last four paras have no bearing whatsoever with the preceding episodes and by the time the story peters out it has deteriorated into a pastiche of meaningless rhetoric. Even allusions to Dadaism cannot redeem it or turn it into a short story in any conventional sense. Of the various unrelated incidents, the one about Kallu Mehtar's son dying of snake bite and the young educated son of the master coming to visit the poor sweeper's smelly hovel (and later

---

[29] The Urdu poet has made several allusions to Gabriel and Satan. Iqbal, in a conversation (*Gibril-o-Iblis*) between the two, makes Satan say mockingly, '*Main khatakta hoon dil-e-yazdan main kaante ki tarah/Too faqat Allah hu Allah hu*' (While I pierce the Almighty's heart constantly like a thorn/All you can do is say Allah is, Allah is.) The revolutionary poet Josh Malihabadi too asks, '*Tu kaun hai? Gibril hoon. Kyon aaye ho?*' (Who are you? I am Gabriel. Why have you come?). Neither was blamed of irreligiosity.

washing his hands and covering his nose with a cologne-drenched handkerchief) could have been turned into a full-fledged story. We have seen similar treatment of upper-class people 'engaging' with the lower castes in Premchand's *Doodh ka Daam* (The Price of Milk) and Krishan Chandar's *Kalu Bhangi* (Kalu the Sweeper). The two examples are pertinent because they show how an idea can be transformed into a powerful short story in the hands of gifted storytellers and writers who had honed their craft with diligence. At the stage of writing *Angarey*, Sajjad Zaheer could claim to be neither. He was simply a man with an idea. He was also a man in a hurry.

Two Stories by Ahmed Ali

Let us now look at the two stories by Ahmed Ali: the first, *Baadal Nahin Aate* is somewhat similar to *Neend Nahin Aati* in terms of style and content, but Ahmed Ali, being by far the most gifted writer of the *Angarey* quartet, shows how the same idea, using the same stream of consciousness technique, can be used to better advantage. The story begins with a realistic description of a searing Indian summer that resembles a hellish inferno where the protagonist is unable to sleep. Meandering through a thicket of popular phrases and idioms (*muhawre*) in the old-fashioned dastan tradition (refashioned by Intezar Husain[30] several decades later for an altogether different purpose), one story emerges out of the belly of another. Coiled within one idea is another, seemingly unrelated one, and together they paint the image of a languid, lackadaisical society. Ahmed Ali speaks to us in the *taksali zubaan* (a language that rings true, has the genuineness of a mint or *taksal*) of Dehli or Dilli (as Delhi was called by its inhabitants before the British changed the name, pronunciation, and everything else about the city) with its typical coinages, turns of phrase and peculiarities of idiom, and abundant play on words which no translation can sufficiently carry across. And, most significantly, the choice of

---

[30] Intezar Husain has also written a story on the missing clouds, called '*Badal*'. His treatment is from the point of view of a young boy who goes looking for the elusive rain-bearing clouds and how the clouds, when they do come, turn his dusty little world into a cool, green, fresh place. See my translation of this story in Intezar Husain's *Circle and Other Stories* (New Delhi: Rupa & Co., 2004). It is to be noted that Intezar Husain belonged to the group of writers who, in contrast to the progressives, owed their allegiance to *jadeediyat* or modernism.

words and expressions gives an indication that the narrator's voice is a woman's. This is reinforced when the current of thought suddenly and inexplicably turns towards the difference between the hair styles of men and women and how wonderfully light one would feel if one could also have short hair, like men.

Somewhere in the coiling, twisting, turning heap of words are some images that stand out: a cave high up on a mountain top, its mouth covered by a huge boulder, hiding the clouds in its belly; maulvis crouched over the Holy Book, reading and rocking, reading and rocking, incessantly repeating the Truth of God like parrots; maulvis prescribing talismans, prayers, and offerings at the graves of saints to the women who flock to them; curses upon the British for teaching English and turning people into non-believers and eunuchs; the lot of women living behind purdah and being in many ways worse than animals; and hard-working, obedient, loyal, child-bearing women who live by men's adage (*'Bujha diya to bujh gaye, jala diya to jale rahe'*, almost like a candle that stays lit or unlit depending on whether it is snuffed out or allowed to remain lit). Sexual abuse of married women, verging on marital rape, is brought out in shocking detail:

The devil is driving you all the time; you see neither day nor night. Defeat, why don't you kill me, kill me with a dagger. You have twisted my wrist, broken it. Where are you running off to? Cling to my breast and lie down. Come and taste the delights of the dagger. There go your hands to my breasts crushing them with your hard fingers. The wretch pressed the knobs so hard that I could not even move. May he die young, the scoundrel, people don't behave like this even with prostitutes. I am a weak thing. I lay down as he took out all his anger over the heat at me. Why are you lying like a corpse? Don't you have any life? Harder, my lovely, my lover-ly. My daaar-ling. And I? I could do nothing.

And close on the heels of the sense of defeat and helplessness is anger and the first stirrings of awareness:

Why can't we do anything? If we had our own money why would we have to tolerate such humiliation? We could have done whatever we wanted whenever we desired. We don't even have the permission to earn our own money. We are rotting away behind the *purdah*. Our lives are worse than slaves, worse even than animals. We are lying in our cages, lying in captivity. There isn't even the space for us to spread our wings.

As for the men, all they do is smoke huqqas, gossip, play chess, or cards. And in the evenings, if nothing else, they go to Chawri[31] on the pretext of listening to music and next morning making their wives burn with jealousy. Burning reminds the narrator of the terrible heat that is scalding everything and everybody for 20 hours in a day. Springing in the midst of this all-pervading self-pity, which scalds her like the ever-present heat, is the comparison with the Hindus who are a lot better-off and the Christian women who are way above any comparison with Muslim women.

Christian women can dance, watch movies, cut their hair. Why was I born in a Muslim household? May such a religion catch fire! Religion, religion, religion! Satiation of the spirit is only for men. Who thinks of poor women! They [referring to the men] grow five-finger long beards and think they have become Muslims.

The narrative then shifts to her childhood: how she was studying in the eighth standard when her father died and she was pulled out of school, and almost instantly she was 'tethered' to this 'fat lout with a beard'. Of her husband she says, 'The man is a devil. Forget freedom, he doesn't even brook a woman giving an answer.' Her thoughts then turn to the wayward, still-missing clouds and throw up a new dimension: a fear of the British that is keeping the clouds away. She was taught in school that clouds are made of vapour. She imagines the clouds going to the seaside, drinking up all the water greedily like sponges, being driven away in the winds and then, out of fear of canon fire, beginning to pee. Whatever they teach in geography at school is wrong, she surmises, only the fear of the British is true. And what do the British do: they beat you like a dog; in fact, treat you worse than a cur. After this the narrative lapses into fragments of childish verse. In the end, there is an overwhelming sense of anti-climax. It reminds you of T.S. Eliot's 'The Hollow Men' (1925): 'This is the way the world ends/This is the way the world ends/This is the way the world ends/Not with a bang but with a whimper.'

Ahmed Ali's second story *Mahavaton ki Ek Raat* is located in a totally different landscape: it is cold and wet, not dry and searing hot. But human misery, especially the lot of women, remains unchanged whether it is cold or hot, wet or dry. Once again, we hear a woman's voice in the form of an

---

[31] Chawri Bazaar in Delhi once housed the prostitutes' quarter. It now has a wholesaler's and hardware market.

interior monologue, but this time the narrative is reasonably straightforward and while there is still no attempt at plot or characterization, there is a rudimentary storyline. A woman and her children are huddled in the biting cold night, in a rundown, cramped, impoverished, 24 × 24 feet hovel. In fact, it is raining so hard that it seems as though with every clap of thunder the skies will burst open. The sagging roof, already leaking like a sieve, is showing every sign of coming down over their heads in the next gust of winter rain. The woman rues her lot, bemoaning why God has made her poor and, worse still, had once made her see better days. While she does not much care for herself, she is worried sick about her children—the four of them huddling in one bed under one sodden quilt. And then she is reminded of her better days: her palatial home, the servants, her room with the four-poster bed with velvet sheets and chenille pillowcases that could instantly lull her to sleep, and the satiny quilts with real gold lace, and the maids waiting to press her feet and, in front of her, Sleep wearing shimmering starry clothes waiting to take her to magical places. At this point, one wonders if there genuinely was such a marvellous past or is it, like the archetypal Muslim escape into an imaginary glorious past, a figment of her imagination? From here onwards the so far linear narrative lapses into a stream of consciousness fantasy. The poor woman is rudely wrenched back into her miserable present by an ominous clap of thunder that wakes her children. The three poor mites are huddled under one sopping-wet quilt. Her cold, wet, miserable children—the daughter clinging to her, the two boys entwined like snakes around a tree—evoke a litany of existential questions in her:

Why doesn't God listen? Does He even exist or not? What is He? Whatever He might be, He is very cruel and very unjust. Why are some rich? And some poor? It is His wisdom, and what a strange wisdom it is! Some writhe in the cold, without a bed to lie in, with no clothes to wear. They shiver in the cold, brave the rain, suffer without food, and yet death doesn't come to them. Some have lakhs, they enjoy every manner of good things and know neither want nor suffering. Will it hurt them if they give us a little of what they have? Many poor lives will be saved. But why should they care? Who created us? God? Then why does He not care for us? Why did He make us? To know sorrow and experience suffering? What justice! Why are others rich and why are we poor? We shall find recompense in the afterlife—that is what the maulvis say. But what after life? Let the afterlife go to hell! The suffering is now. The need is now. The fever is raging now and the medicine will be given ten years later? To hell with such an afterlife!… God is merely an excuse, a deception, a consolation for staying poor in one's poverty, for keeping a hopeless hope alive during times of hopelessness, and a means to stay content in troubled times. God? Nothing more than a screen of deception! And religion, it teaches you the same thing. And then they say it is a treasure trove of knowledge and an excuse for poverty. It is the wisdom of fools, it pulls back those who are learning more or making progress.

A long rambling soliloquy on inequality, injustice, and suffering of the poor is broken by the woman's children who wake up, hungry and cold, asking for food. It appears that the woman takes in some sewing and makes a little money or else some kind soul from the neighbourhood gives them a little food. The woman's helplessness is believably drawn, 'How long can I go on begging? People get tired of giving.' The woman, her name is suddenly revealed as Mariam, finds a piece of roti in the house, soaks it in some water and feeds her five-year-old son who has not eaten since the previous day and is incessantly demanding food. The boy leaves a few mouthfuls and goes back to sleep; hungry Mariam cannot help herself. She devours those few morsels, eating a little at a time. As she goes back to lie with her little daughter she is reminded of her husband who is no more. The words, 'If only he were here', run like a refrain through a long passage describing his virility and strength. How he pampered her with delicacies, how her every need was met, how lush and green was her life with him in it! The analogy of a tree—solid, sheltering, full of sap—is evocative of man as a protector in a woman's life:

If only he were here! Two legs, a lush green tree, flesh and bone and marrow. Its sap warmer than blood, its bark softer than flesh, its trunk strong and slender, its branches … its branches grafted onto another, entwined with each other, so much into each other that they had become alike, together, attached to each other, giving life to each other, and then the expectation of a third life, the treasure of a full life, the wealth of a fleeting moment, the strength of being in non-being....

This near-perfect existence is shattered and Mariam is left 'leafless, alone'. She is reminded of the rope swings on which she rode higher and higher in some magical garden of her long-ago youth. The author seems to imply that the rope that makes the swing also makes the noose: both offer escape. If life is so full of defeat and despair, is death the only escape? Why not, then, the last paragraph seems to suggest, go to the devil who is trying to seduce everyone? Doomsday is here. There is no help, no one to extend a hand. The night is dark and fearsome. And into that fearsome night we must all go. In the ending of this story, Ahmed Ali, to my mind, shows evidence of the German philosopher Nietzsche (1844–1900) and his theories on the 'Death of God' and nihilism.

A Story by Mahmuduzzafar

The only story by Mahmuduzzafar—possibly his only known Urdu short story published anywhere—is *Jawanmardi*, a tale of man's pride, vanity, and wilfulness. Literally meaning 'young manhood', it can include notions of virility, bravery, gallantry, courage. It begins thus: 'That wife of mine, she passed away.' The man's wife had been sick for a long time and had become 'no more than a bundle of bones'. Her dead eyes are filled, not with love or tenderness for him, but with aloofness, even hatred. And the cause of this hatred is the stillborn child whose head can still be seen stuck in her hip bones. 'Who could have thought,' the man wonders, 'that my wife would have such hatred for me when she was dying?'

What follows is the portrait of an early and loveless marriage between two people who are poles apart: 'My wife walked on old-fashioned dark and dingy alleys while I like the modern, clean, broad, and pucca streets.' The man has lived abroad, seen the world and its ways, and indulged in meaningless affairs. In keeping with time-honoured sequestered spaces for men and women, his wife has led a pure, sheltered life, cloistered in her strong citadel. In a 'flashback' we hear her voice in a letter written to the husband while he is abroad. She sounds long-suffering, patient, loving, caring, and giving. She writes longingly of imagining him to be a *kamil dumsaz*, a perfect companion. The man reads her letter and, in a rush of homesickness, decides to come back home. These, incidentally, are familiar tropes in both Urdu/Hindi fiction and Hindi films and seem little more than stereotypes. But even as the narrator is on his way, his feelings undergo a dilution. Other, more worldly matters intrude on his desire to come back to his sick wife's bedside. By the time he reaches home, he finds himself in a dark, dirty, cramped world filled with injustice and ignorance. Most of those who have come to meet him at the station are the base, bad-mannered, narrow-minded, and idle sort. He finds their company and humour not to his taste. Equally unappealing is his wife's appearance: her hair sticky with oil, her emaciated body, her ashen complexion. Yet, after the guests have dispersed, he finds time to sit beside her bed. She lives not in his home, but with her own parents who tend her and indulge her. The reader is never told exactly what is wrong with the wife, but again one is struck by the perpetuation of the stereotype as the narrator tries to speak to her, telling her how he was moved by her letter, how he has come back because he thinks he can be that perfect companion that she had written so longingly about, and how she must, now that he is back, speak to her. She declines to speak, saying she has nothing to tell. He, on the other hand, has travelled and seen the world; so, instead, he should tell her about his experiences. This expression of self-abnegation on the wife's part and espousal of interest in the husband's world instead of drawing them closer convinces the man that he and his wife are as distant as they always were. The distance and the long years of separation have not brought them any closer. They stand on the two opposite banks of a river like two strangers. But life carries on. He now makes little effort to come close to her or talk to her. Gradually, he goes back to his old ways and old friends. Cards, drinking, and women—these consume his attention. Soon he develops an interest in music and becomes a patron of the most well-known singers of the town. Under the circumstances, it is natural that he too has begun to 'keep' a woman of his own. Such are the ways of living a meaningless and purposeless existence: 'And those of us who had travelled to foreign lands would tell the others stories of our virility and amorousness in an attempt to impress them.'

For all his hedonism the narrator now begins to find his wife's condition to be a real nuisance. Friends and relatives offer advice and suggestions regarding her health, letters pour in offering unsolicited advice, commiseration, and sympathy, and his mother too becomes insistent that he marry again. His family gets split in two camps: those who want him to marry again and those who oppose it. He resists his mother's entreaties and steadfastly refuses to marry again. But people begin to question his virility and start to gossip. Finally, he decides to do something. He tells his in-laws that there is nothing the matter with his wife and that he will take her away with him and that they are only making her out to be ill so that they can hold on to her. He takes his wife away to the mountains where the fresh mountain air improves her health somewhat. Then, he brings her back home. His friends are surprised to see them together, but still not fully satisfied. To fully allay their suspicions, and establish his virility beyond the shadow of doubt, he realizes he must do something more. Having realized what form that must take (that is, a child sired from his loins), he is willing to provide that proof: 'Slowly, slowly, as month passed after month, my wife's belly began to grow bigger and bigger.... My state was like the gardener's who is delighted to see the buds burst into blooms on the trees he has planted. With every passing day, with every minute, my success became more apparent.'

It must be noted that he uses the word 'success' above and not happiness. His wife, however, becomes quieter and more withdrawn with every passing day. He dismisses it, thinking it to be no more than anxiety about the impending childbirth. 'Finally, her pains began. They lasted for hours. Her body writhed in pain. Even her soul seemed to convulse with pain, asking for release. But her pain and anguish and her cries—all of them were giving proof of my virility. By the grace of God, the sound of her pain-filled groans is still echoing in my ears.'

This vile man, stuffed with false pride, partly redeems himself with his last line: he confesses to feeling some relief when those offering (false) sympathy tell him that his wife had a smile on her lips as she was dying. He knows that her eyes held nothing but aloofness, even hatred, but just as planting a seed in her sick womb bolstered his pride and reinforced his virility in the eyes of his friends and family, so too these false and token words of consolation offer balm to his guilty heart. The man, then, is not utterly contemptible; he is weak and typical of his class and background. There are traces of potential though. He could, perhaps, have been a better specimen of manhood had society not exerted its corrupting influence on him. Left to himself he had an innate goodness that might have seen him through. We can only conjecture; we shall never know. Mahmuduzzafar is content to paint a picture of a society that is as sick and ailing as the man's wife. He offers no cures.

While one can concede a certain degree of self-awareness on the part of the male narrator, to my mind, to invest the story with any real examination of issues of gender or credit Mahmuduzzafar with psychological astuteness and perspicacity seems to place too heavy a burden on this somewhat slender story. Mahmuduzzafar's contribution to *Angarey* can be seen, at best, as a self-deprecatory admission of the 'evil that men do'; this valuable male intervention will be picked up in later years by women writers such as Rashid Jahan, Ismat Chughtai, Khadija Mastur, and others.

A Story and a Play by Rashid Jahan

Finally, let us look at the two pieces by the only woman in this quartet, namely, *Dilli ki Sair* and *Parde ke Peechche* by Rashid Jahan. *Dilli ki Sair* is a cryptic short story that packs quite a punch in its brevity and compactness and relies for effect on all that it leaves unsaid. The very title is redolent with irony; the word 'sair' used conjunctively in spoken Urdu with *sair-o-tafri* is indicative of a touristy fun-filled journey, yet the story is about an abortive tour, a journey that ended before any sights could be seen. A simple story simply told, *Dilli ki Sair* has few claims to literary excellence. All of three pages long, it begins with a woman regaling her women friends with her day trip to Delhi from Faridabad, then a small town, a short train ride away from the big city. On the surface, the story seems an unlikely contender for any sort of incendiary intent. Malka Begum, a young housewife, is the first one from among her acquaintances to have sat on a train and gone all the way to Delhi. She has already recounted the story thousands of times, but there is always a ready audience to hear it yet again possibly because none of these suburban housewives have ever travelled to Delhi or sat in a train. Naturally enough, Malka Begum milks the story for all it is worth because her trip to Delhi has given her a certain standing among the other women. When someone tries to get familiar with her or tease her about the men who pass comments on her, Malka Begum instantly uses her superior status to issue a threat, 'Don't interrupt if you want to listen'. And she is met with complete silence as her audience listens to her attentively with no further interruptions. 'After all, how often does one get treated to such juicy, delicious talk in a place like Faridabad. No wonder women come from far away to listen to Malka Begum's tale.'

It matters little to the listeners, some of whom have heard her story many times before, that the trip to Delhi, memorable though it was, was not a particularly enjoyable one for the narrator. For, as soon as Malka Begum and her husband alight at Delhi, at the railway station itself Malka Begum's husband meets an acquaintance, some station master, and goes off on his own leaving her to guard the luggage.

Wrapped in her burqa, sitting atop her luggage, she waits on the platform for hours watching the world go by. She has to endure the stares of the wretched men who love to stare at a woman sitting by herself, especially one who is burqa-clad. Some cough suggestively as they hover; others pass lewd comments. One even says suggestively, 'Show us your face....' Terrified at being thrust in the middle of this strange

[32] This early story can be compared with Rashid Jahan's *Mera Ek Safar* (A Journey of Mine), written in 1937, where the narrator is more comfortable in

crowd,[32] she is also tormented by pangs of hunger. Her observations to her friends are in the homely, simple language of a small-town woman. Impressed by the station, the only 'sight' she sees in Delhi, she remarks, 'The station at Delhi is as large as a fortress—it stretches as far as the eye can see'. More than the predatory, inquisitive men who are circling her, she is terrified of the coal black men in the engines. One woman from the audience of rapt listeners cuts Malka Begum's monologue short to ask who these men living in the engines are. Malka Begum's answer is childlike in its innocence: these men, some with beards, others clean shaven, dressed in blue clothes, swing onto moving trains by holding on to the railing with one hand. Clearly, she is referring to the coolies or porters. She is also awestruck by the English *mems* and *sahebs*; so many that they cannot be counted, talking among themselves in their strange *'git-pit'* lingo. Like her, fellow Indians too stare at them in wide-eyed wonder. And the hawkers, she marvels at their clean clothes, so different from the sort you see in Faridabad, selling paan, cigarettes, *dahi vadas*, toys, sweets. She describes the commotion that erupts when a train stops at a platform: the deafening noise, the coolies running about, the passengers piling on top of each other, the hawkers darting in between among the crowds, bent upon selling their wares. And she, a poor thing by her own admission, sits in the midst of this jostling crowd, sitting on top of her luggage in the middle of a crowded bustling platform, getting jostled and pushed by the milling crowd, mumbling prayers to keep herself safe from harm. As the train begins to pull away from the station, she describes the arguments that break out between the coolies and passengers haggling over money. By the time her husband returns, two hours later, twirling his moustaches, dripping machismo, looking not in the least repentant about abandoning her, she has lost all zest for seeing the sights and only wants to return home. Carelessly, he asks her, 'I can get you some *puris* if

---

appropriating a public space and negotiating her way in it. Here, for Malka Begum, as for any other woman from a sheltered background, the space outside her home is viewed as alien and, therefore, essentially hostile. Priyamvada Gopal makes a convincing case of public spaces being 'masculinised' as opposed to private ones and this story being about the 'sexual politics of public spaces'. Priyamvada Gopal, *Literary Radicalism in India: Gender, Nation and the Transition to Independence* (Oxon: Routledge, 2005), p. 53.

you are hungry? Will you eat? I have already eaten at the hotel.'³³ By now thoroughly fed up and at the end of her tether, she asks only to be taken home. 'No one would want to go even to heaven with you!' she answers angrily. The train for Faridabad happens to be ready to leave from the station. The husband seats Malka Begum on it and sullen faced says, 'As you wish.... Don't see the sights if you don't want to'. And with that the story ends.

The two-page story says more about the lack of concern shown by many husbands than voluminous novels by far more articulate authors. The story is a brief but penetrating meditation on life behind the all-encompassing 'veil' and the blindness of male privilege towards the experience of women behind the purdah. Worse still, in using the device of a woman telling the story of her aborted trip to a group of women friends and neighbours, there is a sense of bonhomie: men *are* like that; women know it and can do nothing about it. Urdu critic Khalilur Rahman Azmi has called it a '*mazmoon-numa kahani*'³⁴ ('an essay-like story'). Indeed it is one; but it is brimful with inference and meaning.

The other piece by Rashid Jahan is a one-act play called *Parde ke Peeche*. Here, she digs deep not only into her experiences in dealing with female patients, but also the time she had spent in the Old Delhi neighbourhood of her maternal grandparents' home. She employs authentic, idiomatic speech to portray life in the cloistered confines of the women's quarters of a typical Muslim household in Delhi. She also describes the setting in minute detail: floor covered with *sozni* with sausage-shaped pillows called *gau-takhiya*s scattered about for easy reclining, *paandan, ugaldan, surahi*, and on the ceiling a pink-frilled hand-pulled cotton fan. Two women sit, chatting and cutting betel nut. The older is about 40 years of age; her name is Aftab Begum. The younger, looking harried, tired, and depressed, is Muhammadi Begum. We are told she was born the year Queen Victoria died; that makes her 32, but she looks nearly double her age. A lady doctor who comes to examine her is dumbfounded by the discrepancy between

---

[33] Brief though the story is, it makes a convincing case of spaces being gendered in a patriarchal society. Just as the station is a masculine space, so is the hotel where Malka Begum's husband has eaten. He can *get* her some puris, but he cannot *take* her to a hotel to eat with him and his friend. The hotel, clearly, is a space where men like him go with their male friends.

[34] Azmi, *Urdu mein Taraqqui Pasand Adabi Tehreek*, p. 181.

her biological age and her prematurely withered looks.[35] Married at 18, Muhammadi Begum has borne children in all the years since; except twice, that is, once when her husband was abroad and once when they had fought. She suffers from pyorrhoea and has had several teeth pulled out and that too because her husband came back from abroad and told her that her breath stank. Her children are pale, thin, emaciated, querulous, under-nourished, ill-kempt, and rowdy. She has several ayahs who nurse the smaller kids and try to keep peace among the older ones. She herself has never been allowed to nurse a child since her husband has a voracious sexual appetite. 'Doesn't matter if it is night or day, he wants his wife. And not only his wife. He goes the rounds to other women too.'[36] She means prostitutes. And she is fed up with the ayahs; the last one had a venereal disease which she passed on to Muhammadi Begum's four-month-old baby who eventually died a painful death with pus-filled blisters all over his body. We hear more about men being worse than animals when it comes to assuaging their sexual appetite in a manner reminiscent of Ahmed Ali's *Baadal Nahin Aate* and Mahmuduzzafar's *Jawanmardi*. As in the latter story, Muhammadi has been running a fever of 100 to 101 every evening for months, yet her husband forces himself on her. Again, exactly like *Baadal Nahin Aate*, Muhammadi says, 'We'd have been better off if we'd been Christians.' Aftab Begum, of course is horrified by such talk, especially because her own son has gone off and married a Christian much against her wishes. Their gossip about a certain doddering Mirza who has married a young and poor girl is interrupted by the squabbling children.

---

[35] Clearly, Rashid Jahan has drawn from her own experiences as a 'lady doctor' for these intimate and exact details. She will do so again, more explicitly, in later stories such as '*Voh*' (That One). The lady doctor who comes to examine Muhammadi Begum (an alter-ego of Rashid Jahan herself) comments on the co-relation between frequent pregnancies and the patient's poor health to which Muhammadi tells the doctor:

Oh miss, you are all right. You earn your living; you eat well and sleep soundly. It's not like that with us. These fellows [referring to men like her husband] don't care whether they go to heaven or to hell when they die. They know what they want here. They don't care whether their wives, poor wretches, live or die. Men want their satisfaction.

[36] All translations of 'Behind the Veil' are from Ralph Russell, *Hidden in the Lute: An Anthology of Two Centuries of Urdu Literature* (New Delhi: Viking, 1995), pp. 34–46.

The children, grubby and garrulous, are driven away by the irate mother who has neither the time nor the patience to rear them properly; there are too many of them and despite the abundance of wet nurses and servants, they are always underfoot.[37] Then comes the real blow—Muhammadi's lecherous husband has been passionately wooing her niece (who is about the same age as their daughter) with the intention of marrying her. When confronted, he is unapologetic, 'I've fallen in love with her. For God's sake help me. It's your duty to help me.' He even reads out verses from the Holy Book telling her what would happen to her in the next world if she does not help him. When that proposal falls through, he goes visiting the prostitutes in Chawri Bazar. This suits Muhammadi fine for 'the day he goes off somewhere I sleep soundly at night'. But six months later he is back to his old ways: complaining about her always being ill and unavailable and threatening to marry again. Moreover, he wants her to arrange his marriage as the Shariat allows a man four wives. About his own insatiable appetite he says, 'What do women know about it? God didn't give them feelings'.

So, all in all, being ill herself and one or other of her large brood of children falling ill, and a husband who wants sex on demand and also wants her to broker his next marriage, poor Muhammadi has no joy left in life. She is only 32 years old. She knows her husband will marry again and lives in perpetual dread of having to share her home with a co-wife. Tiresome and unpleasant though it is, she does everything to keep her husband in the only way she knows. She has even had herself fixed up:

---

[37] It is evident that Muhammadi is a bad manager of her household and many of her troubles are because she is not good at keeping her house in order, especially the children. She is ill and therefore not up to it is one reason, but perhaps she is also not organized and Rashid Jahan has given her plight a feminist twist; she links Muhammadi's troubles with her husband. Being a feminist, Rashid Jahan is not content to merely delineate social injustice; she gives it a gendered perspective. As we have seen in Chapter 1, Nazir Ahmad wrote a tale of two sisters: one good and the other bad. The good sister is above all a good housekeeper and manager of everything including her husband. Nazir Ahmad's book *Mirat al-Urus* (The Bride's Mirror, *c.* 1860) also debates polygamy and marriage in Islam. Rashid Jahan does not labour the point of Muhammadi being a complaining, lazy, fretful woman; she is all this because her husband has made her so and what is worse, the husband revels in the licence given to him by religion.

My womb and all my lower parts had fallen. I got it put right so that he could get the same pleasure as he'd got from a newly married wife. But when a woman has a baby every year how can she stay in shape. It slipped down again. And then he went on at me and threatened me until he got me butchered again. And even then he wasn't satisfied.

Shortly after this alarming and altogether unpleasant disclosure from Muhammadi Begum, the call for the noon prayer is heard and both women break up their tête-à-tête. This blood-curdling account of female violation, rendered in a fairly realistic female speech, emerging from a hitherto sacrosanct female space is left exposed. No attempt is made to bring it into a public space and to examine it or to go beyond the diagnosis stage. That, in fact, is the case with all the *Angarey* stories; their writers rip apart the innards of a sick society; they offer neither balm nor cure. Carlo Coppola, who has extensively studied the *Angarey* episode in the history of the progressive writers, notes that

The special sort of didactism for which Rashid Jahan would later become known is here in these early stories. Though she chooses to merely depict a problem without editorialisation, the didactic intent is inherent in each situation she describes, for clearly, with such all-good and all-bad characters she is attempting to provoke readers to side with the all-goods and perhaps, offer their own solutions to the problems posed. The Indian husband's poor treatment of his wife and childbearing are two recurrent themes in a number of Rashid Jahan's stories. It is also interesting to note that a woman doctor is often presented in later stories as the voice of reason and modernity in the midst of superstition, ignorance and poverty.[38]

I would, however, disagree with Coppola insofar as the all-good characters he refers to. As I have indicated earlier, Rashid Jahan alludes to the shortcomings in Muhammadi's character: she is a sloppy housewife and a slapdash mother, her home is not too well-managed and her children, despite the servants, are ill-mannered and unkempt. But these shortcomings are glossed over in the face of the larger issue: that of multiple pregnancies and the perception of wives as sex objects and progenitors of children, especially sons.

Like Rashid Jahan's other writings, both before and after *Angarey*, the two pieces expose the enclosed and oppressive world of Muslim women.

[38] Carlo Coppola, 'The Angare Group: The *Enfants Terribles* of Urdu Literature', *Annual of Urdu Literature*, vol. 1 (1981), p. 60.

Slaves to their husband's demands and tethered against their will to outworn religious and social dogmas, these women still manage to emerge not as victims but as thinking individuals who have the capacity and the desire to change their lot. All they need is encouragement. *Parde ke Peechche* brings to life not just a mise en scène from the lives of real women, but also speaks to us in a real language about real issues that no respectable woman would bring up in public—second marriages, sexual abuse, child marriages, the vagaries of the reproductive system, the pains and pleasures of breast feeding, the lack of care for contraception, and hence the over-large families. These are conversations that can, strictly speaking, only be heard behind a curtain. Rashid Jahan draws that curtain aside momentarily, showing us the depravity behind the so-called respectability of sharif families. Ending as it does, on a high note with no resolution in sight, the play encourages us to think. We are left to dwell on a bewildering range of issues from family, marriage, sex, morality, husband–wife relations, health, and hygiene to family planning and family politics—all of which have a direct bearing on a woman's emotional and physical well-being.

Rashid Jahan's younger sister, Khurshid Jahan, who became popular as Renuka Devi, the Hindi film actress in the pre-Partition era, writes, 'The story is poignant in its depiction of men's complete lack of concern for women's feelings.... [*Parde ke Peechche*] underscores men's utter disregard for the women in their lives and describes accurately the goings-on in the middle-class Muslim household of the 1930s.'[39] The play portrays the woman as a victim of domesticity, marriage, and sexuality, and becomes, as Gopal says, a 'subversive litany of the wrongs that men do and women endure'.[40] Why subversive? Why not a realistic litany, as realistic as Muhammadi's rant against her oppressive domesticity? We will get our answer in the next chapter when we see why *Angarey* was considered incendiary.

Having examined each of the 10 ensemble pieces that constituted *Angarey*, we will now look at the furore they generated, and the near-manic hatred they incited, for the four contributors. In the next chapter, we will look at the reasons why *Angarey* was considered incendiary. Shabana Mahmud finds *Angarey* not an anomaly or aberration but

a logical conclusion to the intellectual trends of the preceding decade. But the courage, anger and rebelliousness that were expressed in the stories ... ushered in

[39] Kazim, *Woman of Substance*, p. 101.
[40] Gopal, *Literary Radicalism in India*, p. 40.

a new generation that was not afraid to confront and expose issues which had previously been concealed. The shock and condemnation which the book provoked was a salutary one. It drew attention to many serious social issues of the time, and paved the way for the introduction of these issues into the mainstream of Urdu literature.[41]

Raza Imam,[42] a retired professor of English at the Aligarh Muslim University (AMU) and a card-carrying member of the party in later years, recalled for me the 'aura' surrounding *Angarey* and the attraction it had for young readers, especially those who were conversant with Western literary styles and English-language authors:

Angarey reflects the impact of modern English writers like D.H. Lawrence, James Joyce and Virginia Wolfe, who were at that time in a state of revolt against the staid Victorian and Edwardian traditions and were exploring new possibilities in both style and content. The young authors of *Angarey* felt the urge to do something of the kind themselves to expose the hypocrisy and stagnation in their own literature and society. The reaction was not just that of ripples caused by a pebble thrown into a stagnant pool but of a splash caused by a rock. It drew the attention of many a young writer who realized the importance of literature as a tool of social awakening, which facilitated the formation of PWA later on.[43]

In the previous chapter, we have noted some of the events that rocked the world, whose ripples were felt in India, and found a resonance in the heart of the Indian Muslims. We have also seen how some of these events found expression in Urdu literature. Interestingly, no such reflection is to be found in *Angarey*, except briefly and somewhat obliquely in Ahmed Ali's *Baadal Nahin Aate*. While the stories speak of the place of religion in the lives of Indian Muslims, the pathetic lot of women, the injustices that are perpetrated in the guise of religion, even the economic disparities that exist in a feudalistic, capitalistic society, there is no mention of the two major events that rocked the country a decade ago—the khilafat and the non-cooperation movement. Nor is there any political figure in evidence, not even Gandhi

---

[41] Shabana Mahmud, 'Angare and the Founding of the Progressive Writers' Association', *Modern Asian Studies*, vol. 30, no. 2 (May 1996), p. 453.

[42] Raza Imam was critically ill when he gave me this interview; he passed away in January 2012.

[43] Interview with Raza Imam.

who had begun to exercise quite a spell over Muslims and especially the disenfranchised lot that the contributors of *Angarey* seem to have a special affinity for. Similarly, the relations between Hindus and Muslims, the mandir–masjid disputes, the communal riots that had broken out shortly after Gandhi abandoned the civil disobedience movement, and the khilafatists too who had run their course find no mention in these stories. Curiously enough, despite the absence of historical detail or political reference, the collection has come to acquire a historical importance; it is regarded as a historical milestone in the history of Urdu literature, but not a literary one.[44] This is ironic insofar as *Angarey* seems to be written in a political vacuum of sorts and yet is viewed as an intensely radical piece of writing, one that marked 'a sharp break with previous literary currents'.[45] However, as we shall see in the next chapter, reactions to *Angarey* and its ban covered a broad spectrum of literary opinions. Decades after the fire lit by the incendiary book had tuned cold, some believed that it should have been banned for its banalities rather than its obscenities![46] Banal or bold, it was nevertheless a brave book, and an important one. Its importance lies also in the fact that it levelled the ground for later, from a literary point of view, 'more important works' that were superior in terms of craft and technique.[47]

In the next chapter, we shall see how this important milestone (*sang-e-meel*, as it is called in Urdu) cast a long shadow over the literary history of progressive writing in India. We shall also explore the 'culpability' of the four contributors and gauge the extent of their awareness, that is, ascertain whether they were indeed courting controversy when they chose to dub their collection '*Angarey*'. Clearly, they must have known that these live embers would light a fire; whether they knew fully well the extent and fury of its backlash, however, is uncertain.

---

[44] Khalid Alvi, *Angarey ka Tareekhi Pasmanzar aur Taraqqui Pasand Tehreek* (Delhi: Educational Publishing House, 1995), p. 63.

[45] Talat Ahmed, *Literature and Politics in the Age of Nationalism: The Progressive Episode in South Asia, 1932–56* (New Delhi: Routledge, 2009), p. 15.

[46] N.M. Rashid, interview, *Mahfil*, vol. 7, no. 2 (Spring–Summer 1971), p. 6.

[47] Jogindar Paul, 'Taraqqui Pasand Fikr aur Afsana', in Qamar Rais and S. Ashoor Kazmi (eds), *Taraqqui Pasand Adab: Pachas Sala Safar* (Delhi: Naya Safar Publications, 1987), p. 141. Paul refers to the 'big stories' that were to follow in the wake of the *Angarey* stories, such as 'Toba Tek Singh', 'Hamari Gali', etc.

4

The Furore over the Publication of *Angarey*

> *Likhte rahe junoon ki hikayat-e-khoon chakan*
> *Har chand usme haath hamare qalam huaye*
> (We kept writing the blood drenched narratives of that madness
> Although our hands were chopped off in the process)
> —Mirza Ghalib (1797–1869)

We shall begin by looking at the furore created by the publication of *Angarey* and the sequence of events culminating in its ban. The following section will look at the reaction to *Angarey* in the press. It will also take into account the response of those who considered *Angarey* not merely incendiary but blasphemous and its writers a dangerous threat to society counterpoising it with the response of the *Angarey* group who advocated the need for self-criticism on the part of the Muslim community. We will also look at those who wrote, mildly and cautiously, in favour of the *Angarey* group and more openly and positively, with hindsight, in the decades after its publication. The last section will end with biographical sketches of the four contributors and what they did after the publication of *Angarey*. Their literary careers will spill over into the next chapter and, as we shall see in Chapter 5, the contribution of the four young writers continued in the setting up of the PWA and the organization of the first PWM conference in Lucknow on 10 April 1936. Overall, this chapter will show how while *Angarey* heralded a trend of literary radicalism, the first PWA meeting 'points to a crystallisation of radicalizing trends begun in the years before',[1] a trend marked by a declaration of intent, as it were, made through Mahmuduzzafar's letter to the editor of *The Leader* dated 5 April 1933.

Why was *Angarey* Considered Incendiary?

Angarey drew public anger verging on mass hysteria. It was thought to ridicule the Prophet and several rituals, customs, and practices that were dear to the Muslims. Proscribed shortly after publication, it however gave people no time to form an opinion on their own; most of those who vociferously condemned the book—widely perceived as blasphemous— had not read it, and many felt obliged to condemn it simply because other respectable folk all around them were doing so. Public perception was so obviously banked against the book and its authors that the verdict was influenced by popular perception rather than an informed reading of the text. The colonial government, responding to a knee-jerk reaction from a section of Muslims, imposed a ban in—what it considered—the larger good of the community. The voice of the strident illiberals drowned out the saner voices of the liberal, secular Muslims who though a largely silent minority could not be ruled out as being of no consequence.[2] That a ban fuelled paranoia and played into the hands of a relatively small section of hardliners was a truism that eluded the British government in India. It is significant to note that *Angarey* was reprinted in Urdu in India

---

[1] Priyamvada Gopal, *Literary Radicalism in India: Gender, Nation and the Transition to Independence* (Oxon: Routledge, 2005), p. 15.

[2] One is reminded of Nehru writing to Syed Mahmud, a few years after the *Angarey* uproar, in the context of the Urdu–Hindi controversy on 5 October 1936: 'Is it our fate that always the reactionary Muslims should take the lead in everything and the nationalists should follow in their wake like dumb-driven cattle?' See *Selected Works of Jawaharlal Nehru*, vol. 7 (New Delhi: Orient Longman, 1975), p. 398.

as late as 1995.[3] Some of its stories[4] have been translated and published in the *Annual of Urdu Studies*, but the entire book has not been translated into English.

Before we look at the uproar over *Angarey*, let us look at the calm before the storm. The fortnightly report for the end of December 1932 had nothing very startling to report. Prices were stable, and except for small random incidents no major signs of trouble were evident. The total number of convictions arising out of the civil disobedience movement were winding down by now and were pegged at 12,916. Another 1,000 persons were convicted for assorted small crimes.[5] *Angarey* appeared sometime in December 1932 from Lucknow. The next three months saw a torrent of abuse and fatwas against the book and its authors prompting the Government of the United Provinces to ban it on 15 March 1933 under Section 295A of the Indian Penal Code (IPC). The proprietor of Nizami Press, Malik Ali Javed, had already caved in completely after his press had been raided under orders of the city magistrate. He had confessed to his mistake in bringing out the book and apologized in a written statement on 27 February 1933 for insulting the feelings of the Muslim community. He readily agreed to surrender the unsold copies of the book to the government. All but five copies

---

[3] This slightly edited version of *Angarey* was brought out in 1995 by Khalid Alvi and published by Educational Publishing House, Delhi, where the 'objectionable material' had been deleted. Earlier, in 1990, Shakil Siddiqui had brought out a transliterated version in Hindi published by Parimal Prakashan, Delhi. I found a reference to another Hindi edition of *Angarey* in *Ismat: Her Life, Her Times*, edited by Sukrita Paul Kumar and Sadique. According to this reference, the Hindi version appeared in *Samkaleen Dastavez*; however, I could not trace this version. In the absence of a printed version, till 1990, *Angarey* had become somewhat of an urban legend, more talked about than seen or read.

[4] *Garmiyon ki Ek Raat, Mahavaton ki Ek Raat,* and *Phir Yeh Hungama* have been translated by Snehal Shingavi and published in the *Annual of Urdu Studies*, vol. 22 (2007). Rashid Jahan's play has been translated by Ralph Russell, *Hidden in the Lute: An Anthology of Two Centuries of Urdu Literature* (New Delhi: Viking, 1995), pp. 34–46. Priyamvada Gopal has exhaustively studied the two pieces by Rashid Jahan in *Literary Radicalism in India: Gender, Nation and the Transition to Independence* (Oxon: Routledge, 2005), chapter 2.

[5] These figures are from the fortnightly reports for the United Provinces, IOR/L/PJ/12/729.

were destroyed by the police in the raid. Of the five, three were placed in the custody of the Keeper of Records in Delhi (in what is now the NAI) and the remaining two were sent to London. Under the provision of the Press Regulation Act, 1890 (Government of India), the British Museum obtained a copy on 21 June 1933.[6]

Writing the preface to the catalogue of books proscribed by the Government of India, B.C. Bloomfield notes that 'the British normally banned publications for two main purposes: first, they promoted criticism of the British administrations; and second, they promoted religious and/or racial strife. The proscription of publications for moral or sexual reasons seems almost never to have been the case....'[7]

A study of the catalogue reveals how—taken together—the books, pamphlets, periodicals, newspapers, handbills, and posters in all the major Indian languages proscribed by the British government in India provide an invaluable printed archive. There is ample material here for the study of the Indian freedom struggle during its last four decades. The collection at the British Library constitutes perhaps the largest accumulation of primary literature and ephemera relating to the Indian independence movement. There are similar, but smaller collections in the library and files of the Home (Political) Proceedings of the NAI and the state archives in Kolkata. The editors of the catalogue write:

From the establishment of a commercial publishing and newspaper industry in the 1780s up to the Mutiny of 1857, the British authorities in India fluctuated between tightening or loosening their powers restricting the production of books and newspapers ... by the turn of the century the two main categories of proscribed publications had been established: criticism of the British colonial government coupled with increasing demands for self-government, and expressions of communal conflict fuelled by inter-sectarian and inter-religious controversy.[8]

---

[6] For details of the book in its present location in the India Office Collection, see Shabana Mahmud, 'Angare and the Founding of the Progressive Writers' Association', *Journal of Modern Asian Studies*, vol. 30, no. 2 (May 1966), p. 450.

[7] Graham Shaw and Mary Lloyd (eds), *Publications Proscribed by the Government of India: A Catalogue of the Collections in the India Office Library and Records and the Department of Oriental Manuscripts and Printed Books, British Library Reference Division* (London: The British Library, 1985).

[8] Ibid., p. vii.

As we have seen in Chapter 2, the Indian Press Act of 1910 was the government's biggest ally in dealing with the increasing amounts of 'seditious' literature being made available—be it home-grown or produced abroad. The Act pulled the noose around presses that dealt with such material by requiring their proprietors to deposit securities which could be forfeited if they produced 'objectionable' material. When necessary, presses could be impounded and their publishers even jailed. The Act took stronger measures against the importation and circulation of foreign political material by authorizing provincial governments to ban any 'suspect' material and empowering the police to search and seize such literature.

Usually, the great bulk of literature banned by the British dealt with criticism of the British presence in India, its policies, and activities. Occasionally, criticism of native princes or of Western colonialism, religion, and culture generally also came under the purview of the Press Act. Any denunciation of British rule by Westerners such as Annie Besant or W.S. Blunt accounts of revolutionary movements elsewhere (particularly Ireland or Egypt), or of anti-capitalist models such as China which might serve as a model for India too were invariably proscribed. Waffling between eclectic traditions (back home) that favoured a free and frank airing of public opinion and a colonial mindset that was anxious to quell the slightest stirring of discord, imperial proscription policies were remarkable for their ambivalence. The non-cooperation movement mounted in response to the Rowlatt Act led to

the first mass circulation of collections of nationalist poetry. Many of these were banned and copies were preserved in two London collections. Another category of proscription at the time was literature expressing support for the Khilafat movement and pan-Islamism. The tragedy of Jallianwala Bagh probably evoked more anti-British poetry than any other single incident except the execution in 1931 of the revolutionary Bhagat Singh, who on the evidence of proscribed material, rivaled Gandhi in popular literature as the embodiment of the freedom struggle.[9]

The resurgence of non-cooperation and the growth in revolutionary activity in the 1930s led to renewed mass circulation of nationalist poetry. What is interesting is that despite the threat of proscription, there was no let nor leave in the sheer numbers of revolutionary literature that kept appearing. While occasional attempts were made at concealment, by giving

[9] Shaw and Lloyd, *Publications Proscribed by the Government of India*, p. viii.

an innocuous sounding title, by and large the nationalist press, refused to go underground.

Reeling under the Khilafat movement and the non-cooperation agitation, the government decided to adopt a twin-pronged approach of 'coercion and conciliation'. While banning, censorship, and imprisonment were tested ways of retaining political control, another strategy was cultivating allies and conciliating political and religious leaders. Having studied and compiled banned literature in British India, Norman Gerald Barrier notes 'the conflict between cherished British ideological traditions and the demands of control over a non-Western population. Censorship, banning, and other varieties of official interference with freedom of the press also constitute key but little-known elements in India's struggle for independence.'[10]

It is important to see the banning of *Angarey* in the context of the overall strategy adopted by the British. It is equally important, however, to correctly interpret the impulses behind the publication of such a book in the first instance. The overtly sexual references and the attacks on religion draw away from the purpose of the book which was, namely, to introduce another sort of writing, one that was filled with graphic word pictures of a sick, ailing society. It was a self-conscious attempt to shock people out of their inertia, to show them how hypocrisy and sexual oppression had so crept into everyday life that it was accepted with blithe disregard for all norms of civilized society. This sort of writing, if allowed to grow unchecked, *could* become subversive and that would not suit either the religious or the political powers-that-be. It suited the colonial administration, therefore, to thwart, suppress, and malign such writing by encouraging a religious colour to swamp its real intent. Unlike the later work produced by the progressives, here there is no optimism, no attempt at providing solutions, or even advocating change. *Angarey* is a dark, driven documentary of disquiet; we see no attempt whatsoever at social reform. Those who clamoured for banning such a book and those who capitulated were not interested in the impulses that drove these four young people. One set merely saw an affront to their religious identity; the other was solely interested in buying peace. Only a handful saw and appreciated the intent behind the provocation.

---

[10] Norman Gerald Barrier, *Banned: Controversial Literature and Political Control in British India, 1907–1947* (Delhi: Manohar, 1978), p. 3.

Each of the 10 pieces in *Angarey* dealt with the lives of the most disenfranchised, disempowered, and downtrodden. When not shabby and poor, these lives were certainly marked by decay and disintegration and in the case of women, marginalization and exclusion. This attempt at becoming the 'other', speaking in the voice of a completely alien, unrelated other, can be considered *Angarey*'s single most important contribution in strictly literary terms, for it opened the doors for many writers to speak in voices other than their own and yet sound convincing and real. Premchand had done this before the *Angarey* writers, but his characters, while no doubt poor and deprived, lacked this altogether new and earthy vigour. Women like Gangi in Premchand's *Thakur ka Kuan* (The Thakur's Well) had spoken bitterly against the caste-ridden, unjust, unequal society, but done little to break free. Premchand had been largely content with depicting the exploitative, inhuman, debased conditions of those at the bottom of the great Indian pyramid; not so the *Angarey* quartet. They saw, commented and commented without caution or restraint.

A useful comparison can be made between Rashid Jahan's writing and the other writings for women by women novelists or male writers adopting a woman's perspective, such as Rashid ul-Khairi (1968–1910).[11] Khairi and some of the journalists who wrote for women's magazines like *Ismat*, in a sense, presage the adopting of the 'other'—of empowered, educated, aware men and (occasionally) women speaking of illiterate, disempowered, marginalized women, and also of male writers like Khairi himself and Ahmed Ali (in *Mahavaton ki Ek Raat*) speaking in voices not their own—of genteel, well-born women living behind the purdah—and later Manto—impersonating the voice and persona of a pimp or prostitute—to voice concerns that nevertheless are legitimately theirs too. While writers like Premchand,[12] Bharatendu Harishchandra (1850–1885), Sajjad Hyder

---

[11] See Gail Minault, '*Ismat*: Rashid ul Khairi's novels and Urdu Literary Journalism for Women', in Christopher Shackle (ed.), *Urdu and Muslim South Asia: Studies in Honour of Ralph Russell* (New Delhi: Oxford University Press, 1991), pp. 129–38. Khairi started the journal *Ismat* in 1908 from Delhi and wrote a spate of tear-jerker novels about the lot of women. We have discussed Khairi and Ismat in Chapter 2.

[12] Premchand wrote *Bazar-e-Husn* (The Bazar of Beauty) in 1917 in Urdu. Dealing with marriage, women's sexuality, and prostitution, it had to wait till 1924 to find a publisher in Urdu. It was, however, published in Hindi in 1918

Yildrim (1888–1942), and others had written about women's issues—social issues such as widow remarriage, purdah, fallen women who take to prostitution, women's education, child marriage, and so on—no one had hitherto spoken of women's bodies and their needs.

There had existed in Urdu poetry two traditions that are noteworthy here: one, of the poetic genre of *rekhti* where male poets speak in the feminine voice; and two, of courtesan poetry, such as that of the famous courtesan Mahlaqa Chanda of Hyderabad.[13] The only women who had written about women and their needs had so far been 'fallen' women, those outside the pale of society. This is not to say there were no sharif women writers of any note till now; there were several prose writers, such as Rokeya Sakhawat Husain, Hijab Imtiaz Ali, Nazar-e-Sajjad Zaheer, and some who took the name of husbands or fathers, as in 'Mother-of-so-and-so' or 'Wife-of-so-and-so', and wrote on women's issues, but not with any degree of boldness, nothing in fact that could be termed 'obscene'. Women from sharif families also composed poetry, but it was read privately and not meant for public consumption or publication. As Petievich points out, even the great advocates of learning such as Syed Ahmad Khan believed that women should be encouraged to read but not write,[14] which resulted in a disparity between women's readership and authorship. 'For authorship,' Peteivich says with commendable perspicacity, 'is agency, and there were already a number of—perhaps too many—competing agents in the social space under negotiation in post-1857 British India.'[15] While the British India of the 1930s was gradually allowing a space for real voices of women (instead of the 'phoney' women-like voices of the rekhti poets), the climate

---

under the title *Sevasadan* (The House of Service). For further details, see the Introduction by Vasudha Dalmia in *Sevasadan*, translated by Snehal Shingavi (New Delhi: Oxford University Press, 2005).

[13] For a detailed analysis of the feminine voice, see Carla Petievich, 'Feminine Authorship and Urdu Poetic Tradition: *Baharistan-i Naz* vs *Tazkira-i Rekhti*', in Kathryn Hansen and David Lelyveld (eds), *A Wilderness of Possibilities: Urdu Studies in Transnational Perspective* (New Delhi: Oxford University Press, 2005); and *When Men Speak as Women: Vocal Masquerade in Indo-Muslim Poetry* (New Delhi: Oxford University Press, 2007).

[14] See Gail Minault, *Secluded Scholars: Women's Education and Muslim Social Reform in Colonial India* (New Delhi: Oxford University Press, 1998).

[15] Carla Petievich, 'Feminine Authorship and Urdu Poetic Tradition', p. 242.

was still not suitable for women's voices that interpreted 'real' women's hearts and bodies. The distinction between existing proponents of *écriture féminine* ('writing the feminine') and the *Angarey* writers is precisely that the latter, for the first time, addressed female sexuality head-on.[16] As we shall see in the next section, the uproar over the so-called obscenity stemmed from sheer surprise at this unexpected assault on virgin territory. Here were four young people—one of them being a woman—who were going where no one had gone before. They were appropriating a space that no one knew even existed.

Georg Lukács (1885–1971), the noted Marxist intellectual, observed that a writer's awareness can be subdivided into awareness about reality, critical awareness about reality, and socialist awareness about reality. These three planes of reality have also been described as realism, critical realism, and socialist realism.[17] Lukács developed a coherent theory of realism which started with the dogma that all literature is a 'reflection of reality' (a phrase which Lukács repeated over a thousand times in the first volume of his *Aesthetik*, published in 1962), and that literature can become the truest mirror of society if it fully reflected the contradictions of social development, that is, in practice, if the author showed an insight into the structure of society and the future direction of its evolution. Man as a social animal in the best Aristotelian tradition, was interpreted by Lukács to mean man as being 'rooted' in history and society. Most writers of seemingly 'realistic' fiction may reflect awareness about a given social reality, but they might not have a 'critical' attitude towards it. The writers of *Angarey* showed an acutely critical awareness of the world around them. Moreover, they gave it a socialist interpretation. They saw with an unblinking unsparing gaze, recorded the minutest detail in the most forthright and unflinching manner

---

[16] Perhaps it is only with the benefit of several decades of hindsight that Ali Jawad Zaidi writes that while the *Angarey* writers 'repudiated, even ridiculed the well-established traditional ideas on sex, social norms and rites and rituals in a rather uncontrolled and emotional manner ... they served the purpose of awakening the average writers' intellect and observation to the surrounding chaos, social inertia and economic stagnation'. Ali Jawad Zaidi, *A History of Urdu Literature* (New Delhi: Sahitya Akademi, 1993), p. 392.

[17] For an interpretation of some of Lukács's works, see Max Rieser, 'The Aesthetic Theory of Social Realism', *The Journal of Aesthetics and Art Criticism*, vol. 16, no. 2 (1957), pp. 237–48.

and above all, commented on things that most Muslim writers would shy away from in squeamish horror. Despite their liberal, Western-style education, all four display a remarkably astute understanding of Muslim manners and mores. Their depiction of a way of life, in almost every way far removed from their own, is spot on.

In this context, it would be appropriate to comment on the myth of homogeneity and the tendency to view the Indian Muslim as an unvariegated, monolithic mass. We have already seen in the previous chapters that the Muslim response to 1857, Gandhi's non-cooperation movement, the First World War, and other world events that impacted India were never uniform. Historians such as Mushirul Hasan have repeatedly contested the myth of Muslim unity and of pan-Islamism and stressed the healthy presence of pluralism and multiculturalism among the Indian Muslims.[18] Hasan also makes a point of stressing that even on the Khilafat issue there were differences of opinion. It was the Muslim publicists who upped the ante of pan-Islamism and homogeneity of the Muslim masses to suit their own purposes; this perception, no matter how flawed and far removed from the truth, suited the British interests too. 'Though British functionaries continued to perpetuate the myth of the pervasive influence of Pan-Islamism, overseas writers visiting India, including the Turkish writer Halide Edib, thought differently.'[19] In the course of her travels through India (in early 1935), Edib found that Muslim allegiance to England during the First World War belied 'a strong historical myth—it showed that political pan-Islamism was a mere bogey. The attachment of the Indian Muslim to the interests of his country was a greater reality than his solidarity with Muslims outside India. It may be useful for Western powers with Muslim colonies to realize that there is a distinct sense of nationhood.'[20]

---

[18] The subject is taken up repeatedly in many of Hasan's writings, most notably in 'Redefining Boundaries: Modernist Interpretations and the New "Intellectual Structures"', in *Legacy of a Divided Nation* (New Delhi: Oxford University Press, 1997), pp. 223–52; and 'The Myth of Unity: Colonial and National Narratives', in David Ludden (ed.), *Contesting the Nation*, South Asia Seminar Series (Philadelphia: University of Pennsylvania Press, 1996), pp. 185–208.

[19] Hasan, 'Myth of Unity', p. 192.

[20] Halide Edib, *Inside India* (New Delhi: Oxford University Press, 2002), p. 317.

Also, at this point it must be noted that the wave of communistic ideas was spreading across India, especially among the youth. By 1930, youth associations had spread to different parts of the country though they were most active in Bengal, in the Bombay presidency, in the United Provinces, and in Punjab; in the Punjab the Naujawan Bharat Sabha began getting students to fill the ranks of its newly formed Comrades' Corps. Occasionally, some of these student wings would be incited to violence, as, for example, the Youth League at Etah where during a meeting in July 1930 mention was made of the Chittagong and Calcutta outbreaks and much abuse was levelled at the police.[21] The colourful figure of Kamaladevi Chattopadhyay became increasingly active at youth conferences since she was frequently invited by students and young writers where she would make repeated assertions of war on England and on imperialism.

To return to the *Angarey* quartet, it must be remembered that their self-image (as indeed of the great many progressive writers) was not of *being* Muslim. If anything, *being* Muslim figured very little in their stream of consciousness, nor did they believe that they belonged to a larger ummah. Unlike other middle-class educated Muslims who either belonged to the charmed circle of colonial bureaucracy or were so deeply steeped in religious theocracy that they could neither correct these stereotypes nor instigate debates, these people were deeply committed to setting their own house in order. Insofar as busting myths and breaking stereotypes was concerned, the *Angarey* group came like a breath of fresh air in a closed fetid room. The group was representative of the internal, moral, political, and social tensions within the Indian Muslims and the disruptive effect these tensions could have once brought out into the open. The Muslim intellectuals of the day were so busy setting the record straight on Hindu–Muslim relations and on the Indian Muslims' commitment to nationalism *or* pan-Islamism (depending on their creed) that few bothered to turn the gaze inwards. Few bothered to look at the Indian Muslim community—how 'static' it had become, 'sunk in torpid medievalism, insulated from the winds of change, influenced by the diktat of the mullahs'.[22] Socially conscious, politically aware nationalist Muslim writers were busy enlisting the Indian

---

[21] *Youth Movements in India: Intelligence Reports*; IOR/L/PJ/12/60, File 4968 (g) 21, Dec 1928–Oct 1936.

[22] Hasan, 'Myth of Unity', p. 197.

Muslim as co-partners in the nation-building process that was underway.[23] Intent upon building bridges between Hindus and Muslims, though they were addressing issues that seemed important to them such as the Hindi–Urdu debate or the mandir–masjid dilemma, they, however, failed to see the chasms that cleft the Muslim community. They were blind to the fact of the ummah divided into small isolated sections and the gulf that separated the rich from the poor, the landed classes from their feudatories, the small elite of the Western-educated liberals from the large mass of Muslims who either had no formal education or had emerged from traditional madrasas that had equipped them with a limited, if not narrow, world view. In contrast, the *Angarey* quartet had an altogether different perspective—influenced by their privileged family background, education in English, their friendship and camaraderie with Western-educated, liberal, left-leaning intellectuals. All four had, in different ways and degrees, been exposed to socialism which had widened their intellectual horizon and made them more willing to question and probe beneath the layers of civilized society. We have noted in Chapter 2 how the much-awaited renaissance failed to take place among the Muslims, how reform movements such as those that touched thousands of Hindus in Punjab and Bengal failed to find fertile ground among the Muslims, how both the Aligarh School and the ulama of Deoband failed the Indian Muslim, failed that is, in giving them realistic ways of seeing themselves.[24] The *Angarey* quartet was quick to seize this lacuna, and to fill it with their rough-and-ready home-made dynamite, a literary equivalent of a Molotov cocktail. They were expecting some sparks, yes, but even they could not have imagined its explosive after-effects.

But how did this fiery combination meet? What made them produce such a book? We get a small clue in Zaheer's *Roshnai*: 'While I was a

---

[23] W.C. Smith, *Modern Islam in India: A Social Analysis* (Delhi: Usha Publications, 1979), p. 257.

[24] There are instances of some purely Muslim organizations that drifted away from the nationalistic Congress and began to set up regional groupings in the early 1930s such as the Ahrar Party in the Punjab and the Krishak Praja Party in Bengal; though politically and socially progressive, they were unwilling to look at religion or religious issues with any degree of objectivity. If anything, the Ahrar leaders relied upon quotations from the Holy Quran and incidents from the early history of Islam to appeal to, what Smith calls, 'religious emotional idealism'; see Smith, *Modern Islam in India*, p. 271.

student in England, I had returned to India for six months in 1931 and stayed in Lucknow. I had met him [Ahmed Ali] then, and together we had brought out *Angarey*.'[25]

We get another clue from Ahmed Ali, writing years later in 1993, in his introduction to a reprint of *Twilight in Delhi*:

And yet, rising from within, a tide of revolt led some of us to contemplate the state of inanity and indifference into which the social order had sunk. It was the beginning of the third decade, almost a hundred years since the infamous Minute of 1835.[26] A few of us, filled with dreams of freedom and independence, made bold to publish in 1932 a collection of our short stories in Urdu, *Angaray* (Burning Coals) to show a mirror to society. Our enthusiasm was immediately dampened by a cold shower of denunciations, from the pulpit down to the social and political platforms. Though it made us famous overnight, the government banned the book as subversive, and our names were listed in the Intelligence Bureau as communists and dangerous characters. The mirror had warped our own image into its reverse. The social order we had set out to reform, pronounced us West-stricken devils![27]

[25] Sajjad Zaheer, *The Light: A History of the Movement for Progressive Literature in the Indo-Pak Subcontinent*, English translation of Sajjad Zaheer's *Roshnai* by Amina Azfar (Karachi: Oxford University Press, 2006), p. 6.

[26] Referring to Lord Thomas Babington Macaulay's Minute of 1835 which set about a new agenda of anglicizing the colonized in order to produce the brown sahebs: 'a class of persons, Indian in blood and colour, but English in taste and character, in morals and intellect'.

[27] Ahmed Ali, *Twilight in Delhi: A Novel* (New Delhi: Rupa & Co., 2007), p. xiv. Ali goes on to make a case for finding his true identity as an Indian and not a brown Englishman by writing about his family and the city of Delhi where he had grown up. 'The story of my immediate ancestors held the key to a treasure trove of mysteries.' In 1935 he wrote a short story in Urdu '*Hamari Gali*' (Our Lane). In 1940, he produced his seminal work, *Twilight in Delhi*, written in English and published by Hogarth Press, London. Maurice Collis, writing in *Time and Tide*, 30 November 1940, wrote about *Twilight*, 'It may well be that we shall not understand India until it is explained to us by Indian novelists of the first ability, as it was that we understand nothing of Russia before we read Tolstoy, Turgenev and others. Ahmed Ali may well be at the vanguard of such a literary movement.' No such judgement was pronounced for Ahmed Ali's contributions to *Angarey*. Why? Because it was in Urdu? Did it provide a less-than-adequate understanding of India? How did the tide turn for Ahmed Ali from 1932 to 1940? We will seek answers in the concluding chapter.

Clearly drawing on the benefit of hindsight and longevity compared to his three comrades, Ali was to write in later years: '[W]e dreamed of winning for Urdu and the regional languages the same respect and for the Indian people the same dignity which other civilised languages and societies enjoyed.'[28] Shabana Mahmud quotes a personal interview with Ahmed Ali in Karachi in February 1987, wherein Ali said there was no 'set goal' except to present a collection of stories in one collection. The book was published 'as a result of a creative urge of a few young writers ... its direction being determined not by any foreign influence but by social conditions and the degrading state of society.'[29] He goes on to say that 'all but three of the stories in *Angarey* were written independently of each other', and that the four did not know each other at the time of writing their pieces, and 'it was co-authorship that led to the group and not the group to the co-authorship'. Ahmed Ali, in the same interview, also asserts that the idea of publishing the stories was his and was discussed between himself and Zaheer during the summer of 1932. Of the four, Ahmed Ali was the only established writer at the time; not only had '*Mahavaton ki Raat*' already appeared in print in the journal called *Humayun* published from Lahore in January 1932, but Ahmed Ali was a well-regarded name in literary and academic circles. Also, he was the only one amongst the four who had a long innings and went on to establish a formidable literary and academic reputation in later years.

Zaheer (known to friends and family as Banne Bhai) is brief about *Angarey* to the point of being dismissive. In the only reference to *Angarey* in the entire book, *The Light*, he goes on to give a brutally honest assessment of the book:

Most of the stories in this collection lacked depth and serenity, and contained a good deal of anger and agitation against obsolete and retrogressive values. In some cases where the focus was on sexuality, the influence of D.H. Lawrence and James Joyce was apparent. The reactionaries had used these weaknesses to make *Angarey* and its writers the subject of harsh propaganda. As usual resolutions

---

[28] Ahmed Ali, 'The Progressive Writers' Movement and Creative Writers in Urdu', in Carlo Coppola (ed.), *Marxist Influences and South Asian Literature* (East Lansing: Michigan State University Press, 1974), p. 36.

[29] Mahmud, 'Angare and the Founding of the Progressive Writers' Association', p. 452.

were passed in mosques. Maulvi Abdul Majid Daryabadi challenged us to battle. We received death threats. And, finally, the UP government confiscated the publication.[30]

It is worth noting that in later years, while Zaheer talked of the PWA, of having a preliminary meeting of the PWA (long before the first AIPWA Conference) at his father's home in Allahabad which was attended by city luminaries including Vijaylakshmi Pandit, and of discussing 'his' proposal to launch a countrywide PWA with Nehru, Acharya Narendra Dev, JP, and Ramkrishna Benipuri (all of whom liked 'his' idea), there is no mention of *Angarey*.[31] It is almost as though he wished to distance himself from the infamous book if not disown it altogether.

Given the provocative title and the deliberate defiance of existing literary norms by the four young writers, the book unleashed a storm of controversies and marked a turning point in the history of Urdu literature. Literary critics panned it for its crudeness and immaturity, its lack of literary finesse, and its largely borrowed literary sensibility. Religious leaders expressed outrage and outright condemnation, some maulvis going so far as to issue fatwas against the book and its authors. Newspapers and journals published angry editorials and articles denouncing the book, calling it a 'filthy pamphlet … which has wounded the feelings of the entire Muslim community … and which is extremely objectionable from the point of view of both religion and morality'.[32] Ahmed Ali wrote:

We knew the book would create a stir, but never dreamt it would bring the house down. We were condemned at public meetings and private; bourgeois families hurried to dissociate themselves from us and denied acquaintance with us, especially with Rashid Jahan and myself … people read the book behind closed doors and in bathrooms with relish but denounced us in the open. We were lampooned and satirized, condemned editorially and in pamphlets.… Our lives were threatened, people even lay in wait with daggers to kill us.[33]

---

[30] Zaheer, *Light*, p. 6.

[31] Interview for the NMML's Oral History Project.

[32] Resolution passed by the Central Standing Committee of the All-India Conference, Lucknow quoted in, *Hindustan Times*, 21 February 1933.

[33] Quoted by Carlo Coppola, 'The Angare Group: The *Enfants Terribles* of Urdu Literature', *Annual of Urdu Studies*, vol. 1 (1981), p. 61.

The notion of obscenity in literature is a delicate one. What constitutes obscenity? Legally speaking, it must be prurient in nature; completely devoid of scientific, political, educational, or social value; and it must violate the local community standards. Coming from the Latin word *obscenus*, meaning 'foul, repulsive, detestable', obscenity is that which offends the prevalent sexual morality of the time, is a profanity, or is otherwise taboo, indecent, abhorrent, or disgusting, or is especially inauspicious; ill-omened. The definition of obscenity differs from culture to culture, among communities within a single culture and also among individuals within those communities. Many cultures have produced laws to define what constitutes obscene, and censorship is the preferred tool to suppress or control things that are deemed obscene under these definitions. However, the parameters of obscenity change with time. For instance, D.H. Lawrence's *Lady Chatterley's Lover* (1928), banned for obscenity, would fail to raise any eyebrows today. Neither would James Joyce's *Ulysses* banned in 1922, Henry Miller's *Tropic of Cancer* (1934), John Steinbeck's *Grapes of Wrath* (1939), or George Orwell's *1984* (1949). Clearly, what constitutes obscenity today may or may not do so tomorrow.

Incidentally, the progressives' own views on obscenity changed with time and circumstance. While they put their weight behind the *Angarey* writers, they were less than generous with a poet like Miraji whom they excluded from their charmed circle on charges of the explicitly sexual nature of his poetry.[34] While we will discuss the events related to the PWM in detail in subsequent chapters, here—at the cost of skipping our narrative forward by a decade—it is important to draw attention to the PWA's public stance on obscenity. At the All-India Urdu Progressive Writers' Conference held in Hyderabad in October 1945, the organizers wanted to pass a resolution 'against' obscenity. They were not successful in getting the motion passed because the maverick Hasrat Mohani, always the dissenter, proclaimed that if the subject was raised he would insist on proposing an amendment. While Mohani agreed that obscenity should be condemned, he had no objection to literary portrayal of *latif havasnaki* ('refined sexual desire'). Eventually, the organizers chose not to put up the motion at all.[35]

---

[34] For details see Geeta Patel, *Lyrical Movements, Historical Haunting: On Gender, Colonialism, and Desire in Miraji's Urdu Poetry* (New Delhi: Manohar, 2005), p. 75.

[35] Russell, 'Leadership in the All-India Progressive Writers' Movement', p. 126.

Before we move on to examining what the newspapers had to say about *Angarey*, it might be pertinent to look, briefly, at other samples of radical writings in Urdu as well as some of the other major Indian languages, namely, Hindi, Marathi, and Bengali. 'The period between the two wars,' writes Ale Ahmad Suroor, 'sees literature coming into its own, freed from the clutches of politics and religion.'[36] While the writers mentioned by him (in the context of wit and satire) cannot be compared with the *Angarey* quartet, it might be worthwhile to note the work of others during this period who were similarly inclined to cock a snook at the traditionalists. Suroor mentions Sajjad Ansari, an essayist who considers the devil delightful company and paradise a bore and 'is angry with mystics and maulvis and asserts the freedom of literature from the tyranny of morals'. Suroor goes on to praise Ansari for attacking 'the philosophical attitude of Abdul Majid with his lofty airs of high seriousness'. Suroor also praises Qazi Abdul Ghaffar who, in *Laila ke Khutoot* (The Letters of Laila), 'lashes out against men for their cruelty to women, with the savage indignation of Swift'. Ghaffar,[37] who wrote some finely crafted columns for *Payaam* (a journal he edited from Hyderabad), is also credited with exposing 'with merciless wit the double standards in our life and the stifling yoke of convention'.

By most accounts, the first Urdu story to deal with the issue of sex and sexual matters was 'Kharistan-o-Gulistan' (The Land of Thorns and the Garden, in the collection entitled *Khayalistan*, The Land of the Imagination) by Sajjad Hyder Yildrim, the father of noted Urdu novelist Qurratulain Hyder.[38] The

[36] Ezekiel, *Indian Writers in Conference*, p. 212.

[37] There is a delightful reference to Qazi Abdul Ghaffar and his beautiful wife in Hameeda Akhtar Husain Raipuri's *My Fellow Traveler*, translation of *Humsafar* (Karachi: Oxford University Press, 2006). It was the year 1936 when she first meets Ghaffar and mentions how Akhtar Husain Raipuri 'campaigns' for a job in *Payaam* for his friend Sibte Hasan, another socialist from their Aligarh days and a leading light of the PWM. In the same book, Hamida talks of how she had borrowed a copy of *Laila ke Khutoot* from a friend and read it secretly for fear of being reprimanded by her mother (p. 84). *Laila ke Khutoot* and its sequel *Majnun ki Diary* (The Diary of Majnun) (both novelettes written in the form of a diary) are remarkable examples of the psychoanalytical mode in Urdu; together, they established Ghaffar's reputation as a prose stylist.

[38] Mentioned by Khalid Alvi, *Angarey ka Tareekhi Pasmanzar aur Taraqqui Pasand Tehreek* (Delhi: Educational Publishing House, 1995), p. 63.

writings of Niyaz Fatehpuri (1884–1966)[39] also come close to the *Angarey* brand in what can be termed bold, radical, even daring. In an article entitled '*Urdu mein Firauniyat*' (The Pharoahs of Urdu), Premchand calls him 'an iconoclast concerning traditional ways and customs, and a rather vocal proponent of reform in current [standards of] scholarship. Every once in a while, he displays his own freedom of expression in sallies against religious truths and ethical values'.[40] His novel, *Shahab ki Sarguzashti* (The Autobiography of Shahab), has 'the same tone of bitter cynicism as is to be found in Huxley's works.' The hero, Shams, has 'seen through the shams and pretenses of society and has little or no illusions left about anything'.[41]

In the period before the publication of *Angarey*, the influence of Russian masters such as Chekhov, Tolstoy, and Turgenev can be clearly seen in the writings of men like Muhammad Mujeeb, Hayatullah Ansari, Mushir Ahmad Kidwai, and Khwaja Manzur Husain.[42] Also, by the 1920s, we begin to see a flood of translations—of English, French, Russian, and Turkish writers into English. The role of translations in the dissemination of new ideas, styles, and genres has never been fully appreciated; it needs to be studied to appreciate how 'open' Urdu was to outside influences. Occasionally, these new influences took the form of translations, but some were trans-created to adapt to the Indian scenario. They introduced, to the Indian reader, not just new notions of liberty, equality, justice, change, but also newer ways of looking at things. Along with revolutionary ideas

---

[39] Niyaz Fatehpuri is best known for the monthly journal, *Nigar*, launched by him at Bhopal in February 1922 and then moved to Lucknow in 1927, editing, publishing, and often writing the entire issue himself. He was also an important figure among the so-called 'aesthetes' in Urdu. Frequently involved in literary and religious controversy, he also gained many admirers all over South Asia. After living in Lucknow until late in his life, he moved to Karachi with his magazine, where he died not long after. C.M. Naim, *Annual of Urdu Studies*, vol. 18 (2003), p. 487. The other Urdu 'aesthetes' listed by Naim include Lam Ahmad Akbarabadi, Mian Bashir Ahmad, Hijab Imtiaz Ali, Majnun Gorakhpuri, and Sajjad Ansari.

[40] Translated by Naim in *Annual of Urdu Studies*, vol. 18, p. 488.

[41] Shaista Suhrawardy, *A Critical Survey of the Development of the Urdu Novel and Short Story* (Karachi: Oxford University Press, 2004), p. 181.

[42] Qamar Rais, '*Urdu Afsane mein Angarey ki Riwayat*', in Ali Sardar Jafri (ed.), *Guftagu* (Conversation) (Taraqqi Pasand Number) (Bombay: Wadera Publications, 1980), p. 47.

inspired by the great revolutions in France and Russia, they introduced Freudian insights into human character and behaviour.[43]

Reactions in the Press

The case for banning *Angarey* was an unusually piquant one for the 'other' community, that is, the non-Muslims who could sit back and enjoy the drama; for the Muslims it was a galling experience and a bitter pill to swallow at the hands of one's own people. So far, attacks on Islam or the Muslims' religious practices had come from the 'other' community;[44] it was rare for Muslims to criticize their own practices. In this, the contributors of *Angarey* were a novelty. The disbelief generated by their book among members of their own community was closely followed by outrage that four young Muslims, that too from eminently respectable shurfa families, should be so misguided!

A 'Note on the Press' from the Native Newspapers[45] for the week ending 4 February 1933 reveals the first inkling of the ferment that was brewing under the following bold headlines: 'A Mischief in the sphere of religion: A new spark in the storehouse of religious tenets: Desecration of Islam at the hands of the sons of Islam: Muslim press should direct its attention towards this.'

The same report goes on to mention that the *Sarfaraz*, a Shia newspaper from Lucknow, had strongly condemned the 'extremely indecent and slanderous' language of the book and appealed to the Muslims to put a united demand for the proscription of this 'heart-rending' book and to take no rest unless and until the government issued necessary orders.

---

[43] Muhammad Sadiq, *Twentieth Century Urdu Literature* (Karachi: Royal Book Company, 1983).

[44] *Vichitra Jivan* (A Strange Life), written by Arya Samaj preacher and polemicist Pandit Kalicharan Sharma in 1925; a tract in Urdu called *Rangila Rasul* (The Merry Prophet) by an unknown author published by a Lahore bookseller, Rajpal, in 1927; and an article entitled 'A Trip to Hell' published in the *Risala-e-Vartman* (The Journal of Today) elaborating the Prophet Muhammad's sufferings in hell were some of the prominent examples of ridiculing Islam and its Prophet by the 'other' community. They were all banned. Not so Dante Alighieri's *Inferno* which dealt with much the same subject.

[45] 'Note on the Press', 1933, United Provinces of Agra and Oudh, No. 2 of 1933, NAI.

On 10 February 1933, a certain Mullah Shahadmi wrote a satirical play entitled *Aag Khaaein* (Let Us Eat Fire) in the *Khasaf Nama*.[46] The four contributors to *Angarey* featured in the play with the syllables of each contributor's name slightly altered and given an Anglo-Saxon intonation. For instance, Zaheer became Mistar Sejad and was described as 'a fashionable saheb'; Mahmuduzzafar appeared as Mistar Memad, 'a romantically inclined gentleman'; Ahmed Ali was identifiable as Mistar Emad, an 'up-to-date professor'; and there was no doubt whatsoever about the identity of Miss Razida, 'a lady doctor'. An illustration appeared with the play showing the men wearing Western clothes and two of them—Sejad and Emad—also wearing hats. Mistar Sejad is clutching Miss Razida and all four are looking fearful. All around them are what appear to be flames and the simple, almost crude, line drawing is entitled '*Ek Awaaz*' (A Voice). The author relied upon much black humour to show these creatures as foolish, ridiculously Westernized heathens who shall 'eat fire' for their blasphemous views when they are consigned to hell.

From then on, the movement against *Angarey* gathered momentum. Three days later, on 13 February 1933, the *Medinah* from Bijnor carried a set of three articles on the objectionable book. The first report, entitled '*Angarey: Ek Fahash aur Malhadanah Kitab*' (*Angarey*: A Pornographic and Atheistic Book), began with the following ponderous assertions:

We are grateful to exalted God that he has allowed us to live in a remote township to perform the duties of journalism, a township which is safe from the piety-destroying and faith-removing elements of civilization, where neither the gaieties and frivolities of youth and poetry strike with lightning the granary of patience and steadfastness, nor the tumultuousness of beauty breaks the bonds of faith, and where the fierce and fiery winds of atheism and apostasy cannot burn the rose-garden of faith and religion.

No calamity can reach the seclusion of solitude

In our little world there are neither theatres nor cinemas, nor gatherings of dance and music, nor the tumult of atheism and apostasy. There are no reprehensible attempts at distressing the religious nor are there throngs of thieves and highwaymen intent on robbing us of the wealth of our dear faith. Praise be to God that we are to a large extent protected from the frivolities of the world. Alas from time to time journalism acquaints us with some of the mischiefs to which the sons of

---

[46] A copy was given to me by Urooj Ahmed Ali from Ahmed Ali's exhaustive collection of the press cuttings related to the *Angarey* episode.

Adam are prey, and after making their acquaintance it becomes difficult for us to sustain our patience and steadfastness....

... We could not find in them [the stories] anything intellectually modern except immorality, evil character and wickedness. To mock at the creator of the world, to ridicule religious beliefs and to make indecent jokes are the main characteristics of this bundle of filth. There is no regard for the greatness and majesty of God nor any respect for the sanctity and honour of prophets, nor any respect for human dignity. Instead one finds a bold and shameless display of every kind of foul language.[47]

The *Hindustan Times* of 21 February 1932 carried a report entitled 'Urdu Pamphlet Denounced: Shias Gravely Upset.' It mentioned that the Central Standing Committee of the All-India Shia Conference 'strongly condemns the heart-rending and filthy pamphlet[48]... which has wounded the feelings of the entire Muslim community by ridiculing God and His Prophets and which is extremely objectionable from the standpoints both of religion and morality. The Committee further strongly urges upon the attention of the U.P. Government that the book be at once proscribed.'[49]

Lucknow and Aligarh soon emerged as active centres of agitations against *Angarey* with festive book burnings being organized to draw the government's attention to the filthy contents of the book. Given the substantial and influential Shia population in Lucknow, the government felt compelled to take notice, especially when the matter was raised in the UP Legislative Council by Khan Bahadur Hafiz Hidayat Hussain, asking whether the government was aware that the book had 'created resentment among a wide circle of the Muslim intelligentsia'. In response, Home Minister Sir Ahmed Sayed Khan (the Nawab of Chhattari) informed the house that 'action to be taken is under the consideration of the government'.[50]

---

[47] Mahmud, 'Angare and the Founding of the Progressive Writers' Movement', pp. 448–9.

[48] It is interesting that many newspaper reports and articles described the book as a 'pamphlet'. Apparently many of those who wrote excoriating critiques against it had not read it and therefore did not know that it was a work of fiction.

[49] Alvi, *Angarey ka Tareekhi Pasmanzar aur Taraqqui Pasand Tehreek*, p. 104. Unless otherwise specified, all translations from the Urdu press clippings are mine.

[50] UP Legislative Council, *Proceedings*, no. 47 (16 February–9 March 1933), p. 310, NMML.

A report in the Native Newspapers for the week ending 18 February 1933 mentioned the *Sarfaraz* deploring the government for not taking any action against the 'obscene and nonsensical collection'. It also mentioned the *Rozana Akhbar* lending support to the protests of the *Sarfaraz* as well as the *Tamir* that made a strong case for the book's proscription. The *Rasti* was the only paper to differ; it believed that no useful purpose would be served by proscription as the *Sarfaraz* had already given it enough publicity. The *Sarfaraz* would have done better to prove its religious enthusiasm had it asked for the prosecution of the authors and publishers. The *Rasti* claimed to be opposed to the 'half-way' action proposed by the *Sarfaraz*.

The *Sarfaraz*, a *sahroza* or paper that came out every three days, wrote mostly about the Shia community and its concerns. Its chief editor was Khwaja Asadullah Asad. While the *Angarey* controversy was raging, the *Sarfaraz* was battling on different fronts. Reports from the Native Newspapers show that at about the same time it was also protesting against the government's policy of curtailing Shia holidays such as the 21st of Muharram and reducing the number of holidays given to schoolchildren from 10 to 5 during Muharram in the Awadh region. On 13 February 1933, it carried an article entitled '*Angarey*' by Maulvi Mohammad Ali Kamoonpur terming the book '*duniya-e-mazhab mein ek fitna*' ('a storm in the world of religion'). The *Sarjuzasht*, on 24 February 1933 under the headline '*Aag dekhi, pani dekha aur angarey dekhe*', carried the following first-person account:[51] The author claims to have seen the much-talked about book *Angarey* which was also on display in a bookstall at the Aligarh *numaish*.[52] Friends show him (the author) a copy of the book, he tries to read a few pages, but after a while his eyes refuse to see, his brain becomes hot, his eyes shut of their own accord, and the 'dirty book' falls from his hands. He comes home from the numaish ground, lies down on the bed, and his mind is swamped with all sorts of thoughts. The uneasiness in his heart grows with the darkness of the night.... The author then goes on to compare the stories in *Angarey* with those of Niyaz Fatehpuri, which were absurd and obscene, but at least had some glimmerings of literary quality and intelligence. This collection, on the other hand, showed nothing except

---

[51] Alvi, *Angarey ka Tareekhi Pasmanzar aur Taraqqui Pasand Tehreek*.

[52] The numaish (meaning 'exhibition') was an annual touring fair that travelled (still does) to many cities in UP. In Aligarh, it was a high point in the university's social and cultural calendar.

the poor upbringing of the contributors. He goes on to ask some questions since this (referring to the publication of such a book) has gone beyond hurting religious sentiments and the parameters of law. The Muslims should now find out why people are doing such things? After all, why are such debased writings appearing in print? And why did something appear in the market everyday which hurt one's religious sentiments? For, if one knows the real reason for these occurrences, how should one then set about removing them? And if there is nothing within the constitution of the present government to stop/curb religious and moral *gumrahi*, what should the religious world do to protect its rights? The article then makes a plea for self-introspection:

Angarey is not the first attempt to mock religion and religious rituals. Earlier, others too have published their writings mocking religious practices, but their writings at least had the semblance of research or study of religion and they adopted a mode of discussion on the subject. And in this they were somewhat successful. Whereas *Angarey*'s purpose is neither reform nor study.... When things have come to such a pass that God, the Prophet, the angels, the rituals of religion, and moral principles are ridiculed only and only for the sake of cheap humour, then one should think about why things have become so bad and how they can be rectified. In our opinion this is due to the bad upbringing of those young people who have turned their face away from morality and *sharafat* because sharafat can never tolerate ridiculing or hurting others' feelings.... And in reality it is not the fault of Syed Sajjad Zaheer but of his well-known and well-placed father who did not take appropriate measures for the correct upbringing of his recalcitrant child. Whatever is happening today is due to the negligence or *ghaflat* of the parents and elders....

Note: It is the highest sin to buy or make a reference to this dirty book. It should be banned forthwith and a correct picture of Islam should be immediately put forth.[53]

Similar sentiments were echoed by *Sach* (Truth), Lucknow, on 10 March 1933, in an essay entitled 'Disgraceful Book':

Haqiqat, *Haq*, and a few other newspapers have written about this disgraceful book. Angry meetings were held at different places, so much so that at the Legislative Council Hafiz Hidayat Hussain saheb even raised a question about banning it. No one had ever heard of these writers before the publication of the book, or

---

[53] Alvi, *Angarey ka Tareekhi Pasmanzar aur Taraqqui Pasand Tehreek*, pp. 86–7; translation mine.

afterwards. At best the book would have come out, people would have read a page or two and put it away because the book was a collection by unknown writers unworthy of attention. It is so common and vulgar that it would not have garnered the slightest attention, but unfortunately this didn't happen. The writers achieved their goal; they became famous. They became so famous and their book so talked about that they got more publicity than they would have had they spent Rs 1,000 on it. This is what they wanted; this is what they got. Unfortunately, something that had limited appeal became famous. My modest opinion on the strong reaction of the Islamic press is given above.[54]

The writer then goes on to insinuate that Zaheer, being the son of Sir Wazir Hasan, has wandered into this unknown territory; otherwise his real turf is the red light district of Lucknow where the other effete and debauched young men of his ilk are to be found. 'The same language, style, low thinking, vulgar, and cheap arguments are found here; even from the point of view of literature, these stories are senseless and worthless.'[55]

Maulana Abdul Majid Daryabadi (1892–1977), an Islamic scholar and writer of some repute, authored the above tirade. He was amongst the most vocal and virulent critics of the book and its writers. As editor of the Urdu weekly, *Sach*, he mobilized public opinion against *Angarey*. The issue of *Sach* dated 24 February 1933 panned the book for its

dirty and *bazari* language and cheap and low style of narration with vulgar insinuations against religion which despite much searching yields no literary beauty. In fact, it is awash with gross inaccuracies of language and syntax; the book is not worthy of being mentioned in civilized society. The attacks on religion caused a Shia newspaper from Lucknow, *Sarfaraz*, to launch a tirade against it. The owner of the printing press immediately acknowledged his mistake but the young writer [who is also the publisher] is apparently out of the country. There is a great deal of disquiet in Lucknow; in fact by the time this appears in print demonstrations and protests might begin.[56]

The same issue of *Sach* went on to express sympathy for Sajjad Zaheer's father and brother (the latter being a member of the Legislative Council, municipal commissioner of the city, and one of the most successful barristers of Awadh) who are both deemed 'fine, upright gentlemen and pillars

[54] Ibid.; translation mine.
[55] *Sach*, Lucknow, 10 March 1933.
[56] Ibid.; translation mine.

of society'. The next day's issue of *Sach*, that is, dated 25 February 1933, carried the following poem by some unknown poet instead of an editorial. Entitled '*Laga di Aag Angarey ne Duniya-e-shariat main*' (*Angarey* Has Set the World of Shariat on Fire), it makes a piteous lament:

> O you who torture the Prophet in his grave
> On what basis have you torn the religion of righteousness into shreds
> Had it interfered in any ways with your irreligiosity....

With *Sarfaraz* and *Sach* leading the pack, other papers joined the fray, such as *Maarif* and *Khilafat*. A report in the Native Newspapers[57] for the week ending 4 March 1933 showed agitation for the proscription of *Angarey* spreading to other newspapers like a wildfire. The *Hindi Jadeed* declared the authors of *Angarey* to be no better than Rajpal, of *Rangeela Rasool* notoriety, in its assault on Muslim sensibilities. The *Haq* complained that *Angarey* had ridiculed God, the prophets, angels, religion, and religious beliefs in a most disgraceful and blasphemous manner and there ought to be a united demand on the part of Muslims for its proscription. The *Sarpanch* viewed the book as a specimen of 'obscene and irresponsible writing' and its 'insult of God and His Prophet showed that its writers were not in their proper senses'. The *Sach* found the language of the stories to be 'vulgar, indecent and profane' and the contents to be 'much more filthy and profane from the moral than the religious point of view'. It goes on to make a case for the law itself to be amended if the contents of the book do not fall within the existing standards of obscenity. The *Rasti* repeated its assertion that the *Sarfaraz* was giving undue publicity to *Angarey* and its authors and proscription would be akin to 'closing the stable door after the horse is stolen'.[58]

---

[57] Native Newspapers, NAI.

[58] In the same week, that is, the week ending 4 March 1933, the Report from the Native Newspapers showed the *Haqiqat* regretting that in spite of persistent agitation the Muslims were not being appointed in adequate numbers to higher railway posts and appealed to the railway board to adopt a firm attitude. And the *Mazdoor* from Kanpur was fervently exhorting the labourers to flock under the banner of the local trade union and urging them to declare a general strike until the minimum wages were fixed. Almost all other Urdu newspapers were engrossed with the Congress session in Calcutta (which had 900 delegates from UP alone), the 'White Paper' on the forthcoming reforms that would establish 'czardom in the guise of viceroydom' as well as demands for 33 per cent reservation for Muslims in government jobs.

The report from the next week, the week ending 11 March 1933, showed the *Hamdam* inciting Muslims in the following manner: 'It is Muslims and not the authors of *Angarey* who deserve punishment as the former have become so shameless that they keep quiet for fear of the law while their Creator is insulted.'

The writer of the above report claimed he had not seen the book nor did he wish to. He was also scathing about those Muslims who 'shamelessly' appeal to the government for redress 'like women'. The *Barham* declared that since *Angarey* was offensive to *all* religions, people of all faiths should join in securing the prosecution of its authors. Meanwhile, in the same week, the intrepid *Nigar* was praising Kamal Mustafa's move to have the Azaan and Khutba as well as verses from the Quran read in Turkish instead of Arabic. Drawing a comparison, Fatehpuri derided the Indian scenario where the ulama insisted that the 'word of the maulvi occupy the position of the word of God'.[59] Incidentally, both Majid Daryabadi and Hafiz Hidayat Hussain had earlier criticized Niyaz Fatehpuri's *Nigar* which had carried sacrilegious articles.

Writing on 17 March 1933 in *Sach* in a long essay entitled 'Gandagi ka Ek Qadardan' (A Connoisseur of Filth), Majid Daryabadi began with quotes from *Angarey*:

If only my hair could be cut. The nape of my neck burns, still I cannot cut my hair.... If only I were a boy I would chop off my hair with a blunt knife, in fact cut them from the roots. If one has no nose where is the fear of having it cut? God does not give nails to a bald person. Is God too made out of sperms in a womb?

A longish extract from Ahmed Ali's *Baadal Nahin Aate* followed. Majid Daryabadi then went on to say that somehow by keeping a tight control over his feelings and praying all the while, he had managed to provide the extract, but beyond that he could not permit any young person from a good family to even glance at the book. Such was the vulgarity and obscenity of the other sentences that he did not have the courage to quote the rest. He forbore to either take the name of the book or its authors, but simply referred to it as a 'dirty book' and hoped that by the time his article appeared in print it would have been banned thanks to the efforts of Hafiz Hidayat

[59] *Angarey* was banned on 15 March 1933. Oddly enough, the report from the Native Newspapers for that week makes no mention of the ban. Instead, it talks of the lathi charge on hajis in Bombay and the proposed reforms.

Husain, member of the Legislative Council and his '*ghairat-e-imaani*'. He then went on thus:

There can be only two suitable places for this 134-page long bundle of filth: either these paper embers should be thrown into a fire or they should be taken apart page by page, trampled underfoot and thrown into a garbage heap far away from human habitation. The entire Islamic press of Hindustan has thought this book to be fit for precisely this fate. But there has been one exception and this exception has made one believe that this connoisseur of filth should be revealed to the rest of the Muslim community. This honour goes to a monthly journal. It carried a semi-laudatory, three-page review and in true western style managed to give adequate publicity to both the book and its writers. If you are surprised and want to know who can be the journal that praises filth? Can it be *Nigar*? In answer you will be saddened to hear that the journal in question is not Niyaz Fatehpuri's *Nigar* but the journal of your most national, Muslim, and educational institution, namely the journal, *Jamia*, of the Jamia Millia Islamia. *Inna lillahae* ...[60] if the reviewer, M saheb, was so troubled by pangs of friendship he could have revealed his filthy nature along with revealing his full name. But publishing this review in the same style as others in the *Jamia* can only mean that the Jamia Millia Islamia too is in agreement with the terms of the book, if not in its entirety than partly. And on top of that to announce—with no trace of shame of *jamiat*, *millat* or *islamiat* or even shying away from morality, civility and gentility—that the book can be bought at the Maktaba Jamia![61] If the seller's instinct of the Maktaba Jamia Millia Islamia has stooped to such depths [then] why should it not take up the distribution of the writings of Lekhram and Rajpal[62] and the dispensers of quack medicine? ... As God is my witness, whenever I have had to take up my pen to write against the Jamia it has caused me immense pain. Let the advocates of Jamia tell me how one can stay silent at such a time? ... Does [the Jamia] not care for the feelings of the eight crore Muslim population of India? ... While the reviewer has acknowledged

---

[60] '*Inna lillah e wa inna ilayh i rajioon*'. Roughly translated as 'We belong to Allah and to Him we return', it is usually recited at someone's death.

[61] The publishing arm of Jamia Millia Islamia, the Maktaba Jamia, stocked and distributed books by other publishers as well. In contradiction to the above report, there is a reference in Carlo Coppola's article to a letter in Ahmed Ali's possession from the 'Jamia Millia Book Depot, Delhi, dated 27 February 1933' who for fear of 'irrepairable damage' to their business had returned copies of *Angarey* 'without so much as displaying it in their shops.' Coppola, 'Angare Group', p. 62.

[62] Lekhram and Rajpal had written scurrilous books disparaging Islam and its Prophet.

the obscenity of certain sections in the book, he has also praised some parts, especially of the person who has written the bulk of the book [that is Sajjad Zaheer].... I challenge the Jamiawallahs to show me any one page which has correct language, good description, any trace of literary beauty, any moral worth.[63]

Daryabadi squarely blamed the writer of the review, the editor and assistant editor as well as the vice-chancellor of the University for this open attack on good taste.[64] The article in *Sach* carried a note at the bottom that said that soon after the journal had gone to press, news came of the banning of the book. *Alhamdullillah* (Praise Be to Allah), sighed Majid Daryabadi. Incidentally, the same Daryabadi, champion of Islam, wrote in his autobiography that in his BA admission form at the Aligarh University, under the column for 'Religion', he had written 'Rationalist'. In 1917, he wrote *Psychology of Leadership* which was published from London. From 1918 onwards, his attraction towards Islam started. Perhaps his zeal in attacking *Angarey* was the zeal of the neo-convert. However, in his condemnation of *Angarey* he used such intemperate language that the Urdu critic and humourist, Rashid Ahmed Siddiqui, felt constrained to coin a new term, 'Majidiyat', meaning 'vile abuse'.[65]

The reviewer who had earned the ire of Majid Daryabadi was none other than Muhammad Mujeeb, the historian who in later years would become the vice-chancellor of Jamia Millia Islamia. Known for his liberal, humane views, he had done the unthinkable: he had reviewed *Angarey* as one would an ordinary book, though albeit under a single initial 'M' instead of his full name. Writing in 1933 in the journal *Jamia* (vol. 20) he comments on the patchy, uneven quality of its contents using the analogy of a beautiful woman stepping out in the company of ugly ones (referring to the stories by Zaheer which shine in contrast to those of the other three

---

[63] Alvi, *Angarey ka Tareekhi Pasmanzar aur Taraqqui Pasand Tehreek*, pp. 86–7; translation mine.

[64] The fact of the matter, however, was that Daryabadi's attack on the Jamia, its journal, its vice-chancellor, and others (especially the dig about *Jamia's* tendency to ask for donations from Muslims from all over the country to keep itself afloat) actually stemmed from somewhere else; in the past *Jamia* had refused to print Daryabadi's book on the life of Mohamed Ali in toto and had stipulated certain changes.

[65] There are references to Daryabadi's prolonged jihad against *Angarey* and its writers in Siddiqui's letters. Munibur Rahman drew my attention to this coinage in the course of an interview at Aligarh.

contributors). Mujeeb had earlier helped place two of Zaheer's stories in *Jamia*. He is disparaging of the stories of the other three, calling them drab, tasteless, and vulgar.

Ale Ahmad Suroor, a student of MA at Aligarh in 1933 and the editor of the University's prestigious journal *Aligarh*, also wrote an article on the book that was at the heart of a storm. Evidently, not all Urdu writers and newspapers took the hard line. Someone wrote a letter in the daily *Star* from Allahabad on 27 February 1934, making an appeal from the literary point of view and stating religion should be kept away from literature. In response, a very stern letter appeared in the same daily. The *Payam* from Aligarh, on 5 March 1933, too urged moderation, though it did so after first upbraiding the authors for spreading sensationalism: 'The newspapers have found something handy and the factories for churning out *kufr* are working once again. From the point of view of style, I too find it objectionable. Pornography is not acceptable under any condition. This is not an indication of open-mindedness but of gratifying sexual appetite.'[66]

Having said that, *Payam* made a case against proscription:

In this respect the attitude of religious leaders is exceedingly misleading and incorrect. Condemnation, proscription, and legal action are no answer to blasphemy and atheism. How ironic that the very people who claim the right to free speech from the Government are not willing to concede the same right to their countrymen. The result of this is that fire keeps kindling unnoticed and bursts into flames when it gets a chance. If the truth is with religious leaders, why do they get flustered by one attack of heresy and blasphemy? If the religious belief of the common man is such that he gets misled by a handful of people, then the responsibility for this load of sin cannot be placed on anyone's shoulders except those of the religious leaders. The irreligious cannot be opposed with these weapons. When a man has no plausible answer to a question he gets annoyed and enraged. Such anger and rage can silence criticism for some time but the question still remains. The progress of the human mind cannot depart from the path of research. This is a futile effort.

It is hoped that the leaders of the community will try to provide satisfactory answers to the problem underlying *Angarey*....[67]

---

[66] Alvi, *Angarey ka Tareekhi Pasmanzar aur Taraqqui Pasand Tehreek*, pp. 86–7; translation mine.

[67] Mahmud, 'Angare and the Founding of the Progressive Writers' Movement', p. 449.

But by then it was already too late. Maulvis had begun to issue fatwas against the book and its authors, copies of the book were being burnt, and funds were being collected across much of upper India for the prosecution of the authors. Punishments ranging from death by stoning to hanging by the neck were suggested. The voices of moderation—few and faint as they were—went unheeded. A respectable paper such as *Payam*, while acknowledging the charge of blasphemy and heresy, also made an eloquent and urgent plea for self-introspection. Akhtar Husain Raipuri, under the pseudonym 'Naqqad' (Critic), wrote a long 15-page article on *Angarey* in the venerable magazine *Urdu*, published from Aurangabad and edited by the equally venerable Maulvi Abdul Haq (known to posterity as Baba-e-Urdu). Munshi Daya Narayan Nigam too wrote in its defence in *Zamana* from Kanpur in May 1933.

Section 295A of the IPC, under which *Angarey* was banned, stipulated

Whoever, with deliberate and malicious intention of outraging the religious feelings of any class of His Majesty's subjects, by words, either spoken or written, or by visible representations insults or attempts to insult the religion or the religious beliefs of that class, shall be punished with imprisonment of either description for a term which may extend two years, or with fine, or with both.[68]

Sufficient pressure was exerted on the government and efforts were made to convince the British that the continued availability of *Angarey* posed a serious life-and-death situation and proscription of the offending book was the only way to maintain peace. The government gave in. The Proscription Order[69] was served by the police department on 15 March 1933 stating

---

[68] Act XLV 1860, V/8/349, referred to in Shabana Mahmud, ibid.

[69] Incidentally, along with *Angarey*, some of the other proscribed works mentioned for the first quarter of 1933 by the UP government were: posters in Urdu entitled 'Paigham Janab Maulana Qadri Mohammad Ishaq saheb', 'Dictator Panjam Jamiatul Ulama', 'Zila Saharanpur'; several issues of a news-sheet in Hindi entitled 'Shankh Nad'; leaflets in Hindi entitled 'Khun chusne wale hatyare Viceroy ka bahishkar kijiye' and 'Rashtrapati Shri Rajendra Prasad ka vaktavya'; a cyclostyled Hindi magazine entitled *Bundelkhand Kesari*; two books in Hindi on Éamon de Valera; a Hindi leaflet headed 'Prantiya Congress Committee ka kisanon ko lagan ka ek paisa na do'; and a Hindi leaflet entitled 'Congress Bulletin'. IOR/L/R/7/75.

In exercise of the power conferred by Section 99A of the Code of Criminal Procedure, 1898 (Act V of 1898), the Governor in Council hereby declares to be forfeited to His Majesty every copy of a book in Urdu entitled 'Angare' written by Sayed Sajjad Zahir, Ahmed Ali, Rashid Jahan and Mahmudal Zafar, published by Sayed Sajjad Zahir, Butlerganj, Lucknow and printed by Mirza Mohammad Jawad at the Nizami Press, Victoria Street, Lucknow on the ground that the said book contains matter the publication of which is punishable under section 295A of the Indian Penal Code.[70]

The storm generated by *Angarey* had abated somewhat after its proscription, but on 21 April 1933, *Sach*, quoting a 'highly placed and most reliable source' announced that a teacher of the AMU was selling copies of the 'disgraceful book'. The University authorities, upon due investigation, however, denied any such activity according to the report. The writer of *Sach* expressed his satisfaction that the report was untrue; moreover, it noted now that the book had been banned, it would require courage to sell it. According to Khalid Alvi, the purported teacher at Aligarh could possibly have been Professor Habib, elder brother of Professor Mujeeb.[71]

Aligarh was not just an important centre of protest in the *Angarey* outcry; it was also the home of Rashid Jahan. Her father, Shaikh Abdullah was the founder of the Girls' College and this is where he lived with his wife Wahid Jahan and the rest of the family. Rashid Jahan's younger sister, Khurshid, recalls:

When *Angarey* came out, I was involved in preparing for the annual examinations and had no idea of the public reaction. There were defamatory articles written against the writers in the Muslim press every day. One day, as I was climbing the steps of the verandah after a strenuous game of badminton, a girl called out loudly to another one as I was passing by: 'Do you know, a vulgar book called *Angarey* has come out. Rashida Apa has also written in it and the Muslims have threatened to chop off her nose.' My lovely sister's face minus her nose swam before my eyes, everything blacked out for a minute, and I sank on the steps in a dead faint.[72]

---

[70] *United Provinces Gazette*, 1933, IOR/V/11/1511.

[71] I found no reference to any such controversy in a search through the records of the Sir Syed Archives in the Maulana Azad Library at Aligarh, and have, therefore, not been able to establish any proof of Alvi's assertion.

[72] Lubna Kazim (ed.), *A Woman of Substance: Memoirs of Begum Khurshid Mirza (1918–1989)* (New Delhi: Zubaan, 2005), p. 102.

Later, when Khurshid learnt that it was 'only a threat and not a fait accompli' she requested a day scholar to get her the book. 'I read *Angarey* with a group of students and sighed with relief. There was nothing vulgar in Apabi's [Khurshid's way of addressing Rashid Jahan] stories, and so I did not bother to finish the book.'[73] Her family, however, received innumerable threats from those who had not bothered to read the book, but were willing to commit murder over it. Again, we have Khurshid's testimony:

My parents had faced public threats all their lives. First when Shaikh Abdullah changed his religion from a Kashmiri Brahmin to a Muslim. Then, later, when he advocated education for Muslim women in India and alienated even Syed Ahmad Khan, whom he respected greatly. Then, providing hostel accommodation to young Muslim women became a bitter controversy, although it facilitated education for women who came from all parts of India. So, when it came to the agitation over *Angarey*, my parents were angry but unfazed by the threats.

A blackmailer by the name of Ahrari[74] decided to exploit the situation and targeted Shaikh Abdullah as the father of one of the writers of *Angarey*. All through the year 1933, he kept writing scurrilous articles in a local newspaper saying that the morals of the girls in Shaikh Saheb's school were questionable and that the daughters of Shaikh Abdullah were setting a bad example by writing 'filthy' stories. He pleaded that the Trusteeship of the Muslim Girls College be taken away from him. We later learnt he was a dismissed employee of the university. This man sent his emissaries to Papa [Shaikh Abdullah] demanding a bribe of Rs 2000 to contradict his own accusations. Of course, Papa was not going to give into coercion, and refused to pay.[75]

Rashid Jahan's father, instead, took the blackmailer to court by filing a defamation case against him in 1934. 'Ahrari lost his case and was awarded 16 months of hard labour in jail and a fine of about Rs 5,000,' records Khurshid.

We get another recollection about the '*Angarey* days' from Ismat Chughtai, the incorrigible enfant terrible of Urdu literature and one of the leading lights of the PWM. Ismat admired Rashid Jahan in particular and has acknowledged being influenced by her—both as a writer and as a person. In her autobiography, *Kaghazi Hai Pairahan* (The Clothing

---

[73] Ibid.

[74] Khurshid Jahan has the name slightly wrong. It was actually Shahid Ahrarvi.

[75] Kazim, *Woman of Substance*, p. 103.

Is Made of Paper), she reminiscences about her days as a boarder in Aligarh when she first heard of *Angarey*. She begins by marvelling how these 'smouldering crackling' embers could have been published in Urdu 'the language over which Muslims have a feudal hold', and then goes on to substantiate Khurshid Jahan's account of the uproar fuelled by Ahrarvi who 'launched an attack on the Girls' College. He brought out a paper to launch a tirade against the Abdulla family. According to him the Girls' College was a whorehouse and it should be closed down immediately. He also published obscene caricatures of Rashida apa and other writers.' Intrigued by all the fuss, Ismat writes, 'I had not read the book, but Ahrarvi made me want to read it.' Someone smuggled in a copy and the girls 'lit lanterns, hung quilts over windowpanes' and read the book overnight.[76] However, Ismat writes, 'we were faced with a dilemma. We looked hard for obscenity and filth, and couldn't find it.' But such are the pressures of respectability upon sharifzadis, she rues, that 'no one had the guts to say that *Angarey* was not obscene. A respectable girl saying that *Angarey* was not obscene would have been considered shameless.'[77] And therein, perhaps, lies a clue to the blanket condemnation of *Angarey* both in the press and in private.

But Ismat, always the rebel, chose to speak up. She wrote a long and impassioned letter challenging Ahrarvi: 'As it is Muslim girls are backward and deprived; on top of that bigots like Mullah Ahrarvi have become our enemies. By all means close down the college, but only our dead bodies will go out from here.'[78] The article, published in the *Aligarh Gazette*, appealed

---

[76] Interestingly enough, Kaifi Azmi, another founder-member of the PWM, describes encountering *Angarey* for the first time in much the same way: behind closed doors in an atmosphere of prurience and secrecy. In his version of the first encounter, the place is not a room in a girls' hostel but in a small room in the Shia seminary, the Sultanul Madaris, where his maulvi saheb lay in bed and two or three other boys sat huddled around him reading the book. The secrecy about the book, and the desire to read it despite the directives (both religious and lay) not to, added to the intrigue and drama behind *Angarey*.

[77] Sukrita Paul Kumar and Sadique (eds), *Ismat: Her Life, Her Times* (New Delhi: Katha, 2000), p. 77. A complete translation of Ismat's *Kaghazi Hai Pairahan* has since appeared; translated by M. Asaduddin, it is called *A Life in Words: Memoirs* (New Delhi: Penguin, 2012).

[78] Kumar and Sadique, *Ismat*, p. 78.

to 'our six thousand brothers, our senior professors and teachers' to not 'sit back quietly'. In her autobiography, Ismat noted with not unjustified glee that the boys of the university gave Mullah Ahrarvi such a beating that he disappeared soon afterwards. And, best of all, her beloved Rashida apa, who was fast becoming some sort of idol, praised her a lot.

The most important rejoinder to the fuss and fury over *Angarey* came from the four contributors themselves. Drafted by Mahmuduzzafar but signed by all four, a statement appeared in *The Leader* from Allahabad, dated 5 April 1933, a little over four months after the publication of the book. Entitled 'In Defence of *Angarey*: Shall We Submit to Gagging', it deserves to be quoted in full:

Some five months back four young authors, among them a young woman, brought out a collection of short stories in Urdu under the title *Angarey*. I happened to be one of the contributors to this collection. This book at once raised a storm in Moslem circles. It was said to be a shameless attack on Islam and everything decent in society. The book has already been proscribed by the U.P. Government under Section 295A of the I.P.C. It is even said that funds are being collected to start the prosecution of the authors. Shall we submit to such gagging? That is the question I wish to raise here. Coming to the contents of the book itself, the stories of my friend S. Sajjad Zaheer are concerned chiefly with the criticism and satire of the current Moslem conceptions, life and practices. His attack is directed primarily against the intolerable theological burden that is imposed from childhood upon the average Moslem in this country—a burden that leads to a contortion and cramping of the inquisitive or speculative mind and the vital vigours of body of both man and woman. Ahmed Ali essays into the realms of poverty, material, spiritual and physical, especially the poverty of the Moslem woman, and imagination and admirable boldness breaks through the veils of convention to expose the stark reality. Rashid Jahan, who is also a Doctor of Medicine drawing on her practical experience, also portrays vividly the ghastly plight of the woman behind the purdah. My own single contribution is an attack on the vanity of man which seeks to find an outlet at the expense of the weak and defenseless womanhood. Nobody can deny the truthfulness of those portraits, and anyone who chooses to exert himself can see that they are not drawn for the sake of literary 'flair', but spring from an inner indignation against 'this sorry scheme of things'. The authors of this book do not wish to make any apology for it. They leave it to float or sink of itself. They are not afraid of the consequences of having launched it. They only wish to defend 'the right of launching it and all other vessels like it' ... they stand for the right of free criticism and free expression in all matters of the highest importance to the human race in general and the Indian people in particular. They have chosen the particular field of Islam, not because they bear any 'special' malice, but because, *being born into that particular society, they felt themselves better qualified to speak for that alone. They were more sure of their ground here.* Whatever happens to the book or to the authors, we hope that others will not be discouraged. Our practical proposal is the formation immediately of a League of Progressive Authors, which should bring forth similar collections from time to time, both in English and the various vernaculars of our country. We appeal to all those who are interested in this idea to get in touch with us. They may communicate to S. Ahmed Ali, M.A., Jalal Manzil, Kucha Pandit, Delhi.[79]

Quite apart from revealing an embryonic version of the *Manifesto* that would appear fully formed a couple of years later, several things stand out in this statement: its tone of quiet vehemence; its refusal to back down; its declaration of the authors' right to freedom of expression; its utter lack of apology or regret; and most significantly its assertion of the authors' perfectly bona fide right to self-criticism. Their identification with the Muslim community is also made in clear, unequivocal terms.

Even at the worst of times, the book was not entirely without supporters. The Marxist critic and lexicographer, Akhtar Husain Raipuri, in a long review in the *Urdu* gives us another way of viewing the debacle in the press:

The crusade against this book in some quarters is no more than a species of fretful humiliation.... No doubt there are cynical references to the current concept of religion, God and social forms in the book, but it appears that the real object of the writers is to record their disapproval of the decrepit system of life in vogue amongst us. To condemn them without due consideration would serve no useful purpose. The forces working in the sub-soil and in human nature cannot be silenced by anathemas and imprecations. What is really needed is that we should study the viewpoint of the writers in a spirit of sympathy and cooperation and attempt to evolve values acceptable alike to the young and old. But if the emperor of Reaction continues to frown indignantly upon the world from his place of pride, the insurgents would end by deposing him sooner or later.[80]

In the light of the above, it is important to not allow simply the reaction of the local press to guide our impression of *Angarey* and its impact on

---

[79] Quoted in Mahmud, 'Angare and the Founding of the Progressive Writers' Movement', pp. 450–1; italics mine.

[80] Quoted in M. Sadiq, *Twentieth Century Urdu Literature* (Karachi: Royal Book Company, 1983), p. 210.

popular imagination. Eighty-one years after its publication, it is important to view *Angarey* in the right perspective and to assess its significance also in the light of the PWM. As Carlo Coppola notes, it brought together and 'solidified' a group of individuals who would shortly lay the foundations of a movement that would revolutionize Urdu literature.[81] Writing with hindsight, the literary historian, M. Sadiq observed:

Angarey [was] an act of defiance pure and simple. But it was also a sign of the times; and the rebels were successful because all those who were repelled by middle-class tyranny flocked to their banner. Some of the best journals were on their side; and, for once, in spite of all their alarums and excursions the custodians of public morality had to acknowledge defeat. The book was banned, but the moral victory lay with the rebels.[82]

Urdu critic and a pillar of the progressive movement in recent times, Qamar Rais too valued the book because it demolished the existing feudal values, but more importantly 'in its mirror the realities of the times to come could see their face. After Premchand, in the new field that opened up in the Urdu short story, the new trends that began to become discernible, *Angarey* can be called the forerunner, nay the *sar chashm*.'[83]

What the *Angarey* Quartet Did Thereafter

Marx wrote in the *Theses on Feurbach*, 'Philosophers have only interpreted the world in various ways; the point, however, is to *change it*'. The *Angarey* quartet set out to change the world not only through their writings, but also through everything else they undertook in life. We shall examine their literary careers in due course; let us first see what they did in the immediate aftermath of what was, evidently, a defining moment of their life.

Writing in *Roshnai* many years after the dust had settled, Zaheer noted, 'Probably alarmed by the furor, Ahmed Ali had adopted a practically reclusive lifestyle for two years or so'.[84] This is refuted by Ahmed Ali who claimed that it was not him but Zaheer who disappeared from the scene till the dust settled down:

---

[81] Coppola, 'Angare Group', p. 63.
[82] Sadiq, *Twentieth Century Urdu Literature*, p. 209.
[83] Jafri, *Guftagu*, p. 47.
[84] Zaheer, *Light*, p. 6.

The publication of *Angarey* in December 1932 was followed by an all-India agitation against the book and its authors ... by reactionary parochial forces. As a result Sajjad Zaheer disappeared from the scene, and took up residence in London as early as February or March 1933. On 5th April we published our 'Defence of *Angarey*' statement announcing the formation of the League of Progressive Authors, which was renamed in 1936 'All India Progressive Writers Association'. Our statement was, thus, the first manifesto, as *Angarey* was its first manifestation.[85]

One of Majid Daryabadi's diatribes against *Angarey* also referred to Zaheer being abroad.[86] As does Carlo Coppola, according to whom Zaheer 'had left the country, ostensibly for a cure of his tuberculosis in Switzerland before proceeding to London for his law studies'.[87] It is also possible that his influential and wealthy family packed him off post haste to avoid further mishaps.

Mahmuduzzafar had very little to do with Urdu literature after *Angarey*. He wrote one play *Amir ka Mahal*, which was possibly his last piece of writing in Urdu.[88] In 1934, he married Rashid Jahan and moved to Amritsar where he taught history and English as vice principal of the M.A.O. College from 1934–7. Afterwards, he became a full-time worker for the CPI, editing the Urdu edition of the CPI's journal *Chingari* (Sparks) from late 1938. In 1948, he became general secretary of the CPI in UP and was thereafter forced to go underground when the party was banned. His major work is

---

[85] Ahmed Ali in the 'Afterword' to his *The Prison-house*, p. 164, an English translation of his stories published in 1986, referred to in 'Professor Ahmed Ali and the Progressive Writers' Movement' by Zeno, *Annual of Urdu Studies*, vol. 9, pp. 39–43.

[86] *Sach*, 24 February 1933.

[87] Coppola, 'Angare Group', p. 62. Coppola goes on to say that 'According to Ahmed Ali, he [Zaheer] had secured a promise of marriage from Rashid Jahan and left her in the care of his friend Mahmuduzzafar. A relationship developed, and they got married in 1934.' Zaheer, in his interview for NMML's Oral History Project, claimed to have spent close to a year in a sanatorium in Switzerland shortly upon arrival in England to pursue his BA; this was before *Angarey*.

[88] Reference found in Khalilur Rahman Azmi, *Urdu mein Taraqqui Pasand Adabi Tehreek* (Aligarh: Educational Book House, 2002 [1957]), p. 181. And in Sudhi Pradhan (ed.), *Marxist Cultural Movements in India (1936–1947)*, vol. I (Calcutta: National Book Agency, 1979), where the play is referred to by its English title.

the travelogue *A Quest for Life* (1954),[89] in which he describes his travels in Russia where he had gone with Rashid Jahan, who was at the time terminally ill with cancer. Rashid Jahan died on 29 July 1953, three weeks after their arrival in Moscow; Mahmuduzzafar stayed on and travelled throughout the Soviet Union and recorded his impressions. We will look more closely at his activities in the context of the PWM in subsequent chapters. Here, a short quote from the reminiscences of Dr Sarwat Rehman,[90] his neighbour in Dehradun, captures the aura of this most unusual young man who had come back home in 1931 after spending 14 long years studying in England: 'The accomplished young man, product of an aristocratic and almost purely occidental education, came back with revolutionary ideas of social change. How much his idealism, his artistic gifts, his youthful good looks and distinguished Oxford accent must have appealed to his numerous girl cousins and other ladies of his generation!'[91]

Mahmud, who had studied economics and history at Balliol College, Oxford, was also a keen painter. In fact *A Quest for Life* carried some fine

---

[89] Published by PPH in 1954, this is an unabashed, almost naive, account of the author's complete adoration of all things Soviet. For a well-travelled man, Mahmud's unquestioning and childlike admiration for the land and its people is a trifle over the top. He gushes over 'Moscow, the city of our dreams!' its wide roads, modern architecture, and energetic people. In the course of his five-month stay, he travelled to Georgia, the Black Sea, Stalingrad, and Uzbekistan; visited institutions, theatres, art galleries, etc., in Moscow; and attended the XIX Congress of the Communist Party of the Soviet Union (Bolsheviks) where he met several leading figures from the worldwide communist movement.

[90] I went to Dehradun to interview Sarwat Rehman on 24–25 March 2010. She is a sprightly 87-year-old living an intellectually and socially charged life and has a fund of memories about Rashid Jahan and Mahmuduzzafar who were older than her, but since her family home, 'Shameem', was close to Mahmud's house, called 'Nasreen' (which has since been bought by the Welham Girls' School), she had several occasions to meet them. Dr Sarwat Rehman's reminiscences will crop up again in this book.

[91] Lola Chatterji (ed.), *Autobiography: Hamida Saiduzzafar (1921–1988)* (New Delhi: Trianka, 1996), p. 61. Hamida Saiduzzafar, an opthalmologist of some repute, worked at the Gandhi Eye Hospital at Aligarh. Her autobiography also has reminiscences from her contemporaries and friends; some of them are useful for the purpose here because they throw valuable light on the personal and professional lives of Mahmuduzzafar and his wife Rashid Jahan.

drawings causing his sister, Dr Hamida Saiduzzafar, in her *Autobiography*, to lament how Mahmud had neglected his painting and could have been a fine painter had he chosen art as his calling: 'He had a great talent for sketching.... Sad to say, Mahmud neglected this gift of his, and later in life devoted his time and energy to politics rather than drawing, painting and sculpture where his real talent lay.'[92]

Hamida Saiduzzafar remembers her much older brother being full of nationalist ideas after he returned to India in 1931. Despite a severely English education, upon his return, Mahmud 'wore a Gandhi cap, wanted to wear *khadi* clothes, and tried hard to speak Urdu (or Hindi) rather than English'. He also gave his sister, then barely 10 years old, Gorky's *Twenty-Six Men and a Girl* much to the chagrin of her snooty governess (who was 'of French descent' and disapproved of Mahmud's 'progressive' ways).[93] Sarwat Rehman remembers Mahmud coming to their home to learn to read and write Urdu from her mother. Zaheer too noted Mahmud's great desire to learn Urdu and how whenever the rest of them 'quoted Persian or Urdu poetry, or discussed a subtle literary point of our own language, an expression of sadness would suffuse his face'; Zaheer goes on:

Mahmud was always troubled by the fact that he was not proficient in his mother tongue. He used to write poetry in English and sometimes even wrote short stories and literary essays, but he was well aware that no matter how hard we try, we can never produce a major creative work in a language that is not our own.

Mahmud was not just literary; his English upbringing and his study of philosophy, logic, and economics had endowed him with the ability to work untiringly and systematically.[94]

Eventually, Mahmud chose to devote himself wholeheartedly to the CPI, and 'putting his ideas into practice distributed his lands and inherited villages to the peasants and reduced himself to the status of an ordinary worker of the Communist Party'.[95] Elsewhere, in Hamida's *Autobiography*,

---

[92] Chatterji, *Autobiography*, p. 18.

[93] Mahmud's cousin, Hajra Begum, who later married Dr Z.A. Ahmed, in an interview with the NMML's Oral History Project revealed how she was attracted towards communism by Mahmud and other relatives. They gave her Bernard Shaw's *The Intelligent Woman's Guide to Socialism and Capitalism*.

[94] Zaheer, *Light*, p. 14.

[95] Ibid., p. 62.

one of her contemporaries, Dr Ranjana Sidhanta Ash, remembers Mahmud as 'the most polished and charming communist who would come round on his cycle to the [Lucknow] university intelligentsia selling "progressive literature". *I hope that genre of writing still finds its way to school-girls from the middle classes growing up in a world that rigidly silences Marxism.*'[96]

Dr Ash remembers Mahmud as being 'not merely the bearer of Marx and Lenin, Gorky and the Gollancz Left-book Club orange volumes',[97] but also as the husband of Dr Rashid Jahan and how the two 'charming and charismatic people', a 'wondrous couple', were her 'idols'.

Others too have commented on Mahmud and Rashida (as Rashid Jahan was popularly called) being an 'ideal couple'. She was untidy and unmethodical, whereas her husband was orderly and organized; yet the two were firm friends who appreciated the good and selfless qualities of the other. Zaheer wrote:

The union of Rashid Jahan and Mahmud was really a meeting of opposites. Rashida hated orderliness. It used to astonish her friends and acquaintances that she was such a good doctor, and they could not understand why she was so popular with her patients. Losing and misplacing her belongings was a daily occurrence with her, while Mahmud never forgot anything. He remembered not only his own but also his friends' responsibilities and plans for work ... he would always smoothen out the confusion spread by Rashid Jahan. Yet the golden chain of love that tied them together was a sight worth seeing. Both seemed to have substituted the care of humanity for their own selves. A serene domestic life was not in their stars. For Mahmud, the future held imprisonment, hard labour, and anxiety related to his work for the homeland. For Rashida it held long periods of solitude, financial problems, and physical stress. But ... whenever one went to their house one felt that it was suffused with happiness—the kind of happiness that springs like a clear pool of water from the meeting and harmony of

---

[96] Chatterji, *Autobiography*, p. 36; italics mine.

[97] Ghulam Rabbani Taban records a similar memory of how in the 1930s, when he was studying at St. Johns' College in Agra, the CPI had been banned, but some party workers established contacts with students. They brought books with them and set up a Secret Study Circle. Taban notes that the 'psychology of an enslaved people' is such that he and his fellow students 'enjoyed the thrill of doing something illegal' by 'flouting the regulations of the enslavers'. Reference found in article entitled 'Some Thoughts on Soviet Russia', Ghulam Rabbani Taban Papers, NMML, 1957–99, pp. 446, 78.

two hearts and minds. It was a happiness that enlivened sad spirits, and brought lushness and music into their life.[98]

While Mahmud's career as an activist and party worker is of interest to us in the context of the PWM, Rashid Jahan's mercurial, charismatic persona and her brief but volatile literary career deserves to be the subject of a separate, book-length study. After *Angarey*, she published *Aurat wa Digar Drame wa Afsane* (Woman and Other Stories and Plays); a collection of short stories came out after her death at the untimely age of 47 in 1953 and was called *Shola-e-Jawwala* (Sparks of a Volcano).[99] Writing about her sister, Khurshid Jahan says forthrightly enough that

Dr Rashid Jahan was better known as a progressive writer than as a medical practitioner. The writer's group that she was a part of, comprising Mahmuduz Zafar, Sajjad Zaheer, and Prof. Ahmed Ali, wrote against social conventions and the false interpretation of religion that had become the monopoly of a particular class of Muslim scholars. These precocious young intellectuals brought about a cultural as well as an artistic revolution in Muslim society because of their ability to see things clearly. They wrote stories without mincing their words and meanings, choosing sensitive topics that were not discussed.... Their unique and bold style of writing and vocabulary gave a new impetus and vitality to Urdu literature. Rashid Jahan's writing was appreciated in literary circles for being energetic and lively, and for the introduction of colloquial speech into the narrative that made it immediately accessible to the reader, breaking with the conservative and formal mode of earlier writing. Later, Ismat [Chughtai] perfected this style in her literary works.[100]

The third and most proactive person in the quartet of *Angarey*, Zaheer, did several very remarkable things soon after the book's appearance: almost immediately upon arrival back in England, he collected a group of likeminded Indians in England who helped him draft a manifesto; returning to India, he helped organize the first PWA in Lucknow; became its chief secretary, set up the first Marxist journal in Urdu called *Chingari* (with the help of Sohan Singh Josh in Saharanpur), wrote a novel called *London*

---

[98] Zaheer, *Light*, p. 14.
[99] I am grateful to Professor Aulad Ahmad Siddiqui for giving me his copy of this out-of-print book.
[100] Kazim, *Woman of Substance*, p. 100.

ki Ek Raat (1935), *Nuqush-e-Zindan* (Impressions of Prison), a collection of letters to his wife from the prisons of Lucknow and Allahabad (1944), *Zikr-e-Hafiz* (Some Thoughts on Hafiz), a critical look at the works of the legendary Persian poet Hafiz (1958), and a collection of poems in vers libre called *Pighalata Neelam* (Melting Sapphire, 1964), but remained, primarily, an organizer and party worker. Called 'Banne Bhai', he was at the heart of a group of devoted party workers, some of whom, till this day, can brook no criticism of his 'dominance' in the PWA.[101]

Ahmed Ali was the only one of the *Angarey* group who had what can safely be called a vast and varied literary oeuvre. Yet, it is his linkage with the PWM that will merit some scrutiny in later chapters. In word and print, Ahmed Ali maintained that he remained a part of the movement; yet it is widely believed that he was the first to drift away. In later years, he—unlike Zaheer who seldom mentioned *Angarey* or downplayed its publication— constantly referred to the book as the precursor to the formal movement, going so far as to state that 'The most earth shattering utterances of the Movement are to be found in *Angare*, which, in spite of it adolescence and immaturity, exposed discredited doctrines and dogmas which no one had dared attack, and set into motion a whole chain of actions and reactions'.[102]

---

[101] In response to my question regarding Zaheer's domination being one of the causes of the decline of the PWA, Raza Imam was quick to correct me thus:

Contrary to what your question implies, Sajjad Zaheer always played a very constructive and positive role in guiding the PWM. While he was critical of the writers who wallowed in self-pity and psychological squalor for its own sake and of those who considered the description or mention of the living conditions of the toiling masses as something non-literary, he was equally critical of those progressive writers who rejected literary heritage and laid too much emphasis on political correctness. His book *Zikre-e-Hafiz* and critical essays emphasize the need to value the literary tradition and uphold the literary values. He was also not averse to experimentation. *Angarey, London ki ek Raat*, and *Pighalata Neelam* are all innovative in style and content. *Pighalata Neelam* has even a number of prose-poems which are quite symbolic—something that the puritans among the progressive writers would have frowned at. As a matter of fact, if the PWM has survived today, it is mostly due to the efforts of Sajjad Zaheer after his return from Pakistan.

I found a near-similar reaction from Arif Naqvi who is willing to look critically at almost all aspects of the PWA, but will not brook the slightest criticism of 'Banne Bhai'. Arif Naqvi lives in Berlin, but I was able to have extended interviews with him in the course of his recent visits to Delhi.

[102] Ali, 'Progressive Writers' Movement and Creative Writers in Urdu', p. 40.

To conclude, let us look briefly at the 'other' side of the coin. While there is no denying its impact on Urdu literature, let us ask whether *Angarey* did lasting good or damage to Urdu literature? While no one denies that *Angarey* was a ground-breaking piece of work, its contribution as a piece of literature is up for scrutiny. Equally, its place in the canon of progressive literature needs to be understood. In the absence of any significant body of critical writings—either on *Angarey* or on the early history of the PWA—one falls back on Zaheer's *Roshnai* (published in 1956 in Pakistan and in 1959 in India). Written while Zaheer was imprisoned in Pakistan, it strongly reflects the author's commitment to Marxism. However, all we have by way of documentary evidence is his word and his perspective has been largely unchallenged. A dissenting viewpoint was offered by the only member of the *Angarey* quartet blessed by longevity—Ahmed Ali—in an interview published in the *Journal of South Asian Literature* in 1995 as well as in an article in Carlo Coppola's edited volume entitled *Marxist Influence in South Asia*. It would be illustrative to juxtapose the two opposing perspectives regarding these early years of the PWM and also look at the infighting and disagreements that occurred shortly after the first meeting of the AIPWA at Lucknow, and the eventual acrimonious parting of the ways of these two once-close friends. However, these are small albeit interesting details and one must not be guilty of missing the woods for the trees.

In hindsight, most critics agree that *Angarey* was a phenomenon that was waiting to happen. Looking back at the time in which it was written, M. Sadiq writes, 'And now who should appear on the scene, but a most intrepid band of heroes and heroines who boldly walked up to the dragon and trod on its tail with such malicious joy that it rose in all its fury, spitting fire and brimstone, to scorch them to death'.[103]

This intrepid band were not scorched to death; some of them lay low for a while, others went away to recoup their losses, but eventually they regrouped to launch a fresh assault on the citadel of literary morality. Showing the interconnection between literature and morality, *Angarey* questioned, for the first time, what was acceptable and what was not in purely literary terms. Someone who described himself as 'A Friend' while writing a memorial tribute to Rashid Jahan, drew a correlation between the severity of the attack by the detractors of *Angarey* and its impact: 'The intensity of the scandal ... was a measure of the fact that

---

[103] Sadiq, *Twentieth Century Urdu Literature*, p. 209.

the protest had struck deep in the layers of the congealed hearts of the feudal order.'[104]

Others took the opposite view and felt that the lack of moderation did more harm than good. The 'absence of circumspection and unprincipled extremism'[105] was an essentially destructive object and nothing constructive could come out of it. Aziz Ahmad goes so far as to assert that the PWM could have gone further than it did were it not for the grievous body blow inflicted upon it by *Angarey* during its infancy. He believed that many writers chose to stay away from any formal association with the movement precisely because they did not wish to be tarred with the same brush as the *Angarey* group. Taken in the balance, both groups—those who run down *Angarey* for its lack of literary merit and its unprincipled attacks on religion and morality as well as those who agree that despite its literary merits it paved the way for a new sort of writing—can marshal enough arguments to prove their respective cases. The presence of a still inconclusive verdict is illustrative of an ongoing debate on intellectual and emotional landmarks in the history of Urdu literature. There will always be the traditionalist versus the modernist point of view just as there will always be those who pour scorn on existing morality and others who uphold prevalent moral and religious doctrines.

The question we must ask at this point is: did the publication of *Angarey*, which was nothing short of a rebellion against existing literary norms, amount to anything substantial or was it just a flash in the pan, no more than 'a brave and adolescent book'?[106] Was it a tossing of hats at the windmills of convention and little more than youthful fervour and nonchalance on the part of writers largely unmindful of the consequences of their actions? We hope to explore these questions in subsequent chapters.

---

[104] *Indian Literature*, vol. 1 (Bombay, 1952), p. 1. The 'Friend' could possibly have been Jafri, the editor of *Indian Literature*.

[105] Aziz Ahmad, *Tarraqui Pasand Adab* (Delhi: Khwaja Press, 1945), p. 44.

[106] Ali, 'Progressive Writers' Movement and Creative Writers in Urdu', p. 35.

5

Setting up the All-India Progressive Writers' Association

Hum akele hi chale they janib-e-manzil magar
Log saath aate gaye aur karvaan banta gaya
(We had set off towards our destination on our own
But others joined us and a caravan was formed)
—Majrooh Sultanpuri (1919–2000)

To begin with, we shall look at the circumstances that lead to the drawing up of the Progressive Writers' *Manifesto* in London in the winter of 1934. The next section shall look at the interim period—the middle of 1935 when Zaheer returned to India with the document and circulated it among prominent Indian literary figures—as well as the underground activities of the CPI which had been banned since 1934 and the nation-wide signature campaign launched by Zaheer to draw support for the setting up of an AIPWA across the spectrum of India's literary fraternity. The *Manifesto* found an immediate champion in Premchand, one of the most respected figures in Hindustani literature, who published its Hindi translation in the October 1935 issue of his journal *Hans* (Swan). Subsequently, its English version was published in the February 1936 issue of the *Left Review* in London. Though it is said that Premchand 'watered down' the Hindi version (we shall see, among other sources, Carlo Coppola for a study of the differences between the Hindi and Urdu translations of the *Manifesto*), the Hindi and Urdu writers set aside their differences over the Hindi–Urdu debate and found common cause in the setting up of AIPWA.

The years 1934–6 deserve close scrutiny because they show how a movement came to be formed, who guided its formation and laid down its definition, and who, in the years to come, exercised control over its growth. The last section of this chapter will look at the first All-India Progressive Writers' Conference in Lucknow on 10 April 1936, detailing the efforts of Sajjad Zaheer, Rashid Jahan, Mahmuduzzafar, and Ahmed Ali, among others in this seminal gathering, along with abstracts from Premchand's inaugural address as well as the presentations of several others. It will conclude with a brief political overview of the late 1930s, outlining some of the key incidents that stand out as milestones in the history of the PWM, a movement that, as we shall see, was next in importance only to the Aligarh movement in the history of the Indian Muslims. Here, as elsewhere in this book, I have deliberately cast the net wide to include social, political, economic factors because the PWM was not merely a literary movement, but, in its broadest, truest sense, also a social and political one. Therefore, a history of the PWM cannot be merely a literary history drawn exclusively from literary sources.

Drawing up the *Manifesto* in London

In the immediate aftermath of the controversy over *Angarey*, far from being cowed down, its authors published an eloquent defence in *The Leader* dated 5 April 1933, stating: 'Our practical proposal is the formation immediately of a League of Progressive Authors, which should bring forth similar collections from time to time, both in English and the various vernaculars of our country. We appeal to all those who are interested in this idea to get in touch with us.'[1] This was borne out by Ahmed Ali, writing years later: 'On 5th April we published our "Defence of *Angarey*" statement announcing the formation of the League of Progressive Authors, which was renamed in

---

[1] Quoted in Shabana Mahmud, 'Angare and the Founding of the Progressive Writers' Association', vol. 30, no. 2 (May 1996), pp. 450–1.

1936 "All India Progressive Writers Association". Our statement was, thus, the first manifesto, as *Angarey* was its first manifestation.'[2]

Ahmed Ali also maintained that the movement was 'really born in enthusiastic discussions preceding and followed by the publication of *Angarey*, that brave, adolescent book' and that *Angarey* 'grew into the Progressive Movement'.[3]

We have also seen in the previous chapter that Sajjad Zaheer went back to England as early as February or March 1933 after the storm broke over *Angarey*. Almost 29 years old, with one BA degree from the University of Lucknow (1924) and another from Oxford (1931), he was sent back by his father ostensibly to study law. While Zaheer took to London like a duck to water and found himself in the thick of the Indian student community, he harboured few illusions either about a career as a barrister or serving His Majesty's government like his father and brothers. In his *Yaadein*, he writes how *Angarey* had made him famous among the literary community towards which he naturally gravitated rather than the company of budding lawyers:

The fame of *The Embers* had reached the Indians in London. I was happy that my first literary effort had shocked the old, bearded fogeys. I was glad that the *Urdu* of Dr Abdul Haq praised my stories, though I had no illusions about my literary abilities. In this literary tumult, I began my novel *A Night in London* (*London Ki Ek Raat*) to save my conscience.[4]

---

[2] Ahmed Ali, 'Afterword', *The Prison-house*, p. 164, referred to in Zeno, 'Professor Ahmed Ali and the Progressive Writers' Movement', *Annual of Urdu Studies*, vol. 9, pp. 39–43.

[3] Ahmed Ali, 'The Progressive Writers' Movement and Creative Writers in Urdu', in Carlo Coppola (ed.), *Marxist Influences and South Asian Literature* (East Lansing: Michigan State University, 1974), p. 35.

[4] Sajjad Zaheer, *Yaadein*, translated from the Urdu by Khalique Naqvi, in Sudhi Pradhan (ed.), *Marxist Cultural Movements in India: Chronicles and Documents (1936–47)*, vol. I (Calcutta: National Book Agency, 1979), p. 39. *Yaadein* was written when Zaheer was in the Deoli detention camp in 1940, and first published in *Naya Adab*, the journal edited by Ali Sardar Jafri from Bombay, in the January–February issue of 1941. *Yaadein*, together with *Roshnai* (published in Pakistan in 1956 and in India in 1959), provides a valuable history of the early years of the PWM. That some parts of *Roshnai* are contested by others, notably, Ahmed Ali,

And so while he entered the Lincoln's Inn in 1935, he was in constant touch with the Indian student community in London. He also began writing *London ki Ek Raat*, a rambling story of several young Indians, men and women like him who have crossed the seas in search of a better education that will make them doctors, lawyers, or teachers.[5] In the process, they encounter prejudices and humiliations in the imperialist metropolis, but also meet good, upright working-class people who meet and interact with them without the 'baggage' of culture or race. The novella portrays nearly all the stereotypes associated with overseas students: bashful Azam in love with blonde Jane who keeps him on tenterhooks; stolid working-class Jim and Tom who meet Azam and his belligerent friend Rao in a workers' pub; Naim who loves Sheila who loves Hiren; the foppish Arif who is preparing for the Indian Civil Services and dresses like a dandy in a 8–10 guinea suit and the bird-like Karima in her pink brocade sari; and Khan who gets drunk and picks a fight with Singh. Then, there are irascible landladies who break up rowdy drunken parties in shabby students' digs, long conversations besides crackling fires and inside pubs, and the general gloom of a winter's night in London. The young people discuss the new film by the French actor Maurice Chevalier, listen to gramophone records, and dance the rumba. It is easy to get riled by these superficialities and dismiss the novella as a simple, even banal, piece of writing. While it has none of the vim and vigour of the *Angarey* pieces, it does occasionally make some sharp observations about Indians vis-à-vis their colonial masters. For instance, English newspaper headlines that scream 'Ten English soldiers stop ten thousand natives from rioting; One white injured and 15 natives killed' evoke anger and scorn among nationalistic students. 'Just think,' one of them tells the other, 'less than a lakh English are happily ruling over 35 crore people.' Elsewhere, there is derision for the so-called well-wishers of the country—those who spin the charkha (like Gandhi), set out in search of the Truth, aspire to become ministers or members of councils, participate in conferences on untouchability or social reform, look for government jobs, or join the Hindu Mahasabha or the Muslim League—all

---

will be discussed in Chapter 8. It must be noted that *Roshnai* was written when Zaheer was incarcerated in Pakistani jails and had no access to notes or reference materials; its Afterword says: 'Central Jail, Much, Baluchistan, 17 January 1954'.

[5] What follows is a synopsis of the novella culled from Noor Zaheer (ed.), *Sajjad Zaheer: Pratinidhi Rachnain* (Shahadra: Medha Books, 2006).

supposedly to 'serve' the country. All along, there is also the awareness that the colonizers have their own problems to deal with; jobless workers take out processions in Hyde Park and the labour unions are up in arms.

Much of the 'action' during that one night in *London ki Ek Raat* happens in and around Bloomsbury, a London neighbourhood made famous by the Bloomsbury Group[6] of writers whom Zaheer admired and who were, partly, the inspiration for the readers' group he hoped to start as a precursor to the PWA. Like the Bloomsbury Group, Zaheer and his friends were fiercely anti-imperialist and anti-fascist (however, unlike them, there is no evidence of the progressives being at all sexually permissive).

The early 1930s had seen the rise of Hitler and the strengthening of fascist forces in many European countries. On 27 February 1933, the Nazis conspired to set fire to the Reichstag, the German Parliament in Berlin, and falsely accused the communist leaders of doing so. With civil liberties suspended, the government instituted mass arrests of communists, including all communist parliamentary delegates. With them gone and their seats empty, the Nazis swept through the elections and thus allowed Hitler to consolidate his power. A popular leader of the communist party of Bulgaria,

---

[6] The Bloomsbury Group was a group of writers, intellectuals, and artists who held informal discussions among themselves during the first half of the twentieth century. This collective of friends and relatives (many were related to each other by marriage) lived and worked near Bloomsbury. Its best-known members were Virginia Woolf, John Maynard Keynes, E.M. Forster, and Lytton Strachey, though at different times Duncan Grant, Vanessa Bell, Clive Bell, Leonard Woolf, and Roger Fry were also associated with it. Their work deeply influenced literature, aesthetics, criticism, and economics, as well as modern attitudes towards feminism, pacifism, and sexuality. The group did not hold formal or informal discussions on particular topics, but talked about a range of topics and their views influenced the cultural scene. Much work on Bloomsbury continues to focus on the group's class origins and alleged elitism, their satire, atheism, oppositional politics, and liberal economics, their non-abstract art, their modernist fiction and literary criticism, and their non-nuclear, non-traditional family, and sexual habits and personal 'arrangements'. During the Second World War, they became conscientious objectors which of course added to the Group's controversies. Politically, the members of Bloomsbury were divided between liberalism and socialism—as can be seen in the respective careers and writings of Maynard Keynes and Leonard Woolf. But they were united in their opposition to the government that involved them in the war and later in what they deemed an impermanent peace.

Georgi Dimitrov, was in the eye of the fascist-generated storm. The case of Dimitrov and his valiant fight to prove his innocence caught the imagination of the world in what came to be known as the Leipzig Trial. The unrest spilling out from Hitler's Germany spooled all over Europe as men like Albert Einstein and Thomas Mann were hounded out of their own country. Scores of German scientists, intellectuals, artists, musicians—many forced into exile by the Nazis—helped raise the banner of protest and fuel a rising anti-fascist movement. These refugees—to France, England, and America—carried with them terrible stories of tortures and repressions. It was in this Europe, awakening to the power, as yet not fully tested, of the people, that Zaheer returned ostensibly to complete his education, but actually to discover the enormous power of the pen to rouse the people. For him, one world was coming to an end: the world of carefree student days and naïve idealism; the other, more brutal and complex, was waiting to draw him and his comrades fully into its tumult and misery. He wrote:

We were gradually drifting towards socialism. Our minds searched for a philosophy which would help us to understand and solve the difficult social problems. We were not satisfied with the idea that humanity had always been miserable and would always remain so. We read Marx and other socialist writers with great enthusiasm. As we proceeded with our studies, solved the historical, social and philosophical problems through mutual discussions, our minds became clear and our hearts contented. After the end of our university education this was the beginning of a new and unlimited field of education.

Most of the members of our small group wanted to become writers. What else could they do? We were incapable of manual labour. We had not learnt any craft and our mind revolted against serving the imperialist government. What other field was left?[7]

The group of young Indian students included M.D. Taseer, Mulk Raj Anand, Jyotirmoy Ghosh, and Promod Sengupta.[8] Of these, Mulk Raj

---

[7] Sajjad Zaheer, 'Reminiscences', in *Marxist Cultural Movements in India: Chronicles and Documents (1936–47)* (Calcutta: National Book Agency, 1979), pp. 36–7.

[8] M.D. Taseer became the principal of the M.A.O. College at Amritsar and walked a short distance with the progressives before parting ways; Jyotirmoy Ghosh, born in Ghasiara, Bengal, was educated at the universities of Calcutta and Edinburgh, retired as the principal of Presidency College, Calcutta, and wrote several books in Bangla and English; Promod Sengupta stayed on in Europe till 1946 and was the secretary of the London PWA.

Anand (1905–2004) was shortly going to make a name for himself with *The Untouchable* (1935) followed by *The Coolie* (1936); he too, like the others, had socialist leanings. *The Untouchable* is a story based on the life of the most downtrodden, despised, and oppressed section of Indian society, the outcastes—those at the bottom of the caste hierarchy. This story is based on a single day in the life of Bakha, a latrine cleaner and sweeper boy. The readers follow him on his daily chore of cleaning up the shit of the rich and powerful, who despise him. When he walks down the streets he has to signal an alarm with his voice as he approaches so that the 'pure' are forewarned to avoid even allowing his shadow to be cast upon them. On one occasion, he does 'pollute' a caste Hindu and is chased, abused, and attacked all day long for this defilement. With a Preface by E.M. Forster, the book was well-received, and Anand became the toast of literary circles in London. While not a communist at any point in his life, Anand's politics as well as his writings expressed a keen desire for social transformation and political change.

Zaheer's own radicalization—which had begun during his student days in the politically active Lucknow University—had intensified when he joined the Indian Students Cell of the CPGB during his undergraduate days at Oxford.[9] The noted British Marxist historian, Victor G. Kiernan (1913–2009), who entered Cambridge in 1931, commented on the large numbers of Indian students (over a 100 in Cambridge itself!) and the 'growing body of communists' among young people: 'In Britain Marxism was having a modest growth in the 1930s and interest in India was kindling at the universities, especially in London, Oxford and Cambridge where Indian students were most numerous, all of them nationalists, and some turning towards socialism.'[10]

Jyoti Basu (1914–2010), the veteran communist leader who, like many other young men born into well-to-do middle-class families, went to England in 1935 to study law and take the Indian Civil Service exam, and became instead the first editor of the London Majlis[11] and was inexorably drawn towards communism. Basu wrote:

[9] In an interview with Hari Dev Sharma for NMML's Oral History Project, Zaheer claimed to have joined the CPGB in 1930.

[10] V.G. Kiernan, 'The Communist Party of India and the Second World War', in Prakash Karat (ed.), *Across Time and Continents* (New Delhi: LeftWord Books, 2003), p. 209.

[11] Like the India League, this too was a community of overseas Indian students. Basu wrote in his memoirs *Jatadur Mone Pore* (Memories: The Ones That

Politics was a hot topic of discussion at all the Universities in England. Professor Harold Laski was drawing huge crowds with his anti-fascist lectures. I had also become one with the progressive forces. I was reading a lot on Fascism. We Indian students were at the same time trying to generate public opinion on the movement back home.... We met Britain's top communist leaders Harry Polit [sic], Rajani Palme Dutt, Ben Bradley[12] and others. The British communist leadership actively helped the India League and the Indian Students.[13]

Zaheer recaptured the mood of the mid-1930s in England, a mood that contributed to the formation of the PWA in London, when he observed:

I was staying in London to study which was now something of very little importance. Before my eyes was the panorama of Europe in particular and the world in general that was changing daily. It was the picture of a world dying and a new world being born. It was not because I was a young man of any exceptional understanding or that my heart was moved by the vision of an unhappy world. A large

---

Have Lasted, translated by Abhijit Dasgupta), serialized in www.ganashakti.com from 16 November 1998 to October 1999: 'My job was to create public opinion for India's cause and collect subscriptions.'

[12] Harry Pollitt (1890–1960) was the head of the trade union department of the CPGB, a charismatic orator and activist, and the general secretary of the party for more than 20 years. He worked with Indian communists like Shapurji Saklatvala and Rajani Palme Dutt (1896–1974). The latter, best known as R. Palme Dutt, was a leading journalist and theoretician in the CPGB. Dutt also played an important role for the Comintern by supervising the CPI for some years Together with Ben Bradley (1898–1957) he wrote 'The Anti-Imperialist People's Front in India', popularly known as the Dutt–Bradley thesis, which was published in *Inprecor* on 29 February 1936. Bradley, an accused in the Meerut Conspiracy Case, had spent some time in Indian jails. Saklatvala wanted to have no truck with the British and was militantly anti-imperialist. 'India does not want to come to the Round Table Conference as she has nothing to do with Parliament, excepting for a peace treaty on an independent basis.' On the same occasion, a certain Begum Mit (Meenakshi) Faruki, BA, while condemning the repressive laws and police severity, observed: 'The same minded people in India still want to be within the British Empire, but not as an inferior nation—as a Dominion or absolute equality with other Dominions in the British Empire.' All references are from IOR/L/PJ/12/405.

[13] Basu, *Jatadur Mone Pore*.

number of educated young men and women were thinking on similar lines. It was the logical reaction of the stresses of the times.[14]

It would not be inappropriate here to mention the influence of British socialism on the young Indians who went to study at British universities. That this influence was far more pronounced than that of the exiled Central European intellectuals—those who had seen at first hand the servitude of the totalitarian state and therefore advocated libertarianism and free enterprise—meant that the founders of the future free India showed a marked tendency towards socialism and state control in the early days of the republic. This perhaps explains the enormous influence of men like Harold Laski[15] on an entire generation of Indians who had been educated abroad, prompting a wag to comment, in the 1950s, that 'in every meeting of the Indian Cabinet there is a chair reserved for the ghost of Professor Harold Laski'.[16] A staunch advocate of India's freedom, Laski argued in works such as *The State in Theory and Practice* (1935) that the economic difficulties of capitalism might lead to the destruction of political democracy, and increasingly came to view socialism as the only alternative to fascism.

Zaheer and his band of young Indian students had an older English friend, Ralph Fox (1900–1937). Fox impressed upon them the need for workers and intellectuals to come closer like never before. He told the

---

[14] Zaheer, 'Reminiscences', p. 33.

[15] Harold Laski (1893–1950) taught political science at LSE, where he was hugely popular among his students some of whom included Kingsley Martin, Ralph Milliband, and K.R. Narayanan, the former president of India. Apart from his academic work at the LSE, Laski was a brilliant speaker, theorist, and executive member of the socialist group, the Fabian Society during 1922–36. In 1936, he co-founded the Left Book Club along with Victor Gollancz and John Strachey. A prolific writer, he produced a number of books and essays throughout the 1920s and 1930s; his influence on men like Sajjad Zaheer, K.M. Ashraf, Nehru as well as V.K. Krishna Menon, P.N. Haskar, B.K. Nehru, who were his students and in one way or another shaped Indian policies, is important. According to John Kenneth Galbraith, American Ambassador to India, 'the center of Nehru's thinking was Laski' and 'India the country most influenced by Laski's ideas'; reference in Sanjeev Sabhlok, *Breaking Free of Nehru: Let's Unleash India* (Delhi: Eastern Book Corporation, 2009).

[16] Reference in Ramachandra Guha, 'The LSE and India', *The Hindu*, 23 November 2003.

young band of Indian nationalists and budding socialists how the millions of workers who had traditionally been barred from real cultural activity had an immense thirst for knowledge, health, and beauty, which only socialism could satisfy. The demand of these millions for schools, laboratories and clinics, new modes of travel, art, literature, and music meant, in turn, a new and splendid future for scientists, artists, doctors, and teachers. Fox died a hero's death in the Spanish War, but not before he had left his mark on the group of young writers who were keen to set up a first-of-its-kind all-India writers' association. As Harold Laski noted, Fox's death was, 'a fulfillment. It was, for him, simply a necessary service to his ideal'.[17] Fox, in his combination of qualities, his devotion to the Communist Party, and his intellectual ardour, was able to foreshadow the alliance between mental and manual worker in the fight against fascism and war, which he saw as the destroyers of culture. Sajjad Zaheer credited Fox with sensitizing the young Indian students to the dangers of sectarianism and prejudice. And, so the group that sought to set up the AIPWA actively tried to draw members from different parts of India and encouraged writers from different regional languages to read their works to each other. Sajjad Zaheer wanted a progressive-minded young woman to be a part of their London group, one who would be useful when the group reassembled in India, and so Hajra Begum[18] was co-opted.

---

[17] Harry Pollitt, *Ralph Fox: A Writer in Arms* (London: Lawrence & Wishart, 1937). Biographical information and quote from Harold Laski taken from Marxists Internet Archive (2006).

[18] A cousin of Mahmuduzzafar, like him also a member of the extended royal family of Rampur, Hajra Begum was a divorcee with a small son when she travelled to London to do a Montessori Teachers' Training course. She married Dr Z.A. Ahmed on 20 May 1936 and played an active role in the CPI as a full-time member. Her nikah was performed by Dr Ashraf and Zaheer was a witness. The very next day she and her husband went to meet Nehru to offer their services. Dr Ahmed was put in charge of the economic department of the All India Congress Committee (AICC) and Hajra, instead of working with Vijaylakshmi Pandit (Nan) as Nehru suggested, chose to set up the Railway Coolie's Union at Allahabad. In the interview, she revealed how those with communist leanings had to work either with the Congress or the Congress Socialist Party (CSP) and wait to be 'contacted' by the CPI during the period when the party was banned. The transcript of her interview at the NMML as part of the Oral History Project revealed a fund of information on the working of the CPI. Hajra Begum was the elder sister of the stage and cinema actor, Zohra Segal.

To begin with, a group of no more than six or seven met informally in Zaheer's room in 1935 where it was decided that before they proceeded any further, a manifesto should be drafted to formulate the aims and objectives of this fledgling group. Zaheer recorded:

Four or five persons were commissioned to do this job. Anand prepared the first draft, which was very long. Later this work was entrusted to Dr Ghosh who presented his draft before the committee. I was asked to re-write the drafts of Anand and Ghosh (which we had discussed repeatedly for hours together) and prepare a final draft. After many disputes and long discussions about every sentence and every word, the committee finally approved the draft.[19]

A version of the *Manifesto*, said to be the one adopted in London, is found in the intelligence files in the India Office Library (IOL). It is as follows:

(1) The establishment of organisations of writers to correspond to the various linguistic zones of India; the co-ordination of these organisations by holding conferences, publishing magazines, pamphlets, etc.; the establishment of close connexion [sic] between the central and local Indian organisations and the Indian organisation.
(2) To co-operate with those literary organisations whose aims do not conflict with the basic aims of the association.
(3) To produce and to translate literature of a progressive nature and of a high technical efficiency, to fight cultural reaction; and, in this way, to further the cause of Indian freedom and social regeneration.
(4) To strive for the acceptance of a common language (Hindustani) and a common script (Indo–Roman) for India.
(5) To protect the interests of authors; to help authors who require and desire assistance for the publication of their works.
(6) To fight for the right of free expression of thought and opinion.[20]

It was then decided to begin regular meetings. The owner of a Chinese restaurant, the 'Nanking' on Denmark Street, offered the back room of his restaurant free of charge.

This small, unventilated cellar could accommodate forty to fifty people with difficulty. Our regular meeting was held there. Mulk Raj Anand was elected president and on behalf of the committee we presented the draft of the manifesto

[19] Zaheer, 'Reminiscences', p. 38.
[20] IOR/L/PJ/12/499, File 70/36.

which was adopted after a few amendments. Four or five of us, elected to the executive committee were very satisfied with the meeting. It was an achievement to collect about 30 to 35 Indians in London. Further, the drafting of the manifesto had helped to clarify scattered ideas. What is progressivism? What is the aim of progressive writers? How should they work? The Manifesto tried to answer these questions, however tentatively, which was an important achievement. *When I find a discussion on these issues still raging in our magazines (1940) which is, of course, desirable, the comprehensiveness of our first manifesto becomes all the more apparent.*[21]

While no published evidence is to be found of the first draft, a study can be made of the two extant versions of the *Manifesto*: the version that was approved in London at the Nanking restaurant towards the end of 1935 and subsequently published in *The Left Review* (in February 1936, from London) and the one that was eventually adopted as the official version at the second AIPWA conference in Calcutta in December 1938.[22] Both versions begin thus: 'Radical changes are taking place in Indian society. Fixed ideas and old beliefs, social and political institutions are being challenged. Out of the present turmoil and conflict a new society is arising. The spirit of reaction, however, though moribund and doomed to ultimate decay, is still operative and is making desperate efforts to prolong itself.'

Zaheer sent the approved version to litterateurs in India, including K.M. Ashraf and Abdul Alim (who taught History and Arabic, respectively, at Aligarh), Mahmud and Rashid Jahan (who were both in Amritsar by now), Hiren Mukherji (in Calcutta), and Premchand (who was so smitten by its contents that he reproduced a slightly diluted version in the *Hans* in October 1935). Since the three versions of this document have been produced in toto in Annexure IV, it should be suffice here to make three brief points about it: (*a*) In all three versions, the *Manifesto* can be understood

---

[21] Sajjad Zaheer, 'Reminiscences', p. 38; italics mine.

[22] For a detailed discussion on the differences between the two versions of the *Manifesto*, see Ralph Russell, 'Leadership in the All-India Progressive Writers' Movement, 1935–1947', in B.N. Pandey (ed.), *Leadership in South Asia* (New Delhi: Vikas Publishing House, 1977), pp. 104–27; and between the English and Hindi version in Carlo Coppola (ed.), 'The All-India Progressive Writers' Association: The European Phase', in *Marxist Influences and South Asian Literature*, pp. 6–10. The *Manifesto* adopted at the Calcutta Session of the AIPWA in 1938 is given in Annexure IV. The same Annexure reproduces pp. 6–10 from Coppola's study.

to be a declaration of Socialist Realism;[23] (*b*) its architects had appropriated for themselves the task of commenting, creatively and critically, on all aspects of Indian life; and (*c*) there was no doubting that the cause of Indian freedom and social regeneration would be vital to their concerns. A close reading, however, showed the communist training of those who had drafted it. Here, I shall highlight those phrases, expressions, and statements that, camouflaged between other seemingly general or sweeping statements, carry portents of the shape of things to come:

- 'The spirit of reaction, however, though moribund and doomed to ultimate decay, is still operative and is making desperate efforts to prolong itself.'
- 'Indian literature, since the breakdown of classical literature, has had the fatal tendency to escape from the actualities. It has tried to find a refuge from reality in spiritualism and idealism. The result has been that it has produced a rigid formalism and a banal and perverse ideology.'
- Draws attention to the 'mystical devotional obsession' of existing literature, its 'furtive and sentimental attitude towards sex, its emotional exhibitionism and its almost total lack of rationality'.

---

[23] For a detailed study of socialist realism, see speech by A.A. Zhdanov in *Soviet Writers' Congress, 1934: The Debate on Socialist Realism and Modernism in the Soviet Union* (London: Lawrence & Wishart, 1977). Briefly, at the heart of socialist realism was the furtherance of socialism and communism. At the same time, it was also focused on keeping people optimistic because the soviet ideologues believed that optimism was important for productiveness. It was adopted as a state policy when the Union of Soviet Writers was set up by Stalin on 23 April 1932. The Union restricted people from expressing alternate geo-political realities that differed from the policy laid down as socialist realism. This state policy was further endorsed at the Congress of Socialist Writers in 1934 and thereafter ruthlessly enforced by the Stalinist regime. Those who strayed from the official line were marginalized if not severely punished. According to the terms of the laid-down policy, form and content were not merely regulated, but also limited. For instance, erotic, religious, surreal, or expressionistic forms were forbidden. As we shall see, in the context of the PWM, a similar exclusion happened in the case of Miraji, Manto, and Ismat on similar grounds. The Indian progressives, perhaps taking a cue from the Union of Soviet Writers, became increasingly intolerant of deviations and transgressions from the aims and objectives outlined in the PWA's *Manifesto*, which underwent several modifications, but remained the 'Bible', as it were, for the times.

- Takes upon themselves the task of criticizing 'ruthlessly, in all its political, economic and cultural aspects, the spirit of reaction in our country'.[24]

The core group had actively spread the word among Indian students with literary interests. Soon meetings began to be held once or twice a month where the group would read and critique each other's work; Zaheer read his one-act Urdu play *Beemar* (The Sick Man). Occasionally, a visiting Indian professor or writer would be invited. The subjects were eclectic ranging from the use of Roman script[25] (by one Dr Suniti Kumar Chatterji, a professor from Calcutta University) to the revolutionary significance of the poetry of Kazi Nazrul Islam (by a Bengali member). Looking back on those days, we have a valuable testimony from Anand:

It is almost uncanny to look back upon those dark, foggy days of the year 1935 in London when after the disillusionment and disintegration of years of suffering in India and conscious of the destruction of most of our values through the capitalist crisis of 1931, a few of us emerged from the slough of despond of the cafes and garrets of Bloomsbury and formed the nucleus of the Indian Progressive Writers' Association.[26]

The group began to meet once or twice a month, reading and critiquing their works to each other. And so it went on till the summer of 1935 when

---

[24] All references to the *Manifesto* are taken from the version published in the *Left Review*.

[25] The progressives all along maintained that the use of Roman script was the only way out of the ugly Hindi–Urdu debate. Zaheer wrote in his 'Reminiscences':

The idea of one script for the entire country was very attractive and in London the fire of prejudice and sentiments which blazes at the mention of this problem in India was completely absent. Hindi and Urdu speaking people, Madrasis, Bengalis, Gujratis, in short, young men from every part of India, were present there and all of them unanimously decided that the Progressive Writers' Association should propagate for Roman script.

In Pradhan, *Marxist Cultural Movements in India*, vol. I, pp. 38–9. Later, Zaheer wrote a long article entitled 'Hindi, Urdu aur Hindustani' which he read at the Hyderabad conference in 1945.

[26] M.R. Anand, 'On the Progressive Writers' Movement', in Sudhi Pradhan (ed.), *Marxist Cultural Movements in India: Chronicles and Documents (1936–47)*, vol. I (Calcutta: National Book Agency, 1979), p. 1.

Zaheer decided to return to India and start in real earnest the work of setting up the AIPWA. He wrote:

We knew from the beginning that living in London we can neither influence Indian literature nor create any good literature ourselves. Side by side with our realizing the advantages of forming the association in London, this feeling was strengthened. A few exiled Indians could do little more than draw up plans among themselves and produce the orphanlike [sic] literature under the influence of European culture. The most important thing that we learnt in Europe was that a progressive writers' movement could bear fruits only when it is propagated in various languages and when the writers of India realize the necessity of this movement and put in practice its aims and objects. The best that the London association could do was to put us in contact with the progressive literary movements abroad, to represent Indian literature in the West and to interpret for India the thoughts of Western writers and the social problems which were profoundly influencing western literature.[27]

The vacuum left by Zaheer was recorded by Jyoti Basu in the following words:

Hiren Mukherjee, Sajjad Zahir [sic], Dr. Z.A. Ahmed and Niharendu Dutta Majumdar had left Britain for India in the meantime. Their absence was felt by us dearly; in fact, our enthusiasm had ebbed somewhat. We realized that the void had to be filled. Indian students at London, Cambridge and Oxford formed their own communist groups. The British leadership advised us not to hold public meetings because the British Raj in India had already banned the Communist Party. We started attending Marxist Study circles. Our teachers were Harry Pollitt, Rajani Palme Dutt, Clemens Dutt and Bradley. The entire world was by then in a tizzy. There was a civil war in Spain; all progressive forces were coming together against the dictatorial rule of Franco.... Marxist literature and the contemporary political happenings of the world were fast pulling me into the mainstream of politics.[28]

A most valuable document for the purpose of this study proved to be the file on the Indian Progressive Writers' Association (IPWA) containing reports on its members and their activities in India.[29] It opens with an

---

[27] Zaheer, 'Reminiscences', pp. 39–40.
[28] Basu, *Jatadur Mone Pore*.
[29] IOR/L/PJ/12/499, File 70/36, January 1936–October 1941.

extract from the weekly report of the DIB from New Delhi dated 2 January 1936 entitled 'Foreign Intelligence':

Amongst the more recent activities of the London Students' Secret Communist Group in London, mention must be made of the development of the Progressive Writers' Movement. The association responsible for the conduct of this movement is a literary organisation formed in November 1934 by S.S. Zahir [sic] and Promode Ranjan Sen Gupta, the latter being the Secretary. Although the organisation actually took shape in November 1934, the germ from which it sprang is to be found in 1932 when Zahir, then in India, and two or three other young persons of like thought produced a collection of stories called *Angare*. This aroused a stormy protest because of its anti-religious nature. The authors retaliated with protests against the suppression of their work and announced that they intended to form a League of Progressive Authors in order to secure the publication from time to time of works of a similar nature both in English and in the various Indian vernaculars.

The membership of the association is believed to number about twenty, most of whom probably do not realise that they are merely the tools of those behind the scene and that the association is, in fact, merely a recruiting ground for members of the Indian Students' Secret Communist Group in London. Now that Zahir has returned to Allahabad, it is to be expected that branches of the Association will be formed in India which will be used to disseminate quasi-socialist propaganda amongst the intelligentsia of this country.[30]

The intelligence report on the activities of the young progressives in London concludes dourly:

How far this purely Indian association is connected with the Writers' International (which is, of course, a Moscow-sponsored concern) or with the British branch of that International, it is difficult to say. But so long as B.F. Bradley remains in charge of Indian Communist activities in England, it is likely that the Progressive Writers' Movement will be conducted in close conjunction with the British movement on similar lines; and this will give these budding Indian litterateurs access to the good offices of such publishing houses as Messrs. Martin Lawrence & Co. and Messrs. Wishart & Co., whose main business is the production of Communist publications and books of a 'progressive' kind.[31]

From 21 to 26 June 1935, a conference of world writers was held in Paris under the tutelage of a galaxy of literary giants, namely, Maxim Gorky,

[30] IOR/L/PJ/12/499, File 70/36, Serial no. 64.
[31] Ibid.

André Gide, E.M. Forster, and André Malraux,[32] among others. This, in turn, led to the formation of the International Association of Writers for the Defense of Culture against Fascism with the intention of helping to sharpen a new awareness of the role of writers in a world besieged by forces of repression. A host of affiliated organizations offered solidarity and support; these included the League of American Writers, League of Left Writers in China who were battling Japanese imperialism, the French writers who were a part of the United Front against fascism established in 1933, a delegation from Soviet Union with representatives from different nationalities like Tatar, Uzbeks, and Tajik, among others. Zaheer happened to be in Paris, staying with his friend Shaukatullah Ansari[33] and trying to complete the novella *London ki Ek Raat* begun almost a year ago. He attended the conference held in Balboulille,[34] where thousands attended even though entry was by ticket, and recorded his impressions in great detail. He mentioned the great intellectuals of the day—in particular Louis Aragon (1897–1982), the French poet, novelist, and editor—who met the participants and conversed with ease and informality, the stress

[32] Maxim Gorky (1868–1936), founder of social realism in literature and a huge influence on a broad spectrum of writers in the twentieth century; André Gide (1869–1951), staunch anti-colonialist and fellow-traveller of the communists though never a member of any party, he won the Nobel Prize for literature in 1947 and also translated Tagore's *Gitanjali* into French; E.M. Forster (1879–1970) examined class differences with the eye of a miniaturist whose appeal to humanity (expressed in his novel published in 1910, *Howard's End*), serves as an epigraph to his entire literary oeuvre and world view: 'Only Connect'; André Malraux (1901–1976) a vocal critic of French colonialism in Indo-China and a champion of Republican forces in Spain, he was instrumental in setting up the 1935 conference in Paris. Regarded by some as an adventurer, Malraux nonetheless did a lot for focusing the world's attention on Spain and the fight against fascism being waged there.

[33] Shaukatullah Ansari (1908–1972) studied at Aligarh, Switzerland, and Paris. When Sajjad Zaheer stayed with him in Paris, Ansari was studying medicine. Later, Ansari abandoned medicine for a career as a diplomat and government servant. His last post was the Governor of Orissa. He was married to Zohra, the daughter of Dr M.A. Ansari.

[34] Zaheer calls the Balboulille 'a famous hall in Paris' in his 'Reminiscences'. According to Coppola, however, the meeting took place in the Palais de la Mutabilité in Paris.

laid by every speaker on freedom of thought and opinion, the need for writers to defend themselves by becoming a part of the People's United Front for freedom and the presence of large numbers of workers in keeping with the newly formed relationship between writers and workers. Writing in his *Yaadein*, Zaheer rues that while all other countries were adequately represented, India was regrettably represented by Miss Sophia Wadia.[35] Clearly regarding her as a literary (and political) lightweight, even though she spoke passionately against the colonization of India, the inference Zaheer draws from her inclusion is that had there been an independent association of writers, surely someone of a greater stature could have been sent. He, therefore, used the opportunity to affiliate the proposed Progressive Writers' Association (yet to be formed in India) with the international forum established in Paris after the conclusion of the conference.

'It is in the nature of Fascism to be a nation; it is ours to be a world', André Malraux famously declared in his speech at the 1935 conference before going on to spell out the intention of this new association:

> [E]very work of art becomes a symbol and a sign, but not always of the same thing. A work of art implies the possibility of a reincarnation. And the world of history can only lose its meaning in the contemporary will of man. It is for each of us, in his own field and through his own efforts, and for the sake of all those who are engaged in a quest of themselves, to recreate the phantom heritage which lies about us, to open the eyes of all the sightless statues, to turn hopes into will and revolts into revolutions, and to shape thereby, out of the age-old sorrows of man, a new and glowing consciousness of humankind.[36]

The second conference of the International Association of Writers for the Defence of Culture was held in London from 19 to 23 June 1936. Anand attended this conference on behalf of the AIPWA.[37] A proposal was put

---

[35] Sophia Wadia was married to B.P. Wadia, founder of the United Lodge of Theosophists. Born in Bogata of French parentage, Ms Wadia spoke in French at the Paris conference. The Wadias were among the first members of the International PEN and started the Indian PEN periodical for which, incidentally, she wrote to Zaheer asking for a copy of Premchand's inaugural address at the first AIPWA.

[36] André Malraux, 'The Work of Art', in Maynard Solomon (ed. and commentary), *Marxism and Art: Essays Classic & Contemporary* (Detroit: Wayne State University Press, 1979 [reprint]), from the Marxists Internet Archive.

[37] Details found in Anand, 'On the Progressive Writers' Movement', p. 13.

forward by the international writers' community to prepare an encyclopaedia of world culture. However, the civil war in Spain in July 1936 drew attention away from the encyclopaedia and the third conference was held in war-ravaged Madrid in the summer of 1937. As a gesture of solidarity with the beleaguered people of Spain in their fight against fascist forces, the intellectual fraternity descended from different parts of the world. André Malraux, Stephen Spender, W.H. Auden, Ernest Hemingway, and John Dos Passos leant their weight to the Spanish War. Sajjad Zaheer attended this conference too and later Jawaharlal Nehru, a member of the AIPWA, visited the trenches of Spain as a gesture of solidarity.

Intelligence reports on the activities of the students at Oxford and Cambridge[38] show that they tended to invite rather a lot of communist leaders. The Cambridge Majlis, which had for years been the honoured meeting place for Indians, was gradually captured by the left and began to be used as 'propaganda' centre, according to the secretary and supervisor, Indian Civil Service probationers, H.L.O. Garrett. The Oxford Majlis held meetings on Sunday evenings during term time. Among those who had attended the society were W.B. Yeats, Bertrand Russell, Rabindranath Tagore, Mahatma Gandhi, Jawaharlal Nehru, E.M. Forster, Rev. C.F. Andrews, George Lansbury, the marquis of Zetland, and Lord Lytton. The Cambridge Society carried on in a similar fashion, except that under the influence of its two leading lights, Rajni M. Patel and S.M. Kumaramangalam, who if not actual communists, had 'very definite communist affiliations' by 1937.[39] Unfortunately, the files for the previous years have been destroyed so one could get no information on the years that Sajjad Zaheer and others were part of these activities. However, the name of Mulk Raj Anand crops up again and again, among the speakers or those who helped get speakers for the student community.

Another intelligence report entitled 'The Indian Progressive Writers Association' and marked 'Secret' dated 2 July 1936 notes:

Since the departure of S.S. Zaheer for India, the London end of the Indian Progressive Writers' Association has been run by Dr Mulk Raj Anand as President, with Promode Ranjan Sen Gupta as Secretary. The association maintains close contact with Zaheer and M.D. Taseer (now in Amritsar). There is now no doubt

---

[38] 'Indian Students and Societies at Oxford and Cambridge: Scotland Yard Report', IOR/L/PJ/12/4, File 1290/17, February 1936–April 1946.

[39] Ibid., report by Mr Silver, 23 November 1937.

whatsoever that this organization was designed and built up by Zaheer as a cover for communist activities and as a recruiting ground for members of the secret Communist Students' Group. As might be expected, it is a fairly broad organization and includes semi- and non-communists, likewise persons who cannot truthfully be described as 'progressive' writers at all, but who are known to be communists or to have communist sympathies. Zaheer claims to have held a successful Conference of Indian Writers in Lucknow (simultaneously with the session of the Indian National Congress), and to have established branches in various parts of India.

In London the Association has very friendly relations with the communist intelligentsia. There is also evidence that it is in touch with the League Against Imperialism, the National Council for Civil Liberties and the Indian Journalists' Association over the question of ordinances relating to the Press in India. There is no evidence that it is subsidized by the Communist Party of Great Britain and it is believed that B.F. Bradley is not in contact with M.R. Anand. (*The latter is not a member of the Indian Communist Students fraction, for the reason that P.R. Sen Gupta considers him rather indiscreet in his conversation.*)[40]

The same report goes on to mention that amongst those who attended the London meetings of the IPWA, which were held fairly regularly, was Christabel George, the fiancée of M.D. Taseer, and the sister of Alys who later married Faiz, who was known to act as a link between Taseer and members of the association. Others who, according to the report, may be mentioned as playing 'some' part in the affairs of the IPWA in England were R.M. Patel (at St Catherine's College, Cambridge, who had undertaken the sale of the *New Indian Literature* and canvassing for subscriptions), Iqbal Singh (closely connected with the India League, and himself an author), and Sasadhar Sinha (who employed Promod Sengupta at his bookshop where *New Indian Literature* was prepared for issue).

About Mulk Raj Anand, the report mentions his two books, *The Untouchable* and *Coolie*, both of which were published by the 'communist firm' of Wishart–Lawrence (which was an amalgamation of Wishart & Co. and Martin Lawrence & Co.) The report also mentions that '*Untouchable* had been translated into Russian, and a considerable sum in roubles awaited Anand's disposal in Moscow. He intended to visit the Soviet Union in order to spend his money, but for some reason the trip appeared to have been postponed. Two further novels, *An Indian Tragedy* and *All Men Are*

---

[40] IOR/L/PJ/12/499, File 70/36; italics mine.

Equal, were shortly due for publication.'[41] These works of fiction were 'readable', according to the report, and were on the whole a 'fair' picture of the lives of the lower classes in India, though the report concludes that these books might offend Indian susceptibilities for much the same reason as Miss Mayo's *Mother India*.

The report also mentions that Anand had been engaged on behalf of Wishart–Lawrence in editing a collection of Marx's writings on India. R. Palme Dutt, who was asked to write an Introduction to this book, declined because

[although] he is convinced of Anand's good intentions, he does not think him qualified to expatiate on Marx. Dutt recommended that the book be thoroughly checked by Marxian experts before it appears, lest coming from the firm of Wishart-Lawrence it should cause a scandal in communist circles. Dutt was also said to be at a loss to understand why such an important part of Marx's work should have been entrusted to the mercies of such a tyro. From this it may be gathered that though Anand's sympathies are with the communists, he is not yet a qualified communist theoretician.[42]

Further reports on the activities of the IPWA and London Majlis can be found in the Scotland Yard Report No. 201, dated 3 September 1941. It mentions two meetings held at the 'Bengal India Restaurant' on 13 Percy Street, W 1. The first was advertised by means of a cyclostyled memorandum circulated through post by Anand from 16 Little Russel Street, WC 1 'proposing the formation of a small publishing concern to issue books on various subjects designed to further the Indian struggle for Independence'.[43] This meeting was attended by 60 people, most being Indians, and was chaired by V.K. Krishna Menon with Anand and Jyoti Basu (secretary of the London Majlis) on the platform. Anand explained the purpose of the scheme which he said had originated in a previous meeting attended by Iqbal Singh, P.N. Haksar, Islam ul Haque, and himself. A sum of £ 25 had already been subscribed and appealed for further donations. Menon was not enthusiastic about the proposed project and foresaw limitations imposed by the Defence of India Regulations. A second meeting, immediately after, was to commemorate the death of

[41] IOR/L/PJ/12/499, File 70/36.
[42] Ibid.
[43] Ibid.

Rabindranath Tagore. It was chaired by A. Subramanian and the speakers were M.R. Anand, S. Sinha, I. Singh, and T.C. Ghosh. Others present at this meeting were a barrister called Asha Bhattacharya Sen and a law student called Mulla.

The last intelligence report dated 1 October 1941 on the activities of the IPWA in London mentions a meeting of the members to discuss the publishing of a small book by K.S. Shelvankar on the defence of India.

Back in India: The Build-up to the First AIPWA

Before we come back to the exploits of Sajjad Zaheer and his spadework in setting up the AIPWA, it would be useful to understand the increasing stronghold of communism in India, especially among peasants' and workers' groups and students. The country had been rocked by strikes and lockouts all through the late 1920s, prompting the viceroy to order countrywide arrests of all militant trade union and communist leaders on 20 March 1929. The jails were filled with communists and their sympathizers from where they emerged further 'indoctrinated' and 'radicalised' due to the abundance of propaganda literature churned out by the underground comrades. Intelligence reports in the British Library point the finger towards Moscow with proof of remittances from the USSR to, for instance, the All-India Railwaymen's Union Federation of Calcutta in 1927 and the claims of Moscow-trained communists such as M.N. Roy who announced that the Comintern had set aside substantial sums of money for the eastern operations.[44]

By the mid-1930s, there seemed a definite parting of ways between the communists and others: where the Congress and socialist parties increasingly adopted the path of revolutionary struggle for reform and constitutionalism, the CPI gave the call for revolutionary nationalism and mass struggle. Perhaps taking its cue from Russia, it termed the Congress a 'National Bourgeoisie'. It rallied the nation for what it called the 'final struggle' which would combine strikes and armed demonstrations resulting in a violent

---

[44] 'Communist Influence in India's Trade Unions', IOR/L/PJ/12/137, File 6835 (E)/23; Shipment of Gold & Silver to India: Suspected Funding for Russian Propaganda in India, IOR/L/PJ/12/100, File 6262/22; Russian Communist Influences in India: Agents, Recruitment, Training & Propaganda, IOR/L/PJ/12/117, File 6533/122.

insurrection against the state leading to civil war and the establishment of a Soviet style socialist republic. This plan, prepared in Moscow in 1930 under the title 'Draft Platform of Action',[45] prophesied that in the end there would be a dictatorship of the proletariat. The cue from Moscow was taken up by the Indian communists (prominently by Adhikari who published the 'Draft' illegally and had it distributed) along with a slew of propaganda literature through the party's official organs as well as leaflets, posters, and handbills.

This call from the party ideologues was interpreted in different ways by different people before the formation of the PWA. A look at Urdu literature, especially poetry of the mid-1930s, shows how the message of the Russian Revolution trickled down from the party high command to the workers and handlers and percolated amongst the sympathizers as vague, inchoate dreams of revolution. The Urdu poet took his cue from the message that was blowing in the wind before the PWA came along to give form and direction to a laid-down ideology. It must be emphasized that there was a progressive current of thought evident in Urdu poetry *before* the word progressive came to be coined. In the late 1920s, Ram Prasad Bismil (1897–1927), the revolutionary hero and martyr of the Kakori Case, was advocating armed insurrection:

> The desire to have our heads chopped off is in our hearts
> Let us test the strength of the enemies' murderous hands.

Saghar Nizami in his *'Qaumi Geet'* (National Songs) was proclaiming 'Every Hindi should be the owner of Hind', and Seemab Akbarabadi had his pulse to his age when he was proclaiming the dawn of a new age in *'Ahd-e-Nau'* (The New Age):[46]

> The time for the new revolution has come
> The time for testing our mettle has come
> The time for singing fiery songs has come
> The time for raising the flame of life has come.

Majaz was dreaming of *'Inquilab'* (Revolution) in 1933:

> The reign of capitalism is about to end
> The workers' passion for revenge is about to show results

---

[45] Found in Appendix II in *India & Communism*, IOL/L/PJ/12/671.

[46] Muzaffar Abbas (ed.), *Urdu mein Qaumi Shairi* (Lahore: Maktaba Aaliya, 1978), p. 239.

> Winds, laden with the scent of blood, shall come from the jungles
> There will be blood everywhere....

Hasrat, the old rebel, was laying down fresh challenges:

> Let us see how long this tyranny will succeed
> Let us see how long the patriots do not awaken from their sleep.

Josh Malihabadi, the *shair-e-inquilab* (revolutionary poet) was laying down a stern warning in 'East India Company ke Farzandon se' (To the Sons of the East India Company):

> Time will write a new story on a new topic
> Whose redness will need its colour from your blood.

And in 'Shikast-e-Zindaan ka Khwaab' (Dream of a Vanquished Prison), comparing India to a prison, Josh was looking forward to the day its prisoners would rise in revolt:

> The prison of India is quaking as the shouts of victory rent the air
> Some prisoners have risen in revolt and are clanking their chains.

Quick to sense these scattered, diffused sentiments, the CPI wanted to harness and channelize this inchoate desire for revolution. It wanted to dragoon the dispersed groups into a structured, bureaucratic, infallible model based on the Soviet model. It wanted to put in place systems that would help in the flow of information from the party high command to the lowest grass root worker leaving no room for deviation or aberration. On 10 September 1934, the first issue of *Chingari* (Spark) appeared from Saharanpur. This was the cyclostyled English organ of the UP Committee of the CPI, edited by Sohan Singh Josh and Sajjad Zaheer. Its subsequent Urdu version was meant to supplement the organ of the Central Committee of the CPI and to deal with problems specific to UP. Culled from material that had appeared in the short-lived *Communist* from Bombay and *Inprecor*, *Chingari* made the first serious contribution—since the inauguration of the Meerut Conspiracy Case in 1929—towards the introduction of pure communism into agrarian India, outside the Sikh areas of the Punjab. *Chingari* also revealed the nominal existence of the UP Committee of the CPI that under the charge of Sajjad Zaheer would increasingly play a wider role with the establishment of the PWA.[47]

---

[47] From 1938, the task of editing *Chingari* increasingly fell upon Mahmuduzzafar.

The CPI was banned in 1934. The Revolutionary Movements Bill was framed the same year to combat the 'menace' of communism and its provisions depended on the definition of 'unlawful organisations' in Clause 2 of the Bill.[48] An Ordinance was further enacted which allowed the government to take action against persons 'acting in furtherance of the objects of an unlawful organisation', that is, the government could take action irrespective of whether they were acting individually, or as members of any organization or as part of a 'particular subversive movement'. Earlier, the General Communist Notification of the Sea Customs Act of 16 September 1932 allowed custom authorities to withhold certain books, open up luggage, mail, etc., and extract 'objectionable' literature.[49] The Special (Emergency) Powers Act already conferred wide powers on the Executive. But this was not considered to be effective for it could only be enforced in a state of emergency such as total lockout. Something had to be done to take preventive action. One measure was the use of the Criminal Law Act of 1908 (as amended in 1932) to be used against communists. This had 'proved of great value in the past in dealing with revolutionary organizations of an extreme type'.

On the subject of 'Communist Legislation', the secretary to the Government of India M.G. Hallett wrote on 16 May 1934 that 'it may be hoped that the results of the recent strikes will tend to discredit them rather than increase their influence'. An earlier intelligence report dated 13 July 1933 stated that 'it would appear that Moscow is scared of the Bombay type of Communist working through trade unions, and is at present relying more on members of the Ghadr Party to carry out their work in this country'.[50] But as it turned out, despite the ban on the CPI, the communist activities continued unabated. By 1939, the government was forced to consider adopting a Revolutionary Movements Ordinance which conferred special powers on the chief commissioners of the provinces for 'the purpose of preventing a grave menace to the peace and tranquility of the Province'.[51]

---

[48] 'Communism & Communist Agitation in India, Revolutionary Movements, Bill & Supplementing Ordinances', IOR/L/PJ/8/584, 1933–40.

[49] Year-wise lists of books seized under this Act are found in IOR/L/PJ/12/20-24, File 3907 (B).

[50] All of the above taken from 'Communism & Communist Agitation in India, Revolutionary Movements, Bill & Supplementing Ordinances', IOR/L/PJ/8/584, 1933–40.

[51] Ibid.

By the time Sajjad Zaheer returned to India, there was such a profusion of terrorist, communist, left-wing, anti-British organizations active and flourishing in different parts of the country as to make sharply defined distinctions impossible. The CPI's influence was measured not so much by its size as by its ability to guide other groups and movements. A study of the obscurer nationalist papers, especially the vernacular press, leaves little doubt that by the mid-1930s there appeared a trend towards communistic ideas in many parts of the country.[52] Increasingly, the open activities of the communists or direct influence of the CPI was not something which worried the government as the 'insidious and seditious manner in which communists penetrate other organizations and the indirect hold which communist teachings exert over the national movement'.[53] This was evident from the ease with which communists used the Congress as a cover to capture political power—first through the CSP[54] and ultimately in the Congress itself. In fact, both Mahmuduzzafar and Sajjad Zaheer had brief stints in the mid-1930s working as private secretaries to Jawaharlal Nehru; in later years Nehru would speak with dry bitterness of those who embed themselves in the Congress and then undermine its basic creed.[55] As part of the communist training imparted to Sajjad Zaheer, he was to initially devote himself to legitimate activities such as making contacts with 'unmarked' members of the intelligentsia (being a writer helped), holding private study circles, and openly aligning himself with trade union activities.

An intelligence report entitled 'A Promising Communist' describes Sajjad Zaheer thus:

---

[52] DIB reports, 1930–7, IOR/L/PJ/12/430.

[53] 'Growing Menace of Communism in India', *The Statesman*, 6 December 1939.

[54] It is important to note that the socialists soon developed differences with the communists leading to a lasting acrimonious feud.

[55] Nehru, *Selected Works*, vol. 14 (New Delhi: Orient Longman, 1981), pp. 16–17, 523–47. Nehru dwells at great length on the 'self-contradictory role' of the CPI and the relations between the Congressmen and communists in an interview with Dr Z.A. Ahmed, in a letter to Gerald Peel (an Australian communist party leader) and in a report dated January 1946 when he recommends that Zaheer, Ashraf, Sohan Singh Josh, etc., be expelled from the primary membership of the Congress.

There is little doubt that during his stay in England, he succeeded in impressing B.F. Bradley and some other British communist leaders with his energy and ability, for there are few Indian students who have shown a greater degree of consistency in their devotion to underground communist activity than he. Whether he has gained the complete confidence of the hierarchy in Moscow is another question. Those of his kind who have already returned to India have done little to justify themselves in Moscow's eyes or in the eyes of the CPGB. Kiron Basak has attempted a little underground work but has achieved practically nothing; Nirmal Sen Gupta has been an even greater disappointment; and even Niharendu Dutta Mozumdar, though he has been imprisoned for his activities, is considered ideologically unsound (though sincere) and is now not in receipt of assistance, financial or otherwise, from the CPGB. Thus, Zaheer, the son of a member of the wealthier classes, has much to live down, and the official communist attitude towards him may be said to be one of *hope tinged with skepticism*.[56]

The Seventh World Congress of the Comintern was held in Moscow in 1934. Money came via Britain for the dispatch of Indian students for training and to pay for the Indian delegates to attend the Congress. The Moscow Congress officially recognized the Central Committee of the CPI and the proposal to set up three strong provincial committees was passed—in Bengal, Bombay, and UP. Zaheer, who was still in Europe at the time of the Congress, is not known to have visited Moscow. Although there was considerable time between his 'disappearance' from England and his embarkation in Italy for India in the autumn of 1935, although too his heavy luggage arrived in Bombay by one Lloyd Triestino boat and he by the next, there was no evidence on his passport or elsewhere that he visited Russia before he returned to India. However, his avowed plans of setting up the AIPWA, based as they were on 'the assumption of financial and moral support from abroad, seem to bear upon them the stamp of authority higher than his own. He had not left England when B.F. Bradley returned from the Seventh World Congress in Moscow and possibly this, or a clandestine discussion somewhere in Europe'[57] provided the explanation.

The same intelligence report mentions 'a source which has hitherto proved reliable' that had some idea of Zaheer's future activities. It talks of the directive from Moscow to 'penetrate all working-class organisations

---

[56] Weekly Report, DIB, New Delhi, 30 January 1936, No. 4; IOR/L/PJ/12/430; italics mine.

[57] Ibid.

with a view to their ultimate capture'. Other organizations, especially those in which there are young people, especially *sewa samiti*s, youth congresses, and the like were to be similarly permeated with communists with the intention of drawing recruits for study circles. The report mentions a sum of Rs 1,500 being given to Zaheer (sanctioned from Moscow, but sent through 'the usual channel') to start a magazine along with a gestetner and a typewriter in three different languages. Zaheer did, indeed, start the *New Indian Literature* from his father's house in Allahabad. The report mentions 'a subsidy of £4 a month' towards the cost of production and Zaheer's plans to visit Calcutta and Bombay in order to discuss details regarding its publication with local communists and also to get in touch with Philip Spratt with a view to securing his advice. In addition to these activities, the report mentions Zaheer's hope of organizing branches of the League against Imperialism in Bombay and Calcutta. The report concludes with a grim prognosis for Zaheer:

Zaheer has a growing reputation as a writer and it seems likely that, if, as I believe, his new plans are forwarded on instructions received from Moscow, the Comintern have decided to use his talents in this direction while satisfying themselves about his bona fides. If he survives the test, it is probable that he will be employed on the more important communist work for which his training in England and Germany has fitted him. Till then, it seems he will be expected to confine his activities within the limits suggested above and to the formation of the PWA.

Two things may be concluded from the intelligence reports (cited in such detail above because one seldom gets to see them in real perspective). One, they stress a link between Sajjad Zaheer and Moscow, if not directly than definitely through the CPGB which played the role of a via media for Indian communists; and two, Sajjad Zaheer, once set on the trajectory he had sketched for himself with some inspiration from Moscow and the rest from London, executed his 'part' brilliantly to the last detail.

However, it must be stressed that while the weekly reports of the DIB of the Home Department (an institution of diligent and intelligent policing) provide ample evidence of the ground gained by communism in India, they contain *no actual proof of direct Soviet involvement or interest in Indian communist affairs after the mid-1930s*. In fact, some reports admit that financial assistance from Moscow had stopped coming into India by the late 1920s; others make largely unsubstantiated surmises about unknown methods such as through gifts or transmissions to bogus firms. With the ever-vigilant Sea Customs Act routinely proscribing 'objectionable' literature, communists and their sympathizers began to devise ever-ingenious ways of getting propaganda material into India. Publishers abroad were instructed to send books and papers by ordinary mail within covers of safe literature or to unmarked persons and addresses. *While there is evidence of publicity material coming in, there is no evidence of a money trail between Moscow and India.*

To return to Sajjad Zaheer and the setting up of the PWA, we once again find rich pickings in the intelligence reports in the IOL. A report dated 16 April 1936 looks back at the formation of the AIPWA in London in 1934 and notes that 'the Comintern had decided to use Zaheer's talents as a writer until they had satisfied themselves about his bona fides, has been amply confirmed by information received during the past three months'. This refers to Zaheer's efforts in organizing the first of its kind association of Indian writers across language divides. The report then goes on to give a potted version of Sajjad Zaheer's activities in India since his return:

Zaheer, as the association's chief organizer for India, has spent this period in working up the Association's membership, in forming subsidiary groups in the provinces, in circulating literature (much of it printed or cyclostyled in London) to members and to persons likely to be interested, and in attending to a considerable correspondence from what may be termed earnest seekers after truth. A typical example of this kind of inquirer is a Madrassi[58] who wrote in the middle of March[59] to say that he had been 'groping towards some such thing for some time past' and that he was 'very much heartened by the prospect of a conference coming so soon'. This correspondent went on to say, 'I'm afraid unless some active interest in our new way of life is insisted upon, our members may drift into a kind of artistic individualism, much like Sidney Hook's Marxism.[60] ... I believe that with the co-operation of the several trades-unions we may embark upon a countrywide

---

[58] Who this Madrassi might have been has not been ascertained. No likely reference has been found among Sajjad Zaheer's own writings.

[59] All through these intelligence reports one finds ample evidence that the correspondence of all those who were deemed 'revolutionaries' was routinely intercepted and studied. The reports carry frequent and unabashed references to personal/domestic correspondence as well.

[60] Sidney Hook was a Marxist philosopher who by the mid-1930s had become fervently anti-Communist and pro–Cold War.

educational programme for the five or six million proletariats [*sic*] of our land.' In conclusion, he advocated a one-year plan for teaching the illiterate workers to read and write, so that the Association might win for itself 'millions of readers who will eagerly listen to our songs and fill our theatres'.[61]

The intelligence report then goes on to comment on the fact that Zaheer, on behalf of the progressives, had kept Anand in London informed of the progress they had been making and had received the felicitation of the London group on the amount of work he had managed to do, eliciting the response from Anand: 'If you go on at that rate, we shall have conquered the whole of India in one year.'[62]

It must be noted that it could not be 'mere coincidence'[63] that Zaheer should think of setting up an association of Indian writers a mere two years after the creation of the Union of Soviet Writers. The Central Committee of the Soviet Communist Party had passed a resolution on 23 April 1932 to create a single, highly focused, and structured body, which actually came into being in 1934 and soon acquired a formidable reputation as the custodian of socialist realism. Zaheer was either instructed to do something similar or decided on his own to establish an association modelled on Soviet lines. He therefore spent the better part of 1935–6 travelling all over India, making contacts, showing the *Manifesto* of the PWA (copies of which he had already mailed from England prior to his departure) and generally getting a signature campaign going.

We get an account of this period in Sajjad Zaheer's *Roshnai*. Virtually upon setting foot on Indian soil, Zaheer asked his friend Huthi Singh to introduce him to Gujarati and Marathi writers in Bombay. He met Kanaiyalal Maniklal Munshi (1887–1971) and his wife Leelavati, both established writers in Gujarati. Munshi had been co-editor of *Young India* with Gandhi and was to set up the Bharatiya Vidya Bhawan in 1938. The meeting, however, was not fruitful as Zaheer thought Munshi was 'trying to revive the ruins of Somnath'[64] whereas he (Zaheer) wanted to look ahead,

[61] IOR/L/PJ/12/499, File 70/36.

[62] Ibid.

[63] Hafeez Malik, 'The Marxist Literary Movement in India and Pakistan', *The Journal of Asian Studies*, vol. 26, no. 4 (August 1967), p. 649.

[64] Sajjad Zaheer, *The Light: A History of the Movement for Progressive Literature in the Indo-Pak Subcontinent*, English translation of Sajjad Zaheer's *Roshnai* by Amina Azfar (Karachi: Oxford University Press, 2006), p. 5.

not backwards. From Bombay, Zaheer went to Allahabad, where his parents lived. There he met Ahmed Ali whose house became an office where they met, made plans, and wrote copious amounts of letters. Ahmed Ali introduced Zaheer to Firaq Gorakhpuri (1896–1982), the sharp-tongued, sharp-witted poet-critic-teacher at Allahabad University; Ehtesham Husain (1912–1976), then doing an MA in Urdu who would become one of the most respected progressive critics; Shivdan Singh Chauhan and Narendra Sharma who would both become prominent Hindi writers and active in the Allahabad branch of the PWA.

All of the above pledged support to the Association, as did Amarnath Jha, the vice-chancellor of Allahabad University and Dr Tara Chand, the educationist. Fortunately, there was a large gathering of Hindi and Urdu writers in Allahabad in December 1935, organized by Tara Chand under the aegis of the Hindustani Academy. This afforded an excellent opportunity to meet a galaxy of writers—Premchand, who instantly offered his unstinting support; and Maulvi Abdul Haq, who had been running a phenomenally humongous dictionary project from Hyderabad and proved to be just as cooperative in appending his signature to the *Manifesto* Zaheer had shown him. The others who came for the Hindi–Urdu conference and pledged their support included Josh Malihabadi, the poet who sang sweetly and robustly of revolution and Munshi Daya Narayan Nigam, the editor of *Zamana* from Kanpur. Soon, letters began to pour in from other cities where other men had been doing a similar canvassing on behalf of the PWA. Sibte Hasan reported from Hyderabad that he had managed to get signatures from many prominent writers including the influential Qazi Abdul Ghaffar, the editor of *Payam*. From Bengal, Hiren Mukherjee wrote to say that he was getting a group of writers together in Calcutta. The PWA, known among Urdu writers as the Anjuman (short for Anjuman-e Taraqqui-i-Urdu), soon evoked interest in many cities apart from Allahabad—Bombay, Ahmedabad, Calcutta, Hyderabad, and Aligarh.

Rashid Jahan, who now lived in Amritsar with her husband and had also travelled to Allahabad for the Hindi–Urdu conference, suggested that Zaheer meet the writers of the Punjab. In January 1936, Zaheer went to Amritsar and stayed with Rashid Jahan and Mahmuduzzafar where he met Faiz Ahmed Faiz for the first time. Together, the four of them travelled to Lahore (to stay in the home of Mian Iftikharuddin) where they hoped to secure more signatures and establish a branch of the PWA. Faiz introduced the young progressives from UP to the writers of Lahore—Sufi Ghulam Mustafa Tabassum, Akhtar Shirani, Abdul Majeed Salik, Chiragh Hasan Hasrat, Mian Bashir, and Firoz Din Mansoor. Zaheer recorded in *Roshnai* how he read out the *Manifesto* and fielded questions on what constituted 'progressivism', what was the progressive view on Shakespeare and Ghalib, how the progressives classified classical love poetry, whether or not it was necessary for a progressive to be a socialist or a communist, what was the progressive stance on religion, and so on.

While there could be no clear or satisfactory answers to these questions, there appeared to be unanimity on the goals of the proposed Association laid down in the *Manifesto*. Without further ado, a branch of the PWA was established in Lahore and Sufi Tabassum was appointed its secretary. Zaheer recorded this momentous event thus:

But it did not occur to any of us that this, the first step taken in the land of the Punjab, would reap a golden harvest in Urdu literature. Only a few years later, writers and poets like Krishan Chander, Faiz, Rajinder Singh Bedi, Ahmed Nadeem Qasmi, Mirza Adeeb, Zaheer Kashmiri, Sahir Ludhianvi, Fikr Taunsvi, Arif, Hans Raj Rahbar, Upendranath Ashq had raised the banner of progressive literature so high that its radiant heights became the envy of writers in other parts of our homeland.[65]

The time was ripe for the various branches of the PWA, in conjunction with individual supporters to meet and set up a central committee. It was decided to hold an All-India Conference on the sidelines of the annual session of the Congress which would be presided over by Nehru in Lucknow.[66] By common consent, Premchand was asked to preside over the first AIPWA. With characteristic modesty, this doyen of Hindi literature demurred, suggesting instead the name of Pandit Amarnath Jha or K.M. Munshi and Nehru or Zakir Husain. While Munshi was not acceptable due to his links with rich capitalists in Gujarat, Zakir Husain and Nehru (despite their known sympathies for the PWM) were not acceptable due to their active role in politics. Once Premchand was prevailed upon to agree to preside, attention was turned to the agenda. It was decided that language issues would be given as much importance as literary ones. The other issues

[65] Zaheer, *Light*, pp. 25–6.
[66] At this 49th Congress Session, the Constitution of the INC was amended.

on the agenda were linkages with overseas literary associations, how best to protect the democratic rights of writers from government restrictions, to raise a collective voice against the usurpation of peoples' freedoms worldwide, whether it was in the case of imperialist Japan's attack on China or Italian fascists invasion of peaceful Abyssinia.

Zaheer's parental home, the palatial Wazir Manzil, became the camp office for the first AIPWA. The Rifah-e-Aam Hall, venue for the Khilafat Conference in 1920 and witness to many a bonfire of foreign-made cloth, was secured for the Conference with the help of Anand Narain Mullah, a lawyer, poet, and future progressive. Ale Ahmad Suroor was appointed convenor.[67] Rashid Jahan and Mahmuduzzafar came from Amritsar to pitch in. Chaudhry Mohammed Ali Rudaulvi, a man of good taste and an influential talukdar from the Barabanki district, was chosen as chairman of the Reception Committee. Chaudhry sahab's donation of Rs 100 was a welcome addition to the Rs 150 that had been gathered so far as donations (of which the largest individual amount had been the princely sum of Rs 10!). No more than 30 or 40 delegates from outside Lucknow were expected: 2 from Bengal, 3 from Punjab, 1 from Madras, 2 from Gujarat, 6 from Maharashtra, and another 25 from different parts of UP. It appeared that most of the 300 chairs that had been hired for the hall would remain empty. To mobilize an audience, Mahmuduzzafar went around sticking posters announcing the conference in different parts of the city. Rashid Jahan, who was well-known in Lucknow on account of her medical practice, sold 3-rupee tickets for the reception committee among all and sundry. The progressives' real hope rested with the thousands who were expected to attend the Congress session. Among them, they were especially hopeful of the Congress socialists such as Acharya

---

[67] There is no mention of Suroor in Zaheer's account of the first AIPWA in *Roshnai*. Such deletions and effacements of people who were actively associated with the PWA in its infancy but later moved away is borne out by Ahmed Ali who (in the context of Majrooh Gorakhpuri) noted with tart asperity: 'Other critics and writers, who were most active in the Movement during the 1930s and who were Progressive in any wider sense of the word, have been bypassed by Sajjad Zaheer, or at best slurred over and slandered, in his account of the Movement.' Ahmed Ali, 'Progressive Writers' Movement and Creative Writers in Urdu', p. 40. I was told by Suroor's brother, Aulad Ahmad Siddiqui, about Suroor's formal role as convenor of the Lucknow conference.

Narendra Dev (1889–1956)[68] and Jayaprakash Narayan (1902–1979),[69] as well as women of substance within the Congress such as Kamaladevi Chattopadhyay (1903–1988)[70] and Sarojini Naidu (1879–1949).[71]

Since money was short, some delegates were put up in the homes of friends and sympathizers; others made do with whatever arrangements had been made for the Congress session. Mahmuduzzafar was given the task of typing out resolutions, programmes for each session, and other administrative tasks; Rashid Jahan and Hajra Begum were entrusted with selling tickets at the door of the hall and ushering people to their seats. Years later, Hajra Begum would recall a sexist bias, claiming she and Rashid Jahan would end up doing 'all the work which nobody else liked to do like putting on stamps, writing addresses and so on and we ran around, in fact so much so that when Munshi Premchand came, he asked Sajjad Zaheer: "What is this Banne, you are using these two girls?"'[72]

Soon, the hall began to fill—delegates from different provinces, visitors who had been charmed by Rashid Jahan into buying tickets, students from Lucknow University, office workers with a penchant for literature, trade union activists, even farmers. At 10.30 when the hall was almost two-thirds full, Maulana Hasrat Mohani showed up causing a frisson of excitement. The proceedings began with Chaudhry Mohammed Ali making his welcome address from a spartan dais, unadorned save for red

---

[68] A leading theorist of the CSP, he was drawn to satyagraha under the influence of B.G. Tilak and Aurobindo Ghosh. Active in the Hindi Movement and the All-India Kisan Congress, he was at various times a member of the UP Legislative Assembly.

[69] Widely known as JP or Loknayak (Leader of the People), he, along with Ram Manohar Lohia, Minoo Masani, Achyut Patwardhan, Ashok Mehta, and Yusuf Desai, formed a socialist caucus, the CSP, a left group within the Congress in 1934, with Acharya Narendra Dev as president and Narayan as general secretary.

[70] She was married to Harindranath Chattopadhyay, the well-known poet-actor and brother of Sarojini Naidu. She set up the All-India Women's Conference in 1927, became the first woman to be arrested in connection with the salt satyagraha in 1930, and became the president of the CSP in 1936.

[71] The first woman president of the Congress, and a poet herself, she was especially sympathetic towards writers.

[72] NMML, interview.

banners proclaiming 'All-India First Progressive Writers Conference' in Urdu, Hindi, and English.

The arrangements may have lacked in finesse, but they more than made up in the dynamism of its organizers and the sheer magnetic appeal of the message that was being conveyed from the Rifah-e-Aam Hall. For, after Gandhi's call for satyagraha, the most important mass movement unfurled from within its portals. A literary movement, unlike any other in the history of this country, came into being, a movement that was to shape the responses of a whole generation of Indian intelligentsia, one that would continue to influence creative writing, in one form or the other, long after those who put it together had fallen apart.

The Successes of the First AIPWA Conference, Lucknow

Premchand, who was unanimously elected president of the conference, read out his presidential address from a prepared text. This address, entitled '*Sahitya ka Uddeshya*' (The Aim of Literature)[73] written in unadorned Urdu, was heard by a rapt audience. In simple but powerful words, the greatest storyteller of his time told his audience how good literature can only be founded on truth, beauty, freedom, and humanity, and that his definition of literature was simply 'the criticism of life'. And since literature is nothing but the mirror of its age, its definition, scope, and contents just as much as its aims and objectives must change with time. Given the turmoil and change in the world, the present-day reader was no longer content with the wondrous tales of love and escape that were the staple fare of the fasana and dastan of yore. 'Currently, good literature,' he maintained, 'is judged by the sharpness of its perception, which stirs our feelings and thoughts into motion.'[74] The main aim of literature, then, was to 'refine' the mind of the readers. And while undoubtedly the aim of art was to strengthen one's sense of beauty, art too must be weighed on the same scale of usefulness as everything else in life. The time had come, he declared with the quiet assurance of a messiah, to redefine the parameters of beauty.

Calling language a means and not an end, and while conceding that a writer is born, not made, Premchand stressed that a writer's natural gifts

---

[73] The full text, translated by Francesca Orsini, can be found in *The Oxford India Premchand* (New Delhi: Oxford University Press, 2004).

[74] Orsini, ibid., Appendix; no page number is given.

could be enhanced with education and curiosity about the world around him. 'Literature,' he said, 'is no longer limited to individualism or egotism, but tends to turn more and more towards the psychological and social. Now literature does not view the individual as separate from society; on the contrary it sees the individual as an indissoluble part of society.' Deeming 'a quick mind and a fast pen' not enough, a writer must also be abreast of the 'latest scientific, social, historical, or psychological questions'—as was the case in international literary conferences. In India, Premchand maintained, we shy away from such matters and thus the need for far more socially engaged literature becomes more urgent than ever: 'We will have to raise the standard of our literature, so that it can serve the society more usefully ... our literature will discuss and assess every aspect of life and we will no longer be satisfied with eating the leftovers of other languages and literatures. We will ourselves increase the capital of our literature.'[75]

Speaking not merely as president of the inaugural session, but identifying himself completely with the aims and objectives of the PWA (the address is replete with references to 'our association', 'our ideal', 'our aim'), Premchand spoke about opening centres in 'each province and in each language': 'To water them and to strengthen their aim is our goal.' The 14-page text is not merely an eloquent plea on behalf of the PWA; it is significant for other reasons as well: here is the doyen of Hindi literature, rising above the thorny issue of language (Hindi–Urdu–Hindustani) and talking about what concerns, or *should* concern, all writers irrespective of language. He urged writers to discard individual and personal concerns and, instead, speak in a collective voice taking upon themselves public and political roles. Literature, which had hitherto been content to entertain or at best educate, must now, given the exigencies of the times, advance human knowledge and freedom.

This call for freedom was taken up by other speakers in this two-day conference, most notably by Raghupati Sahai (aka Firaq Gorakhpuri) in his paper entitled 'The Indian Renaissance at the Parting of Ways'. Being a lecturer of English at the Allahabad University and already a poet of some eminence, Firaq brought a wealth of erudition and made a convincing case of linking Indian renaissance with burgeoning nationalism. The Hindu and Muslim universities set-up by social reformers, the various reform movements, the work of cultural institutions, after the first flush of enthusiasm,

---

[75] Ibid.

soon became mired in despondency and sloth, Firaq observed. The forces unleashed by Gandhi, by the post-war global scenario, and the growing anti-imperialist movement, Firaq prophesied, could only be rekindled by the spark of socialism to produce a real and lasting renaissance. Known for his brilliant wit and repartee, celebrated as an aesthete-scholar, Firaq however, unlike the progressives, never sought to break away from the past. In his speech, he said

> The new Indian renaissance will both destroy and fulfill. In positive dynamics it will reflect both the inter-dependence and the uniqueness of Indian culture. Our artists, poets, … will annex and assimilate those abiding elements in the culture of India's past and of other people and places which have life and survival value in them and shall transform and trans-substantiate them.[76]

Mahmuduzzafar, the diligent note-taker, general factotum, and silent lynchpin of the conference too took time off from his administrative tasks and read a paper entitled 'Intellectuals in Cultural Reaction'.[77] It gave a glimpse into his orderly mind when it shows Mahmuduzzafar insisting that it was 'not enough to form an Association or sign a Manifesto'. Instead, he believed, 'We must also come to an understanding as to what we mean by progressivism, and also what we intend to do after we have understood'. Placing the intellectual firmly within the 'essential part of the whole we call society', he, more than anyone else, drew the audience's attention most strongly to the threat of fascism. And given the nature of the threat, he believed it became more important than ever before to understand what did and did not constitute progressivism in literature. He listed 'all tendencies towards sympathy with reaction, with imperialism, with feudal superstitions, with fascism, imperialist aggression and war' as patently non-progressive, which must be 'mercilessly attacked and rooted out'. Similarly, all tendencies towards 'irrationalism, mysticism, introversion, sex-perversion or obsession, over-concern with the fate of the individual as against society as a whole, dreams of the irrevocable golden age or the never-to-be-realised future' too were to be regarded as dangerous because 'they are the indirect allies of reaction'.

Mahmuduzzafar's short but succinct speech is a luminous example of the clear-sightedness of the early progressives which dimmed and eventu-

---

[76] Pradhan, *Marxist Cultural Movements in India*, vol. I, p. 65.

[77] Ibid., pp. 84–9.

ally got lost in the murky waters of party politics. In the light of this clear denunciation of imperialism, fascism, and war, one wonders what men like Mahmuduzzafar would have made of their party's support of Great Britain in the Second World War calling it a 'people's war'. However, more on the differences between now and then, between the beginning and the end, between what was or could have been, and what eventually became of the PWM and the progressives themselves in the concluding chapter.

Ahmed Ali's name has cropped up in previous chapters as the dissenting voice among the progressives. In his address, 'Progressive View of Art',[78] having elaborated at some length on 'only that art which is the outcome of the highest consciousness, which reflects social reality' being progressive, he went on to define 'progressive'. While not synonymous with revolutionary, he maintained that progressive meant 'trying for the betterment of social life', it implied the 'banishment of mysticism' and 'all that which stands in the way of attaining freedom'. Deeming the poetry of Tagore and Iqbal 'morbidly escapist', he concluded by making a strong case for nationalist literature. Progressive literature, he maintained, could only be a literature of opposition. And as progressive writers, his duty and that of others like him, he felt was 'to produce literature which will not be bloodless and anemic, but pulsating with fresh blood, throbbing with new life.' (This sort of extremist view had been earlier aired by Akhtar Husain Raipuri and, in the longer run as we shall see later, did more harm than good to the movement.)

Another paper found in the volume edited by Sudhi Pradhan is entitled 'Tendencies in Contemporary Bengali Literature' by Surendra Nath Goswami of Calcutta University. An otherwise straightforward overview, it makes an interesting observation about the 'Kallol' group of writers who consciously revolted against Tagore's 'romantic humanism'. These radical writers, including Nazrul Islam, were successful in their depiction of the lowest classes because the post-war economic crisis had brought about disruption of traditional structures.

The formal paper-reading session was followed by informal speeches. Kamaladevi Chattopadhyay gave a fiery speech in praise of this new movement, while Sarojini Naidu sent a message encouraging those behind this new initiative. Hasrat Mohani, delivering the valedictory address, expressed his complete agreement with the aims and objectives of the *Manifesto* and

---

[78] Ibid., pp. 67–83.

added that the Association must now devote itself to national freedom. Being progressive was not enough; it must be revolutionary, it must uphold socialism and communism for, he believed, there was no essential difference between Islam and socialism. Among the prominent writers present at the conference were Faiz Ahmed Faiz, Mian Iftikharuddin, Yusuf Meher Ali, Indulal Yagnik, Jainendra Kumar, and Saghar Nizami.

Since the conference was organized at short notice (three weeks according to Zaheer[79] and 'the papers read at the conference were few and hurriedly written'), its significance lies not so much in the issues it raised or the number of people it attracted, but the impact it nevertheless managed to have on literary sensibilities. Also, in its first-ever gathering of writers from different languages and different parts of the country, it became a landmark of sorts. In its stress on literatures in different Indian languages being made accessible, it was a clarion call for the need for translations, a need that was stressed by the progressives in the years to come, but never fully addressed.[80]

After the paper reading, the conference formally adopted the constitution of the AIPWA (drafted by Zaheer, Mahmuduzzafar, and Abdul Alim), passed resolutions (one, against Mussolini's barbaric attack on Abyssinia, and the other, a demand to the imperial government for freedom of speech), and elected office bearers. An intelligence report dated 16 April 1936 found in the IOL reads thus:

The Association's first conference began on the 10th April, when representatives and sympathizers from most Indian provinces assembled in Lucknow. As an observer on the spot has put it, 'the proceedings were attended by a number of Congress adherents and a sprinkling of lettered men' but it may be mentioned that the fair sex was also represented. Notices which Zaheer had circulated in connexion [sic] with the conference had referred to the existence of definite branches

---

[79] See 'A Note on the PWA' in Pradhan, *Marxist Cultural Movements in India*, vol. I, pp. 48–51.

[80] Incidentally, despite this well-meaning intervention, it was eventually left to the central government under a personal directive from Jawaharlal Nehru to set up the Sahitya Akademi with various state units under its umbrella, to look seriously into the question of translations from and into regional languages and truly make bhasha literatures intelligible to a national audience. The Sahitya Akademi was set up in 1954 with one of the staunchest Hindi progressives, Prabhakar Machwe, as its first secretary.

of the Association in Lahore, Delhi, Allahabad, Aligarh and Calcutta, but the list of those who had been induced to sign the manifesto (which had been slightly modified and published; it is now more carefully worded in order to conceal the Association's communist origin and proclivities) revealed 'contacts' also in Benares, Aurangabad, Cawnpore, Waltaira, as well as in London, Oxford and Paris. Those who eventually went to Lucknow represented a still wider field, including Amritsar, Satara (Bombay Presidency), Bangalore, Madras City, and Lucknow itself as well as Bolpur Santiniketan in Bengal. The resolutions passed adopted the new manifesto; demanded freedom of thought and expressions; condemned imperialist wars as 'a brutality and a serious menace to human culture'; urged the authorities of Indian universities to allow their students freedom to develop political organizations and journals; extended hearty greetings to a 'universal gathering for peace' which is to be convened in Geneva in September under the presidentship of the well-known Frenchman Romain Rolland; and denounced the intention of the educational authorities to restrict higher education in accordance with the recommendations of the Sapru Committee. S.S. Zaheer was formally elected as the PWA's general secretary.[81]

The report goes on to say that every effort is being made to

conceal the Association's communist inspiration and intentions, but the veil has been lifted a little by a press announcement which summed up the proceedings of the conference and declared that the new literature of India must deal with 'the basic problems of existence today—the problems of hunger and poverty, social backwardness and political subjection—and characterize all that drags us down to passivity in action and reason as reactionary'.... It may be presumed that this is the line adopted in four or five new books by members of the association which are almost ready to be placed on the Indian market. It is not the case with the Party's London journal, *New Indian Literature*, copies of which have recently been intercepted. Although the first issue of this journal contains articles by prominent members of the Association including Dr Mulk Raj Anand and S.S. Zaheer, their writings on this occasion are comparatively mild. In fact, were the journal to be judged on this issue alone and without reference to the Party's known intentions, it might be allowed free circulation ... but it would obviously be unsafe to believe what is displayed before our eyes when it is known, that for the present, the whole policy of the Association is carefully to disguise its activities and its literature behind an innocuous front. The word 'progressive' in the Association's title is most

---

[81] 'IPWA Reports on Members and Activities in India', IOR/L/PJ/12/499, File 70/36, January 1936–October 1941.

significant in this connexion; it may be taken that its literature and policy will be 'progressively' reactionary.[82]

Writing later, Sajjad Zaheer spoke of the 'consciousness, in many cases vague and unidentified'[83] of the world and its ways that led to the formation of the PWA and how a need was being felt for the last two or three years: 'In many parts of India groups of writers, mostly young, were feeling the need of making a break with the supine and escapist literature with which the country was being flooded; of creating something more real, something more in harmony with the facts of our existence today, something which will make our art full-bodied and virile.'[84]

The idea of holding the first AIPWA in Lucknow—on the sidelines of the Congress session—was neither as simple nor as literary as it is made out by Zaheer, who remains the only chronicler of the early history of the PWA.[85] Intelligence reports in the IOL reveal a deeper motive. The Conference allowed a perfect opportunity for conversations and meetings between communists, socialists, and their sympathizers. The prominent official or declared communists present on the occasion were S.A. Dange, S.V. Ghate, P.C. Joshi (all active in the Bombay presidency), J.H. Bukhari (Ahmedabad), G.M. Mote (Nagpur), Sohan Singh Josh (Lahore), Sundarma Reddy (Madras), and Ajoy Kumar Ghosh (Kanpur). Enormous amounts of communist literature were produced for the occasion and distributed inside the Congress pandal by male and female volunteers. This included several proscribed publications in English, Hindi, and Urdu. A

---

[82] Ibid.

[83] Sajjad Zaheer, 'A Note on the PWA', in Sudhi Pradhan (ed.), *Marxist Cultural Movements in India*, vol. I (Calcutta: National Book Agency, 1979), p. 48.

[84] Ibid.

[85] Apart from Zaheer's accounts, the first critical history of the PWM is provided by Aziz Ahmad's article entitled 'Taraqqui Pasand Adab' published in *Urdu* (1942), which placed the movement in the context of social realism. This was followed by Jafri's book-length study, *Taraqqui Pasand Adab* (1951 [2nd ed. in 1957]) which was a largely one-sided and laudatory account. The most balanced history, and also the best researched, is Azmi's *Urdu mein Taraqqui Pasand Adabi Tehreek* (2002 [1957]). There is also Hansraj Rahbar's *Taraqqui Pasand Adab: Ek Jaiza* (Delhi: Azada Kitab Ghar, 1967), but that is more in the nature of re-evaluation and a search for what went wrong. Rahbar's views will be taken up in Chapter 8 when we look at the reasons for the decline of the PWM.

cyclostyled edition of the 'Draft of the Provisional Statutes of the CPI', which had first appeared in *Inprecor* of 11 May 1934, was circulated in the Congress camp, as was a new issue of *The Communist* (no. 7).[86]

With a fairly successful first All-India Conference under their belt and newer branches opening up in newer cities—Poona, Ahmedabad, Benaras, Patna, and Delhi—besides those that existed before the conference, the organizers could afford to sound pleased. Writing a few years later, Zaheer noted, 'We do not pretend that we have in this short time effected any change in the course of Indian literary life; but we do assert that we have succeeded in creating the organization and the necessary atmosphere which will help to bring about this change.'[87]

For all their smugness, however, the progressives did not believe in letting the grass grow under their feet. The ink was barely dry on reports of the big conference they had organized on the sidelines of the Congress conference when the grapevine was abuzz with reports of the first issue of *New Indian Literature* dated Spring 1936, which was to be the official organ of the PWA. Published at 38 Canning Road, Allahabad, it declared that all communications in connection with it were to be addressed to Mulk Raj Anand at 53, Woburn Place, WC.[88] Unfortunately, differences developed between the editorial team comprising Anand, Abdul Alim, and Ahmed Ali and the journal folded up after two issues.

Another weekly report of the DIB of the Home Department dated 20 August 1936 describes an All-India Students' Conference held at Lucknow on 12 and 13 August under the presidentship of M.A. Jinnah: 'It was convened by the United Provinces University Students' Federation, and if the political complexion of its organizers is any guide, its chief object was to bring the student community into the "anti-imperialist United Front".'[89] Of the 50-odd members of the Subjects Committee,

---

[86] This section has been built from IOR/L/PJ/12/430. The same file talks of the Trojan Horse Policy of the Communists in infiltrating the Congress at all levels. It gives the example of Sajjad Zaheer and of K.M. Ashraf who was appointed secretary of Nehru's new Political and Economic Information Department in June 1936. The report also mentions Zaheer distributing left-wing literature, on behalf of the AIPWA, at the Faizpur session of the Congress in January 1937.

[87] Zaheer, 'Note on the PWA', p. 51.

[88] IOR/L/PJ/12/499, File 70/36.

[89] IOR/L/PJ/12/60, File 4968 (g) 21.

'thirty are said to have openly declared themselves to be either revolutionaries or communists'. In a similar report dated 31 October 1936 entitled 'Students and Socialism', there is mention of a 'so-called all-India organisation' set up under the name of the All-India Students Federation, again with Lucknow as its headquarters.[90] 'The communist attack in the United Provinces,' the report goes on to substantiate Zaheer's assertions in *Roshnai* and other writings, 'seems mainly to consist of the establishment of study circles and night schools. A number of these, with prominent communists in charge, have been formed in Cawnpore, Lucknow, and Allahabad and also in the Banaras Hindu University where a strong Communist Party is said to exist under the control of a resident professor of economics.'

Aligarh, so far aloof from such activities, is reported to have been 'contaminated' too. 'Communist pamphlets have also made their appearance in the Aligarh University, but it is difficult to determine how far this form of activity is prompted by the expectation of results and how far by animosity towards the present vice-chancellor.'[91] A branch of the PWA functioned

---

[90] Just a few weeks ago, on 10–11 October 1936, the Maharashtra Youths Conference had been organized by S.A. Dange in Poona.

[91] The vice-chancellor of Aligarh, Dr Ziauddin Ahmed, wrote the following scathing critique of communism in his capacity as editor of *The Muslim University Gazette* on 8 June 1937:

Communism and Fascism which are diametrically opposite to each other in all respects except that they are both opposed to democracy and stand in the way of independent growth of democratic institutions. Fascism, which is a form of dictatorship, is not concerned with India because we never hope to face it in any conceivable future. But Communism is much nearer to India because the propagandist literature of its exponents is being daily dinned into the ears of our young men and it is the duty of educationists to present the other side of the picture to enable the young men to make up their own mind. There may be some good points but three of its fundamental principles are definitely opposed to Islam and these are:

1. Denial of God and revolt against religion;
2. Discarding matrimonial ties; and
3. Abolition of property.

This issue of *The Muslim University Gazette* is found in the Sir Syed Collection of the Maulana Azad Library, AMU. The vice-chancellor's views are symptomatic of wilful ignorance and mistrust of communism among a large section of educated Muslims.

in Aligarh from early 1936; its first event was held in the house of Khwaja Manzoor Husain. Sardar Jafri, then a student at Aligarh from where he was shortly expelled, read a paper on *'Jadeed Adab aur Naujawanon ki Rujhaniyat'* (The Interest of the Youth in Modern Literature) which was subsequently published in *Aligarh Magazine*, then edited by Jan Nisar Akhtar. However, to give a sense of the different poles of opinion among Aligarh students it must be mentioned that while the left was represented by liberals such as Majaz, Hayatullah Ansari, Akhtar Husain Raipuri, K.A. Abbas, Shahid Latif, and Sibte Hasan, there were some students who were impressed by Hitler's Nazism and had set up the German society to promote fascism.[92]

Jawaharlal Nehru had been active among the youth organizations from the late 1920s, and was known to talk of the Russian revolution where 'a very few men and women had worked a miracle, and converted this very wretched human material into a hardworking and virile race. I am sure this can be done here despite our leaders....'[93] An intelligence report of 8 January 1938[94] attributes the increased activity in the left-wing direction to the Lucknow session of the Congress in 1936 and Nehru's open patronage of the communists. Another report, dated 12 June 1937, speaks of Zaheer's role, as general secretary of the PWA, in spreading communist ideas among students:

The activities of the PWA, the moving spirit of which is S.S. Zaheer, are extending. Branches now exist in most university and college towns, to foster an interest in 'progressive' literature, but the true objects of the organisation are more properly indicated by the political views of certain important branch members. Amongst Zaheer's most ardent supporters are a number of well-known Communists, and there is reliable information to show that the Association proposes to supply Socialist and Communist literature to student bodies in many parts of the country. The Association's bulletin [referring to *New Indian Literature*] has suspended publication for the time being but, meanwhile, Zaheer is engaged in subversive activities of a more practical aspect. In April [1937] he visited Bengal, in May the Kottapatnam Socialist summer school in Madras, and after a short stay in Allahabad, he visited the Punjab. Each of these occasions provided the opportunities

---

[92] K.M. Ashraf, 'The Political Life of Aligarh', *Aligarh Magazine* (Aligarh Number), 1954, p. 170.

[93] IOR/L/PJ/12/60, File 4968 (G) 21.

[94] IOR/L/PJ/12/61, File 4968 (G) 21.

he sought, of carrying to students and young men generally his message of communism, and of advancing plans for their further corruption.[95]

The All-India Students Federation too had grown with branches in almost all the important educational centres in UP and the three presidencies. It was reported to be under the influence of the 'intellectual' communists, especially those who were regarded as Nehru's protégés in the AICC's secretariat at Allahabad, and much had been done to familiarize students with extremist doctrines through the medium of study circles and training classes (in which Sajjad Zaheer and other members of the PWA had taken active part) conducted according to the recognized principles of communist practice.

A DIB report[96] reveals a reference to Mahmuduzzafar Khan[97] who worked as Jawaharlal Nehru's personal secretary and visited London in the autumn of 1936 where he discussed the possibility of collaborating with the firm of Victor Gollancz and furthering the scope of the activities of the Left Book Club.[98] The purpose of such a venture was to evade the restrictions under the Sea Customs Act and to publish Indian editions of left books from manuscripts which would be sent over from England. Gollancz himself had a 'lively interest in the dissemination of communist literature in India' and was determined to popularize the Left Book Club in India. A Left Book Club Discussion Group already existed in London for Indian students, under the charge of Promod Sengupta (one of the original signatories to the *Manifesto*). Another reference to Mahmuduzzafar is found in a DIB report dated 27 November 1937. Described as an 'intellectual' communist, he is said to have expressed his opinion (upon returning from Europe) that the CPI was growing in

[95] IOR/L/PJ/12/61, File 4968 (G) 21.

[96] IOR/L/PJ/12/430.

[97] In the NMML interview, Zaheer stated that Mahmud lived in Anand Bhawan for almost two years while he worked for Nehru and he was joined by his wife, Rashid Jahan. Mahmud wrote a note on the election tour which Nehru undertook in 1937. We find a reference to it with Nehru pointing out instances where he disagrees with Mahmud. See *Selected Works of Jawaharlal Nehru*, vol. 8 (New Delhi: Orient Longman, 1976), pp. 41–2.

[98] Hamida Saiduzzafar, writing in *Shola-e-Jawwala*, mentions that Mahmud travelled with his wife to England to seek medical treatment for lumps in her throat.

confidence, and was in a strong position as regards the Congress since many of its adherents, such as Dr Ashraf, Z.A. Ahmed, and Sajjad Zaheer were working in the Congress 'inner circle'. According to the report, this 'clique of intellectuals', most of whom were personal friends of the Meerut Conspiracy Case accused and were at one time members of the Secret Indian Students Communist Group in London, exert influence on the affairs of the Congress Central Committee, which is 'hard to distinguish from active membership'. B.F. Bradley, the bête noir of the intelligence agencies, is described as the group's 'chief technical advisor' and 'confidant abroad' who had endorsed the 'open tactics' adopted by the Indian communists and advised 'full speed ahead' along the triple line comprising workers, peasants, and student groups.

Sajjad Zaheer returned to India in November 1935 and joined, almost immediately thereafter, the AICC and the CSP as well as got in touch with P.C. Joshi and R.D. Bhardwaj (both of whom were then underground). An acknowledged communist, he was nevertheless appointed secretary of the Allahabad Congress Committee in 1935 (with Nehru as its president) and plunged whole-heartedly into the peasants' movement.[99] In June 1937, he was arrested in Mussoorie for delivering a speech at the Unnao Kisan Conference. On 29 June 1937, he wrote to Nehru (both his immediate boss and family friend given the overlapping ties of legal fraternity and neighbourliness between their families) informing him that he had been released on bail, and that the hearing of his case would be in July 1937. Nehru (addressing him as 'My Dear Banne') assured him legal help by getting either the eminent lawyer Katju or Kapil Deva to appear for him. The affectionate letter concluded thus:

I hope you are none the worse after a few days in the lock-up. My own opinion is that it is a very desirable part in a person's education and far from minding it, you should almost welcome it! But of course you should fight this case out on larger

---

[99] In the NMML interview, Zaheer stated that one of his earliest tasks was to organize an all-India hartal against the new constitution which gave autonomy to the provinces but not to the centre. His other duties were to go door to door, mohalla to mohalla in Allahabad in a bid to increase Congress membership. He addressed street corner meetings to press the demand for real freedom and not the fake assurances of the constitution that the British were trying to impose. Within six months of his arrival from England, he was arrested on charges of sedition but released two days later due to his father's influence.

grounds of principle. I am glad to learn the nature of the speech you delivered. That will make it a good test case.[100]

However, the next transgression was not viewed with the same affectionate tolerance. A month later, on 25 August 1937, Nehru wrote asking about a demonstration Zaheer had lead in front of the *kutchery*. Tenants who had been forcibly ejected from their lands in Allahabad district, had marched in procession (under Zaheer's guidance) shouting slogans against the zamindars.[101] This prompted Nehru to write a mild reprimand: 'Some important questions of principle are involved in this matter, such as the desirability of Congressmen demonstrating against and condemning the Congress ministries and the Congress.'[102]

Nehru also protested, mildly, about the use of red flags on such occasions. However, despite Nehru's growing disenchantment with communism and his occasional impatience with the young comrades in his own party, his relations with Zaheer and with the PWA remained cordial. In November 1937, he addressed the PWA session in Allahabad. Perhaps, Nehru saw groupings such as the PWA as furthering the cause of nationalism, the cause dearest to his heart. Admitting that in the West progressive groups have a longer history, but in Asia, where such groups have recently come into existence, the issue is often 'clouded by the nationalist issue'.[103]

Matters came to a head between Congress and the communists over the latter's unqualified support of the Muslim League's support for Pakistan and the, equally untenable, support for the British war effort.[104] Zaheer

---

[100] *Selected Works of Jawaharlal Nehru*, vol. 8, p. 851.

[101] In the NMML interview, Zaheer said: 'At that time our main objective was to create a situation for a big mass anti-imperialist movement in our country and that, we thought, could only be done if more and more demands of peasants, workers and the middle-classes were included in the national movement and let it become, say a politico-socio-economic movement and an anti-imperialist movement.'

[102] *Selected Works of Jawaharlal Nehru*, vol. 8, p. 307.

[103] Presidential Address at the Conference on Peace and Empire, London, 15 July 1938. *Selected Works of Jawaharlal Nehru*, vol. 9, p. 63.

[104] *Charges against Communist Members in the Congress*, filed on 21 September 1945, AICC, File No. G-23 (Part I) 1945–6, pp. 79–97, NMML; and *Selected Works of Jawaharlal Nehru*, vol. 14 (1981), pp. 528–47.

was eventually expelled from the Congress (along with K.M. Ashraf, Sohan Singh Josh, S.G. Sardesai, and others) in 1945.[105] Given the closeness of their families, given that their fathers had had flourishing legal careers in Allahabad, given also that Nehru was remarkably tolerant of the left-leaning young intellectuals such as K.M. Ashraf (to whom he had entrusted his Muslim Mass Contact Programme) and Dr Z.A. Ahmed (who served on the Congress's committee on economic affairs),[106] the ties between Nehru and Zaheer were never entirely broken. The two had, earlier, been imprisoned in the Central Jail in Lucknow where, when Nehru joined in April 1941, he found Banne had been there for 13 months as a detenue. As we shall see, in the last chapter, Nehru once again answered the call of friendship and family ties when Zaheer wanted to come home to India from the Pakistani jail.

We get a glimpse of the communist 'infiltration' in the Congress and the CSP in an interview with Hajra Begum.[107] Not a writer herself, she nevertheless served as secretary of the Allahabad PWA as part of the party's directive to work with the city's intellectuals: 'So, in the guise of the PWA, I would go to them and, in that way, approach them also for whatever help the Party needed and that was one of my tasks, which was not openly known—openly I was doing work for the PWA.'

She was the 'contact' on behalf of the party for a year and a half and approached well-known sympathizers in Allahabad University such as Firaq, Satish Chandra Deb, and Ejaz Hussain. She also admitted that, as a party worker, one was expected to do propaganda on the lines adopted

---

[105] *Selected Works of Jawaharlal Nehru*, vol. 14, p. 547.

[106] Zaheer, in his interview with the NMML's Oral History Project, recalled how Nehru was proud of the Muslim members in the core group of the AICC—Mahmuduzzafar, Dr Ashraf, Dr Z.A. Ahmad, and Zaheer himself. However, according to Zaheer, the right-wing within the Congress resented the presence of the left and kept a watchful eye on the young comrades, reporting their activities to Gandhi and Patel. Hajra Begum, in her interview at the NMML, corroborated this and added that Acharya Kriplani was the link between the goings on at the AICC and Gandhi. During these days in the AICC, Zaheer organized a series of lectures at Swaraj Bhawan and invited Nehru, Acharya Narendra Dev, Jayaprakash, P.C. Joshi, and K.M. Ashraf to speak on different aspects of the present situation in the country

[107] NMML, Oral History Project.

by the party. Later, she worked with party colleagues active in UP, such as Romesh Tandon and O.P. Singhal; she also worked 'through' the All-India Women's Conference for the CPI. In the interview, Hajra Begum was candid enough to admit, 'I feel that as a writers' movement, it [PWM] should have been a broader movement. It did become sort of dominated by people of one way of thought, that is, the communist thinking or having revolutionary ideas and to be a very good writer, it is not necessary that you should have revolutionary ideas.'

Meanwhile, a repeat of the *Angarey* furore was adroitly averted by the government. The Muslims were up in arms against the publication of H.G. Wells's *A Short History of the World* published by Heinemann as long ago as in 1922, with Muslim organizations in Kampala, Nairobi, and different parts of Africa suddenly finding the book objectionable and expressing outrage. In the East End of London, a group of Indian Muslims consigned the book to flames, organized a procession on 18 August 1938, and demanded that the book be proscribed.[108] A body called the Jamiat-ul-Muslimin, an East End Muslim association, coordinated the activities by mounting pressure on the Indian high commissioner, Sir Firoz Khan Noon. Lord Zetland wrote to Sir Noon expressing his sympathy and regret: 'I have no power to secure a modification of the passage to which exception has been taken.'[109] And there the matter rested. Oddly enough, neither the book nor the offending passages raised similar protests in Muslim countries of the Middle East. In India, agitation in the press regarding the chapter 'Muhammad and Islam', lead the provincial government of Sind to take action against the book under Section 26 of the Indian Post Office Act, 1898. The book came to the notice of the CID which reported that it would inflame Muslim feelings, and the government ordered detention of all copies of the said book as objectionable literature in March 1939. The whole matter was thus dealt with adroitly and a repeat of the *Angarey* furore was nipped in the bud.

We will conclude this last section by looking briefly at certain other events that directly and indirectly affected the PWM. We will look at the differences that began to creep in by the time of the Second World War and the distinction that many Indians began to make between communism (especially the highly organized party-based system) and socialism, and

---

[108] *Manchester Guardian*, 13 August 1938, IOR/L/PJ/12/ 614.
[109] IOR/L/PJ/12/ 614.

began to express their preference for the latter. A quote from Nehru, in a statement made to the press on 9 June 1936, encapsulates this ambivalence:

I prefer to use the word socialism to communism because the latter has come to signify Soviet Russia.... I am not afraid of the word communism. Constituted as I am, all my sympathies go to the underdog and to him who is persecuted most. That in itself would be sufficient to incline me towards communism when all the power of the state and of vested interest tries to crush it.[110]

Prominent socialist leaders such as Acharya Narendra Dev and Jayaprakash Narayan, despite their pronounced sympathy with Marxism, became openly hostile to the CPI due to its connection with Moscow. The communists in India, for their own part, were marred by inter- and intra-group jealousies and petty rivalries, and constant threats of encroachment on their turf both from the Congress and the socialists. Looking back on the communists' support of Pakistan, Ram Manohar Lohia makes the following blistering denouement of communism vis-à-vis nationalism: 'Communism is partitionist, only when it is not in power, in order to weaken its foe in the shape of a strong nationalism. When it can itself represent nationalism, it ceases to be partitionist.'[111]

Intelligence reports in the British Library reveal that funds from Moscow had dried up altogether by 1938 (though the Comintern was officially dissolved in 1943, its influence had begun to decline after 1935 when its last Congress was held) and funds from the CPGB too had reduced to a trickle.[112] A report for 27 July 1939 states that while no direct link seems to exist between the CPI and Comintern, there was an active link between CPI and CPGB. The Comintern, which the report calls the 'handmaiden of Soviet foreign policy' and the active promoter of communist revolution in neighbouring countries, had 'receded' from the current politics of India. Occasional private subscription such as from Indian Students' Secret

---

[110] *Selected Works of Jawaharlal Nehru*, vol. 7 (1975), p. 283.

[111] Rammanohar Lohia, *Guilty Men of India's Partition* (New Delhi: B.R. Publishing Corporation, 2000), p. 3.

[112] Paltry sums continued to come their way from sympathizers in Britain with small amounts of cash sent through visitors. A report dated 26 February 1938 mentions £100 sent by CPGB to Dr Adhikari for printing and circulating a large amount of communist literature. There is no evidence that money came regularly or in sufficiently large amounts from the CPGB in later years; IOR/L/PJ/12/431.

Communist Group helped keep the CPI journal *The National Front* afloat. In stark contrast to the heady years of the Meerut Conspiracy Case, now the intellectual rather than the violent type of British Communists began to visit India and take up employment, such as K.H. Platt[113] and his wife.

A report entitled 'Growing Menace of Communism in India' theorized that Comintern continued to operate in India through British communists who were not 'parlour socialists or drawing-room Bolsheviks', but highly committed individuals who genuinely believed that only through chaos can one construct a classless society. The report went so far as to warn:

> What appears as a nationalist movement and has behind it all the impetus of patriotism can be permeated with communism and perverted into a socialist revolutionary movement, a nursery for strikes, sabotage and terrorism … the direct influence of the CPI which call for serious attention as the insidious and seditious manner in which communists penetrate other organizations and the indirect hold which communist teachings exert over the national movement.[114]

The agitators active in the peasant and workers' trade unions eked out a largely hand-to-mouth existence and some also earned the reputation of being professional rabble-rousers who would even stoop to extortions from mill-owners, landlords, and the hated capitalists.

Meanwhile, as Hitler's aggression turned towards the Eastern Front and the Soviet Union got drawn into the war amphitheatre, the Indian communists' anti-war stance began to change. As early as 1939 (before the German invasion of June 1941), the Comintern advice to the CPI, conveyed through the CPGB, was as follows: 'The War against Hitler today is not an imperialist war of the 1914 type. This war is being fought by the people in defence of their rights, and it is these new forces that must be and will be finally victorious.'[115]

Promptly taking the cue, the CPI dubbed it a 'people's war' and with Britain aligning with the USSR against the fascist forces, the complexion of the war suddenly changed. What had so far been a conflict of imperialisms had, overnight, through the leaven of Russian involvement, become a cause worthy of unqualified support. Its effects were felt in India with the

---

[113] Platt taught Mechanical Engineering at Banaras Hindu University in 1938.

[114] *The Statesman*, 6 December 1939.

[115] *Colonial Information Bulletin*, 13 September 1939, p. 58; IOR/L/PJ/12/431.

lifting of the ban on the CPI on 23 July 1942. With the legalization of the CPI, certain things were brought out in the open, such as the existence of political schools and study circles. Underground arrangements, on which the party had survived eight years of the ban, were also overhauled and improved. However, while for the majority of the communists or their sympathizers fear and hatred of the fascists outweighed all other considerations, the party's about-turn and sudden pro-war policy made many waver. Careful not to hinder war production, the CPI, the indefatigable organizer of strikes and lockouts, even took a no-strike line!

Meanwhile, Gandhi's Quit India campaign, launched during October–December 1942, dented the CPI's pro-war slogans and made many erstwhile sympathizers decide to put their faith in Gandhi and the Congress. Communists stood aloof from the Quit India disturbances that rocked the nation not only because they disapproved of the Congress action as playing into the enemy's hands, but also because they did not want to risk police action and imprisonment. The pro-war policy helped restore the CPI's political fortunes when they were at their lowest ebb, but drove a wedge that further disintegrated its already quarrelling and fractious camps. At about the same time as Gandhi's mass movement, the CPI, in a bid to save face and reclaim lost ground, launched the Unity Campaign, projecting a united Congress and Muslim League as a panacea of all ills. The Muslim League, on its part, appreciated the communists' recognition of the Muslims' right to self-determination, but was essentially and fundamentally wary of the CPI, mostly on political grounds, but, for the more religious among the Leaguers, also due to the communists' godlessness.

In the following two chapters, we shall cover the contested terrain between the Congress, Muslim League, and CPI (which had begun to call itself the 'third largest political party in India' or the 'young patriotic party') in the last decade leading up to the Partition. However, after this densely political chapter, drawn as it is from primary sources, we shall once again turn our attention to literary sources. In the next two chapters, we shall reconstruct the history of the PWM—first from progressive Urdu poetry and then from prose. Historical events, both connected with the PWM as well as Indian national history, will run as the warp in the weft of Urdu sources to weave the richly layered and complex tapestry of the freedom movement. The picture that will emerge will, hopefully, show the intersections between the PWM and the Indian national movement which is as much the concern of this study as the recreation of a literary history.

6

From *Shabab* to *Inquilab*
Progressive Poetry from 1930s till 1950s

> *Kaam hai mere taghiar naam hai mera shabab*
> *Mera naara inquilab o inquilab o inquilab*
> (My work is change, my name is youth
> My cry is revolution, revolution, revolution)
> —Josh Malihabadi (1898–1982)

'It was the best of times; it was the worst of times', wrote Charles Dickens in the opening lines of *A Tale of Two Cities*. He was alluding to the French Revolution, but it could just as well be said for the progressive upsurge of the late 1930s, for in its progress lay the seeds of its decline and in its beginning lay, coiled, its end. In this chapter, we will analyse the work of some of the major Urdu poets associated with the PWA during the 'high noon' of the movement and assess their work, both individually and in the light of their association with the movement. In the process, we shall also look at the cities that emerged as major hubs of the PWM—Lucknow,

Aligarh, Delhi, Bombay, Hyderabad, and Lahore.[1] Lahore and Hyderabad will feature largely in the context of Faiz and Makhdoom, respectively, but the other cities will recur in our study of Majaz, Jafri, Kaifi, Jan Nisar Akhtar, Akhtarul Iman, and a host of other progressives.

But before discussing individual poets, we shall take up the history of the PWM where we left it in the previous chapter and in a brief section, entitled 'The Glory Days (1936–1947)', look at some of the highlights of the heady years from 1936 till 1947. Majaz died in 1955—the year that has been set as the cut-off year for this study of the PWM—as did Manto, whom we shall study in the next chapter. The other writers in this group continued to be active till the end of their lives. They acknowledged their role in the PWM, wrote about the movement and its shortcomings, and generally came to be identified with the finest literary output among the progressives. We will set out the changes that appeared in their writings in the years after 1955. Simultaneously, we will also examine their poetry in the light of national and international events. We will attempt to establish how important milestones in the freedom struggle impinged upon their consciousness, how, faithfully or otherwise, they wove it into their writings, and how their own affiliations with the PWM waxed and waned in the light of some of these events. We shall also study, for the first time, some of those who were associated with another contemporary literary coalition called the Halqa-e Arbab-e Zauq (Circle of the Men of Good Taste) and see how, in the early days, the PWA and the Halqa were loose groupings with overlapping memberships. We shall continue to pay close attention to these interstices between groups which began with fluid, changing membership and only later fossilized into structured organizations. In so doing, we shall look at the literary careers of several Urdu writers who were, in one way or the other, connected with the PWM up till the 1950s.

[1] I am indebted to a section entitled '*Jin Dayaron se Karvaan Guzra*', in Qamar Rais and S. Ashoor Kazmi (eds), *Taraqqui Pasand Adab: Pachas Sala Safar* (Delhi: Naya Safar Publications, 1987) for an understanding of the growth of the PWM in the different cities and provinces. The section contains articles by Farigh Bukhari, Brij Premi, Rafiq Ahmad Naqvi, Kamal Ahmad Siddiqui, Syed Aquil Rizwi, Sulaiman Athar Javed, Yusuf Nazim, M.A. Nasr, S. Akhtar, Rifat Sarosh, and Atiq Ahmad on NWFP, Kashmir, Aligarh, Lucknow, Allahabad, Hyderabad, Calcutta, Bihar, Bombay, and Karachi, respectively.

The Glory Days (1936–1947)

Travelling to India for the first time in 1949, Ralph Russell observed that almost every Urdu writer of any note was a progressive.[2] The observation is neither fanciful nor exaggerated. The PWM enjoyed an uninterrupted spell of over a decade when its influence, extent, and character were most pronounced. Virtually from the beginning, the progressives had found friends in high places that helped the movement gain momentum. Premchand was an early convert though he died a few months after the first AIPWA conference in 1936.[3] However, his endorsement of the progressives' credo laid the grounds for Hindi and Urdu writers to meet and discuss the common issues that confronted them without the acrimony of the script and language debates. Maulvi Abdul Haq lent his gravitas to the cause whenever he could. Influential Urdu critics such as Aziz Ahmad, Ehtesham Husain, and Ale Ahmad Suroor wrote about the movement and its adherents in literary journals. As early as July 1935, Akhtar Husain Raipuri wrote 'Adab aur Zindagi' (Art and Life) for Maulvi Abdul Haq's *Urdu*, spelling out the place of realism in life and by extension in art. The article caused a sensation in literary circles because it showed a new way of looking at literature and was sternly critical of old literary concerns. In April 1936, days after the AIPWA conference in Lucknow, Raipuri read his version of a 'manifesto' at the Bharatiya

---

[2] 'My most numerous contacts were with the Progressives. This is not mainly because I myself shared much of their ideology (which I did) but because most of the prominent writers of that time were progressives.' Ralph Russell, *Annual of Urdu Studies*, no. 11 (1996), p. 29.

[3] In these short months, Premchand did a great deal for the progressives' cause: he published the Hindi version of his inaugural address in *Hans* (July 1936), encouraged Hindi writers from Benaras, Patna, Nagpur, etc., to join the PWM, talked about the movement from public platforms, be they Congress events or Hindi Sahitya Parishad functions. In a letter dated 10 May 1936 (published in *Naya Adab*, January–February 1940), he wrote to Zaheer asking him to send copies of the *Manifesto*, membership forms as well as Urdu and English translations of his inaugural address, and copies of the report of the conference proceedings. He writes about speaking to fellow Hindi writer, Sampurnanand, about a paper in every language, including English, devoted to the progressive cause. In the letter, Premchand spoke of the need for haste and urgency in the matter.

Sahitya Parishad's conference in Nagpur whose aims and objectives were much the same as the PWA's, but he also added:

We have decided the outline of literature but have not decided what will be its shape and colour. First we must decide what to say, and who to say it to. How to say it will be addressed later. Literary issues cannot be separated from other issues of life. Life is a complete unit; it cannot be divided into the pigeonholes of literature, philosophy and politics. Literature is the mirror of life; it is also the guide for the caravan of existence. Literature must not only be the companion of life but must also show it the way.... Today when there is a war between the forces of progressivism and reactionaries, can literature remain impartial?[4]

Alarmed by the growing importance of the progressives, M.G. Hallett, the home secretary, sent a notice (which soon acquired notoriety as the Hallett Circular) in 1936 advising concerned authorities to keep a stern watch on the activities of the PWA which despite its professedly 'innocuous' objectives was 'advocating policies akin to those of the communists'. While the government did not regard the PWA as a 'subversive or revolutionary organisation', it did feel the need to watch it with some suspicion and dispense 'friendly warnings about this association to journalists, educationists and others who might be attracted to its ostensible programme'.[5] Undeterred by the local government's tight vigil, the PWA continued to attract new adherents.

Sohail Azimabadi helped set up the Patna branch of the PWA as early as 1936, and Hasrat Mohani took charge of the Kanpur branch. However, from 1936–8, the movement was largely confined to Urdu, Hindi, and Bengali writers and the overwhelming majority of members were drawn from the Urdu intelligentsia. Hindi and Urdu writers held three major conferences in 1937, 1938, and 1939, the first two in Allahabad and the third in Lucknow. The first was organized by Shyam Kumari Nehru;[6] it was held in the marquee set up for a swadeshi exhibition thus sparing the

---

[4] *Adab aur Inquilab* (Literature and Revolution) (Bombay: National Information and Publishers Ltd.), p. 2.

[5] Sudhi Pradhan (ed.), *Marxist Cultural Movements in India: Chronicles and Documents (1936–47)*, vol. I (Calcutta: National Book Agency, 1979), pp. 344–5.

[6] A member of the Nehru clan, a writer (as was her mother, Uma), the first woman from UP to do an LLB and practice law, she had participated in the civil disobedience movement and gone to prison.

PWA the cost of venue, lights, etc.[7] Zaheer recorded in *Roshnai* how Shyam Kumari managed to collect a tidy sum as donations from university professors and lawyers. Unlike the Lucknow conference, here it was decided to have a presidium where writers of more than one language could preside; the presidium comprised Maulvi Abdul Haq, Acharya Narendra Dev, and Pandit Ram Naresh Tripathi. This conference was attended by Shivdan Singh Chauhan, Narendra Sharma, Ramesh Chandra Sinha, Om Prakash Singhal, among other notable Hindi writers. Maulvi Abdul Haq sent a presidential address that spoke of the need for freshness above all else in literature and the need to get rid of the old and fetid.

The second Allahabad conference in 1938[8] was organized by Bishambar Nath Pandey (secretary of the Allahabad branch of the PWA), again during the swadeshi exhibition and on its grounds. This was more representative (in that it had representatives from Punjab and Bihar apart from UP) and had discussions on different literary genres; it also looked critically at the organizational weaknesses that were by now evident, such as the lack of a central office. Its presidium included Josh, Anand Narain Mulla, and Sumitranandan Pant. Nehru, an honoured guest, spoke on the occasion as did Kaka Kalelkar and Maithili Sharan Gupt. Faiz came as a delegate from Punjab. Premchand's son, Amrit Rai, came from Benares along with several young Hindi writers.

[7] As in the first Lucknow conference this was to become a habit. While indeed it saved trouble and expense, it was a considered decision on the part of Zaheer to 'open up' the proceedings and allow more people—including non-literary types—to participate. It strengthens the belief that in Zaheer's mind the PWA was never a purely literary association; it was a political body which planned to use literature for specific ends. Those of its members who thought otherwise were bound to be later disillusioned. On the decision to hold the conference on the sidelines of the swadeshi exhibition, Zaheer wrote, 'The Movement for Progressive Literature too was after all a "Swadeshi" movement, so it could be said to have the right to be held under the same marquee.' Sajjad Zaheer, *The Light: A History of the Movement for Progressive Literature in the Indo-Pak Subcontinent*, English translation of Sajjad Zaheer's *Roshnai* by Amina Azfar (Karachi: Oxford University Press, 2006), pp. 110–11.

[8] There appears to be a discrepancy in the dates of the Allahabad conference mentioned by Zaheer in *Roshnai*. Nehru's selected works mention his address to the PWA in Allahabad on 14 November 1937. The text of his speech was published in the *Leader*, 18 November 1937. Khalilur Rahman Azmi too gives the date of the second Allahabad conference as March 1938.

Zaheer, Abdul Alim, and Bishambar Nath Pandey made an impassioned plea for a common Roman script to put an end to the corrosive Hindi–Urdu debate which was vehemently opposed by Kalelkar. However, the proudest moment was when the message from Rabindranath Tagore was read out, advising writers to mingle with the people and to know them, for 'literature that is not in harmony with mankind,' the seer warned, 'is destined for failure'. Tagore went on to caution that 'creative literature exacts tribulations. If you want to find beauty and truth you must throw off the slough of egoism.'[9] The egoism that Tagore referred to was the exclusivity and sequestering that writers, especially of the higher classes imposed upon themselves; this was evident when he confessed: 'I understand now the mistake I made by staying away from society, and that is why I am giving you this counsel.'[10]

Nehru's address, more informal but equally heartfelt, stressed the role of the progressive writer. He also touched upon the Hindi–Urdu debate by saying an academic discussion was more likely to find a solution than politicians who can be relied upon to generate more heat and distrust rather than genuine debate! He urged the association to include only writers and not 'allow among yourself politicians like me'; else the creative and artistic side of their work would suffer, Nehru warned. Emphasizing his point about keeping politicians at bay, he gave the example of European and American associations of progressive writers and writers like Voltaire whose writings influenced not just the French Revolution, but the whole world for over a hundred years. Stating that a writer must contribute to the progress of a nation, Nehru showed his clear support for socialism and communism insofar as the liberty it allowed for individualism:

When everyone is given an opportunity to think, read and write, then how can individualism be prevented from developing? It is therefore a mistaken belief that individualism gets suppressed under a socialist or communist set-up. Everybody should have an opportunity to rise and that is possible when the basis of society is socialist or communist. Progressive writers should, therefore, show to the people the way to reach ideals.[11]

[9] Zaheer, *Light*, p. 122. The speech was published in *Naya Adab* (January–February 1941). A copy is also found in Sardar Jafri (ed.), *Guftagu* (Taraqqui Pasand Number) (Bombay: Wadera Publications, 1980); it does not mention a date.

[10] Ibid.

[11] *Selected Works of Jawaharlal Nehru*, vol. 8 (New Delhi: Orient Longman, 1976), p. 860. It is worth noting that by the 1940s many former progressives were

By 1937, the PWA was gradually acquiring a pan-Indian look with branches opening in Sylhet, Guwahati, Nagpur, Poona, Ahmedabad, Mysore, Bijwada, and Malabar as well as more and more writers from other languages becoming a part of the movement. While an all-India conference of writers could not be organized, the all-India council of the PWA met twice—in Delhi in the winter of 1936, and in Haripur in Bombay district in April 1937—both on the sidelines of the annual convention of the Congress. The Delhi meeting was attended by 10 or 15 council members including Faiz, Indulal Yagnik, Somendranth Tagore, and Abdul Alim. The Haripur meeting was larger but still informal. Sarojini Naidu made a presidential speech and writers from different parts of the country reported on the progress their branches had made in their states.

During 14–15 May 1938, a most unusual conference took place in Faridabad. Organized by Syed Muttalibi Faridabadi (1890–1964), this was a gathering of poets from the rural areas surrounding Delhi who wrote in Brajbhasha or Haryanavi or the countless other dialects that broadly came under the category of 'Hindustani'. Faridabadi had been active with the peasants and workers in the Gurgaon, Alwar, Bharatpur, and Rohtak regions, and was convinced that big literary events in big cities did not address the needs of people closer to the soil, and the continuing distinction between 'high' and 'low' culture meant that the urban was necessarily high and the rural (which included the folk) was always low. He had written a verse drama, *Kisan Rut*, in a style redolent of the sights and smells of the countryside, but using a pleasing mixture of Urdu and Haryanavi.[12] His derelict haveli in Faridabad became the venue for a large gathering of rural poets. Peasants squatted on the ground, while on a makeshift dais sat Faridabadi, Ahmed Ali, and Zaheer, representing the central committee of the PWA. A sprinkling of teachers and students from the Jamia Millia Islamia, some political workers from Delhi and its neighbourhood listened to the peasant poets who often sang their compositions to the beat of folk

---

accusing the PWA of suppressing individualism. We shall study this in greater detail in the section titled 'Makhdoom Mohiuddin and the Others' in this chapter and in Chapter 8. We shall also see how Ahmed Ali, began to move away from the PWM by 1939, citing its overtly political character as the reason for his withdrawal.

[12] I am grateful to Ali Javed for procuring a photostat copy of this book for me, presently unavailable in India.

instruments. While the subjects were topical—even overtly social and political—the style was the time honoured *bara masa*.

Zaheer waxed eloquent on this peasants' conference in *Roshnai* calling it a step in the right direction of making the PWA a truly comprehensive movement of people's literature. He also spoke of Ahmed Ali writing an 'excellent and detailed report of this conference in English' and translating some of the peasant poetry. We get an altogether different picture from Ahmed Ali,[13] a picture that shows his less-than-enthusiastic reception of peasant poetry, his reservations about poets and peasants sharing the dais and the rifts that marred the surface unity of the PWM as early as 1938 on the issue of the PWA becoming a custodian of peasants' and workers' rights, barely two years after its inception.[14]

The second conference of AIPWA was held in Calcutta in December 1938, a full two years and nine months after the first one in Lucknow. Its purpose was to take stock, secure new directions, and address the weaknesses and shortcomings that were coming to the fore despite the many successes. The Calcutta conference was a 'proper' conference, especially since the Bengal PWA was the most well-organized and influential in the country, and because the city of Calcutta boasted a vigorous literary life. Maulana Abdur Razzaq Malihabadi, editor of the influential Calcutta

---

[13] Carlo Coppola (ed.), *Marxist Influences and South Asian Literature* (East Lansing: Michigan State University, 1974). Oddly enough, Ahmed Ali wrote a report entitled 'The Village Poets and Indian Revolution' for *The New Age* (May 1939), pp. 513–24. There is nothing in this report to indicate Ahmed Ali's disagreement or disapproval of such a venture. I found a copy of this issue of *The New Age* among Ahmed Ali's papers and am grateful to Urooj Ahmed Ali for giving me a copy. In Ahmed Ali's account, the conference and mushaira were held under a *shamiana* (cloth canopy) erected in a school; he also mentions Zaheer and S.M. Oyama (the painter) travelling from Delhi to Faridabad by car to attend the conference.

[14] An apocryphal story, attributed to Josh Malihabadi, has Josh exclaim: '*Ghoron se humdardi hai to kya ghora ban jayein?*' (If I have sympathy for horses, must I become a horse myself?). This was narrated to me, in his inimitable style, by Shahryar, who in the course of helping me understand many things about the history of Urdu literature, used *latife* and *qisse*, many apocryphals such as this one, to illustrate a point. The implication of the above being that established poets, regardless of their sympathies for the downtrodden and marginalized, saw themselves as separate and distinct from the plebeian masses.

Urdu daily *Hind* too came. Zaheer described the Maulana's unusual politics thus:

[He] was one of those strict modern religious scholars in whose view it was necessary for a poet to be a socialist. In those days, therefore, he passionately supported in his paper, the Communist movement and Soviet Russia from an Islamic point of view. However, his general politics was that of nationalist Muslims. The Maulana was a sympathiser (of the PWM) and took a leading part in organising the Calcutta conference. The office of his newspaper became the hub of Calcutta's Urdu writers of the Progressive Movement.[15]

Delegates came from Assam, Andhra, Orissa, and Tamil Nadu. Three representatives of Hindi came from Bihar and Calcutta. Balraj Sahni (then teaching Hindi at Shantinekatan, later to become an active member of IPTA in Bombay) and his wife Damyanti too came, as did Krishan Chandar who represented Punjab. A newly married Zaheer ran away with his bride, Razia, from the formalities of post-wedding ceremonies and introduced her to his circle of friends and admirers. The *Manifesto* was finally adopted, the constitution completed and approved, and a new all-India executive committee chosen with Alim replacing Zaheer as general secretary. What was still worrying was the emphasis on organizational matters and the consequent neglect of literary issues vital to a conference, such as the dearth of written papers, academically sound discussions, or debates on creative writing. This was rectified at the two next conferences—in Hyderabad in 1945 and in Lucknow in 1947.

The All-India Urdu Progressive Writers held their conference in Hyderabad in December 1945.[16] Its presidium comprised Firaq Gorakhpuri, Tara Chand, Krishan Chandar, Ehtesham Husain, and Akbar Wafakhani. Its highlights included: Zaheer's paper on the problems of Urdu-Hindi-Hindustani; Sibte Hasan's paper on Urdu journalism which was a historical and critical survey of the past 150 years; and Jafri's critical essay was titled 'Iqbal: The Social Background to His Poetry'. Later at the mushaira, Kaifi and Jafri regaled the audience with recitations from their new poems. They had revived the classical masnavi, but had given it a political twist by writing, respectively, '*Election Nama*'

---

[15] Zaheer, *Light*, p. 143.

[16] The details that follow have been built from Pradhan, *Marxist Cultural Movements in India*, vol. I, pp. 323–5.

(dealing with the electoral politics of Congress, League, CPI, etc.) and *'Jumhoor'* (meaning the people, dealing with the wealth and beauty of India and the immortality of its people). Kaifi also read from another political masnavi called *'Khana Jangi'* (civil war) dealing with communal riots. Jafri read from *'Nai Dunya ko Salam'* (Greetings to the New World) where he drew from the classical masnavi tradition of Rumi and Firdousi. In Jafri's hands, the old masnavi form had been infused with a new dramatic element and the rhymed verse had been interspersed with blank verse; also in this epic poem of 2,000 lines, Jafri had used six different metres and the poem's theme too was startlingly different for a masnavi: the birth of a child was symbolic of the birth of a nation, the struggle of the parents symbolized the struggle against imperialism and slavery, and the pangs of parturition were the pangs of partition. Interspersed with the story of the child were references to historical events, the rise and fall of Rome, the peasants' uprising in medieval Europe that led to a new social order, French and Russian revolutions, as well as instances of struggle in India such as the naval uprising[17] and mass movements in Kashmir, Travancore, and Hyderabad. Krishan Chandar wrote a reportage of the conference's proceedings entitled *'Pauday'* (Sapling) detailing the significance of the movement and its achievements so far.

The increasing militancy and politicization of the PWA can be traced to the Fourth All-India Conference held two years prior to the Hyderabad one, from 22 to 25 May 1943 in Bombay, where a revised version of the *Manifesto* had been adopted. Held in the Marwari Vidyalaya Hall, this was a grand affair attended by a virtual who's who of the Urdu literary world: Zaheer was there with his wife Razia (an increasingly prolific writer and active member of the Lucknow PWA), Abdul Alim, K.A. Abbas, Jafri, Saghar Nizami, Krishan Chandar, Sibte Hasan, among others. The highpoint of this conference was the adoption of another modified *Manifesto* which proclaimed: 'In this hour of grave peril, it is the supreme task of Indian progressive writers to spiritually sustain the nation.'[18] Urging the writers to come out of their ivory tower and take full social responsibility,

---

[17] The Royal Indian Navy's uprising on 22 February 1946 caused Krishan Chandar to write a short story entitled *'Teen Goonde'* (Three Goondas) exposing imperialist tyranny and national leadership and the heroism of the Indian people.

[18] For full version of this *Manifesto* see Pradhan, *Marxist Cultural Movements in India*, vol. I, pp. 348–50.

it went on to declare: 'Soviet example tells us how revolution gives men the chance of bringing dignity and civilisation into the common possession.'[19]

This version of the *Manifesto* was markedly different from the London, Lucknow, and Calcutta ones in its sharply political tone, specific references to food shortages, and biting critique of imperialist policies; in short, it sounded more as a wake-up call from a political economist rather than a manifesto of a literary association. Speaking at the resolution to pass this *Manifesto*, K.A. Abbas and Zaheer were at pains to stress that it did not 'restrict but widen the scope and appeal of our literary activities'. Emphasizing that the document would 'serve as a basis for the united front of all Indian writers who claim to be patriotic', they invited writers of 'all shades and schools, humanists, romanticists, Marxists and even religious writers' into the PWA. The inherent duality of their statement does not seem to have struck them though the invitation to S.A. Dange to deliver the inaugural address seemed to many a clear giveaway of the political underpinnings of what Zaheer was still at pains to call a 'cultural movement'.[20] Comrade Dange used the PWA's platform to defend the CPI's 'people's war' stand thus: 'Can we remain neutral and not be against fascism and belie our whole past, our greatest of poets, our whole national and patriotic leadership? We cannot. We stand against fascism and its complete destruction in this war. We chose to side against fascism and for the liberation of all nations and peoples of the world.'[21]

Declarations of friendship with Soviet Union and China were made and writers such as Pearl S. Buck, Lin Yu Tang, and Upton Sinclair were hailed as role models. By calling upon 'all genuine and honest intellectuals to unite' and by constant references to patriotism, the speakers were flinging a gauntlet in the face of the Indian intelligentsia—those not with us are against us and, by extension, for reactionary right-wing forces. Zaheer was

---

[19] Pradhan, *Marxist Cultural Movements in India*, vol. I, pp. 348–50.

[20] In most reports presented by Zaheer of the PWA's activities, there is a noticeable stress on culture; he refers to the PWA as a cultural organization. He also credits the local PWA units with achieving the main tasks of the association, namely, helping members 'develop' their 'creative and critical faculties', see 'The All-India Progressive Writers' Association (1943–1947): A Report', *Golden Jubilee Brochure*, p. 62. A copy of the *Brochure* was found among the Ghulam Rabbani Taban Papers, NMML.

[21] Pradhan, *Marxist Cultural Movements in India*, vol. I, pp. 118–19.

again elected general secretary, Bishnu Dey and K.A. Abbas became joint secretaries, Mama Varerkar took over as treasurer, and the central office of the PWA moved from Lucknow to Bombay. The IPTA held its foundation conference on the same occasion.

As the movement grew and the IPTA spawned a host of cultural squads, PWA functions became lively, energetic occasions with songs and dances interspersed with academic discussion and poetry readings. The progressives wrote plays and songs which were shown to peasant and working-class as well as middle-class audiences in different parts of the country. Despite the early heady success, the perception that the progressives were against tradition grew and this, many felt, was like throwing the baby out with the bathwater. In an editorial penned for the inaugural issue of *Naya Adab* (New Literature), the three young editors, Sibte Hasan, Majaz, and Jafri, tried to defend the charge:

It is wrong to say that the term progressive literature denotes protest and hatred of all old things. Progressive literature sees all things in their proper perspective and historical background; this very fact is the touchstone of literary achievement. Progressive literature does not break off relations with old literature; it embodies the best traditions of the old and constructs new edifices on the foundations of these traditions. In fact, progressive literature is the most trustworthy guardian and heir of ancient literature... In our view, progressive literature is that which keeps in view the realities of life; it should be a reflection of these realities; it should investigate them and should be the guide to a new and better world.[22]

Asrarul Haq Majaz (1909–1955)

Born in Rudauli, a qasba in Barabanki district in the erstwhile United Provinces on 19 October 1909, Asrarul Haq, or Majaz Lucknowi as he called himself, was the people's poet par excellence. He burst upon the Urdu literary firmament and caught the imagination of all those who had wearied of the Urdu poet's angst over the *shama-parwana* and the gul-o-bulbul. He introduced a new sensibility and new literary concerns through startlingly new images and conceits, and above all a new sort of prosody—the nazm which resembled the ghazal in its close approximation of rhyme

---

[22] Quoted by Ali Husain Mir and Raza Mir in *Anthems of Resistance* (New Delhi: Roli, 2006), pp. 35–6; translated from the Urdu by the authors.

and metre but was free of the two-line constraint of the ghazal.[23] While his early poetry showed the influence of Josh Malihabadi's wordy resonance and the symbolist melancholy of Fani Badayuni,[24] soon Majaz evolved a lexicon that was uniquely his own yet completely in tune with his times. Fresh, sparkling, and lilting as a mountain brook, Majaz's poetry acquired near-universal acclaim in Urdu-speaking circles.

For Majaz, the Urdu critic, Jafar Ali Khan said, 'A Keats was born to Urdu poetry but the progressive wolves ran away with him!'[25] There were others too who accused the progressives of hijacking Majaz, of touring with him as one might with a lucky mascot banking upon his reputation of being a sure-fire hit on the mushaira circuit and of using his popularity for their own ends, ends that Majaz was ill-equipped to fully comprehend or endorse. However, whatever the depth of Majaz's ideological moorings or the extent of his intellectual engagement with socialism or communism, there was no denying his emotional affinity to the cause of freedom, change, and progress.

In many ways, Majaz can be taken as the finest example of sharif culture, the sort of culture that was inextricably linked with the qasbas of upper India. The qasbati culture could lay claim to a unique ambience, one that was naturally conducive to the development of a liberal, enlightened ethos. The qasba of Rudauli, in particular, produced some fine men and women.[26] Majaz was born in one such uncloistered, educated

---

[23] Rahi Masoom Raza, who in later years gained fame as a scriptwriter for film and television, made a stern distinction between ghazal and other poetic genres in 'Tanquid-e-Ghazal', in Ale Ahmad Suroor (ed.), *Tanquid ke Buniyadi Masail* (Aligarh: Aligarh Muslim University Press, 1967), pp. 212–13. He goes so far as to say, 'Only those verses that deal with love can remain in the House of the Ghazal; there is no place for others.' Some progressives, such as Majaz, popularized the geet and nazm to express newer concerns; others, such as Faiz, employed the ageless idiom of the ghazal but refashioned its usage to express radical ideas.

[24] His near-contemporary at St John's College, Agra, Fani influenced Majaz with the overwhelming despondency of his poetry.

[25] Quoted in Khalilur Rahman Azmi, *Urdu mein Taraqqui Pasand Adabi Tehreek* (Aligarh: Educational Book House, 2002 [1957]), p. 128.

[26] For a detailed study of the qasbati culture, see Mushirul Hasan, *From Pluralism to Separatism: Qasbas in Colonial Awadh* (New Delhi: Oxford University Press, 2004).

middle-class family.[27] He gained his early education in Lucknow, then went on to St John's College, Agra in 1929, and then to Aligarh where he finally completed his BA (after losing two years due to shortage of attendance) in 1935. Never one for books or academia, Majaz was an indifferent student, but a dazzling performer on the mushaira circuit where he had already acquired an enviable reputation from his Agra days. At Aligarh, that reputation grew to such an extent that he was a popular figure both among his peers and teachers.[28] Unwilling to join the hurly-burly of the world outside the campus, he embarked upon an MA in Urdu he could never finish.

Majaz's last years at Aligarh were the heyday of the PWM and he was swept in the fervour of heady optimism. For a man with an open, receptive mind like his, it was natural for him to gravitate towards progressivism. He joined Marxist study circles and gradually became aware of the red tide that was swamping the horizon. In him, like in countless educated young men, the skeins of nationalism, revolutionary ardour, dreams of a new dawn, became so intertwined that it was difficult to separate them. Like countless other young men of his age, he might have remained unnoticed had it not been for the magic of his poetry which took root in the hospitable soil of Aligarh, an Aligarh that was emerging from the influence of tradition and classicism and opening its windows to the new winds blowing in from the West. Aligarh was not only quick to recognize his genius, it also nurtured his talent allowing it to expand and flourish.

Due to financial reasons, Majaz had to abandon his MA and leave the cloistered easy-paced life of Aligarh for the hustle and bustle of Delhi where he found employment as sub-editor for a journal called *Awaaz* (Call)[29] started at the new radio station set up by an Englishman named Feldon. However, Feldon soon left and his place was taken by the mercu-

---

[27] All his siblings were well-educated: his brother Ansar Harwani was a journalist and Member of Parliament; his sister Safiya, a writer of some note herself, was married to Jan Nisar Akhtar, a progressive poet and their son is Javed Akhtar, also a progressive; the youngest sister, Hamida, the first woman to do an MA from Aligarh, wrote a luminous account of her family entitled *Hum Paanch They* (We Were Five).

[28] The venerable Rashid Ahmed Siddiqui of the Department of Urdu, a man of infinite good taste, grounded as he was in the sternest, most classical of traditions, appreciated Majaz's poetry though he would have no truck with the progressives or their movement in the years to come.

[29] The name, *Awaz*, was suggested by Majaz. *Awaz* lasted for 30 years.

rial Pitras Bukhari (with whom Saadat Hasan Manto was to cross swords a few years later) who brought in his younger brother Zulfiqar as assistant director. Majaz soon developed differences with the brothers and chose to leave rather than submit to their demanding ways and authoritarianism.[30] Majaz's first, some say only, major romantic encounter happened in Delhi and it was here that he got habituated to drinking.[31] It was here also that he got more actively drawn into the PWM through its Delhi branch which was run by Shahid Ahmed Dehelvi, editor of the prestigious *Saqi*. Majaz attended these meetings as did Josh (then living in Delhi and running the *Kaleem* [The Speaker]), Raipuri (who had left the work of the Anjuman-e Taraqqui-i-Urdu in Hyderabad), Jafri (studying at the Delhi College after being expelled from Aligarh), and Abid Husain (a teacher of philosophy at the Jamia Millia Islamia who brought students and colleagues to these meetings and helped set up an active progressives' group at his university). Shahid Dehelvi also started a literary journal called *Shahjahan*, especially devoted to progressive literature, but it soon folded up after the secret police intimidated him and Dehelvi lost interest in the Delhi branch.[32] In

---

[30] Jafri gives an account of the circumstances in which Majaz left AIR in his *Lucknow ki Paanch Raatein* (Five Nights in Lucknow), and how Majaz got entangled in the politics between Punjabis and non-Punjabis at the station. See Ali Sardar Jafri, *Lucknow ki Paanch Raatein aur Doosri Yaadein* (Lucknow: Nusrat Publishers, 1964), pp. 78–9.

[31] Much of Majaz's poetry is personal and romantic, but that part of his oeuvre or personality does not concern us here. We talk of his drinking insofar as it impinged upon his life, altering it irrevocably as he slid deeper on a downward spiral of despair and frustration. His friend Farhatullah Ansari reveals in *Majaz: Kuchch Baatein, Kuchch Yadein* (Some Accounts, Some Memories) that Majaz had already acquired a fondness for drinking while at Aligarh, but since he lived with his parents it perforce remained under control. In Delhi, however, his drinking habit grew uncontrollably and took hold of his life.

[32] The Delhi branch was inactive, after Dehelvi's desertion, till 1942 when Qazi Mohammad Ahmad became its general secretary. Masudul Haq, of the Department of Education at the Jamia Millia Islamia, described to me in the course of a freewheeling interview how a progressive group continued to meet regularly even during the inert phase, reading their work to each other. In 1946, the Delhi association began to show signs of life due to the presence of Shivdan Singh Chauhan and Shamsher Singh Narula who held meetings in hired halls in the city.

this context, a brief digression is necessary to understand the tugs and the pulls within the PWA and how these forces pulled what for many of its members was essentially a literary organization into the turbulent seas of political activity. The incident also illustrates how Zaheer and an increasingly small coterie of like-minded people controlled the movement as early as 1936 and brooked no difference of opinion.

In the *Roshnai*, Zaheer described the setting-up of the Delhi branch by Dehelvi and mentioned the secret police that had begun to sniff around and was infiltrating the meetings with informers.

[E]ager to prove the entirely 'literary' and 'non-political' nature of the Association, [Dehelvi] told the members of the secret police that they could attend its meetings regularly in order to satisfy themselves regarding its harmlessness. Subsequently, on the invitation of the Association's Secretary an Intelligence inspector attended one or two of the meetings openly to act as a censor for the organization.[33]

Roshnai carried a two-page diatribe against Dehelvi's 'moral weakness and cowardice'. While it was no doubt wrong, even naïve, of Dehelvi to invite intelligence people to sit in on their meetings, perhaps he did so because he genuinely believed that theirs was a purely literary and therefore 'harmless' association. Zaheer knew it was anything but that; hence his annoyance with Dehelvi. Hence also the decision to keep only a very small core group of like-minded people in charge of the association's activities. Increasingly, this core group shrank to include only committed communists and party members. In the last chapter, we will return to this point, especially the reaction of those who were not party men and therefore began to feel left out and marginalized.

Majaz stayed in Delhi for close to two years of which he worked at the AIR for one year and spent the rest of the time looking for another job. However, unable to find any means of employment, unlucky in love, having tasted failure both in *gham-e-dauran* and *gham-e-jaanan*, Majaz had no choice but to seek shelter under his parents' roof who had by then moved to Lucknow. This Awadhi city, dedicated though it was to tradition, feudalism, and aristocratic decadence, was fast emerging as the beating heart of the PWM. Many progressives had made it their

---

[33] Zaheer, *Light*, pp. 101–2.

home[34] and it was here, in the Wazir Manzil, that Sajjad Zaheer too periodically came home to roost from his wanderings.

Swept up by the nation-wide wave of revolutionary fervour, along with Jafri (who had moved to the Lucknow University to pursue an MA in Urdu) and Sibte Hasan (who had found work as sub-editor at the *National Herald* and of whom Zaheer said 'Sibte Hasan owed his importance in our movement to his optimism'), Majaz founded *Parcham* (Pennant), a magazine for the progressives in Lucknow. The first (and only) issue was a handsome affair with an eclectic collection of poetry on nationalism and freedom. The collection was so good that the Congress, which had established a provincial government in 1937, bought the issue of *Parcham* and decided to cull the poems from it and publish them as a separate volume entitled *Azadi ki Nazmein* (Poems of Freedom). After *Parcham* closed mysteriously, the trio started *Naya Adab* in March 1939.[35]

---

[34] Ale Ahmad Suroor, Abdul Alim, and Ehtesham Husain taught at the university. Hayatullah Ansari was bringing out the weekly *Hindustan* which given Ansari's friendship with Nehru, caused Zaheer to comment: '… [it] was being brought out under progressive guidance, and editorship. But we were gradually beginning to distrust its ties with Congress.' Zaheer, *Light*, p. 164. Jafri completed his BA from the Delhi College in 1938 and went to Lucknow. Moin Ahsan Jazbi too went from Delhi in 1939 and so did Josh Malihabadi; the latter took on the mantle of mentor to the young progressives, especially Majaz with whom he was to later have an acrimonious and public falling out. Another progressive, Sikandar Ali Wajd, had come to Lucknow from Hyderabad for training. In *Lucknow ki Paanch Ratein*, Jafri wrote: 'While our group was largely in agreement over most matters, we were divided over Gandhi, Nehru and Subhash Bose. No one disagreed with socialism' (p. 35).

[35] *Naya Adab* fared better than other progressive journals. However, it is worth noting that the history of the PWM is littered with short-lived literary journals that shut down as abruptly and as frequently as they started. The reason can only be paucity or irregularity of funds since most ran on subscriptions with the editors in most cases dipping in their pockets for start-up capital. This was unlike *Chingari* which was an official organ and was funded by the party, or the other Urdu magazines (both literary and non-literary) that had private sponsors and therefore more assured funds and longer lives. Zaheer gave the date for starting *Naya Adab* as the beginning of 1941. He also wrote: 'Officially, *Naya Adab* was not the organ of the Association of Progressive Writers, but informally and in reality, it very soon became the mouthpiece of our Movement.' Zaheer,

In December 1938, Majaz travelled to Calcutta to attend the second AIPWA; there, he stayed in the home of Sudhindranath Dutta, editor of the well-known Bengali monthly *Parichay* and president of the reception committee of the conference.[36] Majaz's rousing poetry struck a chord with Calcutta's labouring classes, many of whom did not understand Urdu. These lines from *Hamara Jhanda* (Our Flag, 1938) became an anthem of sorts for urban labour:

> We are tigers, we roar as we stride
> We hover and amass like clouds,
> We sing the sweet songs of life
> We hold our flag in our hand.[37]

Majaz fought a lifelong battle with chronic depression; he had three long spells of what can euphemistically be called mental ill-health—in 1940, 1945, and 1952. However, he pulled himself from the maw of

---

Light, p. 167. *Naya Adab* carried the best of progressive writing of its period in Urdu as well as translations from Russian and Chinese. One issue carried translations of Chinese stories by Tamannai (from Patna) which were later published as an anthology entitled *Zinda Cheen* (Living China). Zaheer's comment 'it strung together our whole movement in its early period' (Zaheer, *Light*, p. 168) showed the importance of an organ like *Naya Adab* in not only reaching out to a dedicated readership in a sustained way, but also putting across a sustained point of view in a systematic manner. It revealed the dedication and organizational ability of men like Jafri who were committed party members and were thus trained in a more rigorous manner. When the *Kaleem*, edited by Josh, was incorporated into *Naya Adab*, Josh's name appeared as editor-in-chief. According to Zaheer, however, the real work was done by Sibte Hasan, Jafri, and Majaz. Other magazines with a pronounced progressive tilt were *Adab-e-Latif* (Literature and Elegance) from Lahore and *Shameem* (sweet, light fragrance) from Patna.

[36] Zaheer narrated an amusing incident in *Roshnai* which showed that Majaz was not only affable and good natured, but gifted with a sharp sense of humour too. Due to a shortage of space, Majaz had to share the rather wide bed given to him in Dutta's house with the bearded and portly Abdul Alim. The next morning Majaz was heard plaintively humming the following line from one of his own poems: '*Jawani ke hasin khwabon ki hasratnak tabeerein*' ('The dismal interpretation of youth's beautiful dreams'). Zaheer, *Light*, p. 146.

[37] *Ahang* (New Delhi: Maktaba Jamia, 2002), p. 118; translation mine. Interestingly, in Zaheer's *Roshnai*, 'our flag' became 'red flag'!

melancholia and self-destruction and moved to Delhi to stay with friends Shaukat Ansari and K.M. Ashraf. Here, for want of anything better on offer, he accepted employment in the Hardinge Library[38] and began to live in a small flat found for him by Kulsum (Ashraf's wife) in the Fountain area of Chandni Chowk, a short distance from the library.

Meanwhile, the PWA had grown sluggish, its branches inert, its members committed but largely rudderless. In March 1942, Zaheer came out of jail after two years' incarceration. Abdul Alim, the general secretary of the PWA after Zaheer's two-year term, had been released in 1941. Together, they began to gather the scattered flock. The third AIPWA conference was held in Delhi in the hall of the Hardinge Library in 1942. Majaz attended it as did Faiz. Six months later, in May 1943, Majaz travelled to Bombay to attend the fourth conference of the AIPWA.

Majaz suffered his second nervous breakdown in 1945. Evidently, he could no more bear the terrible duality of his life: on the one hand, there were the Olympian heights of the mushaira where the skies would be rent by loud cries of *wah wah* when he stood up to recite his mesmeric poetry and, on the other hand, the ignominy of his clerical duties at the Library. Little did he know that for all his straightened circumstances, in the eyes of those who knew him such as his friend from Agra and later Aligarh, Ale Ahmad Suroor, Majaz was rich beyond measure. His heart broken, his spirit bruised, his body frail, his pockets empty, Majaz remained for his friends the epitome of tehzeeb and sharafat.[39] Good opinions such as these, generally held by all those who knew Majaz remotely or well, could not save him. Like Manto, the demon of drink drove him to destruction and madness. Chaudhry Mohammad Ali, an early patron of the progressives, a

---

[38] His contemporaries have variously described his job as 'assistant librarian' and 'clerk'. Whatever be the exact nature of his duties, it was evidently a far cry from the adulation he was used to receiving at Aligarh and Lucknow, especially in the mushairas where even in a company of greats he invariably received the loudest applause.

[39] This is borne out by the many hagiographical accounts of Majaz's life available in Urdu; it is also emphasized by those who knew Majaz. Majaz's friend, Akhilesh Mitthal, testified to his essential goodness. Mitthal also told me that Majaz suffered from schizophrenia; it was diagnosed by an English doctor, a Colonel Davis, who treated him in Ranchi and with whom Mitthal discussed Majaz's medical prognosis over telephone. The doctor advised a lobotomy which Mitthal severely discouraged.

man of refined sensibilities, one who did not frown upon drinking, a poet of no mean standing himself, a fellow native of Rudauli, and an admirer of Majaz, took him away. Majaz's stay in Rudauli with this extremely amiable, cultured, genteel, old world yet liberal aristocrat proved beneficial. He recovered somewhat, shed some of the delusions of grandeur he had acquired in Delhi (partly due to the uninspiring work at the Library) and a month later returned to his parents' home in Lucknow where he stayed briefly before moving on to Bombay.

Several progressives had made Bombay their home by the early 1940s and Majaz too gravitated there lured no doubt by dreams of finding the pot of gold at the end of the rainbow. Majaz stayed with Zaheer and his wife while he looked for work in the Bombay film industry, but without much luck—unlike the scores of young Urdu-knowing men who found employment in the film industry. When freedom came on the midnight of 15 August 1947, it found Majaz literally dancing on the streets of Lucknow with Jafri and others. But the sight of blood and gore that came in its wake was intolerable for someone like him and once again he hurried back to the relative calm of Lucknow.

From 1947, Majaz became a full-time poet and made no further attempts to look for a proper job. He blew up whatever he earned on the mushaira circuit in drinking coffee at the old Indian Coffee House in Hazratganj[40] or cheap country liquor in ramshackle working-class *sharab khanas*.[41]

---

[40] The coffee-house culture was an essential part of the progressive culture with its emphasis on simple living, high thinking, and intense discussions among like-minded people. Sharib Rudaulvi gives a life-like account of this culture so unique to Lucknow with its tables laid out for regulars that included some of the best and brightest from the university, courts, and the old city. A student of MA (Urdu) at the University and a regular at the Coffee House (being a student he could never sit at the same table as the greats), Rudaulvi describes the strict code of behaviour in this otherwise liberal space. His account of Majaz in the Sahitya Akademi's Urdu monograph (in the Makers of Indian Literature series), 2009, is the most lucid, balanced, and comprehensive account and stands out substantially from the other, mostly hagiographical, Urdu sources.

[41] Majaz had named one such place the Lorry's Top (*Laary ki Chhat*) in Lal Bagh as it had an open roof where he and his drinking cronies escaped to get away from the crush of poor, working class people from the no-frills establishment downstairs. Majaz, dressed in a kurta and waistcoat, spent a winter's night in a

Majaz was the life and soul of these gatherings (*jaan-e-mehfil*, as testified by Sharib Rudaulvi and Akhilesh Mitthal) and every night someone or the other from his vast circle of friends would put him—dead drunk—in a rickshaw. At home, his family would leave his food on a tray along with some money for the rickshaw.

Despite the prodigious influx of refugees and exodus of large chunks of its population, post-independence Lucknow retained an active branch of the PWA and many former progressives were still around. Zaheer had left for Pakistan, under the party's instructions to set up the CPP, but his wife Razia was still there; as were Rashid Jahan,[42] Abdul Alim, Ehtesham Husain, Mumtaz Husain, Shaukat Siddiqui, Mohammad Hasan, Anand Narain Mulla, Salam Machchlishahri, Hasan Shahir, Manzar Salim, Kamal Ahmed Siddiqui, Noorul Hasan Hashmi, and Ale Ahmad Suroor. Soon regular meetings were resumed in the home of Ale Ahmad Suroor at 7 Barrow Road.[43] By the 1950s, the group had expanded to include younger faces: Ratan Singh, Abid Sohail, Sharib Rudaulvi, Arif Naqvi,[44] Agha Sohail, Iqbal Majeed, Hasan Abid, etc. D.P. Mukerji or Munibur Rahman would join them whenever they came

---

drunken stupor here and died as a result of the chill he caught on this very rooftop. The next morning when the shop's servants went up to the roof to collect empty bottles, they found Majaz lying unconscious.

[42] Mahmuduzzafar, who was a full-time party member, had to go underground when the CPI fell foul with the new Indian government. He too attended some of these meetings when he could; at other times he stayed with friends such as Suroor whose family had to observe utmost secrecy and not allow servants or neighbours to guess the identity of the mysterious guest who stayed locked up in a room for days and whose food was delivered on a tray by the host himself!

[43] My mother, Mehjabeen, who is the daughter of Ale Ahmad Suroor, remembers sitting in at numerous such meetings where the likes of Prithvi Raj Kapoor would show up and read a story or a play. She also remembers the home-made delicacies prepared for these regular meetings that turned their home into a festive place with much to-ing and fro-ing of important writers and litterateurs who nevertheless took the time out to talk to her.

[44] Arif Naqvi has given a luminous account of his association with the progressives in a collection of essays, sketches, and reminiscences entitled *Yaadon ke Chiragh* (New Delhi: Modern Publishing House, 2005). I have also had the occasion to speak with Arif Naqvi in the course of his recent visits to Delhi.

to Lucknow as would Kali Parshad, head of the psychology department at the University.

In January 1951, Majaz travelled to Karachi for a mushaira and then on to Lahore. By now he was a broken man, a shadow of his former self. His voice gone, his body racked, he was a far cry from the young poet who had broken hearts at the Aligarh Girls' College. His third, and severest, attack of mental ill health came upon him while he was in Delhi in 1952. While still not fully recovered, he travelled to Calcutta to attend the Peace Conference. This is yet another evidence of his commitment—even in his precarious mental and physical state—to world peace, humanity, and freedom. However, excessive drinking, being in a new place, and the hurly-burly of a large international conference brought him to such a pass[45] that his brother, Ansar Harwani, and friend, Yusuf Iman, rushed to rescue him. He was taken to Ranchi, by air (an unheard of luxury in those days), on the pretext of being taken to a mushaira. Once there, his friend and fellow progressive, Sohail Azimabadi, took charge of him and admitted him to the Ranchi mental asylum[46] where, incidentally, the beloved poet of Bengal, Kazi Nazrul Islam, too was undergoing treatment at the same time. After three months of treatment, Majaz returned once more to Lucknow.

Meanwhile, Zaheer returned to India in 1955 after four years in Pakistani jails over the trumped-up Rawalpindi Conspiracy Case (discussed in detail in the last chapter). Among the first things he undertook was the organization of the first-ever Students' Urdu Convention in Lucknow on 3–4 December 1955.[47] A deluge of the greatest living Urdu writers descended upon Lucknow: Ismat Chughtai, Sahir Ludhianvi, Jafri, Niyaz Haider apart from locals such as Hayatullah Ansari, Nihal Rizwi, and scores of others. The city had turned into a carnival and among those who trooped into Lucknow there were scores of Majaz's friends from his

---

[45] Majaz's sister, Safiya, in a letter to her husband described Majaz's condition as being practically reduced to begging on the streets of Calcutta.

[46] A description of the Ranchi days is found in Mohammad Hasan's *Gham-e Dil, Wahshat-e Dil* (Delhi: Takhliqkar Publishers, 2003).

[47] The chairman of the Organizing Committee was Aaliya Imam (nee Askari) and Sharib Rudaulvi was its general secretary. A sea of young talent—which included Arif Naqvi, Zaki Shirazi, Shakeb Rizvi, Haider Abbas, Khwaja Raiq, Hafiz Nomani—worked under the guidance of Zaheer and Ehtesham Husain who had sent letters of invitation to many from the old flock.

younger, happier days. K.M. Munshi, inaugurated the convention.[48] At the mushaira afterwards, Majaz read the following sher:

> It is difficult to set the world in order
> It is not like the tangles in your tresses.

The delegates' session continued the next day at the Ganga Parshad Hall in Aminabad. A group photo was taken which showed Majaz amidst a sea of students from the University standing along with Zaheer, Jafri, Abdul Alim, Mohammad Mehdi, Niyaz Haider, Baqar Mehdi, Ehtesham Husain, and Ismat Chughtai. On 5 December 1955, as the open session of the convention was underway, with Zaheer, Ismat, and Ehtesham Husain in the chair, word came that Majaz had been found on the Lorry's Top and taken to Balrampur Hospital. His friends declared the convention closed and rushed to his bedside. Majaz breathed his last at 10.22 pm on 5 December 1955. He was only 46 years old.

Majaz's condolence meeting was held on 7 December 1955 in the Rifah-e-Aam Hall, the venue of another meeting of progressives from all over the country 20 years ago. One of Majaz's ghazals was sung by Hasan Abid. Speeches were made by old comrades like Ismat, Ehtesham Husain, Jafri, Yashpal, and Hayatullah Ansari. Majaz's young nephew, Javed Akhtar (the son of Majaz's sister Safiya and her husband Jan Nisar) presented one of Majaz's ghazals in his uncle's inimitable style. Reminiscent of that historic conference 20 years ago in April 1936, Lucknow had once again hosted the first-of-its-kind literary gathering. Once again, the biggest names in Urdu literature had gathered here—names that were familiar from the radio and from countless magazines. But now the occasion was a sombre one. The ebullience of youth was replaced with the certainty of death. The wheel had come full circle. The past 20 years had seen not just the rise and fall of Majaz and his beloved Lucknow, but also the birth and decline of a movement.

Majaz lies buried in a Lucknow cemetery; the epitaph on his grave has a verse from one of his ghazals written in 1945:

> And after this there is morn and the new morning Majaz
> With me ends the eve of sorrows of Lucknow.

---

[48] This time, unlike the first AIPWA on 10 April, there was no Premchand to save the day for Zaheer. Moreover, as governor of UP and chancellor of Lucknow University, this time there was no escaping K.M. Munshi.

And, indeed, with Majaz gone an entire way of life changed; the Lucknow of his days changed beyond all recognition, and the PWM lost a strong ally. Majaz had become a 'myth' in his own lifetime; his early death simply fuelled it, keeping alive his memory, his persona, and most of all his poetry for years to come. His poetry had been 'appropriated' fairly early on in his literary career by the progressives and the progressive critics—who had a formidable reputation for destroying young talent that deviated from the trajectory they had mapped for 'their' literature—chose to heap nothing but encomiums upon him. Equally, they could, when they chose or when it suited the larger purposes of the movement, build or enhance reputations. I suspect they chose to 'build' on Majaz's already substantial reputation for reasons that I shall discuss in detail below.

Majaz wrote compulsively but much of what he wrote never got published, for it was written on wayward scraps of paper and indiscriminately handed over to admirers and friends. Therefore, his oeuvre is today established by little other than the slender *Ahang* (*awaz* or call), first published in 1938 with a Foreword by Sajjad Zaheer. Already a popular and well-loved figure among students and fellow poets, this volume established Majaz's reputation as the poet who sang sweetly of love and sorrow and social change earning him the sobriquet of 'the Keats of Urdu poetry' and securing a place of honour both on the mushaira circuit and as an iconic figure among young men and women in campuses across northern India.[49] Looking at his oeuvre, it now seems as though his revolutionary poetry too stemmed from his essentially romantic temperament.

Ahmed Ali, friend turned foe of the PWM, makes a vital distinction between the 'creative' and 'political' section of the Movement. In the former, he places Faiz and Majaz; in the latter his bête noir, Sajjad Zaheer and the unnamed 'orthodox':

[T]he work of the two outstanding poets of the group consistently acclaimed by the orthodox—the political—section of the Movement as progressive is curiously not 'progressive' in the ideological sense espoused by the custodians of the movement. It is essentially romantic ... there is (in the works of Majaz and Faiz) an awakened sense of wonder at the discovery of a new, vast field of approach to man

---

[49] Ismat Chughtai has described how her fellow students at the Girls' College at Aligarh would sleep with a copy of *Ahang* under their pillows and write their names on slips of paper and pick one to decide who would be the lucky girl chosen as a bride for Majaz!

and art, a new awareness of life and politics, social problems and slavery to convention. They have used imagery derived from life around them and have written with a deeper consciousness of self and fellow-beings, giving a new interpretation to old symbols and ideas.[50]

Representing the period of 1931–52, the second edition of *Ahang* has 60 nazms and 41 ghazals.[51] Among these there are few that can be called strictly revolutionary in the style popularized by Josh, Jafri, Kaifi, or Niyaz Haider. Of the 60 nazms, only 18–19 can be called revolutionary or even political and of these only 8 that are loudly or overtly radical in their call for revolution, fight against capitalism, or setting the world on fire. These nazms are: *'Inquilab'* (Revolution, 1933); *'Sarmayadari'* (Capitalism, 1937); *'Hamara Jhanda'* (Our Flag, 1937); *'Mazdooron ka Geet'* (The Workers' Song, 1938); *'Ahang-e Nau'* (New Call, 1942); *'Bol Ari o Dharti Bol'* (Speak, o Earth, Speak, 1945); *'Bideshi Mehman se'* (To a Foreign Guest, date not known); and *'Ahang-e Junoon'* (The Call of Madness, date not known). There are other nazms too, which are politically aware. These include: *'Andheri Raat ka Musafir'* (Traveller in the Dark Night, 1937); *'Naujawan se'* (To a Young Man, 1937); *'Naujawan Khatoon se'* (To a Young Woman, 1937); *'Tafli ke Khwaab'* (Childhood Dreams, 1938); *'Ek Jilawatan ki Wapsi'* (The Return of an Exile, 1938); *'Khwab Sehar'* (Dawn's Dream, 1939); *'Mujhe Jaana Hai Ek Din'* (I Must Leave One Day, 1945); *'Pahla Jashn-e-Azadi'* (The First Independence Day Celebration, 1947); and *'Fikr'* (Thought, 1950). Some of these poems were pegged on definite political events such as *'Bideshi Mehaman se'* which was written on the Quit India Movement. And another, not included in *Ahang*, was the *'Pakistan ka Milli Tarana'* (The National Anthem of Pakistan). Whether it was written in response to the communists' support for Pakistan and the right of self-determination or simply out of his own conviction for Muslim separatism and nationalism is hard to tell.[52] His niece, Sahba Lucknowi, described the marches led by Majaz in the streets of Delhi reciting this anthem:

[50] Coppola, *Marxist Influences and South Asian Literature*, p. 37.

[51] I am indebted to Sharib Rudaulvi for his incisive analysis of the revolutionary content of Majaz's poetry. This section has been built from his monograph for the Sahitya Akademi.

[52] I asked Mitthal about Majaz's political convictions and the extent of his understanding or commitment to CPI policy. Mitthal recited these lines from

> On the horizon of the Khyber shines the bright crescent
> Lo and behold the freedom-lovers are calling us.
> Our soldiers march upholding the green flag …
> Say one, say all
> This Pakistan is ours.[53]

For the purpose of this study, we shall look only at Majaz's *inquilabi shairi* which—as has been pointed above—was less fiery than his contemporaries and fewer in number in his already slender oeuvre. What then is the reason for his immense popularity or his near-universal acceptance in progressive circles as one of their own?

Majaz, it must be clarified, was never a party man; nor was he an ideologue. He was simply a man who was buffeted by the storms of life, unlucky in love, never able to hold a proper job for long, increasingly dependent on a circle of friends and admirers, increasingly given to spells of depression, and increasingly dependent on alcohol. And, yet, there was no denying his mesmeric way with words. He gave voice to the frustration and angst of a generation that yearned for freedom. His rejection of the world around him—whether it was in the angst-ridden 'Kyun?' (Why?) or the ballad-like geet he wrote for the workers of the world—reflects his deep longing for a better, more humane, more just world. Among his many poems exhorting upheaval and change, there is '*Inquilab*', written in 1933:

> And on this red-hued horizon, amidst a thousand splendours
> Shall arise the sun glittering with the country's freedom.[54]

Ehtesham Husain,[55] who single-handedly evolved a canon of progressive criticism, noted in the context of '*Raat aur Rail*' (Night and the Train, 1933), how Majaz used traditional romantic props, but magically transformed them to speak of the war of light upon darkness, the fight between India and its oppression. This seemingly depressing poem, in the progressive's lexicon,

---

Ghalib by way of answer: '*Chalta hoon har ek rahguzar ke saath / Pahchanta nahin kissi rahbar ko main*' (I walk along the way with every wayfarer / Though I don't recognize my fellow travellers).

[53] Sahba Lucknowi (ed.), *Majaz ek Ahang* (Karachi, 1956), pp. 684, 37–8.

[54] Majaz, *Ahang*, p. 68; translation mine.

[55] Ehtesham Husain, 'The Romantic in Majaz's Poetry', *Naya Adab*, no. 3, Karachi.

became a triumphant proclamation of faith with the train hurtling in the darkness becoming a metaphor for change and rebellion:

> Going ahead fearlessly with a typhoon-like thunder
> A rebellion in each motion,
> Singing songs of mankind's greatness.[56]

Another early poem, 'Nazr-e Khalida' (Ode to Khalida), dedicated to the Turkish writer Khalida Edib who visited Aligarh during Majaz's student days, while not an ostensibly political poem, let alone a revolutionary one, is hailed as evidence of Majaz's political sensitivity. Here, Majaz salutes Edib as an embodiment of secular democracy, a role model, and an honoured guest. The poem reads like an ode, not a panegyric; it is good poetry and not propaganda. For me, 'Nazr-e Khalida' is remarkable for its unabashed celebration of a woman and fellow writer. More importantly, it shows how Majaz's essentially classical mindset and catholic world view never allowed him to either abandon his literary sensibilities or sacrifice them at the altar of his political sensibility. This is, essentially, what sets him apart from Kaifi, Jafri, and some of the other progressives who put policy over poetry, and in the same league as Faiz. One is reminded of the distinction made by Urdu critic, Atiqullah, between poetry for the sake of subject (*mauzoo*) and subject for the sake of poetry and how the former (*shairi barai mauzoo*) is nothing more than sloganeering.[57]

A soft, seemingly romantic poem called 'Nazr-e-Dil' (To My Heart, 1936), which carries an unexpected punch in its subversive last couplet, is in many ways characteristic of Majaz's enduring appeal, especially to the youth:

> Let us together bring about a new revolution
> Spread ourselves over the world so that all eyes are on us.[58]

Majaz wrote on women and about women too. His address in 'Naujawan Khatoon se' (To a Young Lady) has been adopted as the slogan for the women's' movements across South Asia:

---

[56] Translation by Coppola (ed.), *Marxist Influences and South Asian Literature*, p. 43.

[57] Atiqullah, 'Taraqqui Pasand Nazm: Nazrayati Kirdar ki Tausih', in Qamar Rais and S. Ashoor Kazmi (eds), *Taraqqui Pasand Adab: Pachas Sala Safar* (Delhi: Naya Safar Publications, 1987), p. 419.

[58] Majaz, *Ahang*, p. 81; translation mine.

The veil that covers your forehead looks lovely indeed
But it'd be better still if you turned your veil into a pennant.

Majaz wrote of both love and revolution, of the need for social change and the delights of an idealized beloved. Spurning the newly emerging *azad nazm* (vers libre), he wrote lilting lyrical poetry which was full-bodied and flavoursome of the vigour and radicalism of his time and age. It reflected, in ample measure, the currents of social change and the winds of socialism sweeping across India on the brink of independence. At the same time, his nazms were as disciplined and immaculately constructed as his ghazals. Not for him the looseness of metre or the laxity of craft adopted by the progressives—in the name of a Larger Cause—with such devil-may-care abandon by some of his fellow progressives. It is this that has made Majaz's legacy endure; it is this, also, that made the progressives quick to identify him as their poster boy. He got along with everybody, had no disputes, literary or otherwise, and was, by and large, an amenable and easy-going person. He was also, apparently, perfectly content to be hijacked by the progressives. He believed in their cause, was happy to lend his name to their movement, was willing to travel with them to their conferences and mushairas, yet it seems doubtful whether he felt as strongly about the progressive cause as Zaheer or Jafri evidently did. *Roshnai* carried a brilliant pen portrait of Majaz, his bony, angular face and his personality:

He was sweetness itself, extremely humble, shy and taciturn. The wit and subtlety of Majaz' temperament appeared only in the informal company of close friends. If Jafri was a cavalier in the field of debate, Majaz had never been touched by its atmosphere, even though thanks to his intelligent mind, he was fully aware of the scholarly and philosophical viewpoints of socialism as well as the current political thought.[59]

In the same section of *Roshnai*, Zaheer recalled hearing Majaz recite 'Andheri Raat ka Musafir' in Hayatullah Ansari's ancestral home in Firangi Mahal.[60] While deeming the poem 'weak' insofar as 'the goal of revolution is vague, the forces of revolution have not been clearly visualised, and the concept of endeavour for bringing about revolution is weaker than the enthusiasm for it', Zaheer conceded that flaws were not unique to

---

[59] Zaheer, *Light*, p. 159.
[60] The Ansaris of Firangi Mahal (the hallowed abode of the Lucknow ulama) were the new breed of alim—patriotic, nationalist, and educated.

Majaz's poetry, but 'existed in the whole revolutionary movement of the time'.[61]

Majaz could build a wonderfully rousing effect through the use of sonorous wordplay that simulated the excitement of the coming revolution. He also wrote eminently sing-able, extremely lyrical songs such as *'Bol ari o dharti bol'* (Speak, O earth, speak)[62] and the near-cultish *'Nazr-e-Aligarh'* (Ode to Aligarh), written in 1936, with its passionate, impetuous, foot-tapping beat that was adopted as the anthem by the AMU and for generations has brought Aligarians to their feet and close to tears. Its rousing, dramatic appeal to the young remains, to this day, unmatched as does its call to rise for the nationalistic cause:

The clouds that arise from here shall rain upon the entire world.

Like good poetry the world over, some of Majaz's poems transcend their time and place and can be read again and again by newer audiences. *'Awara'* (Vagabond) is one of them. Written towards the end of the active phase of his life, in 1937, before the demons of drink and despair pulled him down, it has all the brilliance of a lamp that will be snuffed out. Majaz was dubbed a 'martyr to romanticism'[63] and *'Awara'* bears witness to that description. It uses similes and metaphors that had never been used in Urdu poetry to describe a new restlessness and despair that had a generation in its thrall. The moon that had hitherto been compared to all manner of fanciful objects was now likened to the mullah's turban and the moneylender's ledger. *'Awara'* ends with a welling up of rebelliousness

---

[61] We have already seen how fellow-Marxist Ehtesham Husain found a revolutionary echo in the use of traditional romantic images in the same poem.

[62] Lyricists played an important role in the PWM. They helped popularize the movement's ideas and stances on certain issues and reached out to larger audiences, especially students, peasants, and workers. The PWA nurtured an entire generation of lyricists, many of whom eventually drifted towards the Bombay film industry such as Sahir, Jan Nisar, Kaifi, Akhtarul Iman, etc. Some lyricists resisted the hold of the party; others became tools of propaganda and often wrote lyrics as command performances. Shaukat Azmi's *Kaifi & I* mentions how Kaifi was often asked to write a poem on a specific subject under the instructions of the party high command. Javed Akhtar uses the same example—of a lyricist having to first dig a grave and then find a body to fit it! Akhtar also credits the film lyricists of the 1940s and 1950s with advancing the progressives' cause.

[63] Ale Ahmad Suroor, *Aligarh Magazine* (Majaz Number), 1956.

bordering on anarchy with the poet, frustrated beyond endurance, wanting to

> Reach out and turn this glorious assembly to cinders.

Writing the Foreword to the second edition of *Ahang*, Faiz Ahmed Faiz praised Majaz's poetry for its wonderful mix of diverse qualities and appended one of Majaz's own verses as an epigraph:

> Look, it is a sword, it is a musical instrument, a goblet of wine
> If you raise the sword it shall become a mighty achievement.

Other revolutionary poets beat their chests and make loud proclamations, Faiz said, but they cannot sing because they see only the horror of revolution, not its beauty. Majaz, on the other hand, could do precisely that: he could sing about the coming revolution because he saw it as a thing of beauty, a joy to behold and to rejoice in.

Faiz Ahmed Faiz (1911–1984)

We have seen in Chapter 1 how politics and history are commensurate. At the worst of times when upheaval and change are the order of the day, so are politics and poetry. There can be no better example of this axiom in the twentieth century than the poetry of Faiz Ahmed Faiz. Like Majaz, he too matured from a callow romantic to a revolutionary poet, but unlike Majaz he had a longer innings and a far more complex, more nuanced oeuvre. Faiz wrote, prolifically and compellingly, on the events that shaped the destiny of the subcontinent; apart from his prodigious output as a poet, he also wrote newspaper editorials and articles and gave interviews on a range of subjects that, taken together, reveal a highly political mind beneath the poet's persona with an astonishing range of concerns and interests. However, here in this book, I will look at his career largely in connection with the PWM and only up till 1955, though the crop of what can be called his most seasoned offerings ripened in later years.

His father had been educated abroad—in Cambridge and Lincoln's Inn—but not him. Born into straitened circumstances on 13 February 1911 in Sialkot, Faiz received his early education at the city's Murray College (a landmark institution run by the Church of Scotland, where Iqbal too had studied). He then joined the Government College in Lahore where he studied Arabic, English literature, and philosophy. In those hallowed portals, amidst its quadrangles and courts reminiscent of Oxbridge, he drank slowly but thirstily from the cup of knowledge, drinking in new ideas about the world and its ways. In college, he met people who would have a lasting influence on his life: Pitras Bukhari, M.D. Taseer, Sufi Ghulam Mustafa Tabassum, Imtiaz Ali Taj, Chiragh Hasan Hasrat, Hafiz Jallundhri, Akhtar Shirani.

In 1935, he joined the M.A.O. College at Amritsar. Run by Muslims, along the same lines as the college in Aligarh, but owned by a family of Punjabi landowners, the college also employed M.D. Taseer,[64] Mohibbul Hasan,[65] the historian who had moved from Calcutta, and of course Mahmuduzzafar as the vice principal. In Amritsar, Faiz was drawn to the vice principal's wife, the charismatic Rashid Jahan who deemed him the only sensible 'boy' in the entire college! In her home[66] he met communists and their sympathizers—both from the Punjab as well as visitors from Aligarh, Lucknow, and Mahmuduzzafar's friends from England. *Roshnai* has several light-hearted references to the young Faiz who seemed a trifle bemused by Rashid Jahan's forthrightness and easy self-assurance. Zaheer also wrote in *Roshnai* how when he first met Faiz in January 1936, neither he nor his hosts knew that this shy young man wrote poetry. Mahmuduzzafar merely regarded him as a young teacher with good taste in books since he borrowed Stephen Spender and W.H. Auden from his collection.

We have seen in the previous chapter how Zaheer travelled to Lahore in the company of Faiz, Mahmuduzzafar, and Rashid Jahan, met Mian Iftikharuddin and other prominent Punjabi writers, and how Faiz helped Zaheer in setting up the Lahore branch of the PWA. This marked the beginning of Faiz's association with the progressives. During the Amritsar days, he got drawn into the trade union and civil liberties' movements— concerns that would occupy him for the rest of his life. And it was here that he got drawn into the great debate of his day: Art for Art's Sake

---

[64] The two were related by marriage; their wives were sisters. In later years, their politics differed widely as Taseer became increasingly an establishment man.

[65] In an interview, Faiz's wife recalls learning Urdu from Mohibbul Hasan and teaching him French. See Sheema Majeed (ed.), *Coming Back Home: Selected Articles, Editorials and Interviews of Faiz Ahmed Faiz* (Karachi: Oxford University Press, 2008), p. 143.

[66] Rashid Jahan's only surviving sister, Birjees Kidwai, told me about meeting Faiz in her sister's home in Amritsar and going for picnics in the surrounding countryside with an eclectic group of writers and intellectuals.

versus Art for Life's Sake. It was possibly in Amritsar too that Faiz read the *Communist Manifesto*, banned in India, but smuggled in by communist groups and made available in universities. It marked a turning point in his life. Of his days in Amritsar, Faiz said: 'It was a time of great creativity and the opening of new perspectives. I think the first lesson I learnt was that it was impossible to detach oneself from what was happening externally.... What is important is the larger human equation of pain and pleasure. As such, internal and external experiences are two sides of the same coin.'[67]

One is tempted to draw parallels with Majaz and view both Faiz and Majaz as good-natured, easy-going young men, shy with strangers, but equipped with a ready wit in the company of friends, given to a liberal left inclination, but neither fully radicalized nor showing any leaning towards organized communism. Both were heavily influenced by classical Persian traditions and both evolved, in unique ways, their own prosody and vocabulary that was at once contemporary yet exquisitely musical. Again, in the case of both, once nationalism began to colour all else, we see the emergence of a distinct poetic voice. Like Majaz, Faiz too began to use the nazm for increasingly political, even revolutionary, purposes. Unlike Majaz, however, Faiz had an academic bent of mind. Being a teacher, he retained a scholarly disposition which he brought to all subsequent vocations and callings. Another useful comparison would be between Faiz and Iqbal. Both from the Punjab, they took to Urdu (not their mother tongue) as a bird takes to song. They wrote poetry that was at once passionate, direct, impetuous, that appealed with a startling near-prophetic call to the collective consciousness of their readers. Both used traditional poetic forms such as elegy, ode, and anthem and infused them with a fresh note of social consciousness. And, eventually, Faiz took the message of Marx where Iqbal had left it and carried it to a younger generation of Muslims who were, in the light of the growing importance of the PWM, more receptive to its egalitarianism, concern for the poor, and advocacy of change. Faiz remained a Marxist long after the decline of the PWM, but never an in doctrinaire one, nor was he ever a member of the Communist Party.

Apart from the help in setting up the Lahore PWA, Faiz lent his weight to the progressive cause whenever called upon to do so. He, along with Krishan Chandar, emerged as a leading light of the Punjab progressives.

---

[67] Translated from the Urdu by Khalid Hasan in *The Unicorn and the Dancing Girl* (New Delhi: Allied Publishers, 1988), pp. li–lii.

He organized the Punjabi Progressive Writers' Conference in Amritsar in the historic Jallianwala Bagh on the same venue as the annual meeting of the Punjab Kisan Committee in February–March 1940. Denied permission to hold their conference in the M.A.O. College (where Faiz taught and where Taseer was by now the principal), Faiz sought permission from the organizers of the kisan conference to use their marquee. Sitting on grimy rugs under a torn canopy, an eclectic group of intellectuals from all over the Punjab responded to Faiz's call: Chiragh Hasan Hasrat, Firoz Deen Mansoor, Teka Ram Sukhan, Mohibbul Hasan, Taseer, Raghuvansh Kumar Kapoor, Raghupati Chopra, Sanat Singh, Faiz himself, and Zaheer and Ashraf in the unlikely role of representatives from the UP sent to attend the kisan conference!

Faiz produced seven volumes of verse, of which only the first three concern us here. His first collection, *Naqsh-e-Faryadi* (Imploring Imprints, published in 1941 while he was still in Amritsar, but written over a period of 10 years), shows a strange intermingling of the romantic and the revolutionary. It reflects the aches of a sensitive, somewhat sheltered young man but also the sorrows of the world. The early poems have a haunting, dreamlike quality, such as '*Mere Nadeem*' (My Friend), '*Husn aur Maut*' (Beauty and Death), and '*Aaj ki Raat*' (Tonight). This trance was broken as he came in contact with Marxists and became increasingly influenced by social realism. In '*Mujhse Pahli si Muhabbat Mere Mahboob Na Mang*'[68] (My Beloved, Don't Ask Me to Love You as I Once Did), for instance, the poet acknowledges the heart-tugging beauty of the beloved but talks of the other sorrows of the world which claim his attention. He juxtaposes the beloved's beauty against the miseries and ugliness of the world, a world which has hunger, disease, and deprivation, a world that can never let him love her as he once did, for a love that is divorced from social reality is too individualistic, too meaningless:

> There are other sorrows too apart from love
> And other pleasures too apart from that of union.[69]

Another poem, '*Chand Roz aur Meri Jaan*' (A Few Days More, My Dear), again has the poet addressing his beloved and comforting her that the days

---

[68] Aulad Ahmad Siddiqui, younger brother of Ale Ahmad Suroor, narrated a conversation with the historian, Mohibbul Hasan in which the latter told him that '*Mujhse Pahli si ...*' was written for Rashid Jahan. Apparently, Faiz counted himself as one of her many admirers and visited her Dehradun home.

[69] Translation mine.

of cruelty, oppression, and helplessness are about to end. The humiliations inflicted by strange hands (the British), he assures her, shall be short lived:

> We are constrained to breathe in the shade of tyranny
> Bear it just a little longer, endure thus oppression
> This suffering that is our inheritance, and we are helpless ...
> But now the days of cruelty are numbered.[70]

Other poems from *Naqsh-e-Faryadi* that bear the stamp of progressivism are '*Raqeeb Se*' (To My Rival), '*Tanhai*' (Solitude), '*Bol ke Lab Azaad Hain Tere*' (Speak, For Your Lips Are Free), '*Mauzoo-e-Sukhan*' (Subject for Creation), '*Hum Log*' (We People). If in '*Bol*' he is inciting his people to speak up and reminding them that they are free despite their fetters:

> Speak, for your lips are free
> Speak, for your tongue is still yours
> Your supple body is still yours
> Speak, for your life is still yours.[71]

In '*Hum Log*', he seems to be chastising them for the fear, regret, and sorrow that do not let them rise in revolt:

> Clasping a row of snuffed out candles in the niches of our hearts
> Scared even of the light of the moon, wearied of all things
> Like the remembrance of love's beauty now faded
> Clutching our darkness, and being cloaked by it.[72]

In '*Mauzoo-e-Sukhan*', he makes the most direct statement of what should concern a poet: should it just be the darkness of a beloved's tresses or the delicate tracery of henna on her pale hands or should it be all that has happened to the sons and daughters of Adam and Eve from time immemorial and all the tragedies and misfortunes that shall continue to happen? Should he not ask:

> The countless souls who inhabit these glittering cities
> Do they live simply with the desire to die one day?
> These beautiful fields whose youth is bursting forth
> Why does only hunger grow in them?[73]

---

[70] Ibid.
[71] Ibid.
[72] Ibid.
[73] Ibid. All subsequent translations of Faiz are mine, unless otherwise specified.

The next two volumes, *Dast-e-Saba* (The Breeze's Hand, 1953) and *Zindah Nama* (Poems from Prison, 1956), buttressed his reputation as one of the leading intellectuals of his day. The first of the 'prison poems'—written during the four years of incarceration in the infamous Rawalpindi Case (which will be discussed in detail in Chapter 8)—remains the best-known among his early works long after the details of the so-called conspiracy are forgotten:

> Why should I mourn if my tablet and pen are forbidden
> When I have dipped my fingers in my own blood?

In 'The Execution Yard (A Song)', he seems to be consoling himself and all others who face oppression:

> Where the road of longing leads us, we will see tomorrow
> This night will pass, and this too we will see tomorrow.

In the same poem, he goes on to speak of the Street of Scorn, a familiar trope in Urdu poetry, used to refer to the wrong side of the street where the prostitutes lived; in Faiz's altered landscape it becomes any street anywhere in Pakistan where the summons can come for anyone at any time.

Sometime in the summer of 1951, Faiz wrote 'Subah-e-Azadi' (Freedom's Dawn), his first, and only, poem that directly addresses independence and makes an allusion to the trauma of partition:[74]

> This patchy darkness, this night-bitten dawn
> This is not the dawn of freedom we had waited for.

---

[74] Akhilesh Mitthal, who knew Faiz in London and met him several times in India, narrates a conversation with Faiz's daughter, Salima. Mitthal asked Salima why her father never wrote anything on the Partition which was, after all, the greatest tragedy to befall the subcontinent. Salima, according to Mitthal, did ask her father and his response was: 'Because it was too Big.' Subsequently, I posed the same question to Salima. In an email message dated 17 March 2011, she corroborated it thus:

In a chat with Abba I mentioned that in terms of cinema, World War II spawned movies galore.... But curiously not Partition.... I asked him directly why there was only the one poem from him? He looked very pensive … and I think his exact words were … 'It was too big.... We couldn't cope'.... The last part of the sentence I am certain of, i.e. 'we couldn't cope' not so sure of the word 'big' but I seem to remember that was more or less it. It struck him deeply.... And am sure he must have asked it of himself too … but then he was writing very little at the time. The business of survival around him was acute … '71 hurt him equally.... I watched him brooding for ever so long … '65 made him angry.

Such subversive poems created a stir not just among the progressives (who were of course quick to hail them and embrace their writer as one of their own), but also in literary circles where the connoisseurs of Urdu were quick to notice the promise of greatness and the use of classical tropes in the high tradition of Hafiz and Rumi. Ale Ahmad Suroor, writing the Foreword to the Indian edition of *Zindah Nama*, praised not merely the melodiousness of his poetry, but also its technical finesse. But what really struck a chord with millions of lay Urdu readers was the manner in which Faiz was voicing ageless concerns, but also pointing out new ones. Not only was he drawing the readers' attention away from the ecstasy and agony of love, he was also no longer content to talk of *deen* or *qaum* in a narrow sectarian way.

Faiz brought a new internationalism to Urdu poetry, for though the Urdu poet at the turn of the century had spoken of tremors in the Muslim world—as we have seen in Chapter 2—it was only insofar as it concerned the Muslims of India. Faiz was saying it was as much his concern as anybody else's when someone somewhere oppressed the weak, or the mighty 'system' crushed the lone voice of dissent. Inspired by the letters of Julius and Ethel Rosenberg, who were sent to the electric chair in 1953 on charges of being Soviet agents in America, Faiz wrote his hauntingly evocative '*Hum jo tareek raahon mein mare gaye*' (We Who Were Executed in the Dark Lanes):

> As the evening of tyranny dissolved in your memory
> We walked on as far as our feet could carry us
> A song on our lips, a lamp of sadness in our hearts
> Our grief bore witness to our love for your beauty
> Look, we remained true to that love
> We who were executed in the dark lanes.[75]

Similarly, his ode to Africa, '*Aa Jao Africa*'[76] (Come Africa, 1955) is an ode to oppressed people anywhere; it was to show the way towards increasing internationalism in the progressives' range of interests:

---

[75] Mir and Mir, *Anthems of Resistance*, p. 78.

[76] Africa exercised a powerful spell on the Urdu writers, especially the progressives. Jafri in an article in his *Naya Adab* entitled '*Taraqqui Pasand Shairi ke Baaz Masail*' (Some Issues Concerning Progressive Poetry), urged the poets to draw the readers' attention to people's movements in other parts of the world. Consequently, in the early 1950s it was decided to start an Afro-Asian Conference to draw poets

Come, for I have raised my forehead from the dust
Come, for I have peeled off the film of grief from my eyes
Come, for I have freed my arms from the grip of pain
Come, for I have thrown away the web of helplessness.

In later years, Faiz would write with equal passion about Palestine, Nambia, and Chile and justify it thus:

[A]s a writer or an artist, even though I run no state and command no power, I am entitled to feel that I am my brother's keeper, and my brother is the whole of mankind. And this is the relevance to me of peace, of freedom, of detente and the elimination of the nuclear menace. But out of this vast brotherhood, the nearest to me and dearest are the insulted and the humiliated, the homeless and the disinherited, the poor, the hungry and the sick at heart.[77]

Faiz's use of classical imagery for political themes, according to Gopichand Narang,[78] is in the same tradition as Chakbast and Hasrat Mohani—whom we have briefly studied in Chapter 2. In fact, one can go further and trace Faiz's progressive poetry to the centuries-old shehr ashob tradition in Urdu. Unlike the dirge-like laments that were the

---

from the developing world. Jafri wrote his hugely popular *'Jangal jangal phool chune, Bhai ke paaon lal gulab'* as a mark of solidarity: 'This African, my brother/Picks flowers in forest after forest/My brother, whose feet are red/Red as roses.' Similarly, when Patrice Lumumba, the first prime minister of Congo was deposed and murdered in January 1961, the Urdu poets wrote in white heat in support of this staunch supporter of anti-imperialism. Makhdoom spoke up for all the progressives when he wrote *'Chup Na Raho'* (Don't Be Silent): 'On a high scaffold, hope was hanged again in the desert/And another drop of blood fell from the eyes of the morn/Let the celebration of martyrs continue, be not silent/The execution grounds cry out: be not silent, do not be silent.' Sahir Ludhianvi too wrote about the slain African in his powerful poem *'Khoon phir Khoon Hai'* (Blood, However, Is Blood): 'Tyranny is but tyranny; when it grows, it is vanquished; Blood, however, is blood; if it spills, it will congeal.' Translations from Mir and Mir, *Anthems of Resistance*, pp. 79–81.

[77] Faiz Ahmed Faiz, 'The Role of the Artist', *The Ravi*, vol. 71, no. 2, pp. 1–2, quoted in Adeeb Khalid, *Annual of Urdu Studies*, vol. 23 (2008), p. 264.

[78] Gopichand Narang, 'Tradition and Innovation in Faiz Ahmad Faiz', *Urdu Language and Literature: Critical Perspectives* (New Delhi: Sterling Publishers, 1991), pp. 102–3.

shehr ashob, Faiz broadened the scope of time-honoured images and symbols and infused a new life and urgency in them. Narang sets out, in tabular fashion, what he calls the 'three-dimensional elements of Faiz's poetic structure'. Briefly, some of the most commonly used terms in Faiz's poetry, as identified by Narang, are: *ashiq* which is, of course, used for any lover anywhere, but by constant usage becomes synonymous with a patriot and revolutionary also. By extension, the *mashuq* (beloved in the conventional sense) is used for the country or people; *raqib* meaning rival is used interchangeably for imperialism, capitalism, tyranny, exploitation; *ishq* (love) becomes revolutionary zeal; *visal* or *deedar* (union with the beloved) becomes revolution or social change; *hijr* or *firaq* (separation) becomes oppression by the state; *rind* (libertine) becomes rebel; *sharab, maikhana, pyala, saqi* (wine, tavern, cup, cup-bearer) become sources of social and political awareness; *mustasib* (censor) becomes the colonial system or the capitalist state; *junoon* (sublime madness) becomes zeal for social justice; *haq* (truth) becomes socialism; *khirad* (empirical knowledge) becomes capitalism or the establishment; *mujahid* (fighter) becomes freedom fighter; *zanjir* (chain) becomes the chain of slavery; *hakim* (ruler) becomes unjust ruler or colonial master; *zindan* or *dar-o-rasan* (prison) becomes political imprisonment; *bulbul* (nightingale) becomes not just the poet but the nationalist poet; *gul* (rose) becomes the political ideal; and finally *baghban* (gardener) becomes the usurper of the corrupt system.

Against this template, Faiz's poetry rises aeons above the lament of a lover for his beloved; it becomes the agonized call of the conscience. The ghazal below, written in the spring of 1951 from a prison cell when the threat of a death sentence hung above him like the sword of Damocles, illustrates Faiz's ability to use classical idiom to speak of new, urgent concerns, and in the process also write what Carolyn Forche[79] has called the 'poetry of witness'—from behind the bars of a prison cell:

> This hour of chain and gibbet and of rejoicing
> Hour of necessity and of choice
> At your command the cage, but not the garden's
> Red rose-fire, when its freshest hour begins:

---

[79] Carolyn Forche (ed.), *Against Forgetting: Twentieth Century Poetry of Witness* (New York: W.W. Norton & Co., 1993).

No noose can catch the dawn wind's whirling feet,
The spring's bright hour falls prisoner to no net.
Others will see, if I do not, that hour
Of singing nightingale and splendid flower.[80]

Faiz called his second and third volumes a 'tribute' to captivity: 'Confinement, like love, is a fundamental experience. It opens many new windows on the soul.'[81] Deprived of pen and paper in the early days of solitary confinement, he wrote *qatas* that he could memorize; later he evolved a complex system of images, drawn from the classical Persian tradition that seemed on the face of it 'harmless' enough.[82] Shortly before his death, while addressing the Asian Study Group, he revealed the subtle ways he was forced to evolve to evade censorship. For instance, when speaking of *ehd-e-junoon* or *chaman ki udasi*, he was actually referring to oppression and injustice.[83]

Khalilur Rahman Azmi holds Faiz and N.M. Rashid responsible for bringing modernism—the sort influenced by contemporary English poets such as Spender and Auden—into Urdu poetry. Even in an outright political poem, such as the poem above, Faiz can be philosophical, even mystical; he can appeal to the senses and also stir one's thoughts; he can use imagery that is at once oblique, even radically new. The tangled skeins of modernism (*jadeediyat*) and progressivism (*taraqqui pasandi*) run through not just Faiz's poetry, but in many of his contemporaries, at least in the early years. We can see it in the range of literature published in the popular (not owned or run by progressives) journals of the 1940s—*Saqi* and *Jama* (from Delhi), *Nigar* (Lucknow), *Adab-e-Latif* (which Faiz edited intermittently from 1938–46), *Humayun*, *Dastan*, and *Shahkar* (all three from Lahore), and *Preet Lari* from Amritsar.

---

[80] Translated by V.G. Kiernan, quoted in Narang, 'Tradition and Innovation in Faiz Ahmad Faiz', p. 105.

[81] Hasan, *Unicorn and the Dancing Girl*, p. lii.

[82] See Ted Genoways, '"Let Them Snuff Out the Moon": Faiz Ahmad Faiz's Prison Lyrics in Dast-e-Saba' for a detailed study of the lexicography evolved by Faiz to evade detection and censorship in prison, in *Annual of Urdu Studies*, vol. 5 (1989), pp. 117–25.

[83] As reported in *Dawn* (13 March 1984), http://dawn.com/events/Mughal/1984.htm.

Faiz, while being a part of the progressives, was also a part of another literary grouping—the Halqa-e Arbab-e Zauq[84] which flourished in Lahore in the early 1940s. The Halqa was a loose coalition of like-minded young men which demanded nothing of its members save a vaguely defined aestheticism that did not shy away from individualism and subjectivity (both, incidentally, anathema to the 'hard-core' progressives).[85] Several Punjab progressives such as Rajinder Singh Bedi, Krishan Chandar, and Faiz attended the Halqa meetings, read their works, and listened to close, careful critiques from some of the more ardent members such as Miraji. While it never acquired the shape or momentum of a movement, its influence was tremendous over some of the important Urdu writers of modern times, such as Yusuf Zafar,

---

[84] Originally known as the Bazm-e-Dastango (The Assembly of Storytellers), it began in 1939 as the brainchild of two Lahore-based writers, Nazir Ahmad Jami and Sher Mahmud Akhtar, who felt the need for a non-political, purely literary organization. By October 1939, from its second meeting onwards, its name was changed to the rather pretentious-sounding Halqa-e Arbab-e Zauq. The rift with the PWM became more pronounced as the members of the Halqa became increasingly and studiously non-conformist and the PWA began to insist upon conformism above all else from its members. See Geeta Patel, *Lyrical Movements, Historical Hauntings: On Gender, Colonialism, and Desire in Miraji's Urdu Poetry* (New Delhi: Manohar, 2005) for details of the Halqa as well as an absorbing study of Miraji and his oeuvre. About the overlapping concerns with the PWA, Patel writes: 'The Halqa encouraged collaboration between social realist writers of prose and fiction, the more modernist experimental poets who wrote prose poetry, and those poets who were reorienting older forms like the ghazal to political concerns' (p. 59). In an interview to Mahfil, N.M. Rashid however credits the birth of the Halqa to the city of Delhi where it was set up as a 'substitute' for the Delhi Cultural Society and where members like Miraji were keen to focus on both Hindi and Urdu writers; with time, its focus turned exclusively to Urdu writers though, as Rashid claims, its doors remained open to all kinds of writers.

[85] 'The Halqa had no slogan. All it insisted on was, that any literary movement, must first be literary.' Akhtarul Iman, *Iss Abad Kharabe mein* (New Delhi: Urdu Academy, 1996), p. 113. Iman also mentions that the Halqa produced an annual compendium of poetry which included the entire spectrum of contemporary Urdu poets from Josh to, say, Shad Arfi; it never, even inadvertently, made a distinction between progressive and non-progressive poetry.

N.M. Rashid,[86] and Miraji. The influence of the Halqa and its members on Faiz's poetry remained long after the group had waned; we can see it in the obliqueness of some of the imagery, in the erotic, mystic, even spiritual connotations that run as a parallel track and, above all, in the use of symbols that transcend their accepted meaning and speak of new concerns. An early poem, 'Sarud-e-Shahanah' (Nocturne) is a densely symbolist poem redolent with the sort of imagery one associates with Miraji, yet a closer reading can make it yield new meanings. For instance, *mahfil-e-hast-o-bood* can refer to old and new political ideologies, just as 'desire' can be understood as personal choice.

The War in Europe affected India and Indians in strange ways. After the Nazi invasion of the Soviet Union in 1941, Faiz's pacifism underwent a change.[87] He joined the welfare department of the British army in 1942 and was put in charge of publicity. He served in the army till 1947 and was given an MBE for his services and raised to the rank of a lieutenant-colonel. He wore a uniform and served His Majesty's government not for guts or glory, but simply because he believed fascism had to be fought at all costs and by whatever means one could. However, his decision was viewed with misgivings from those within the PWA and outside. It prompted Majaz to say

> *Afghan nahi, Turk nahi, Hur nahi hoon main*
> *Shair hoon main aur uroose-e-sukhan hoon mani*
> *Karnal nahi hoon, Khan Bahadur nahi hoon main*[88]
> (I am not an Afghan, or Turk or Hur/
> I am a poet and a lover of poetry/
> And nor am I a Colonel or a Khan Bahadur)

The last line is a dig at Faiz and Hafiz Jallundhari, who were rewarded with the rank of a colonel and title, respectively.

---

[86] N.M. Rashid (1910–1975) was a curious case of being a progressive, yet not being part of either the movement or the association. He believed that literature must necessarily have a social content, but he refused to clothe his concern for the world in an ideological garb. Averse to the 'personality cult' of the leftists, he wrote a critique of Stalin in a poem called '*Hama Oost*' (Pantheism). Incidentally, Faiz chose to have the foreword of *Dast-e-Saba* written by N.M. Rashid, where, according to the latter, Faiz 'stands at the junction of romanticism and realism'.

[87] After leaving Amritsar, he had taught, briefly, at the Hailey College of Commerce and edited the *Adab-e-Latif* from Lahore.

[88] Quoted by Akhilesh Mitthal, who knew Majaz from 1951–3 in Lucknow.

Whatever be the rumblings within the PWA in distant Lucknow or Bombay, Faiz's relationship with the progressives remained warm as ever. While some comrades such as Jafri tried to play down some of the poignant and pathos-laden poetry at the expense of his more political offerings, Faiz himself brooked none of this specious double-speak. Just as Art for Art's sake could be the wrong maxim to adopt, he believed Art for Rebellion's sake could be just as misleading. Using the analogy of a beautiful face to go with a healthy body, he spoke of the due importance of aestheticism and social realism in poetry whereby good poetry is that which passes the test of both life and literature.[89]

Though never a member of the communist party, Faiz remained organically linked to the motherland. He travelled to the Soviet Union for the first time in 1958 to attend the first Afro-Asian Conference in Tashkent; he went again in 1962 to receive the Lenin Peace Prize. By then *Dast-e-Saba* had already appeared in Russian and Faiz was treated as a literary superstar. Here, Faiz forged bonds of friendship with Nazim Hikmet and Pablo Neruda as well as Russian intellectuals such as Rasul Hamza and Oljas Suleymenov.[90] Faiz wrote 'Maah-o-Saal-e-Aashnai' (Months and Years of Friendship), as a gesture of solidarity from a fellow-traveller. While this may be viewed as 'propaganda' literature, the powerful nazm 'Leningrad ka Goristan' (The War Cemetery in Leningrad) in the omnibus entitled *Nuskha-e-Wafa* (Inventories of Fidelity, 1984) is not a command performance. In later years, during the repressive regime of Breznev, Faiz's views on the Soviet Union were to undergo a change. In the last years of his life, Faiz's concern was only with his *laila-o-watan*, his beloved country.

On his relationship with the PWA, he once said in an interview[91] that he, like many others, was drawn to the movement because of two reasons: one, it was powered on the engine of independence, and two, its emphasis on the social priorities of those times; on both there was no difference of

---

[89] Faiz Ahmed Faiz, 'Shair ki Qadrein', in Qamar Rais and S. Ashoor Kazmi (eds), *Taraqqui Pasand Adab: Pachas Sala Safar* (Delhi: Naya Safar Publications, 1987), p. 211.

[90] For details of the Soviet connection, see Ludmila Vasileva, *Parvarish-e-Lauh-o-Qalam: Faiz, Hayat aur Takhliqat*, translated from the Russian by Usama Faruqi and Ludmila Vasileva (Karachi: Oxford University Press, 2007).

[91] Transcript of a conversation with Muzaffar Iqbal in Saskatoon, Canada, 4 June 1981, published in Hasan, *Unicorn and the Dancing Girl*, p. liv.

opinion among the members. The differences cropped up later: once independence was achieved, there arose the question of how best to reach the goal of 'true independence'. There were differences also, Faiz said, on how best 'to portray life and its problems realistically in literature'. We will come back to these differences in the section on the PWA in Pakistan in the last chapter.

In early 1947, the Pakistan Papers Limited[92] was established in Lahore by Mian Iftikharuddin and Faiz became the first editor of *Pakistan Times*, and head of its sister publications, the Urdu daily *Imroze* and the literary and political weekly *Lail-o-Nahar*. As the editor of *The Pakistan Times*, the English-language left-leaning newspaper from Lahore, he wrote on an array of issues from 1947 until his arrest in the Rawalpindi Conspiracy Case in 1951. In an editorial entitled 'What Price Liberty?' written in April 1948, we see Faiz at his most trenchant:

There are no halfway houses between liberty and thraldom. The public have to choose and decide whether they are going to permit this and similar inroads on their hard-won freedom [referring to the infamous Public Safety Act that gave unbridled powers to the State] or whether they are content to live in daily fear for their freedom and honour. The weapon of the Safety Act that they have placed into the hands of their Government is a dangerous weapon and is not a fit thing for children or sadists to play with. It should either be taken back or the people entrusted with it should be taught its proper use. It must be realized that a weapon like this cannot be used properly either by men who are cursed with the vindictiveness of an elephant and the ferocity of a wolf or by men who lack the guts of a rat and the courage of a sparrow.[93]

Faiz's English prose, much like his Urdu poetry, is hard-hitting and passionate and concerned deeply and ardently with the past and the present; like his poetry it looks at the future with hope and not just a little foreboding. However, unlike the poetry—and one says this with some trepidation for someone of Faiz's stature—the prose is occasionally long-winded and just a trifle ponderous. Where the Urdu poetry enchants and beckons, spilling

---

[92] In 1958, Pakistan Papers Ltd was taken over by Field Marshal Ayub Khan and merged with the National Press Trust, thus ending Pakistan's brief flirtation with a free, frank, and secular press.

[93] Majeed, *Coming Back Home*, pp. 4–5. All subsequent references to Faiz's editorials are from this collection.

out a kaleidoscope of images and metaphors, calling out to the readers to find common cause against injustice, exploitation, and a host of social and political issues, the English prose is occasionally weighed down by its own rhetoric. Where the poetry lilts and soars with effortless ease, conjuring up the most evocative and lyrical images to record or condemn the most grisly events in the history of the subcontinent, the prose harks back to an older style of writing that was self-consciously pedantic, even arcane sometimes. Having said that, one must admit the comparison itself—between prose and poetry—is unfair and the two, even from the same pen, are by their very nature as unalike as apples and oranges.

Of this period, perhaps the most moving is the editorial of 23 March 1949 titled 'Progress of a Dream'. Declaring the Partition as a way 'to end the vertical division that separated the two major peoples of the sub-continent ... by a horizontal division so that the divided halves could each develop an internal harmony that the undivided whole lacked,' he says, 'The dream is as yet unfulfilled. The division has come but neither half is as yet completely at peace, either with itself or with its neighbour.' Faiz saves his strongest words of criticism for those 'selfish packs of men' who 'mock at the nobility of freedom'. However, it seems hard to reconcile the glowing tribute to Muhammad Ali Jinnah, captioned 'To God We Return', written upon the Quad-e-Azam's death on 13 September 1948 with the poet who wrote '*Yeh daagh daagh ujala, yeh shab-gazida sehar, yeh woh seher to nahi tha inteza jiska?*' (This patchy light/ This night-bitten dawn/ This is not that dawn we had waited for?). Was it the same man who lamented in the poem '*Subah-e-Azadi*' the 'stained light and the night-bitten dawn' that greeted those who had yearned for freedom? For a man like Faiz to write such an unqualified obituary of a political leader whom he calls 'friend and counsellor, the guide and confidante, the comrade and leader all combined into one' seems excessive to say the least. Moreover, in comparing the loss of India and Pakistan who were 'in quick succession deprived of the two wisest and most humane men in the sub-continent' (referring to Gandhi and Jinnah in the same breath), he goes on to say incredibly enough: 'Ours is very much the greater and the more grievous loss.'

There is plenty in Faiz's prose writings that seems not quite in consonance with the liberal, progressive ideology that runs like a shaft of translucent light all through his poetry. In real life, however, while Faiz had his sympathies with the poor and the downtrodden, he was clearly never one of them. Constrained to walk a tightrope between ideology and good taste, between art and propaganda, between his role as an editor and a free thinker, between being a citizen of a Pakistan increasingly moving in the direction of sectarianism and fundamentalism and a world whose borders were dissolving, Faiz 'made himself known as an opponent of oppression'.[94] Despite all his scathing editorials on the goings on in the government and his hauntingly evocative ghazals on the bloodbath in East Pakistan by the West Pakistani armed forces, and his many years in exile, Faiz was a nationalist. He remained one no matter where he lived—in Lahore, London, or Beirut. He may not have written any rousing national anthems, but his epochal poem on the 1965 war, 'Uttho Ab Maati se Uttho, Jago Mere Lal' (Rise from the Earth, Wake Up, My Son), is a tribute to the soldier who lays down his life fighting for the country. It is a fine example of progressivism, of the poet's humanity and concern for the individual life that is precious. His elegy is for all the soldiers who die in war—any war. Once again, it illustrates his humanism which was the essence of his progressivism.

Faiz's association with the PWM continued after independence; we will study his role in the context of the PWA in Pakistan and his arrest and subsequent detention on charges of conspiracy in the section on Pakistan in the last chapter.

Makhdoom Mohiuddin and the Others

The seeds of progressivism had been planted in Hyderabad as early as 1935 by Sibte Hasan who secured the signatures of several of the city's notables for Sajjad Zaheer's *Manifesto*.[95] Among the early supporters of the progressive cause was Mohiuddin Qadri Zore (1905–1962) who had attended the Hindustani conference in Allahabad and Qazi Abdul Ghaffar (1888–1956),[96] editor of the *Payam* (1934–46); though in later years Zore

---

[94] Naomi Lazard, *The True Subject: Selected Poems of Faiz Ahmed Faiz* (Lahore: Vanguard Books, 1988), p. xi.

[95] Sulaiman Athar Javed, 'Hyderabad aur Taraqqui Pasand Tahrik', in Qamar Rais and S. Ashoor Kazmi (eds), *Taraqqui Pasand Adab: Pachas Sala Safar* (Delhi: Naya Safar Publications, 1987), p. 268.

[96] See Chapter 4 for more details on Ghaffar's career. He worked closely with Mohammed Ali Jauhar during the Khilafat movement, travelled to West Asian countries to raise support for Turkey, and after the collapse of the Khilafat worked with M.A. Ansari, Sarojini Naidu, and Hakim Ajmal Khan. He trained a whole

too drifted away and Ghaffar set up his own Urdu Congress in disagreement with the increasingly pronounced communist slant of the PWA. In the previous sections, we have seen the growth of the PWA in Lucknow, Allahabad, Aligarh, and Lahore; now we shall see its rise in Hyderabad and intertwined with a study of the PWM in the city we shall look at the life and career of a most remarkable man—Makhdoom Mohiuddin.

Born into a god-fearing family of teachers and scribes in the Medhak district of Andhra Pradesh, Makhdoom was struck from an early age by the disparities he saw all around him. Where, on the one hand, the Nizam government encouraged education and extra-curricular activities (such as compulsory boys' and girls' scouts training under the 'Bluebird' movement), on the other hand, it fostered a grossly unequal social system. Given Makhdoom's natural talents and keen interest in sports, theatre, and writing, he found direction and guidance from enlightened teachers at the Osmania University. While still a graduate student in 1935, he staged a play based on Bernard Shaw's *Widower's Houses*, which he translated along with his friend Meer Hasan into Urdu as *Hosh ke Nakhoon* (The Nails of Consciousness). It was staged at the University's Annual Day celebrations and watched by Sir Haidery, the prime minister of Hyderabad, Sarojini Naidu, and Rabindranath Tagore.[97] Makhdoom went on to write another play, *Murshid-e-Kamil* (The Perfect Teacher) in 1936 when he was studying for his MA in Urdu; this was staged to raise funds for the victims of the earthquake in Quetta. In both plays, Makhdoom not only wrote the excellent script in Urdu (inflected with a sharp Deccani flavour), but also played

---

generation of Urdu journalists and also wrote biographies on Abul Kalam Azad, Hakim Ajmal Khan, and Jamaluddin Afghani. Ghaffar took over the work of the Anjuman-e-Taraqqui-i-Urdu from Maulvi Abdul Haq when the latter moved to Pakistan. He brought the Anjuman to Aligarh in 1947 and worked as its general secretary till his death in 1956. Thereafter, Ale Ahmad Suroor took over the Anjuman.

[97] Tagore was very popular in Hyderabad. Makhdoom himself had written an essay entitled '*Tagore aur Unki Shairi*' which was published by the Idara-e-Adabiyat-e-Urdu, Hyderabad, in 1935. At the Annual Day celebrations, Tagore was warmly welcomed by the students and the Jana Gana Mana was sung for the first time in Hyderabad. Tagore invited Makhdoom to come to Shantiniketan, but the latter was discouraged by Maulvi Abdul Haq who felt his services were required in Hyderabad.

the central character. His third and last play, *Ban Phool* (Wild Flower), was an adaptation from Chekov; thereafter he devoted his time to writing poetry, trade union movement, and party work.

After completing his MA in Urdu from Osmania in 1936, Makhdoom spent the next two years searching for a job, doing odd jobs such as a stint at the *Payam* and another at the Records Office till he finally found employment as a lecturer at the prestigious City College in 1939. Here, Makhdoom's Urdu classes where a huge hit with the students since he lectured on Urdu literature and Indian politics with equal gusto. It was during one of these classes, in the classroom itself, that he wrote *Andhera* (Darkness), at one go. Makhdoom published his first collection *Surkh Savera* (Red Sunrise) in 1944; it made him a hero among peasants' and workers' groups as well as heralded the arrival of an exciting new voice in literary circles. One of its nazms, *'Inquilab'* (Revolution) not just created a storm in Hyderabad, but its ripples reached the entire Urdu-speaking world. The nizam's government took serious objection to its incendiary contents. The incitement to open rebellion became steadily more pronounced in poems like *'Baghi'* (Revolutionary):

> I am thunder, I am lightning
> Restless mercury, never still
> Self-respecting, self-appraising,
> Bending others to my will.
> And the sword which cut the tyrant was my own;
> And the spark, which burnt the wheat-stock
> Is from me and me alone.[98]

In another nazm entitled *'Jang-e-Azadi'* (War of Independence),[99] he announced the imminent dawn of a new day, a dawn that he was convinced would be a red one:

---

[98] This translation is from David J. Matthews, Christopher Shackle, and Shahrukh Husain, *Urdu Literature* (Islamabad: Alhamra, 2003), p. 179. All other translations, unless specified, are mine.

[99] Raza Imam, in an interview, recalled for me his earliest memory of the progressives thus:

My earliest memory of reading anything written by a progressive writer goes back to Makhdoom's *Yeh jang hai jang-e-azadi*. It was in some publication meant for the promotion of war efforts. I liked it for its rhythm, simple diction, and its emphasis both on India's freedom and the fight against Hitler, who seemed to me an epitome of evil. But it was in the late

Look, the red dawn is coming, the red dawn of independence
Singing the red anthem of liberty, freedom and independence
Look, the flag is waving, of liberty, freedom and independence.

For all its revolutionary ardour, *Surkh Savera* also contained some exquisitely sweet, romantic ghazals, ghazals that established Makhdoom's reputation as a romantic poet par excellence. As we have seen in the careers of Majaz and Faiz, in Urdu poetry it was entirely possible for a poet to be passionately romantic in one breath and espouse revolt and rebellion in the next breath, or to be sweetly sentimental in one poem and breathe fire and brimstone in another. Makhdoom's oeuvre reflects these dualities; he can be lyrically extravagantly lovelorn in exquisitely fashioned ghazals such as:

Once again, we began to speak of flowers last night
What a night it was—like a bridal procession of flowers.

And from the same pen he can produce anthems of revolt and resistance:

I am fire, yes, a blazing, roaring fire
I am fire; let me set everything on fire.

And, as we have seen in the case of Faiz, Makhdoom too relied upon an established tradition of classical Urdu and Persian poetry that allowed the poet to use time-honoured tropes to speak of radical, even revolutionary, themes. Like romantic poets the world over, Makhdoom used nature as living prop in many of his poems. The ode to the Telangana maiden ('*Telangan*') is reminiscent of Wordsworth's 'Solitary Reaper' and the Lucy poems:

Wandering and swaying on the edges of the fields
Showering sweet and gentle gurgles of laughter
Playing with her bangles, yet shy and bashful
Don't fall silent in front of strangers; sing on
Sing on, O beauteous Telangan maiden, sing on!

In 1936, Makhdoom was instrumental in setting up the Hyderabad branch of the PWA with the active support of Sarojini Naidu who offered

---

1940s, from class 7 to 10, that I came in touch with the progressive fiction writers, thanks to my well-stocked school library. Among the writers that I read at that time were Krishan Chandar, Manto, Ismat Chughtai, and Sajjad Zaheer. These writers did not tell just stories but seemed to be narrating experiences that I myself was undergoing in my surroundings and at that age.

her house, the 'Golden Threshold', as the venue for the group's meetings and in 1939 the Hyderabad unit of the then-banned CPI. The Nizam government had banned the setting up of political parties so Makhdoom and his comrades had to work under extreme secrecy and, again, clandestinely have their fledgling organization affiliated with the CPI.

A people's movement had been slowly gathering among the peasants of the Telangana[100] region from the 1940s. It was supported by the intellectuals of Hyderabad—men like Sibte Hasan, Akhtar Husain Raipuri, N.M. Jaisurya, and Makhdoom. In 1942, Makhdoom left the City College to fully devote himself to party work. The period of 1946–51 was not merely the high noon of the Telangana movement and growth of communism in Andhra, it was also the time when Makhdoom was forced to go underground and work in extremely hazardous circumstances. After the toppling of the Nizam government in the face of severe police action in 1948 and its merger with the Indian union, while the objective of the nationalist movement was met, the aim of the Telangana movement remained a far cry. If anything, the CPI faced a lot of flak for its perverse stand on the annexation of princely states with the Indian union (in the name of a specious argument on the right to self-identification) and its subsequent fostering of armed insurrection against the Indian state among the peasants of Telangana. In both cases, the CPI's about-turn seemed to fly in the face of logic: having aided and abetted the nationalist

---

[100] Comprising eight districts on the eastern half of Hyderabad state and populated mostly by Telugu-speaking peasants, the Telangana region had suffered under an oppressive agrarian system. By 1946, the CPI had set up communes and leftist poets were holding up the Telangana as a model for revolutionary uprisings in other parts of the country. Zaheer Kashmiri exhorted the Telangana model thus:

> Today, communes are sprouting from the land of Telangana
> Today, the scorched earth is bearing varieties of beautiful life
> Today, Men of Telangana are spreading the glad tidings of conquering love,
> Today, Men of Telangana are giving the blessed news of the renaissance of East
> Today, Men of Telangana have joined in the struggle of Java and Greece.

The above translation is by Hafeez Malik, 'The Marxist Literary Movement in India and Pakistan', *Journal of Asian Studies*, vol. 26, no. 4 (August 1967), p. 657. See, also, Zaheer Kashmiri, 'My Life, My Art', *Annual of Urdu Studies*, vol. 25 (2010).

movement, its refusal to lend support to a united Indian state at a crucial time seemed perverse to say the least.[101]

In the wake of the Indian government's crackdown on communists, Makhdoom was arrested in 1951, but released a year later, along with other communist leaders, so that they could participate in the general elections—the country's first in 1952. Makhdoom stood for both the assembly and Lok Sabha elections from Hyderabad as a candidate of the People's Democratic Front, a new alliance of left parties forged to face the mighty Congress in Andhra Pradesh. He lost both, though he later won the by-election from Huzoor Nagar in Hyderabad. He faced defeat the second time round, in 1952, though this time he was appointed leader of the opposition in the state assembly. Makhdoom remained actively involved in the trade union movement, where he worked closely with V.V. Giri, who became the fourth president of India. In fact, Makhdoom died in Delhi, while attending a night-long celebration organized by the left parties to celebrate Giri's appointment to the country's highest office.

The Kul Hind Taraqqui Pasand Mussanifin (All-Indian Urdu Progressive Writers) conference held in Hyderabad in October 1945 was the highpoint of progressivism not only in the city but in the history of the PWM. We get a delightful account of this momentous event from Shaukat Azmi, a Hyderabad lass who met her future husband, Kaifi Azmi, during the conference and was swept up in a life of poetry, politics, and progressives. Struck by the lack of affectation in the group that had come from Bombay, she writes: 'The young progressive writers were a refreshing change; they wore their fame so lightly that I was overwhelmed.'[102] No progressives' conference was ever complete without a mushaira; this one had an assembly of greats. Majrooh Sultanpuri struck the opening notes, in his inimitable *tarranum*:

> My destination hove into sight and the wind too changed direction
> As your hand came in mine and a thousand lamps lit up my path.

Shaukat goes on to describe Jafri's rendition of 'The Caravan of Life' from his long poem in the masnavi tradition, 'Greetings to the New World':

---

[101] For an enunciation of the CPI's stand on Telangana, see *Documents*, vol. VII (1948–50) and vol. VIII (1951–6).

[102] Shaukat Azmi, *Kaifi & I: A Memoir*, edited and translated by Nasreen Rehman (New Delhi: Zubaan, 2010), p. 27.

Travellers who set out for new horizons,
Carrying with them the flame of time
These nights of rebellion and armies of revolution
Have their feet on the ground, their sights on the sky
Arise, and join these wanderers
For whom time is the dust that blurs their path.

At a previous mushaira, Kaifi had recited *'Taj'* (Crown), a powerful attack on monarchy and injustice, which required some fearlessness in the city of Nizams. Now he recited *'Aurat'* (Woman):

Arise, my love, for now you must march with me
Flames of war are ablaze in our world today
Time and fate have the same aspirations today
Our tears will flow like hot lava today
Beauty and love have one life and one soul today
You must burn in the fire of freedom with me.

By 1944, a large number of progressive writers had begun to flock to Bombay. Josh Malihabadi, Akhtarul Iman, Krishan Chandar, and Saghar Nizami were in Poona, but the lure of the silver screen drew them to the city that was home to the biggest film industry in Asia. By the time the war ended, some of the most dynamic writers of the age had flocked to Bombay: Urdu writers like Bedi, Sahir, Hameed Akhtar, Jafri, Kaifi, Jan Nisar Akhtar, Majrooh Sultanpuri, Rifat Sarosh, Niyaz Haider, Hajra Masroor, Khadija Mastoor, Manto, Miraji, Vishwamittar Adil, Upendranath Ashk, Ismat Chughtai, and her husband Shahid Latif; Hindi writers Nemichandra Jain, Amritlal Nagar, Balraj Sahni, Prem Dhawan; Marathi writers Mama Varerkar and Anna Bhau Sathe; and Gujarati writers Bakulesh Swapnath and Bhogilal Gandhi. They were all members of the Bombay branch of the PWA which was then the most active in the country.[103]

---

[103] Rifat Sarosh, who reached Bombay in August 1945 to take up a post at All India Radio (AIR), lists himself and the following as most faithful attendees of all PWA meetings: Zaheer, Jafri, Kaifi, Zoe Ansari (summoned from Delhi to 'replace' Sibte Hasan after the latter left for America), Krishan Chandar, Mahindarnath, Majrooh, Akhtarul Iman, Vishwamittar Adil, Sahir, Ibrahim Jalees, Hajra Masroor, Khadija Mastoor, Hamid Akhtar, Madhusudan, Niyaz Haider, Qudoos Sehbai, and Captain Anwar. See Aziz Ahmad, *Taraqqui Pasand Adab* (Delhi: Khwaja Press, 1945), p. 298.

It was to this Bombay that Kaifi, a full-time party member, brought his Hyderabadi bride, to live in the commune in Andheri. Shaukat notes her first impressions thus:

Katthal, banana and mango trees stood with giant banyans. A swing was hanging from one of the trees and the air was filled with the scent of mogra and juhi. A few years earlier, this idyllic setting had been the home of the Cultural Squad, a wing of the Communist Party. Many artists and dancers had lived here.... In 1943, during the Bengal famine, artists from the Communist Party of India had toured the length and breadth of the country and collected two lakh rupees for relief work. Their theme song, *Bhuka hai Bengal* (Bengal is hungry), written by Wamiq Jaunpuri, became very well known throughout India.

We went to Kaifi's tiny room in which there was a loosely strung jute charpai with a dhurrie, a mattress, a sheet and a pillow. In one corner there was a chair and a small table on which there were some books, piles of newspapers, a mug and a glass. The simplicity of this room touched my heart....

Lunch in the commune was unlike anything I had seen. Everyone had an aluminium plate, two bowls, and two low wooden chaukis (one for sitting and one to use as an improvised table). The cook served the food which was a daal, a vegetable, four chapattis with ghee, some rice, salt, onions, a slice of lemon, and I think, some pickle on the side. Everyone washed their own utensils and put them away.[104]

Shaukat provides a luminous account of her new life in the company of gregarious comrades: Zaheer and his wife Razia and their two daughters, the affable duo of Muneesh and Mahdi,[105] Jafri and his wife Sultana who

---

[104] Azmi, *Kaifi & I*, pp. 43–4.

[105] In a lengthy interview with Mahdi, who now lives in Aligarh, I was able to get a corroboration of Shaukat's account. Like Shaukat, he blamed B.T. Ranadive, who took over from Joshi in 1947, for the infighting and bitterness that marred the post-1947 years. Mahdi also told me how he, Muneesh, and Kaifi formed a trio in the commune. In the course of a rambling chat, he described the party leadership as being puritan, bent upon keeping the party away from *badnami*. He also described how bohemianism was not tolerated by the party, nor were 'deviations' such as homosexuality. One of Mahdi's assigned tasks was to distribute the Urdu weekly *Naya Zamana* in the Muslim areas of Mohammed Ali Road and Bhindi Bazar. Bitterly critical of Ranadive, he claimed, the sectarianism fostered by him eventually led to the split in the party. In contrast, he praised Joshi for his inclusive policies. He described Joshi as critical of the national leadership, but not anti-nationalistic the way Mahdi perceived Ranadive's policies to be. Joshi, he believed,

took Shaukat under her wing and taught her the ways of coping in a commune, the parsimonious party treasurer, Comrade Ghate (who nevertheless grudgingly parted with Rs 100 to the newlyweds), and P.C. Joshi who was the general secretary of the CPI during 1935–47 and comes across in her narrative as a benevolent despot. Shaukat's nikah with Kaifi was witnessed by nearly all the progressive writers from Bombay; it was followed, naturally enough, by a mushaira with Majaz reciting *Aaj ki Raat* (Tonight) and the bride being presented a copy of the groom's first collection of poetry, *Aakhr-e-Shab* (The End of the Night), dedicated to her. Shaukat describes Kaifi and his friends, who would become her fellow-travellers, thus: 'They were enlightened and humane individuals who were struggling to create a new world for the poor, the destitute and the hungry. Although they were from different parts of India, these people were like one family where everyone was addressed as "Comrade", which at the time meant an evolved human being.'[106]

Kaifi earned Rs 40 as monthly salary from the party; from this he had to give Rs 30 towards his wife's boarding expense. To earn some extra money, he wrote a column for the Urdu daily *Jamhuriat* (Democracy).[107] Shaukat got drawn into the IPTA partly to lighten the burden on Kaifi and partly in response to P.C. Joshi's command that 'the wife of a communist should never sit idle'.[108] Her first role was in Ismat Chughtai's *Dhani Bankein* (Green

---

did not want to cut off the communist movement from the nationalist movement and kept his links open with Gandhi and Nehru. Ranadive, on the other hand, was vehemently opposed to this; he called independence a 'false freedom'.

[106] Azmi, *Kaifi & I*, p. 49.

[107] From 1956 onwards, Kaifi had a fairly successful stint as a film lyricist with films like *Yahudi ki Beti, Kaaghaz ke Phool, Haqeeqat, Pakeezah, Heer Ranjha, Hanste Zakhm, Garam Hawa, Razia Sultan,* etc.

[108] IPTA was launched on May 1943 in Bombay with P.C. Joshi as president and Anil de Silva as general secretary with the aim of using the stage and other traditional arts to portray the problems facing the country. Joshi had earlier begun the practice of gathering the country's prominent writers, journalists, artists, economists, historians, film, and stage actors to rally around the party organ, *National Front*, and later *People's War* and *People's Age*. He commissioned Sunil Jana to take photographs of the Bengal famine and document people's movements elsewhere such as in Telangana. Joshi understood, and capitalized on the need to use culture as a living tool. While the catalyst for IPTA was the Bengal famine, it continued to be active long after the PWA declined. IPTA is still functional.

Bangles), a play on the Hindu–Muslim riots that were tearing the fabric of a newly independent India. Here, Shaukat got drawn into the country's most vigorous cultural movement that had the likes of Zohra Segal, Uzra Butt, Bhishm Sahni, and Prithviraj Kapoor, among its stalwarts.[109]

IPTA, PWA, and the Bombay film industry were like three inter-linked circles, with overlapping memberships and a host of common concerns. Foremost among these was a socially transformative agenda which would fulfil the needs of a fledgling nation. For this they sought inspiration not only from Marxist tomes and ideologues, but also from Nehruvian socialism that hailed schools, colleges, dams, and factories as the 'temples of modern India'. Members of the IPTA and PWA—some of whom worked in the film industry as actors, directors, scriptwriters, lyricists, technicians, etc.—worked in tandem to produce a radically new set of images, metaphors, vocabulary, even aesthetics that influenced several generations of film-goers.[110] Their most visible and immediate effect was the introduction of a non-sectarian ethos, one that rose above the narrow confines of caste, creed, and religion and worked as a balm on a national psyche that had been traumatized by the communal outrages before, after, and during the Partition.

Among the Bombay progressives, Sahir Ludhianvi was the most successful film lyricist. His lyrics in simple but chaste Hindustani touched a chord with millions of Indians in films like *Pyasa* (Thirsty, 1957). Here, we shall concentrate on his career till 1955 where his reputation rested largely on his progressive poetry for the mushaira circuit and his first collection entitled *Talkhiyan* (Bitterness, 1943). In later years, he came to be regarded as a lyricist[111] rather than poet and, like most progressives, learnt to make

---

[109] We get two wonderful accounts of the IPTA in Zohra Segals' autobiography, *Close-Up: Memoirs of a Life on Stage and Screen* (New Delhi: Women Unlimited, 2010) and Kiran Segal's biography of her mother, *Zohra Segal: 'Fatty'* (New Delhi: Niyogi Books, 2012)

[110] For a study of 'The Progressive Tradition and the Film Industry', see Talat Ahmed, *Literature and Politics in the Age of Nationalism: The Progressive Episode in South Asia, 1932–56* (New Delhi: Routledge, 2009), pp. 164–71.

[111] A collection of his film lyrics, *Gaata Jaye Banjara* (And the Gypsy Sings On) continues to be popular even today. For a nuanced understanding of the distinction between lyrics, especially film lyrics and conventional poetry see Nasreen Munni Kabir, *Talking Songs: In Conversation with Javed Akhtar* (New Delhi: Oxford University Press, 2005).

compromises giving in to the demands of film-makers—a practice Kaifi once compared with digging a grave and then looking for a corpse to fit in! Perhaps aware that the *adeeb*, literary connoisseurs, had judged him and found him wanting, Sahir wrote the following sher, boldly declaring that he wrote for the masses, not the classes:

> I do not regret that people do not consider me an artist
> The traders of thoughts and words do not consider my verses verses.

For all its bravado, the above sher underlines the tension between the literary tradition (of which the progressive poets were acutely aware since every single one of them had their roots in the soil of the classical tradition and almost all had a good grasp over Persian and Arabic[112]) and the demands of socialist realism. How much of this tension arose from the party's diktat and how much from the progressives' own rather stringent observation of Western experiments in aesthetics and people's poetry (especially in the Soviet countries) is hard to tell. While there are references to party member-poets like Kaifi and Jafri producing poetry that is clearly in the nature of 'command performances', the extent of the pressure on other progressives is not certain. It may well be that some progressives felt the need to be more loyal than the king simply in order to remain in the inner circle, or as in the case of Makhdoom or Faiz, out of genuine conviction of the party's stand on national and international events. We can see propaganda replace poetry—in direct proportion—whenever there is the slightest dilution of the poets' belief in certain stated positions. Wherever the poets speak with conviction, their words have the ring of honesty; they might lack in craft, but not in clarity.

In the case of Sahir in particular, and the other progressive lyricists in general, it would be useful to make a distinction between their film and non-film poetry; the former was more need-based, more tailored to the exigencies of the trade rather than the times and the latter was, as Mir Ali

---

[112] In the next chapter, we shall see this tension was largely missing in the prose writers. Manto, Ismat, Bedi, Krishan Chandar, and Rashid Jahan crafted a new lexicon with blithe confidence because the Urdu short story was putty in their hands. The absence of an evolved literary canon for the Urdu short story empowered them instead of intimidating or curbing their natural instincts for a new kind of self-expression.

Raza puts it, more 'programmatic and manifesto-driven'.[113] And it was this latter kind of poetry that allowed poets like Sahir to ask more acerbic, more trenchant questions as in '26 January':

> Come, let us today ponder on this question
> Whatever happened to those beautiful dreams we had dreamt?
> Not a shroud to cover the helpless nakedness
> Whatever happened to those promises of silk and brocade?[114]

Sahir's poetry has proved to be the most popular, longer lasting, and with greater recall-value than his comrades'; it is still sung, broadcast, and remembered by more Indians than any of the other Urdu heavy-weights, yet, both the Urdu critic and the Western scholar of Urdu literature has been quick to dismiss Sahir as a publicist for the PWM. Deeming this unfortunate, Mir Ali Raza makes a larger point about the progressives: 'In the specialised world of Urdu criticism in English, there appears to be an implicit agreement that the works of the PWA writers, while they may be lauded as devices of organising, are aesthetically inferior, and even harmful to Urdu poetry's classical traditions.'[115]

I would agree only partly with such an assessment: while a great deal of progressive poetry (the same cannot be said for prose) was indeed purposeful art and some of it was, it must be accepted, 'aesthetically inferior', good, bad, or indifferent, it could never be 'harmful'. As I have repeatedly shown through a sampling of Majaz, Faiz, and Makhdoom, progressive poetry drew from classical poetry all its strengths; its weaknesses, and there were many, were entirely its own. The progressives not only introduced freshness and vigour into Urdu poetry, they strengthened it in much the same way as cross-breeding strengthens the genetic pool and in-breeding weakens it.

In the high noon of the Bombay days, every Sunday the progressives would meet at Zaheer's house in 7 Sikri Bhawan at 96 Walkeshwar Road, not far from the Hanging Gardens. The Bombay branch of the PWA was not only the most active, but, given its location, boasted a cross-section of great writers from Urdu, Hindi, Gujarati, Marathi, and English. They would meet jointly where the barrier of language would be overcome with

---

[113] 'The Poetry of No', *Outlook*, 29 July 2004.
[114] *Kulliyat-e-Sahir*, '26 January' (Delhi: Hashmi Book Depot, 1994).
[115] 'The Poetry of No'.

working translations in English or Hindustani as well as in separate language groups such as Gujarati or Urdu. The Bombay PWA also organized day-long celebrations devoted to pan-Indian icons such as Premchand, Tagore, Sarat Chandra Chatterjee, Iqbal, and Shibli, as well as Gorky Day, Russian Revolution Day, and Romain Rolland Day.[116] Reminiscent of the Oxford Majlis days, Zaheer also invited an array of visitors including E.M. Forster, the English novelist and Ould Herman, secretary of the International PEN. Members of the Bombay PWA also formed the Cultural Workers' Committee for Fighting Famine and volunteered to work during communal riots. One of the most diligent members, Hamid Akhtar, began the practice of taking notes at the weekly meetings and publishing them in the *Nizam*.[117] In the regular meetings, the writers would read from their works, which would then be discussed freely and frankly by all present, with Zaheer playing the dual role of umpire and attendance taker.[118]

Stern and benevolent by turns, Zaheer had no patience with those who came infrequently or showed deviations from a laid-down party line. While ostensibly these meetings were in the nature of 'open house', they gradually became tools of marginalization. While Zaheer's *Roshnai* depicted this as a Bloomsbury-in-Bombay sort of group, we get a sharply

---

[116] Culled from a report on the Bombay PWA in Pradhan, *Marxist Cultural Movements in India*, vol. I, pp. 317–21.

[117] Hameed Akhtar subsequently collected and published his reports as *Roodad-e-Anjuman: Anjuman Taraqqui Pasand Mussanifin ki Roodad (1946–7)* (Lahore: Bright Books, 2000). A photocopy of this book was given to me by Akhtar's comrade from the Bombay days, Mahdi, when I went to interview him in Aligarh. The book deserves a serious study for it holds a mirror to the concerns, tensions, groupings, and politics of the Bombay group.

[118] Rifat Sarosh describes the 'pattern' of these meetings: a poem would be read, followed by a short story and an essay; each would evoke vigorous debate with Zoe Ansari being the most voluble dissenter. Jafri would make a brief speech in his decisive style (*faislakun andaaz*) and when the members became too volatile or the discussion too acrimonious, Zaheer would step in and deflect the course of debate. Sarosh credits Zaheer with being the most stable, sober, and far-sighted senior in the group. With gravitas, Zaheer kept his flock together and also invited non-progressives to attend their meetings. Sarosh mentions Jigar Moradabadi, Yagana Changezi, Zulfiqar, and Pitras Bukhari being invited despite their avowed non-leftist leanings. These meetings, attended as they were by a cross-section of intellectuals, had a profound effect on the pre-partition Urdu literature.

conflicting version from Akhtarul Iman,[119] another young progressive who began to feel left out largely due to a small core group that demanded strict adherence to laid-down policies that brooked neither debate nor dissent. Here, it must also be said that by the late 1940s, the Urdu canon had been commandeered by the progressives and it was they who henceforth decided what comprised the canon and what was beyond the pale. For instance, at the Hyderabad conference in 1945, a move was made (primarily by Abdul Alim) to pass a resolution to condemn the writings of Ismat, Manto, and Miraji on grounds of obscenity and preoccupation with sexual matters which was thought to contravene the aims of the PWA. Fortunately, Hasrat Mohani and Qazi Abdul Ghaffar disagreed vigorously and the resolution could not be passed.[120] Miraji, who was present in Hyderabad, tasted first-hand public ostracization from a 'community of writers to which he thought he belonged'; he was subsequently kept away from the meetings of the progressives in Bombay who had declared an 'all-out war'.[121]

While Miraji's was the most extreme form of ostracization (especially since he was emotionally and financially the weakest and most vulnerable), others too were marginalized, mocked, or blanked out in different ways or different degrees. We will study some of these ways in the next chapter in the context of Ismat and Manto; in the last chapter we will examine how this politics of exclusion eventually became one of the reasons for the decline of the movement itself. At this point we must note the change that came about in the Bombay group almost immediately after independence. From a large, genial, well-read, well-meaning group, it dwindled and deteriorated into a shadow of its former self. The times were such that the intricacies of

---

[119] Iman worked as a scriptwriter for Shalimar Pictures in Poona. He moved to Bombay shortly before Partition and started, with Miraji, a literary journal called *Khayal* (Thought). Zoe Ansari, on the journal's board of supervisors, condemned Miraji's publications and insisted that *Khayal* stop publishing his work. For Iman's version of the fate of *Khayal*, see Patel, *Lyrical Movements, Historical Hauntings*.

[120] See Azmi, *Urdu mein Taraqqui Pasand Adabi Tehreek*, p. 96 for details. Also, Ralph Russell, 'Leadership in the All-India Progressive Writers' Movement, 1935–1947', in B.N. Pandey (ed.), *Leadership in South Asia* (New Delhi: Vikas Publishing House, 1977). It has been noted by both that the same group that defended *Angarey* on grounds of social realism now wished to target Ismat, Manto, and Miraji for their so-called obsession with 'deviance'.

[121] Patel, *Lyrical Movements, Historical Hauntings*, pp. 70–3.

literature were not discussed in the salons of the literati, but in the public debates in Nagpada and Madanpura where young men like Abdul Jabbar made fiery speeches about the usefulness of literature.[122] On the other hand, the police began to keep an increasingly watchful eye on the progressives. Niyaz Haider and Majrooh were arrested on flimsy charges. Jafri spent over eight months in the Arthur Road Jail where he wrote poems like *'Patthar ki Diwar'* (The Wall of Stones). His long incarceration prompted his friends such as Ramesh Sinha and Shahid Latif to launch a 'Free Sardar' campaign.

The name of Ali Sardar Jafri (1913–2000) has cropped up repeatedly in the history of the PWM. While still an undergraduate student at Aligarh in 1936 (from where he was expelled for leading a protest march), he got involved with the Aligarh branch of the PWA. Long before he became known as a fiery poet and a fine orator, he wrote a collection of short stories entitled *Manzil* which landed him in jail for eight months. Thereafter, poetry, propaganda, and progressivism became the mainstays of his life. His first collection of nazms and ghazals, *Parvaz*, published in 1943, established him as a force to reckon with in Indian literary circles; this early and formidable reputation was shored up with a string of collections, each more powerful, more rousing, more visionary than the other: *Nai Duniya ko Salam* (Greetings to a New World, 1948), *Khoon ki Lakeer* (The Line of Blood, 1949), *Asia Jaag Utha* (Asia Has Woken, 1951), *Patthar ki Diwar* (The Rocky Wall, 1953), *Pairahan-e Sharar* (The Garment of Embers, 1966), *Lahu Pukarta Hai* (The Blood Calls, 1965), and *Navambar, Mera Gahwara* (November, My Cradle, 1998). A dynamic and industrious person, he also made documentaries, a highly successful TV serial on the lives of seven Urdu poets called *Kahkashan* (Galaxy), besides writing sundry articles, editorials, and essays voicing progressive concerns. At various points in his career, he edited journals that were a vehicle for progressive ideology: *Naya Adab* from Lucknow and *Guftagu* from Bombay.

---

[122] This section has been built from Rifat Sarosh's essay on Bombay in *Taraqqui Pasand Adab: Pachas Sala Safar*, p. 302. He writes of the slips of objective (*maqsadiyat*) being pasted on the forehead of every writer; some succumbed to the demands, others resisted, but the casualty both ways was good poetry. Sarosh also mentions how, after Zaheer's departure for Pakistan, the meetings were held at the Deodhar Hall at Opera House. Miraji attended some of these meetings at Deodhar Hall and Ismat read her 'Pompom Darling' article here for the first time and a critique of Manto's *Siyah Hashiye* (Black Margins).

A member of the CPI and a dedicated party man, Jafri was among those who saw the PWA as a vehicle of spreading communism both among intellectuals and workers. He swiftly rose to be one of the leaders of the PWM (along with Zaheer) and guided the PWM away from purely literary issues towards overtly political concerns. He wrote two plays *Yeh Khoon Kis ka Hai?* (Whose Blood Is This? 1943) and *Paikaar* (1944)—both on communal riots. His urgent desire for the country's independence was coupled with his equally strong yearning for a freedom that would bring equality and dignity to the proletariat. A dedicated Marxist, for him the world was polarized between two conflicting extremes: rich/poor, colonizer/colonized, exploiter/exploited, capitalist/proletariat, and so on. This black-and-white, doggedly bipolar world view coloured much of his poetry all through the 1940s–1950s. It is this, also, that made his early poetry unidimensional, one-sided, and, to my mind, stridently rhetorical; its grandiloquence, fervour, and posturing caused many to view him as a propagandist for the progressives, a competent poster boy and talented lyricist at best, but not a revolutionary poet in the league of Faiz or even Makhdoom.[123] While the fiery rhetoric and impassioned urgency earned him 'wah-wahs' in the people's mushairas that the progressives had taken to organizing in such abundance, especially in industrial hubs and among peasants and workers' groups, the more discerning were unmoved by Jafri's brand of message over manner, style over substance, theme over aesthetics.[124] Whatever be the opinion of the critics, Jafri continued till the end of his career to be a popular poet, lavishly awarded by successive governments (earning the country's highest literary award, the Jnanpith in 1999); more importantly, he became the most powerful person in the PWA, the 'sole spokesman' as it were, especially after Zaheer went away to set up the CPP after Partition.

There is a great deal in Jafri's vast oeuvre that cannot be dismissed as sloganeering or pandering to ideology alone.[125] Given Jafri's profound scholar-

---

[123] 'To inflate their numbers, the progressives began to praise even inferior writers who could not be called more than *mauzu-go shair* (propagandists)', Iman, *Iss Abad Kharabe mein*, p. 114. Jafri was guilty of patronizing such poets and encouraging such poetry.

[124] Iman goes on to say how, a time came, when literature seeped out; what remained was the mention of Russian buildings and Russian leaders.

[125] For details of Jafri's poetry and career, see Irfan Ahmad, *Seminar*, no. 494 (October 2000).

ship, his eclectic reading, and his command over the classical Persian idiom and imagery, he can paint the most graphic word pictures and speak of ageless concerns when he so chooses, as, for example, in his eponymous *Mera Safar*:

> I am a fleeting moment in the enchanted house of time
> I am the restless drop that travels
> From the pitcher of the past to the wine-cup of the future
> I sleep and get up and again go to sleep
> I am a play that is many centuries old
> I expire and become immortal.[126]

Or in the hauntingly evocative *Asia Jaag Utha*:

> This soil of Asia, this womb of civilization, this land of culture
> This is where the sun first opened its eyes
> This was where the first dawn of humanity unveiled itself
> This is where the ancient ages lit their lamps of science and wisdom.[127]

In his later collections, the uncompromising radical and diehard Marxist moved to a study of Kabir and the Bhakti-Sufi poets who too had brought about a people's movement centuries ago. In a collection of critical writings, *Paighambaran-e-Sukhan* (The Prophets of Art, 1970), Jafri the rebel acknowledged the significance of Mir and Ghalib, the true masters of Urdu poetry. His pacifism moved him to write *Kaun Dushman Hai* (Who Is the Enemy?) in the wake of the Indo-Pak war of 1965 making him the undisputed anti-war publicist; however, in 1999, he confounded his many admirers by presenting a collection of anti-war songs, *Sarhad* (Boundary), to the then right-wing prime minister A.B. Vajpayee. In the last chapter, we will come back to the dualities that marred the rosy optimism, the twists and turns in the uncompromising idealism of the early days, and the pragmatism and jingoism that seeped into the careers of the best of the progressives.

If all major Urdu poets and writers were either card-carrying progressives or sympathetic to the progressive cause, who were those who steadfastly remained outside the charmed circle? What were their compulsions? Considering that the CPI put its weight behind the call for Pakistan, a separate homeland for the Muslims, what was left to disagree over? What

---

[126] Translation mine.
[127] Ibid.

then was the agenda of those not in the charmed circle of the progressives, these 'others' who were regarded as traditionalists at best or reactionaries at worst? Among them can we count someone like Hafeez Jallundhari who not only wrote the *qaumi tarana* (national anthem) of Pakistan (*Pak sar zameen shaadbaad / Kishwar-e-haseen shaad baad / Tu nishan-e-azm aalishan / Arz-e-Pakistan*), but also a poetic history of Islam in three volumes called *Shahnama-e-Islam*? Upon the death of Jinnah, Jallundhari wrote:

The saviour himself was lifted by the hand of God
The martyr was enveloped by the shawl of His mercy.

Apart from the issue of Pakistan, by 1947, one is hard-pressed to find any major Urdu poet who, regardless of his affiliation with the PWA, was not voicing progressive concerns. There was near-unanimity in the poets' celebration of azadi, freedom from the imperial yoke, sadness at the price of this hard-won freedom, but also hope and optimism for the future. So, we see Moin Ahsan Jazbi, a lapsed member of the PWA who had worn the cloak of silence during the heydays of the progressives, picking up his pen once again to welcome a new age in *Naya Suraj*.

Very similar to '*Yeh daagh daagh ujala*' by Faiz, there was Ibadat Barelwi warning of the worse that lay in store:

Yes, the bitterness among the people will increase, still more
Yes, the perpetrators of cruelty will keep struggling against cruelty.

A traditionalist like Jigar Moradabadi was voicing his disappointment with an independent but truncated India:

The gardeners still have time to mend their ways
And still the spring they angered might return.

Perhaps, the effectiveness of the PWM may be judged by the proliferation of progressive thought among large numbers of poets and it may be said that it was a consequence of the acceptance of progressive views that poets, even ghazal writers, could no longer afford to keep their eyes closed to their social environment and to the problems of mankind as a whole.[128]

---

[128] N.M. Rashid, Interview, *Mahfil*, vol. 7, no. 2 (1971), p. 7. See also, S.R. Kidwai, '*Taraqqui Pasand Tahrik aur Ghazal*', in Qamar Rais and S. Ashoor Kazmi (eds), *Taraqqui Pasand Adab: Pachas Sala Safar* (Delhi: Naya Safar Publications, 1987) for a study of how the ghazal too, given its constraints, was 'used' by the progressives to reflect new concerns.

However, the pen that wrote eloquently of the coming revolution fell silent once faced by the immense human tragedy of the Partition. By and large, the Partition numbed the Urdu poet by its sheer scale and horror, unlike the Urdu prose writer. In the next chapter, we shall look at the horrors of the Partition that the progressive prose writers probed with all the delicacy of a camp surgeon, laying bare a sick, ailing society like 'a patient etherised upon a table'.

7

From *Fasana* to *Afsana*

A Study of Progressive Prose from 1930s till 1950s

Iss ahad ko na jaane agla sa ahad Mir
Woh daur ab nahi woh zameen aasman nahin
(Do not think this age to be like the age before
The times have changed, the earth and sky have changed)
—Mir Taqi Mir (1723–1810)

One of the greatest contributions of the progressives was to the development of Urdu prose which, in comparison to poetry, had been somewhat a neglected child.[1] Ale Ahmad Suroor, a progressive himself who in later years distanced himself from the movement, gives us a clue as to how this

---

[1] Majnun Gorakhpuri traces the evolution of Urdu prose in '*Nazm se Nasr Tak*', in Ale Ahmad Suroor (ed.), *Tanquid ke Buniyadi Masail* (Aligarh: Aligarh University Press, 1967). He speaks of the spurt in Urdu prose in the post-1857 period, in the greater freedom enjoyed by prose in terms of scope for expression, form, and content, as well as the greater attention it began to attract from the literary critics who had hitherto lavished all their attention on poetry.

change came about: 'Progressive writing came in Urdu with a bang and its tall claims and its prophetic poses soon earned for it a good deal of ridicule. Satire has often been the weapon of the conservative, against the romantic and the rebel. But gradually the rebel was accepted and became part of a tradition.'[2]

Looking at the work of some of the major prose writers associated with the PWM and assessing their work, both individually and in the light of their association with the movement, we shall see that the concerns at the forefront of the progressive agenda were women, independence, and a third that the writers appropriated for themselves, namely, partition. Why did the progressive writers give especial importance to the partition? Their predilection for focusing on the communal violence that spiralled out of the partition raises some disturbing questions.[3] Did they do so out of the conviction that it was 'bad' or 'wrong'[4] or from any real understanding of the long-term consequences of partition? Or, was it because the only meaningful reality for them was the present, and the present contained violence and degradation and misery in such ample measure? While some modern critics such as Muhammad Hasan Askari believed rioting and violence cannot become the subject of true literature,[5] the progressives believed that violence was a natural consequence of the ill-will sown by the Cabinet Mission Plan of 16 February 1946 and the Mountbatten Plan of 3 June 1947.[6] Interestingly, while modernists like Intezar Husain chose to

---

[2] Nissim Ezekiel (ed.), *Indian Writers in Conference: The Sixth PEN All-India Writers' Conference* (Bombay: PEN, 1964), p. 214. Suroor goes on to say that

Krishan Chandar, apart from his short stories dabbled in satire and humour and made fun of the old order. Manto with his clear vision could discern the grim humour which is akin to tears, in the tragedy of partition and plunder. He laughs away the iron in his soul and brings out the sordidness and savagery of that harrowing time much more poignantly than many a sentimental and tearful account.

[3] M.U. Memon, 'Partition Literature: A Study of Intizar Husain', *Modern Asian Studies*, vol. 14, no. 3 (1980), p. 381.

[4] Given the progressives', especially the committed communists', support of Pakistan, their later criticism of the partition is inconsistent. This tendency has been discussed in detail in the second section of Chapter 8.

[5] Quoted by Mumtaz Shirin in *'Pakistani Adab ke Char Saal'*, *Mayar* (Lahore: Naya Idara, 1963), p. 171.

[6] Memon, 'Partition Literature', p. 386.

view the partition as hijrat in the sense of a recurrent historical partition that allowed the writer to explore the past while laying bare the present, for the progressives the partition was an opportunity to dwell on the present. For, it was in the present that there was hardly any Muslim family that had not lost one member (if not more) or whose lives had not been affected by the trauma in some way or the other. It was no wonder that the violence seized the imagination of the people and '… its memory haunted them and kept them tormented, even after they had made it to the safety of a promised land. Thus the fiction that emerged during and soon after the heat and chaos of the partition presents little more than variations on the all-pervasive theme of communal violence.'[7]

In the first two sections of this chapter, we shall reconstruct the social and intellectual history of two writers who contributed most significantly to progressive prose—Manto and Ismat Chughtai. The last section is in the nature of an overview of what was being written by almost all the major Urdu writers who could, loosely, be defined as 'progressives'.

Saadat Hasan Manto (1912–1955)

One of the finest Urdu short story writers—provocative, outrageous, scandalous, sometimes even blasphemous—Manto was the original enfant terrible of Urdu literature. Cocking a snook at society, literary norms, and most notions of propriety, Manto touched the hearts of many with his convincing and utterly original portrayal of human fallibility. In an impudent epitaph[8] written for himself shortly before his death, he wrote: 'Here [Manto] lies buried—and buried in his breast are all the secrets of the art of story-telling. Even now weighed down by mounds of earth, he is wondering if he is the greater story teller or God!'[9] Immodest, yes, but

---

[7] Ibid., p. 380.

[8] Aamir Mufti has dwelt at length on the semantic baggage of his self-chosen epitaph. He sees it as a 'reflection of Manto's ironic relationship to the culture of Indian nationalism, in particular the bourgeois universalism of its "moment of arrival", which Partha Chatterjee has identified with the figure and influence of Jawaharlal Nehru'. See Partha Chatterjee and Pradeep Jeganathan (eds), *Community, Gender and Violence* (London: C. Hurst & Co., 2000), p. 3.

[9] Quoted by Abu Said Quraishi, '*Rahm Dil Dahshat Pasand*' (The Kind-hearted Terrorist), *Nuqoosh* (Manto Number), Lahore (1955), p. 13.

by no means outrageous, for it is true that whatever the merits of Manto's style and craft, he had the rare gift of being able to narrate the most blood-curdling events with faithful accuracy and an unsparing eye for detail.

Dismissed variously as a voyeur, a purveyor of cheap erotic thrills, a scavenger of human misery, a compulsive scraper of the wounds of a sick and ailing society, or at best a mere rapporteur and no more, Manto upset every conceivable notion of literary propriety and licence. An under-achiever all through school and college (he even flunked twice in Urdu in the matriculation examination!),[10] Manto drifted through various jobs in AIR and the Bombay film industry before he found his true calling as a storyteller. Like his near contemporary, Ismat Chughtai, he too loved to handle bold and unconventional themes that had so far been taboo in Urdu literature.[11] However, unlike Chughtai's homely and colourfully idiomatic language, Manto chose a stark, spare, almost staccato style, unembellished and unaffected, deliberately shorn of all appendages of style and convention.

[10] Manto studied at the Muslim High School and the Hindu Sabha College in Amritsar and, having failed to complete his BA, took admission at the Aligarh University in 1934. His contemporaries at Aligarh were some of the most promising young men of his age—Jafri, Akhtar Husain Raipuri, Sibte Hasan, Hayatullah Ansari, Majaz, Suroor, Jan Nisar Akhtar, Shahid Latif, and others. Manto left Aligarh nine months later, after he was diagnosed with tuberculosis. He met many of his Aligarh friends in Bombay in the course of his work with the film industry and during his on–off relationship with the Bombay progressives. Shahid Latif was instrumental in helping Manto join Filmistan Studio where Manto worked on several films with the noted actor Ashok Kumar. He remained friends with Shahid Latif and his wife, Ismat Chughtai, throughout his waxing and waning career.

[11] A case of obscenity was filed (by one Chaudhry Mohammed Husain) against Manto and Ismat in a court in Lahore in 1944 for their stories *Boo* and *Lihaf*, respectively. The case dragged on and was eventually dismissed for lack of evidence. There is a delightful account of their trips to Lahore to attend the protracted court trial by Ismat in an essay entitled 'Un Byahtaon ke Naam' (In the Name of Those Married Women), in Sukrita Paul Kumar and Sadique (eds) *Ismat: Her Life and Times* (New Delhi: Katha, 2000). There is also a reference to Mohammed Husain in Sajjad Zaheer, *The Light: A History of the Movement for Progressive Literature in the Indo-Pak Subcontinent*, English translation of Sajjad Zaheer's *Roshnai* by Amina Azfar (Karachi: Oxford University Press, 2006), p. 109. Ismat and Manto were defended by Harilal Sibal, father of Kapil Sibal, in Lahore.

Never the one to impose his own interpretation of events, Manto could look at people and events with a consciousness uncoloured by notions of nationalism, religion, morality, and, least of all, sentimentality. He wrote what he saw and felt, and he wrote compulsively and prodigiously. In the 43 years that he lived, he published 22 collections of short stories, 1 novel, 5 (7, according to some) collections of radio plays, 3 collections of essays, and 2 collections of sketches of famous personalities (one called, rather evocatively, *Ganje Farishte* [Bald Angels])! Though much of his writing was in the nature of 'command performances'—to feed the twin demons of drink and acute, chronic poverty—there is still a great deal in his vast and variegated oeuvre that is touched by greatness. Incidentally, these 'command performances' were at the behest of editors and publishers, not the party as in the case of some progressives! Of his various collections, many stories appear in more than one collection, occasionally appearing under different names. Always hard up, Manto was known to sell his stories to different publishers at different times, sometimes he would tweak a story or its ending to make it somewhat different.[12]

Manto, meaning 'weight' in Kashmiri, belonged to a family of wealthy Kashmiri traders who had come to the plains and settled in Lahore. His grandfather, a dealer in pashmina, moved to Amritsar where the family prospered, but remained deeply, quintessentially, religious. Manto's father, Maulvi Ghulam Hasan, married twice and had 12 children in all. Manto, born from the second wife, was in awe of his stepbrothers who were not only older, but much better educated. While he was fond of his mother, his relations with other family members remained distant. He lived in especial dread of his father, who had retired as a sub-judge from Samrala, a town near Ludhiana, and returned to Amritsar to live in the Kucha Vakilan neighbourhood of the old city. Manto's rebellious streak can be traced to living under threat from the sharp edge of his father's acerbic tongue and authoritarian ways. Harshly critical of films, theatre, music, and other forms of plebeian entertainment, Maulvi Ghulam Hasan wanted Manto to study hard and do as well as his other sons, who had studied abroad and become barristers. He despaired of Manto's growing irreligiosity and impertinence. Yet, despite all his chaffing against his father's harshness, Manto dedicated his first collection of short stories, *Aatish Parey* (Slivers of

---

[12] These details have been culled from Waris Alvi, *Saadat Hasan Manto, Makers of Indian Literature* (New Delhi: Sahitya Akademi, 2000).

Fire), to his father and hung his somewhat grim and disapproving portrait in his room.[13]

Bent upon ploughing his own furrow from an early age, Manto's early waywardness and wilfulness soon took the form of an idiosyncratic individuality. Having failed twice in the intermediate exam, Manto embraced a life of hedonism with single-minded dedication. Gambling, drinking, smoking charas, keeping the company of idle but idealistic and impetuous men like himself, these were Manto's trivial pursuits all through the early 1930s. Things would have continued along this trajectory of despair and dissipation had Manto not met Bari saheb, editor of *Mussavat*. Bari saheb introduced Manto to the great Russian novelists, to the skilfully crafted stories of Oscar Wilde and Maupassant, to Victor Hugo's *Les Misérables*, and, most significantly, the curious possibility of earning a living by wielding the pen. Manto took to dabbling in revolutionary poetry, writing articles for magazines, translating Wilde and Hugo with the enthusiasm of a neo-convert. His introduction to Russia and its revolution too can be traced to this period when he edited and translated stories for the 'Russian Number' of the Lahore-based literary journal, *Alamgir*.[14] When Manto translated Oscar Wilde's play *Vera*, he and his friends put posters all over Amritsar which proclaimed

> Horrifying end to brutal and tyrannical Russian rulers
> The sounds of revenge echoes in the streets of Russia
> The last nail in the coffin of the czars![15]

---

[13] Alvi, *Saadat Hasan Manto*.

[14] Manto translated several Russian stories for *Alamgir* and *Humayun*; these were published as *Rusi Afsane* (Russian Stories). It included Tolstoy's 'Three Questions', Chekov's 'The Maid' and 'An Offspring', Gorky's 'Twenty-six Men and a Girl', as well as Manto's own original stories '*Tamasha*' (Spectacle) and '*Mahgir*' (Fisherman). '*Tamasha*', his first short story, dealt with the Jallianwala Bagh massacre. About '*Tamasha*', Manto's mentor Bari sahib, writing the Introduction to *Rusi Afsane*, noted: 'After a study of Russian literature, the translator has written a Russian style short story. The locale of the story seems more like Moscow than Amritsar.' Reference in Leslie Flemming, *Another Lonely Voice: The Life and Works of Saadat Hasan Manto* (Lahore: Vanguard, 1985), p. 36.

[15] Reference found in *Ganje Farishte*, p. 101. In the same essay entitled 'Bari Saheb', Manto writes of his fascination with Russia, of looking at the world map, with his friend Hassan Abbas, and planning to use the overland route to travel to Russia. Manto wrote: 'We imagined the streets and lanes of Amritsar as Moscow, and we wanted to see the terrible end of tyranny.' Ibid., p. 103.

While Manto's way of crafting a story showed the influence of European writers, in particular Maupassant, the content of the stories of the early years showed the influence of the Russian writers such as Gogol, Turgenev, Chekhov, Pushkin, Dostoyevsky, Andreyev, and Gorky. Apart from the translations he did for the special issue of *Alamgir*, he also wrote articles and essays on the Russian Revolution. One such article entitled *Surkh Inquilab* (Red Revolution) was about the freedom of women; another on Gorky made the following observation:

Before writing his stories, Gorky looks all around him and observes the smallest, most trivial details as though it might be of use somewhere. The hotness of the sauce, the snow sticking to the man's boot, the snowflakes entangled in the hair of some woman, the woodcutter cutting wood, the coarse language of the farmhands, the drifting notes of a piano, the bestial glint in the eyes of a sentry, the dirt flying in the bazaars, and the black smoke billowing from the chimneys of factories—he notes down all this and more.[16]

This early exposure to Russian writers had a lasting influence. Manto's lifelong interest in low life, in the harsh, even sordid realities of life, in the complex relationship between men and women can also be traced to this formative period.

Manto was 23 or so when he was struck by tuberculosis. Initially, he tried to stifle the pain by drinking more country liquor than usual, but when even that did not serve to dull the ache in his chest, he was packed off to the mountains. Born to Kashmiri parents but raised in the Punjab, this was Manto's first visit to Kashmir. Though he never managed to go beyond Batot, he was clearly enchanted by the land of his forefathers and its people. He also had his first, and some believe his only, romantic experience with a tantalizing shepherd girl. Many of his stories draw on the time he spent among these idyllic hills and vales. In *Ek Khat* (A Letter), he spoke (presumably) of her as a girl who was 'young and totally young … one who left some beautiful inscriptions on the pages of my life'.

Manto went to Bombay in search of work sometime in 1936, landing a job as editor of a weekly called *Mussavvir* (The Creator). The glamour and gaiety of the city's high society, as also the grit and grime of its underbelly,

---

[16] From *Manto ke Afsane*, p. 246, quoted in Khalilur Rahman Azmi, *Urdu mein Taraqqui Pasand Adabi Tehreek* (Aligarh: Educational Book House, 2002 [1957]), p. 188; translation mine.

provided ample fodder for a man of Manto's disposition. The red light district of Forres Road, the chawls of Nagpara, the paanwallas, taxi drivers, washermen, Parsi landladies and Jewish hotel keepers, the editors of motley Urdu newspapers—all became rich sources of inspiration. Manto wrote prolifically and some of his most memorable characters were drawn from the people he met in these halcyon days in Bombay from 1936 to 1948. Manto hobnobbed with film stars, first as a film journalist and then as a scriptwriter, made money and frittered it all away on drinking, gambling, and the good life. He did, briefly, live in Delhi for a year and a half (1941–2) when he worked at AIR, but irreconcilable differences with the legendary Pitras Bukhari, the station director, and colleague and fellow progressive, Upendranath Ashk, made him give up the only job he enjoyed, one that also fetched him a regular salary.

During the radio days, he met many progressives, such as Chiragh Hasan Hasrat (whom he had known from his journalist days in Amritsar), Akhtar Husain Raipuri, Ashk, Miraji, and Krishan Chandar. Miraji, also a neighbour, became his constant drinking companion and inspired him to write a darkly witty sketch entitled '*Tin Gole*' (Three Balls) in *Ganje Farishte*. Manto also wrote a rather wickedly funny story, '*Taraqqui Pasand*' (Progressive), based on Rajinder Singh Bedi and Devindar Satyarthi. The story is about a young postal clerk (Bedi) who wants to become a writer and whose home is taken over by an older writer and itinerant collector of folk songs (Satyarthi). The postal clerk, who fancies himself as the country's pre-eminent progressive writer, is initially in awe of his illustrious guest, but soon tires of his self-absorption. Bedi and Satyarthi got back at Manto by writing a radio story about him! Manto's relationship with Ashk was mercurial, causing the latter to write a litany of complaints entitled '*Manto Mera Dushman*', published ironically enough in a special issue on Manto published posthumously.

This short spell at AIR was an exceptionally productive one with Manto dashing off plays, features, sketches on his Urdu typewriter at breakneck speed; he is said to have published four collections of radio plays during these 18 months.[17] It was during the Delhi days that he wrote and published the controversial collection entitled *Dhuan* (Smoke). Upon his return to Bombay, Manto's association with the progressives began to weaken as the content of his stories was seen to be increasingly at odds with the avowed

---

[17] For details, see Flemming, *Another Lonely Voice*.

aims of the PWA. The years till 1947 saw Manto stubbornly writing precisely the sort of stories he wanted to write despite opposition from critics and his friends among the progressives.[18]

No one quite knows why Manto went away to Pakistan. Was it in a huff or on a whim? Was it to seek a better future, broken as he was by chronic drinking and acute poverty? Was it the thought of starting afresh, on a clean slate as it were, that attracted him whenever he did think of his wife and three daughters whom he loved dearly? Was it out of genuine disenchantment with the increasingly strident and communally charged atmosphere of the so-far bohemian film industry? Or, was it, as some suggest, the dream of owning an 'allotted' mansion the moment he crossed over? One gets a glimpse into Manto's state of mind when he made the journey across in *Sahay* and in *Zehmat-e-Mehr-e-Darakhshan*,[19] but with Manto there never were any clear answers.

Manto migrated to Pakistan in 1948 and lived there for the next seven years. These were years of hard drinking, acute penury, a near hand-to-mouth existence, and a time of ever-mounting frustrations and humiliations. The mansion of his dreams did not materialize, nor did he, by all accounts, seriously pursue the 'allotment' issue. The film industry in Lahore was in the doldrums and there was very little work for a writer who wanted to write his own sort of stories. Yet, Manto wrote like a man possessed, often producing one story a day, a bit like a hen laying an egg a day![20] Some of his finest work was produced during these years of near-manic productivity, poverty, and profligacy. Shunned by the Pakistani progressives like their counterparts in India before partition, Manto turned to the Halqa-e Arbab-e Zauq. At the Halqa's meetings in Lahore, he read

---

[18] Flemming has pointed out that Manto was never quite at home in the countryside, which is why unlike Ahmad Nadeem Qasmi or even Krishan Chandar, he has not written about peasants or rural folk. Ibid., p. 48.

[19] From the verse by Mirza Asadullah Ghalib,

Larazta hai mera dil zehmat-e-mehr-e-darakhshan par
Main hoon voh qatra-e-shabnam ke ho khaare-e-bayaaban par
(My heart trembles at the trouble taken by the shining sun
I am the drop of dew that rests on the desert thorn)

[20] In an autobiographical essay entitled 'Saadat Hasan Manto', Manto has himself used the analogy of a hen in his description of the way he normally wrote—sitting in a squatting position atop a chair, like a hen about to lay an egg.

his stories, found friends and admirers in men like N.M. Rashid (whom he had known during his radio days in Delhi) though it is unlikely that Manto, no matter how straitened his circumstances, could ever subscribe to the Halqa's ideology of Art for Art's Sake. It is possible that Manto's closeness to the Halqa and its members was in defiance of the progressives' increasing politicization of literary ideals. However, his rebelliousness and his individualism could not let him belong wholeheartedly to either grouping. Manto died on 18 January 1955 in Lahore of cirrhosis of the liver. His last wish, literally made with his dying breath, was for a drink of whiskey.[21]

Manto's legacy constitutes a formidable body of work. There is more to Manto than *Thanda Gosht*, *Khol Do*, or *Kaali Shalwar*—stories that offended many (including the progressives) on grounds of perversion and obscenity. While these stories have been most anthologized and are therefore most well-known, they are by no means representative of Manto's writings. Most of these provocative stories belong to the last years of his life when the shadows were darkening not just in his personal life, but also over the subcontinent, and when Manto's demons had begun to trouble him to the extent of driving him briefly to a mental asylum. These are dark stories, unrelieved by even a tinge of the humanity and liberalism that one sees in his early work. Unfortunately, it is these stories that are understood, in popular perception, to define Manto's oeuvre. The truth, however, is that his world is peopled by the good as much as the bad; if anything, Manto possesses the rare knack of making the reader share his delighted discovery of goodness and beauty whenever he comes across it in the midst of wickedness and ugliness. Maybe it was the age he was born in, or the circumstances of his own life that made Manto see the darkness more acutely than others. But Manto was not blind to light. He cherished goodness whenever he stumbled upon it. More importantly, in his diagnosis of a sick and ailing society lay his prognosis.[22] For, only when we see ourselves for what we are and what we have become can we set about bringing a change for the better. Manto could hold a mirror up to society more faithfully and more brutally than many of his contemporaries. It is this—more than any ideology or the lack of it—that made him a progressive.

---

[21] Manto's nephew Hamid Jalal has given an account of the last few days of Manto's life in 'Manto Mamu ki Maut', *Nuqoosh* (Manto Number), Lahore (1955).

[22] This section has been built from my Introduction to Saadat Hasan Manto, *Naked Voices: Stories & Sketches* (New Delhi: Roli/India Ink, 2008).

If we are to view Manto's relationship with the progressives, it can be said that the progressives had an ideology, while he had a world view; both had their roots in the Russian Revolution. In the early years, the progressives were willing to ignore his lack of ideology since he kept churning out story after story about the working class, especially the outcast, the marginalized, and what Ibadat Barelwi called the 'little person'.[23] Also, given the nature of Manto's European and Russian influences and given his own personal predilection, his stories could be viewed as purposive literature and were remarkably free from any trace of romanticism (the same however cannot be said of the work of the other progressives, especially Krishan Chandar who was consistently praised by Sardar Jafri in his *Taraqqui Pasand Adab*).

Taken in the balance, perhaps that is why till the 1940s the progressives were content to let Manto be; while they were happy enough to appropriate the political stories in his first two collections—*Aatish Parey* (1936) and *Manto ke Afsane* (1940)—trouble began to brew with the third collection, *Dhuan* (1942). One story, *Boo* (Smell), in particular, irked the progressives, causing Sajjad Zaheer to publicly condemn it at the Hyderabad conference in October 1945. Justifying his censure, Zaheer later wrote:

We felt the need for such a statement all the more because some Urdu writers (for example Saadat Hasan Manto) whose work had some elements of progressiveness, and who wrote some good progressive short stories, were at times inclined towards obscenity. Moreover, in European literature, anarchist conservatism was making its appearance in the form of obscenity, immorality, and revolts against all kinds of cultural discipline. Some undiscerning intellectuals were copying this foul innovation of decaying capitalism, thinking it was progressive.[24]

The irony of Zaheer, the author of *Angarey*, taking the high moral ground on grounds of 'cultural discipline'[25] seems to have escaped the progressives, just as much as the perils of 'selective' appropriation. Quick

---

[23] Ibadat Barelwi, '*Manto ki Haqiqat Nigari*', Nuqoosh (Manto Number), Lahore (1955), p. 274.

[24] Zaheer, *Light*, p. 252.

[25] The version of the *Manifesto* published in the *Left Review*, London, February 1936, criticized existing literature for its 'furtive and sentimental attitude towards sex, its emotional exhibitionism and its almost total lack of rationality.' Manto's writing was far removed from these qualities, yet he was attacked on grounds of obscenity.

to appropriate the early part of Manto's oeuvre, the progressives wanted to discard or disown some of the later stories. A story like *Naya Qanoon* (New Law) was in fact widely acknowledged by the progressives and found a place in the many anthologies edited by progressive critics and editors. The story's central character, Mangu the Coachman, who believes a new law has been passed that has given independence to India, takes on an English Tommy and in the process becomes an emblem of the subaltern's desire for freedom. In his unlettered, untutored, instinctive defiance of British rule and in his impetuous headlong rush to throw off the imperial yoke, Mangu became the progressives' version of Everyman. Manto's later stories, especially those that dealt with women or sex, probably caused ruffled feathers among the progressive ideologues who felt much harm had been done to their cause by charges of obscenity during the *Angarey* period.

In their keenness to put the *Angarey* episode behind them, Abdul Alim had been drafted to move a resolution against obscenity at the Hyderabad conference in 1945, a move that was scuttled by Hasrat Mohani and Qazi Abdul Ghaffar. Thwarted in passing a unanimous resolution, a core group within the PWA began to marginalize Manto along with Ismat and Miraji. For his part, Manto initially tried to put up a defence by saying that his intention was neither pornography nor titillation, but simply to show certain important and stark realities of life: 'If it is obscene to even mention a prostitute then her existence is also obscene. If one is forbidden to mention her, then her profession too should be forbidden. Remove the prostitute; her mention too will end.'[26]

Manto was many things, but he was not a poseur. He wrote what he saw or felt; his stories, therefore, cover many subjects. There is, of course, the Partition and the communal divide that left a gash on not just men like Manto, but on millions who were affected by the terrible events before and after 1947.[27] Some writers shape their oeuvre; others have it shaped by events and circumstances larger and beyond them. The cataclysmic events of the Partition influenced many writers who lived during that period. So, while Manto wrote almost obsessively about the events that lead to

[26] From Manto's article '*Mujhe Kuch Kehna hai*' (I Have to Say Something) in *Manto ke Mazamin*, quoted in Azmi, *Urdu mein Taraqqui Pasand Adabi Tehreek*, p. 189; translation mine.

[27] Aamir Mufti talks of the 'enormous historical density within Manto's life and career', in *Community, Gender and Violence*.

the division of the subcontinent and the terrible suffering it inflicted on innocent people, he wrote on other subjects as well. Most notably on sex! So much so that those who do not see Manto's prolific outpouring over a period of 20-odd years, often regard him as a writer unhealthily obsessed with sex. It is important to see stories like *Thanda Gosht, Khol Do, Kaali Shalwar, Boo, Hatak* (Insult), or any of the other prostitute-related stories in their context and also their place in Manto's oeuvre. While it is true that Manto's prostitute is a far cry from Mirza Ruswa's Umrao Jaan or Qazi Abdul Ghaffar's Laila, who were victims, creatures more sinned against than sinning, women like Sugandhi, Sultana, and countless unnamed others seem willing participants in the trade of their bodies.

Khalilur Rahman Azmi, commenting on the increasing emphasis on sex and sexual matters in the later part of Manto's career seems to lay the blame partly on Manto's critics.[28] He finds Manto's behaviour like a wilful naughty child who, upon being taken to task, becomes more wilful, more intent upon doing that which brings censure. In the collection of sketches called *Siyah Hashiye* (Black Margins), one can find Manto bent upon rebellion, willing to cross the limits of brutality, jeering the proponents of social realism to do their worst. Fortunately, Manto was able to check himself and once he found his own voice over the din of partition, he wrote some of his finest stories leaving us with some memorable characters just before his end: Babu Gopinath, Mozelle, Toba Tek Singh, Mammad Bhai, Janki, Neelam, Mummy, Hafiz Manzoor, Qadir the Butcher, among others. To match these characters and their real, living contexts, he gave us an equally living, equally real language, the sort of Urdu that had never been written before, but one that sounded perfectly believable in the mouth of these characters. Fifty years later, Toba Tek Singh's famously unintelligible diatribe has become a telling commentary on the madness of the partition: *Oper di, gurgur di, anx di, bay dhiana di, mung di dal di, of Pakistan government.*

Manto's relentless individuality continued to pose a problem for critics, both progressive and otherwise. While the erudite and old-world Rashid Ahmed Siddiqui was disdainful of what he saw as Manto's 'exploitation' of a woman's sexuality, others like Ibadat Barelwi and Mumtaz Shirin were able to take a more balanced view of his strengths and weaknesses. Manto, for his part, hated and dreaded all criticism of his work and was especially touchy about the progressive critics. Writing the introduction to *Chughad*

---

[28] Azmi, *Urdu mein Taraqqui Pasand Adabi Tehreek*, p. 190.

(Idiot), the first collection of stories published in Pakistan in 1950, Manto was at a loss to explain why Jafri, Krishan Chandar, and other progressives who had heaped praises on his *Babu Gopinath*, later turned against it: 'But suddenly God only knows what kind of reversal took place, that all the progressives disavowed the greatness of this story. To start with, it was criticized quietly. In whispers, it was reviled. But now all the progressives of India and Pakistan openly consider this story as reactionary, immoral, wounded and depraved.'[29]

In the same introduction, he went on to wonder whether the progressives' ire directed against him and his last collection, *Siyah Hashiye*, was due to his proximity to Muhammad Hasan Askari who was a vocal critic of the PWM. He concluded by feigning nonchalance about 'progressivism' though he admitted that 'the back and forth leaps of the famous progressives hurt a lot'. Jafri, a famous progressive and an influential critic, was guilty of precisely the sort of back and forth leaps that proved Manto right. In the introduction to *Chughad*, Manto recalled Jafri praising *Khol Do* as a masterpiece of its period, yet a year later when Jafri wrote his seminal study of the PWM in which he made a distinction between healthy and sick, chaste and dirty, beautiful and ugly love, and the political and social content of good literature, he criticized Manto's stories for bitterness, restlessness, and lack of realism: 'Krishan Chandar's story *Garjan ki ek Shaam*, *Shahtoot ka Darakht*, and *Poore Chand ki Raat*; Majaz's *Nora, Aurat, Purdah* and *Ismat*; Faiz's *Raquib* and *Aaj ki Raat* are examples of heart-warming and chaste literature but Manto's story "*Boo*" and Rashid's poem "*Intiqam*" (Revenge) are sick and repulsive things. Their repulsiveness makes them reactionary.'[30]

Drawing a comparison between Manto and Krishan Chandar—to my mind, a comparison between chalk and cheese—Jafri wrote: 'The difference between Krishan's and Manto's stories is this, that Manto's heroes are mutilated men, therefore they cannot be representative.... Krishan's heroes are courageous and conscious builders of life. They express evolution....'[31]

Ahmed Ali, himself at the receiving end of the progressives' short stick too is critical of Manto's predilection for the unsavoury:

[29] Quoted in Flemming, *Another Lonely Voice*, p. 30.

[30] Ali Sardar Jafri, *Taraqqui Pasand Adab* (Aligarh: Anjuman-e Taraqqui-i-Urdu, 1957), 239.

[31] Flemming, *Another Lonely Voice*, pp. 28–9.

[But] after the first few brilliant flashes of deeply-felt social wrongs and intense desire for social justice, Manto ended up, due to his own peculiar psychological predilections, in the preoccupation with the world of the socially wronged and sexually exploited woman, whether she was the heroine of the 'Black Shalwar' or the red-light district of Bombay itself, and became the protagonist of erotic literature and perverted tastes apparent in Urdu writing today.[32]

I would disagree with Ahmed Ali and say that Manto wrote about human nature in all its diversity. And he wrote about all sorts of people. While he wrote with particular empathy about women, simulating a certain naturalness in speech and behaviour that can only come from close interaction and minute observation, he wrote with astonishing perspicacity about fellow men as well. And all sorts of men—writers, film-makers, photographers, social workers, office workers, tinsmiths, tongawallahs, washermen, water-carriers, pimps, shopkeepers. In short, he could claim a nodding acquaintance with every form of low life, high society-types, and those in the middle rungs as well.

A broad-based sampling of Manto's work will reveal a wide range of stories. There will be dark stories of the evil that lies hidden in the hearts of men. There will be stories of exploitation, double standards, greed, corruption, lust—in short every imaginable vice and venality; astonishingly enough, there are some romantic stories as well such as *Mausam ki Shararat* (The Weather's Playfulness), *Misri ki Dali* (A Lump of Rock Candy), *Begu*, etc. *Shaheedsaaz* (The Maker of Martyrs) and *Haarta Chala Gaya* (Loser All the Way) are light-hearted spoofs on man's degeneracy and moral bankruptcy. But there are other stories of goodness too that Manto saw in men who lived less-than-exemplary lives, like the pimp in 'Sahay'. Then, there are stories such as *Sharifan* when otherwise decent men are forced to commit acts of bestiality; the culprit here is not the men, but the circumstances that they find themselves in. The horrors of Partition are central in some stories such as *Sharifan* and incidental in others such as 'Khuda ki Qasam' (By God). In *Hundred Candle Watt Bulb* a woman kills her pimp because she has not slept for a long, long time, while he keeps forcing her to serve customers. No one knows how long the woman's torment has been

---

[32] Ahmed Ali, 'The Progressive Writers' Movement and Creative Writers in Urdu', in Carlo Coppola (ed.) *Marxist Influences and South Asian Literature* (East Lansing: Michigan State University Press, 1974), p. 40.

going on, who the woman is, or how she came into her pimp's clutches. Nothing matters in the explosive end when the woman, agonized beyond endurance by her lack of sleep, clobbers the pimp with a brick and finally sleeps, her head covered with her dupatta, lying in the blinding glare of a hundred-candle-watt bulb blissfully oblivious. What does this woman want from life? Sleep. And the pimp stands in the way of her and sleep. So she kills him.

Like sleep, sex too is a fact of life and therefore the subject of many of Manto's stories. In *Nangi Awazein* (Naked Voices), Manto paints a very realistic picture of a group of robust but hard-working families living on the fringes of poverty and dealing with not just the demands of their bodies, but also the constraints of communal living. What is a man to do when the instinct for privacy is as strong as the instinct for sex? How does one consummate a marriage behind a screen of sack cloths strung on a bamboo frame in the midst of a sea of sleeping, coughing, copulating couples crowded on a tiny roof top on a summer night? Only Manto would consider this a perfect scenario for a short story. And only Manto could do justice to it. Just as he portrayed an ordinary young man's obsessive-compulsive need for a woman, any woman, in *Darpok* (Coward). Despite his fantasies, when the young man eventually cannot pluck the courage to go up to the seedy brothel of a soiled, sorry-looking prostitute, he takes solace as only a coward can: by occupying the high moral ground and seeking the sanctuary of religion that would have deemed his act, had he committed it—a sin!

There are many stories that reveal Manto's take on contemporary politics: *1919 ka Ek Din* (A Day in 1919) is a recasting of the terrible slaughter visited upon the poor benighted city of Amritsar in the wake of the Jallianwala Bagh massacre. Drawing upon popular accounts of the French Revolution, which ascribe the first bullet fired in the revolution hitting a prostitute, here Manto makes a 'hero' out of the good-for-nothing brother of the city's two most famous prostitutes. An early story, this was a fairly sophisticated one and showed Manto's propensity for busting myths and forcing his readers to revisit both past shames and legacies. *Kirchein aur Kirchiyan* (Slivers and Slivereens) had a needle-sharp take on politics and politicians, especially the murky politics of Kashmir, Manto's home state. Not a story in the conventional sense, since it had no beginning, middle, or end, not even a plot or character, it was striking nevertheless for its staccato sound and the slivers of biting satire.

A gentle story, most unusual for the Manto of popular imagination, was *Yazid*. It showed a glimmer of the pacifist in Manto, the man who hated wars, who espoused reflection and contemplation, who urged his fellow men to look within. By placing his protagonist in a rural setting, Manto also made a point about rough-hewn country folk being repositories of the wisdom distilled from the ages. Karimdad, who decides to call his newborn baby Yazid, is an evolved man, willing to think outside the straightjacket of convention and stereotype, and name his child after one of the worst offenders in Islamic history. 'What's in it? It's only a name!' he tells his horrified wife, reasoning thus: 'It needn't be the same Yazid. He had closed the river; our son will open it.'

Manto wrote about women in a way that no other writer from the Indian subcontinent had or has till today. *Sadak ke Kinare* (By the Roadside) was a beautiful elegy to a mother forced to abandon her baby. Here Manto, quite literally, got under the skin of a woman, and described the very physical changes that took place in a woman's body as it prepared to nurture life deep inside it—and the equally 'real' physical trauma when the baby was snatched from her and tossed on a rubbish heap by the roadside, possibly because it was illegitimate. And again in *Shahdole ka Chooha* (The Rat of Shahdole), he talked of a mother's despair in giving up her son as *mannat* at a saint's shrine where a perfectly healthy baby was 'miraculously' disfigured and mutilated into a rat-boy before being sold to an itinerant *tamashawala*. A scathing attack on the shrines that thrive on poor, desperate, and superstitious people, the story derived its punch from a mother's steadfast desire to keep her son's memory alive inside her heart.

Similarly, *Khuda ki Qasam* was a mother's refusal to accept that her daughter may have been killed in the riots. Old, blind, and half-crazed with grief, she cannot believe anyone can kill a girl as beautiful as her daughter. In the end, she finds peace in death when she spots her daughter unexpectedly on the street one day, married though she is to the man who had abducted her. A most unexpected story was *Dhandas* (Comfort). A young widow is raped at a family wedding. Initially angry and inconsolable, she finds comfort in the arms of another man, the one who offers comfort immediately thereafter!

In several stories, the woman was both 'subject' and 'predicate'. In *Bismillah*, a woman by the strange, eponymous name was the object of a man's lust, though she appeared to be the legally wedded wife of another man. Saeed is attracted, in equal measure, by Bismillah's large, sad-looking eyes as well as the lush fullness of her breasts and finds himself torn between voyeuristic delight in a woman's body and the prick of his own conscience. In the end, it turns out that the sullen, sphinx-like young woman is not his friend Zaheer's wife; she is a Hindu girl who got left behind during the riots and is being forced into prostitution by Zaheer who had been, all along, posing as a loving husband and budding film-maker.

Manto wrote a great deal of non-fiction too. Of these, the autobiographical pieces served to shed light on Manto's complex love–hate relationship with himself and the world at large. 'Saadat Hasan', for instance, revealed the schizophrenia that lay at the heart of Manto's self-image: between the man called Saadat Hasan and his far-more (in)famous alter-ego, the writer who masqueraded as Manto or vice versa, that is, the less-than-likeable man called Manto who pretended to be a great writer. *Zehmat-e-Mehr-e-Darakhshan* was a rambling account of his early days in Pakistan plagued as he was by penury and the threat of punitive damages imposed by harsh judges bent upon browbeating him into submission. A delightful series called 'A Letter to Uncle Sam', ostensibly written by a fawning nephew in awe and admiration of his vastly superior uncle, was a trenchant critique of the Pakistani judicial system. It took several impertinent swipes at Uncle Sam who had recently begun to woo the newly established Islamic Republic of Pakistan drawing it towards the hedonistic pleasures of capitalism in the early 1950s.

Rebutting the progressives' charge of voyeurism and sacrilege, Manto wrote

> I am no sensationalist. Why would I want to take the clothes off a society, civilization and culture that is, in any case, naked? Yes, it is true I make no attempt to dress it—because it is not my job; that is a dressmaker's job. People say I write with a black pen, but I never write on a black board with a black chalk. I always use a white chalk so that the blackness of the board is clearly visible.[33]

And that is precisely what he did in story after story.

Ismat Chughtai (1911–1991)

The remarkable career of Ismat Chughtai exemplified how the conservative Muslim response to *Angarey* shaped the literary sensibility of an entire

---

[33] Saadat Hasan Manto, *Lazzat-e Sang* (Lahore: Naya Idara, 1956), p. 20.

generation of Urdu writers. Ismat clearly looked upon Rashid Jahan as a role model; in an interview she has said how the good doctor 'spoiled' her: 'She was bold, and used to speak about all sorts of things openly and loudly.'[34] Impressed by her open-mindedness and free thinking, Ismat joined the PWM. In the *Mahfil* interview, she claimed to have been present at the first AIPWA conference in Lucknow (though other members of the PWA have made no mention of her presence) and admitted to having had a rocky relationship with the progressives, yet not being overly concerned about it: 'Sometimes they would praise me and sometimes they would condemn me. I didn't take it very seriously in any case. Neither the praise, nor the condemnation.' About her association with the movement, she said: 'I was with the progressives from the start. But I was much too frank to be trusted. I was much too open hearted and too bold for any party to make me a member.'[35]

While Ismat wrote voluminously till she was diagnosed with Alzheimer's disease in 1988, for the purpose of this study, we shall concern ourselves only with her output till 1955, which included *Ziddi* (Stubborn, 1939, her first novella) followed by *Kaliyan* (Buds, 1941, her first collection of short stories), *Chotein* (Wounds, 1941, a collection of stories, sketches, plays), *Tehri Lakir* (Crooked Line, 1945, a novel), *Dhani Bankein* (Green Bangles, 1948, a play), *Ek Baat* (One Matter, 1952, a novel), *Chhoi Mooi* (The Delicate One, 1952, a collection of stories, essays, reportage), and *Shaitan* (The Devil, 1955, a collection of radio plays). She also wrote 14–15 stories, dialogues, and scenarios for the Hindi film industry, of which *Ziddi*, *Sone ki Chidiya* (The Golden Bird), and *Darwaza* (Doorway) were successful. While she did not write anything that can be described as overtly sexual, the spectre of *Lihaaf* (The Quilt)[36] haunted Ismat for the rest of her career and, rightly or wrongly, coloured everything she wrote thereafter.

Much of her non-film writing was autobiographical. If not directly related to her own life, it certainly stemmed from her own experiences as a woman, especially a middle-class Muslim woman. Some critics, like Aziz

---

[34] *Mahfil*, Asian Studies Center, Michigan State University, East Lansing, Michigan, vol. 8 (1972), p. 172.

[35] Ibid.

[36] Written in 1942, it dealt with a lesbian relationship as witnessed by a young girl. It created a storm in literary circles and, as we have seen in the previous chapter, even landed Ismat in court.

Ahmad, have viewed this as a flaw rather than strength, objecting to the constant, overwhelming presence of Ismat herself in all that she wrote.[37] Regardless of Ismat's own larger-than-life persona, while it is true that her interest was primarily in women, it is also true that she saw women in the larger social context. She wrote stories (*Jadein* [Roots]) and plays (*Dhaani Bankein* [Green Bangles]) on the communal tensions, issues that did not concern women alone, but issues that can be viewed from a unique perspective because they come from a woman's pen. She used wit and satire as tools to sharpen her depiction of social realities and give an extra edge to her pithy, flavoursome, idiomatic language, the *begumaati zuban* that she herself knew so well. In her hands, Urdu acquired a new zest, an added spice that made it not only more readable, but also better equipped to reflect new concerns, concerns that had been hitherto considered beyond the pale of literature.

Ismat wrote bold stories that challenged traditional morality and worn-out notions of a woman's 'place' in society. Given her interest in sexual matters, comparisons between her and Manto have always been inevitable. Like Manto's *Boo*, she faced terrible flak for *Lihaaf*, published in *Adab-e-Latif* in 1942. Noted writer and critic Intizar Husain drew an interesting parallel between these two enfant terribles of the Urdu short story: 'Where Ismat moves away lightly after making a passing reference to (such) a subject, Manto is like the naughty boy who flings open the door, claps his hands and says, "Aha! I have seen you!"'[38]

Ismat found some supporters after the storm created by *Lihaaf* broke over her head: Majrooh Sultanpuri, Krishan Chandar, and Manto came out openly in support of her.[39] In *Kaghazi Hai Pairahan* Ismat confesses to being nervous when the court summons arrive: 'Though I put up a courageous front, I felt quite embarrassed.... I was quite nervous, but Manto encouraged me so much that I forgot all my misgivings.'[40]

---

[37] Aziz Ahmad, *Taraqqui Pasand Adab* (Delhi: Khwaja Press, 1945), p. 104.

[38] Intizar Husain, '*Shair aur Biddat*', *Adab-e-Latif*, Lahore (September–October 1947), quoted by Azmi, *Urdu mein Taraqqui Pasand Adabi Tehreek*, p. 194.

[39] Ahmad, *Taraqqui Pasand Adab*.

[40] Translated by M. Asaduddin, *A Life in Words: Memoirs* (New Delhi: Penguin, 2012), p. 24.

She goes on to admit that while she was torn to shreds over *Lihaaf* in some quarters, some people 'also wielded their pens in my support', whereas the same consideration was not shown to Manto: 'I am fortunate that I have been appreciated in my lifetime. Manto was driven mad to the extent that he became a wreck. The progressives did not come to his rescue. In my case, they didn't write me off, nor did they offer me great accolades.... I continued to remain a follower of the progressives and endeavoured to bring about a revolution!'[41]

Years after *Lihaaf*, and the progressives themselves had become a distant memory, Faiz wrote an essay on Ismat, pointing out the reasons for her enduring appeal: the first, according to him, was 'the strong sex appeal of her writing', the second was her command over her language, and third was her choice of theme.[42] In a society which still practiced rigorous seclusion of the sexes, Ismat's writings opened a window into the life of the 'other' and allowed her male readers a glimpse into the zenana with all its intrigues, excitements, and sorrows. Placing Ismat in the context of the PWM, Faiz wrote:

When Ismat Chughtai's name started appearing in magazines the debate regarding progressive writing had grown stale. Some people were fed up with it. Some were exasperated. There were two big groups. One followed the dictum of art for art's sake and the other believed in art for salvation ... while one group was complaining of the obscenity in progressive literature, the other group complained that its writers were not uninhibited. When Ismat Chughtai started writing both groups became active once again.[43]

But as Faiz rightly observed, Ismat refused to conform to either group and continued to write stories culled largely from her own experiences and her own understanding of the world. While the progressives were pleased by the realism of Ismat's writings and her depiction of everyday lives, they continued to have misgivings about what Faiz had called the 'sex appeal' of her writing. We get a glimpse of Ismat's own feelings about the progressives in several essays. In '*Taraqqui Pasand Adab aur Main*' (Progressive

---

[41] Ibid., p. 40.
[42] Faiz Ahmed Faiz, 'Ismat Chughtai', in Sukrita Paul Kumar and Sadique (eds), *Ismat: Her Life, Her Times* (New Delhi: Katha, 2009), pp. 189–92.
[43] Ibid.

Literature and I), she recalled her many friends in Bombay who while part of the PWM were also active in the Bombay film industry, the CPI, theatre, and other creative and intellectual pursuits. She described the Bombay progressives as a group of 'undisciplined revolutionaries—careful, happy-go-lucky and very interesting people. I remember spending very exciting moments in the company of these outspoken, candid, crazy but intelligent people.' Typically her interest in them was on grounds of compatibility and camaraderie rather than party affiliations, even less so on any real understanding of the CPI's policies: 'I have never seriously taken it to be my mission to reform society and eliminate the problems of humanity; but I was greatly influenced by the slogans of the Communist Party as they matched my own independent, unbridled, and revolutionary style of thinking.... What wonderful get-togethers, arguments and scuffle of words we had!'[44]

Going on to address the difference between her writing and the 'rigid policies of the progressives', she wrote:

If my writings have not measured up to the set standards of the progressives, I have not panicked. I shunned dogmatism, the very idea of getting tied to codes and norms is hateful to me.... What is and what is not progressivism has been discussed so much that the very topic somewhat perturbs me. I despise the four walls and I am also irritated with the idea of a stamp or a label. The pens should be free. That is the reason why I am not one with the critics—whether they are progressive or modern. They remind me of surgeons whose only interest is dissection.[45]

In '*Bombay se Bhopal Tak*' (From Bombay to Bhopal), she describes a train journey to Bhopal in January 1949 to attend a progressive writers' conference. The journey and the experiences in Bhopal become symbolic of the disarray among the ranks of the Bombay progressives after partition—while many had left for Pakistan, some like Jafri had been arrested following the clampdown on the communists; others like Kaifi and Niyaz Haider went underground. In Ismat's description of the goings-on in Bhopal in the company of Krishan Chandar, Mahindarnath, Majrooh Sultanpuri, Josh Malihabadi, Adil Rashid, Shahid Latif, Jan Nisar Akhtar and his wife Safiya, the progressives seem like a bunch of

[44] Faiz, 'Ismat Chughtai', p. 127.
[45] Ibid., pp. 133–4.

a merry—sometimes chaotic, occasionally comic—cast of talented but idiosyncratic characters.

Unlike most other progressive prose writers, Ismat also wrote novels, not exceptionally long ones, but certainly where she allowed herself a bigger canvas and several more strands to create a more nuanced, more colourful tapestry. *Tehri Lakir*, written when she was pregnant with her daughter and sick all the time, is an ideal example of the early part of her career.

Among Ismat's non-fiction writings, some are of especial interest to us for this study. She wrote a biting satire on Qurratulain Hyder entitled 'Pompom Darling' deriding a world of hyper-anglicized Shoshos and Fofos who swam and danced and played, a world of charming people cast in the same mould. Less serious criticism and more a tirade against the literary values of the modernists who were heaping praise on this new rising star in the firmament of Urdu literature, Ismat's rants against Hyder typify the progressives' worst ire for writers (like Hyder) who recreated a world of lost glory. In contrast, her essays on Manto, Krishan Chandar, and her own writer brother Azim Beg Chughtai are brimful with warmth and understanding of other kinds of writings. Her essay entitled '*Fasadat aur Adab*' (Communal Violence and Literature) describes the trauma of partition in words very similar to Manto's: 'The flood of communal violence came with all its evils and left, but it left a pile of living, dead and gasping corpses in its wake. It wasn't only that the country was split in two, bodies and minds were also divided. Moral beliefs were tossed aside and humanity was in shreds.'[46]

Rajinder Singh Bedi, Krishan Chandar, and Others

Due to reasons of space, Bedi and Chandar—the two pillars of the Urdu short story (Ismat and Manto being the other two)—are being clubbed together; each deserves to be studied in detail on their own, as do some of the other short story writers associated with the PWM who shall only be mentioned very briefly here. Towards the end of this section we will also look briefly at other forms of prose writings associated with the

---

[46] Translated by Tahira Naqvi and Muhammad Umar Memon, *Annual of Urdu Studies*, no. 15, part 2, p. 445. '*Fasadat aur Adab*' is actually Ismat's most nuanced writing on communal violence; it shows a clear-headed and clear-sighted writer who is abreast of literary and political currents.

progressives, such as criticism, drama, character sketches, reportage, radio plays, translations, diary writing, profiles, and essays.[47]

Like Ismat, Krishan Chandar (1914–1977) can also be said to be an instinctive progressive, that is, one by inclination rather than indoctrination. However, Krishan Chandar was the only progressive who remained associated with the movement till the end of his days and, more importantly, the only one who was consistently praised by fellow progressives for being one. He courted neither controversy nor criticism and we see never a dip or deviation in his commitment, nor a public disagreement with the laid-down policies—possibly because he, along with Jafri and Zaheer, decided the form and content of those policies. A prolific writer, he continued to write stories and novels dealing with explicitly social and political themes. Like many of his contemporaries, he came to write revolutionary fiction through an early phase marked by acute emotionalism and sentimentality. Writing an introduction to a selection of Krishan Chandar's short stories translated into English, Gopichand Narang admits that while these stories lack some of the qualities of Manto and Bedi, 'no one can deny Krishan Chandar's contribution to Urdu literature': 'The typical features of his stories are fundamental humanism and abounding wit, as well as charm of style and suppressed poetry ... he is significant for his combination of story telling, idealistic approach and a personal, happy tone. The tone reflects his own kindliness and good humour.'[48]

A novel like *Shikast* (Defeat) showed a young Krishan Chandar depicting a world cleft by social and economic injustices and inequalities with all the ardour of a romantic. His first collection of short stories, *Tilism-e Khayal* (The Magic of Thoughts), while plagued by romanticism, did not advocate escapism; instead it talked with fervour and touching idealism of changing the world and making it a better place. His next collection, *Nazare* (Sights) took him closer towards the realism being preached by the progressives and set him on a lifelong course of purposeful, socially engaged

---

[47] In the context of Manto, we have already looked at translations which were an important part of the literary agenda of the progressives and had been mentioned in the *Manifesto*. And in the previous chapter, we have seen the role of journalists and editors in shaping the progressive canon.

[48] Jai Ratan (trans.), *Krishan Chander: Selected Short Stories* (New Delhi: Sahitya Akademi, 1990), pp. 7–8.

literature.[49] Stories like *'Be-rang-o-bu'* (Without Colour or Smell), *'Jannat aur Jahannum'* (Heaven and Hell), *'Khooni Naach'* (Bloody Dance), *'Do Furlang Lambi Sadak'* (Two-Furlong Long Road), *'Dil ka Chiragh'* (The Lamp of the Heart), *'Garjan ki Ek Sham'* (An Evening of Thunder), and *'Balcony'*, were praised both by critics and readers for their social realism, a reputation that was bolstered by *'Kalu Bhangi'* and *'Annadata'* (The Giver of Food), the last especially for its portrayal of the Bengal famine. Krishan Chandar's ability to write on extremely topical events made him a poster boy for the progressives for he could be relied upon to churn out plays, novels, reportages, and short stories on the latest 'cause' adopted by either the party high command or the progressives. These offerings, marked as they were by emotionalism and poetic fervour, lacked depth and profundity; stories in the collection entitled *Hum Wahshi Hain* (We Are Beasts) can be viewed today as examples of *waqti adab* (topical literature).[50]

Rajinder Singh Bedi (1915–1984) earned a place for himself in the canon of Urdu short stories with his first collection, *Dana-o-Dam* (1940). He was also actively involved with the film industry like many of his fellow progressives, but his interest led him from writing the dialogue and screenplay of over 27 films to producing and directing memorable films like *Garam Coat* (Warm Coat), *Dastak* (knocking), and *Phagun* (the last month of the Indian lunar calendar).[51] Women occupied a central position in a great deal of Bedi's writings and he has etched some memorable female characters: the eponymous Kalyani and Lajwanti, Indu in *Apne Dukh Mujhe De Do* (Give Me Your Sorrows), Rano in *Ek Chadar Maili si* (A Slightly Soiled Sheet), and Ma in *'Banj'* (Barren Woman). Details of everyday life, no matter how small, found a place in his stories and became reflections of a larger social reality. Bedi's stories survive the test of time because they hinge on the common and the commonplace that transcend time and circumstance. Human desires and aspiration just as much as human foibles and frailties neither change nor date; they are ageless and eternal. Stories like *'Lajwanti'*, *'Zainul Abideen'*, *'Garhan'* (Eclipse), *Garam Coat* are testaments to the

---

[49] Azmi, *Urdu mein Taraqqui Pasand Adabi Tehreek*, p. 184.

[50] Azmi marks 1947 as a high-water point in the career of Krishan Chandar; thereafter, he sees a decline in his craft as a writer. Azmi, *Urdu mein Taraqqui Pasand Adabi Tehreek*, p. 187.

[51] See Leslie A. Flemming, 'Progressive Writer, Progressive Filmmaker: The Films of Rajinder Singh Bedi', *Annual of Urdu Studies*, vol. 5 (1985), pp. 81–97.

human condition; they do indeed conform to the prevalent literary more of realistic writing, but they are as meaningful today as they were in the heydays of the trend towards socialist realism. However, the same Bedi who was hailed by the progressives as a champion of their cause for his portrayal of lower-middle-class working people, later distanced himself due to his unwillingness to conform to communism and the soviet brand of socialist realism—the two factors increasingly stressed by Zaheer, Jafri, and Anand.[52]

Jafri, while expressing admiration for *Garam Coat* and *Jhola*, both early works, summed up the progressives' disapproval of Bedi when he alluded to the bitterness that had begun to creep into his writing, pushing it towards despair and melancholia.[53] The weft of bitterness that Jafri objected to does indeed run through the weft of life that is none-too-easy and offers neither immediate hope nor progress in stories like *Man ki Man Mein* (Silently within the Heart), *Apne Dukh Mujhe De Do* (Give Me Your Sorrows), *Ghar mein Bazar mein* (At Home and in the Market), *Quarantine*, etc. However, one also finds flashes of love, humanity, and compassion illuminating Bedi's grim landscape making life worth living.

Let us now look briefly at some of the other progressive short story writers. Devindar Satyarthi lived the life of a vagabond, travelling through Ceylon, Burma, Nepal, and different parts of the country, gathering folk songs, translating them and weaving stories around them. These songs which grew like wild flowers in deep dark forests told stories about real people and real lives and therefore deserve a special place in the history of the PWM. Khalilur Rahman Azmi wrote: 'When his first collection, *Main Hoon Khanabadosh* (I am a Vagabond) was published, Urdu readers came to know of the vast literary treasures that lie hidden in the meadows of Kashmir and Punjab, in the paddy fields of Bengal, in the forests of the Santhal and Gond tribals.'[54] Stories like '*Diya Jale Saari Raat*' (The Lamp Burns All Night), '*Laachi*', '*Kavita Sasural Nahi Jayegi*' (Kavita Won't Go to Her In-Laws), '*Hirni*' (The Female Deer), '*Jangli Kabootar*' (Wild Pigeon) were in the nature of experiments in Urdu short story writing.

[52] For details, see Bedi's interview in *Journal of South Asian Literature*, vol. 6 (Summer–Fall 1972), p. 143.

[53] Jafri, *Taraqqui Pasand Adab*, p. 245.

[54] Azmi, *Urdu mein Taraqqui Pasand Adabi Tehreek*, p. 201. Much of this section on the lesser known progressive short story writers is built from a reading of Azmi's perceptive analysis.

Comparable with Satyarthi's portrayal of folk India, there was Ahmad Nadeem Qasmi's portrayal of rural Punjab. From the land of Heer Ranjha and Sassi Punnu, Qasmi eked out stories of brutal realism in collections such as *Bagole, Gardab, Aable, Sailab, Aanchal*, and *Talwa-o Gharub*. Despite being located in small local communities, Qasmi's stories spoke of universal concerns in much the same way as Thomas Hardy's novels set in rural England.

Another very unusual writer was Akhtar Orainvi, who wrote about the poorest and most disenfranchised, those who occupied the lowest rung of India's social pyramid along with the myriad problems they face such as hunger, debt, and debilitating court cases that sap them of whatever remained after zamindari, and how landless labour and family feuds suck their life blood dry. Orainvi's characters are coolies, bakers, farmers, rickshaw-pullers, and petty labourers in stories such as *'Andhi Nagri'* (The Blind City), *'Boodhi Maa'* (The Old Mother), *'Do Maain'* (Two Mothers), *'Aakhri Ikanni'* (The Last One-anna Coin), *'Jeene ka Sahara'* (A Prop for Life), *'Bail Gadi'* (Bullock Cart), *'Gande Ande'* (Rotten Eggs), *'Golewala'*, etc. Unlike Manto's stories about the same set of characters, in Orainvi there was a sentimentality and emotionalism. His most successful novelette, *Kaliyan aur Kaante* (Buds and Thorns), was based in a sanatorium and was marked by its realism and psychological insight into human nature.

In the early, purer days of the movement, Akhtar Husain Raipuri, who later not only got more involved in linguistics rather than literature, but also steadily distanced himself from the PWM, wrote some short stories too. Some of the notable stories in his first collection were *'Mujhe Jaane Do'* (Let Me Go), *'Marghat'* (Cremation Ground), and *'Mera Ghar'* (My House).

Like Raipuri, Upendranath Ashk belonged to the early generation of progressives whose first collection, *Nau Ratan* (Nine Jewels), published in 1930, received praise from no less a personage than Premchand. His reputation was shored up by the second collection entitled *Aurat ki Fitrat* (Woman's Temperament), published in 1933. The stories of these two collections were marked by reformism and idealism. Ashk's progressive phase started with *Daachi* with stories reflecting the Congress's satyagraha phase and other political events. Ashk's emphasis on plot and characterization set him apart stylistically and temperamentally from the other progressives. His last collection in Urdu, before he began writing in Hindi, was *Chattan* (Rock); Azmi ranked it as his finest contribution to the Urdu progressive short story.

Another significant short story writer, and like Ashk an active member of the PWA in Bombay, was K.A. Abbas. His first collection, entitled *Ek Ladki* (A Girl) was perhaps his best effort; later collections, each more political than the other, were more in the nature of essays and diatribes. '*Ek Payali Chawal*' (A Cupful of Rice), about the Bengal famine; '*Zindagi*' (Life) about Gandhi ji; '*Sardarji*' about communal riots; '*Zafran ke Phool*' (Saffron Flowers) about the Kashmir problem, are some examples of the progressives' failure to marry craft with ideology. On the other hand, a writer like Hans Raj Rahbar was more successful in the craft and technique of story writing yet inexplicably less popular. His stories include '*Gadolta*', '*Raja Ram*', '*Naya Ufaq*' (New Dawn), '*Ab aur Tab*' (Now and Then), and '*Gorki Nagri*'.

Unlike the other Urdu progressive writers, Abbas was bilingual; it is often difficult to tell whether he first wrote a particular story in Urdu or in English as he translated his own stories or rewrote them. In many stories, he blurs the boundaries of fiction and journalism, possibly because he believed that both stem from realism. In his autobiography, *I Am Not an Island*, he noted

good, imaginative, inspired journalism has always been undistinguishable from realistic, purposeful contemporary literature. There was a special correspondent called Karl Marx whose despatches to *New York Herald Tribune* are now part of the scriptures of communism. Steinbeck wrote his *Grapes of Wrath* as he scoured the United States to investigate the causes of the great depression. Hemingway wrote *For Whom the Bells Toll* as he covered and fought the Spanish Civil War.[55]

An unabashed admirer of Nehru, he embraced the nation-building projects with great enthusiasm. In a preface to an early collection of short stories, he noted:

A few stories may provoke high-brow critics living in isolated ivory towers to utter the dreaded word 'Propaganda'. But these stories are not about plans, projects and policies of the government. They are about men and women, our contemporaries, the people of a new India, and how their subjective 'inner life' ... in which the positive values of socialism (even where hesitantly and half-heartedly adopted by our government) are playing their own part.[56]

---

[55] Suresh Kohli (ed.), *An Evening in Lucknow: Selected Stories by K.A. Abbas* (New Delhi: HarperCollins, 2011).

[56] Ibid.

Another progressive writer, Mahindarnath wrote about sexual matters in a collection entitled *Chandi ke Taar* (Silver Strands) which dealt with the frustrations of young men, especially in stories such as *'Akela'* (Alone) and *'Khala'* (Vacuum), and in a later story called *'Jahan Main Rahta Hoon'* (Where I Live). Akhtar Ansari, who was active even before the inception of the PWA and whose writings show the stamp of Qazi Abdul Ghaffar (of *Laila ke Khutoot* fame), wrote on similar subjects though in a more satirical, far more experimental fashion. His fame in the progressive canon rests on a novelette called *Lo Ek Qissa Suno* (Here, Listen to a Story) where stories tumble out of each other like images from a kaleidoscope and form new patterns. Others who made their mark, in different ways and different degrees, were Ibrahim Jalees, Shamsher Singh Narula, and Ramanand Sagar.

A valuable contribution of the progressives was in hitherto neglected or totally unknown literary genres such as reportage, travel writing, and writing of essays, diaries, and character sketches. Of these, reportage soon became very popular with the progressives: often topical, written either for easy name or quick money, it has escaped the scrutiny of literary historians or been dismissed as literary flotsam. But some forms of reportage have lasting value. Zaheer's *Yaadein*, for instance, is invaluable for its record of the early history of the PWM, as is Krishan Chandar's account of the Hyderabad conference entitled *'Paudey'* (Saplings). Ibrahim Jalees's *'Bombay'* brings alive the Bombay of the progressives and *'Do Mulk Ek Kahani'* is a valuable account of partition and the communal violence that came in its wake. Some excellent reportage focused on communal violence: Fikr Taunsvi's *'Chhata Darya'* (The Sixth River) alludes to the river of blood that flowed in the land of five rivers and Tajdar Samri's *'Jab Bandhan Toote'* (When the Bonds Broke) speaks of suffering endured by the common people whose humanity and brotherhood was challenged by the partition.[57]

---

[57] M.U. Memon makes a convincing case when he suggests that for the Urdu writer the division of India and the subsequent creation of Pakistan 'had no deeper meaning'. They failed to view the Partition in a historical and cultural context and the bulk of writing of this period gives the impression that the writers were not trying to describe reality, but avoid it by focusing their attention on 'intrinsically less significant element'. The writers' desire to sound impartial causes the treatment to remain 'superficial and artificial' and the hero is 'forced to react not according to the dictates of his personality and nature, but according to an ideal superimposed upon his personality'. Memon, 'Partition Literature', p. 381.

We have been taking up the issue of partition intermittently throughout this chapter. Early in this chapter, in the introduction itself, we had noted how the progressives wrote extensively on the partition, choosing to focus exclusively on its violence and trauma, often with melodramatic, even unrealistic or idealistic effect. We will conclude our observations on the progressives predilection for violent, exaggerated depiction of partition by suggesting that perhaps they did so because they wished to evoke, in the reader, their own sense of 'disgust and indignation'.[58] They seldom, if ever, questioned the motivation behind this violence and that is perhaps why the bulk of writing of the late 1940s had a knee-jerk quality and occasionally 'lack depth and conviction'. Added to this, the progressives' very earnest desire to appear even-handed and impartial pushed them further away from reality.[59] Some of these shortcomings were rectified by the generation that came immediately after; writers like Intizar Husain concentrated not so much on the blood and gore, but on the long-term consequences. Unfortunately, it is still being left to the historian to offer the reasons behind the partition; the bulk of the Urdu writers—progressive and modern—preferred to look at the consequences rather than the causes.

A compulsive scraping of wounds, a cataloguing of unimaginable horrors, and a depiction of a sick, momentarily depraved society (as in several of Manto's stories) seems to be the creative writer's only way of exorcising the evil within. It may have served the needs of its times in a rough and ready sort of way, but it was patchy, uneven, often incoherent in its pain or anger or bewilderment. In hindsight, also worrying is the lack of historical awareness among some of the writers. References to political events, resolutions, statements, etc., are vague; the focus is on the 'impact' of partition on the common people rather than *why* the political leaders failed to resolve their disputes over power sharing and ended up carving the country along religious lines. By and large, the writers seem content to write of consequences rather than reasons, effects rather than causes, of partition.

---

[58] Memon, 'Partition Literature', p. 390.

[59] Krishan Chander's collection *Hum Wahshi Hain* is replete with examples of brutal depictions of communal violence which, somehow, fail to move the readers despite their graphic contents. His story *Andhe* (Blind) mimics Manto's *Sharifan* and *Thanda Gosht*, but the call for balance and humanity gets lost in the blind violence.

Alok Bhalla, one of the ablest and most diligent chroniclers of the many partition narratives, points out the 'real sorrow' of the partition, namely, that it 'brought to an abrupt end a long and communally shared history'.[60] In his deeply insightful introduction to the four volumes of partition-related stories, he shows a clear-eyed understanding of the tensions within the communities which occasionally burst into spurts of outrage yet did not, he believes, impair 'the rich heterogeneity of the life of the two communities'. That is, till the partition; at the 'ordinary and local levels, even as late as 1946,' Bhalla notes, the daily life of the Hindus and Muslim remained 'so richly interwoven as to have formed a rich archive of customs and practices, that explains why there is a single, common note which informs nearly all the stories written about the partition and the horror it unleashed—a note of utter bewilderment.' And it is this bewilderment that is common across barriers of ethnic, linguistic, and cultural identities, not to say religious ones, that comes out in his selection of stories translated from Urdu, Hindi, Punjabi, Sindhi, and Bengali.

The progressives, who encouraged the participation of women in all walks of life, had a fair sprinkling of women writers amidst their ranks. We have earlier looked at the contribution of Rashid Jahan in the setting up of the PWA, and we have noted Ismat's testimony to the sort of influence she exerted on young and impressionable women. Her stories and plays reflect the currents of contemporary thought and the testimony of those who knew her show her as a strong-willed, outspoken, independent-minded woman. Brief though her life was and slender her literary output, together they serve to illustrate the fact that Rashid Jahan single-handedly paved the way for other women writers. Equally importantly, she opened a window of immense possibilities for young Muslim women.

Razia Sajjad Zaheer, who grew steadily more active as a writer after her husband's departure for Pakistan, attended the Peace Conference in Calcutta and wrote *'Aman ka Carvan'* (Caravan of Peace). While Ismat was the tallest among the women writers of her generation, those who also made their mark were Hajra Masrur, Khadija Mastur, Siddiqa Begum Seoharvi, Shakila Akhtar, and Sarla Devi. None of these women, however, matched the vim and vigour of Rashid Jahan or Ismat Chughtai.

---

[60] Alok Bhalla (ed.), *Stories about the Partition of India*, vols I–IV (New Delhi: Manohar, 2012).

No survey of progressive prose can be complete without a look at two important components: satire and humour, and literary criticism. Humour and satire have been the weapons of the subaltern from the earliest days of Urdu literature even though only one generic term *hasv* included the different strands of wit, humour, and satire. The Awadh Punch school of humourists thrived in the half century after 1857 when satire and parody of the *angrez sarkar* was closely followed by barbs directed at the slavishness and herd mentality of the 'brown sahibs'. We see examples of gentle humour and squeaky-clean wit in the writings of Rasheed Ahmed Siddiqui and Pitras Bukhari, but in the hands of the progressives, humour acquired a sharper, darker, blacker hue as in Fikr Taunsvi's *Tir-e-Nimkash, Badnam Kitab, Adha Admi,* and *Akhiri Kitab*. Kanhaiyyalal Kapoor's collection entitled *Sang-o-Khisht* contained essays such as '*Apne Watan mein Sab Kuch Hai Pyare*' and '*Qaumi Libas*', the latter being a spoof on the correspondence between Gandhi and Jinnah. Kapoor turned his pen towards his fellow writers parodying the fare being passed off as 'new poetry' in '*Ghalib Jadeed Shoara ki Ek Majlis mein*' (Ghalib in an Assembly of Modern Poets). Several contemporary literary, social, and political issues became the target of Kapoor's satire, including the PWM itself, in a letter-like essay '*Taraqqui Pasand Dost ke Naam*' (To a Progressive Friend).

We have discussed in previous chapters the clout and command of the progressive critics in making and breaking the literary canon. With the spurt in literary activity and the profusion of literary journals, meetings, conferences, and writers' groups, literary criticism too blossomed as the PWM gained momentum. The Urdu critic increasingly began to move from the fringes of the literary consciousness to occupy a place at the centre of the stage. Ehtesham Husain, the presiding deity in the pantheon of Urdu critics, not merely defined approaches to Urdu criticism, but ensured they were abided by a process of strict control and a keen eye on who was writing what. His own immaculate scholarship and erudition lent weight to his views on what constituted good literature and his unwavering and unequivocal advocacy of Art for Life's Sake helped define the parameters of progressive literature. The other prominent name among the progressive critics, Ale Ahmad Suroor, showed the influence of modern critics like T.S. Eliot and Ian Richards in the early part of his career, but refused to be straightjacketed as a modernist or a progressive, and retained a lasting aversion to the use of labels in literary criticism. Some of his prominent critical writings include *Tanquidi Ishare* (Critical Signposts, 1942), *Tanquid*

Kya Hai? (What Is Criticism? 1947), and *Adab aur Nazariya* (Literature and Perspective, 1954), among others. A lifelong advocate of moderation and balance, he decried any form of one-sidedness. In the Preface to *Naye aur Purane Chiragh* (New and Old Lamps, 1946), he wrote:

It is not good for a critic to put himself into pigeonholes. A writer or critic should not be defined by his party.... In India people still believe in only day or only night, only white or only black. As Kingsley Martin says, things are not only good or only bad; they can be good and bad at the same time.[61]

Another progressive theoretician, Aziz Ahmad, conducted the first-of-its kind survey of progressive writing in Urdu as early as 1945; amongst his several useful findings was how the progressives lavished all their care and attention on the short story and neglected the novel. The reason for this was ascribed to haste and lack of time.[62] The progressives were, as has been said before, people in a hurry to change the world; they had neither the time nor the leisure to pursue their craft. Even in the years after the first flush of excitement, the progressives found it easier to write good short stories rather than good novels. Bedi has offered a very interesting reason why very few Indian writers generally preferred to write novels rather than short stories. Apart from the obvious reason of haste to write as much as possible in as little time (often due to financial reasons), he believed Urdu writers were 'mindful of the content' but still 'unaware of the form'. A novel, he said, is not an extended harangue where the author produces hundreds of pages of invective, implying that heaping invective was easier than a nuanced and sustained scrutiny.[63] Ale Ahmad Suroor too, while agreeing that the short story like the ghazal is a difficult art form precisely because of its compactness, expressed alarm at the profusion of short stories being written.[64] As he pointed out, can there be real talent in this haystack of frenzied feverish activity?

We shall conclude this overview of progressive prose with two observations: one, not everything that emerged from the progressives' pen was

---

[61] Quoted in Azmi, *Urdu mein Taraqqui Pasand Adabi Tehreek*, p. 298.

[62] Ahmad, *Taraqqui Pasand Adab*, p. 155.

[63] *Mahfil*, interview, vol. 8 (1972), p. 140.

[64] Ale Ahmad Suroor, 'Maujooda Adabi Masail', in *Tanquid Kya Hai?* (New Delhi: Maktaba Jamia, 1972), p. 131.

uniformly, consistently good literature; and two, irrespective of its score on the literary yardstick, it was nonetheless necessary literature. The progressives were articulating concerns that needed to be voiced. That they were not too concerned with literary niceties should be the concern of literary critics. For literary historians, their writings hold a faithful mirror to their times. And for the purpose of this study, their writings offer another way of reconstructing history. What emerged from the progressives' pen was not a magisterial survey of Urdu literature from the 1930s till the 1950s, but a series of small, compact, minutely etched cameos that *together* give us a comprehensive way of reviewing the most tumultuous period of Indian history. Also, the bird's-eye view of history usually adopted by conventional historians does not take into account the silenced, the marginalized, or the under-represented. A study of the cumulative output of the progressives corrects this anomaly, which is precisely the purpose of this study.

8

The Decline of the Progressive Writers' Movement

> *Buland ho to tujh pe khule raaz pasti ka*
> *Isi zameen mein darya samaye hain kya kya*
> (From the heights you shall know the secret of the depths
> In this very earth so many rivers have gone underground)
> —Yagana Changezi (1884–1956)

In this concluding chapter, we shall once again look at the political underpinnings of the PWM, and its linkages with the CPI (which had increasingly come to the fore during the War years). The second section shall look at the creation of Pakistan, the exodus of some progressives to the new country, and their activities leading up to the Rawalpindi Conspiracy Case which drove the last nail in the coffin of progressivism in Pakistan. The last section, also in the nature of a conclusion to this study, shall encapsulate the reasons for the early and widespread success of the PWM followed by reasons for its decline

Political Ramifications of the PWM

It is a truism much acknowledged that minorities often exercise an influence unrelated to their actual size.[1] So too the communists in India. And since public opinion is obstinately averse to anything savouring of that bugbear of democratic functioning—suppressive measures—suppression invariably leads to a peculiar sort of flowering. We can see that in the growth of communism in India all through the 1930s and 1940s.[2] The history of the CPI during the period under scrutiny (1935–55) was a period of gains and losses, ups and downs, highs and lows, backward and forward flips. As we have seen in Chapter 5, the considerable gains of the 1930s were lost by the 1940s when the CPI decided to support the allied war effort. The war years saw the party reduced to a marginal player at a crucial period in Indian history when the sheer force of Indian nationalism demanded nothing short of complete independence—war or no war! The Congress socialists, unlike the communists, did not support the war and defied the Defence of India Act by widespread anti-recruitment propaganda, boycott of British goods, organizing of peasant agitations and fomenting of general strikes among the workers. The All-India Students Federation too was involved in anti-war propaganda.

Soon after the war, the CPI—which had enjoyed a brief stint of freedom when the ban had been lifted from July 1942 to December 1946—reverted, albeit briefly, to its role of 'loyal opposition' to Nehru's interim government. By 1946, in the broader political field the ground had shifted awkwardly for the communists. It had been well enough when Britain had been the target of excited political attack, to aid, abet, and influence anything which tended towards disorder because out of chaos might emerge the rule of the mob and communism. However, with the transfer of discord, through the establishment of a national government, support of disorder cut at the roots of nationalism. The communists found themselves in the unusual position of peacemakers. They were compelled to sway hate back into the channel which offered the greatest advantage, that is, the channel of anti-British antagonism.

---

[1] In 1942, the CPI claimed a membership of 30,000 (including supporters in the students unions, trade unions, as well as kisan organizations) and declared itself to be the third largest party after the Congress and Muslim League. Other estimates put the actual membership in the range of 16,000.

[2] The CPI was more successful and more popular when it worked underground rather than in the four-and-a-half years of its legal existence.

In themselves, the public manifestations of the movement—'the strident denunciations of governmental policy, the savage pamphleteering campaigns on any and every subject, the quasi-libellous articles, the subversive speeches and resolutions, even the strikes and demonstrations—had a certain legitimacy as the outward and visible signs of the party system.'[3] Having said that, there was evidently also an element of self-deception in the majority of young Indians who confessed sympathy for communism or Marxism, for there was little in their own background that was conducive to the lifelong fostering of such an ideology. A society that was essentially class-based exercised a spell over its members to fall back on lines of class and privilege. We shall come back to this when we discuss the reasons for the decline of the PWM; first, let us take up the history of the CPI where we left it in Chapter 5.

The turning point in the growing popularity of the CPI came in August 1942 when Gandhi launched the biggest mass movement the country had yet seen: the Quit India agitation. Rattled by Gandhi's growing popularity, the newly legalized CPI accused Gandhi of decimating the revolutionary vanguard that had been built so assiduously by its cadres. Adhikari, writing *A Review of Gandhism*, went so far as to declare that Gandhi's line 'shorn of its moral embellishment is the line of the cowardly and compromising bourgeoisie'.[4] Faiz, though not a member, displayed his loyalty when he wrote 'Siyasi Leader kay Naam' (To a Political Leader)[5] in 1942:

> You don't like that the darkness conquers everything
> But you want that these hands are chopped off
> And the day that pulsates in the hideout of the East
> Gets buried under the steely corpse of night.[6]

The years before and during the war were difficult times for the progressives. With every change in the CPI's war policy, the progressive poets turned round and round like bewildered weathercocks. When the British government in India announced Indian participation in the war, the pro-

---

[3] *Communism and India*, IOR/1/PJ/12/671.

[4] Quoted in *Selected Works of Jawaharlal Nehru*, vol. 14 (New Delhi: Orient Longman, 1981), p. 532.

[5] Faiz confirmed that this was written for Gandhi in an interview with his biographer Ayub Mirza. The context was Gandhi's non-cooperative Quit India Movement which was obstructing the British war effort against the Nazis.

[6] Faiz Ahmed Faiz, *Dast-e-Saba* (Aligarh: Educational Book House, 1990), p. 14; translation mine.

gressives jumped to express their pacifism. Jafri, the most eloquent of the progressives, spoke for his comrades when he put the blame squarely on the door of the Allied:

> This lightning was nurtured in your home
> This dagger was sharpened by your hand ...
> Your imperialism has been shaken to its core
> Lovers of freedom rejoice at your plight.[7]

When the war reached Russian soil, it ceased to be a war of imperialism; it was now a revolutionary war against fascism. Sajjad Zaheer, in detention in the Deoli camp, issued a statement—along with the other jailed communists—urging the writers and intellectuals to support the anti-fascist cause.[8] Makhdoom, who had earlier written the anti-war *'Sipahi'* (Soldier), now exhorted his readers thus with the *'Jang-e-Azadi'*:

> This war is a war of freedom
> This war is a war of the people of India
> Under the banner of freedom.[9]

The first All-India Congress of the CPI was held in Bombay from 23 May to 1 June 1943.[10] Zaheer, who upon his release had been elected to

---

[7] Translated by Hafeez Malik, 'The Marxist Literary Movement in India and Pakistan', *Journal of Asian Studies*, vol. 26, no. 4 (August 1967), p. 655.

[8] A report on the 'Demands Made by the Jailed Leaders' is found in the P.C. Joshi Archives, JNU, File No. 1941/43, dated December 1941. An introductory note ranks this demand at par with the Dutt–Bradley Thesis as providing a blueprint for future action. The Joshi Archives also contain confidential reports on Zaheer's medical problems and his interviews with the CID during his detention at the Central Prison in Lucknow during January 1942. The report reiterates Zaheer's affirmation that the war was a 'people's war'. See File No. 1942/61, p. 3.

[9] Makhdoom Mohiuddin, *Bisat-e-Raqs* (Hyderabad: Urdu Academy Andhra Pradesh, 1986), p. 100.

[10] According to the *People's War* (June 1943), 139 delegates attended this first Congress accompanied by an equal number of party members. The delegates comprised an interesting cross-section of Indian society: 86 from the intelligentsia; 25 peasants; 22 working class; and 18 women. Eighteen per cent of the delegates had been to jail, half worked underground, none was illiterate, a few knew English; 48 were matriculate and 57 graduates; and most of them were under the age of 35! It was also reported that in May 1943 the CPI boasted of having 41,100 women members. Sourced from IOR/L/PJ/12/431.

the Central Committee, used this opportunity to hold an all-India conference of the PWA (the fourth so far) from 22 to 25 May 1943. We have looked at the decisions taken during this conference in the first section of Chapter 6; here, we will establish how this conference, with S.A. Dange as president, met with the primary purpose of mobilizing writers to support the war effort. The decision to ask Comrade Dange, a party man, to preside over the conference marked a departure from the practice of inviting literary personages beginning with Premchand. Dange's speech was a fiery invocation for art to mobilize and unify people; it also made no bones about pointing out where the sympathies of the progressive writers ought to lie: 'If you believe that the victory of the nations led by the Soviet Union is no concern of yours you are not paving the way for freedom from your national enslaver, you are aiding a worst slavery to take place, you are aiding not only your own annihilation but the annihilation of all people, all culture.'[11]

Like the changing war policy, confusion was further compounded by the communists' support of the two-nation theory on the grounds of self-determination. The Indian communists were taking their cue from Lenin's definition of national self-determination which held 'By examining the historical-economic conditions of the national movements we must inevitably reach the conclusions that the self-determination of nations means the political separation of the nations from alien national bodies and the formation of an independent national state.'[12]

A secret document entitled 'Communist Survey' dated January–March 1943 found in the India Office Records (IOR) reveals the naïve assumptions ('wishful conjectures') on the part of the communist ideologues:

While recognizing the validity of the Pakistan demand they (communists) are, however, careful to express the hope that once the other parties concede the principle, Muslims will be content to forego the right to secede. The Muslim leaders, on the other hand, remain entirely unmoved by these unsolicited concessions

---

[11] Sudhi Pradhan (ed.), *Marxist Cultural Movements in India: Chronicles and Documents (1936–1947)*, vol. I (Calcutta: National Book Agency, 1979), p. 119.

[12] V.I. Lenin, *Critical Remarks on the National Question* (Moscow, 1971), p. 41. It must be pointed out that Lenin praised, for instance, the separation of Norway from Sweden on the above grounds.

and wishful conjectures and are still inclined to regard the communists as self-appointed agents of Congress.[13]

Despite the support of Pakistan, Muslim membership of the CPI remained less than 5 per cent in 1943, spurring the party to begin actively wooing the Muslims. Special issues of *People's War* began to be published in Urdu. Notwithstanding its overtures to the Muslim League, Jinnah refused to find common cause with the CPI. In an address to the Punjab Muslim Students' Federation's annual session on 19 March 1944, Jinnah asked the CPI to keep its hands off the Muslims who, he declared, wanted no other flag than the League flag and whose guide and complete code of life was Islam.[14] Danial Latifi, Sohan Singh Josh, and K.M. Ashraf tried to meet Jinnah to convince him it was not so, but met with little success. Liaqat Ali Khan made it clear to Sajjad Zaheer that any communists wishing to join the League would have to first resign from the CPI.[15] Towards the end of June 1944, Danial Latifi and Abdulla Malik resigned from the CPI and joined the Muslim League in Punjab knowing perhaps fully well that they would be thrown out once they had served their purpose. Meanwhile, the CPI's relations with the Congress too were irretrievably severed when the Congress decided in December 1945 to exclude communists from elective office in Congress bodies. Prominent Congress leaders had already been baying for the comrades' blood and charging the communists of treachery to the national cause and of stabbing the Congress in the back by not supporting the Quit India disturbances. The CPI had the option of humbly admitting its mistake in not joining the nation when it responded to Gandhi's call for civil disobedience at an unprecedented scale, or sticking to its guns. It not only chose the latter, but also launched a tirade against the Congress.

P.C. Joshi, the right-hand man of Spratt and one of the original accused in the Meerut case, had all along displayed great energy and organizational ability in building up the party. His tenure as general secretary from 1939 to

---

[13] IOR/L/PJ/12/431, p. 98.

[14] Ibid.

[15] This did not deter Zaheer from writing a largely flattering book called *Muslim League aur Azadi* (Bombay: PPH, 1944). Other similar books by Zaheer during this period were *Light on League-Unionist Conflict* (Bombay: PPH, 1944) and *Punjab ki League-Unionist Jhagre ka Rahasya* (Bombay: Jan Prakashan Griha, 1944). All are to be found in the P.C. Joshi Archives, JNU.

1948 saw the party consolidate its strengths on many fronts. The American correspondent, Snow, in a dispatch to the *Saturday Evening Post* from New Delhi, on 3 July 1943, wrote:

The Quad-e-Azam is now getting reinforcement from an unexpected quarter—the CPI. Its youthful Secretary, Mr. P.C. Joshi told me that Pakistan fits in neatly with the communist principle of 'self-determination' for national minorities, so that the party can whole-heartedly back up Mr. Jinnah. The latter, an expert at opportunism, is not averse to utilizing energy from wherever it comes. He has said publicly that he would unite with the Devil if it would bring him Pakistan. He has invited some of the young Reds to join the League, and help him to organize Muslim youth.... But the marriage has its benefits for the communists too. Like Mr. Jinnah they have been haymaking while Mr. Gandhi's star is down. Party membership shot up from 9000 to 16,000 and Mr. Joshi predicts it will double again this year.... The communists already dominate the Trades Union Congress, India's largest working class organisation, and likewise they rule the great Kisan Sabha to which hundreds of thousands of poor peasants regularly pay their dues.... While old-line Congressmen have during this period been immobilized and frustrated, the army of Indian communists has been capturing many new streets of power. Its national following has cut across Class, Race, Religious and even party lines, with Hindu, Sikh, Moslem, Bengali, Parsi and Christian boys and some hundreds of girls and young adults making the network. It includes more fulltime paid workers than the Congress party and the Muslim League combined.[16]

On 24 August 1944, in a secret letter written by R. Tottenham, additional secretary to the Government of India, we get a glimpse of the pragmatism on the part of both the British and the communists:

When the war has been won, the communists will be faced with the need of finding a new platform; and though their post-war activities may well be given a specious cloak of socialism or communism, we have no reason to believe that their long-term revolutionary goal has ever been set aside ... the majority of the party are revolutionaries first and communists second (and they will bound to take advantage of the troubled situation).[17]

As the war dragged on, the communists' pro-war policy began to cost the party dearly. Opposition mounted in the kisan and students' wings;

---

[16] Ibid., pp. 115–6.
[17] IOR/L/PJ/8/681, January 1942–5.

clearly the policy had outlived its usefulness. Propaganda, which had always been the most powerful weapon in the armoury of the communists, was now turned towards reaping the benefits of a decision that had been controversial to begin with. The end of the war in June 1945 was hailed by communists as a victory for the forces of democracy led by USSR which had sounded the death knell of world imperialism and heralded the dawn of freedom for all peoples. The Indian communists gave the Red Army most of the credit for defeating Germany in a series of articles in the *People's War*. Communist propaganda, in the form of pamphlets, leaflets, newspapers, as well as party organs in the various languages, glorified Russia as the only true friend of India devoted to the cause of freedom of the Asiatic people. With no evidence of any direct or indirect guidance emanating from Russia, the CPI found itself left to its own devices. In the immediate aftermath of the war, it found itself confronting two major issues: (*a*) how best to maintain and extend its influence over worker, peasant, and student groups in the face of a powerful and hostile Congress which was eyeing the same groups with hungry eyes; and (*b*) how to continue its self-appointed role of strident opposition on the national platform. The latter was especially tricky since its influence was out of all proportion to its strength—as was displayed by its poor showing in the first elections when the Congress swept past to form an interim government.[18]

However, the four-and-a-half years of its legal existence were not wasted; the CPI infiltrated different organizations, secured sympathizers and supporters, strengthened its position both financially and politically, and above all perfected its propaganda apparatus in its minutest detail.[19] It produced vast amounts of oral and written propaganda and while its views often went unheeded in the larger arena of nationalist politics, it was able to command public attention by exploiting local grievances or bringing the authorities into disrepute or launching anti-government campaigns. Its literature and party organ was printed in every major Indian language and reached the masses in the remotest corners through an efficient system of party units. While it recorded some measure of success with the middle classes, its propaganda, however, appealed most to the masses because it preached undiluted hatred for the capitalists and landlords. It succeeded in

---

[18] Built from a reading of Gene D. Overstreet and Marshall Windmiller, *Communism in India* (Bombay: Perennial Press, 1960).

[19] IOR/L/PJ/8/681, January 1942–5.

maintaining a high pitch of discontent and disaffection among the workers and peasants. Shortly after the war, in anticipation of the ban being re-imposed, the party decided to send prominent members underground armed with typewriters, cyclostyled machines, and stenographers.[20]

The CPI also ran the PPH from Bombay and several smaller printing presses in the provinces. The PPH sold several reputable bestsellers as well as English publications of the state publishing house in Moscow and some magazines like *International Literature* and *Moscow News*. Its motto—Not for Profit, but for Patriotism—was reflected in the low cost of its publications. In Bombay, the material was printed at the New Age Printing Press; and while some of it was written in India, much of it was translated from other languages, especially texts and treatises on Marxism published in Moscow and articles written by Soviet writers that were supplied by TASS. Many Indian communists and several members of the PWA (including Bedi) maintained close contacts with the Indian branch of the pro-Soviet organization called the Friends of the Soviet Union. The PPH evidently functioned with some small help in the procuring of paper from the CPI; for the rest it managed on its own.[21]

The Bombay Conference left little doubt that the PWA was indeed closely aligned with the CPI. Yet, both the IPTA and PWA maintained an avowedly non-political stance. The PWA functionaries remained in the closest touch with not just the CPI, but also TASS in Delhi as well as the Moscow and Kabul agencies of the Society for Cultural Relations with Foreign Countries, known by its acronym VOKS, which was affiliated to the Comintern. The *People's War* carried laudatory stories of the achievements of writers and artists in Soviet Union and China and held up the examples of Indian writers, such as Saghar Nizami's homage to China and Makhdoom's anti-Japanese poems;[22] yet, the PWA maintained that it was a non-political, purely cultural body.

Like the Urdu PWA, the Hindi PWA was inextricably linked with the party. A note on the Hindi Party Writers' Conference called by Comrade Ramesh Sinha, dated 24 October 1946, was prepared by Mahmuduzzafar in his capacity as provincial secretary; it clearly mentions the 'important

---

[20] Ibid.

[21] There is a reference in the IOR to the astronomical sum of Rs 375,000 given by Subodh Mangaldas Shah of Ahmedabad to the PPH. IOR/L/PJ/12/772.

[22] *People's War*, 6 June 1946.

part played by the Party' in the upsurge in Hindi literature.[23] A 'Note for Comrades on the Writers' Front' further establishes the directions being given from the party to writers and journalists, 'whether working on our own papers or in other journals' to 'carry forward the battle for freedom of thought' and to guard against 'bourgeois compromises'.[24] Yet another document, 'Draft Statement on Tasks of Indian Progressive Writers: For Discussion by the All-India Executive Committee of the IPWA', warns progressive writers of Anglo-American imperialist plans of sowing 'distrust and suspicion between Indian people and their Soviet and Chinese neighbours'.[25]

As the time of partition approached, the communists wanted the 17 'Indian national homelands' to have the right to exercise self-determination through assemblies elected by universal adult franchise. The CPI took an ultra-revolutionary unrealistic stand regarding the princely states, saying that people must *first* overthrow the princely ruler, set up a people's democratic rule, and then decide how to accede and merge with the Indian union. Such a radical approach lead to setbacks in Andhra Pradesh where the communists had actively fuelled the glorious Telangana struggle for land reform and where the peasant workers felt betrayed by the communists leaving them in the lurch, as it were. Irrespective of other differences, all communists were in favour of a 'final struggle'. The CPI possessed the most efficient body of well-trained labour agitators and strike engineers in the country who, in turn, were guided by experienced communist leaders, some of whom had been trained in communist schools in Russia. Their policy was one of disruption to facilitate a mass revolution and the political and economic conditions in India at this time were not unfavourable to their purpose. High cost of living, rampant profiteering, and hoarding during the war years gave the communists enough reasons to incite the workers. A wave of strikes, unrest, and agitation continued from late 1946 till mid-1947. The communist cadres also stepped up agitation among the peasants due to the Congress Party's election manifesto that promised abolition of the zamindari system and distribution of land among the ryots. While most of the strikes were against British imperialism, the communists also fomented other strikes for better living conditions, and successive

[23] File No. 1946/13, P.C. Joshi Archives, JNU.
[24] File No. 1946/14, P.C. Joshi Archives, JNU.
[25] File No. 1946/10, P.C. Joshi Archives, JNU.

waves of anti-landlord peasant struggles in different parts of the country broke out under the stress of post-war burden of exploitation: tehbhaga in Bengal, bakasht in Bihar, and Warli adivasi in Maharashtra.[26] While the mass movement that had resulted in freedom subsided after 1947, in its place a new movement based on the discontent of the masses was taking shape. The communists seized this discontent and directed it towards the new government.

Commenting on the bitter conflict between nationalism and the imperialist situation, Nehru had written as early as 12 August 1945 to R. Palme Dutt: 'They have become full-blooded supporters of Jinnah's demands (unspecified and vague as they are) and in the name of Congress-League unity they demand a complete surrender by Congress to Jinnah. I have no doubt that they have worsened the communal problem by their attitude. Communists who have joined the League appear to be more rabid Leaguers than others.'[27]

Writing to V.K. Krishna Menon on 2 December 1945, Nehru expressed his disappointment with the communists thus:

It is exceedingly unfortunate that the Communist Party in India has drifted further away from the nationalist movement. Their position today is one of absolute hostility to the Congress and of practical alliance with the Muslim League.... Communists here have become terribly isolated and have developed the complexes and narrowness of outlook and isolationism. They take one wrong step after another in trying to justify themselves.[28]

In an interview with Nehru on 28 June 1945, on the deteriorating relations between Congressmen and communists, Z.A. Ahmed accused the communist-baiters of taking full advantage of Nehru's statements, some of which charge the communists of 'being on the other side'.[29] The Socialist Party of India, particularly Jayaprakash Narayan, had all along accused the communists of being agents of a foreign country branding them undependable and unreliable. Like the socialists, many others too began to view the communists as traitors who had betrayed the country in its hour of need

---

[26] Mohit Sen (ed.), *Documents of the Communist Party of India*, vol. VIII (1951–56) (New Delhi: PPH, 1977), p. 326.

[27] *Selected Works of Jawaharlal Nehru*, vol. 14, p. 526.

[28] Ibid., p. 362.

[29] Ibid., pp. 523–4.

and as people who did not work in the interests of the country but according to the dictates and commands of a foreign power.

However, even their worst detractors could not fault the communists over their efforts to control communal riots and in their steadfast resolve to disallow any split in their ranks on communal grounds. The communists remained consistently anti-communal because they believed that communalism tended to weaken the working class. The few Muslims who had remained in the CPI after partition felt that the CPI was the best placed to defend the just interests of the minorities against communal forces.[30] From supporting the idea of a separate homeland, the CPI executed yet another about-turn in its policy on the Pakistan issue. When partition became a fait accompli and resulted in widespread disorder, mass murder, and acute estrangement between India and Pakistan, the CPI began urging the cessation of strife and emphasizing the need for national unity if the Indian subcontinent was to be preserved from anarchy. From an unabashed advocate, it became critical of Jinnah's intransigent policy while being accommodating towards the Indian government till the end of 1948. It also lashed out at militant Sikhism and the reactionary Hindu Mahasabha which it felt was destroying national cohesion.

There has been a great deal of speculation on the role and reaction of Moscow towards the developments in India. As has been stated in Chapter 5, a thorough study of intelligence reports in the IOR reveals no direct link between the Indian communists and their so-called Russian masters. While the Indian comrades bent over backwards to glorify Russia which they saw as the land of pure applied communism, there appeared nothing to indicate that India scored very high in the Russian scheme of things. S.A. Dange visited Russia in 1946 and reported that there was no likelihood of a new international communist organization being revived. He also admitted that Russian newspapers showed little interest in Indian affairs though TASS in Delhi maintained links with communists such as Rahul Sankratayan in Leningrad. However, a study of the press clippings in Russian press *after partition* reveals that in Moscow there was widespread criticism of *both* the governments in Delhi and Karachi for their 'reactionary' tendencies. There was also a harping on the need to unite both India and Pakistan and the urgent need to destroy communalism if India was to advance politically and

[30] M. Farooqi, *The Communist Party and the Problems of Muslim Minority*, no. 2 (New Delhi: Communist Party Publications, 1969).

economically. In equal measure, critics of Moscow (as gleaned through a reading of the intelligence reports and the British press) accused it of 'communist imperialism', of fomenting trouble in the border areas, and looking for opportunities whereby it could intervene in NWFP and Kashmir. The eagerness to fasten the imperialist boot on British legs was seen by the British as just a masquerade for the Soviets' own interests in the geopolitics of that region. In the immediate aftermath of independence, Nehru was keen to build bridges of friendship with the Soviet Union and was confident that the Soviet policy had changed vis-à-vis India and the new communist dispensation was more favourable to the Indian government.[31]

The CPI held its Second Congress from 28 February to 6 March 1948 in Calcutta. It was attended by 632 delegates representing 89,263 members, showing a growth of membership among the intelligentsia as well as peasants and workers. Delegates also came from Yugoslavia, France, Australia, Burma, and Ceylon. Admitting that it had made some serious mistakes in the past, the Central Committee outlined the agenda for the future which included liquidation of feudal states, nationalization of banks and industry, and setting up of an independent communist party in Pakistan; the last entailed shifting of its Muslim members to Pakistan. Just before the Second Party Congress in Calcutta,[32] the South East Asia Youth Conference was held. According to intelligence reports in the IOR delegates from communist countries carried instructions for the Indian communists. As we shall see in the next section, the Indian communists were receiving directives that resulted in their dramatic volte-face.[33]

---

[31] Letter to K.N. Katju in *Selected Works of Jawaharlal Nehru*, vol. 26 (New Delhi: Oxford University Press, 2000), p. 519.

[32] At the Calcutta Congress Rudovan Zugovic (a representative from Yugoslavia at the Southeast Asian Youth Conference and thought to be a member of Cominform) proposed that the communists would over-run China, and having done that would turn their attention to Burma and India. Zugovic's active presence at both events lent credence to the belief that the mantle of mentorship to the Indian communist had fallen from Britain to Yugoslavia. Incidentally, at the Calcutta Congress, the politburo decided to shift the party headquarter from Bombay to Calcutta and to begin concentrating on white-collar members in its membership drives.

[33] According to reports found in the IOR, Indian communists also received guidelines from *New Times*, a Soviet weekly mainly for foreign consumption, distributed in English to Bombay and other Indian cities by TASS.

From being an enthusiastic supporter of Nehru's government, the CPI overnight began to accuse the government of supporting an Anglo-American bloc. Evidently a scapegoat was needed to justify this about-turn. The moderate P.C. Joshi was replaced by the extremist B.T. Ranadive[34] as general secretary. In tandem, almost as though synchronized, Moscow began to attack Nehru for belonging to the 'anti-progressive camp'.[35] The first clear indication that Moscow had changed its line of benevolent neutrality towards India came in a strong attack on the Indian government. A Moscow newspaper, *Literary Gazette*, carried an article entitled 'Labourite Aggression'.[36] We find a blistering critique of Nehru's foreign policy by A. Dyakov entitled 'Anglo-American Plans in India'.[37] While praising the establishment of communist rule and the 'great historic victory of the Chinese people', Dyakov said that 'The post-war dismemberment of India was a result of a deal between the Indian big bourgeoisie and landowners, and British imperialism.' The revolutionary movement of the Indian masses (referring to the communists) posed a threat, according to Dyakov, not only to British domination in India, but also to class interests of the Indian landowners and capitalists. He went on to criticize Home Minister

---

[34] According to Mahdi, Ranadive attacked Joshi on grounds of 'reformism'; in this he was supported by Sajjad Zaheer. In the course of an interview in Aligarh, Mahdi also told me that Ashraf was asked to set up the Communist Party of Pakistan (CPP), but he refused; Ranadive then decided to send Zaheer to Pakistan. Mahdi also said that as part of the 'Ranadive Line', weekly meetings of the Bombay PWA were disrupted whenever any member showed the slightest sign of 'deviation'. Attacks were orchestrated on K.A. Abbas and Saghar Nizami whenever they strayed from the party line. Also, as Mahdi observed, once writers were 'ordered' to write, some like Ismat and Bedi began to stay away from these meetings. Ismat openly rebelled when she was told to write about peasants and workers. Mahdi, who was active in student mobilization and later in the IPTA (where he dramatized Rashid Jahan's story 'Chor') and attended the many meetings of the Bombay progressives, believed that the PWA was never a movement; it was merely a forum, a platform that allowed the consolidation of a trend, a trend, he stressed, that already existed even before 1936. Mahdi believed that Zaheer suffered 'a loss of credibility' when he was patronized by Ranadive in the post-Joshi period; in contrast Ashraf suffered no such loss and Mahdi described him as a *khara aadmi*.

[35] *Trud*, 20 March 1948.

[36] IOR/L/PJ/12/772.

[37] *Pravda*, 25 November 1949. Found in IOR/L/PJ/12/773, File 683/49.

Patel's acts of clamping down on trade union activities and mass arrests of striking labour, as well as American President Truman's offer of technical aid to India. He ended with accusing the Nehru government of 'making India the Anglo-American gendarme in the East'.

Nehru was at pains to explain through the press that his government's actions were directed against individual communists (those who were planning nation-wide sabotage and arson) and not against communism per se or the CPI: 'I have sympathy for their (the communists') principles but we had to put them down because the communists of India are aiming to create unrest among the people and seize power by creating chaos in the country.'[38]

As the situation steadily worsened and communist strikes brought the country to the brink of a civil war, the clampdown became fiercer, and Nehru's attitude towards the communists too showed a hardening. In a speech in Allahabad, he took the communists to task for repeating old lessons. Saying that the world had changed greatly since Marx (who in any case wrote about conditions in Europe), Nehru repeated a charge that many were levelling against the progressives: 'It is absurd to say that we must blindly accept everything that Marx wrote about economic or political matters ninety years ago.' Going on to accuse the communists of having dogmatic rigid minds, Nehru pointed out how even Russian communists had changed their policies to suit changing circumstances while the Indian comrades were stuck in an old rut. He also questioned the communists' avowed aim to break up everything and rebuild on a clean site: 'How can we plant a garden by first cutting down all the trees?'[39]

Many years later, when the CPI was to take stock, party ideologue G. Adhikari admitted to the serious mistakes of 1942 and the 'wrong attitude' to the national struggle:

Rightist mistakes of the CPI such as support to Pakistan, rigid anti-strike and anti-peasant struggle stand did serious damage to the party by isolating it from the rest of the anti-imperialist elements in the national movement and also split our mass base.... Our attitude of keeping away from the movement was both theoretically and tactically wrong. Was the neutralist and conditional stand of the national leadership pro-fascist and opportunist? Or was it basically anti-fascist and anti-imperialist? ... Our wrong stand vis-a-vis this turn in the national movement arose

[38] The Hindustan Times, 7 April, 1948.
[39] Selected Works of Jawaharlal Nehru, vol. 26, pp. 43–4.

from our dogmatic understanding of proletarian internationalism and sectarian attitude towards the national movement.[40]

To return briefly to the PWA, which was increasingly being seen as an 'important front organisation'[41] of the CPI, we must record here the changes being wrought in its functioning after Ranadive took over as general secretary. The first PWA conference after partition was held from 27 to 30 December 1948 in Lucknow. To make the meeting 'more fruitful', it was decided that party workers who were not writers would also be invited. This meeting coincided with an all-India conference of Indian Muslims organized by Maulana Abul Kalam Azad to take stock of the issues facing the community. As always, the progressives used the existing venue, the Ganga Prasad Memorial Hall, where for three days deliberations were held on a variety of issues and culminated with a mushaira. Maulana Azad had been invited to inaugurate, but since he could not come at the last minute, Dr Syed Mahmud was roped in. Qazi Abdul Ghaffar presided over the open session and spoke on the role of the progressive writer in the context of partition, communal riots, and the new political scenario. Hansraj Rahbar read a paper on Premchand; Ibadat Barelwi on new inclination in modern criticism; Khwaja Ahmad Faruqi on *Ghubar-e-Khatir*; Akhtar Ansari on modern ghazal; and Masud Ali Zauqi on the poetry of Fani. One special session, devoted to language, was presided over by Niyaz Fatehpuri; it had papers by Sajjad Zaheer, Zainul Abedin, Dr Ashraf, Hayatullah Ansari, Firaq Gorakhpuri, Abdul Alim, Ale Ahmad Suroor, Ehtesham Husain, and Hasrat Mohani. The only major administrative decision was to open a branch in Bombay and appoint Sardar Jafri as an honorary general secretary. This conference was largely attended by Urdu writers. The proceedings of this conference and the poetry read during the mushaira were published by Sehba Lukhnowi in a special issue of the journal *Afkar* from Bhopal.

Soon after partition, the biggest issue facing the Urdu progressives was one of language. In April 1949, the UP progressives held a state-level

[40] G. Adhikari, *Communist Party and India's Path to National Regeneration and Socialism (For Members Only)* (New Delhi: Communist Party Publications, June 1964).

[41] Overstreet and Windmiller, *Communism in India*, p. 432. The expression 'cultural front' is used repeatedly in the reports on the activities of the PWA found in the P.C. Joshi Archives.

conference to thrash out this one issue that rose above all else. The language question was now no longer being seen as an academic one, but as part of a sharp class battle.[42] The Urdu progressives who attended this conference were Abdul Alim, Ale Ahmad Suroor, Majrooh Sultanpuri, Sahir Ludhianvi, Mumtaz Husain, and Majaz. The Hindi group was represented by Ram Bilas Sharma, Prakash Chandrgupt, Amrit Rai, Laxman Shastri, Narottam Nagar, etc. The following resolution was passed: 'The UP Progressive Writers' Conference announces that every language has the right to progress freely and without hindrance. It opposes any move to impose a *sarkari* language on the speakers of other languages.'[43]

Apart from language, there was also the issue of Right Reformism; 'A Note on the PWA Fraction' prepared by Comrade Ismail noted: 'The Right Reformist deviation in literature appears in the garb of formalism and a defence of reactionary bourgeois writers. In both forms this deviation hampers the growth of progressive writings. It denies the partisan character of literature and blunts the edge of Marxist criticism.'[44]

Worries among the comrades that the cultural fronts were getting progressively divorced from mass struggles and becoming 'drawing-room coteries' caused the fourth conference of the AIPWA, held from 27 to 29 May 1949, to be organized in Bhiwandi, an industrial hub with a large population of migrant labour from eastern UP.[45] Ismat, as chairperson of

[42] A detailed report on the April 1949 conference is found in File No. 1949/77, P.C. Joshi Archives, JNU. The report presented by Comrade Sinha in the December 1948 conference, dubbed the RB Thesis, came up for discussion; Comrade Ismail criticized the line adopted by Comarde Sinha that 'there can be no proletarian intelligentsia till after the Democratic Revolution'. Amrit Rai pointed out the existence of 'two camps in culture: one bourgeois and decadent, the other democratic and popular', and the UP government's anti-communist committee. Many others began to point to the increasingly 'middle-class nature' of the PWA.

[43] Khalilur Rahman Azmi, *Urdu mein Taraqqui Pasand Adabi Tehreek* (Aligarh: Educational Book House, 2002 [1957]), p. 88.

[44] File No. 1949/76, P.C. Joshi Archives. The report states that the

crisis inside the Party on the cultural front in UP is basically a crisis of petty bourgeois leadership, which refuses to base itself on Marxism, on the working class, on class struggle; which tries to cut itself off from the struggles of the working class and other sections, out of fear of repression and lack of faith in the masses.... All this has to be radically changed.

[45] Detailed report on the conference found in *Golden Jubilee Brochure*, p. 64. Found among the private papers of Ghulam Rabbani Tabban at the NMML.

the reception committee, exhorted writers to thwart the attacks on cultural organizations. Bedi read out messages of solidarity from other countries, including one from the Pakistan PWA. A new executive committee was elected with Ram Bilas Sharma as its general secretary. Sharma, who taught English at the Balwant Rajput College in Agra, was vociferously against the 'corrupting' influence of American and British imperialists. His speeches show the influence of the combative Ranadive and Soviet ideologues of the late 1940s who, similarly, spewed venom against Anglo-American hegemony. Sharma also decried the present trend among Hindi writers to combine Marxism and Freudian philosophy, terming it unscientific. The conference denounced the arrest of several progressives in the popular uprisings in Bengal and Telangana. Deeming the 1936 *Manifesto* inadequate to deal with the changed situation, it announced a new version, one that would better reflect the concerns of a world poised on the brink of a third World War.[46]

All was quiet on the progressive front for the next four years,[47] till the fifth conference of the AIPWA met in Delhi from 6 to 8 March 1953 under the charge of Krishan Chandar who had taken over from Sharma. The manifesto prepared during the previous conference came up for review and, after much discussion, was eventually passed.[48] Krishan Chandar claimed the PWM was a 'revitalising force' in the cultural life of the country and the basic task of the progressives was 'to defend and enrich the national culture by creative writing' while also defending 'our culture from

---

[46] The entire text of the new *Manifesto* is given in Azmi, *Urdu mein Taraqqui Pasand Adabi Tehreek*, pp. 89–95. It was published in *Naya Parcham*, Bombay, June 1949.

[47] Reports in the P.C. Joshi Archives for the years 1950–3 show the in-fighting among the Urdu and Hindi PWA. One sees some attempt at self-analysis and self-criticism for their 'isolation, disorganisation and inactivity', but by and large there is a repetition of the Party line and the increasing presence of comrades who are non-writers at these meetings. There are also constant references to writing in Party-approved papers such as *Hans, Naya Sahitya, Nai Chetana, India Today, Shahira, Alochana, Naya Parcham,* etc.

[48] S.R. Kidwai has made a useful study of the various manifestos of the PWM entitled '*Taraqqui Pasand Tehreek: Manshuron ki Roshni mein*', in Qamar Rais and S. Ashoor Kazmi (eds), *Taraqqui Pasand Adab: Pachas Sala Safar* (Delhi: Naya Safar Publications, 1987).

Indian fundamentalists'.[49] The conference passed a resolution mourning the death of Stalin and marched to the Soviet embassy in New Delhi to pay homage to the departed leader. Krishan Chandar, who had begun to churn out stories at a furious pace, stories that were published in commercial journals like *Shama* or *Beesween Sadi*, no longer had the credibility to head the PWA. The association slowly began to break up into several small, breakaway groups and camps.

Moreover, as Azmi notes in his history of the PWM, many writers were disgusted by the extremism shown by some of the progressives during the 'hardliner' days of the late 1940s. A stylistic change came to be noticed shortly after the 1953 conference. After a long time of writing nazms under the progressives influence, the Urdu poet picked up his pen to once again write the ghazal. The days of nazms such as *Naya Parcham* and *Surkh Savera*, as Azmi points out, seemed to be waning. The advocates and architects of progressivism now began to openly decry sloganeering. In the annual conference of the Aligarh branch of the PWA, Abdul Alim made the following startling declaration: 'Those who turn social or political events into poetry without measuring up to the parameters of literature can become progressives but not good writers.'[50]

This brutal announcement caused many writers to take stock. Those who had written solely in the light of the progressives' beacon suddenly found they were rebels without a cause. Used to the stings and barbs from the non-progressives, this frontal attack from no less a person than Dr Alim caused consternation among the ranks.

Since 1950, the debate between the hardliners and moderates among the PWA on right-wing reforms and left-wing deviations had gathered strength. Writers found themselves grouped in two mutually exclusive categories: progressives and reactionaries. Given the acrimony between the two groups and the hostility to the use of the word progressive, by 1950 suggestions were made to change the name of the PWA to All India Union (or Federation) of Democratic Writers.[51] Meanwhile, a Central Cultural Commission was set up to help the Central Committee of the CPI 'in

---

[49] The text of Krishan Chandar's speech is reproduced in the *Golden Jubilee Brochure*.

[50] The Annual Report of the Aligarh PWA, *Mahaul*, Delhi, nos 13–14; quoted in Azmi, *Urdu mein Taraqqui Pasand Adabi Tehreek*, p. 102.

[51] File No. 1950/279, P.C. Joshi Archives.

guiding the cultural work of the Party'—not at a national level, but by taking into account the specific demands at the provincial level. Comrades were inducted from the various provinces and language groups. Jafri, as convenor, presented a report dated 8 September 1952, which stressed the importance of the party: 'We fail to realize that only the party can lead. It must assert itself. Without it there is no possibility of individual comrades guiding and organizing the work.'[52]

Meanwhile, Sajjad Zaheer was released from Pakistan and returned home in 1955. Some of his old comrades in the PWA and some young Turks urged him to revive the defunct PWA. In March 1956, a gathering of progressive writers was organized in Mau in Azamgarh district; its agenda was to decide whether to keep the PWA alive or not, and if at all it was to be kept afloat should it retain the same name. While much discussion took place, no decision could be reached because not many progressives were present on this occasion. It was, therefore, decided that Ehtesham Husain would be appointed convener of a committee and he would initiate correspondence with all the major writers and come to a decision regarding the fate of the PWA. A circular was passed which, among other things, asked

1. if there is a need for a separate association of Urdu progressive writers and
2. should the name 'Anjuman-e-Taraqqui Pasand Mussanifin' remain, or should it be changed.[53]

Shortly thereafter, the All-India Urdu Conference was held in Hyderabad in May 1956. It was attended by several Urdu progressive writers. Here too, the same questions were raised. Zaheer and Abdul Alim maintained that the 'progressive' view had become so common and wide-based that there was no need for a separate association to 'preach' it. Both maintained that in the changed scenario, literature was faced with other more important issues than ideologically sound literature. New India needed constructive programmes that would gain the approval of the widest possible cross-section of people. Moreover, they stressed, the issue of language had become more important than ever before. Abdul Alim, once the votary of exclusion, now spoke of the need to be inclusive. Harking back to the original *Manifesto*,

---

[52] File No. 1952/22 B, P.C. Joshi Archives.
[53] Azmi, *Urdu mein Taraqqui Pasand Adabi Tehreek*, p. 103.

he reminded his audience how the founders of the PWA had drafted a document that was wide-ranging and all-embracing. Gradually, he rued, the inclusiveness had leached out and the proponents of progressiveness had begun to stick labels of 'progressive' or 'reactionary'. As a result, Alim maintained, membership had shrunk alarmingly, and by 1949 there were so few progressives left that there was no need for a separate association for them. Instead of debating whether to revive and modify the scope of the existing PWA, he felt that the assembled writers should instead form an All-India Association of Urdu Writers. Joining and merging with a larger association would help writers reach larger audiences. 'Reactionarism cannot be faced by staying away; it can only be contested by coming together.' Alim's call for merger was echoed by Zaheer. He confessed that he had initially thought of reviving the PWA, but had changed his mind given the prevailing atmosphere in the country. What the country needed was an association of writers that would strengthen its cultural and literary life. Interestingly enough, Zaheer declared

Our association will not be a political one. Our aims shall be reflected through the medium of literature. Writers may disagree in their opinions and these differences can remain even while being a part of a movement. There is no harm in this as long as the differences are aired in a democratic manner. We must reduce our differences. We must go forward as a group, no matter what name we give our movement.[54]

The last significant achievement of the AIPWA was the Asian Writers' Conference in New Delhi in December 1956 where a large number of delegates arrived from Korea, Mongolia, Nepal, Syria, Pakistan, Indo-China, USSR, Ceylon, and China. Thereafter, several offshoots of the PWA came up from time to time, such as the Urdu Writers' Cooperative Society in Maharashtra in 1960, but their purpose was more to safeguard the livelihood of Urdu writers than to lay down literary, social, or ideological guidelines.

A sixth AIPWA conference was held from 28 December 1966 to 1 January 1967.[55] It had 150 participants representing different languages,

---

[54] Report of the Conference of Progressive Writers, *Saba*, Hyderabad, June–July 1956. Quoted in Azmi, *Urdu mein Taraqqui Pasand Adabi Tehreek*, p. 105.

[55] A detailed report of the conference by Zaheer is found among the Golden Jubilee Brochure in Ghulam Rabbani Tabban Papers, NMML.

a gigantic presidium with exactly a dozen writers as well as foreign delegates from USSR, USA, Mongolia, and Arab League. Interestingly, the very same Jafri who had denounced Bedi and Hyder spoke of the importance of Bedi's Sahitya Akademi award-winning novel *Ek Chadar Maili si* and Qurratulain Hyder's bestselling *Aag ka Dariya*, both of which, in his opinion, were 'outstanding contribution' of progressive writers to Urdu literature! Clearly, the Pompom Darling had become a darling of the progressives.[56] Amrit Rai spoke of the writer's role in society and Hansraj Rahbar, who had recently written a book in Hindi criticizing the PWM, made a hard-hitting speech condemning the progressive leaders for being opportunists.[57] 'He demanded a proletarian, revolutionary literature and had no use for writers who differed from his ideology. Few seemed to agree with him; yet all realized that the main task ahead was to unite, in spite of our differences.'[58] The next few days saw charges and counter charges—both against the movement and individual writers. Zaheer presented a critical review of the movement. More heated discussion yielded yet another version of a manifesto and a new constitution for the AIPWA. Zaheer was once again elected general secretary, and Namwar Singh, Karanjeet Singh, and Taqui Haider as joint secretaries and K. Damodaran as treasurer.

For all the talk of unity and forging ahead, the PWA was lost in the muddy waters of personal rivalries, feuds, and uninspiring leadership. While it never ever regained its lost glory, the PWA continued to exist in some sort of nominal fashion. Yet another AIPWA conference was organized, the seventh so far, in Gaya from 6 to 9 May 1975, but now it

---

[56] It must be stated that Hyder maintained a safe distance from the progressives and justified it thus: 'My concerns were very different from those of the progressives. They were involved in changing and analyzing the present life, the span from one's birth to one's death. My concerns were different. I was interested in life as a whole.' Interview with Noor Zaheer, in Rakhshanda Jalil (ed.), *Qurratulain Hyder and the River of Fire: The Meaning, Scope and Significance of Her Legacy* (Delhi: Aakar, 2010), p. 26.

[57] Rahbar followed this with a book-length critique of the movement entitled *Taraqqui Pasand Adab: Ek Jaiyza* (Delhi: Azad Kitab Ghar, 1967). In a chapter entitled 'Ghalti dar Ghalti' (Mistake upon Mistake), he finds no fault in linking literature with politics; he, however, objected to the manner in which the two were yoked together and the methods employed by the 'opportunists' (p. 169).

[58] *Golden Jubilee Brochure* in Ghulam Rabbani Tabban Papers, NMML, p. 68.

was renamed the 'First Conference of National Federation of Progressive Writers'. A new set of writers had emerged: Bhisham Sahni was elected general secretary and now the focus was on people, culture, and the role of non-commercial magazines in propagating literature. Subsequent conferences, of what was by now being called National Federation of Progressive Writers, met in Jabalpur on 26–28 October 1980 and in Jaipur on 26–27 December 1982, but these were lacklustre events. What is more, these were purely literary gatherings. A PWA still exists. A national conference, held at Begusarai, Bihar, in April 2008 was inaugurated by Habib Tanvir; it was attended by Asghar Ali Engineer, Namwar Singh, and writers from several languages as well as a few foreign delegates. Namwar Singh was elected national president, Kamla Prasad general secretary, and Ali Javed deputy general secretary. The Urdu wing of the PWA held a national conference at Azamgarh in November 2008; Ali Javed currently serves as its general secretary, and also as one of the secretaries of the Afro-Asian Writers Conference, whose 'revival conference' was held in Cairo in December 2012. In April 2012, the 15th national conference of the AIPWA was held in New Delhi and attended by over a thousand delegates.[59]

The PWA in Pakistan

Let us briefly recapitulate that the communists had favoured the separate electorate granted to Muslims in 1909 and the Lucknow Pact agreed to by the Congress and Muslim League in 1916.[60] By the same measure, they had criticized the Nehru Report (presented in 1928) for failing to accommodate what they deemed the 'genuine demands' of Indian Muslims and refuted the 'Congress patriots' who regarded the demand for Pakistan as a blackmailing device of 'reactionary' Muslim leaders to secure greater concessions. As early as 1944, Zaheer, in keeping with the communist line, tried to stress the 'progressive' nature of the Muslim League and made an eloquent plea for Congress–League unity: 'Congressmen generally fail to

---

[59] As revealed by Ali Javed.

[60] For a background to the role of the CPI and the demand for Pakistan, I have relied upon Shri Prakash, 'CPI and the Pakistan Movement', in Bipan Chandra (ed.), *The Indian Left: Critical Appraisals* (New Delhi: Vikas Publishing House, 1983), pp. 215–57.

see the anti-imperialist, liberationist role of the Muslim League, fail to see that the demand for self-determination or Pakistan is a just, progressive and nationalist demand, and is the positive expression of the very freedom and democracy for which Congressmen have striven and undergone so much suffering all these years.'[61]

Zaheer went on to assert that the conception of Indian unity was based on the denial of the fundamental right of self-determination. Right of secession, be it in the case of a separate homeland for the Muslims or the rights of the 17 princely states, he asserted did not mean balkanization: 'Behind that lurid visualization—of the balkanization of India—lurked the imperialist consciousness that India could only be kept together by force.'[62]

At the Calcutta Congress of March 1948, Sajjad Zaheer[63] was entrusted with the onerous task of setting up the Pakistan operation, made more arduous because the bulk of Muslim opinion was against communism for its widely perceived godlessness. It did not help matters that communism was identified with Russia and communists both in India and Pakistan looked towards Russia for guidance. And the Russians had a poor image among some Muslims because the Muslim peoples of Central Asia and the former Turkish empire had suffered grievously at their hands. Zaheer's task in Pakistan was made more uphill by the fact that before Partition, most Muslims who were communists were generally from the educated classes, and being town-bred their experiences were naturally somewhat limited; it had not been so among the communist workers in undivided Punjab who had included a large number of Sikhs and Hindu comrades active in the rural areas. There were some Muslims among the labour class too, but they seemed to be in the party mainly for what they hoped to get through a structured party framework that gave them leverage rather than any faith in the communist credo per se.[64]

---

[61] Sajjad Zaheer, *A Case for Congress-League Unity* (Bombay: PPH, 1973), p. i.

[62] Ibid., p. 12.

[63] Intelligence reports found in the IOR show that Zaheer was already in Lahore on 22 February 1948 to set up the party office, *before* the Calcutta Congress.

[64] Ibid.

The communist party office in Lahore had always been situated in the Lady Fazl-i Husain Building on McLeod Road.[65] Some six weeks before Partition, Teja Singh Suthanthar—helped by Fazl-i Ilahi Qurban[66] and his group—rented a house on Montgomery Road and established a Pakistan Communist Party. The venture, however, was disowned by the CPI and the formal establishment of the CPP is understood to be under the stewardship of Sajjad Zaheer in February 1948. Firozuddin Mansur, Muhammad Husain Ata, and Abdulla Malik were important communists active in the Punjab at the time. The party office was continued, after the Hindus and Sikhs had left, by Eric Citrine,[67] a retired Christian teacher from Peshawar. An office of the PPH[68] had been established in Lahore by 1946. Run by

[65] I found a delightful reference to Pakistani historian K.K. Aziz's *The Coffee House of Lahore: A Memoir, 1942–57* in a blog run by the indefatigable Raza Rumi. Aziz's book, published in 2008 shortly before his death, makes the link between the 'coffee house culture' and leftism in Lahore. Situated on the Mall Road, the Coffee House entertained more leftists than at the Communist Party office on McLeod Road. The leftist visitors here included luminaries such as Sajjad Zaheer, Sibte Hassan, Abdulla Malik, Safdar Mir, Zaheer Kashmiri, and many others. The Coffee House changed many sites, but remained at the Alfred Building till the end. It was 'for over 30 years, the single most important and influential mental powerhouse which moulded the lives and minds of a whole generation, and its legacy affected the careers of the succeeding generation.' Its old site, off Mall Road, was later the location for Pak Tea House, which survived until the turn of the last century.

[66] Fazl-i Ilahi Qurban was among those muhajirin who were picked up for training and indoctrination. He was arrested in the Peshawar Conspiracy Case in 1924 and sentenced to three years' imprisonment. The only one among the Muhajir recruits who continued to be active till the 1950s, he was one of the leading lights of the CPP.

[67] Eric Citrine (in some places mentioned as Cyprian) and Muhammad Husain Ata attended the Calcutta Congress in 1948.

[68] A variety of communistic literature was published by the PPH in Lahore. It was printed at Talimi Press, Cooperative Capital Press, and the Gilani Press. These were usually cheap reprints of texts published by Lawrence & Wishart, Faber & Faber, or the Communist Party Bookshop, London. Some books were also published by the Progressive Publishers Club, 114 McLeod Road, Lahore. Communistic literature from Bombay, Calcutta, and the USSR found its way through different routes; popular among these were *People's Age, Nai Zindagi,*

Abdul Rauf, brother of Abdulla Malik,[69] it had functioned as a sister concern of the Bombay branch. Representatives of the PPH, Bombay, visited Karachi in March 1949. They met the manager of Paramount Bookstall (the principal retailer of communistic literature in Karachi) and promised greatly accelerated delivery of such literature, especially *New Times* (from Moscow), which they promised to supply free except for freight charges from Bombay to Karachi.[70]

As early as 1948, the Karachi communists had been finding it heavy going since the arrest of J. Bokhari—a CPI veteran from the Bombay days—for fomenting labour trouble. While cosmopolitan Karachi proved inhospitable for organized communism to take root, the CPP could claim some support among the Muslim labour in the Port Trust, Tramways, and Electricity Corporation. There was no organizational branch of the CPP in NWFP because of the strong presence of Islam. In West Pakistan, activities of the CPP were largely confined to Lahore, Rawalpindi, and Sialkot, the latter with its substantial cottage industry of sports goods and manufacture of medical instruments had a large population of semi-skilled workers.[71] An active communist party flourished in East Pakistan which had a sizeable population of Hindu intelligentsia and a long tradition of anti-government agitation. Were it not for the overwhelming presence of religion, both East and West Pakistan abounded with excellent material for communist agitation: agrarian unrest, antiquated landowning systems, masses of refugees, spiralling unemployment, squalid rehabilitation camps.

Opposition to the communist movement was present from the Pakistani government virtually from the start, as well as from rival political

---

Ilm-o-Danish, and Rajani Palme Dutt's *Labour Monthly*. Detailed information on the PPH was found in a letter from the Office of the High Commission, Lahore, dated 7 January 1949. IOR/L/PJ/12/773.

[69] Before Partition, Abdulla Malik had tried to seek permission under the Press Registration Act to start a women's journal, but permission had been denied. After Partition, he started a communist newspaper called *Naya Zamana*.

[70] Freight charges were 1.5 annas per copy; it was retailed for 8 annas. In consultation with the Bombay group, it was decided to open two more branches of its Pakistani distribution agency—National Book Agency (which already had one branch in Lahore)—in Dhaka and Chittagong.

[71] According to intelligence reports in the IOR, the strength of the members in all of Punjab was no more than 150–200.

parties, religious leaders, and a feudal system which held large parts of the country in its thrall. Also, since there was limited industry in Pakistan, there were no large hubs of industrial labour that the communists could adopt. There was, however, the Punjab Railway Men's Union which had had a long history of executing lightning-swift strikes. In the absence of a clearly marked-out terrain, the Pakistani arm of the communist party looked towards India and Moscow for guidance. A 13-page article by M. Alekseev entitled 'The Indian Union and Pakistan since the Partition of India'[72] was taken to be a directive from Moscow for future political campaigns in the two newly established countries. Bitterly critical of the Mountbatten Plan (published on 3 June 1947), Alekseev maintained that partition according to religious-communal considerations disregarded the national composition of the population, economic connections, and even territorial integrity. Deeming the new dominions as highly artificial state formations, he accused the Indian leaders of striking a compromise with the British Labour government. Banking being a powerful instrument of colonial exploitation, the article attempted to establish how both India and Pakistan were no better than colonies, how the 'meagre' land reforms had brought about no change in the lot of the peasants, and how landlords and usurers continued to exploit peasants. This article was almost in the nature of a directive to the communist parties in India and Pakistan telling them what was important and what they must strive to achieve. The importance given to Kashmir and the NWFP was marked.

In February 1948, the newly established CPP set about making certain demands of the government: a truly democratic constitution, nationalization of key industries, and the repeal of all repressive laws. It also offered a proposal for the reorganization, on a linguistic basis, of the federating units of the constitution, each of which should have the right of self-determination. While the CPP tried to woo the Muslim League by using its old rhetoric of self-determination, the powerful League was in no mood to tolerate the pesky communist presence. Antagonism flared between the two, especially in Punjab where the major communistic efforts were directed. Punjab became the hunting ground of the communists in Pakistan because of the large numbers of intellectuals, students, teachers, and writers in Lahore, as well as the industrial proletariat in Lahore's factories and railway workshops. The CPP also tried to take advantage of

---

[72] *Bolshevik*, no. 11 (15 June 1948). Found in IOR/L/PJ/12/773.

the lack of cohesion in Punjab politics, especially the rivalry between the Muslim League and the Unionist Muslims.

Mian Iftikharuddin (1907–1962), scion of a wealthy landed family of the Punjab and president of the Provincial Muslim League, was known to Sajjad Zaheer from their days in England and January 1936 when Zaheer had toured the Punjab. While Iftikharuddin did not associate openly with the communists, he was known to be a 'fellow traveller'. He had been the president of the Punjab chapter of the Congress party till he jumped ship and joined the League in 1946. Shortly after Zaheer's arrival, he set up the *Pakistan Times* as a counterbalance to the only other popular English-language newspaper, the *Dawn*, from Karachi, which was not only centrist, but also a mouthpiece of the League. With Faiz at its helm, the *Pakistan Times* routinely drew attention to matters close to the communist heart: land reform, abolition of zamindari, etc. *Imroze*, its sister publication, was a successful attempt at raising the technical level of a vernacular newspaper; it too held the USSR in high esteem.[73]

A study of the intelligence files in the IOR shows that while British intelligence could not do enough to stress the danger of communism to India and was forever prodding the Government of India to increase her caution against the red menace, it did not feel the same level of threat perception in Pakistan. An intelligence report which establishes, for instance, a connection between PPH in Bombay and communist publishing houses in London and Moscow is not able to produce similar evidence to establish a connection between Lahore and London or Moscow. The file notes: 'The Pakistan Communist Party having only a shadowy and nominal existence counts for little or nothing in the eyes of the British communists.'[74]

The Lahore branch of the PWA had been active since the 1930s. After Partition, it came under the charge of Abdulla Malik who held weekly meetings where papers were read and new work shared. It had 60–70 members of whom a handful were members of the communist party. A new cell of the PWA was started in Okara. The first All-Pakistan Congress of Progressive Writers was organized in Lahore from 11 to 13 November

---

[73] Interestingly, though, while we find several references to the popularity of communistic literature either produced in Russia or sponsored by the Soviets, when the distributors of Soviet films tried to screen two very successful Russian films, they met with no success in Lahore

[74] IOR/L/PJ/12/772, p. 111.

1949.[75] It was presided over by Faiz in his capacity as acting president of the Pakistan Trades Union Federation, and attended by delegates from Peshawar, Karachi, Multan, and other cities. Weeks before the conference, a campaign was launched by Agha Shorish Kashmiri, editor of the weekly *Chattan* and the daily *Ehsan*, denouncing the progressives for being against Islam and enemies of Pakistan. Encouraged by their editorials, some maulvis began to issue fatwas denouncing the progressives as kafirs. Preparations were in place to disrupt the proceedings by unruly demonstrations. However, the presence of Ahmad Nadeem Qasmi[76] and Faiz, both enormously popular writers in the traditional mould, ensured the involvement of a cross-section of writers and thinkers who were drawn possibly not so much for ideological reasons as their intellectual and emotional sympathy for social and economic justice.

While ostensibly a literary gathering, an openly communist note was struck from the first day of the Congress. Revolutionary messages from the Punjab committee of the CPP were read as was a message from Sajjad Zaheer who was then in hiding due to a warrant of arrest. The Soviet Union sent four delegates—two Russians and two from the Muslim areas of Central Asia. The conference hall was decorated with large portraits of Maxim Gorky, Paul Robeson, Howard Fast, Vladimir Mayakovsky, and the missing-in-action Zaheer. Abdulla Malik presented a manifesto which contained a detailed analysis of contemporary literary trends in Pakistan and how, given the exigencies of the times, the writers could not afford to be neutral to the revolutionary struggle that was evident all around them in their own milieu as well as in newly emerging nations all across the globe.[77] The manifesto pledged its members against war and condemned the Marshall Plan[78] and the Atlantic Pact.[79] Speaker after speaker spoke

---

[75] This delegation of Soviet writers on its way to Lahore was denied Indian entry visa to attend the All-India Conference of Partisans of Peace in Calcutta on 24 November 1949.

[76] Qasmi has provided a revealing account of his transformation from a young man born into a deeply religious family to a devout Marxist in a long essay entitled 'Tamhid' in *Jalal-o-Jamal* (Lahore: Naya Adara, 1946), pp. 1–40.

[77] For details see Malik, 'Marxist Literary Movement in India and Pakistan', pp. 661–2.

[78] From 1947–51, the Marshall Plan offered American aid to the European nations affected by the war.

[79] Following from the Marshall Plan, the Atlantic plan (NATO) was a military alliance among America and European countries signed on 4 April 1949.

about the wave of awareness that had risen in the countries of Asia, Africa, and Latin America (countries that would shortly be termed the developing world) in the wake of the Second World War. Attention was also drawn to the successful people's revolution in China and the rising tide of public opinion in Indonesia, Malaya, Vietnam, and Burma as well as the unrest among the Arab countries of West Asia against British domination. A resolution was passed against right-wing 'deviationists' who included many former progressive stalwarts such as Ahmed Ali, Akhtar Husain Raipuri, Mumtaz Shirin, Manto, as well as those the Indian progressives had been increasingly reviling such as N.M. Rashid, Shafiqur Rahman, Qurratulain Hyder, M.D. Taseer, and Muhammad Hasan Askari.

In passing such a sweeping resolution condemning a large chunk of the country's most influential writers and critics as 'bourgeois' and going so far as urging the editors of progressive literary magazines not to publish their work, the Pakistani progressives perhaps painted themselves in a box.[80] They not only made some powerful enemies, but also alienated a large group of those budding writers who, while attracted by the principles of socially engaged literature, were not willing to accept Marxism–Leninism as the bedrock of their literary ideology.[81] The breakaway faction, already labelled deviationist, led by Askari and Manto joined the Halqa which welcomed them with open arms. And it was here where they exercised considerable influence in shaping a new literary sensibility. A much-depleted stock rallied around Qasmi and Faiz, the only upholders of the faith who now devoted their attentions to the openly progressive journal called *Savera* (Morning) which soon became a semi-official organ of the Pakistani progressives.[82]

[80] In retaliation of the resolution to 'boycott' government publications, M.D. Taseer launched a tirade against the progressives; see Atiq Ahmad, '*Taraqqui Pasand Tehreek aur Karachi*', in Qamar Rais and S. Ashoor Kazmi (eds), *Taraqqui Pasand Adab: Pachas Sala Safar* (Delhi: Naya Safar Publications, 1987), pp. 317–18.

[81] Hafeez Malik points out that for many writers there was also the financial reason of earning a living and those, freshly transplanted from India, were looking to the government for jobs in radio, publishing, teaching, or the various newly set-up public relations departments. Such writers were not willing to make the enormous sacrifices that a fully fledged progressive writer was required to make in Pakistan. Atiq Ahmad makes the same point in '*Taraqqui Pasand Tehreek aur Karachi*', p. 308.

[82] M.U. Memon looks at several issues of *Savera* to study the rise and fall of progressivism in Pakistan; see 'Partition Literature: A Study of Intizar Husain', *Modern Asian Studies*, vol. 14, no. 3 (1980), pp. 377–410.

To return to the Lahore conference, let us look briefly at some of the resolutions passed on the last day of the meeting which carried the seeds of not merely their isolation from other literary associations in Pakistan, but also their confrontation with the government which would, in a few short years, lead to the demise of organized progressivism in Pakistan. Some of these resolutions were:

1. Condemnation of the Provincial Government's Public Safety Act and the Public Safety Ordinance of the Government of Pakistan.[83]
2. Condemnation of PEN International[84] as a 'reactionary' writers' organization.
3. Support to writers in the provincial dialects.
4. Official recognition of the People's Republic of China.
5. Declaration to take active part in the international struggle for peace.
6. Withdrawal of arrest warrant for Zaheer.
7. Disapproval of the Pakistan Newspaper Editors' Conference's condemnation of only those parts of the Pakistan Safety Ordinance which applied to newspapers.
8. Moral support to the staff of *Sindh Observer* who were battling their management.
9. Appreciation of the efforts of the Indian PWA and condemnation of the terror tactics adopted by the Nehru–Patel government.
10. Condemnation of repressive policies of capitalist countries against their progressive writers.
11. Recommendation to bring literature in the closest possible contact with the people.

Later, Abdulla Malik published a report on the conference with a Foreword by Ahmad Nadeem Qasmi, the general secretary of the Pakistan

---

[83] These draconian laws were also bitterly criticized by Faiz in an editorial entitled 'Murdering Freedom' in *The Pakistan Times*, 11 October 1949; see Sheema Majeed (ed.), *Coming Back Home: Selected Articles, Editorials and Interviews of Faiz Ahmed Faiz* (Karachi: Oxford University Press, 2008).

[84] As we had noted in Chapter 6, Zaheer had invited Ould Herman, secretary of PEN International as a guest speaker during the halcyon days of the PWA in Bombay.

PWA, entitled *Mustaqbil Hamara Hai* (The Future Is Ours).[85] Expressing his anguish at the mud-slinging indulged in by the reactionaries, Qasmi wrote that the purpose of holding the conference had been to bring literature close to the people—those who were in the clutches of the factory owner and the landlords—and include them in the activities of the literati. However, the tone and tenor of the 11-point manifesto was such that it alienated more people than it attracted. Moreover, Zaheer's ignorance and inexperience in building a party from scratch—that too in such a hostile terrain—proved to be the undoing of both the PWA and the CPP. Had the militancy been less pronounced, had the progressives decided to take everyone along instead of alienating influential writers, had they exercised moderation and not indulged in blatant name-calling (*dhandhorchi adeeb* or drum-beating writers being the politer terms of reference used by the progressives against those they disapproved of); in short, had they been less confrontationist, the literary history of Pakistan might have been different. On the other hand, the PWA did not survive much longer in India either where there was lesser overt repression. Perhaps the time for openly, aggressively, nakedly purposive literature was over. Perhaps, people in both Pakistan and India wanted a literature that was less intertwined with political ideology.

The Lahore press, already humming with fatwas and editorials in the weeks leading up to the Congress, was quick to condemn the resolutions. Raising the cry of 'Islam in Danger', a series of articles began to appear in the months following the November Congress in the vernacular press that the speakers had proclaimed superiority of communism over Islamic doctrines. Widespread indignation culminated in the passage of resolutions condemning communist activity in over 40 mosques in Lahore on the Friday following May Day.[86] This demonstration of the ease with

---

[85] I am grateful to Asif Noorani, a senior journalist from Karachi, who sent me copies of Abdulla Malik's *Mustaqbil Hamara Hai* (Lahore: Al-Jadid, 1950). Asif saheb scanned pages upon pages from the book and emailed them to me as a chain of attachments; at my end I took printouts and am now the proud owner of an entire copy of a book I could never have accessed without the kindness and ingenuity of friends. This section on the Lahore PWA's conference is built largely from Abdulla Malik's reportage and supplemented from reports in the IOR. Some material has been gleaned from Hafeez Malik's article and has been duly acknowledged.

[86] Details of the outcry found in a dispatch from the Office of the High Commissioner, Karachi dated 3 June 1949. IOR/L/PJ/12/773.

which the Pakistani public could be rallied to the defence of Islam against (perceived) attacks by communists was not likely to have been lost to the Pakistani authorities. This perhaps explains why the government was able to get away with its grossly unlawful actions in the Rawalpindi Conspiracy Case.

On 9 March 1951, on the eve of the first election to the provincial assembly in the Punjab on the basis of adult suffrage, Liaqat Ali Khan, who was both the prime minister and defence minister of Pakistan, made the following startling announcements on the floor of Parliament regarding a conspiracy that had been unearthed a few days ago:

The conspirators seemed convinced that there was no possibility of achieving their objective through popular support or by the use of democratic or constitutional means. They planned, therefore, to resort to force with the support of the armed forces. The plan envisaged the removal of high military officers and civilians, and the seizure of effective power. The country was to be brought under a military dictatorship, when existing authorities, both civil and military, had been eliminated. The Government was thereafter to be patterned on the communist model but under military domination. For this purpose, economic and constitution-making missions were to be invited from a certain foreign country.[87]

The disclosure left almost as much unsaid as it revealed, though the involvement of the CPP seemed evident in the arrest of Faiz and Zaheer, two leading left intellectuals. It seemed so incredible that not only the opposition press in Pakistan but the sober British newspapers also expressed doubts and misgivings. The *Manchester Guardian* of 10 March 1951, normally charitable in judging the policies and actions of the Pakistan government, found the news 'very puzzling' and added that the arrests constituted 'a melodrama of a kind new to Pakistan politics'. 'The coming bitter elections,' its correspondent went on to observe, 'may supply an answer'.[88]

American journalist, Andrew Roth, writing in the *Sunday Observer* of 11 March 1951 made a similar observation: 'It is noteworthy that announcement of the plot came on the day before the beginning of the

---

[87] IOR/L/PJ/12/614.

[88] Ibid. The *Manchester Guardian* also carried a letter by the lawyer Michael Foot who wrote to mobilize support for the accused. Munibur Rahman told me how Foot had visited India during the Telangana movement and was willing to take on the job of defending the Rawalpindi accused.

Punjab elections—the first open electoral contests in Pakistan.' Altogether 16 people were arrested including Sajjad Zaheer who was picked up shortly after the first high level army officers had been arrested.[89] Those arrested were neither allowed to contact their families nor make efforts for their own defence. Instead, the government—everyone from the prime minister of Pakistan to the government spokesperson—did everything to prejudice the public mind by making wild and sensational charges without producing a shred of evidence to substantiate their case. The Pakistani government seemed determined to set aside all legal safeguards to which everyone is entitled as it built a case whereby Faiz was said to have invited Zaheer to Rawalpindi to meet some disaffected army officers with the intention of toppling the civilian government. Apparently, the group had, indeed, met in Rawalpindi and decided against taking any action whatsoever as the time, they believed, was not ripe for any action. However, since the 'conspiracy' was unearthed, a 'case' was suitably built and facts were stretched.

On 13 April 1951, the government introduced a bill in the constituent assembly—reminiscent of medieval measures of repression, oppression, and persecution—to set up a special tribunal empowered to try the case in camera. In justifying such legislation, the prime minister once again invoked national security and stressed the need for secrecy in view of the nature of the conspiracy. Several speakers spoke out in favour of a public trial which they felt would strengthen Pakistan's stability. Mian Iftikharuddin, one-time president of the Punjab Muslim League and now heading the Azad Pakistan Party, urged the government to consider an open trial as that would strengthen the hands of the authorities, but the suggestion was rejected by the prime minister. The travesty of a trial commenced on 15 June 1951, where the evidence was not even recorded, only a memorandum of the substance of evidence was produced. Requests of counsel for adjournments were refused.

The case raised vital issues of interest to everyone interested in the preservation of elementary human and civil rights. According to the Universal Declaration of Human Rights by the United Nations Organisation, in the

---

[89] BBC journalist Wiqar Ahmad told me in the course of a rambling chat in his home in Harrow, England, how Zaheer narrated the events leading up to the Conspiracy Case to him. According to Wiqar Ahmad, Zaheer was thoroughly 'fed up' of a life on the run from Pakistani authorities and by March 1951 he was simply 'waiting' to be arrested.

drafting of which the Pakistan representative took an active part, 'Everyone is entitled to full equality to a fair and public hearing by an independent and impartial tribunal to the determination of his rights and obligations and of any criminal charge against him.' The manner in which the accused of the Rawalpindi Conspiracy Case were tried represented a clear and flagrant violation of this right.

Calling it a test case of international importance, Munibur Rahman, secretary of South-East Asia Committee who drafted an appeal and launched a signature campaign to raise awareness about the trial, prophesied (unwittingly) the future of trials in Pakistan:

If the Pakistan authorities are able to work their will in this case, then the cause of civil rights and democratic liberties will have suffered a major setback. For it will encourage reactionary governments everywhere to order the arrest of innocent people on vague and fictitious charges of conspiracy, to withhold all evidence from the public by trying people in secret by means of special courts whose verdict is not subject to appeal, and thus bypass the normal process of legal trial.[90]

Munibur Rahman made a passionate appeal to all men and women of goodwill everywhere, whatever their political views, on behalf of the 16 people—men who faced death—to sign the appeal appended at the back of the pamphlet and send it directly either to the prime minister of Pakistan or to the committee's office in London.

On 5 January 1953, almost two years after the arrests and after a protracted trial, 14 of the 16 accused in the Rawalpindi Conspiracy Case were convicted and sentenced. D.N. Pritt, King's counsel, called the trial 'both a tragedy and a scandal' and went on to make a scathing denouement of this travesty of justice: 'To this point has secrecy brought us that we cannot even be sure who is being tried.'[91] The cloak of secrecy parted to reveal the names of those under trial: Faiz Ahmed Faiz; Major-General Akbar Khan, chief of general staff, and his wife; Brigadier M.A. Latif, brigade commander, Quetta; Air Commodore A.K. Janjua; Lieutenant-Colonel Niaz Muhammad Arbab; Captain Zafarullah Poshni; Lieutenant-Colonel Ziauddin; Major Hasan Khan; Major Ishaq Muhammad; Captain Khizr

---

[90] *The Pakistan Trial*, South East Asia Committee Paper No. 1, published by South-East Asia Committee, 1 Hampstead Hill Gardens, London NW3, price 2 pence.

[91] *Manchester Guardian*, 23 July 1951.

Hayat; Brigadier Siddiq Khan; Sajjad Zaheer, secretary of the Pakistan Communist Party; Muhammad Husain Ata; Lieutenant-Colonel Mohiuddin Siddiq Raza; and Major Khwaja Muhammad Eusoph Sethi. The last two turned approvers and were granted pardon.

Behind the massive walls of the jail at Hyderabad (Sindh) in a specially air-conditioned room, these people were put on trial on the flimsiest of evidence. Had its details become public, it could have become as famous as the Reichstag Fire Trial. Unlike the trial of Dimitrov and others that was held in full public view and the international press had full access to its hearings and was in no small measure instrumental in rousing world opinion which exercised a restraining influence on the Nazis, the Pakistan government was extending no such courtesies to the world at large and none whatsoever to the accused. By a law, passed retrospectively, it set up a special tribunal denying the accused the right to trial by jury and the right to appeal; it also enforced the most exceptional measures of secrecy denying both the public and the press access to the trial. Also, according to the new law, 'any person in possession of documents of information or information by virtue of his participation in the proceedings of the said case, shall not disclose them to a person not officially connected with its preparation ... and a breach of these provisions is punishable under the Official Secrets Act'. Even the counsels had to take permission from the tribunal and were subject to the said act. Even in Pakistan, where the laws were never lenient nor the normal processes anything but opaque, this iron curtain of secrecy was excessive, to say the least. By its sheer excessiveness, it choked the life out of the fledgling communist movement in Pakistan and deterred any substantial people's movement ever to see the light of day.[92]

While the accused in the Rawalpindi Conspiracy Case were spending their days in solitary confinement,[93] a second conference of the All-Pakistan

---

[92] The Pakistani communists regrouped themselves and set up the APP in 1954 with Mian Iftikharuddin as its head, but they were never able to establish a national presence. In 1957, the banned CPP got together with other left-leaning parties and merged the APP to form a larger body called National Awami Party. In East Pakistan, the banned CPP worked with the Awami League and the Ganatantri Dal to form a United Front which was, relatively speaking, more successful. In 1958, the Kul Pakistan Kisan Association was formed.

[93] I had the occasion to meet Zafarullah Poshni in Karachi and talk about his days spent in the company of Faiz, Zaheer and the other accused while they served the jail term. Poshni presented me a copy of his book which gives a detailed

PWA took place. Held in the Sir Abdullah Haroon Muslim Gymkhana, Karachi, on 12–13 July 1952, it was a tame affair.[94] The government had pulled the wind out of the leftists' sail after the Lahore conference followed by the blatant violation of human rights in the Rawalpindi Conspiracy Case. The fissures within the movement itself had grown into chasms. A sizeable section of the country's intelligentsia had been alienated by the 'exclusive' nature of the manifesto adopted in Lahore. To make matters worse, the already-truncated PWA found itself a house divided as differences emerged between Faiz and Qasmi. The narrow interpretation of progressivism adopted by Qasmi led to some short-sightedness. In later years, Faiz acknowledged the error in excluding writers like Manto, N.M. Rashid, and Qurratulain Hyder (then living in Pakistan).[95] N.M. Rashid himself, while crediting the progressives with fostering a much-needed sense of social awareness among Indian writers was critical of the stronghold of ideology that imposed restrictions upon creativity.[96]

---

account of the so-called conspiracy and the flimsy nature of the charges against him; for details, see Poshni, *Zindagi Zindan Dilli ka Naam Hai: Rawalpindi Muqadama Sazish ke Aseeron ki Sarguzasht-e-Aseeri* (Life Is the Name of Surviving Prison: A Memoir of the Prisoners in the Rawalpindi Conspiracy Case), 4th ed. (Karachi: Fazli Sons Pvt. Ltd, 2001).

[94] Atiq Ahmad gives a detailed account of this conference as well as a lively portrait of the Karachi progressives and the Café George in the Sadar Bazar area which was a haunt of middle-class Karachi intellectuals. Progressives such as Mujtaba Husain, Riaz Rufi, and Ahmad Husain set up the Sindh branch of the Anjuman in April–May 1948 by holding its first and second meetings in the flat of Shahab Ansari. The third, and bigger, meeting held in Burns Garden was attended by Jamiluddin Aali, Shanul Haq Haqqi, Salim Ahmad, Arif Jalali, Aziz Asri, and others. After the next meeting, this venue too was unavailable: the CID had ordered the manager to discontinue these gatherings. With the efforts of Comrade Ashraf and his brother, who was active with the dockworkers' union, a tiny office was found in Muhammadi Building on Bund Road. A CID man, dressed as a *malang*, was parked in the small shrine across the road keeping an eye on the goings on. An informer, Haji Abdul Ghaffar, posing as a regular attendee, faithfully 'reported' the weekly (Sunday) meetings from 1948–54. I am grateful to Kamran Asdar who showed me Burns Garden and the area around Muhammadi Building during my visit to Karachi. Café George has since closed.

[95] Interview with Muzaffar Iqbal in Majeed, *Coming Back Home*, p. 98.

[96] Interview, *Mahfil*, vol. 7, nos 1–2 (Spring–Summer 1971), Asian Studies Center, Michigan State University, East Lansing, Michigan, p. 7.

In the opening session held on 12 July 1952, Maulvi Abdul Haq, who had migrated to Karachi to set up the Pakistan wing of the Anjuman-e Taraqqui-i-Urdu, presided as Qasmi, in his capacity as general secretary of the Pakistan PWA, read a report on the activities of the PWA in the past two years. Acknowledging the association's mistakes, he admitted that the 1949 manifesto was wrong in its resolve to boycott individuals and organizations. He also read out a milder, toned-down version of the new manifesto which urged the government to remove the 'political label' from the PWA. The Anjuman-e-Taraqqui Pasand Mussanifin (or PWA) resolved, henceforth, to be a purely literary association having no truck whatsoever with any political party. The second day's session, chaired by Maulana Abdul Majeed Salik, stressed the writers' role in society and their responsibility in maintaining world peace. As always, the proceedings wound down with a mushaira in the evening. But this mushaira was presided over by Pir Hisamuddin. Evidently, the message blowing in the wind was reconciliation, moderation, low-key, and purely literary confabulations.

The CPP was declared illegal in July 1954; the Pakistan PWA existed, but it was a harassed, harried lot forever looking over its shoulder anxious for any crumbs of largesse provided by the government.[97] In the few short years of its official existence, the CPP set up offices in Gujranwala, Lyalpur, Rawalpindi, Peshawar, Karachi, Sikkur, Hyderabad, Multan, and Rahim Yar Khan.[98] Sajjad Zaheer was allowed to return to India after his release in 1955, upon an order of the Lahore high court, after serving four years in prison. Faiz too emerged from jail in 1955, but as the saying goes '*Chhute aseer to badla hua zamana tha*' (the captives emerged from prison but found themselves in a changed world). The Progressive Papers Ltd, that had once employed Faiz and scores of the country's bright young left-leaning intellectuals, was accused of collaborating with a foreign power and its assets forcibly auctioned off. In one fell stroke, the Ayub government dealt a

---

[97] Successive left-wing revolutionary poets from Faiz, Faraz, Fahmida Riaz, Kishwar Naheed, and others accepted government positions and occupied high offices in literary and cultural establishments set up by the very government that broke the back of the fledgling communist movement in Pakistan.

[98] Sibte Hasan provides a detailed account of the CPP under Zaheer's charge in *Mughanni-e Aatish Nafas, Sajjad Zaheer* (Karachi: Maktaba Daniyal, 2008). I am grateful to Asif Noorani for sending a copy of this book to me by post.

bodily blow to the last haven of progressive writers and editors as well as the Pakistan PWA and the fledgling communist movement.

The Rise and Fall of the PWA in India

Reasons for Success

Before we proceed to look at the reasons for the decline of the PWM, it might be instructive to go over, once again, the reasons for its success. Why did the PWA win the allegiance of so many so quickly? How did established veterans like Premchand, Maulvi Abdul Haq, and Hasrat Mohani, all in the autumn of their lives, take to the ideas of the Young Turks? How did the progressives manage to get a patient hearing from men like Iqbal and Tagore, who, unfortunately, both died before they could actively help the movement? It might, perhaps, have been because no one, really, could find fault with the progressives' avowed intention of harnessing literature to social and political change. In their own way, after all, writers as diverse as Premchand and Iqbal were already doing precisely that when the progressives burst upon the scene. Even before them, the didactic element had never been absent in Indian literature and the Indian reader was perfectly accustomed to being told in unceremonious terms all that was wrong in society and all that must be done, individually and collectively, to bring about change. By the 1920s, this didactic and hectoring streak had taken the form of an open espousal of social reform and revolt against imperialism. Literature, the progressives stressed, must serve the cause of the people and the biggest cause at that time was the liberation struggle of the Indian people. An argument such as this drew everyone who regarded themselves as patriotic. So whether it was political leaders like Sarojini Naidu, Nehru, or Azad who were known to take interest in cultural and literary matters or Congress socialist leaders like JP—everyone who believed in the cause of freedom lent their support to the movement.

As we have seen in the first two chapters, the writers just before the progressives stoked the fires that had been lit over a hundred years ago and harnessed the burst of political consciousness. Far from being escapist or moribund, as the progressives declared in their original manifesto, Indian literature just before the formation of the PWA was bursting with new ideas, forms, styles, and genres. Yet, few questioned the sweeping generalizations and mistaken assumptions of the hot-headed young men who had drafted the manifesto of the AIPWAs. Most, instead, were willing to jump to the rescue; the rescue of a literature that the progressives believed had degenerated in the hands of priestly, academic, and decadent classes. Strictly speaking it was not so. Urdu literature, just before the advent of the progressive episode, was infused with fresh ideas from a young breed of journalists, politicians, editors, and professional writers who were none of the above. Possibly, all those who offered instant loyalty to the progressive cause were touched by one singular quality about this new movement: its aim to do everything possible to lead the country to a 'new life', one that would be free of the problems of hunger and poverty, social backwardness and political subjugation.[99]

The progressives' repeated assertions of dealing with 'the problems of today' was possibly its single-most rousing, most instantly attractive quality for even the most cynical, weary, and blasé among Indian writers and critics who could not turn their face away from the shining optimism of the progressives. Moreover, there was the example of Soviet Russia held out by the progressives as a system that worked, and worked, moreover, in favour of the poor and the oppressed. An unexpected bonus came from the official hysteria about Soviet Russia and communism in the British Indian administration. Communism, and by extension the progressives who, in popular perception, were *all* left-leaning, got some unearned prestige among fellow Indians for being opposed to British rule. Indian progressives made full use of their 'martyrdom' and while none of them (save Zaheer who was an office holder in the Central Committee of the CPI from 1942) exerted a very direct or powerful influence on the party or its policies, nevertheless played an important role in swinging the Indian intelligentsia's outlook towards the left.

Another reason for the initial success and widespread support for the PWM was suggested by Ralph Russell. He believed it was the political atmosphere in the India of 1935, more than anything significant in the message of the progressives themselves, that allowed a movement formed by avowed communists to take root and allowed a cross-section of intellectuals—from the left, Congress, Gandhians, socialists, as well as men 'of not very articulate political views at all'—to come together within a few months. Comparing the political atmosphere in India in 1935 to that in Britain during the Second World War, Russell notes: 'In those years the

---

[99] This point has been repeatedly made in Chapters 1 and 2; examples from Urdu literature have been used to demonstrate the assertions being made here.

necessities of war against fascist Germany, Italy, and Japan fought in alliance with the Soviet Union and with a China in which nationalists and communists were formally in alliance, made communism respectable and evoked ardent expression of radical populism from even the most unlikely quarters.'[100]

Russell goes on to draw attention to the dissatisfaction with Gandhian methods and an increasing articulation—if not sympathy—for modern, leftist Marxist-influenced solutions to India's protracted detente with its imperial masters. Nehru, an early supporter of the PWM, recognized this growing dissatisfaction and leant his weight not only to the movement, but also initiated several radical measures such as the Muslim Mass Contact Programme in 1937,[101] whose charge he gave to Ashraf, a communist theoretician.

Another reason for the early success of the movement, one that the progressives would never deign to acknowledge, was the existing feeling of reform and radicalism already current in the literature of the 1930s. Far from being 'anaemic in body and mind' as asserted by the *Manifesto*, Zaheer and his friends were exceptionally lucky to find a favourable soil and climate for the sapling they wished to plant. More importantly, and this must be stressed, far from being the exotic hybrid brought from foreign climes by a group of foreign-educated, English-speaking young men, progressivism was in vogue. Indian literature was experiencing an exceptionally healthy and vigorous growth. Far from being reactionary, the Urdu writers of that period were perfectly amenable to the idea of harnessing literature to social change. There was no dearth of intellectuals who, regardless of their sympathy for communism, saw the merit of purposive literature and were prepared to find common cause with the progressives, many of whom were known to be communists. Iqbal, Josh, Firaq were already singing songs of rebellion and revolt when the progressives came along.

---

[100] Ralph Russell, 'Leadership in the All-India Progressive Writers' Movement', in B.N. Pandey (ed.), *Leadership in South Asia* (New Delhi: Vikas Publishing House, 1977), p. 107.

[101] For details, see Mushirul Hasan, 'Muslim Mass Contacts Campaign: Analysis of a Strategy of Political Mobilisation', in Richard Sisson and Stanley Wolpert (eds), *Congress and Indian Nationalism: The Pre-Independence Phase* (Los Angeles: University of California Press, 1988).

The above argument finds support from a most unexpected ally: Ismat Chughtai who believed that the movement lived long before the progressives gave it a name. In calling Kabir a progressive, she reveals how many progressives, including her, viewed progressivism. Clearly seeing progressive literature as that which is concerned with humanity, social awareness, and humanism, she said, 'I think all those who have said something good and nice for the good of humanity are progressive writers. And they didn't start in '35 or '36 only. They existed in the past, only this name was not applied to them.'[102]

This broad, generous definition of 'progressivism' also explains why so many were initially so enamoured by it. Also, as Ismat went on to declare in the same interview, in the early days of bonhomie and good cheer, the writers benefitted from their association with the organization; it afforded them opportunities to meet informally and in a conducive atmosphere (usually the home of a fellow writer), discuss their work, learn about (as Ismat called them) 'the new values of life' (by which she possibly meant the new literary and social trends as well as world affairs that influenced literature).

The strongest gain recorded by the PWA, one that was acknowledged even by its detractors, was the unity fostered between the bickering Hindi–Urdu groups due to the efforts of the progressives. The three Hindi–Urdu conferences in Allahabad and Lucknow in the early days did a great deal to bridge the distance between these warring camps of intellectuals and at the same time reflect the growing strength of the PWA. Another significant gain was the conscious inclusion of writers from different languages giving the movement a pan-Indian outlook, as well as the consequent attention to translations—something that had never been attempted before. It is a different matter that while the subject of translation from and into the various regional languages was repeatedly raised at the various PWA functions, nothing tangible was done; it was left to the Sahitya Akademi to do so from the 1950s onwards.

And, lastly, the PWA's efforts to draw the common man into the ambit of literary endeavour came to be both its success and the reason for its decline. One of the aims of the original *Manifesto* had been 'to bring the arts into the closest touch with the people'. The progressives set out to do precisely this, first with the meeting of the Punjab PWA in the historic

---

[102] *Mahfil*, vol. 8, p. 172.

Jallianwala Bagh on the sidelines of the Punjab Peasants' Conference in 1937 and shortly thereafter with a meeting of peasant poets organized by Muttalibi Faridabadi. This was a mixed blessing. While a certain core group within the PWA was viewing its efforts in drawing peasants and workers into the mainstream of literary activity, there was another group that was watching these events with mixed feelings. Encouraged by the response from the predominantly plebeian audience in Faridabad, the progressives organized mushairas in working-class industrial hubs and invited workers to share the dais with established poets. Moreover, by 1942 the IPTA had been formed and as in the Bombay Conference of May 1942, PWA functions were followed by folk performances, plays, and other forms of folk theatre where actors from IPTA performed alongside folk artists.

A section within the PWA began to view such activities with increasing alarm. While some poets like Kaifi were hugely popular at the revolutionary peoples' mushairas, such as the one organized in Malegaon (Maharashtra) for textile workers from Azamgarh, some of the more conventional poets shrank with distaste at these plebeian gatherings. Both sides, in fact, were acutely aware of the differences rather than the commonalities: the conventional poets of their highbrow, classical tradition, refined diction and sophisticated vocabulary and clever wordplay, and the worker-poets of their own shortcomings when compared by the yardstick of the former and altogether different language, idiom, and conventions. The progressives, however, revelled at all such occasions which allowed them to create a maximum impact over as wide an audience as possible.[103] With this intention, they also began to have short story readings where writers like Krishan Chandar read their stories. Inferior by most literary standards, these stories were nevertheless lapped up by the working class audience. Some of Krishan Chandar's particularly unfortunate examples of increasingly jingoistic and propagandist writings proved to be most popular with

---

[103] Akhtarul Iman, who did not approve of such gatherings, noted: 'To increase their numbers, the progressives began to praise even inferior writers who could not be called more than *mauzu-go* (topical) writers.' In the same vein, Iman believed the progressives to be 'victims of fear and persecution'. As the 'first and second rung of writers distanced themselves from the progressives, what remained were the third and fourth rung who remained faithful to the slogan of the progressives.' Akhtarul Iman, *Iss Abad Kharabe mein* (New Delhi: Urdu Academy, 1996), p. 114.

mass audiences. However, not all propagandist literature was crass or crude. Progressives kept writing stories and poems condemning communal violence and somewhere their ceaseless efforts must have had an impact on the huge audiences they were able to effortlessly rustle up. Overall, the progressives began to score as many hits as misses and a pronounced unevenness began to mark their output.

Reasons for Decline

Notwithstanding the early successes and the wide support base, soon the inherent weaknesses of the association came to the fore. These included, primarily, organizational weaknesses, loss of direction, an ambivalence on the part of many who professed loyalty to the PWA but could not muster the same loyalty to its parent organization (the CPI) or the same unqualified support to the militant positions adopted publicly by some of the progressives especially in retaliation to a hostile reactionary press. The hostility in the press came from both the vernacular papers as well as some of the more pro-British papers such as the *Statesman* which carried a government-inspired attack on the PWA in two long instalments (quoted from at length in Chapter 5). The hostility also came from those within the writing fraternity. It was not lost to the progressives. Wondering why there should be such antipathy, derision, and outright rejection of progressive thought and ideology in literature, Ehtesham Husain maintains that 'The proponents of progressivism make no claim that is contrary to the claims of nature, civilisation, culture or etiquette. It isn't correct to consider it strange or different because everyone must obey the laws of change—regardless of whether change is right or wrong....'[104]

While few would deny the truism that change is the only constant in life and that change is usually met with resistance, it can also be said that any change or revolutionary movement, be it in literature or society, needs much more than youthful fervour and devotion; it needs consistency and guidance, the two things lacking in the PWA. As we shall see ahead, its policies waxed and waned with the laid-down policies of the CPI which in turn sought guidance from an often contradictory Soviet Union.

---

[104] See Ehtesham Husain, 'Urdu Adab mein Taraqqui Pasandi ki Rivayat' in his collection of essays entitled *Tanquidi Jaize* (Lucknow: Ahbab Publishers, 1978), p. 13.

The progressives wanted to hunt with the hounds and run with the hare; naturally enough, it caused some amount of uncertainty both among members of their own flock and in their perception by the world at large. We get a glimpse of the cross-currents that would, in less than a decade, sweep the ground from under the progressives' feet given the contradiction between some of their own positions and those they derived from the party. Nehru, invited to the third conference of the AIPWA held in Delhi on 19–20 May 1942, sent a message, which carried a polite but firm note of caution:

Seldom, if ever, was it more necessary for people to think correctly and understand world conditions as well as the different forces struggling for mastery as it is today. Effective action cannot come out of a vacuum; it must grow out of clear thinking. Unless that clear thinking is there to govern our actions, all our energy and enthusiasm may well run waste. It is obvious that it must be the especial duty of the thinkers and writers of today to give a lead to others in regard to clear thinking.[105]

Nehru's message went on to a rebuttal of the progressives' advocacy of the war as a people's war on the grounds of it being against fascism:

Fascism is bad; no argument is needed to prove that it is the enemy of human freedom and progress. Imperialism is bad as all of us know, not merely in theory but in practice. We want to be rid of both.... This war has demonstrated afresh that in every country nationalism is still the most powerful urge.... In a subject country like India the importance of nationalism and the hunger for freedom is even more important. It is for writers to balance these two urges, that of nationalism and that of internationalism, and thus to evolve a resultant force which derives strength from the nationalist sentiments of the people and is in harmony with the international objectives of today.[106]

Nehru's plea went unheeded by the core group of hardliners within the progressives, and the distance between Congress and the progressives steadily widened after the war. However, not all writers were deaf to Nehru's call for placing the demands of nationalism above international loyalty. The 1942 conference saw many avowed progressives denounce the

---

[105] *The Hindu*, 22 May 1942.
[106] Ibid.

war effort; they were willing to fight for Indian independence, but saw no reason why they should be dragged into Stalin's war.[107]

The 'hegemonic ideological force'[108] of the PWA did not dissipate overnight. For over two decades, it sustained a national consciousness that was multi-lingual and pan-Indian. According to Aijaz Ahmad, it survived the partition but was defeated, almost a decade later, by a combination of contributing factors:

[T]he defeat of Telangana, the stabilization of the Partition and its consequences, the further communalization and deepening of the Hindi–Urdu divide, the emergence of new clusters of Rightwing literati on both sides of the border, the retreat of the communist movement in Pakistan as well as the Gangetic heartlands of India, not to speak of the great industrial cities of Bombay and Kanpur, two of the historic homes of progressive thought in modern Urdu.[109]

Ahmad sees a link between the erosion of progressive thought and the gradual abandonment of the national project itself and the lowering of the left-of-centre tone of Urdu writings in the post-partition period in contrast to the heady days of the national movement. Though 'gradual' and 'ambiguous', the erosion of the progressives' hegemony can be linked with the erosion and abandonment of the leftist thinking prevalent in mainstream politics; Gandhi and Nehru's inability (or unwillingness) to press for Hindustani, the abandonment of Gandhian politics by the Congress itself, and the factionalism and regionalism within the communist movement lead to a re-structuring of the national project.

Also, there was a sizeable section of the Urdu intelligentsia that was growing steadily weary of the extreme topicality of some of the progressive writings, deeming it *waqti adab* and therefore not likely to stand the test of time.[110] Inevitably, as happens with literature produced in times of great stress, some of these writings were indeed shoddy, hastily produced if not outright inferior.[111] The charge of propagandism increasingly began to be

---

[107] Iman, *Iss Abad Kharabe Mein*.

[108] Aijaz Ahmad, *In the Mirror of Urdu: Recompositions of Nation and Community, 1947–65, Lectures 102–5* (Shimla: Indian Institute of Advanced Study, 1993), p. 28.

[109] Ibid., p. 29.

[110] Azmi, *Urdu mein Taraqqui Pasand Adabi Tehreek*, pp. 69–71.

[111] Anand Narain Mulla, a successful lawyer, a modernist poet of some standing, and an excellent raconteur, said: '*Hungama-e-surkh inquilab hamne suna to tha*

levelled at the progressives given their penchant for producing high-octave works designed to pump adrenaline rather than leave any lasting impact. Written often as a knee-jerk response to topical events that caused mini earthquakes on the progressives' richter scale, but caused no real ripples in the rest of the country, were some of the worst examples of waqti adab. We have looked at these examples in the work of Makhdoom, K.A. Abbas, Krishan Chandar, and several others in Chapters 6 and 7.

In the early days, the PWM drew many writers to its fold because there seemed nothing in its agenda that they could disagree with. On the face of it, the movement subscribed to two basic beliefs: nationalism and literature that could become an instrument of change. However, with the PWM's advocacy of the CPI's line—whether it be on Pakistan, pro-war policy, the abandonment of strikes during the war (so that they do not interfere with the war effort), and the resumption of strikes thereafter—certain members such as Zaheer, Anand, and Jafri began to demand greater ideological fidelity from its members. This was reflected in stricter adherence to the principles of socialist realism, communism, and the style and manner of functioning of writers' bodies in the Soviet Union. At the same time, there was a group within the PWA that was pulling in a contrary direction; influenced by the writings of Freud they were looking more closely at sexual behaviour. The works of Manto, Miraji, Ismat, etc., drew flak from mainstream critics. The progressives, on their part, already perturbed by the lack of ideological commitment in writers like Manto and Ismat were quick to distance themselves from them citing their so-called obsession with sexual matters as a deviation from the aims and objectives of the PWA. The ideological purity of one group was at odds with the ideological fluidity of the other. N.M. Rashid, a staunch defender of Miraji, made a larger point about progressivism per se when he insisted that any poet who represented a modern consciousness is a progressive; and insofar as Miraji was eminently qualified to be included. Moreover, Rashid maintained, Miraji's poetry was a protest against the havoc created by moralism. Regrettably, the progressives chose to invest Miraji with an altogether sinister set of qualities—negativism, defeatism, morbidity, eroticism, obscenity, ambiguity. This, Rashid believed, the progressive theorists

---

magar / Jaam-o-suboo ke paas paas, daar-o-rasan se door door' (I had heard of the revolutionary ferment of the Left / Staying close to the cup that cheers and far away from the noose that hangs). The barb here is directed at the progressives who enjoyed their drink at the expense of other concerns.

did because there was 'no drumfire in his [Miraji's] poetry to advance the leftist cause, or any cause for that matter'.[112] In a blistering critique of the progressives' tendency to marginalize those who did not fit the bill (a bill, which meant leftist or overtly political), Rashid went on to observe rather tartly: 'Considering that the progressives themselves have over time qualified their definition to include Ghalib and Iqbal, there is hope for Miraji. It would not help Miraji but it might enrich the progressives.'[113]

Years later, Hajra Begum, not a writer herself, but a dedicated party worker, was able to show both sides of the coin when, on the one hand, she admitted that those who came under the progressives' umbrella were moved by the exploitation they saw all around, and on the other, how differences cropped up when one set of people began telling the other group the way out.[114] Having served as secretary of the PWA, she was uniquely placed to observe how one group began to vociferously present their point of view (which was the party's point of view) so that their literature became not so much a purely literary exercise, but a kind of propaganda which some people did not like and some resisted. Taken in the balance, she said, while 'one of the good points about the PWM was that from the north to the south and from east to west, people were introduced to each other' the movement had its weaknesses too: 'I feel that as a writers' movement, it should have been a broader movement.' She also felt that, perhaps unconsciously, one group within the PWA burdened the other with the weight of their ideology: '[I]t didn't happen in a conscious way but somehow because they were enthusiastic and of a particular point of view.' About those who were sidelined or silenced within the PWA, she said: 'We did not realize we were driving them away from us. This understanding came much later. By that time, there were already different groups.' On the reasons for the movement's decline, Hajra Begum is unambiguous: there was, she believed 'no clear understanding as to what should be the object of this movement'. Her assessment of Zaheer is similarly frank. While 'he could be put amongst intellectuals, he was not a practical person at all'.

Apart from Manto and Ismat (whom we have studied in Chapter 7), there was also the distancing of other erstwhile progressives such as Ahmed Ali and Bedi. Ahmed Ali developed differences with the

---

[112] N.M. Rashid, interview, *Mahfil*, vol. 7, p. 10.

[113] Ibid.

[114] In the course of an interview for the NMML's Oral History Project.

progressives as early as 1936 itself, first over the publication of the PWA journal *New Indian Literature* (discussed in Chapter 5) and the holding of the first people's mushaira in 1937.[115] In later years, Ahmed Ali was at pains to establish two things: one, that he never dissociated himself from the PWA, and two, the original intention of the *Angarey* quartet was to establish a literary association, 'with no forecast of any affiliation with any political ideology or thought other than the right of free criticism and free expression'[116] as enunciated in the letter published in *The Leader* in 1933, which he considered to be the 'real' statement of intent of the progressives and not the *Manifesto* crafted a year later in London. Also, Ahmed Ali believed that for a majority of writers—and readers—the PWM was essentially a revolutionary, not political, movement. Terming the PWM as 'essentially an intellectual revolt against the outmoded past, the vitiated tendencies in contemporary thought and literature, the indifference of people to their human condition, against acquiescence to foreign rule, enslavement to practices and beliefs, both social and religious, based on ignorance, against the problems of poverty and exploitation, and complete inanity to progress and life', Ahmed Ali made a crucial distinction. He saw the PWA as divided into two groups: the orthodox or political group and the creative or non-political in which he included himself. Bitterly critical of Zaheer and others who, he believed, had hijacked the progressives' agenda and stamped a political ideology on what was essentially a literary and cultural movement, he wrote: 'The ideological interpretation was superimposed on the movement after the first formal conference on an all-India basis in 1936 by the political section, which has remained in control ever since, but was not part of the movement when it was originally started in 1932.'[117]

---

[115] According to Carlo Coppola, who has written extensively on Ahmed Ali and also interviewed him at length, the rift between Ahmed Ali and the other members of the *Angarey* group was as much on personal differences as on 'disagreement on the function of art and the artist in society'. See Carlo Coppola, 'Ahmed Ali (1910–1994): Bridges and Links between East and West', *Annual of Urdu Studies*, vol. 9 (1944), p. 50.

[116] Ahmed Ali, 'The Progressive Writers' Movement and Creative Writers in Urdu', in Carlo Coppola (ed.), *Marxist Influences and South Asian Literature* (East Lansing: Michigan State University Press, 1974), p. 35.

[117] Ibid.

While the pan-Indian reach of the PWA no doubt tried to draw writers from different parts of the country making it more broad-based, according to Ahmed Ali, it nevertheless shrank in space, becoming a political platform which, in turn, caused many of the creative writers to move away. Zahida Zaidi,[118] in the course of an interview, told me how in 1949 'orders came' to criticize Jazbi's poem '*Maut*' (Death). Jazbi was a leftist and fellow-traveller of the progressives, but not a party member; Zaidi perforce did one, but it was taken apart by a non-progressive but influential writer such as Khurshidul Islam. This criticism for the sake of a writer's professed lack of ideology disillusioned many. Jazbi himself has written how he increasingly withdrew from literary activity and how his pen was silenced for a while in the face of such overt hostility.

To return to Ahmed Ali, he was also very critical of Zaheer's *Roshnai* which he considered a biased account that eschews the real beginnings of the progressive movement in India: 'What had gone on before 1936 was not entirely political and labeled with a stamp, thus not worth

---

[118] She was active in the Aligarh branch of the PWA from her student days, served as its joint secretary in the late 1940s, and, when it was revived in Aligarh decades later, served as its president in 2002. A member of the student cell of the CPI in Aligarh, Zaidi recounted how she and her sisters worked actively for the local unit under the guidance of 'Lal Siddiq'. Their assigned task was to disrupt the university convocation with black flags. She spent two to three months in the Banaras jail in 1950. She, along with her sisters, gave speeches on the occasion of May Day while still in jail, and was hurt in a lathi charge. In protest, the agitators went on a 21-day hunger strike and were kept in solitary cells. She went to Cambridge in 1956 and upon her return in 1958 did not rejoin the party. She spoke of her disillusionment with the party system and how the party did not look after them once they went to jail. She described the jail term as 'salutary'. She also described the party as 'intellectually weak'. She spoke of gaining the necessary discipline to think for herself as she grew older and of learning to like the discipline, but not the orders. She, however, still sympathizes with the Leftist–Marxist ideology. Asked how she would define herself (as a progressive or modernist), she replied, as a post-modernist and existentialist and 'not a Shubkhoon brand of modernist'. Her novel, *Inquilab ka Ek Din* (A Day of Revolution, 1997) is partly autobiographical; her young female protagonist is torn between her loyalty to the Students' Federation of India (SFI) and her yearning for intellectual freedom. Consequently, she feels suffocated. Zahida Zaidi passed away in 2011.

acknowledging officially.' The group that had produced *Angarey*, whom he calls the main figures of the movement, shared many interests that young people of their class and educational background did. Among these he included

a love of sombreros, bright shirts and contrasting ties, collecting candlesticks and gargoyles, Bach and Beethoven, and an admiration for James Joyce and D.H. Lawrence and the *New Writing* poets, as well as Chekov and Gorki. Whereas we were ardent nationalists and anti-British, Marxism was not a ruling passion, though a progressive outlook was inherent in the revolt; and as the group expanded, leftist leanings vague in some and pronounced in others, did become apparent, for there seemed no other way out of the social and political morass.[119]

The 'creative section', as Ahmed Ali termed it, or the non-political faction was moved by the social, moral, and intellectual backwardness they saw all around them; their stories and poems in turn moved a whole generation of Indians. The ideologists, however, insisted on a complete identification with the worker and the peasant alone and a strict adherence to the doctrine of socialist realism.[120] It was this insistence on accepting one set of beliefs that irked Ahmed Ali and others. He wrote: 'Accepting one set of dogmas and sticking to it is the very negation of progress, and that is not what many of us had asked for or believed in, although that is what the custodians of the movement persisted in reiterating.'[121] Several progressives were also beginning to question the very definition of 'progressive'. In his

---

[119] Ali, 'Progressive Writers' Movement and Creative Writers in Urdu', p. 36.

[120] As discussed in previous chapters, the doctrine of socialist realism developed in Russia in the early 1930s demanded that literature be used only for utilitarian purposes. Art must portray the superiority of the collective way of life (rather than the individual, personal, or idiosyncratic) and depict the Stalinistic line of work ethic where the worker and the peasant are glorified above all others. Freudian analyses of the self and the 'inner world' were anathema to the practitioners of this doctrine. Naturally enough, the Indian communists intensified their purges against those who either wrote on sexual matters or deviated from the larger good to the individual self-interest. In *Marxist Influences in South Asia*, Carlo Coppola, referring to socialist realism as the 'literary handmaiden' of Marxism, speaks of its profound influence on not just Urdu literature, but all of modern South Asian literatures.

[121] Ali, 'Progressive Writers' Movement and Creative Writers in Urdu', p. 37.

speech at the first AIPWA conference in Lucknow in April 1936, Ahmed Ali had given his definition (see Chapter 5). In the Afterword to the fourth collection of fiction, *Maut se Pehle* (Before Death),[122] Ahmed Ali set out yet another definition of the term which, though radical, was neither overtly Marxist nor based on the creed of socialist realism.

Like Ahmed Ali, Bedi also voiced a distaste for the ideology that was being propagated through the writers, many of whom were unmindful of it in their writings. He too talked of a disillusionment that had crept in along with the formalism that came to replace the early spontaneity of the PWM.[123] Bedi traced the beginning of formalism to 1942 when the communists within the PWA intensified their ideological stance in the face of Gandhi's Quit India Movement:

They wanted us to conform to a particular type of ideology but some of us revolted against it because we had read the later Russian literature and were not at all impressed by it as we were with the pre-revolution writing. The later works were not very good at all; they were very formal. Similarly, we were told to write about hot steel is smelted [sic] and other things. Earlier, we did realize that we should write about resurgent India and how we were trying to throw off this yoke of imperialism; to that extent we concurred with the movement. But when we were told everything Stalin had done was grand, we revolted.

Bedi is candid enough to admit that they meekly submitted to these high-handed directives: 'We thought then we had to belong to a group or be thrown out.' But when the world began to talk about Stalin's excesses,[124] some of the Indian progressives realized that their misgivings were true. Moreover, some like Bedi wanted to write about the life of the mind, the inner world that the progressives frowned upon, but that they had found so evocative in the writings of French existentialists like Camus and Sartre.

[122] Ahmed Ali, 'Art, Siyasat aur Zindagi' (Art, Politics, and Life), in *Maut se Pehle* (Delhi: Insha Press, 1945), pp. 47–71.

[123] Interview, *Mahfil*, vol. 8.

[124] Stalin's death in 1953 triggered a bitter power struggle and a de-Stalinization campaign launched by Nikita Kruschev which eventually led to the great 'Thaw'—a reversal of many Soviet policies in the field of foreign affairs, literature, culture, and the arts. Kruschev's speech, 'On the Personality Cult and Its Consequences', delivered on 25 February 1956 opened the floodgates to the horrors of Stalinist Russia.

Another reason ascribed by Bedi to the disillusionment and distancing from the PWM was the persistent demand to write about the lower classes, the mill worker, and the peasant that a writer like Bedi could not conform to. Bedi had been a postal clerk for seven years before he began his literary career and he could—and indeed did—write with empathy about the lower middle class to which he himself belonged, but he had no direct experience of a factory worker's life. He stopped writing altogether for a while and eventually took to writing for films.

Qurratulain Hyder, mocked and derided by the progressives, looked at them with empathy and balance. In an interview, she said

The period of giving shock treatment to society to jerk it out of its lethargy was over. *Angarey*, the early stories of Rasheed Jahan, Saadat Hasan Manto and Ismat Chughtai had already become works of the past. You must also remember that things were moving at a tremendous pace. More events crowded a month in that period than happened in several years just a couple of decades back. With so many issues at hand, it is but natural that the main thrust of any organization would be to survive as an establishment. With that, … the untimely death of Premchand and the removal of Sajjad Zaheer from the literary scenario, the punch had gone out of the PWA. It was now merely an organization, like so many others and no longer a movement that nurtured creative experiments.[125]

Hyder went on to stress the difference between a movement and an organization thus:

A movement has a flow that should be forwards. An organization is the gelling of that movement. It is like the stream flowing into the lake. The focus then becomes the lake, which is considered the life source. Dams are built, banks fortified, *ghats* constructed to make it accessible, de-silting planned. The lake lies there, clean, clear, cool and deep—but stagnant. In the process, the stream that is feeding the lake is neglected. That is why new movements, new streams have to continue to be born, to keep the flow, the life alive.

Once the PWA became a concrete organization, it was but natural that all that was conventional would seep into it. The infighting, the politics, the hierarchy and most importantly the dominance of the office bearers, who were more often than not non-writers, might have kept the organization alive but it killed the movement. Unfortunately, nothing else replaced it.[126]

---

[125] Interview with Noor Zaheer, p. 25.
[126] Ibid.

Some progressives, such as Mumtaz Husain,[127] switched tracks though they never publicly disowned their association with the movement. A short story writer of some repute during the heydays of the PWM, he abandoned creative writing altogether and turned to literary criticism. In an interview he said '... I was more interested in ideas and their presentation rather than just a portrayal of life. Whenever I wrote short stories, I did so under pressure of ideas and I thought that was not the right approach.'[128] While denying that those stories bordered on pamphleteering, he admitted that the ideological content was overwhelming—not only in his own, but also in fellow progressive Krishan Chandar's. This, Mumtaz Husain clarifies, was not peculiar to all progressives. For instance, there is no overwhelming burden of ideology in the stories of Manto, Ismat, and Bedi, and in Faiz, who though subscribed to an ideology, was careful to never let it impair his poetry. Similarly, the 'non-progressives' too were willing to give Faiz the credit for not turning his poetry to serve a purely functional purpose. Though belonging to the other 'camp', Rashid admired Faiz for not directly catering to the proletariat and refraining from oratorical outbursts.[129]

A generation of critics who had the benefit of hindsight spoke of the intellectual paucity of the progressives. While admitting that the PWM—in tandem with the struggle for independence—popularized modern political and economic concepts among the Urdu-speaking people, and the proponents of the movement did indeed bring about a degree of social consciousness among their readers, on the whole the movement failed to engender intellectual creativity compared to, say, Iqbal who single-handedly took Urdu poetry to great heights. Making a distinction between revolutionary slogan-mongering (by Josh and his followers) and startlingly original creative thought such as Iqbal's, a modern critic and philosopher such as Waheed Akhtar rued the limitations of the progressives: 'Undoubtedly this movement made significant contribution in the realm of the novel, short story, verse and criticism. In effect, it transmitted new intellectual and literary attitudes into Urdu but its

---

[127] He joined the PWM in 1938 as a student at Allahabad University where he read Christopher Caldwell, Ralph Fox, and Alec West, and became enamoured with the Marxist interpretation of life. After Partition, he became the general secretary of the Karachi branch of the Anjuman-e-Taraqqui Pasand Mussanifin.

[128] In an interview with Asif Noorani for the *Herald*, Karachi, June 1990.

[129] Rashid, Interview, *Mahfil*, vol. 7, p. 9.

political extremism, rigidity and mechanical approach pre-empted any meaningful contribution in moving it to a level where the foundations of any creative thought are laid.'[130]

To be fair, Waheed Akhtar also noted that Marx and Freud, the two 'epoch-making thinkers' who were introduced to the Urdu world, failed to generate any 'sound works of a high caliber'. He, therefore, held the progressives and the modernists equally negligent in contributing to the intellectual growth of Urdu.

Another reason for the decline, purely in a literary sense, was the commensurate rise of modernism or jadeediyat as it was called in Urdu with many erstwhile progressives turning into modernists. Etymologically, a modernist too ought to be progressive and vice versa, but in the Urdu lexicon, taraqqui pasand and *jadeed* (modernist) became antonyms used to signify those who occupied opposite ends of the literary spectrum. The modernists not only gave greater importance to the individual rather than the collective experience, they also interpreted the social function of literature differently. Not only did the modernists revolt against the watertight compartmentalization of ideas, they did it also against literary etiquette and ideologies, state patronage, even against the ethical, philosophical, religious, social, or political conventions that had come to represent convention. A group of young writers who styled themselves as the *nai nasl* (new generation)—which comprised Balraj Komal, Baqar Mehndi, Qazi Salim, and some lapsed progressives such as Khalilur Rahman Azmi as well as several brand new voices on the Urdu firmament such as Ibne Insha, Nasir Kazmi, Shaaz Tamkanat, Jafar Tahir, Waheed Akhtar, Shahab Jafri—mounted repeated attacks on the citadel of 'organized' progressivism. This wave of new poetry was continued by the post-1960 generation which comprised Shahryar, Zafar Iqbal, Ahmad Mushtaq, Nida Fazli, Kumar Pashi who revelled in defying labels and classifications.

The modernists were in revolt not only against the past, but they refused to worry too much about the future; the present was all that mattered. As the writer became the centre of gravity for the modernists, notions of social or political reform fell by the wayside and a peculiar passiveness took hold of the writer. The *jadeed parast* (lover of modernity) was writing simply to

---

[130] Waheed Akhtar, 'Intellectual Tradition in Urdu', in B.N. Rao and Kadir Zaman (eds), *Modern Thought and Contemporary Literary Trends* (Hyderabad: Committee on Modern Thought and Contemporary Literary Trends, 1982).

satisfy his ego and ease the burden of his soul. In the words of a modern critic, Abid Raza Bedar

With an utter disregard for any kind of social responsibility and having little respect for ideals and reforms, he (the modernist) has been going deep into the layers of his own self, becoming a victim of loneliness and faithlessness.... Since he is in search of some new values and some new relationships with his surroundings and since the centre of his gravity has shifted from society to the individual, he is apparently quite communicative with himself, though often unintelligible to his readers. That is what he calls the tragedy of communication.

In an interview with modern Urdu poet Shahryar, the word 'communication' cropped up again and again as the nub of the debate on jadeediyat. According to him, modernist critics like Shamsur Rahman Faruqi stressed individualism and the evolution of personal symbols and a complicated idiom that, in any case, made communication futile. Faruqi's seminal essay entitled *Tarseel ki Nakaamiyabi ka Alamiya* (The Tragedy of Non-communication) advocates Art for Art's Sake and sees no need for social commitment in literature. Among the modernists too there were different shades of opinion. If Faruqi occupied one end of the spectrum, others like Khalilur Rahman Azmi were not so adamantly against communication, though Azmi, once a progressive himself, by the early 1960s had turned against the canon that had come to define the progressive view of art. Shahryar used the example of the rise of jadeediyat to coincide with the fall of taraqqui pasandi to illustrate how change in literature is always against the literary canon. The progressives changed the classical idiom calling it reactionary and harmful; the jadeed pasand had no space for progressivism. Such is the inevitability of literary movements.

Raza Imam, a communist, a retired professor of English, and in many ways a 'representative' of the sort of young men who found themselves in the thick of the PWA, summed up for me the dualities of the movement and the agony and the ecstasy of being a progressive. On what drew him, he said

When I first read the progressive writers, I did not know that they belonged to any movement. To me they were writers who, apart from telling stories, crystallized for me some of my own vague feelings and ideas. They also provided me a better and wider understanding of things outside my ken. I came to realize that some of the attitudes and values in my environment that I had taken for granted were based on hypocrisy and injustice. As I gradually became aware of social and political movements, my reading of progressive writers, with some help from Gorky, drew me towards Marxism and Communism.[131]

On why the PWM failed to live up to the glory of the early days, he says

Before the Independence, the PWA was a broad-based organization which included all writers who were generally opposed to British imperialism and to the values and structure of the colonial-feudal society. They could write the way they liked on the themes of their choice as long as they exposed the oppression in the existing order and/or gave expression to their longing for an equitable society without any kind of oppression. But, after Independence, several things happened that affected the cohesion of progressive writers. Foremost, one important event was the change in the opinion of the CPI with regard to independence in 1948. The party declared that independence was no more than a sham and the Nehru government was nothing more than an agent of imperialism. Those writers who were party members had to rigidly follow this line. Consequently, the PWA, because of the large presence of writers who were close to the CPI, also adopted a rigid line. Just as the party thought that the communist revolution in India should follow the path of Russian revolution, the PWA thought that progressive literature should be produced on the line of the Soviet concept of socialist realism. This entailed making literature subservient to the existing political line of the party and using no other technique or style except that of straightforward realism. Because of this, a number of writers were either forced out of the organization or became disassociated with it. Later on, when the party realized its mistake, effort was made to re-infuse vigour into the PWA, especially after the return of Sajjad Zaheer from Pakistan. But, by then, the entire communist movement was set on a course of split. When the CPI finally split into CPI and CPI (M), the writers who were sympathetic to the CPI (M) formed a new organization called Janwadi Lekhak Sangh (Democratic Writers Association). Some of these writers moved further to the left when CPI (M–L) was formed. All this had an adverse impact on the morale of the progressive writers and the intensity of their enthusiasm.

An added factor that influenced the young writers and poets to move away or keep away from the PWA or its breakaway organizations was its insistence on using just one mode of expression, i.e., realism. It naturally did not suit young writers who wanted to experiment and use different modes of expression, especially those who wanted to give expression to a sense of confusion, alienation and meaninglessness of existence on account of growing industrialization, creeping urbanization and conflict between new and old values. In the early fifties, such

---

[131] Raza Imam, interview. He passed away in January 2012.

writers were ferociously criticized by adherents of progressivism. For example, the upcoming Qurratulain Hyder was savagely mauled by Ismat Chughtai in 'Pom-pom Darling' for using English words and 'stream of consciousness' technique to reveal the inanities of the life of Indian youth belonging to leisured classes. It was quite ironic that the movement that was heralded by the innovative *Angarey* should oppose any further innovation. If the PWA had retained its initial broad outlook, Ms Hyder might well have been hailed as a writer exposing the hollowness of Indian upper middle class life.

In the case of Urdu, two more factors operated to dilute the attraction of PWA to young poets and writers: one was the general decline in the number of Urdu readers after the partition of India on account of Urdu losing its position as an official language and a major subject at school, the other was the emergence of some influential critics who were ideologically hostile to the PWM. The former led many writers to vie for official patronage and rewards, creating new kinds of groupings and lessening the fervour to build any movement. The latter, in the name of modernism, attracted those young writers who wanted to experiment with new styles and themes.[132]

To coincide with these various changes in the literary arena, one very significant thing also altered the fate of the PWM. Once the goal of the national freedom struggle was achieved, writers began to move from the outer to the inner world, from the material to the psychological realm, and from social to personal matters. They began to take greater interest in themes such as the alienation of the self, the ennui and angst of modernism, the flux and migration caused by rapid urbanization, as well as the problems of increasing westernization and industrialization. Issues of state and society began to give way to matters of the heart and mind, especially in the light of new developments in psychology. Already, Muhammad Hasan Askari had launched a bitter campaign against the progressives, openly sided with the progressives' black sheep Manto, and championed Jungian analysis and the new concept of the Collective Unconscious. Notions of nihilism, narcissism, and anarchism swirling in the new currents seemed far more attractive to many young writers of the 1940s and 1950s than the lot of mill workers or the joys of building dams, bridges, and factories. It is a different matter that many modernist writers too soon fell prey to fads and formulas, in much the same way as the progressives had become ensnared by slogans and propaganda. They were guilty of producing as

[132] Raza Imam, interview.

much cosmetic or artificial literature as the progressives had during their worst days of excess and wilful indulgence.

Some of the writers associated with the Halqa-e Arbab-e Zauq[133] staged a revival of interest in symbolism and romanticism. The French symbolists such as Mallarme and the romantics such as Baudelaire had been anathema to the progressives, but we see them profoundly influencing the work of N.M. Rashid and Miraji who, in turn, influenced an entire generation of modernists. The progressives, who had dubbed the Halqa's members retrogressive and decadent and kept them at bay for almost 20 years, could no longer contain the growing popularity of some of its most prominent members, most notably N.M. Rashid. While the progressives stood for a 'complete suspension of choice' on the part of the writer, the Halqa encouraged its members to write in the light of individual perceptions alone. In a war of words with the progressives accusing modernists like Rashid of extreme independence and a deliberate use of obscure or ambiguous images and diction, and the modernists retaliating with accusing some progressives (such as Jafri) of haranguing and preaching and the movement itself being tainted with totalitarianism and regimentation, the rift was split wide open. In *Iran mein Ajnabi* (Stranger in Iran), Rashid objected to the progressive ideology being linked to a political doctrine imposed from outside. While admitting that literature cannot be created in a vacuum, nor can it exist to serve a vacuum, Rashid objected essentially to the progressives' denial of personal will for that, he believed, was tantamount to denying the creative process and the raison d'etre of all creative activity. Years later, while admitting that there was 'some resemblance' between him and the progressives at the time of his first collection *Muawara* (That Which Is Beyond, 1940), the differences cropped up due to their different approach to life and its problems: 'My criticism of the progressives stems from the view that literature is not and should not be produced under external direction to serve a specified ideology or a specified group.'[134]

Dismayed by those who wished to dictate the course of literature (once again, the target of the modernists' ire was Jafri and to a lesser extent, Krishan Chandar) through manifestos, the modernists saw no reason why

---

[133] For an understanding of the Halqa and especially its relationship with the PWM, I am indebted to Yunus Jawaid's *Halqa-e Arbab-e Zauq* (Lahore: Majlis-e-Taraqqui-e-Adab, 1984).

[134] Rashid, interview, *Mahfil*, vol. 7, p. 6.

one group of people should take it upon themselves to tell others what to write, think, or feel so that literary production may serve a larger purpose, no matter how laudable its aims. Chaffing against the tyranny of form and content imposed by the progressives, these writers revelled in the freedom of creative expression that they believed was the birth right of every creative writer. These poets wanted to write as an individual rather than a 'type' and increasingly the Self began to reign supreme in the new literature of the mid-1950s and politics, society, and the larger common good receded from the artist's consciousness. There were some writers who wished to belong to neither group and wanted to be left alone to write regardless of affiliation with any movement, literary or socio-political. Abdullah Hussein's *Udas Naslein* (The Weary Generations), published in 1963 expressed this desire to break away from established norms and chart new paths. Before that, Qurratulain Hyder's *Aag ka Darya*, published in 1959, had attempted something similar.

While there is no doubt that the PWA eventually declined in popularity, the movement disintegrated, and many of its members drifted away, the movement itself cannot be regarded as a failure. In hindsight, and taking into consideration all its highs and lows, strengths and weaknesses, hits and misses—one can only regard it as a success. It succeeded in

- introducing a new literary sensibility, one that was more attuned to the common man than ever before;
- holding up a more faithful, more ruthless, more accurate mirror to society than had hitherto been the practice;
- bringing together more people, especially the intelligentsia, than any other movement with the exception of the Aligarh movement;
- driving its tentacles deep into different parts of the country and drawing a response from the common man;
- having a lasting effect on literary values decades after its decline;
- playing a vital role in inculcating the values of liberty, equality, and justice;
- drawing attention to crucial issues of hunger, poverty, inequality, exploitation, gender, justice, education, human rights; and
- most importantly, providing an impetus to the national freedom movement by focusing attention on nationalism, love for the country and freedom from foreign rule.

Do ideas die when movements decline? No, one would imagine not. According to Plato, ideas are the Principal Reality. In contrast to individual objects or material things which undergo change and flux, Plato believed that ideas are perfect, eternal, and immutable. Indeed, notions of Liberty, Equality, and Justice continue to ring true centuries after the French Revolution. Movements propelled by ideas may die or end or be curtailed, but ideas, such as the idea of progressivism itself does not die.[135]

As we have seen in the first section of this chapter, a meeting of the Urdu progressive writers in Hyderabad in 1956 declared the end of the movement. A group led by Zaheer and Abdul Alim—the founder-members and architects of the PWA—announced that the movement had completed in meeting the objectives it had set for itself and in the light of new issues facing Urdu language and literature, it would be better if a new association were to take the place of PWA. This new association, they opined, should have the space for people belonging to different literary and political points of view. However, a few years later, the progressives again changed their mind and decided to revive the PWA, but the world had changed. Only a handful of the old progressives remained; they could neither influence nor dictate terms to the new generation of writers who placed themselves beyond the narrow confines of ideological literature and embraced the hedonism of intellectual freedom. Some of these writers were willing to study progressivism as a philosophy, but they could not be induced to practice it or incorporate its carved-in-stone tenets. Nor were they willing to produce literature that could mechanically fit into a preconceived mould by following a step-by-step formula laid down by master craftsmen.

However, while the movement with its rigid formalism (to turn the words of the original *Manifesto* against those who helped draft it) may be a thing of the past, the spirit of progressivism is not dead and gone. It lives whenever a writer speaks out against injustice, inequality, and oppression.

Writing the Epilogue to *Roshnai*, Zaheer, admitting to the shortcomings of the movement, expressed a similar hope for the future: '[F]laws created by internal differences and shortsightedness can hold up the pace of

---

[135] I posed this question to Mushtaq Yusufi, Urdu humourist and prose stylist, during a chat at his Karachi home. He said ideas do not die nor do movements, but creative writers absorb the most beneficial parts of movements; what remains is leftover, discarded waste. He used the word, *khojad*.

progress. However, a movement that is fuelled by the energy of the masses can neither be suppressed nor ended.'[136]

Regardless of their views on individual progressives, most critics and commentators on the recent history of Urdu literature are unanimous on one thing: 'No other movement had attracted such talent and produced so varied a fare.'[137]

Finally, a word about the world we live in. Elsewhere in the world, governments are concerned simply with keeping the existing social machinery in a smooth, running condition. Not so in India. In India, elected governments have always had the additional task of implementing radical and urgent social change. It is a measure of the magnitude and scale of change required that 60 years after Independence it is still a Work in Progress; we are still coping with effective ways to reduce if not eliminate the bane of poverty, backwardness, and inequality and introduce means or redress that require consensus and cooperation. This can be in the form of reservation (for Scheduled Castes/Scheduled Tribes, Other Backward Castes, and lately women in Parliament), or it could be employment generation schemes, especially in the rural sector such as the Mahatma Gandhi National Rural Employment Guarantee Act (MGNREGA). In the years before independence, even the colonial government was under immense pressure to bring about economic and social change. In India, the task of political parties has traditionally been to be the agents of change, and that of writers to *make known* the need for change. Before independence, this task was coupled with the equally pressing task of throwing off the colonial yoke and working together for freedom. After independence, the writers' role underwent a change insofar as the glue of fighting a common enemy, namely, the colonial masters, disappeared. In its place were a host of issues that did not—could not—drum up the same level of passionate intensity.

Drawing a comparison with China, which like India saw a massive changeover (in China's case a year after, in 1948), one can see two ways in which two somewhat similar Asian giants have sought to bring about economic and social change. The contrast is stark; in India the process has

---

[136] Sajjad Zaheer, *The Light: A History of the Movement for Progressive Literature in the Indo-Pak Subcontinent*, English translation of Sajjad Zaheer's *Roshnai* by Amina Azfar (Karachi: Oxford University Press, 2006), p. 286.

[137] Ali Jawad Zaidi, *A History of Urdu Literature* (New Delhi: Sahitya Akademi, 1993), p. 376.

largely been democratic whereas in China it has worked through an unbroken chain of command extending from the politburo in Peking to the lowest peasant and party worker. Everything, including culture, literature, and the arts, was determined by the communist government and implemented by compulsion. In India, such an approach is untenable. In this chapter, we have seen how the party's diktat vis-à-vis literature was not acceptable or, at the very least, not acceptable in toto by all writers and intellectuals.

This last section has traced the fissures that began to arise both within the PWA and among those who were sympathetic to the progressive cause and ideology. Even those free-floating intellectuals who had sympathy for communism per se and professed adherence to a liberal, left-leaning outlook began to display a definite bias towards free(r) systems. However, for every liberal there was a rigid practitioner of progressivism, and some members of the PWA could not escape the pitfalls of 'excessive devotion to a cause'.[138] Therein lay the seeds of their downfall and eventual decline.

---

[138] Muhammad Sadiq, *Twentieth Century Urdu Literature* (Karachi: Royal Book Company, 1983), p. 351.

Annexure I

Major Writers and Poets Associated with the Progressive Writers' Movement

Short Biographical Notes

ABDUL ALIM (1905–1976): Possibly the most important and powerful ideologue in the PWM, Dr Alim was a much-respected figure in academic circles as well as an impressive orator who could hold forth eloquently on history, politics, and society. Gifted with a rational clear-thinking mind, he helped draft the resolutions and constitution presented at the first AIPWA in Lucknow and served as its general secretary from 1938 till Sajjad Zaheer came out of prison. He can be credited with bringing a scientific rigour to the understanding of contemporary literature; his views on Art for Life's Sake formed the basis of much of the progressives' subsequent campaigns. Interestingly enough, though not a creative writer himself, he was at the forefront of the various progressive moves—whether it was a resolution against obscenity at the Hyderabad conference in 1945 or the dramatic about-turn declaring the end of progressivism as it had been understood all along, also at Hyderabad in 1956. He served as vice-chancellor of the AMU from 1968 to 1974, where he had begun his career in the Department of Arabic.

ABDUL HAQ (1870–1961): Known as Baba-e-Urdu for his exemplary work in the establishment of the Anjuman-e Taraqqui-i-Urdu in 1903, he also initiated serious academic work in linguistics, in the learning, teaching, translating of scientific works, and the production of scientifically compiled Urdu dictionaries. During his student days in Aligarh, he met some of the most illustrious men of the age, namely, Syed Ahmed Khan, Shibli Nomani, Ross Masood, Mohsin-ul-Mulk, Syed Mahmud, Professor Arnold, and Babu Mukharjee. Abdul Haq joined the Indian Civil Service and worked as a chief translator at the Home Department in Delhi before being appointed as the provincial inspector of schools at Aurangabad in the Central Provinces. Having also served the Nizam of Hyderabad, he was appointed secretary of the All-India Muhammadan Educational Conference, founded by Syed Ahmed Khan in 1886 for the promotion of education among the Muslims. He served as the principal of Osmania College at Aurangabad till 1930 after which he devoted himself to the compilation of dictionaries. He signed the manifesto of the proposed PWA presented to him by Sajjad Zaheer in Allahabad in December 1935 in the presence of Premchand, Firaq, and others. In 1937, he sent a presidential address to be read out at the conference of Hindi and Urdu progressive writers held in Allahabad exhorting the progressives to emulate the encyclopaedists of France. This Grand Old Man of Urdu migrated to Pakistan in 1947 where he set up the Anjuman-e Taraqqui-i-Urdu in Karachi.

AHMAD NADEEM QASMI (1916–2006): Starting off as a sub-inspector in the Excise Department, Qasmi (whose real name was Peerzada Ahmad Shah) soon adopted life as a man of letters. A journalist, editor, and writer, his fame rests as a writer of 15 anthologies of short stories and 9 volumes of poetry. At various points in his career, he also edited four highly respected literary journals (*Adab-e-Latif, Savera, Nuqoosh,* and *Funoon*) as well as two weeklies (*Tehzeeb-e-Niswan* for women and *Phool* for children) and a newspaper (*Imroze*). Qasmi's portrayal of rural Punjab is his enduring contribution to Urdu literature. From the land of Heer Ranjha and Sassi Punnu, he eked out stories of brutal realism in collections such as *Bagole, Gardab, Aable, Sailab, Aanchal,* and *Talwa-o Gharub*. Despite being located in small, local communities they spoke of universal concerns in much the same way as Thomas Hardy's novels set in rural England. Along with Faiz, he played a stellar role in organizing the first post-partition PWA in Lahore in November 1949. Qasmi suffered several years of incarceration due to his radical views.

AHMED ALI (1910–1994): Founder-member of the PWA, he first shot to fame as a contributor of two short stories, namely, *Mahavaton ki*

Ek Raat and *Baadal Nahin Aate* in *Angarey*. Educated at Aligarh and Lucknow universities, he taught at the universities of Lucknow and Allahabad during 1932–46 and joined the Bengal Senior Educational Service as professor and head of the English Department at Presidency College, Calcutta (1944–7). Ahmed Ali was also BBC's representative and director in India during 1942–4 and, having migrated to Pakistan, from China to Karachi in 1948. Ahmed Ali worked for the Pakistan Foreign Service, establishing embassies in Morocco and China. He achieved international fame with his novel *Twilight in Delhi*, which was first published by Hogarth Press in London in 1940. He was a distinguished visiting professor of Humanities at Michigan State University in 1975, Fulbright Visiting Professor of History at Western Kentucky University, and Fulbright Visiting Professor of English at Southern Illinois University in 1978–9. He was made an honorary citizen by the state of Nebraska in 1979. From 1977 to 1979, he served as Visiting Professor at the University of Karachi, which later conferred on him an honorary degree of Doctor of Literature in 1993.

AKHTAR HUSAIN RAIPURI (1912–1992): He can be regarded as the earliest serious critic belonging to the PWM, one who brought Marxian philosophy into the ambit of Urdu literature. His long essay '*Adab aur Zindagi*' (Literature and Life) published as early as July 1935 in the journal *Urdu* outlined the goals and objectives of a new, socially engaged literature and had a profound influence on charting the trajectory of fellow progressives. It brought the writings of Lenin, Tolstoy, Gorky, and Romain Rolland into the Urdu lexicon. One of his early stories, '*Muhabbat aur Nafrat*' (Love and Hatred), marks the transitory phase of the Urdu short story from the traditional to the progressive. In the early, purer days of the movement, Raipuri, who later not only got more involved in linguistics rather than literature, but also steadily distanced himself from the PWM, wrote some fine short stories that can be called progressive. Some of the notable stories in his first collection were '*Mujhe Jaane Do*', '*Marghat*', and '*Mera Ghar*'. A polyglot, he also produced some excellent translations, especially the works of the revolutionary Bengali poet Kazi Nazrul Islam, who had a profound impact on modern Urdu poetry. His autobiography, *Gard-e-Rah* (Dust of the Road), documents his remarkable life.

AKHTAR ORAINVI (1910–1977): He wrote about the poorest and most disenfranchised, those who occupied the lowest rung of India's social pyramid along with the myriad problems they face such as hunger, debt, and debilitating court cases that sap them of whatever remained after the zamindari system, landless labour and family feuds that suck their lifeblood out. Orainvi's characters were coolies, bakers, farmers, rickshawpullers, and petty labourers in stories such as 'Andhi Nagri', 'Boodhi Maa', 'Do Maain', 'Aakhri Ikanni', 'Jeene ka Sahara', 'Bail Gadi', 'Gande Ande', etc. Unlike Manto's stories about the same set of characters, in Orainvi there was a greater sense of sentimentality and emotionalism. His most successful novelette, *Kaliyan aur Kaante*, was based in a sanatorium and was marked by its realism and psychological insight into human nature.

AKHTARUL IMAN (1915–1994): Having left his home in the Bijnor district of UP, he entered an orphanage in Delhi and after a circuitous education in different cities landed in Poona as a scriptwriter for Shalimar Pictures in 1944. Two years later he moved to Bombay and became involved in the Bombay progressive circle. His first collection of poetry, *Gardaab* (1943) established him as a poet who sang sweetly of frustration, melancholy, and deeply personal traumas and disappointments. A close friend of Miraji, the two edited a bi-monthly literary journal *Khayal* from Bombay. Among those who also served on the board of the journal was Zoe Ansari, a dedicated progressive who 'sided' with those who wished to marginalize and isolate Miraji on grounds of obscenity and perversion. Like Miraji, Akhtarul Iman's poetry too was highly individualistic, and led to a parting of ways from the progressives, some of whom had been his friends in Aligarh and Delhi. His poetry collections include *Sabrang, Tarik Sayyarah*, and *Yaadein*. During his stay in Delhi in the early 1940s, he worked for the AIR and lived near Tis Hazari in the company of Miraji, Manto, Krishan Chandar, Ashk, and N.M. Rashid.

ALE AHMAD SUROOR (1911–2002): Born in the historic city of Budayun in UP, this poet, critic, and scholar lived to be not just the grand old man of Urdu adab, but also of Urdu tehzeeb. Keenly involved with the PWM and an active member of the Lucknow branch of the PWA, he distanced himself from the movement in later years as some of its excesses began to overshadow its literary output. His critical writings show the influence of modern critics like T.S. Eliot and Ian Richards in the early part of his career; he, however, refused to be straightjacketed as a modernist or progressive, and retained a lasting aversion to the use of labels in literary criticism. Some of his prominent critical writings include *Tanquidi Ishare* (1942), *Tanquid Kya Hai?* (1947), and *Adab aur Nazariya* (1954), among others. A lifelong advocate of moderation and balance, he decried any form of one-sidedness. In the preface to *Naye aur Purane Chiragh* (1946), he wrote 'It is not good for a critic to put himself into pigeonholes'.

ALI SARDAR JAFRI (1913–2000): Perhaps the most fulsomely awarded of all the progressives, Ali Sardar Jafri had an early exposure to communism. Expelled from the universities of Aligarh and Lucknow for political reasons, he was a prolific writer, lyricist, and activist. His first collection of short stories titled *Manzil* was published in 1938, and his first collection of poetry, *Parvaz*, in 1944. In 1939, he became co-editor of *Naya Adab*, a literary journal devoted to the PWM; the journal continued till 1949. With a lifetime devoted to social, political, and literary movements, he was arrested at Bhiwandi on 20 January 1949 for holding the (then) banned Progressive Urdu Writers' Conference despite warnings from Morarji Desai, chief minister of Bombay state; three months later, he was rearrested. His important works include *Dharti ke Lal* (The Jewels of the Earth, 1946), *Pardesi* (Stranger, 1957), *Nai Duniya ko Salam* (1948), *Khoon ki Lakeer* (1949), *Aman ka Sitara* (The Star of Peace), *Asia Jaag Utha* (1951), *Patthar ki Deewar* (1953), *Ek Khwab Aur* (One More Dream), and *Pairahan-e Sharar* (The Garment of Embers, 1966); and *Lahu Pukarta Hai* (The Blood Calls, 1965), which were followed by *Awadh ki Khak-i-Haseen, Subh-e Farda, Mera Safar,* and the last anthology titled *Sarhad*, which became a by-word for Indo-Pak friendship. Jafri also edited anthologies of Kabir, Mir, and Ghalib; wrote two plays for the IPTA; produced a documentary film *Kabir, Iqbal and Freedom,* and two television serials, including the 18-part *Kahkashan*, based on the lives and works of noted Urdu poets, and *Mehfil-e-Yaaran*, in which he interviewed people from different walks of life. He was also the editor and publisher of one of the leading literary Urdu magazines of the subcontinent, *Guftagu*.

ASRARUL HAQ MAJAZ (1909–1955): Known as the 'Keats of Urdu poetry', this quintessential romantic poet was also an ardent revolutionary. It was this combination of pathos-laden romanticism combined with rousing anthems advocating revolutionary social and political changes that made him hugely popular on campuses across the country and, in the process, a virtual poster boy for the progressives. A people's poet par excellence, he burst upon the Urdu literary firmament and caught the imagination of all those who had wearied of the Urdu poet's angst over the shama-parwana and the gul-o-bulbul. He introduced a new sensibility and new literary concerns through startlingly new images and conceits, and, above all, a new sort of prosody—the nazm which resembled the ghazal in its close approximation of rhyme and metre, but was free of the two-line constraint of the ghazal. Majaz evolved a lexicon that was uniquely his own yet completely in tune with his times. Fresh, sparkling, and lilting as a mountain brook, Majaz's poetry acquired near-universal acclaim in Urdu-speaking circles.

EHTESHAM HUSAIN (1913–1973): As the presiding deity in the pantheon of Urdu critics, he not merely defined approaches to Urdu criticism, but also ensured they were abided by a process of strict control and a keen eye on who was writing what. His own immaculate scholarship and erudition lent weight to his views on what constituted good literature and his unwavering and unequivocal advocacy of Art for Life's Sake helped define the parameters of progressive literature. It was to Ehtesham Husain that the progressives invariably turned, for he could be counted upon to provide a scholarly context for every contemporary literary issue. A student of Allahabad University, he taught at his alma mater as well as the Lucknow University and influenced several generations of Urdu litterateurs. The Marxist school of criticism, established by Akhtar Husain Raipuri, was taken to greater heights by him.

FAIZ AHMED FAIZ (1911–1984): Like Majaz, he too matured from a callow romantic to a revolutionary poet, but unlike Majaz he had a longer innings and a far more complex, nuanced oeuvre. Faiz wrote, prolifically and compellingly, on the events that shaped the destiny of the subcontinent; apart from his prodigious output as a poet, he also wrote newspaper editorials and articles and gave interviews on a range of subjects that, taken together, reveal a highly political mind beneath the poet's persona with an astonishing range of concerns and interests. Faiz produced seven volumes of verse, of which only the first three concern us here. His first collection, *Naqsh-e-Faryadi* (1941), was followed by *Dast-e-Saba* (1953) and *Zindah*

Nama (1956). Faiz took the message of Marx where Iqbal had left it and carried it to a younger generation of Muslims who were, in the light of the growing importance of the PWM, more receptive to its egalitarianism, concern for the poor and advocacy for change. Faiz remained a Marxist long after the decline of the PWM, but never an in doctrinaire one, nor was he ever a member of the Communist Party.

FIKR TAUNSVI (1918–1987): A poet and occasional translator who found fame as a writer of witty, humorous pieces as well as regular columns in newspapers, his single greatest contribution to progressive literature is his long reportage *Chhata Darya*, referring to the river of blood that flowed in the Land of Five Rivers. Originally from Taunsa Sharif in undivided Punjab, he moved to India after partition. Remembered for his bitingly satirical column, 'Pyaz ke Chhilke', first in *Naya Zamana* and later in the daily *Milap* (for a sum total of 25 unbroken years!), he was the unsurpassed censor and conscience of his age. Of his adopted home, Delhi, he wrote: 'I have been living in the city of Delhi for the past two decades, one of which has passed in waiting for the DTC bus, the other for socialism.'

FIRAQ GORAKHPURI (1896–1982): One of the founding members of the PWA, a doyen of Urdu literature, a poet of excellent standing, a legendary teacher of English at the Allahabad University, Firaq (whose real name was Raghupati Sahay) was a man of many parts. Just as scintillating as his virtually encyclopaedic knowledge of Urdu poetry and literature was his equally sparkling wit that made him a natural orator and an irresistible conversationalist. Well versed in English, Urdu, Hindi, and Persian, his mastery over the Urdu ghazal remained undisputed. A scholar and an aesthete, Firaq towered over his contemporaries such as Akhtar Shirani and Josh Malihabadi. Despite being, relatively speaking, a non-political poet, his influence on the progressives was profound. While essentially a writer of the ghazal (which he once described most memorably as *intehaon ka silsila* or a 'series of climaxes'), he has also left behind some of the finest examples of the modern nazm: 'Sham-e-Ayadat', 'Aadhi Raat', 'Dhundhalka', and 'Jugnu'.

HAJRA BEGUM (1910–2002): She joined the Indian students' group in London in 1935 during her Montessori Teachers' Training. On her return to India, she worked in the junior wing of the Karamat Hussain Muslim

Girls' School in Lucknow, married Dr Z.A. Ahmed in 1936, and thereafter devoted herself to active political work. A lifelong member of the CPI, she was among the founding members of the first AIPWA conference at Lucknow. She joined the All-India Women's Conference in 1936, was founder-secretary of the Allahabad Railway Coolies' Union in 1937, joined the CSP in 1937, and attended the Faizpur session of the Congress in 1936, in Haripura in 1938, and in Ramgarh in 1940. She was a member and later secretary of the Allahabad District Committee of the CPI from 1937 to 1940, co-editor of *Kisan* weekly and editor of *Prabha*, and secretary of the Allahabad PWA. Her major contribution was as organizing secretary of AIWC in 1943 and as its president in 1944, and later as member of the Central Control Commission of CPI from 1958 to 1982.

HASRAT MOHANI (1875–1951): A firebrand revolutionary, an ethical dissenter, a bit of a maverick, Hasrat Mohani nevertheless had a remarkable and varied career. A romantic poet in the classic ghazal tradition (remembered today for his sweetly sentimental '*Woh tera kothe pe nange paon aana yaad hai*' immortalized by Ghulam Ali), journalist, politician, parliamentarian, and freedom fighter, he was deeply impressed by the Russian Revolution and carried its imprint on all his later writings. A deeply religious man (who went on the hajj 13 times), he saw no contradiction between being a pan-Islamist, a nationalist, and a 'Communist Muslim'. He served as chairman of the Reception Committee at the founding of the CPI on 25 December 1925, and was a member of the CPI till 1927. Along with Azad Sobhani, he set up the Muslim Independent Party in July 1932, but later joined the Muslim League in 1937, leaving that too to join the Congress. He remained in India after partition as an independent-minded, liberal, devout Muslim. He first recorded in prose, and later used as a rallying cry at a labour rally in Calcutta in 1928, the slogan '*Inquilab Zindabad!*' He edited the journal *Urdu-e-Moalla*.

HAYATULLAH ANSARI (1912–1999): Scion of a liberal family of alims from the famous Firangi Mahal of Lucknow, he was an active member of the Aligarh branch of the PWA and later in Lucknow. He launched the *Hindustan* weekly in 1937 and ran it till 1942 often to present the Congress point of view. In 1945, he launched the *Qaumi Awaaz* with which he remained associated till 1967. In 1966, he became member of parliament (Rajya Sabha). His major collections of short stories include

Anokhi Musibat, Aakhri Koshish, Shikasta Kangure, Bhare Bazaar mein, and *Khulasa.* His magnum opus, *Lahu ke Phool,* is a novel in five volumes; it is set against the national freedom struggle and brings to the fore issues such as zamindari, landless labour, corruption, exploitation, etc. He also wrote the story of 'Neecha Nagar', which was turned into a film by K.A. Abbas.

IBRAHIM JALEES (1924–1977): His first collection of short stories published in 1944, entitled *Zard Chehre,* was a sweeping look at the widespread poverty in the country. He wrote several short stories in a somewhat similar vein as Krishan Chandar's. Like him, he then ventured into witty and humorous writings. His first collections of humorous essays, *Chalees Karore Bhikhari,* was very well-received, as were other collections entitled *Oot Patang Kahaniyan, Azad Ghulam,* and *Republic Safety Razor.* Two of his finest reportages include 'Bombay', which brings alive the Bombay of the progressives and 'Do Mulk Ek Kahani', which is a valuable account of partition and the communal violence that came in its wake. He was caught up in the movement for an independent Hyderabad state lead by Qasim Rizvi and the Majlis-i-Ittehadul-Muslimeen; however, after the failure of the movement and the annexation of the state by the Indian union, he left for Pakistan. In Pakistan, he kept falling foul of the authorities for his provocative satirical writings; his book *Jail ke Din Jail ki Raatein* is an account of his life behind bars for writing against the infamous Public Safety Act which, incidentally, aroused the ire of many progressives who had made Pakistan their new home. Jalees travelled to China in 1951 and wrote *Nai Deewar-e Cheen.*

ISMAT CHUGHTAI (1911–1991): Chughtai established herself not just as a writer of immensely popular short stories, but also as the enfant terrible of Urdu literature at a time when women writers were not only few and far between, but wrote on 'womanly' or decorous subjects. Ismat held her own in a company of illustrious writers, many of them being progressives like her and either connected with the PWM or the Bombay film industry, or both. Best known for her acerbic and penetrating short stories, she also wrote sharp and sassy essays, commentaries, film scripts, and pen portraits of her contemporaries. Her wit, irreverence, and sheer iconoclasm occasionally divert attention from her one singular quality, that is, her unfailing ability to hold a mirror to society, an ability she shared with her friend Manto.

JAN NISAR AKHTAR (1914–1976): Beginning his poetic career as a writer of soft, sentimental, romantic ghazals and nazms, he changed his style under the spell of the progressives. One of his earliest nazms, *'Girls' College ki Lari'*, made him very popular with young audiences. Later, he wrote rousing poems like *'Khana Badosh'*, *'Bagola'*, *'Jahan Main Hoon'*, and *'Yeh Ho Kar Rahega'* in the style of the fiery Josh Malihabadi. For him, Khalilur Rahman Azmi had written that if only Jan Nisar Akhtar wrote in his own style, rather than following in the footsteps of his more illustrious colleagues, his contribution to progressive poetry would have been more substantial. Be that as it may, there is near-consensus that Jan Nisar's finest hour as a poet was when he wrote *'Khamosh Awaz'* (The Silent Voice) on the occasion of his wife's death. A collection of letters exchanged between him and his wife, entitled *Zer-e-Lab*, is similarly poignant. Married to Safiya, a writer in her own right and the sister of Majaz, his son, Javed Akhtar carries his legacy forward.

JOSH MALIHABADI (1898–1982): Born to a feudal landowning family of Awadh, Josh always had rebellious views and wrote fiery but extravagantly lyrical poetry. He worked briefly in Hyderabad, but on being banished by the Nizam for expressing radical, subversive views, he moved to Delhi where he launched his own monthly journal, *Kaleem*. Later, Josh moved with the journal to Lucknow where the *Kaleem* was merged with the progressives' *Naya Adab*. While his first collection *Rooh-e-Adab* (1921) established him as a poet of youth and vigour, later years saw him as the undisputed *shair-e-inquilab*, the poet who sang of revolt and rebellion. Devoted to the cause of nationalism, Josh drew his readers towards the heady idea of freedom like no one else hitherto had, using a blend of suggestion and forthrightness, seduction and sermonizing, extravagance and subtlety. Producing a number of collections of poetry, each more lyrical, more rousing, more stirring, Josh's oeuvre has piles upon piles of colourful images tumbling out of a kaleidoscope and dazzling his readers with their astonishing and seemingly inexhaustible variety. Two of his early poems, *'Shikast-e-Zindaan ka Khwaab'* and *'East India Company ke Farzandon Se'*, were picked up by the progressives as anthems of resistance. Josh migrated to Pakistan, but was miserable in his new home and pined for India.

K.M. ASHRAF (1903–1962): Born to a Muslim Rajput family, Ashraf was the product of an eclectic education—from a madrasa in Moradabad to the M.A.O. College to Jamia Millia Islamia and then back again at Aligarh where his academic brilliance impressed the Maharaja of Alwar to fund his education in England. In England, not only did he become an avowed communist, but mentored many young Indian students including Zaheer and Mahmud. On his return to India in 1932, he plunged into the freedom movement, joined the CSP, and took charge of the minorities' cell in the AICC and the Muslim mass contact programme. While his academic work was on the social and cultural conditions in medieval India, Ashraf was a scholar with a wide range of interests and his influence over the communists of his generation was profound.

KAIFI AZMI (1918–2000): Born in Azamgarh district in a family of zamindars, Azmi wrote his first poem at the age of 11 and joined the Communist Party at the age of 19. Subsequently, he wrote for the party paper, *'Qaumi Jung'*. In 1948, he wrote his first lyric for the film industry in Bombay for *Buzdil*, directed by Shahid Latif, the husband of his friend and fellow progressive, Ismat Chughtai, and went on to write some of the most hauntingly evocative lyrics ever written for the Bombay film industry including the memorable *'Waqt ne kiya kya haseen sitam....'* An ardent member of the PWM and a major crowd puller at peoples' mushairas organized by the progressives in industrial hubs, Kaifi was equally active as a spokesperson for several workers' unions. A writer of tender lyrics and rousing anthems displaying an astonishing combination of passion and conviction, Azmi was the quintessential activist-poet. His three major poetry collections are entitled *Jhankar* (1943), *Akhir-e-Shab* (1947), and *Awara Sijde* (1973).

KANHAIYYALAL KAPOOR (1910–1981): His best-known collection entitled *Sang-o-Khisht* contained essays such as *'Apne Watan mein Sab Kuch Hai Pyare'* and *'Qaumi Libas'*—the latter being a spoof on the correspondence between Gandhi and Jinnah. Kapoor turned his pen towards his fellow writers parodying the fare being passed off as 'new poetry' in *'Ghalib Jadeed Shoara ki Ek Majlis mein'*. Several contemporary literary, social, and political issues became the target of Kapoor's satire, including the PWM itself, as in a letter-like essay *'Taraqqui Pasand Dost ke Naam'* (To a Progressive Friend). With great mastery over wit, humour, and satire, he perfected the technique of the anti-climax. One of his finest sketches is *'Tutor'*, which seamlessly blends humour and pathos. The post-partition scene in India gave him ample fodder for sharpening his tools, as in 'Shan Shan Shan', 'Hijrat', 'Gunde', 'Professor Danish', 'Urdu ka Akhri Daur', 'Film Director ke Naam', or 'Sansani'. Using both prose and verse, Kapoor could create delightful parody from even the most tense or fraught of situations.

KHWAJA AHMAD ABBAS (1914–1987): An active member of the Aligarh branch of the PWA during his student days, he graduated effortlessly to becoming an integral part of the Bombay progressives' group during its glory days of the 1940s. Active in IPTA and the Bombay film industry as well as being a prolific novelist, short story writer, and journalist, he made several important films like *Saat Hindustani* (1969) and *Do Boond Pani* (1972). *Neecha Nagar*, based on a story by Hayatullah Ansari, won him the Palme d'Or at the Cannes Film festival in 1946. He began writing the hugely popular column 'Last Page' in 1935 for the *Bombay Chronicle* and when it closed in 1947, he moved the column to *Blitz* where it continued till his death; it was known as *Azad Kalaam* in the Urdu edition. A descendent of Altaf Husain Hali, Abbas's best-known work is *Inquilab*, based on communal violence.

KRISHAN CHANDAR (1914–1977): Despite a master's in English and a degree in Law, he went on to become one of Urdu literature's most prolific writers with over 80 published volumes. Having written innumerable short humorous pieces, romantic short stories, and novels, it was the short story that earned him laurels. Accused of being an incorrigible idealist, even a maudlin sentimentalist on occasion, Krishan Chandar was in some ways a 'flawed' progressive. Stories like *Kalu Bhangi, Mahalakshmi ka Pul, Shikast, Jab Khet Jage* display his socialist concerns and his heartfelt empathy for the poor and downtrodden; however, unlike the other progressives, he was seldom able to free himself from despair and defeat. His most prolific period is said to be during 1955–60 when he published the autobiographical *Ek Gadhe ki Sarguzasht* (The Autobiography of a Donkey) in 1957. He remained an active member of the PWA and was held up as a role model for budding progressives.

MAHMUDUZZAFAR KHAN (1908–1954): Scion of a distinguished family from Rampur and the son of Dr Saiduzzafar, a professor of Anatomy at the Lucknow Medical College, Mahmuduzzafar had lived in England for the greater part of his life. Sent to Sherborune School in Dorset at the age of 12, he completed his graduation from Oxford. Yet, when he returned to India in 1931, he had become an active nationalist, choosing to wear khadi and refusing to sit for the civil services examinations as was expected of someone of his class and privilege. He contributed a story to *Angarey* and got swept up by the rising tide of the PWM. He married Rashid Jahan in 1934, worked as vice principal at the M.A.O. College, Amritsar (1934–7), and thereafter worked full time for the party. In 1948, he became general secretary of the CPI in UP and was forced to go underground when the party was banned. While he edited some issues of the party organ *Chingari* from 1938 onwards, his only major literary contribution is *A Quest for Life*, an account of his travels in the USSR, published in 1954. He was actively involved with the first AIPWA conference held in Lucknow in 1936.

MAJNUN GORAKHPURI (1904–1988): His real name being Ahmad Siddiq, he was one of the leading Urdu *afsana nigar* and *adeeb* of his times. A close friend and associate of Firaq, his major critical works include *Adab aur Zindagi* (1944), *Iqbal: Ijmali Tabsirah* (1945), *Tanquidi Hashiye* (1945), *Nuqoosh-o-Afkar* (1955), and *Sher aur Ghazal* (1962), among others; among fiction his major collections are *Zaidi ka Hashr*, a novel, and *Khwab-o-Khayal wa Doosre Afsane* (1943). Along with Ehtesham Husain, he formalized Marxian criticism in Urdu and put up a valiant defence of the progressive school of criticism against the traditional school represented by the venerable Rashid Ahmad Siddiqui at Aligarh. Emphasizing the historical role of literature, he also cautioned against the excess of Marxian philosophy when applied to the Indian context and gave due importance to realism, creativity, and aestheticism. His short stories probe the contours of the human dilemma laying bare the polarities of good and bad, individual will and fatalism, life and death. Like many other Urdu litterateurs (such as A.A. Suroor), he too began his career by teaching English and then switched to Urdu. He migrated to Pakistan.

MAJROOH SULTANPURI (1919–2000): Born as Asrarul Hasan Khan in Sultanpur in UP, he became first a *hakeem* and then an established ghazal poet before becoming a popular poet on the mushaira circuit. He wrote his first film lyrics for the film *Shah Jahan* in 1946 and then launched upon a highly lucrative career in Bombay. However, his leftist leanings did not leave him entirely and Morarji Desai's government put him in prison for writing anti-government film lyrics. As a film lyricist, poet, and song writer, he dominated the world of both Urdu literature and the music industry. Compared to his more prolific colleagues, both within the film industry and among the progressives, Majrooh's non-film oeuvre is slender. Just one collection, titled somewhat modestly as *Ghazal*, is the sum total of a sensibility that was intrinsically 'progressive' insofar as it is inclusive as reflected in his most often quoted sher: '*Hum akele hi chale they janib-e-manzil magar / Log saath aate gaye aur karvaan banta gaya.*'

MAKHDOOM MOHIUDDIN (1908–1969): Fiery trade union leader and writer of romantic verse and fiercely political poetry, Makhdoom was a committed communist. Born into a god-fearing family of teachers and scribes in the Medhak district of Andhra Pradesh, he was struck from an early age by the disparities he saw all around him. After MA in Urdu from Osmania in 1936, Makhdoom spent the next two years doing odd jobs such as a stint at the *Payam* and another at the Records Office till he finally found employment as a lecturer at the prestigious City College in 1939. His first collection *Surkh Savera*, published in 1944, established him as a poet to reckon with. His reputation was shored up with subsequent collections—*Gul-e-Tar* and *Bisat-e-Raqs*. Having set up the Hyderabad branch of the PWA in 1936, he remained an active member all through his life; he was also actively involved in the Telangana Movement from 1946 onwards.

MOIN AHSAN JAZBI (1912–2005): A contemporary of Majaz and Ale Ahmed Suroor and a protégé of Fani Badayuni at St John's College, Agra, Jazbi acquired an early and formidable reputation as a poet in the classical mould. While his depiction of the human condition, its trials and tribulations, made him popular with the progressives of the early days, his steadfast refusal to write on specific social or political issues earned him their collective ire too. Perhaps being too individualistic, he chose not to write poetry according to anyone's dictates save his own conscience. It led to his marginalization and exclusion during the glory days of the progressives. Another accusation levelled at him by the progressives was the despondent tone of his poetry and his refusal to provide solutions to the misery of the human predicament he presented so well. While giving importance to Marx, Jazbi believed that the social reality of each country was different and the communists' 'one-fits-all' theory was, therefore, not acceptable to him. Jazbi introduced a startlingly new idiom and vocabulary into ghazals that were crafted in the classical mould, yet reflected a modern sensibility that was entirely in sync with the times, as is evident in the unforgettable 'Jab kashti sabut-o-salim thi, sahil ki tamanna kisko thi / Ab aisi shakista kishti par sahil ki tamanna kaun kare'.

MULK RAJ ANAND (1905–2004): One of the original signatories of the *Manifesto* at Nanking Hotel in London, he was never a member of the Communist Party, but always a sympathizer and an avid supporter of the movement all through its tumultuous history. He was elected the first president of the PWA set up by Zaheer and other Indian students in England. He made a name for himself with early successes in England first with *The Untouchable* (1935) followed by *The Coolie* (1936). With a Preface by E.M. Forster, his very first book was well-received and Anand became the toast of literary circles in London. His politics as well as his writings expressed a keen desire for social transformation and political change. Though he lived in London, he was present at several important junctions of the progressive bandwagon, such as the Calcutta Conference of 1938, and remained in constant touch with the Indian progressives, especially Zaheer. He attended the Second World Congress of Writers in Madrid in the summer of 1937 on behalf of Indian progressive writers and came to India to regale Indian progressives with his eye-witness account of the struggle against fascism being waged in Spain.

MUMTAZ HUSAIN (1918–1992): A leading critic in the Marxian mould, he began his career as a teacher at the Colvin Taluqedars College in Lucknow before moving to Bombay to work at the Anjuman-e-Islam Urdu Research Institute as an assistant director. Migrating to Pakistan shortly after partition, he worked briefly as a journalist, but went back to academics. He retired as a principal of the Sirajuddin College in Karachi, but all along remained an influential voice in Urdu criticism. Apart from his work on Ghalib and Amir Khusrau, which have furthered the frontiers of understanding creativity and aestheticism in Urdu literature, he has published several noteworthy collections of critical essays such as *Naqd-e-Hayat*, *Naye Tanquidi Goshe*, and *Naqd-e-Harf*. Dubbed the 'Red Traveller' of Urdu criticism by the progressives, he however had his share of disagreements with the 'extremists' within the movement, especially those who wished to throw the baby out with the water when it came to denigrating or outright dismissing classical literature.

MOHAMMAD HASAN (1926–2010): A younger contemporary of Majaz, he was one of the last of the progressives. He has left behind a nuanced study of not only the progressive upsurge, but a varied oeuvre that includes criticism, poetry, drama, and scholarly essays. His major works include *Dehli mein Urdu Shairi ka Tahzibi aur Fikri Pasmanzar, Mashriqui Tanquid, Urdu Adab mein Romani Tehreek, Qadim Urdu Adab ki Tanquidi Tahrik, Adabi Samajiyat, Mirza Ruswa ke Tanquidi Muraselat, Mere Stage Drame, Naye Drame,* and *Diwan-e-Abru*. A biographical novel, *Gham-e-Dil, Wahshat-e-Dil,* deals with his close association with Majaz.

NIYAZ HAIDER (1920–1989): A good poet who possibly stopped short of being outstanding on account of the extreme topicality of some of his concerns, Niyaz Haider's career illustrates the pitfalls of excessive devotion to a cause. While his role in popularizing Urdu drama and his work for the IPTA are indeed commendable, his poetry is marked by excess. Some examples of his poetry, that fulfilled the progressive creed, are 'Jamal-e-Misr' and 'Qasr-e-Lenin'. In Bombay, he worked closely with Krishan Chandar, Mahindarnath, and Sahir Ludhianvi in furthering the progressive cause. His play *Mitti ki Gadi* was made famous by Habib Tanvir. Along with fellow progressive, Vishwamitra Adil, he wrote the lyrics for *Sarai ke Bahar*, the only film directed by Krishan Chandar.

PREMCHAND (1880–1936): Born Dhanpat Rai, but better known by his nom de plume, he was a pioneering figure in modern Hindi literature. He introduced both realism and the genre of the short story in Indian fiction and single-handedly popularized both like no one else had before him. From 1914 or so, he began to write in Hindi instead of Urdu, and from 1920, as he increasingly came under the sway of Gandhi and the non-cooperation movement, we can discern a stronger thrust towards socially purposive literature. Premchand held a mirror to his times like few other writers had hitherto done; he wrote extensively on untouchability, socio-economic disparities, urban–rural divide, the sorry lot of women, especially widows as well as evil practices such as dowry and child marriages. He presided over the first AIPWA conference in Lucknow, and until his death, remained actively involved in propagating awareness of the newly formed association on which he had pinned many hopes. His own writings—read chronologically—are living proof of a steady growth towards progressivism.

QATEEL SHIFAI (1919–2001): Like many other early progressives, he too was a romantic by temperament who got swayed by the rushing tide of progressivism. Infused with the earthy vigour of rustic Punjab, his nazms are full-bodied and flavoursome and both his ghazals and nazms bear the melodiousness and 'singability' of geet. Like many of his contemporaries, he was essentially interested in writing poetry on women (be they actresses, prostitutes, fallen woman, etc.) though he tried, under the influence of the progressives, to also write on social and political issues. His poetic career shows remarkable similarities with Majaz in its tone and tenor. He worked as assistant editor of the monthly literary journal *Adab-e-Latif* in 1946 where he came in contact with the Lahore progressives. He also worked with the film industry in Lahore as a lyricist and also produced a film in his mother tongue, *Hindko*.

RAJINDER SINGH BEDI (1915–1984): With *Dana-o-Dam* (1940), his very first collection, Bedi earned a place for himself in the canon of Urdu short stories. Beginning his professional life as a postal clerk, Bedi moved to Bombay and got involved with the film industry like many of his fellow progressives, but his interest led him from writing the dialogue and screenplay of over 27 films to producing and directing memorable films like *Garam Coat, Dastak,* and *Phagun*. Women occupied a central position in a great deal of Bedi's writings and he has etched some memorable female characters: the eponymous Kalyani and Lajwanti, Indu in *Apne Dukh Mujhe De Do*, Rano in *Ek Chadar Maili si*, and Ma in *Banj*. Details of everyday life, no matter how small, found a place in his stories and became reflections of a larger social reality. Bedi's stories survive the test of time because they hinge on the common and the commonplace that transcend time and circumstance. However, the same Bedi who was hailed by the progressives as a champion of their cause because of his portrayal of lower-middle-class working people later distanced himself due to his unwillingness to conform to communism and the soviet brand of socialist realism.

RASHID JAHAN (1905–1953): The eldest daughter of Shaikh Abdullah, a pioneer among male reformers and the founder of the Muslim Girls' College at Aligarh, Rashid Jahan studied medicine at Lady Hardinge College. A committed communist and party worker, the epitaph on her grave in Moscow sums up her life quite aptly and succinctly: 'Rashid Jahan: Communist Doctor and Writer'. A key player in the setting up of the PWA, she remained actively associated with it all through her brief life, especially in its Lucknow branch. She published only one collection, *Aurat wa Digar Drame wa Afsane* in her life, though she wrote several short stories, radio plays, skits, etc. A collection entitled *Shola-e-Jawwala* was published posthumously by her sister-in-law. Rashid Jahan's writings opened a window into the life of the ordinary middle-class Indian woman—both Hindu and Muslim. More importantly, she ploughed a virgin field that allowed many women writers—a little younger than her—to walk over a terrain that was not simply contested but unimaginable till she wrote perfectly believable stories about real, though ordinary, people.

RAZIA SAJJAD ZAHEER (1917–1979): Born in Ajmer where her father was the headmaster of a school, she married Sajjad Zaheer in 1938. Pursing a master's degree from Allahabad University, she taught at the Karamat Hussain Girls' College, Lucknow. Encouraged by her husband, she blossomed as a writer and soon became an active member of the PWA in Lucknow and later in Delhi. She published a collection of letters, *Nuqoosh-e-Zindaan*, written to her by her husband from jail, in 1951. She published her first novella *Sar-e-Sham* in 1953 followed by the novels *Kante* in 1954 and *Suman* in 1963. She worked at the Russian Cultural Centre in Delhi and translated over 40 works from English and Hindi into Urdu including Bertolt Brecht's *Caucasian Chalk Circle*. Growing steadily more active as a writer after her husband's departure for Pakistan, she attended the Peace Conference in Calcutta in 1948 and wrote *Aman ka Carvan*.

RIFAT SAROSH (1926–2007): With a long and illustrious career in broadcasting, he was also a poet, dramatist, and an essay writer of some repute. Apart from the lyrics that got him much fame, he also experimented with the opera, with *Jahan Ara* being his most famous play. Some of his major works are *Usi Deewar ke Saye mein: Manzum Drame*, *Shakh-e-Gul: Majmua-e-Kalam*, *Nuqush-e-Raftah: Mazamin*, *Thake na Mere Paun: Safarnama*, *Jahan-e-Raqs wa Naghman: Manzum Drame wa Opera*, *Adab Shanasi: Mazamin*, *Meri Sada ka Ghubar: Sheri Majmua*, among others. In *Harf Harf Bambai: Tassurati Khake*, he brings alive many of the Bombay progressives through lively biographical sketches.

SAADAT HASAN MANTO (1912–1955): Provocative, outrageous, scandalous, sometimes even blasphemous, Manto was the original enfant terrible of Urdu literature. Cocking a snook at society, literary norms, and most notions of propriety, he touched the hearts of many with his convincing and utterly original portrayal of human fallibility. Never one to impose his own interpretation of events, Manto could look at people and events with a consciousness uncoloured by notions of nationalism, religion, morality, least of all sentimentality. He wrote what he saw and felt, and he wrote compulsively and prodigiously. In the 43 years that he lived, he published 22 collections of short stories, 1 novel, 5 (7, according to some) collections of radio plays, 3 collections of essays, and 2 collections of sketches of famous personalities. Though much of his writing was in the nature of 'command performances'—to feed the twin demons of drink and acute, chronic poverty—there is still a great deal in his vast and variegated oeuvre that is touched by greatness.

SAGHAR NIZAMI (1905–1984): A disciple of Seemab Akbarabadi (1880–1952), he too wrote on nationalism and patriotism. Wooed by the progressives for the first AIPWA, he joined the PWA being largely sympathetic and in tune with their cause; however, like many others of his generation and temperament he could not remain within the fold for very long and soon distanced himself from the PWA. A man of many parts, he edited the journal *Asia*, wrote plays such as *Shakuntala* and *Anarkali*, compiled anthologies of his prose writings and produced several collections of his poetry, such as *Sada-e-mashriq, Rang Mahal, Mauj-o-Sahil*, etc. A prolific writer of verse—both historical and film lyrics—he also tried his hand quite successfully at writing radio plays, translations, and literary criticism.

SAHIR LUDHIANVI (1921–1980): A popular romantic poet virtually from his college days in Ludhiana, Sahir lived in Lahore where he edited *Adab-e-Latif, Savera, Pritlari,* and *Shahkar*. Though from the 1950s onwards he came to be regarded as a lyricist rather than poet and, like most progressives who learnt to make compromises by giving in to the demands of film-makers, Sahir embarked on his literary career as a political poet. His poem 'Taj Mahal' is a wonderful ode to socialism with its hauntingly evocative romanticism that is nudged aside by a growing awareness of inequities and injustices of the real world. With his very first collection, *Talkhiyan* (1943), he strode like a colossus across the mushaira circuit during the heydays of the progressives. One of the most successful film lyricists of his generation, his lyrics in simple but chaste Hindustani touched a chord with millions of Indians; they continue to be sung, broadcast, and remembered by more Indians than any of the other Urdu heavy weights.

SAJJAD ZAHEER (1905–1973): The prodigal son of Sir Wazir Hasan, the chief justice of Oudh, Zaheer had one BA degree from the University of Lucknow (1924) and another from Oxford (1931), when he came to India during a visit and published *Angarey* in December 1932 along with three friends. He returned to England, took the bar exam, published the novella *London ki Ek Raat*, and hammered out a manifesto with like-minded Indians and returned in 1935 with the intention of setting up an AIPWA. He was instrumental in spreading awareness about this proposed new association whose first conference he organized in Lucknow in 1936. A dedicated member of the CPI, he nevertheless also joined the CSP and the AICC where he was put in charge of foreign affairs and subsequently expelled for anti-party activities.

SALAM MACHCHLISHAHRI (1920–1973): A writer who virtually slipped from public consciousness and known to none among the present generation, save the serious student of modern Urdu history, Salam Machchlishahri was in many ways a remarkable poet. At the peak of his powers, in the years immediately after Partition, he wrote some excellent poetry. His collections include *Mere Naghme*, *Wasatein*, and *Payal*, the last being a collection of songs which remained his specialty even though he was adept at the ghazal.

SIBTE HASAN (1916–1986): Consistently found in the midst of progressive activity all through the movement's tumultuous history, he was among the earliest to lend his support to the mint-fresh *Manifesto* in 1935. As assistant editor of *Payam* (which was then edited by Qazi Abdul Ghaffar), he was among the early proponents of the PWA in Hyderabad. He had heard about the nascent PWM from Dr K.M. Ashraf, his teacher at Aligarh, and helped mobilize support for the idea of starting a branch of the PWA in Hyderabad. Later, when he moved to Lucknow to work at the *National Herald*, he became co-editor of the progressives' journal *Naya Adab* along with Majaz and Jafri. He went to Columbia University for higher education and joined the CPI in 1942. After Partition, he went to Pakistan where he remained involved with socialist concerns and edited the leftist weekly *Lail-o-Nahar* (part of Mian Iftikharuddin's Progressive Papers Ltd) and wrote a slew of Marxist books such as *Moosa se Marx*

Tak, The Battle of Ideas in Pakistan, Maazi ke Mazaar, Shehr-e-Nigraan, Sukhan dar Sukhan, Adab aur Roshan Khayali, among others. He died of a heart attack in India while attending the golden jubilee celebrations of the PWA.

SYED MUTTALIBI FARIDABADI (1890–1964): In June 1938, he organized the first-of-its-kind peasants' conference and rural mushaira in Faridabad. A gathering of poets who wrote in Brajbhasha, Haryanvi, or the countless other dialects from the rural areas surrounding Delhi and broadly came under the category of 'Hindustani' was a novel idea, one that was seized by the PWA as a template for future such gatherings. Faridabadi had been active with the peasants and workers in the Gurgaon, Alwar, Bharatpur, and Rohtak regions and was convinced that big literary events in the big cities did not address the needs of people closer to the soil and the continuing distinction between 'high' and 'low' culture meant that the urban was necessarily high and the rural (which included the folk) was always low. He had written a verse drama, *Kisan Rut*, in a style redolent of the sights and smells of the countryside, but using a pleasing mixture of Urdu and Haryanvi. His derelict haveli in Faridabad became the venue for a large gathering of rural poets. Peasants squatted on the ground while on a makeshift dais sat Faridabadi, Ahmed Ali, and Zaheer, representing the central committee of the PWA. A sprinkling of teachers and students from the Jamia Millia Islamia, some political workers from Delhi and its neighbourhood listened to the peasant poets who often sang their compositions to the beat of folk instruments. While the subjects were topical—even overtly social and political—the style was the time-honoured bara masa with a robust mingling of Urdu and Haryanvi idiom.

UPENDRANATH ASHK (1910–2002): Like Akhtar Husain Raipuri, Ashk belonged to the early generation of progressives whose first collection, *Nau Ratan*, published in 1930, received praise from no less a personage than Premchand. His reputation was shored up by the second collection, entitled *Aurat ki Fitrat*, published in 1933. The stories of these two collections were marked by reformism and idealism. His progressive phase started with *Daachi* with stories reflecting the Congress's satyagraha phase and other political events. His emphasis on plot and characterization set him apart stylistically and temperamentally from the other progressives. His last collection in Urdu, before he began writing in Hindi, was *Chattan*;

Urdu critic Khalilur Rahman Azmi ranked it as his finest contribution to the Urdu progressive short story.

WAMIQ JAUNPURI (1913–2002): He is best remembered for his *Bhooka Hai Bangal* that became a war cry for a country driven to the brink of famine and mass murders by a greedy, insensitive imperial master. It was picked up by the IPTA and used in innovative ways in the course of their country-wide tours. He published three collections of poetry, namely, *Cheekhein*, *Jaras*, and *Shabtab*. In later years, however, he drifted away from the PWA.

ZAHEER KASHMIRI (1920–1994): Not only was he an active member of the literary activities of the PWA, but, being an active worker in the peasants' and workers' groups, was equally involved in its political 'agenda'. Accused of extremism and ideological intolerance, he chose to give importance to the public over the personal, the social and political over the individual. His penchant for rousing *hungami shairi*—be it on the Telangana Movement or the growing anti-colonialism in Asia—earned him a reputation of being a topical poet, one who wrote only for the moment. He served as one of the editors of the literary journal *Savera* during the 1950s; *Savera* was regarded as a mouthpiece of the progressives.

Annexure II

Some Important Dates in the Progressive Writers' Movement

1914–18	First World War.
26 December 1925	Formation of the CPI.
December 1932	Publication of *Angarey*.
15 March 1933	Banning of *Angarey* by the imperial government.
5 April 1933	'In Defence of *Angarey*: Shall We Submit to Gagging' published in the *Leader* from Allahabad.
10 September 1934	First issue of *Chingari* appears from Saharanpur, UP.
24 November 1934	The *Manifesto* is drawn up in the Nanking Hotel in London by a group of young men, many of whom would continue to support the PWA in some way or another.
July 1935	Akhtar Husain Raipuri publishes 'Adab aur Zindagi' in Maulvi Abdul Haq's *Urdu* spelling out the place of realism in life and, by extension, in art.
1935	Sajjad Zaheer publishes *London ki Ek Raat*.
21–26 June 1935	Conference of World Writers held in Paris; attended by Zaheer.

October 1935	The *Hans* carries a Hindi translation of the *Manifesto* of the AIPWA.
November 1935	Zaheer returns to India.
December 1935	Gathering of Hindi and Urdu writers in Allahabad organized by Dr Tara Chand under the aegis of the Hindustani Academy.
February 1936	*The Left Review* publishes the *Manifesto* of the AIPWA.
January 1936	Zaheer travels to Amritsar and meets Faiz for the first time; with Faiz, Rashid Jahan and Mahmud travel to Lahore to set up a branch of the PWA.
9 April 1936	First All-India Progressive Writers' Conference held in Lucknow; presidential address delivered by Munshi Premchand entitled '*Sahitya ka Uddeshya*'.
May 1936	M.G. Hallett, the home secretary, sends a notice (which soon acquires notoriety as the Hallett Circular) advising concerned authorities to keep a stern watch on the activities of the PWA which despite its professedly 'innocuous' objectives was 'advocating policies akin to those of the communists'.
19–23 June 1936	Second Conference of the International Association of Writers for the Defense of Culture held in London; M.R. Anand attends this conference on behalf of the AIPWA.
1936	First Urdu–Hindi Conference of the PWA, in Allahabad; organized by Shyam Kumari Nehru.
14 November 1937	Second Urdu–Hindi Conference of the PWA in Allahabad; organized by Bishambar Nath Pandey, its high point is the message sent by Rabindranath Tagore.

1936–8	Sajjad Zaheer helms the AIPWA as its general secretary.
1938	Abdul Alim takes over from Sajjad Zaheer as general secretary of the AIPWA.
1938	Sajjad Zaheer and Sohan Singh Josh bring out the first issue of *Chingari* in Urdu.
14–15 May 1938	Syed Muttalibi Faridabadi organized the first-of-its-kind peasant poets' conference and rural mushaira in Faridabad.
24–25 December 1938	Second All-India Progressive Writers' Conference in Calcutta; the *Manifesto* is formally adopted.
February–March 1940	Punjabi Progressive Writers' Conference in Amritsar in the historic Jallianwala Bagh organized by Faiz on the same venue as the annual meeting of the Punjab Kisan Committee.
1939–48	Tenure of P.C. Joshi as general secretary of the CPI.
1939–45	Second World War.
August 1942	Gandhi launches the Quit India Movement.
July 1942–December 1946	Ban lifted on the CPI.
1942	Third All-India Progressive Writers' Conference in Delhi.
23 May–1 June 1943	First All-India Congress of the CPI in Bombay.
22–25 May 1943	Fourth All-India Progressive Writers' conference on the sidelines of the CPI Congress in Bombay.
December 1945	All-India Urdu Progressive Writers Conference in Hyderabad.
February 1948	South East Asian Youth Conference in Calcutta, ahead of the Second Congress of the CPI.

28 February–6 March 1948	Second Congress of the CPI held in Calcutta; among other things decision taken to set up the CPP and P.C. Joshi is replaced with B.T. Ranadive as general secretary.
Last week of December 1948	First meeting of the PWA after partition in Lucknow. It coincides with an all-India conference of Indian Muslims organized by Maulana Abul Kalam Azad to take stock of the issues facing the community.
April 1949	UP progressives hold a state-level conference to thrash out the issue of language.
27–29 May 1949	Fourth conference of the AIPWA is organized in Bhiwandi; a new manifesto is prepared under the supervision of Ram Bilas Sharma, the general secretary of the AIPWA.
11–13 November 1949	First All-Pakistan Progressive Writers' Conference in Lahore.
6–8 March 1953	Fifth conference of the AIPWA in Delhi; the new manifesto is presented by the new general secretary, Krishan Chandar.
1951	India faces its first general election.
1951–4	Sajjad Zaheer and Faiz (with 14 other fellow accused) serve time in Pakistani jails under trumped-up charges in the so-called Rawalpindi Conspiracy Case.
12–15 July 1952	Second All-Pakistan Progressive Writers' Conference in Karachi.
July 1954	CPP declared illegal.
1955	Sajjad Zaheer is released from Pakistan and returns home.
March 1956	A gathering of progressive writers is organized in Mau in Azamgarh district; its agenda is to decide whether to keep the PWA alive or not, and if at all it is to be kept afloat should it retain the same name.

May 1956	All-India Urdu Conference held in Hyderabad where Zaheer and Abdul Alim maintain that the 'progressive' view has become so common and wide-based that there is no need for a separate association to 'preach' it.
December 1956	The last significant achievement of the AIPWA is the Asian Writers' Conference in New Delhi where a large number of delegates arrive from Korea, Mongolia, Nepal, Syria, Pakistan, Indo-China, USSR, Ceylon, and China.

Annexure III

Major Progressive Literature in Urdu (1935–55)

Angarey (a collection of progressive fiction), 1932
Aurat ki Fitrat (short stories), Upendranath Ashk, 1933
'*Adab aur Zindagi*' (essay), Akhtar Hussain Raipuri, in *Urdu,* July 1935
London ki Ek Raat (novel), Sajjad Zaheer, set in Bloomsbury, 1935
Atish Pare (short stories), Saadat Hasan Manto, 1936
Aurat aur Digar Afsane (short stories and a play), Rashid Jahan, 1937
'*Bachpan*' (essay), '*Dheet*' (soliloquy), *Fasadi* (drama), '*Kafir*' (first short story), and *Gainda*, by Ismat Chughtai, begin to be published in *Saqi* and *Naya Adab*, all in 1938
Manzil (short stories), Sardar Jafri, 1938
Ahang (poetry), Majaz, 1938
Ziddi (novella), Ismat Chughtai, 1939
Twilight in Delhi (a novel in English), Ahmed Ali, 1940
Manto ke Afsane (short stories), Saadat Hasan Manto, 1940
Azadi ki Nazmein (poetry), Sibte Hasan (ed.), 1940
Dana-o-Dam (short stories), Rajinder Singh Bedi, 1940
Naqsh-e-Faryadi (poetry), Faiz Ahmed Faiz, 1941
Mavara (poetry), N.M. Rashed, 1941
Yaadein (reminiscences), Zaheer, written in the Deoli detention camp in 1940, published in the January–February issue of *Naya Adab*, 1941
Chotein (short stories), Ismat Chughtai, 1942
Dhuan (short stories), Saadat Hasan Manto, 1942
Tanquidi Ishare (criticism), Ale Ahmad Suroor, 1942

Afsane aur Drame (stories and plays), Manto, 1943
Gardaab (poetry), Akhtarul Iman, 1943
Talkhiyan (poetry), Sahir Ludhianvi, 1943
Jhankar (poetry), Kaifi Azmi, 1943
Yeh Khoon Kis ka Hai? (play), Sardar Jafri, 1943
Paikaar (play), Sardar Jafri, 1944
Parvaz (poetry), Sardar Jafri, 1944
Surkh Savera (poetry), Makhdum Mohiuddin, 1944
Adab aur Zindagi (criticism), Majnun Gorakhpuri, 1944
Tanquidi Jaize (criticism), Ehtesham Husain, 1944
Qaidkhana (short stories), Ahmed Ali, 1944
Terhi Lakeer (novel), Ismat Chughtai, 1945
Annadata (short stories), Krishan Chandar, 1945
Tarraqui Pasand Adab (criticism), Aziz Ahmad, 1945
Maut se Pehle (short stories), Ahmed Ali, 1945
Naye aur Purane Chiragh (criticism), Ale Ahmad Suroor, 1946
Hum Vahshi Hain (short stories), Krishan Chandar, 1947
Akhir-e-Shab (poetry), Kaifi Azmi, 1947
Tanquid Kya Hai? (criticism), Ale Ahmad Suroor, 1947
Nai Duniya ko Salam (poetry), Sardar Jafri, 1948
Chughad (short stories), Saadat Hasan Manto, 1948
Siyah Hashiye (anecdotes), Saadat Hasan Manto, 1948
Khoon ki Lakir (poetry), Sardar Jafri, 1949
Badshahat ka Khatma (short stories), Saadat Hasan Manto, 1950
Asia Jaag Utha (poetry), Sardar Jafri, 1951
Nuqoosh-e-Zindaan (collection of letters), written by Sajjad Zaheer to his wife, Razia Sajjad Zaheer, from the prisons of Allahabad and Lucknow, 1951
Dast-e-Saba (poetry), Faiz Ahmed Faiz, 1953
Chooi Mooi (collection of 14 essays, reportage, and short stories), Ismat Chughtai, 1952
Tarik Saiyyara (poetry), Akhtarul Iman, 1952
Sar-e-Sham (novella), Razia Sajjad Zaheer, 1953
Patthar ki Diwar (poetry), Sardar Jafri, 1953
A Quest for Life (travelogue), Mahmuduzzafar Khan, 1954
Kante (novel), Razia Sajjad Zaheer, 1954
Adab aur Nazariya (criticism), Ale Ahmad Suroor, 1954
Zindah Nama (poetry), Faiz Ahmed Faiz, 1956

Roshnai (history of the PWM), Sajjad Zaheer, 1956 in Pakistan and in India in 1959

Note: Many of the writers continued to be active after 1955, but by then they had either loosened or cut their association with the PWM. In other cases, most notably Kaifi and Sardar, they continued to be active as writers and poets even after 1955 and maintained their links with the Movement. But the list above is illustrative because in the years till 1955, empirically, we can see that the output could have been more voluminous in some cases (as in the case of Makhdoom whose first volume appeared in 1941 and the next in 1961 because of his preoccupations with the party); in those cases where it was voluminous as in the case of Krishan Chandar, it suffered from intellectual paucity.

Annexure IV

Two Versions of the First *Manifesto* of the AIPWA, and a Comparison

The Version of the Manifesto printed in *Left Review*, London, February 1936:

Radical changes are taking place in Indian society. Fixed ideas and old beliefs, social and political institutions are being challenged. Out of the present turmoil and conflict a new society is arising. The spiritual reaction, however, though moribund and doomed to ultimate decay, is still operative and is making desperate efforts to prolong itself.

It is the duty of Indian writers to give expression to the changes taking place in Indian life and to assist the spirit of progress in the country. Indian literature, since the breakdown of classical culture, has had the fatal tendency to escape from actualities of life. It has tried to find refuge from reality in spiritualism and idealism. The result has been that it has produced a rigid formalism and a banal and perverse ideology. Witness the mystical devotional obsession of literature, its furtive and sentimental attitude towards sex, its emotional exhibitionism and its almost total lack of rationality. Such literature was produced particularly during the last two centuries, one of the most unhappy periods of our history, a period of disintegrating feudalism and of acute misery and degradation for the Indian people as a whole.

It is the object of our association to rescue literature and other arts from the priestly, academic and decadent classes in whose hands they have degenerated so long: to bring the arts into the closest touch with the people; and to make them vital organs which will register the actualities of life, as well as lead us to the future.

While claiming to be the inheritors of the best traditions of Indian civilisation, we shall criticize ruthlessly, in all its politics, economic and cultural aspects, the spirit of reaction in our country; and we shall foster through interpretative and creative work (with both native and foreign resources) everything that will lead our country to the new life for which it is striving. We believe that the new literature of India must deal with the basic problems of our existence today—the problems of hunger and poverty, social backwardness and political subjugation, so that it may help us to understand these problems and through such understanding help us to act.

With the above aims in view, the following resolutions have been adopted:

(1) The establishment of organisations of writers to correspond to the various linguistics zones of India; the coordination [sic] of of these organisations by holding conferences, publishing of magazines, pamphlets, etc.
(2) To cooperate with those literary organisations whose aims do not conflict with the basic aims of the Association.
(3) To produce and to translate literature of a progressive nature of a high technical standard; to fight cultural reaction and in this way, to further the cause of Indian freedom and social regeneration.
(4) To strive for the acceptance of a common language (Hindustani) and a common script (Indo-Roman) for India.
(5) To protect the interests of authors; to help authors who require and deserve assistance for the publication of their works.
(6) To fight for the right of free expression of thought and opinion.

***

Comparative Study of the 'London Version' and the Version published by Premchand in *Hans*, taken from Carlo Coppola, 'The All-India Progressive Writers' Association: The European Phase', in *Marxist Influences and South Asian Literature*, South Asia Series, Occasional Paper No. 23, Vol. I, East Lansing: Michigan State University, pp. 6–9.

London Version

1. Radical changes are taking place in Indian society.
2. Fixed ideas and old beliefs, social and political institutions are being challenged. Out of the present turmoil and conflict a new society is arising.
3. The spiritual recreation, however, though moribund and doomed to ultimate decay, is still operative and is making desperate efforts to prolong itself.
4. It is the duty of Indian writers to give expression to the changes taking place in Indian life and to assist the spirit of progress in the country.
5. Indian literature, since the breakdown of classical culture, has had the fatal tendency to escape from actualities of life. It has tried to find refuge from reality in spiritualism and idealism.
6. The result has been that it has produced a rigid formalism and a banal and perverse ideology.
7. Witness the mystical devotional obsession of literature, its furtive and sentimental attitude towards sex, its emotional exhibitionism and its almost total lack of rationality
8. Such literature was produced particularly during the last two centuries, one of the most unhappy periods of our history, a period of disintegrating feudalism and of acute misery and degradation for the Indian people as a whole.
9. It is the object of our association to rescue literature and other arts from the priestly, academic and decadent classes in whose hands they have degenerated so long; to bring the arts into the closest touch with the people; and to make them vital organs which will register the actualities of life, as well as lead us to the future.
10. While claiming to be the inheritors of the best traditions of Indian civilisation, we shall criticize ruthlessly, in all its politics, economic and cultural aspects, the spirit of reaction in our country; and we shall foster through interpretative and creative work (with both native and foreign resources) everything that will lead our country to the new life for which it is striving,
11. We believe that the new literature of India must deal with the basic problems of our existence today—the problems of hunger and poverty, social backwardness and political subjugation, so that

it may help us to understand these problems and through such understanding help us to act.
12.
13. With the above aims in view, the following resolutions have been adopted:
14. (1) The establishment of organisations of writers to correspond to the various linguistics zones of India; the coordination [sic] of these organisations by holding conferences, publishing of magazines, pamphlets, etc.
15. (2) To co-operate with those literary organisations whose aims do not conflict with the basic aims of the Association.
16. (3) To produce and to translate literature of a progressive nature of a high technical standard; to fight cultural reaction and in this way, to further the cause of Indian freedom and social regeneration.
17. (4) To strive for the acceptance of a common language (Hindustani) and a common script (Indo-Roman) for India.
18. (5) To protect the interests of authors; to help authors who require and deserve assistance for the publication of their works.
(7) To fight for the right of free expression of thought and opinion.

Hans *Version*

1. Great changes are taking place in Indian society.
2. And the foundations of old ideas and beliefs are being shaken and a new society is being born.
3.
4. It is the duty of Indian writers that they should give the dress of words and form to the existent changes in Indian life and should assist in putting the country on the path of construction and progress.
5. After the destruction of the ancient civilization, Indian literature, having run away from the realities of life, had hidden in the protection of asceticism and devotionalism.
6. The result is that it has become lifeless and ineffective.
7. Today, in our literature, in both form as well as in content, there has come an excess of devotionalism and asceticism. There is a general exhibition of emotion; reason and thought have been totally ignored—nay!—rejected!

8. In the preceding two centuries, which have been the declining period of our history, most literature which has been produced has been of this very sort.
9. The object of this association is to take our literature and other art forms from the monopolistic control of priests, pundits and other conservatives. It [the association] should bring them [literature and other art forms] nearer the people. They should be made to reflect life and reality so that we may be able to light our future.
10. Preserving the best traditions of India, we will comment pitilessly on the decadent aspects of our country and will depict in a critical and creative manner all those things with which we may arrive at our destination.
11. It is our belief that the new literature of India must respect the basic realities of our present-day life, and these are the questions of our bread, plight, our social degradation and political slavery. Only then will we be able to understand these problems and the revolutionary spirit will be born in us.
12. All those things which take us towards confusion, dissension, and blind imitation is conservative; also, all that which engenders in us a critical capacity, which induces us to test our dear traditions on the touchstone of our reason and perception, which makes us healthy and produces among us the strength of unity and integration, and that is what we call Progressive.
13. Keeping these objectives in mind, the association has passed the following resolutions:
14. (1) To establish organizations of writers in the various linguistic provinces of India; to establish contact and cooperation among these organizations by means of meetings, pamphlets, etc; to produce a close relationship among the organizations of the provinces, the center and London.
15. (2) To establish an association with those literary organizations which are not opposed to the aims of this organization.
16. (3) To create and translate Progressive literature which should be healthy and powerful, with which we may be able to erase cultural backwardness and advance to the path towards Indian freedom and social progress.
17. (4) To propagate the acceptance of Hindustani as the national language and Indo-Roman as the national script.

18. (5) To struggle for freedom of thought, opinion and expression of ideas.
19. (6) To protect the interests of authors; to assist people's authors who may want to publish their books.

***

Amended Version of the Manifesto Adopted by the Second All-India Progressive Writers Conference held in Calcutta during 24–25 December, 1938. Taken from Sudhi Pradhan (ed.), *Marxist Cultural Movements in India: Chronicles and Documents (1936–47), Vol. I* **(Calcutta: Distributed by National Book Agency, 1979), pp. 20–22.**

Radical changes are taking place in Indian society. The spirit of reaction, however, though moribund and doomed to ultimate decay, is still operative and is making desperate efforts to prolong itself. Indian literature, since the breakdown of classical culture, has had the fatal tendency to escape from actualities of life. It has tried to find refuge from reality in spiritualism and ideality. The result has been that it has become anaemic in body and mind and has adopted a rigid formalism and a banal and perverse ideology.

It is the duty of Indian writers to give expression to the changes taking place in Indian life and to assist the spirit of progress in the country by introducing scientific rationalism in literature. They should undertake to develop an attitude of literary criticism, which will discourage the general reactionary and revivalist tendencies on questions like family, religion, sex, war and society. They should combat literary trends reflecting communalism, racial antagonism, and exploitation of man by man.

It is the object of our Association to rescue literature and other arts from conservation classes in whose hands they have degenerated so long; to bring the arts into the closest touch with the people; and to make them vital organs which will register the actualities of life, as well as lead us to the future we envisage.

While claiming to the inheritors of the best traditions of Indian civilisation, we shall criticize, in all aspects, the spirit of recreation in our country: and we shall foster through interpretative and creative work (with both native and foreign resources) everything that will lead our country to the new life for which it is striving. We believe that the new literature of India must deal with the basic problems of our existence today—the problems of hunger and poverty, social backwardness and political subjugation. All that drags us down to passivity, inaction and customs un-reasons we reject as reactionary. All that arouses in us the critical spirit, which examines institutions and customs in the light of reasons, which helps us to act, to organise ourselves, to transform, we accept as progressive.

Glossary

alim	learned men
angarey	live embers
angrez sarkar	colonial government
ashiq	lover
awaz	call
azadi ki hawa	wind of freedom
azad nazm	vers libre
badnami	getting a bad name
baghban	gardener
balwai	rioters
banjara	nomad
bara masa	Hindi geet comprising 12 segments in which a woman yearns for her missing beloved; there is a segment for each of the 12 months of the year
baseerat	insight
bedeeni	irreligiousness
begumaati zuban	idiomatic language spoken by women
bejaan	lifeless
berooh	spiritless
chaman ki udasi	sorrow of the garden
dar-o-rasan	prison
Dar-ul-Harb	house or abode of war, but used to refer to enemy territory

Dar-ul-Islam	abode of Islam
dastan	a prose or verse genre generally dealing with epic battles, romance, chivalry, heroism, magic, or trickery
dastan-go	a teller of dastan
deedar	union with the beloved
deen	faith
deendar	religious men
dhandhorchi adeeb	drum-beating writers
dindari	religious piety
duniyadar	worldly men
ehd-e-junoon	period of obsession
faislakun andaaz	decisive style
fasana	story or tale
fasana-go	a teller of fasana
fiqh	Islamic jurisprudence
firaq	separation
gau-takhiya	sausage-shaped pillow
ghadar	revolt or uprising, used to refer to the first War of Independence of 1857
ghaddaar	traitors in the British army
ghaflat	negligence
ghairat	used variously to mean a sense of self or self-esteem
ghairat-e-imaani	courage of faith
gham-e-dauran	sorrows of this world
gham-e-jaanan	sorrows of this life
geet	song
gul-o-bulbul	the rose and the nightingale, traditional motifs in conventional Urdu poetry
gumrahi	waywardness
hakim	ruler
hakim-e-waqt	ruler of the time/age
haq	truth
haram	unlawful/sinful
hasv	satire
hijr	separation
hijrat	migration or journey
hoor	also spelt as 'houri' in English, extremely beautiful female creatures that will await the believers in heaven to serve them and fulfil their every desire; occasionally their gender is ambiguous
hubb-e-watani	love for the nation

Glossary • 441

i'tikaf	retreat
ibadat	fasting and praying
ibn-ul waqt	a man of his time and age
imarat	edifice
inquilab	revolution
inquilabi shairi	revolutionary poetry
ishq	love
islah	correction
Islami ikhlaq	Islamic culture
jaan-e-mehfil	life and soul of a gathering
jadeed	modern; *jadeediyat* means modernism and *jadeed parast* is lover of modernity
junoon	sublime madness
kaagaz ke phool	paper flowers
kafir	infidel
kakri	a salad vegetable, a slim version of a cucumber
kamil dumsaz	perfect companion
kewra	extract distilled from pandanus flowers, used as a flavouring
khalifa	'representative'; it was used for the Caliphs as a title for the representatives of the Islamic ummah
khara aadmi	genuine man
khilaf	against/opposed to
khirad	empirical knowledge
khudi	self-hood
khushboo	fragrance
kotha	establishment of a courtesan or prostitute in a marketplace or chowk
kufr	sacrilege, a belief or action that is against the essentially monotheistic spirit of Islam
laila-o-watan	beloved country
latif havasnaki	refined sexual desire
latife	jokes or entertaining anecdotes
laundi	slave girl, unlike *naukrani* who is a paid domestic employee
mahfil-e-hast-o-bood	assembly of old and new
maikhana	tavern
malang	wandering sufi
mama	female domestic servant, but one for casual work; she may come and go
mannat	votive

markaz	centre
mashriqiyat	westernism
mashuq	beloved
masnavi	a narrative, often long poem of no fixed length or subject though it could be about romance or chivalry
masnoohi	artificial
matamkhana	mourning chamber
mauzoo	subject
momin	believer
mua mustanda	awful ogre
muhawra	idiom
muhazzab	civilized
mujahid	martyr, or one who bears witness
mujra	song and dance performance by a courtesan for her patrons
munsif	a medium-grade judge
muqqadas divangi	divine madness
musarrat	pleasure
mustasib	censor
nai raushni	new light
naib tehsildar	deputy magistrate, or assistant to the officer in-charge of a tehsil
numaish	exhibition
paandan	box containing all the material for assembling a paan
paighambari	prophetic
pyala	cup
qasbah	a small semi-rural community in the Awadh region
qasidah	a poem in praise of someone, often a patron
qasr-e-azadi	fort of freedom
qata	four-lined rhymed verse
qaum	community
qaumi tarana	national anthem
qisse	anecdotes
raqib	rival
rekhti	poetic genre where male poets speak in the feminine voice
rind	libertine
ruhani sukoon	spiritual solace
sahebzadi	well-born young woman, used for a young lady from a good family
sahiban-i-qalam	men of pen

sahiban-i-saif	men of sword
sair	tour
sair-o-tafri	fun-filled journey
sajda	prostration
sajjadanashin	hereditary administrator of a dargah or hospice, the position is passed on along the male line
salatin	princes
sang-e-meel	milestone
saqi	cup-bearer
savab	blessings
sewa samiti	service committee
Shab-e-Barat	festival celebrated on the 13th or 14th day of Shaban
Shaban	the eighth month of the Muslim lunar calendar, 15 days before Ramadan
shairi baraai mauzoo	poetry without a subject
shama-parwana	the candle and the moth, popular images in Urdu poetry
sharab	wine
sharafat	quality of being sharif
shehr ashob	misfortunes of the city
shireen divangi	sweet madness
shurfa	plural of sharif, meaning members of the genteel or upper class
sozni	cotton covering for the floor or settee
surahi	long-necked clay pitcher used to keep water cool
taksal	mint
taksali zubaan	language with the genuineness of a minted coin; an idiomatic language
tamashawala	one who shows the spectacle
tarah	rhyme pattern
taraqqui pasandi	progressivism
tarmeem	renovation
tarranum	recitation
tawaif	courtesan
tehzeeb	culture
ugaldan	spittoon
ummah	Arabic word meaning nation or community, but used for the Muslim peoples across the world
visal	union with the beloved
waqti adab	topical literature
zamane ki hawa	the wind of the times
zindan	prison

Bibliography

Primary Sources

Private Papers

Ahmed Ali, Karachi, Pakistan
Ale Ahmad Suroor, Aligarh
Ghulam Rabbani Taban, NMML, New Delhi

Transcripts, Oral History Project, NMML

Sajjad Zaheer, File No. 298
Hajra Begum, File No. 613
Begum Iftikharuddin, File No. 53
Hans Raj Rahbar, File No. 629
Shaukat Usmani, File No. 307

Records

India Office Records, Political and Judicial Department Records, L/P&J/1–20, British Library
India Office Records, Political and Secret Department Records, L/P&S/1–20, British Library
Indian Political Intelligence Files, Microfiche, 1912–50, Or. Fiche 648–670, British Library

Home Department/Political Branch, NAI
External Affairs Department, NAI
P.C. Joshi Archives on Contemporary History, Jawaharlal Nehru University, New Delhi

Newspapers

Newspaper Reports/Summaries/Annual Reports, IOR, L/R/5
Native Newspapers, NAI, 1932, 1934, 1936

Interviews

Sarwat Rahman, Dehradun
Munibur Rahman, Aligarh
S.M. Mahdi, Aligarh
Aulad Ahmad Siddiqui, Aligarh
Shahryar, Aligarh
Zahida Zaidi, Aligarh
Zohra Segal, New Delhi
Javed Akhtar, New Delhi
Bano and Naren Gupta, New Delhi
Hamida Salim, New Delhi
Akhilesh Mitthal, New Delhi
Birjees Kidwai, New Delhi
Shahla Haider, New Delhi
Arif Naqvi, New Delhi
Raza Imam, New Delhi
Zehra Nigah, New Delhi and Karachi, Pakistan
Mushtaq Yusufi, Karachi, Pakistan
Intizar Husain, New Delhi and Karachi, Pakistan
Asif Noorani, Karachi, Pakistan
Asif Farrukhi, Karachi, Pakistan
Urooj Ahmed Ali, Karachi, Pakistan
Kamran Asdar, Karachi, Pakistan
Wiqar Ahmad, London, UK
K. Humayun Ansari, Egham, UK

Secondary Sources

Published Books/Articles (English)

Ahmad, Aijaz, *In Theory: Classes, Nations, Literatures* (London: Verso, 1992).

Ahmad, Aijaz, *In the Mirror of Urdu: Recompositions of Nation and Community, 1947–65*, Lectures 102–5 (Shimla: Indian Institute of Advanced Study, 1993).

Ahmad, Aziz, *Studies in Islamic Culture in the Indian Environment* (Oxford: Clarendon Press, 1964).

———, *Islamic Modernism in India and Pakistan, 1857–1964* (London: Oxford University Press, 1967).

———, *An Intellectual History of Islam in India* (Edinburgh: University Press, 1969).

Ahmad, Nazir, *The Bride's Mirror: A Tale of Life in Delhi a Hundred Years Ago*, translated by G.E. Ward (Delhi: Permanent Black, 2001).

Ahmed, Talat, *Literature and Politics in the Age of Nationalism: The Progressive Episode in South Asia, 1932–56* (New Delhi: Routledge, 2009).

Akhtar, Waheed, 'Intellectual Tradition in Urdu', in B.N. Rao and Kadir Zaman (eds), *Modern Thought and Contemporary Literary Trends* (Hyderabad: Committee on Modern Thought and Contemporary Literary Trends, 1982).

Alam, Jayanti (ed.), *Remembering Makhdoom* (New Delhi: SAHMAT, 2010).

Ali, Ahmed, 'The Progressive Writers' Movement and Creative Writers in Urdu', in Carlo Coppola (ed.), *Marxist Influences and South Asian Literature* (East Lansing: Michigan State University Press, 1974).

———, *The Prison-house* (Karachi: Akrash Publishing, 1985).

———, *Twilight in Delhi: A Novel* (New Delhi: Rupa & Co., 2007 [reprint]).

Ali, Mohamed, *My Life: A Fragment—An Autobiographical Sketch of Maulana Mohamed Ali*, ed. Mushirul Hasan (New Delhi: Manohar, 1999).

Ali, Yusuf, 'Muslim Culture and Religious Thought', in Mushirul Hasan (ed.), *Islam in South Asia*, vol. II, *Encountering the West: Before and After 1857* (New Delhi: Manohar, 2008).

Alvi, Waris, *Saadat Hasan Manto, Makers of Indian Literature* (New Delhi: Sahitya Akademi, 2000).

Andrews, C.F., *Zakaullah of Delhi*, introduction by Mushirul Hasan and Margrit Pernau (New Delhi: Oxford University Press, 2003).

Ansari, Humayun Khizar, 'Pan-Islam and the Making of the Early Indian Muslim Socialist', *Modern Asian Studies*, vol. 20, no. 3 (1986).

———, *The Emergence of Socialist Thought among North Indian Muslims (1917–1947)* (Lahore: Book Traders, 1990).

———, 'Making Transnational Connections: Muslim Networks in Early-Twentieth Century Britain', in Nathalie Clayer and Eric Germain (eds), *Islam in Inter-War Europe* (New York: Columbia University Press, 2008).

Asaduddin, M., *Ismat Chughtai: Makers of Indian Literature* (New Delhi: Sahitya Akademi, 1999).

———, *A Life in Words: Memoirs* (New Delhi: Penguin, 2012).

Ashraf, Ali and G.A. Syomin (eds), *October Revolution and India's Independence: Proceedings of the Soviet Land Seminar on 'The Great October Socialist Revolution and India's Struggle for National Liberation', New Delhi, August 20–21, 1977* (New Delhi: Sterling Publishers, 1977).

Ashraf, K.M., 'Ghalib and the Revolt of 1857', in P.C. Joshi (ed.), *Rebellion 1857* (New Delhi: PPH, 1957).

Azad, Abul Kalam, *Masala-e-Khilafat* (Lahore: Maktaba-e-Ahbab, n.d.).

Azmi, Shaukat, *Kaifi & I: A Memoir*, edited and translated by Nasreen Rehman (New Delhi: Zubaan, 2010).

Bailey, T. Grahame, *A History of Urdu Literature* (New Delhi: Oxford University Press, 2008 [1932]).

Banerjea, Surendranath, *A Nation in Making* (Calcutta: Oxford University Press, 1963).

Barns, M., *The Indian Press: A History of the Growth of Public Opinion in India* (London: George Allen & Unwin, 1940).

Barrier, Norman Gerald, *Banned: Controversial Literature and Political Control in British India, 1907–1947* (Delhi: Manohar, 1978).

Bartolovich, Crystal and Neil Lazarus (eds), *Marxism, Modernity and Post-Colonial Studies* (Cambridge: Cambridge University Press, 2002).

Bayly, C.A., *Rulers, Townsmen and Bazars: North Indian Society in the Age of British Expansions, 1770–1870* (Cambridge: Cambridge University Press, 1983).

———, *Empire and Information: Intelligence Gathering and Social Communication in India, 1780–1870* (Cambridge: Cambridge University Press, 1996).

Behl, Aditya, 'Poet of the Bazaars: Nazir Akbarabadi, 1735–1830', in Kathryn Hansen and David Lelyveld (eds), *A Wilderness of Possibilities: Urdu Studies in Transnational Perspective* (New Delhi: Oxford University Press, 2005), pp. 192–222.

Bhalla, Alok (ed.), *Stories about the Partition of India*, vols I–IV (New Delhi: Manohar, 2012).

Blunt, W.S., *India under Ripon* (London, 1909).

Bose, Sugata and Ayesha Jalal, *Modern South Asia: History, Culture and Political Economy* (New Delhi: Oxford University Press, 2004).

Brass, Paul, *Language, Religion and Politics in North India* (London: Cambridge University Press, 1974).

Burckhardt, J.L., *Travels in Arabia* (London: Frank Cass & Co. Ltd, 1968 [reprint]).

Burton, Antoinette M., *Dwelling in the Archive: Women Writing House, Home, and History in Late Colonial India* (Oxford: Oxford University Press, 2003).

Butler, Harcourt, *Collected Speeches* (Rangoon: Government Press, 1927).

Carr, E.H., *The Bolshevik Revolution*, vol. 13 (London: Macmillan, 1953).

Chaghtai, M. Ikram, 'Dr Aloys Sprenger and the Delhi College', in Margrit Pernau (ed.), *The Delhi College: Traditional Elites, the Colonial State, and Education before 1857* (New Delhi: Oxford University Press, 2006).

Chandra, Bipan (ed.), *The Indian Left: Critical Appraisals* (New Delhi: Vikas Publishing House, 1983).

Chatterjee, Partha and Pradeep Jeganathan (eds), *Community, Gender and Violence* (London: C. Hurst & Co., 2000).

Chatterji, Lola (ed.), *Autobiography: Hamida Saiduzzafar (1921–1988)* (New Delhi: Trianka, 1996).

Chaudhury, Sushil, *The Prelude to Empire: Plassey Revolution of 1757* (New Delhi: Manohar, 2000).

Chughtai, Ismat, *The Quilt and Other Stories*, translated by Tahira Naqvi and Saiyeda S. Hameed (New Delhi: Kali for Women, 1990).

———, *Heart Breaks Free and The Wild One*, translated by Tahira Naqvi (New Delhi: Kali for Women, 1993).

———, 'Un Byahtaon ke Naam', in Sukrita Paul Kumar and Sadique (eds), *Ismat: Her Life and Times* (New Delhi: Katha, 2000).

———, *My Friend, My Enemy: Essays, Reminiscences, Portraits*, translated and introduced by Tahira Naqvi (New Delhi: Kali for Women, 2001).

Coppola, Carlo, 'Ahmed Ali (1910–1994): Bridges and Links between East and West', *Annual of Urdu Studies*, vol. 9 (1944), p. 50.

——— (ed.), *Marxist Influences and South Asian Literature* (East Lansing: Michigan State University, 1974).

——— (ed.), 'The All-India Progressive Writers' Association: The European Phase', in *Marxist Influences and South Asian Literature* (East Lansing: Michigan State University, 1974).

———, 'Iqbal and the Progressive Movement', *Journal of South Asian and Middle Eastern Studies*, vol. 1, no. 2 (1977), pp. 49–57.

———, 'The Angare Group: The *Enfants Terribles* of Urdu Literature', *Annual of Urdu Literature*, vol. 1 (1981), pp. 57–69.

Coppola, Carlo and S. Zubair, 'Rashid Jahan: Urdu Literature's First "Angry Young Woman"', *Journal of South Asian Literature*, vol. 22, no. 1 (1987), pp. 166–83.

Dacosta, John, *Remarks on the Vernacular Press Law of India, or Act IX of 1878* (London: W.H. Allen & Co., 1878).

Dalmia, Vasudha, 'Introduction', in *Sevasadan*, translated by Snehal Shingavi (New Delhi: Oxford University Press, 2005).

———, *Poetics, Plays and Performances: The Politics of Modern Indian Theatre* (New Delhi: Oxford University Press, 2006).

Dasgupta, Uma, 'The Indian Press 1870–1880: A Small World of Journalism', *Modern Asian Studies*, vol. 11, no. 2 (1977), pp. 213–35.

Datta, V.N. and B. Cleghorn, *A Nationalist Muslim and Indian Politics: Being the Selected Correspondence of the Late Dr. Syed Mahmud* (Delhi: Macmillan, 1974).

Deol, Harbhajan Singh, *The Romance That Stayed: Window on Select Urdu Progressives* (Ludhiana: Aesthetics Publications, 2008).

Derrida, Jacques, *Acts of Literature* (London: Routledge, 1992).

——, *Deconstruction Engaged: The Sydney Seminars* (Sydney: Power Publications, 2001).

Douglas, Ian, *Abul Kalam Azad: An Intellectual and Religious Biography* (New Delhi: Oxford University Press, 1988).

Duara, Prasenjit (ed.), *Decolonisation: Perspectives from Now and Then*, Rewriting History Series (London: Routledge, 2004).

Dutt, R. Palme, *India Today*. Calcutta: Manisha Granthalaya.

Edib, Halide, *Inside India* (New Delhi: Oxford University Press, 2002).

Encyclopedia of Islam, 2nd ed. (Leiden: E.J. Brill, 1989 [reprint]).

Ezekiel, Nissim, *Indian Writers in Conference: The Sixth PEN All-India Writers' Conference* (Bombay: PEN, 1964).

Faiz, Faiz Ahmed, 'Ismat Chughtai', in Sukrita Paul Kumar and Sadique (eds), *Ismat: Her Life, Her Times* (New Delhi: Katha, 2009).

Farooqi, M., *The Communist Party and the Problems of Muslim Minority* (New Delhi: Communist Party Publications, 1969).

Faruqi, S.R., *Early Urdu Literary Culture and History* (New Delhi: Oxford University Press, 2001).

——, *The Flower-Lit Road: Essays in Urdu Literary Theory and Criticism* (Allahabad: Laburnum Press, 2005).

Faruqi, Ziya-ul-Hasan, *The Deoband School and the Demand for Pakistan* (Bombay: Asia Publishing House, 1963).

Fisher, Michael H., *A Clash of Cultures: Awadh, the British and the Mughals* (New Delhi: Manohar, 1987).

——, 'The Office of the *Akhbar Nawis*: The Transition from Mughal to British Forms', *Modern Asian Studies*, vol. 27, no. 1 (1993), pp. 45–82.

Flemming, Leslie, *Another Lonely Voice: The Life and Works of Saadat Hasan Manto*, short stories translated by Tahira Naqvi (Lahore: Vanguard, 1985).

——, 'Progressive Writer, Progressive Filmmaker: The Films of Rajinder Singh Bedi', *Annual of Urdu Studies*, vol. 5 (1985), pp. 81–97.

Forche, Carolyn (ed.), *Against Forgetting: Twentieth Century Poetry of Witness* (New York: W.W. Norton & Co., 1993).

Foucault, Michel, *The Archaeology of Knowledge*, translated by A.M. Sheridan Smith (London: Routledge, 2002).

George, K.M., *Comparative Indian Literature*, vols I and II (Trichur: Kerala Sahitya Akademi; and New Delhi: Macmillan India Ltd, 1984).

Gopal, Priyamvada, 'Sex, Space and Modernity in the Work of Rashid Jahan Angarewali', in Crystal Bartlovich and Neil Lazarus (eds), *Marxism, Modernity and Postcolonial Studies* (Cambridge: Cambridge University Press, 2002).

——, *Literary Radicalism in India: Gender, Nation and the Transition to Independence* (Oxon: Routledge, 2005).

Gopal, Priyamvada, 'A Forgotten History—From Rashid Jahan to Taslima Nasreen, the CPI (M)', 6 December 2007, available at www.Europe Solidaire Sans Frontiere.com.

Gordon-Polonskaya, L.R., 'Ideology of Muslim Nationalism', Hafeez Malik (ed.), *Iqbal: Poet-Philosopher of Pakistan* (New York: Columbia University Press, 1971).

Graff, Violette (ed.), *Lucknow: Memories of a City* (New Delhi: Oxford University Press, 1997).

Gramsci, Antonio, *The Modern Prince and Other Writings* (London: Lawrence & Wishart Ltd, 1957).

Gupta, D.N., *Colonialism and Nationalism in Colonial India (1939–45)* (California: Sage Publications, 2008).

Habib, Naseer, 'The Tradition of Deoband and the Pragmatism of Ubaid Allah Sindhi', *Third Frame*, vol. 1, no. 3 (July–September 2008), pp. 30–42.

Haithcox, J.P., *Communism and Nationalism in India: M.N. Roy and Cominitern Policy, 1920–1939* (Princeton: Princeton University Press, 1971).

Haq, Q.M. and M.I. Waley, *Allama Sir Muhammad Iqbal* (London: British Museum Publications Ltd, 1977).

Haq, S. Moinul, 'The Story of the War of Independence', *Journal of the Pakistan Historical Society*, vol. 5 (1957), pp. 23–57.

Harcourt, E.S. and Fakhir Hussain, *Lucknow: The Last Phase of an Oriental Culture* (New Delhi: Oxford University Press, 1994).

Hardy, Peter, *The Muslims of British India* (Cambridge: Cambridge University Press, 1972).

Hasan, Khalid (ed.), 'A Conversation with Faiz', *The Unicorn and the Dancing Girl* (New Delhi: Allied Publishers, 1988).

Hasan, Mushirul (ed.), *Communal and Pan-Islamic Trends in Colonial India* (New Delhi: Manohar, 1981).

———, 'Muslim Mass Contacts Campaign: Analysis of a Strategy of Political Mobilisation', in Richard Sisson and Stanley Wolpert (eds), *Congress and Indian Nationalism: The Pre-Independence Phase* (Los Angeles: University of California Press, 1988).

———, 'Resistance and Acquiescence in North India: Muslim Response to the West', in Mushirul Hasan and Narayani Gupta (eds), *India's Colonial Encounter: Essays in Memory of Eric Stokes* (New Delhi: Manohar, 1993).

——— (ed.), *India Partitioned*, vols 1 and 2 (New Delhi: Lotus/Roli, 1995).

———, 'The Myth of Unity: Colonial and National Narratives', in David Ludden (ed.), *Contesting the Nation: Religion, Community and the Politics of Democracy in India* (Philadelphia: University of Pennsylvania Press, 1996).

———, *Legacy of a Divided Nation* (New Delhi: Oxford University Press, 1997).

Hasan, Mushirul (ed.), 'Redefining Boundaries: Modernist Interpretations and the New "Intellectual Structures"', in *Legacy of a Divided Nation* (New Delhi: Oxford University Press, 1997).

———, *From Pluralism to Separatism: Qasbahs in Colonial Awadh* (New Delhi: Oxford University Press, 2004).

———, *A Moral Reckoning: Muslim Intellectuals in Nineteenth-century Delhi* (New Delhi: Oxford University Press, 2005).

———, 'Sharif Culture and Colonial Rule', in Mushirul Hasan and Asim Roy (eds), *Living Together Separately: Cultural India in History and Politics* (New Delhi: Oxford University Press, 2005).

———, *Wit and Humour in Colonial North India* (New Delhi: Niyogi Books, 2007).

——— (ed.), *Towards Freedom: The Documents on the Movement for Independence in India (1939)*, vols 1 and 2 (New Delhi: Oxford University Press, 2008).

Hasan, Mushirul and Asim Roy (eds), *Living Together Separately: Cultural India in History and Politics* (New Delhi: Oxford University Press, 2005).

Hasan, Mushirul and Narayani Gupta (eds), *India's Colonial Encounter: Essays in Memory of Eric Stokes* (New Delhi: Manohar, 1993).

Hasan, Mushirul and Rakhshanda Jalil, *Journey to the Holy Land: A Pilgrim's Diary* (New Delhi: Oxford University Press, 2009).

Hashmi, Ali Madeedh and Shoib Hashmi, *Faiz Ahmad Faiz: His Life, His Poems* (New Delhi: HarperCollins, 2012).

Hilal, Abdul Aleem, *Social Philosophy of Sir Muhammad Iqbal* (New Delhi: Adam Publishers and Distributors, 1995).

Husain, Ehtesham, 'Urdu Literature and the Revolt', in P.C. Joshi (ed.), *Rebellion 1857* (New Delhi: PPH, 1957).

Husain, Intezar, *Circle and Other Stories* (New Delhi: Rupa & Co., 2004).

Husain, S. Abid, *The Destiny of Indian Muslims* (New Delhi: Asia Publishing House, 1965).

Hyder, Qurratulain, *River of Fire* (New Delhi: Women Unlimited, 1998).

———, *A Season of Betrayals*, edited and introduced by C.M. Naim (New Delhi: Kali for Women, 1999).

———, *The Street Singers of Lucknow and Other Stories*, introduction by Aamer Hussein (New Delhi: Sterling Publishers, 2004).

———, *My Temples, Too* (New Delhi: Women Unlimited, 2004).

———, *Fireflies in the Mist* (New Delhi: Women Unlimited, 2008).

Jafri, Ali Sardar, *My Journey: Selected Urdu Poems*, translated by Baidar Bakht and Kathleen Grant Jaeger (New Delhi: Sterling Publishers, 1999).

Jalal, Ayesha, *Self and Sovereignty: Individual and Community in South Asian Islam since 1850* (London: Routledge, 2000).

———, *Partisans of Allah* (Ranikhet: Permanent Black, 2008).

Jalil, Rakhshanda (ed.), *Qurratulain Hyder and the River of Fire: The Meaning, Scope and Significance of Her Legacy* (New Delhi: Aakar, 2009).
Joshi, P.C., *Who Lives If Bengal Dies?* (Bombay: PPH, 1944).
——— (ed.), *Rebellion 1857* (New Delhi: PPH, 1957).
Joshi, Priya, 'Reading in the Public Eye: The Circulation of Fiction in Indian Libraries, c. 1835–1901', in Stuart H. Blackburn and Vasudha Dalmia (eds), *India's Literary History* (Ranikhet: Permanent Black, 2010).
Kabir, Nasreen Munni, *Talking Songs: In Conversation with Javed Akhtar* (New Delhi: Oxford University Press, 2005).
Karat, Prakash (ed.), *A World to Win: Essays on the Communist Manifesto* (New Delhi: LeftWord Books, 1999).
———, *Across Time and Continents: A Tribute to Victor Kiernan* (New Delhi: LeftWord Books, 2003).
Kashmiri, Zaheer, 'My Life, My Art', *Annual of Urdu Studies*, vol. 25 (2010), pp. 165–77.
Kazim, Lubna (ed.), *A Woman of Substance: The Memoirs of Begum Khurshid Mirza (1918–1989)* (New Delhi: Zubaan, 2005).
Khan, Abdul Rashid, *The All India Muslim Educational Conference: Its Contribution to the Cultural Development of Indian Muslims, 1886–1947* (Karachi: Oxford University Press, 2001).
Khan, Shafique Ali, *The Demand for Pakistan and the CPI* (Karachi: Royal Book Company, 1987).
Khan, Sir Syed Ahmad, 'Causes of the Indian Revolt', in Mushirul Hasan (ed.), *Islam in South Asia*, vol. II, *Encountering the West: Before and After 1857* (New Delhi: Manohar, 2008), chapter 9.
Kempson, M., *The Repentance of Nussoh: The Tale of a Muslim Family a Hundred Years Ago*, translated by M. Kempson and edited by C.M. Naim (Delhi: Permanent Black, 2004 [first published by W.H. Allen & Co., 1884]).
Kidwai, Mushir Hosain, *Islam and Socialism* (London, 1913).
Kidwai, Sadiq-ur-Rahman, 'The Poet Who Laughed in Pain: Akbar Ilahabadi', in Mushirul Hasan (ed.), *Islam in South Asia: The Realm of the Secular*, vol. IV (New Delhi: Manohar, 2009).
Kiernan, V.G., *Poems from Iqbal* (London: John Murray, 1955; New Delhi: Oxford University Press, 1999; and Karachi: Oxford University Press, 2004).
———, *Poems by Faiz Ahmad Faiz* (New Delhi: PPH, 1958).
———, 'The Communist Party of India and the Second World War', in Prakash Karat (ed.), *Across Time and Continents* (New Delhi: LeftWord Books, 2003).
Kohli, Suresh (ed.), *An Evening in Lucknow: Selected Stories by K.A. Abbas* (New Delhi: HarperCollins, 2011).
Kumar, Girija, *The Book on Trial: Fundamentalism and Censorship in India* (New Delhi: Har-Anand, 1997).

Kumar, Nita, *Women as Subjects: South Asian Histories* (Calcutta: Stree, 1994).
Kumar, Sukrita Paul and Sadique (eds), *Ismat: Her Life, Her Times* (New Delhi: Katha, 2009).
Lal, Mohan, *The Encyclopedia of Indian Literature* (New Delhi: Sahitya Akademi, 1991).
Lazard, Noami, *The True Subject: Selected Poems of Faiz Ahmed Faiz* (Lahore: Vanguard, 1988).
Lelyveld, David, *Aligarh's First Generation: Muslim Solidarity in British India* (Princeton: Princeton University Press, 1978).
Lenin, V.I., *Critical Remarks on the National Question* (Moscow, 1971).
Liddle, Swapna, 'Azurda: Scholar, Poet, and Judge', in Margrit Pernau (ed.), *The Delhi College: Traditional Elites, the Colonial State, and Education before 1857* (New Delhi: Oxford University Press, 2006), pp. 125–44.
Llewellyn-Jones, Rosie, *A Fatal Friendship: The Nawabs, the British and the City of Lucknow* (New Delhi: Oxford University Press, 1985).
Lohia, Rammanohar, *Guilty Men of India's Partition* (New Delhi: B.R. Publishing Corporation, 2000).
Ludden, David (ed.), *Contesting the Nation: Religion, Community and the Politics of Democracy in India*, South Asia Seminar Series (Philadelphia: University of Pennsylvania Press, 1996).
Lukács, Georg, *History and Class Consciousness* (Cambridge: MIT Press, 1971).
Mahmud, Shabana, 'Angare and the Founding of the Progressive Writers' Association', *Modern Asian Studies*, vol. 30, no. 2 (May 1996), pp. 447–67.
Mahmuduzzafar, S., *Quest for Life* (Bombay: PPH, 1954).
Majeed, Javed, *Muhammad Iqbal: Islam, Aesthetics and Postcolonialism* (New Delhi: Routledge, 2009).
Majeed, Sheema (ed.), *Coming Back Home: Selected Articles, Editorials and Interviews of Faiz Ahmed Faiz* (Karachi: Oxford University Press, 2008).
Majumdar, R.C., *The Sepoy Mutiny and Revolt of 1857* (Calcutta: Firma K.L. Mukhopadhyay, 1957).
Malik, Hafeez, 'The Marxist Literary Movement in India and Pakistan', *The Journal of Asian Studies*, vol. 26, no. 4 (August 1967), pp. 649–64.
Malraux, André, 'The Work of Art', in Maynard Solomon (ed. and commentary), *Marxism and Art: Essays Classic & Contemporary* (Detroit: Wayne State University Press, 1979 [reprint]).
Manto, Saadat Hasan, *Naked Voices: Stories & Sketches*, translated by Rakhshanda Jalil (New Delhi: Roli/India Ink, 2008).
Masani, M.R., *The Communist Party of India: A Short History* (London: Derek Vershcoyle, 1954).
Masselos, Jim, *Indian Nationalism: A History* (New Delhi: Sterling Publishers, 1985).

Matthews, David, Christopher Shackle, and Shahrukh Husain, *Urdu Literature* (Islamabad: Alhamra, 2003).

Memon, M.U., 'Partition Literature: A Study of Intizar Husain', *Modern Asian Studies*, vol. 14, no. 3 (1980), pp. 377–410.

Metcalf, Barbara D., *Islamic Revival in British India: Deoband 1860–1900* (Princeton: Princeton University Press, 1982).

———, 'Maulana Ashraf Ali Thanawi and Urdu Literature', in Christopher Shackle (ed.), *Urdu and Muslim South Asia: Studies in Honour of Ralph Russell* (New Delhi: Oxford University Press, 1989).

———, *Perfecting Women: Maulana Ashraf Ali Thanawi's Bihishti Zewar* (Berkeley: University of California Press, 1990).

———, 'Too Little and Too Much: Reflections on Muslims in the History of India', *The Journal of Asian Studies*, vol. 4 (1995), pp. 951–67.

Minault, Gail, *The Khilafat Movement: Religious Symbolism and Political Mobilisation in India* (New Delhi: Oxford University Press, 1982).

———, '*Ismat*: Rashidul Khairi's Novels and Urdu Literary Journalism for Women', in Christopher Shackle (ed.), *Urdu and Muslim South Asia* (New Delhi: Oxford University Press, 1991).

———, *Secluded Scholars: Women's Education and Muslim Social Reform in Colonial India* (New Delhi: Oxford University Press, 1998).

———, 'Delhi College and Urdu', *Annual of Urdu Studies*, vol. 18 (Chicago: University of Wisconsin-Madison, 2003).

———, 'From *Akhbar* to News: The Development of the Urdu Press in Early Nineteenth-Century Delhi', in Kathryn Hansen and David Lelyveld (eds), *A Wilderness of Possibilities: Urdu Studies in Transnational Perspective* (New Delhi: Oxford University Press, 2005).

———, *Gender, Language and Learning: Essays in Indo-Muslim Cultural History* (Ranikhet: Permanent Black, 2009).

Mir, Ali Husain and Raza Mir, *Anthems of Resistance: A Celebration of Progressive Urdu Poetry* (New Delhi: IndiaInk/Roli, 2006).

Mir, Mustansir, *Iqbal* (New Delhi: Oxford University Press, 2006).

Miroslav, Victor, *Peaceful Transition to Communism in India: Strategy of the Communist Party* (Bombay: Nachiketa Publications, 1969).

Mufti, Aamir, *Enlightenment in the Colony: The Jewish Question and the Crisis of Postcolonial Culture* (Princeton: Princeton University Press, 2007).

Mujeeb, M., *Education and Traditional Values* (Meerut: Meenakshi Prakashan, 1965).

———, *Indian Muslims* (London: George Allen & Unwin Ltd., 1967).

———, *Islamic Influences on Indian Society* (Meerut: Meenakshi Prakashan, 1972).

Naim, C.M., *Urdu Texts and Contexts: Selected Essays* (Delhi: Permanent Black, 2004).

Naim, C.M., 'Ghalib's Delhi: A Shamelessly Revisionist Look at Two Popular Metaphors', in *Urdu Texts and Contexts: Selected Essays* (Delhi: Permanent Black, 2004), pp. 250–73.

———, 'Prize-Winning Adab', in *Urdu Texts and Contexts: Selected Essays* (Delhi: Permanent Black, 2004).

———, 'Shaikh Imam Bakhsh Sahba'i: Teacher, Scholar, Poet, and Puzzle-master', in Margrit Pernau (ed.), *The Delhi College: Traditional Elites, the Colonial State, and Education before 1857* (New Delhi: Oxford University Press, 2006), pp. 145–87.

———, 'Syed Ahmad and His Two Books called "Asar-al-Sanadid"', *Modern Asian Studies*, vol. 45, no. 3 (2011), pp. 669–708.

Naqvi, Tahira, 'Ismat Chughtai—A Tribute', *Annual of Urdu Studies*, vol. 8 (Chicago: University of Wisconsin-Madison, 1993).

Narang, Gopicand (selection and introduction), *Rajinder Singh Bedi: Selected Short Stories*, translated by Jai Ratan (New Delhi: Sahitya Akademi, 1989).

———, *Urdu Language and Literature: Critical Perspectives* (New Delhi: Sterling Publishers, 1991).

———, 'Tradition and Innovation in Faiz Ahmad Faiz', *Urdu Language and Literature: Critical Perspectives* (New Delhi: Sterling Publishers, 1991).

Nehru, Jawaharlal, *An Autobiography* (London: John Lane, 1936).

———, *Discovery of India* (New Delhi: Jawaharlal Nehru Memorial Fund, 1982).

Nelson, Cary and Lawrence Grossberg (eds), *Marxism and the Interpretation of Culture* (London: Macmillan, 1988).

O'Dwyer, Michael, *India as I Knew It, 1985–1925* (London: Constable & Co. Ltd, 1925).

O'Malley, L.S.S. (ed.), *Modern India and the West: A Study of the Interaction of Their Civilisations* (London, 1941).

Oldenburg, Veena Talwar, *The Making of Lucknow: 1856–1877* (New Jersey: Princeton University Press, 1984).

Orsini, Francesca, 'Introduction', in *The Oxford India Premchand* (New Delhi: Oxford University Press, 2004).

Overstreet, Gene D. and Marshall Windmiller, *Communism in India* (Bombay: Perennial Press, 1960).

Pandey, Geetanjali, *Between Two Worlds: An Intellectual Biography of Premchand* (New Delhi: Manohar, 1989).

———, *Patriotic Poetry Banned by the Raj* (New Delhi: NAI, 1982).

Patel, Geeta, *ABlyrical Movements, Historical Hauntings: On Gender, Colonialism, and Desire in Miraji's Urdu Poetry* (New Delhi: Manohar, 2005).

Pearson, Michael, *Pious Passengers: The Hajj in Earlier Times* (London: Hurst & Co., 1994).

———, *The Indian Ocean* (London: Routledge, 2003).

Pernau, Margrit, 'Preparing a Meeting Ground: C.F. Andrews, St Stephens, and the Delhi College', in C.F. Andrews, *Zakaullah of Delhi* (New Delhi: Oxford University Press, 2003).

Peters, F.E., *The Hajj: The Muslim Pilgrimage to Mecca and the Holy Places* (Princeton: Princeton University Press, 1994).

Petievich, Carla, 'Feminine Authorship and Urdu Poetic Tradition: *Baharistan-i Naz* vs *Tazkira-i Rekhti*', in Kathryn Hansen and David Lelyveld (eds), *A Wilderness of Possibilities: Urdu Studies in Transnational Perspective* (New Delhi: Oxford University Press, 2005).

———, *When Men Speak as Women: Vocal Masquerade in Indo-Muslim Poetry* (New Delhi: Oxford University Press, 2007).

Petrie, David, *Communism in India, 1924–1927* (Calcutta: Government of India Press, 1927).

Pollitt, Harry, *Ralph Fox: A Writer in Arms* (London: Lawrence & Wishart, 1937).

Pollock, Sheldon, 'The Cosmopolitan Vernacular', *Journal of Asian Studies*, vol. 57, no. 1 (1998), pp. 6–37.

Pradhan, Sudhi (ed.), *Marxist Cultural Movements in India: Chronicles and Documents (1936–47)*, vols I and II (Calcutta: National Book Agency, 1979).

Prakash, Shri, 'CPI and the Pakistan Movement', in Bipan Chandra (ed.), *The Indian Left: Critical Appraisals* (New Delhi: Vikas Publishing House, 1983).

Pritchett, Frances W., *Nets of Awareness: Urdu Poetry and Its Critics* (Berkeley and Los Angeles: University of California Press, 1994).

Qureshi, I.H., *Muslim Community* (The Hague: Mouton, 1962).

———, *The Struggle for Pakistan* (Karachi: Karachi University Press, 1974 [reprint]).

Qureshi, Naeem, *Pan-Islamism in British Indian Politics: A Study of the Khilafat Movement, 1918–1924* (Leiden: Brill, 1999).

Rai, Lala Lajpat, 'Unhappy India', in B.R. Nanda (ed.), *Collected Works of Lala Lajpat Rai*, vol. XIV (New Delhi: Manohar, 2010).

Raipuri, Akhtar Husain, *The Dust of the Road*, translated by Ameena Azfar (Karachi: Oxford University Press, 2007).

Raipuri, Hameeda Akhtar Husain, *My Fellow Traveler*, translated by Ameena Azfar (Karachi: Oxford University Press, 2006).

Rais, Qamar (ed.), *October Revolution: Impact on Indian Literature* (New Delhi: Sterling Publishers, 1978).

Rajimwale, Anil, 'P.C. Joshi and Indian Cultural Renaissance', *Mainstream*, vol. 45, no. 25 (June 2007).

Ratan, Jai (trans.), *Krishan Chander: Selected Short Stories* (New Delhi: Sahitya Akademi, 1990).

Rieser, Max, 'The Aesthetic Theory of Social Realism', *The Journal of Aesthetics and Art Criticism*, vol. 16, no. 2 (1957), pp. 237–48.

Robinson, Francis, *Separatism among Indian Muslims: The Politics of the United Provinces' Muslims, 1860–1923* (Cambridge: Cambridge University Press, 1974).

———, 'An-Nizamiya: A Group of Lucknow Intellectuals in the Early-Twentieth Century', in Christopher Shackle (ed.), *Urdu and Muslim South Asia: Studies in Honour of Ralph Russell* (New Delhi: Oxford University Press, 1991).

———, *Islam and Muslim History in South Asia* (New Delhi: Oxford University Press, 2000).

———, 'The Muslims of Upper India and the Shock of the Mutiny', in Mushirul Hasan and Narayani Gupta (eds), *India's Colonial Encounter: Essays in Memory of Eric Stokes* (New Delhi: Manohar, 2004).

Roy, Subodh (ed.), *Cecil Kaye's Communism in India with Unpublished Documents from National Archives of India* (Calcutta: Editions India, 1971).

Rubin, David, 'Introduction', in *The World of Premchand: Selected Short Stories* (New Delhi: Oxford University Press, 2001).

Russell, Ralph, 'Leadership in the All-India Progressive Writers' Movement, 1935–1947', in B.N. Pandey (ed.), *Leadership in South Asia* (New Delhi: Vikas Publishing House, 1977).

———, *The Pursuit of Urdu Literature: A Select History* (London: Zed Books, 1992).

———, *Hidden in the Lute: An Anthology of Two Centuries of Urdu Literature* (New Delhi: Viking, 1995).

———, *How Not to Write the History of Urdu Literature: And Others Essays on Urdu and Islam* (New Delhi: Oxford University Press, 1999).

———, 'Strands of Muslim Identity in South Asia', *How Not to Write the History of Urdu Literature and Other Essays* (New Delhi: Oxford University Press, 1999).

———, *Losses Gains*, part 2 (Gurgaon: Three Essays Collective, 2010).

Russell, Ralph and Khurshidul Islam, *Three Mughal Poets* (London: George Allen & Unwin Ltd, 1969).

——— (trans and eds), *Ghalib: Life and Letters* (New Delhi: Oxford University Press, 1994).

Sabhlok, Sanjeev, *Breaking Free of Nehru: Let's Unleash India* (Delhi: Eastern Book Corporation, 2009).

Sadiq, Muhammad, *Twentieth-century Urdu Literature* (Karachi: Royal Book Company, 1983).

———, *A History of Urdu Literature (revised and enlarged)* (New Delhi: Oxford University Press, 1984).

Sahni, Kalpana and P.C. Joshi, *Balraj and Bhisham Sahni: Brothers in Political Theatre* (New Delhi: SAHMAT, 2012).

Saiduzzafar, Hamida, *Autobiography, 1921–1988* (New Delhi: Trianka, 1996).

Saiyid, Dushka H., *Exporting Communism to India: Why Moscow Failed* (Islamabad: National Institute of Historical and Cultural Research, 1995).

Sampath, Vikram, *My Name Is Gauhar Jan: The Life and Times of a Musician* (New Delhi: Rupa & Co., 2010).

Sarin, D.P., *Influence of Political Movements on Hindi Literature (1906–1947)* (Chandigarh: Punjab University Publications Bureau, 1967).

Schimmel, Annemarie, *Gabriel's Wing: A Study into the Religious Ideas of Sir Muhammad Iqbal* (Leiden: E.J. Brill, 1963).

———, *Islam in the Indian Subcontinent* (Leiden: E.J. Brill, 1980).

Sehgal, Anil, *Ali Sardar Jafri: The Youthful Boatman of Joy* (New Delhi: Bhartiya Jnanpith, 2001).

Segal, Kiran, *Zohra Segal: 'Fatty'* (New Delhi: Niyogi Books, 2012).

Segal, Zohra, *Close-Up: Memoirs of a Life on Stage and Screen* (New Delhi: Women Unlimited, 2010).

Sen, Mohit (ed.), *Documents of the Communist Party of India, vol. VIII (1951–56)* (New Delhi: PPH, 1977).

Shackle, Christopher (ed.), *Urdu and Muslim South Asia: Studies in Honour of Ralph Russell* (New Delhi: Oxford University Press, 1991).

Shackle, Christopher and Javed Majeed (eds), *Hali's Musaddas: The Ebb and Flow of Islam* (New Delhi: Oxford University Press, 1997).

Shauq, Sumat Prakash, *Thus Spake Firaq: A Collection of Interviews (1959–1976)* (New Delhi: Allied Publishers, 1992).

Shaw, Graham and Mary Lloyd (eds), *Publications Proscribed by the Government of India: A Catalogue of the Collection in the India Office Library and Records and the Department of Oriental Manuscripts and Printed Books* (London: The British Library, 1985).

Sheikh, Farzana, *Community and Consensus in Islam: Muslim Representation in Colonial India, 1860–1947* (Cambridge: Cambridge University Press, 1989).

Siddiqi, M.H., *Agrarian Unrest in North India: the United Provinces (1919–22)* (New Delhi: Vikas Publishing House, 1978).

Singh, Iqbal, *The Ardent Pilgrim: An Introduction to the Life & Work of Mohammad Iqbal* (New Delhi: Oxford University Press, 1997 [reprint]).

Sisson, Richard and Stanley Wolpert (eds), *Congress and Indian Nationalism: The Pre-Independence Phase* (Berkeley: University of California Press, 1988).

Smith, W.C., 'Modern Muslim Historical Writing in English', in C.H. Philips (ed.), *Historians of India, Pakistan and Ceylon* (London: Oxford University Press, 1961).

———, *Modern Islam in India: A Social Analysis* (New Delhi: Usha Publications, 1979).

Spear, Percival, *Twilight of the Mughals* (New Delhi: Oriental Books Reprint Corporation, 1969).

Suhrawardy, Shaista, *A Critical Survey of the Development of the Urdu Novel and Short Story* (Karachi: Oxford University Press, 2006).

Surjeet, Harkishan Singh, Jyoti Basu, E.K. Nayanar, P. Ramachandran, Koratala Satyanarayana, and Anil Biswas (eds), *History of the Communist Party of India (Marxist)* (New Delhi: CPI [M] Publications in association with LeftWord Books, 2005).

Suroor, Ale Ahmad, 'Humour in Urdu', in Nissim Ezekiel (ed.), *Indian Writers in Conference: Proceedings of the Sixth PEN All-India Writers' Conference* (Mysore: PEN, 1964).

———, 'In Contemporary Urdu Poetry', *Modernity and Contemporary Indian Literature* (Shimla: Indian Institute of Advanced Study, 1968).

Taseer, M.D., *The Oxford India Premchand*, translated by Francesca Orsini (New Delhi: Oxford University Press, 2004).

———, *Articles of Dr. M.D. Taseer* (Islamabad: The Pakistan Academy of Letters, 2009).

Vilanilam, John V., *Mass Communication in India: A Sociological Perspective* (New Delhi: Sage Publications, 2005).

Zaheer, Sajjad, *A Case for Congress-League Unity* (Bombay: PPH, 1973).

———, 'A Note on the PWA', in Sudhi Pradhan (ed.), *Marxist Cultural Movements in India: Chronicles and Documents (1936–47)*, vol. I (Calcutta: National Book Agency, 1979).

———, 'Reminiscences', in Sudhi Pradhan (ed.), *Marxist Cultural Movements in India: Chronicles and Documents (1936–47)* (Calcutta: National Book Agency, 1979).

———, *The Light: A History of the Movement for Progressive Literature in the Indo-Pakistan Subcontinent*, English translation of Sajjad Zaheer's *Roshnai* by Amina Azfar (Karachi: Oxford University Press, 2006).

Zaidi, Ali Jawad, *A History of Urdu Literature* (New Delhi: Sahitya Akademi, 1993).

Zakaria, Rafiq, *Iqbal: The Poet and the Politician* (New Delhi: Viking, 1993).

Zeno, 'Professor Ahmed Ali and the Progressive Writers' Movement', *Annual of Urdu Studies*, vol. 9 (1994), pp. 39–43.

Zhdanov, A.A., *Soviet Writers' Congress, 1934: The Debate on Socialist Realism and Modernism in the Soviet Union* (London: Lawrence & Wishart, 1977).

Published Books/Articles (Urdu)

Abbas, Muzaffar (ed.), *Urdu mein Qaumi Shairi* (Lahore: Maktaba Aaliya, 1978).

Abbasi, Qazi Muhammad Adeel, *Tehreek-e-Khilafat* (New Delhi: Taraqqui Urdu Board, 1978).

Afraheem, Sagheer, *Urdu Afsana: Taraqqui Pasand Tehreek se Qabl* (Aligarh: Educational Book House, 2009).

Ahmad, Atiq, 'Taraqqui Pasand Tahrik aur Karachi', in Qamar Rais and S. Ashoor Kazmi (eds), *Taraqqui Pasand Adab: Pachas Sala Safar* (Delhi: Naya Safar Publications, 1987).

Ahmad, Aziz, *Taraqqui Pasand Adab* (Delhi: Khwaja Press, 1945).

Ahmad, Syed Jafar (ed.), *Shakhsiyat aur Fikr* (Karachi: Maktaba Daniyal, 2005).

Akbarabadi, Makhmoor, *Rooh-e-Nazir* (Lucknow: Uttar Pradesh Urdu Akademi, 2003).

Akhtar, Hameed, *Roodad-e-Anjuman: Anjuman Taraqqui Pasand Mussanifin ki Roodad (1946–47)* (Lahore: Bright Books, 2000).

Ali, Ahmed, *Qaidkhana* (Delhi: Insha Press, 1944).

———, *Maut se Pehle* (Delhi: Insha Press, 1945).

Alvi, Khalid, *Angarey ka Tareekhi Pasmanzar aur Taraqqui Pasand Tehreek* (Delhi: Educational Publishing House, 1995).

——— (ed.), *Angare* (Delhi: Educational Publishing House, 1995).

Anand, Vidya Sagar (ed.), *Jang-e-Azadi ke Awwalin Mujahideen aur Bahadur Shah Zafar* (New Delhi: Modern Publishing House, 2007).

Anjum, Khaliq, *Hasrat Mohani* (New Delhi: Publications Division, 1994).

Ashfaq, Humaira, *Nasr-e-Rashid Jahan* (Lahore: Sang-e-Meel Publications, 2012).

Atiqullah, 'Taraqqui Pasand Nazm: Nazrayati Kirdar ki Tausih', in Qamar Rais and S. Ashoor Kazmi (eds), *Taraqqui Pasand Adab: Pachas Sala Safar* (Delhi: Naya Safar Publications, 1987).

Azhar, Naseeruddin, *Sajjad Zaheer: Hayaat-o-Jehat* (New Delhi: Mazhar Publications, 2004).

Azmi, Kaifi, *Sarmaya* (New Delhi: Mayaar Publications, 1994).

Azmi, Khalilur Rahman, *Urdu mein Taraqqui Pasand Adabi Tehreek* (Aligarh: Educational Book House, 2002 [1957]).

Banarsi, Nazeer, *Ghulami se Azaadi Tak: Qaumi Nazmon ka Majmua* (Lucknow: Uttar Pradesh Soochna Vibhag, 1972).

Barelwi, Ibadat, *Urdu Tanquid Nigari* (Delhi: Chaman Book Depot, 1970).

Chughtai, Ismat, *Majaz (Naye Adab ke Maimar)* (Bombay: Kitab Publishers, 1948).

Faiz, Faiz Ahmed, 'Shair ki Qadrein', in Qamar Rais and S. Ashoor Kazmi (eds), *Taraqqui Pasand Adab: Pachas Sala Safar* (Delhi: Naya Safar Publications, 1987).

———, *Dast-e-Saba* (Aligarh: Educational Book House, 1990).

Faruqi, Khwaja Ahmad (trans.), '*Dastambu*' (Delhi: Allied Publishers, 1954).

Fatimi, Ali Ahmed, *Sajjad Zaheer: Ek Tareekh, Ek Tehreek* (Allahabad: Josh & Firaaq Literary Society, 2006).

———, *Taraqqui Pasand Tehreek: Safar dar Safar* (Allahabad: Idara Naya Safar, 2006).

Gorakhpuri, Majnun, '*Nazm se Nasr Tak*', in Ale Ahmad Suroor (ed.), *Tanquid ke Buniyadi Masail* (Aligarh: Aligarh University Press, 1967).
Hasan, Mohammad, *Gham-e Dil, Wahshat-e Dil* (Delhi: Takhliqkar Publishers, 2003).
Hasan, Sibte (ed.), *Azadi ki Nazmein* (Lucknow: Halqa-e-Adab, 1940).
———, *Mughanni-e Aatish Nafas, Sajjad Zaheer* (Karachi: Maktaba Daniyal, 2008).
Husain, Syed Ehtesham, *Tanquidi Nazariyat*, vol. 2 (Lucknow: Idara Farogh-e-Urdu, 1966).
———, '*Novel ki Tanquid*', in Ale Ahmad Suroor (ed.), *Tanquid ke Buniyadi Masail* (Aligarh: Aligarh Muslim University Press, 1967).
———, *Tanquidi Jaize* (Lucknow: Ahbab Publishers, 1978).
———, 'Urdu Adab mein Taraqqui Pasandi ki Rivayat', in *Tanquidi Jaize* (Lucknow: Ahbab Publishers, 1978).
Hyder, Qurratulain, '*Dareen Gard Sawaar-e-Baashad*', in her collection of Urdu short stories *Raushni Ki Raftaar* (Aligarh: Educational Book House, 1992).
———, *Chaar Novelette* (Aligarh: Educational Book House, 1998).
Illahabadi, Akbar, *Kulliyat*, vols I and II (Lucknow: Adabi Press, 1931).
———, *Gandhi Nama* (Allahabad: Kitabistan, 1948).
Iman, Akhtarul, *Iss Abad Kharabe mein* (New Delhi: Urdu Academy, 1996).
Iqbal, Mohammad, *Shikwa and Jawab-i-Shikwa, Complaint and Answer: Iqbal's Dialogue with Allah*, translated by Khushwant Singh (New Delhi: Oxford University Press, 1981).
Irtiza Karim (ed.), *Qurratulain Hyder: Ek Mutala* (Delhi: Educational Publishing House, 1992).
Ishrat, Islam, *Khalilur Rehman Azmi: Taraqqui Pasandi se Jadidyat Tak* (Patna: Danish Publications).
Jafri, Ali Sardar, *Taraqqui Pasand Adab* (Aligarh: Anjuman-e Taraqqui-i-Urdu, 1957).
———, *Lucknow ki Paanch Raatein aur Doosri Yaadein* (Lucknow: Nusrat Publishers, 1964).
——— (ed.), *Muntakhib Qaumi Shairi* (New Delhi: National Book Trust, 1983).
———, *Taraqqui Pasand Adab ki Nisf Sadi*, Nizam Lectures (1987).
Jahan, Rashid, *Aurat wa Digar Drame wa Afsane* (Lahore: Hashmi Book Depot, 1937).
Jalibi, Jameel, *Tareekh-e-Adab-e-Urdu*, vol. II (Delhi: Educational Publishing House, 1982).
Jamshedpuri, Aslam, *Taraqqui Pasand Urdu Afsana aur Chand Aham Afsananigar* (New Delhi: Modern Publishing House, 2002).
———, '1857 aur Ghalib ke Khutoot', in Vidya Sagar Anand (ed.), *Jang-e-Azadi ke Awwalin Mujahideen aur Bahadur Shah Zafar* (New Delhi: Modern Publishing House, 2007).

Javed, Sulaiman Athar, '*Hyderabad aur Taraqqui Pasand Tahrik*', in Qamar Rais and S. Ashoor Kazmi (eds), *Taraqqui Pasand Adab: Pachas Sala Safar* (Delhi: Naya Safar Publications, 1987).
Jawaid, Yunus, *Halqa-e-Arbab-e Zauq* (Lahore: Majlis-e-Tarraqui-e-Adab, 1984).
Joshi, P.C., *Inquilab 1857* (New Delhi: National Book Trust, 1972).
Kabir, Humayun (ed.), *Azadi-i-Hind: Maulana Abul Kalam Azad* (Azad Kashmir: Arshad Book Sellers, n.d.).
Kamran, M., *Professor Ahmed Ali: Shakhsiyat aur Fan* (Islamabad: Academy of Letters, 2008).
Khaliq Anjum and Mujtaba Husain (eds), *Zabt Shuda Nazmein* (New Delhi: Majlis-i-Jashn-i-Ali Javvad Zaidi, 1975).
Khan, Idris Ahmad, *Daktar Rashid Jahan: Hayat aur Khidmat* (1996).
Khan, Salamatullah, *Majaz ka Ilmiya aur Doosre Mazameen* (Aligarh: Muslim Educational Press, 1969).
Kidwai, S.R., '*Taraqqui Pasand Tehreek aur Ghazal*' and '*Taraqqui Pasand Tehreek: Manshuron ki Roshni Mein*', in Qamar Rais and S. Ashoor Kazmi (eds), *Taraqqui Pasand Adab: Pachas Sala Safar* (Delhi: Naya Safar Publications, 1987).
Lari, Ahmar, *Hasrat Mohani: Hayat aur Karname* (Lucknow: Nami Press, 1973).
Mahdi, S.M., *Chand Tasweerein, Chand Khutoot* (New Delhi: National Council for Promotion of Urdu Language, 2006).
Majaz, Asrarul Haq, *Saaz-e-Nau* (Lucknow: Kitabi Duniya, 1949).
Majaz, Lucknowi, *Majaz ek Ahang* (Karachi, 1956).
———, *Ahang* (New Delhi: Maktaba Jamia, 2002 [reprint]).
Malik, Abdulla, *Mustaqbil Hamara Hai* (Lahore: Al-Jadid, 1950).
Manto, Saadat Hasan, *Lazzat-e Sang* (Lahore: Naya Idara, 1956).
Masood, Tahir, *Yeh Sooratgar Kuch Khwabon Ke* (Karachi: Maktaba Takhliq-e Adab, 1985).
Mirza, Yusuf, *Majaz: Majaz Lukhnowi ki Mukkamal Sawana-e-Hayat aur Urdu Dramae ki Jadeed Tareen Technique* (Bombay: Messrs Mohammedan Enterprises, 1985).
Mohiuddin, Makhdoom, *Bisat-e-Raqs* (Hyderabad: Andhra Urdu Akademi, 1986).
Mohsin, Muhammad, *Saadat Hasan Manto: Apni Takhliqat ki Roshni mein (Ek Nafsiyati Tajurba)* (Delhi: Darul Ashaat, 1982).
Naqvi, Arif, *Yaadon ke Chiragh* (New Delhi: Modern Publishing House, 2005).
Narang, Gopichand (ed.), *Sajjad Zaheer: Adabi Khidmaat aur Taraqqui Pasand Tehreek* (New Delhi: Sahitya Akademi, 2007).
———, '*Tehreek-e-Azadi aur Urdu Shairi*' (The Movement for Independence and Urdu Poetry), in Vidya Sagar Anand (ed.), *Jang-e-Azadi ke Awwalin Mujahideen aur Bahadur Shah Zafar* (New Delhi: Modern Publishing House, 2007).

Nomani, Shibli, *Kulliyat-i-Shibli* (Azamgarh: Maarif Press, 1954).
Parti, Rajesh Kumar (ed.), *Ashob*, vol. 1, *National Archives mein Mahfooz Zabt Sudah Adabiyat se Intekhab* (New Delhi: NAI, 1993).
Parvez, Aslam, '*Bahadur Shah Zafar aur Atthara Sau Sattavan*', in Vidya Sagar Anand (ed.), *Jang-e-Azadi ke Awwalin Mujahideen aur Bahadur Shah Zafar* (New Delhi: Modern Publishing House, 2007).
Pasha, Ahmad Jamal, *Majaz ke Latife* (Delhi: Maktaba Shahrah, 1966).
Paul, Jogindar, '*Taraqqui Pasand Fikr aur Afsana*', in Qamar Rais and S. Ashoor Kazmi (eds), *Taraqqui Pasand Adab: Pachas Sala Safar* (Delhi: Naya Safar Publications, 1987).
Poshni, Zafarullah, *Zindagi Zinda Dilli ka Naam Hai: Rawalpindi Muqadama Sazish ke Aseeron ki Sarguzasht-e-Aseeri*, 4th ed. (Karachi: Fazli Sons Pvt. Ltd, 2001).
Qadiri, Hamid Hasan, *Dastan-e-Tareekh-e-Urdu* (Agra: Agra Akhbar Press, 1957).
Quraishi, Abdur Razzaq (ed.), *Nava-e-Azadi* (New Delhi: Maktaba Jamia, n.d.).
Rahbar, Hans Raj, *Taraqqui Pasand Adab: Ek Jaiyza* (Delhi: Azad Kitab Ghar, 1967).
Rais, Qamar, *Tanquidi Tanazur* (Aligarh: Educational Publishing House, 1978).
———, '*Urdu Afsane mein Angarey ki Riwayat*', in Ali Sardar Jafri (ed.), *Guftagu* (Taraqqui Pasand Number) (Bombay: Wadera Publications, 1980).
———, *Ali Sardar Jafri* (New Delhi: Sahitya Akademi, 2007).
Rais, Qamar and Syed Ashoor Kazmi (eds), *Taraqqui Pasand Adab: Pachas Sala Safar* (Delhi: Naya Safar Publications, 1987).
Raza, Rahi Masoom, '*Tanquid-e-Ghazal*', in Ale Ahmad Suroor (ed.), *Tanquid ke Buniyadi Masail* (Aligarh: Aligarh Muslim University Press, 1967).
Rudaulvi, Sharib, *Asrarul Haq Majaz* (New Delhi: Sahitya Akademi, 2009).
Sadri, Makhmoor, *Urdu mein Taraqqui Pasand Tanqueed* (Delhi: Educational Publishing House, 2008).
Saleem, Ahmad (ed.), *Sajjad Zaheer, Hamari Tehreek-i-Azadi aur Takhliqi Amal: Sajjad Zaheer ki Siyasi aur Adabi Tehreerein, Taqsim-e-Hind se Qabl* (Lahore: Sang-e-Meel Publications, 2007).
Salim, Hamida, *Shorish-e-Dauran: Yaadein* (New Delhi: Har-Anand Publications, 1995).
Salim, Hamida, *Hum Saath They* (New Delhi: Anjuman-e-Tarraqui-e-Urdu (Hind), 1999).
Salim, Manzar, *Majaz: Hayat aur Shairi* (Lucknow: Kitab Publishers, 1967).
Sarwar, Muhammad, *Maulana Obaidullah Sindhi* (Lahore: Sindh Sagar Academy, 1967).
———, *Ifadat-o-Malfuzat* (Lahore: Sindh Sagar Academy, 1972).
Shikohabadi, Muhammad Husain, *Majaz: Sawanah Shakhsiyat aur Shairi* (Aligarh: Aligarh Press, 1980).

464 • Bibliography

Siddiqui, Abdul Hafiz (ed.), *Aligarh Magazine* (Majaz Number) (Aligarh, 1955–6).

Sukhachev, Alexei, *Makhdoom Mohiuddin*, translated from the Russian into Urdu by Muhammad Usama Farooqui (Hyderabad: Maktaba Sher-o-Hikmat, 1993).

Sultanpuri, Majrooh, *Kulliyat* (Lahore: Al-Hamd Publications, 2003 [reprint]).

Suroor, Ale Ahmad (ed.), *Tanquid ke Buniyadi Masail* (Aligarh: Aligarh Muslim University Press, 1967).

———, 'Urdu Tanquid ke Buniyadi Afkar', in *Tanquid ke Buniyadi Masail* (Aligarh: Aligarh Muslim University Press, 1968).

———, 'Iqbal ke Khutoot', 'Maujooda Adabi Masail', and 'Yaadgar-e-Hali', in *Tanquid Kya Hai?* (New Delhi: Maktaba Jamia, 1972).

———, 'Taraqqui Pasand Tehreek Par Ek Nazar', in *Tanquid Kya Hai?* (New Delhi: Maktaba Jamia, 1976 [reprint]).

———, 'Hali ki Muqadama Sher-o-Shairi ki Manviyat', in *Fikr-e-Roshan* (Aligarh: Educational Book House, 1995).

Usmani, Muiza, *Majaz: Shakhs aur Shair* (Allahabad: Daira Shah Ajmal, 1985).

Vasileva, Ludmila, *Parvarish-e-Lauh-o-Qalam: Faiz, Hayat aur Takhliqat*, translated from the Russian by Usama Faruqi and Ludmila Vasileva (Karachi: Oxford University Press, 2007).

Zaheer, Sajjad (ed.), *Angarey* (Lucknow: Nizami Press, 1932).

———, *Muslim League aur Azadi* (Bombay: PPH, 1944).

———, *Light on League-Unionist Conflict* (Bombay: PPH, 1944).

———, *Punjab ki League-Unionist Jhagre ka Rahasya* (Bombay: Jan Prakashan Griha, 1944).

———, *Sajjad Zaheer ke Mazameen* (Lucknow: Uttar Pradesh Urdu Academy, 1979).

———, *Roshnai* (New Delhi: Seema Publications, 1985).

Published Books/Articles (Hindi)

Ahmad, Z.A., *Mere Jivan ki Kuchch Yaadein* (Allahabad: Lokbharti, 2008).

———, *Lahuluhaan Baisakhi* (New Delhi: NAI, 1997).

Parti, Rajesh Kumar (ed.), *Azaadi ke Taraane (British Raj Dwara Pratibandit Urdu Sahitya se)* (New Delhi: NAI, 1986).

Premkumar, *Shaoor ki Dehleez* (Delhi: S.S. Publications, 2009).

Salim, Hamida, *Mera Bhai: Asrarul Haq Majaz* (New Delhi: Prakashan Sansthan, 2012).

Zaheer, Noor, *Mere Hisse ki Roshnai* (Shahadra: Medha Books, 2005).

———, *Sajjad Zaheer: Pratinidi Rachnain*, vols I and II (Shahadra: Medha Books, 2006).

———, *Surkh Karvan ke Humsafar* (Shahadra: Medha Books, 2008).

Documents

Selected Works of Jawaharlal Nehru, NMML.
Towards Freedom, ICHR.
Documents of the Communist Movement in India (Calcutta: National Book Agency Pvt. Ltd), 27 vols.
Adhikari, G., *Communist Party and India's Path to National Regeneration and Socialism (For Members Only)* (New Delhi: Communist Party Publications, 1964).
India and Communism (revised up to 1 January 1935), Compiled in the Intelligence Bureau, Home Department, Government of India (Simla: Government of India Press, 1935).
Zaidi, Z.H. (ed.), *Jinnah Papers*, vol. 1 (part I and II) and vol. 2 (Islamabad: Quaid-i-Azam Papers Project, National Archives of Pakistan, 1993).

Journals (English)

Annual of Urdu Studies, Center for South Asia, University of Wisconsin-Madison, Madison (all issues from 1981 onwards).
The Journal of Asian Studies, Association of Asian Studies, Cambridge University Press, University of California, California.
South Asia: Journal of South Asian Studies, South Asian Studies Association of Australia, Routledge.
Mahfil, Asian Studies Center, Michigan State University, East Lansing (vols 1–8, accessed through Digital South Asian Library).
Journal of South Asian Literature, Asian Studies Center, Michigan State University, East Lansing.

Journals (Urdu)

Aligarh Magazine (Aligarh: Aligarh Muslim University, different issues).
Adabiyat (Faiz Number) (Islamabad: Akademi Adabiyat, 2009).
Fikr-o-Nazar (Aligarh: Muslim University, different issues).
Guftagu (Tarraqui Pasand Number), edited by Ali Sardar Jafri (Bombay: Wadera Publications, 1980).
Irtiqa (Sajjad Zaheer Number) (Karachi: Irtiqa Matbuaat, 2006).
Irtiqa (Makhdum Mohiuddin Number) (Karachi: Irtiqa Matbuaat, 2009).
Kitab (Lucknow: Nizami Press, different issues).
Naya Adab (Lucknow and Bombay, different issues).
Sher-o-Hikmat, edited by Shahryar and Mughni Tabassum (Hyderabad: Makataba Sher-o-Hikmat, different issues).

Index

1919 ka Ek Din 64–5, 320
1857 Revolt/Mutiny xx, 91, 149
    causes of 42n110
    Muslim responses to 20–30
    Urdu poetry and 2–20

Abbas, Khwaja Ahmad 233, 251–3, 332
    Zafran ke Phool 332
Abdali, Ahmad Shah 5, 7, 13n28
Abdullah, Shaikh 36, 39, 176
'*Adab aur Zindagi*' 244
Adab-e-Latif 259n35, 280, 324
Afghani, Jamaluddin 49
Afghanistan xxiv
    Muslims migration in 1920 to 72
Ahang 265n49, 266, 271
Ahl-e-Hadith movement in India 59
Ahmad, Aijaz xiiin1, 110n3, 384
Ahmad, Atiq xxvin34, 375n94
Ahmad, Aziz 30, 30n76, 323–4
Ahmad, Nazir xvii, 2, 25–7, 29, 31, 33–6, 39, 46

Ayama 35
Banat al-Nash 34
Fasana-e-Mubtila 35
Mirat al-Urus 34–5
Taubat-al-Nasuh 34–5
Ahrar movement 74
Ahrar Party 157n24
Ahrarvi, Shahid 177–9
Ain-e-Akbari (Syed Ahmad Khan) xvii
Akbarabadi, Nazir 8–10
    '*Aadmi Nama*' 9
    '*Banjara Nama*' 9–10
    '*Roti Nama*' 9–10
Akhtar, Hameed 292, 298n117
Akhtar, Jan Nisar 233, 243, 255n27, 292, 308n10, 326
Akhtar, Waheed 392–3
Alekseev, M. 365
Ali, Abdullah Yusuf 98
Ali, Ahmed xix, xxii–xxiii, 101–2, 113, 152, 158, 158n27, 159–60, 187, 191–2, 227, 249, 265–6, 318–19, 388–90

Baadal Nahin Aate (*see Baadal Nahin Aate*)
criticism of Zaheer's *Roshnai* 388–9
dislocation from PWA 386–7, 387n115
Mahavaton ki Ek Raat (*see Mahavaton ki Ek Raat*)
reclusive lifestyle 181
Twilight in Delhi 158
views on the PWM 387–8
Ali, Ameer 35, 98
Ali brothers 58, 59, 67
Aligarh movement 29, 30, 191
Aligarh Muslim University (AMU) 144, 176, 270
Ali, Mohamed 56n13, 58–60, 60n27
Ali, Syed Ameer 35
Ali, Wilayat 103
Allahabad University 220, 225, 237, 392n127
All-India Association of Urdu Writers 359
All India Congress Committee (AICC) 88, 199n18, 234, 237n106
All-India Muslim Educational Conference, founded by Syed Ahmad Khan (1886) 37
All India Muslim League, in Dhaka (1906) 63
All-India Progressive Writers' Association (AIPWA) xix, 113n15, 160, 182, 188, 228, 244, 260, 323, 360–1, 383 (*see also* League of Progressive Authors)
build-up to first conference 211–24
drawing up *Manifesto* in London 190–211
success of first conference in Lucknow 224–41

All-India Progressive Writers' Conference, Lucknow (1936) xix, xxv, 191, 224
All-India Progressive Writers' Movement 161n35
All-India Socialist Party 88
All-India Students' Conference, Lucknow (1936) 231–2, 234
All-India Urdu Progressive Writers' Conference, Hyderabad (1945) 161, 250, 291, 358
All-India Women's Conference 238
All-Pakistan Congress of Progressive Writers 366–7
All-Pakistan PWA 374–5
Alvi, Khalid xviin12, 108n1, 148n3
American Republicanism 5
Amman, Mir
Bagh-o-Bahar 32n80
Anand, Mulk Raj 195–6, 209, 231, 385
The Coolie 196
The Untouchable (*see The Untouchable*)
Anand, Vidya Sagar 11n23, 13n29, 15n34
Andrews, C.F. xviin11, 22, 22n50
Angarey 53, 90, 104, 107–8, 112, 119n22, 127, 142–3, 145, 151–2, 154, 157–8, 191–3, 205, 238, 315–16, 322, 396
advocated need for self-criticism on Muslim community part 146
consist of short stories 109
dirty and *bazari* language of 169
influence of Russian masters 163
literary radicalism of 113
newspapers' view on 162
Proscription Order on 175
public anger towards 147–8
quartet 181–9

468 • Index

reactions in press after ban of
   164–81
reflects impact of modern English
   writers 144
reprinted in Urdu in India 147–8
*Angarey ka Tareekhi Pasmanzar aur
   Taraqqui Pasand Tehreek* xviin12,
   xvii, xxi, xxiv–xxv, 39
Anjuman-e-Himayat-i-Islam 34, 37–8
Anjuman-e-Khuddam-i-Kaaba 60,
   68, 89
   founders, Abdul Bari and Maulana
      Shaukat Ali 60
Anjuman-e-Punjab, Lahore 40
Anjuman-e Taraqqui-i-Urdu 376
*Anjuman-e-Taraqqui Pasand
   Mussanifin* xiv
Ansari, Hayatullah 163, 233, 258n34,
   263–4, 269, 308, 354
Ansari, Humayun Khizar xvn6, 99,
   101
anti-capitalist models 150
anti-colonial movement xxvii
Arab League 360
Araish-e-Mehfil (Sher Ali Afsos) 32n80
Arnold, Matthew 31n79
art and civilization, European ideas of
   7n16
Arya Samaj/Samajism 72, 89, 105,
   164n44
Asar us Sanadid 16–17, 17n36
Ashk, Upendranath xvi, 312
   Aurat ki Fitrat 331
   Chattan 367
   Daachi 331
   'Manto Mera Dushman' 312
   Nau Ratan 331
Ashob xxiiin29
Ashraf, K.M. 16, 19, 231n86
Askari, Muhammad Hasan 306, 318,
   396

Atlantic Pact 367
Awadh Punch 42n112
Awadh Punch school of humourists
   336
'Awara' 270–1
Azad, Maulana Abul Kalam 21n49,
   56n13, 71, 75, 94, 354
   *Abul Kalam Azad: An Intellectual
      and Religious Biography* (Ian
      Douglas) 71n61
Azad, Muhammad Husain 31
   Aab-e-Hayaat 22, 40
Azmi, Kaifi xiv, 178, 291, 293
   'Khana Jangi' 251
Azmi, Khalilur Rahman xviin12, 139,
   254n25, 317, 330, 394
   Main Hoon Khanabadosh 330
Azmi, Shaukat 291, 293
   Aakhr-e-Shab 294
Azurdah, Mufti Sadruddin Khan
   11–12

Baadal Nahin Aate 109, 129, 140, 144,
   171
Balkan War of 1912 58, 67
Balkans 58, 69
Banarasi, Nazeer 19
ban of publications by British, reasons
   for 149
Barelwi, Ibadat 29, 303, 315, 317
'Barq-e-Kalisa' 45
Barq, Mirza Muhammad Raza 7–8
   'Marsiya-e-Lucknow' 7–8
Barrier, Norman Gerald 57, 151
Basu, Jyoti 196–7, 204, 210
Bazar-e-Husn 124n25, 152n12
Bazm-e-Dastango 281n84
Bedar, Abid Raza 394
Bedi, Rajinder Singh xvi, 312, 327–38,
   390
   Apne Dukh Mujhe De Do 330

Dana-o-Dam 329
Dastak 329
Ek Chadar Maili si 360
Garam Coat 329–30
Phagun 329
views on/distancing from the PWM 390–1
Behl, Aditya 9
Bhalla, Alok 335
Bharatiya Sahitya Parishad's conference, Nagpur (1936) 244–5
'Bhuka hai Bengal' 293
Bihishti Zewar 25, 26n63
Bismillah 321–2
Bloomfield, B.C. 149
Bloomsbury Group 194n6
Bloomsbury Group of Delhi 2, 194
Bolsheviks 79–80, 82, 183n89, 240
'Bombay se Bhopal Tak' 326–7
Bombay Textile Workers' strike (1925) 84
Boo 300n11, 315, 317–18, 324
bourgeois/bourgeoisie 79, 122, 160, 307n8, 341, 348, 352, 355, 358
Brass, Paul 72n64
British imperialism/imperialists 11, 81, 86–7, 111n8, 348, 352, 356, 395
British imperialistic adventurism 93, 104
British socialism on young Indians, influence of 198
British system of education 91
Macaulay's scheme of 'modern' education in 1835 18

Cabinet Mission Plan (16 February 1946) 306
Central Khilafat Committee 65–7
Chakbast, Brij Narain xvi
'Awaz-e-Qaum' 95
'Khak-e-Watan' 95
'Chal Balkan Chal' 95
Chandar, Krishan xiv, 129, 250–1, 273, 281, 292, 296n112, 306n2, 312, 313n18, 315, 318, 324, 326–38, 356–7, 381, 385, 397
Babu Gopinath 318
Hum Wahshi Hain 329
Kalu Bhangi 129
Nazare 328–9
'Pauday' 251
Shikast 328
Tilism-e Khayal 328
Chattopadhyay, Kamaladevi 156, 227
All-India Women's Conference, set up in 1927 223n70
Chattopadhyay, Virendranath 80n89 (*see also* League against Imperialism, Berlin)
Chelmsford Reforms (1919) 58–9n20
Chughtai, Ismat xviii, xiv, xxii, 265n49, 294, 307, 322–7, 380
'Bombay se Bhopal Tak' (see 'Bombay se Bhopal Tak')
Chhoi Mooi 323
Chotein 323
Dhaani Bankein 324
Ek Baat 323
Jadein 324
Kaghazi Hai Pairahan (see *Kaghazi Hai Pairahan*)
Kaliyan 323
Lihaaf (see *Lihaaf*)
Shaitan 323
Tehri Lakir (see *Tehri Lakir*)
Ziddi 323
civil disobedience movement (1930) xxviii, 84, 148
Comintern 78–9, 80n89, 85–7, 197n12, 211, 216–18, 239–40, 347
Vanguard, magazine 78–9

Communist Manifesto xxiii–xxiv, 80–1
  Urdu translation 75–6
Communist Party of Great Britain
  (CPGB) 85–6, 196, 209, 217, 239
  Indian Students Cell of 196
Communist Party of India (CPI) xxii,
  xxiv–xxvi, 74–91, 185n97, 213,
  215, 223n69, 231, 239–40, 293,
  301, 326
  All-India Congress of 342–3
  banned (1934) 214, 290
  establishment of 53
  growing popularity, turning point
    in of 341
  history during period under
    scrutiny (1935–55) 340
  major issues after 1945 war 346
  Muslim membership of 344
  possessed efficient body of well-
    trained labour agitators 348
  pro-war slogans 241
  public manifestations of movement
    341
  refusal to lend support to a united
    Indian state 290–1
  Second Congress, Calcutta (1948)
    351
  ultra-revolutionary stand against
    princely states 348
  war policy 341
Communist Party of Pakistan (CPP)
  262, 301, 352n34, 364–7, 371,
  376
communists, Indian
  basic tasks of 87
  Russian influence on 88
communitarian politics 66
Conference of Indian Writers,
  Lucknow 209
Congress 67–8, 241, 251, 349, 378
  communist infiltration in 237
  declaration of complete
    independence in 1929 84
  –League unity 361
  Muslims 73
  as 'National Bourgeoisie', termed by
    Russia 211
  socialists 340
  Tilak and Ghosh challenges to 62
  Zaheer's expulsion from 236–7
Congress of Peoples of the East
  India's participation in 77–8
Congress of Socialist Writers (1934)
  202n23

Dadaism 114n16
Dagh, Nawab Mirza 12, 14
Dange, S.A. 85, 343, 350
Daryabadi, Maulana Abdul Majid 160,
  169, 171, 173, 182
'Dastambu' 15–16
Defence of India Act 340
Dehelvi, Shah Waliullah 13n28
Dehelvi, Shahid 256–7
Dehlvi, Zaheer 20
Delhi College 21n49, 23, 33
Delhi Renaissance 18, 22
Deoband school 24, 99–100, 157
de-Stalinization campaign by Nikita
  Kruschev 390n124
Dhandas 321
Dilli ki Sair 109, 136–7
Dimitrov, Georgi 195, 374
Dulari 122–3, 127
Dyakov, A. 352

East–West conflict 74
English
  -educated Indians, politically
    minded 55
  education Indians launched
    newspapers and periodicals in 55

imperialism 79
language newspapers 54
equality, notion of 90, 399

Faiz, Faiz Ahmed xiv, 271–86, 325, 341, 367
  'Aa Jao Africa' 277
  'Aaj ki Raat' 274
  'Chand Roz aur Meri Jaan' 274
  Dast-e-Saba 276, 283
  'The Execution Yard (A Song)' 276
  'Husn aur Maut' 274
  'Mere Nadeem' 274
  'Mujhse Pahli si Muhabbat Mere Mahboob Na Mang' 274
  Naqsh-e-Faryadi 274–5
  recipient of Lenin Peace Prize (1962) 283
  'Siyasi Leader kay Naam' (see 'Siyasi Leader kay Naam')
  'Subah-e-Azadi' (see 'Subah-e-Azadi')
  Zindah Nama (see *Zindah Nama*)
Faridabadi, Syed Muttalibi 248, 381
  Kisan Rut 248
Farrukhsiyar, Emperor 4n7
Faruqi, Shamsur Rahman 45–6, 394
fascist forces
  rise in early 1930s 194
  United Front against 206
Fatehpuri, Niyaz 163, 163n39, 171
First Afro-Asian Conference, Tashkent, 1958 283
First War of Independence (*see* revolt of 1857)
First World War (1914–18) 58–9, 75, 100
Fort William College 32n80
Fox, Ralph 198–9
freedom from foreign rule 104
Fughan, Ashraf Ali Khan 6
Fughan-e-Dehli 11–12, 20

Gandhi, Mahatma 47, 64, 89, 103, 114, 193, 219, 226, 241, 341, 345, 378, 384, 390
  call for satyagraha 62, 224, 331
  Hind Swaraj 62
  non-cooperation movement 65, 150
Gandhi Nama 47
Garmiyon ki Ek Raat 119–22
Ghadar Party 75, 214
Ghaffar, Qazi Abdul 162, 162n37, 299, 316, 354
  Laila ke Khutoot 162
Ghalib, Mirza Asadullah Khan xvii, 15–16, 18, 26, 28, 47
  'Dastambu' (see 'Dastambu')
Ghosh, Aurobindo 62, 223n68
Ghosh, Jyotirmoy 195n8
Gorakhpuri, Firaq 220, 225
Gorakhpuri, Majnooh xvn7
groups by Indian revolutionaries
  Anushilan group 80
  Hindustan Socialist Republican Army 80
  Jugantar group 80
  Naujawan Bharat Sabha 80, 156

Haider, Niyaz 263–4, 266, 292, 300, 326
Hajra Begum 184n93, 199, 223, 237–8, 386
Hali, Altaf Husain xvii, 2, 5n11, 18, 26–8, 36, 41
  Chup ki Daad 36
  Majalis un-Nisa (see *Majalis un-Nisa*)
  Muqadama-e-Sher-o-Shairi (see *Muqadama-e-Sher-o-Shairi*)
  Musaddas: Madd-o-Jazr-e Islam (see *Musaddas: Madd-o-Jazr-e Islam*)
Hallett, M.G. on 'Communist Legislation' 214

Halqa-e Arbab-e Zauq 243, 281–2
  (*see also* Bazm-e-Dastango)
Haq, Chaudhry Afzal 74
Haq, Maulvi Abdul 220, 244, 246, 376
Hasan, Maulvi Ghulam 309
Hasan, Mushirul 35, 88n110,
  107n157, 155
Hasan, Sibte 50, 220, 286, 290
  Azadi ki Nazmein 12n26, 14n30,
    20n46, 50, 53n1, 258
  Zabt Shudah Nazmein 53n1
Hasan, Wazir (Sir) 110n7
hijrat movement 72–3, 307
Hindu–Muslim unity 47, 72
Holroyd, Colonel 40–1
Hundred Candle Watt Bulb 319–20
'Hungama-e-Balqan' 69–70
Husain, Ehtesham 4, 19, 32, 220,
  267–8, 336, 358, 382
Husain, Intezar 129n30, 306–7
Husain, Mumtaz 392
Husain, Sharif 59–60
Hussain, Karamat 37
Hussain, Munshi Sajjad 38, 42,
  42n112
  Haji Baghlol 38
  Kaya Palat 38
Hyder, Qurratulain 327, 360, 368, 391,
  Aag ka Dariya 360

Iftikharuddin, Mian 366, 372
  Rawalpindi Conspiracy Case, arrest
    in 284
  Establishment of Pakistan Papers
    Limited 284
Illahabadi, Akbar 43–8, 114–5
  'Barq-e-Kalisa' (*see* 'Barq-e-Kalisa')
  Gandhi Nama (*see Gandhi Nama*)
Imam, Raza 144, 288–9n99, 394–5
Iman, Akhtarul xviii, 281n85,
  381n103

imperial policy of proscription 57
Indian Communist Defence Committee
  formation (1924) 82
Indian National Congress (INC) 87,
  209
  Kanpur session of 82
  Labour Swaraj Party of 84
Indian-owned English newspapers
  56–7
Indian Penal Code (IPC), ban on
  Angarey 148, 175
Indian People's Theatre Association
  (IPTA) xiv, 253, 294n108, 295,
  347
Indian Progressive Writers'
  Association (IPWA) 203–5,
  210–11
Indo-Pak war (1965) 302
Iqbal, Mohammad 30, 37, 47–51,
  70n59, 71, 77, 92n118, 93, 99, 104,
  128n29
  '*Aurat*' 93, 292
  '*Armaghan-i-Hejaz*' 93
  Baal-e-Jibreel 50
  Bang-e-Dara 71
  Jawab-e-Shikwa 71
  paranoia in poems 92
  '*Punjab ke Dehqan Se*' (*see* '*Punjab ke
    Dehqan Se*')
  Shikwa 71
  Zarb-e-Kaleem 51
Islam 65–6, 89, 107
  history in twentieth century 99
Islam and Socialism (Mushir Hosain
  Kidwai) 76
Islam, Kazi Nazrul 84, 203

'Jab Bandhan Toote' (Tajdar Samri)
  333
jadeed 90, 306–7, 327, 393–4, 397–8
jadeed parast 393–4

Jafri, Ali Sardar xiv, 256n30, 261,
  300–1, 315, 342, 385
  Asia Jaag Utha 300, 302
  'Ghar mein Bazar mein' 330
  Kaun Dushman Hai 302
  Khoon ki Lakeer 300
  Lahu Pukarta Hai 300
  Lucknow ki Paanch Ratein 258n34
  'Man ki Man Mein' 330
  Manzil 300
  Mera Safar (see *Mera Safar*)
  Navambar, Mera Gahwara 300
  Paighambaran-e-Sukhan 302
  Paikaar 301
  Pairahan-e Sharar 300
  Parvaz 300
  Patthar ki Diwar 300
  Yeh Khoon Kis ka Hai? 301
Jahan, Khurshid 143, 176–7
Jahan, Rashid 112–13, 136–45, 186,
  188, 220, 222–3
  Aurat wa Digar Drame wa Afsane
    186
  Comparison with other women
    writers 152–3
  death 183
  Dilli ki Sair (see *Dilli ki Sair*)
  marriage to Mahmuduzzafar 182
  Mera ek Safar 137n32
  Parde ke Peechche (see *Parde ke
    Peechche*)
Jalees, Ibrahim
  'Bombay' 333
  'Do Mulk Ek Kahani' 333
Jamiat-ul-Muslimin 238
Jamiayat-i-Ulama-i-Hind, formation
  (1919) 65
Jannat ki Bashaarat 116–19, 123n24
Jaunpuri, Wamiq
  Bhooka hai Bangal 293
Jawanmardi 134–6

Jazbi, Moin Ahsan 303, 388
  'Maut' 388
jihad 117, 173
Johri, Shah Ayatollah 14
Joshi, P.C. 19, 293n105, 294n108,
  344–5

Kaghazi Hai Pairahan 177–8, 324
Kakori Conspiracy Case 83, 212
'Kallol' group of writers 227
Kanpur Conspiracy Case 81–3, 89
Kapoor, Kanhaiyyalal 336
  'Ghalib Jadeed Shoara ki Ek Majlis
    mein' 336
  Sang-o-Khisht 336
Khairabadi, Fazl-i-Haq 11–13
Khairi, Rashidul 38
Khan, Liaqat Ali 371
Khan, Mahmuduzzafar 234
  A Quest for Life 183–4
Khan, Syed Ahmad 26–7, 29, 40,
  42, 45–6, 51, 76, 104–6 (see also
  Ain-e-Akbari)
  'Aligarh Experiment' 104–5
  Asar us Sanadid (see *Asar us
    Sanadid*)
  founder, All-India Muslim
    Educational Conference (1886)
    37
Khan, Zafar Ali 95n130
  'Mazalim-e-Punjab' 95–6
  'Shola-e-Fanoos-e-Hind' 96
Khilafat movement (1919–22) 67,
  68–9
  offshoot of 88n110
  significant fallouts of 88–9
  Turkish National Assembly,
    abolishment by 68
Kidwai, Sadiq-ur-Rahman 8
Kiernan, Victor G. 93, 196
Kirchein aur Kirchiyan 320

474 • Index

Labour Party in Britain 82
Lahore press 370
Laski, Harold 198–9
   The State in Theory and Practice 198
League against Imperialism, Berlin 80n89, 209
League of Progressive Authors 191–2, 205 (*see also* All-India Progressive Writers' Association [AIPWA])
Left Book Club 198n15, 234
Leipzig Trial 195
Lihaaf 323, 324–5
literary/progressive journals
   Alamgir 310–11
   Aligarh 174
   an-Nizamiya 70
   Awaaz 255
   Chingari 182, 186, 213, 258n35
   Dastan 280
   Guftagu 300
   Hamdam 171
   Hans 190, 201
   Humayun 280
   Jama 280
   Langal 84
   Naya Adab 258n35
   Nigar 163n39, 171, 280
   Preet Lari 280
   Saqi 256, 280
   Savera 368
   Shahkar 280
literary newspapers/magazines
   Al-Hilal 58, 76, 94, 98
   Bande Mataram 88
   Comrade 56n13, 58, 98, 103
   Hamdard 56n13, 60, 97
   Hindustan 258n34
   Imroze 284, 366
   Inprecor 85, 85n100, 87, 231
   Ismat 39
   Jamhuriat 294

Khilafat 170
Lail-o-Nahar 284
The Leader 179, 191, 387
Maarif 170
Manchester Guardian 371
Mazdoor 170n58
Muhammadi 76
Muslim Gazette 56n13, 60
Naya Zamana 364n69
Pakistan Times 284, 366
Parcham 258
Payam 174–5
Sach 168–70, 176
Sarfaraz 164, 167, 169–70
Tahzib un-Niswan, first women's Urdu newspaper 39
Urdu-i-Mualla 56n13, 57
Zamana 76, 220
Zamindar 56n13, 57, 97
Lo Ek Qissa Suno (Akhtar Ansari) 333
London ki Ek Raat 193–4, 206
London Majlis 196
Lucknow Pact (1916) 64n38, 71–2, 361
Ludhianvi, Sahir 278n76, 295–7
   Pyasa, lyrics for 295
   Talkhiyan 295
Lukács, Georg 154

Mahavaton ki Ek Raat 131–4, 148n4, 152, 159
Mahindarnath, 333
   Chandi ke Taar 333
Mahmud, Shabana
   views on *Angarey* 143–4
Mahmud-ul Hasan, Maulana, return from British imprisonment (1920) 65
Mahmuduzzafar 109n2, 112, 182, 226–7, 262n42, 272
   Amir ka Mahal 182

life after *Angarey* 182–3
Jawanmardi
reference in DIB reports 234–5
statement in *The Leader* 179
Majalis un-Nisa 36
Majaz, Asrarul Haq 253–71
    Ahang (see *Ahang*)
    'Awara' (see 'Awara')
    'Inquilab' 212–3, 267
    death 243
    inquilabi shairi 267
    'Nazr-e-Dil' 268
    'Nazr-e Khalida' (see 'Nazr-e Khalida')
Malihabadi, Josh 220
    'East India Company ke Farzandon se' 213
    'Shikast-e-Zindaan ka Khwaab' (see 'Shikast-e-Zindaan ka Khwaab')
Malik, Abdulla 364n69, 366, 367
    Mustaqbil Hamara Hai 370
Manifesto xxv, 180, 186, 250, 356, 380–1
    drawing up in London 191–203
Manto, Saadat Hasan 307–22
    1919 ka Ek Din (see *1919 ka Ek Din*)
    Aatish Parey 309–10, 315
    Begu 319
    Bismillah
    Boo (see *Boo*)
    Chughad 318
    comparison with Chughtai 324, 327
    Darpok 320
    death 314
    Dhandas (see *Dhandas*)
    Dhuan 312, 315
    Ganje Farishte 309, 312
    Haarta Chala Gaya 319
    Hatak 317
    Hundred Candle Watt Bulb (see *Hundred Candle Watt Bulb*)
    job at *Mussavvir* 311
    Kaali Shalwar 314, 317
    Kirchein aur Kirchiyan (see *Kirchein aur Kirchiyan*)
    Khol Do 314, 317–18
    Manto ke Afsane 315
    Mausam ki Shararat 319
    Misri ki Dali 319
    Nangi Awazein (see *Nangi Awazein*)
    Naya Qanoon 316
    'Sadak ke Kinare' (see 'Sadak ke Kinare')
    'Shahdole ka Chooha' (see 'Shahdole ka Chooha')
    Shaheedsaaz 319
    Sharifan 319
    Siyah Hashiye 317–18
    Surkh Inquilab 311
    Thanda Gosht 314, 317
    Yazid (see *Yazid*)
    Zehmat-e-Mehr-e-Darakhshan (see *Zehmat-e-Mehr-e-Darakhshan*)
Marshall Plan 367n78
Marxism
    –Communist tomes in Urdu 77
    influence on Indian literature xxviii–xix
    introduction to Indian intellectuals 78
    sympathy to 239, 341
mass circulation of nationalist poetry 150–1
mass contact campaign, Nehru (1936) 101
Meerut Conspiracy Case 82–3, 240
Mera Safar 302
militant
    nationalism xxiii
    Sikhism 350

minority(ies) 340, 350
    communist principle of self-determination for national 345
    Muslims as silent 147
    rights 29
    Shia consciousness of being 102
Mir, Mir Taqi
    about Delhi 6–7
Mir, Raza, on progressives 297
Mohani, Hasrat 70, 71n60, 82, 161
    'Aine-Soviyat' 94
    founder, *Urdu-i-Mualla* (1906) 56n13
    imprisonment 94
    'Montagu Reforms' 95
Mohiuddin, Makhdoom 286–304
    'Baghi' 288
    Ban Phool 288
    'Inquilab' 288
    'Jang-e-Azadi' 288–9, 342
    Murshid-e-Kamil 287
    'Sipahi' 342
    Surkh Savera (see Surkh Savera)
    'Tagore aur unki Shairi' 287n97
Montague–Chelmsford Reforms (1919) 64n39
Moplahs uprising on Malabar Coast (1921) 73n66
Moradabadi, Jigar 303
Morley–Minto Reforms (1909) 63n35
Mufti, Aamir 307n8, 316n27
Muir, William, publication of 'useful books' 39
Mujeeb, M., assessment of Akbar, Iqbal, Ghalib 47
Muqadama-e-Sher-o-Shairi 28, 40–1
Musaddas: Madd-o-Jazr-e Islam 26–7
Mushafi, Ghulam Hamadani, on Delhi 6
mushairas 40–1, 96–7, 115, 249–50, 254–5, 263

Muslim(s)/Musalman
    anti-imperialism, failure of 68n54
    distinction between two sorts of 60–1
    emergence as religiopolitical community 63
    Indian 68, 106, 157
    influence of 61
    intelligentsia 20, 34, 45, 48, 69, 73, 77, 93, 98, 166
    mass contact programme 237
    measure of self-assurance 72
    nationalists 99
    remain with CPI after partition 350
    revolutionary mass movement for 67
    socialists 102, 105
    as unvariegated, monolithic mass 155
Muslim Independent Party 89n111
Muslim League xxv, 64, 66, 70n56, 88, 193, 236, 241, 365
    electoral politics of 251
    establishment of 72
    Zaheer's stress on progressive nature of 361
Muslim Nationalist Party 73

Naidu, Sarojini 248, 289
    founder, All-India Women's Conference (1927) 223n70
nai nasl writers 393
Nangi Awazein 320
Nanotwi, Muhammad Qasim, founder of Deoband school 24
'Nazr-e Khalida' 268
Neend Nahin Aati 109, 114, 127
Nehru, Jawaharlal xix, xiv, 63, 73, 383–4
    dissatisfaction towards PWM 379

foreign policy 351, 352
on Iqbal 92n119
mass contact campaign (1936) 101
support for socialism 247
Truman's blame on government 353
among youth organizations 233
new lithographic press 23
Nizami, Saghar's 'Qaumi Geet' 212
Nomani, Shibli 60n24
   founder, Dar-ul Mussanifien, Azamgarh 42n111
   'Hungama-e-Balqan' (see 'Hungama-e-Balqan')
   Jawab-e-Shikwa 71
   Musalmanon ki Political Karwat 60
   'Qaumi Geet' (see 'Qaumi Geet')

obscenity in literature, notion of 154, 161, 170
Orainvi, Akhtar 331
   Kaliyan aur Kaante 331
oriental scholarship versus Western learning, merits of 22
Oxford Majlis 111, 208

Pakistan Communist Party, establishment of 363
'Pakistan ka Milli Tarana' 266
Pakistan Papers Limited, establishment of 284
pan-Islamism 48, 99, 155
Parde ke Peechche 143
Partition 62n33, 304, 306–7, 350, 354–5, 363, 384
   Telangana movement 290, 348, 384
Phir Yeh Hungama 127
Pighalata Neelam 187
Premchand 31, 103–4, 191, 224–5, 244n3
   Bazar-e-Husn (see Bazar-e-Husn)

Doodh ka Daam 129
Godan 103
Rangabhumi (see Rangabhumi)
'Sahitya ka Uddeshya' (see 'Sahitya ka Uddeshya')
Shahab ki Sarguzashti 163
Soz-e-Watan 31
Thakur ka Kuan (see Thakur ka Kuan)
press reaction after banning Angarey 164–81
Press Regulation Act, 1890 (Government of India) 149–50
Programme of the Communist International, adoption by First World Congress 90
progressive writers 305–6
   emergence of 30
Progressive Writers' Association (PWA) xiii–xiv, xvii–xx, xxv, 91, 144, 186, 187n101, 194, 212, 219, 225, 232–3, 236, 245, 257, 272–3, 289, 299, 313, 316, 323, 332
   in Pakistan 361–77
Progressive Writers' Movement (PWM) xiii–xiv, xvi, xviii, xxi–xxii, xxv–xxvi, 30, 50, 74, 78, 101–2, 147, 161, 178n76, 181, 183, 186, 189, 191, 230, 297–8, 323, 326
   decline of 339
   decline, reasons for 382–401
   glory days (1936–1947) of 244–53
   major hubs/cities of 242–3
   political ramifications of 340–61
   role of lyricists in 270n62
   success, reasons for 377–82
   writers association with 306
progressivism, notion of 113, 201, 221, 226, 245, 255, 280, 286, 291, 300, 318, 326, 339, 357, 369, 375, 379–80, xvi, xvii, xxii, xxv–xxvi

public library(ies) 53, 54n4
Punjabi Progressive Writers'
    Conference, Amritsar (1940) 274
'Punjab ke Dehqan Se' 49
purdah 130, 139, 152–3, 179

Qadiri, Hamid Hasan 29
Qasmi, Ahmad Nadeem xxin24
    Aanchal 331
    Bagole 331
    Gardab 331
    Sailab 331
    Talwa-o Gharub 331
'*Qaumi Geet*' 212
Quit India campaign/movement 241, 341, 390

Rahbar, Hans Raj 332, 360n57
    Taraqqui Pasand Adab 230n85
Rahman, Munibur 373
Raipuri, Akhtar Husain 175, 180, 290
    '*Adab aur Zindagi*' (see '*Adab aur Zindagi*')
Rangabhumi 103
Rashid, N.M. 281n84, 282n86, 375, 385, 397
    Iran mein Ajnabi 397
    Muawara 397
Rawalpindi Conspiracy Case (1951) xxv–xxvi, 276, 373–5
Red Crescent Medical Mission 60
Reichstag Fire Trial 374
renaissance, Indian 225–6, xix
Revolutionary Movements Bill 214
Robinson, Francis 21, 53n3, 107
Roshnai 181, 192n4, 221, 246, 257, 259n36, 268, 272, 298, 388, 399
Round Table Conference, London (1931) 48
Rowlatt Act (1919) 64, 97, 150–1
Russian Revolution 74, 75

Sadak ke Kinare 321
'*Sahitya ka Uddeshya*' 224
Saiduzzafar, Hamida (Dr) 184
Satyarthi, Devindar 330–1
Sauda, Mirza Muhammad Rafi 6
    Tazheek-e-Rozgar (see *Tazheek-e-Rozgar*)
Sea Customs Act (1932) 214, 218
Secret Indian Students Communist Group, London 235
sedition and immorality, censorship and surveillance, link between 57
servant girl in Urdu fiction 122–3
    Bhag Bhari 122
    Utran 122
Seventh World Congress of the Comintern, Moscow (1934) 216
Shahdole ka Chooha 321
Sharar, Abdul Halim 7n14, 38
    Firdos-e-Barin 38
    Guzishta Lucknow 7n14
    Husn ka Dakoo Mansoor Mohana 38
    Zawaal-e-Baghdad 38
shehr ashob 4
    Hatim 4, 6
    Mir 4
    Sauda 4
'*Shikast-e-Zindaan ka Khwaab*' 213
Shikohabadi, Munir 13
'*Shukriya Europe*' (Hashar Kashmiri) 96
Silk Letter Conspiracy, 100
Simla Deputation (1906) 63
Simon Commission (1928), boycott of 84
Sixth World Congress of Comintern (1928) 87
'*Siyasi Leader kay Naam*' 341
socially engaged literature, appearance of 91–107

Society for the Support of Islam (*see* Anjuman-e-Himayat-i-Islam)
Soviet Union 240, 252, 379
    literature from 81
    Nazi invasion of 282
spiritual socialism 51
Spratt, Philip 86
'*Subah-e-Azadi*' 276, 285
Subhani, Azad 89
successive left-wing revolutionary poets 376n97
Sultanpuri, Majrooh 291
Surkh Savera 289
Suroor, Ale Ahmad 29–30, 222, 277, 305–6
    Adab aur Nazariya 337
    Mussarat se Baseerat Tak 31n79
    Naye aur Purane Chiragh 337
    Nazm se Nasr Tak xvn7, 305n1
    Tanquidi Ishare 336
    Tanquid Kya Hai? 336–7

Tagore, Rabindranath xix, xxiii, 247, 287n97
'*Tarana-e-Jihad*' (Ehsan Danish) 96
'*Tarana-e-Milli*' 48
Tashnah, Syed Ali 14
Taunsvi, Fikr
    '*Chhata Darya*' 333
Tazheek-e-Rozgar 6
Tehri Lakir 327
Thakur ka Kuan 152
Thanawi, Maulana Ashraf Ali 25
    Bihishti Zewar (*see Bihishti Zewar*)
Tottenham, R. 345
trade union movement 84, 89, 272, 288, 291
translation of books for higher education into Urdu 40, 53n2
translations, role in dissemination of new ideas 163

Turkey's sultan, surrender of 74
two-nation theory 343

Udas Naslein (Abdullah Hussein) 398
Umrao Jaan (Mirza Ruswa) 122
Union of Soviet Writers 202n23, 219
The Untouchable 196, 209
Urdu literature xv–xvi, xxiii, xxix, 1, 33, 35, 106, 144–5, 177, 188, 378, 400, xv, xvi, xx
    anti-British ideology 19
    British rule and British Victorian values, impact of 33
    contemporary 20
    Delhi College 23
    development and popularization of 32n80
    effect of revolt of 1857 and its aftermath on 2–20
    embodiment of Victorian values 42
    Islamic historiography 43
    post-1857 19
    in the post-1857 scenario 26
    radicalism in 2
    social consciousness reflected in 1, 26
    socialism, presence in 51
    trends in 1857–1920s 30–51
    wataniyat (nationalism), evolution of 19
    Western imagination seeping into 40
Urdu poetry xxiii, 2, 5, 40, 51, 52n1
    Persian–Arabic tradition 4
    wataniyat (nationalism), evolution of 19
Urdu writers 3, 33, 37, 45, 53, 127, 174, 191, 220, 243–5, 250, 263, 281, 292, 307, 315, 323, 334, 337, 354, 379, xiv, xx

480 • Index

emergence of progressive thought among 2
Muslim xvi
non-Muslim xvi
socialistic ideas influenced cross-section of 53

vernacular
  journalism 57
  newspapers 56
  press 54
Vernacular Press Act 56

Wajid Ali Shah, Nawab 7, 7n14, 7n15
  Huzn-e-Akhtar 7
war of 1965 286
wataniyat, evolution of 19
Western
  imperialism 58
  literature 40
  -style education 24, 43, 155
Western education
  educated Indians access to 53
  introduction of 53
women's education 36, 153
Workers and Peasants' Party 86

Yaadein xxvn32, 111, 192n4, 333
Yazid 321
Yildrim, Sajjad Hyder 152–3, 162
  'Kharistan-o-Gulistan' 162

Zaheer, Sajjad xiv, xixn16, xxiv–xxv, 102n149, 109–11, 113–29, 158n25, 169, 181–2, 186–7, 190–2, 194–9, 203n25, 206, 213, 215–23, 230, 231n86, 235–6, 246, 248–50, 252–3, 257, 315, 333, 335, 342, 358–9, 361–2, 366, 372, 385, 395, 399
  Dulari (see Dulari)
  Garmiyon ki Ek Raat (see Garmiyon ki Ek Raat)
  on Hindi–Urdu debate 203n25
  Jannat ki Bashaarat (see Jannat ki Bashaarat)
  London ki Ek Raat (see London ki Ek Raat)
  Muslim League aur Azadi 344n15
  Neend Nahin Aati (see Neend Nahin Aati)
  Nuqush-e-Zindan 187
  Phir Yeh Hungama (see Phir Yeh Hungama)
  Roshnai (see Roshnai)
  secretary of Allahabad Congress Committee in 1935 235
  Zikr-e-Hafiz 187
Zaidi, Ali Jawad xiiin1, 9n19, 154n16
Zakaullah, Maulvi xvii, 2, 3n6, 18, 20, 24, 27, 29, 33
zamindari system xxvii, 348
Zatalli, Mir Jafar 4n7
Zehmat-e-Mehr-e-Darakhshan 313, 322
Zetland (Lord) 238
Zindah Nama 276–7
Zore, Mohiuddin Qadri 286–7
Zubt Shudah Nazmein xxiiin29
Zugovic, Rudovan 351n32

About the Author

RAKHSHANDA JALIL is a prolific writer, literary critic, and independent researcher. She runs Hindustani Awaaz, an organization devoted to the popularization of Hindi–Urdu literature and culture. Her debut collection of fiction, *Release and Other Stories* (HarperCollins, 2011) received critical acclaim.

Rakhshanda has to her credit over 15 books. Some of these are, the edited volume *Qurratulain Hyder and the River of Fire: The Meaning, Scope and Significance of Her Legacy* (Aakar, 2010; and Oxford University Press, Karachi, 2010), *Journey to the Holy Land: A Pilgrim's Diary* (co-authored with Mushirul Hasan; Oxford University Press, 2009), a collection of essays on the little known monuments of Delhi called *Invisible City: The Hidden Monuments of Delhi* (Niyogi, 2008), a selection by Pakistani women writers called *Neither Night Nor Day* (HarperCollins, 2007), and *New Urdu Writings: From India and Pakistan* (Westland, 2013). Apart from these, she has also published several works of translations. Few recent ones include short stories by Intizar Husain entitled *Circle and Other Stories* (Sang-e-Meel, Lahore, 2012; and Rupa & Co., 2004), *Panchlight and Other Stories*, by Hindi writer Phanishwarnath Renu (Orient Blackswan, 2010), *Naked Voices and Other Stories*, a collection of stories and sketches by Saadat Hasan Manto (Roli, 2008), and a collection of Premchand's short stories for children called *A Winter's Tale and Other Stories* (Puffin, 2007).

A popular blogger, she also contributes regularly to national and international newspapers and magazines, and writes book reviews, opinion pieces, and travelogues. She has recently completed an IGNCA-sponsored book-length study of Dr Rashid Jahan, communist doctor and writer, and is presently engaged in a study of secularism as reflected in contemporary Urdu writings.